John Hughes

Controversy Between Rev. Messrs. Hughes and Breckinridge

Is the Protestant Religion of Christ?

John Hughes

Controversy Between Rev. Messrs. Hughes and Breckinridge
Is the Protestant Religion of Christ?

ISBN/EAN: 9783744660372

Printed in Europe, USA, Canada, Australia, Japan

Cover: Foto ©Lupo / pixelio.de

More available books at **www.hansebooks.com**

CONTROVERSY

BETWEEN

REV. MESSRS. HUGHES AND BRECKENRIDGE,

ON THE SUBJECT

"IS THE PROTESTANT RELIGION THE RELIGION OF CHRIST?"

FIFTH EDITION.

Philadelphia:
PUBLISHED BY EUGENE CUMMISKEY,
NO. 250 SOUTH SIXTH STREET.
1862.

NOTE.

The following correspondence and controversy have been extensively published in the religious newspapers of the day, but as it is believed that many persons wish to possess it in a form more convenient for reference and preservation, this edition is given to the public, with a hope that it will meet with extensive patronage. The whole is copied from "The Presbyterian," and "Catholic Herald," in which it originally appeared, and the public is assured that pains have been taken to make it an exact copy, without alteration of any kind.

CONTROVERSY.

PRELIMINARY CORRESPONDENCE.

To the Rev. John Breckenridge,

Rev. Sir,—I have perused your article on the Roman Catholic controversy published in the Christian Advocate, and feel that you have neither been just nor ingenuous in your observations. I am the more surprised at this because those who know you ascribe to you many of those qualities of mind and feeling, which constitute or adorn the scholar and the gentleman.

Throughout the article you seem to regret that your antagonist is not an "accredited" or responsible authority on the subject; and hence you say, "There are Priests and Bishops, &c. We are prepared to meet any of them, on the broad field of this important and vital discussion; and *hereby* make this disposition known."

Now, sir, I am equally ready to accept this challenge; let it only be conducted in a spirit of Christian charity, and of sincere inquiry after truth. Of course it will be necessary to define certain rules and conditions by which we may understand ourselves and each other, in the discussion of the question.

I hope you will find in the publicity of your challenge a sufficient apology for the liberty I take in addressing you. I shall be ready to receive any communication you may make on this subject, and shall be accommodating as to the time, place, manner, and circumstance, of bringing this topic fairly before the public.

Yours, very respectfully,
John Hughes.

Oct. 3d, 1832.

Philadelphia, Oct. 13th, 1832.

To the Rev. John Hughes,

Sir,—Your communication of the third instant was duly received: and I have used the earliest opportunity, which my present unsettled life allowed me, in giving the necessary attention to its contents.

I am gratified to find that in your estimate of my character you differ from "those who know me." If, as you concede, they are pleased to ascribe to me "many of those qualities of mind and feeling which constitute or adorn the scholar or the gentleman," I leave you to determine whether I ought to be more gratified by their judgment, or distressed at yours.

I confess, however, that I am not a little surprised to find you speaking of my letter published in the Christian Advocate on the Roman Catholic controversy, as embracing an *original* challenge, while charging upon me the want of *ingenuousness*. By a reference to the introduction and close of that publication, you will find that this controversy was forced upon me: and that my reply did not originate the discussion, or embrace a challenge, but attempted to transfer a challenge already given to more equal and elevated ground, and to identify the investigation with the best lights and sanctioned defenders of your faith.

And now, sir, allow me to say, that it gives me hearty pleasure to find you disposed, in a manly form, to meet the question at issue between Protestants and Romanists; while at the same time I fully respond to the wish expressed in your letter, that any controversy which may hereafter be undertaken " may be conducted in a spirit of Christian charity, and a sincere inquiry after truth."

As what you have been pleased to style my challenge was a *written reply* to a previous communication, which was also written, so a written answer from an accredited respondent was requested. The obvious course therefore for you to pursue, in meeting the spirit of this requirement, is to respond from the press, to the contents of my letter, which is now widely circulated through the country. And I, in my place, shall, by the grace of God, stand prepared to give your communications prompt and appropriate attention.

The terms in which you speak of arrangements for the discussion, " defining rules and conditions," are not explicit. If the above suggestion, therefore, does not meet your wishes, I shall be gratified to have them more fully expressed, as to the best method of using the press, to reach the desired end. And that you may be assured of my sincerity, and entire readiness to investigate this great and vital subject, I use this occasion to say, that there are several ministers of the Gospel in this city and vicinity, who stand prepared with me to meet yourself, and any number of your clergy that may be disposed to unite with you, in any way most agreeable to yourselves, that is consistent with decorum, and the grave and sacred nature of the themes.

I am yours, very respectfully,

JOHN BRECKENRIDGE.

The following *rules* were next sent to the Rev. Mr. Breckenridge, by the Rev. Mr. Hughes.

Whereas, the undersigned have agreed to enter on an amicable discussion of the great points of Religious Controversy between Catholics and Protestants,—and whereas such discussions cannot prove either profitable to the parties concerned, or edifying to the public at large, unless they are conducted in the language of decorum, and in a spirit of Christian politeness,—and whereas this object is best attained by adherence to certain rules and conditions mutually agreed to, therefore, the following shall be the rules of said discussion, to the observance of which each of the parties hereby binds himself.

1st. We agree respectively to adhere strictly to the subject of discussion, for the time being: and to admit no second question until the first shall have been exhausted.

2d. Each of the parties shall be the accredited interpreter of his own religion. And neither shall have the right to ascribe to his adversary doctrines, or explanations of doctrines, which the latter disclaims.

3d. The parties shall write and publish alternately in the same paper, never allowing any communication to exceed two columns.

4th. The controversy shall commence by a discussion of the *rule of faith*, to prevent it from being interminable and useless.

Signed,   JOHN HUGHES.

Oct. 23d, 1832.

Philadelphia, Nov. 7th, 1832.

The Rev. John Hughes,

Sir,—I received by the hand of your friend on the 26th ultimo, a series of rules proposed by you as the basis of " an amicable discussion of the great points of religious controversy between (Roman) Catholics and Protestants." When you called upon me yesterday, I informed you that I preferred to settle the preliminaries of the proposed discussion, *in writing*; and that although my answer to your proposals had been delayed by my absence from town, as well as other causes beyond my control ; yet it was in readiness to be sent, needing transcription only. In the extended conversation which was at your particular request then entered into, my objections to your rules were stated at large. I need not now repeat more than the substance of what was communicated then : viz.—1. Your proposals are entirely silent as to any rejoinder to my letter in the Christian Advocate, though in that you find the avowed reason of addressing me on this subject, and though it contains a number of objections to your system of faith and morals, to which answers are requested. 2. The manner in which you propose to conduct the discussion (rule 3d) seems very insufficient, breaking up, as it must do, into so many fractions every leading question, and requiring so much time to reach any adequate result. Besides, you are *local*, and may be always at hand to attend upon the continually recurring details of a controversy, carried on in the columns of a daily paper, for such you seemed, in your conversation yesterday, to prefer. But my present pursuits (I will not say that they were known to you in making out this rule) lead me to every part of our country, and frequently after very short notice. 3. Some of the rules are unfair. I speak not of your intention, but of their tendency. See, for example, rule second. This rule will put it in your power, by a forced construction, to suspend all argument on any question by a private explanation or special disclaimer. The symbols, decrees, bulls, and approved writers of the Church of Rome are now before the world, and many of them have been extant for ages. The distinguishing doctrines of the Reformation and the standards of the Presbyterian Church, have also been fully published to mankind. While due weight should be conceded to our respective explanations, yet the discussion of these doctrines must proceed on the principles of honest interpretation. I feel the more constrained to be explicit here, because you charge me with being both *unjust* and *disingenuous* in the statements of my published letter, though they are all founded in acknowledged facts, and most of them on the authority of your standing symbols or *accredited* writers. I must also add that the explanations of this rule given by you yesterday were not satisfactory Again, the 4th rule, as interpreted by you yesterday, would appear to intimate that our discussion must stop if we cannot agree on what is the rule of faith. The tendency then will be to narrow the argument to this single question. For it is not very probable, however others may be affected by our controversy, that either of us will be convinced by the other.

In the deliberate review of these rules, my conclusion, as communicated to you verbally in our recent interview, is, that your alternative properly is, either to answer my published letter, or to meet me in a public oral discussion of all the leading subjects on which we differ.

You have, however, declined to adopt either of these methods; and you assume the right to choose the manner of conducting the controversy, upon the ground that the challenge came from me. This I disclaim in the sense in which you use it; and refer you for explanation to my former letter. Yet that you may have no just cause for attributing to me the failure of the proposed discussion, I hereby agree to adopt the preamble, with the 1st, 3d, and 4th rules—provided, 1. That after the *rule of faith* shall have been fairly and fully discussed, other topics, to be agreed on hereafter, be taken up in order. 2. That if either party be necessarily hindered by sickness or inevitable calls to be absent, the discussion shall for the time, upon due notice being given, be suspended; and 3. That the paper called "The Presbyterian," published in this city, be the medium of communication with the public.

It is my expectation, Providence permitting, to be stationary, either in Philadelphia or New York, for some months after the first of December. In the interval, though several short journeys will be necessary, not only in the discharge of my official duties, but also to prevent the interruption of the proposed discussion from that quarter, yet any communication from you will receive the earliest possible attention.   I remain, sir, your ob't servant,

JOHN BRECKENRIDGE.

Nov. 12th, 1832.

To the Rev. John Breckenridge,

Sir,—In your letter of the 7th inst. you have stated at length your ideas on the preliminaries of the controversy to which you had challenged the "Priests and Bishops" of the Catholic Church. I shall briefly notice in order all those parts of your letter that seem to require attention.

You begin by setting forth that I should issue a rejoinder to your letter. To this I reply that the challenge is *general,* covering the whole of the disputed ground, and consequently an acceptance of it requires that we should commence with the beginning. Secondly, you object to the manner of conducting it, (as indicated in rule 3d,) and hint, that as I am "local," and you obliged to travel, this rule would give me decided advantage. Now so far as this rule restricts us to two columns and alternate communication, I hereby agree to withdraw it;—leaving you free on that subject.—But with regard to your "present pursuits," I am surprised that you allude to them, since you know that they are precisely the same as when you published your challenge.

You say the 2d rule is unfair. This must be owing to your misapprehension of its meaning. I will submit another in its stead, at the close of this letter, in which I trust you will find nothing "unfair."

Rule 4th, you have adopted with a provision to which I agree. Your second provision had reference to that part of the 3d rule, which you objected to, and which I have agreed to withdraw.

The only difficulty that remains, has reference to the medium of communication with the public. I cannot consent to its being "the paper called the Presbyterian." If we *are to be judged* by the public, it must be by the public generally, and not by a sectarian fragment of the community—which is itself a party in the controversy. If I agreed to that provision, what would be my situation? Why, I should have a Presbyterian antagonist, Presbyterian judges, and receive my license to publish, in every case, at the hand of a Presbyterian editor! This sir, is asking too much:—and is not in good keeping with that courage which prompted you to challenge "Priests and Bishops" to the discussion of these vital points, before the *public*.

Upon a review of your letter and my own, I find that we are agreed upon the preamble and the *first rule* without amendment. Let the second be expressed as follows:

"Rule 2. The questions shall be confined to those points of doctrine and morals which are admitted by the parties, *or found* in the Symbols, Decrees, Bulls, Catechisms, approved writers, Standards, and Confessions of Faith of the churches to which the parties respectively belong. And such points shall in all cases be stated in the precise words or literal translation of the document from which they are extracted, and the reference given."

If you agree to this, and will adopt the natural, obvious, and impartial medium of a public newspaper—then am I ready to answer your challenge. If you prefer an oral discussion under the guidance of these rules, let it be in the presence of twelve enlightened gentlemen, neither Catholics nor Presbyterians—and again I am ready. But I cannot consent to exhibit myself as a theological gladiator for the amusement of an idle, promiscuous, curious multitude.

This, sir, is my last private communication on the subject. I shall await your decision on this letter. If you decline every thing I have proposed, then it strikes me that consistency and candour will suggest to you the propriety of offering a public apology for your challenge; at least some explanation of the private circumstances which tempted you to *publish* it, and to wear laurels without the trouble of deserving them.

Yours, very respectfully,

JOHN HUGHES

Philadelphia, Dec. 3d, 1832.

To the Rev. John Hughes.

Sir,—As I intimated to you in my last communication, I hope to be located in this city or New York for the chief part of the winter, and to enjoy sufficient rest to give you some attention. Having returned home on the evening of Nov. 29th, I now send my answer to your letter of Nov. the 12th.

If the cause you advocate is to be measured by the spirit of your reply, then it is still worse than I had even supposed it. The dignity and Christian decorum with which you professed yourself desirous of conducting the proposed controversy, have, I regret to say, strangely disappeared in the progress of our preliminary correspondence, giving place to severe invective, ungenerous taunts, and bad temper. If I patiently lend myself to these uses, the public will at least not think me *aspiring ;* and the laurels which you imagine me so desirous of possessing, without having won, will scarcely be worth wearing. But indeed, sir, you mistake me in supposing that I wish to *wear laurels.* I desire victory for the truth of God, and the crown for Him whose right it is to rule—and whose prerogative has been usurped by him " who, seated as God, in the temple of God, exalteth himself above all that is called God."—As this will probably be my last communication to you in this way, it is perhaps my duty once more explicitly to state the grounds on which we respectively stand in the matter now at issue between us.

Some two years since, (while a resident in Baltimore,) I was singled out, without provocation, by one of your leading laymen, and required to write a reply to his strictures on a Protestant work, with the alternative of appearing to an esteemed member of the church of which I was pastor (who had been perplexed by his subtlety, and was referred to me for a reply) to be unable to defend our avowed faith. I chose to reply in writing, and at the close, called for a written rejoinder to a number of objections stated in the reply; and insisted on one from a *responsible* author—stating my readiness at the same time, in view of these "objections," to meet such a person on the whole field of controversy between Roman Catholics and Protestants. In the autumn of this year I published that letter—impelled to it in part by the frequent, and sometimes insolent, attacks that were made upon the Protestant churches—and in part by the very unwarrantable course pursued at the consecration of the house of worship in which you officiate. You professed to believe yourself (among others) challenged by me *originally* in this publication; and you take advantage of that assumption to fix the terms, according to which, and which alone, the discussion must be conducted. I proposed to you the obvious and ordinary course, at once the most refined and best adapted to make permanent and wide impressions on the public mind—that you should reply to my letter in a connected form, from the press—promising to write again in answer when necessary. This you entirely and repeatedly declined, for reasons whose weight an impartial community will not find it difficult to estimate. I offered you the option of a public oral discussion. From this also you retreat

—and urge in their stead the use of the daily *political press*—and yet you object to oral discussion on the ground that you "*cannot consent to exhibit yourself as a theological gladiator, for the amusement of an idle, promiscuous, curious multitude.*" How you can see so much unsuitableness in one of these forms, and none in the other, I am at a loss to discover. In view of your unmoved determination to proceed in your own way, I proposed the pages of a weekly religious paper—and having no connexion with your papers, I did all I could, *offered one of ours,* expecting you to reciprocate the arrangement. I was led to this course the more by the conversation which you held with the assistant secretary in our office before my arrival, and by the communications which passed between us, on this subject.—The paragraph, therefore, in which you resent my offer of "The Presbyterian," is truly surprising to me, being, as I recollect, wholly at variance with the spirit manifested by you in our interview! Did you not then *entertain* the idea that the religious periodical presses of our respective denominations, might be properly and effectually used, if they could be obtained, to carry on this investigation before the public? And yet now, when the idea is matured, you charge me with dishonourable proposals! Your proposition to meet me before twelve gentlemen is quite amusing; especially in view of your desire to use a daily paper on account of its *publicity.*

You say "*I am surprised that you allude to your present pursuits, since you know that they are precisely the same as when you published your challenge.*" Now, if when I published my letter, I had proposed, as my plan of controversy, *alternate pieces in a daily paper,* and then when challenged by you on that plan, plead as a reason for declining it, my present pursuits though still the same, there would have been reason in your remark; but the case is this, you know now, if not before, that *my pursuits* prevent me from being long *local;* when therefore you propose and insist on a plan not only *puerile,* but which you know I could not adopt, is it I, or you, who shrink from the manly meeting of the question?

Still more, your posture as to my published letter, gives you no exclusive right above me to decide on the method of discussion, it being only a transfer to another person of a controversy which I did not originate. And still more, while my letter was in progress through the press, and (as I think) that point which contained "the challenge," was not yet published, you did attack Protestant ministers in a daily paper of this city, in a most unwarrantable and injurious manner.

As to the rule substituted by you for rule 2d, to which I had objected, I still decline it. It is both unusual and uncandid to propose it in the form and terms which you use. I wish to be fair but free in my argument, and extend to you the same right. If we misinterpret, or misquote, or bring bad authority, let it be shown in the discussion; it will injure only him who does it.

And now, sir, this is also *my last private* communication in this way. I have therefore to say in conclusion, if you will secure a weekly Roman Catholic paper, as I have the Protestant paper already named by me, I will agree to write and publish, simultaneously, in alternate weeks, with you, our respective pieces, until we have done; or if you can obtain the use, week after week, of some respectable paper devoted to religion and literature, which is neither Roman Catholic nor Presbyterian, I will promptly acquiesce. In the event of your accepting this last offer, I am prepared to have a personal interview with you, to settle the remaining particulars of the arrangement, it being understood, that I still agree to your rules, as qualified by this and my previous letter. If, however, you decline this, having declined the fair and scholar-like method of a connected answer from the press; having declined a public and oral discussion; and having intrenched yourself in the columns of a daily political paper, which can never afford room for a *full* discussion, is no fit place for *such* a discussion, and is a plan, for any length of time, to your knowledge, incompatible with my "present pursuits," I shall feel called on in duty, as well as justified in right, to publish this correspondence, and to begin a series of letters through the press, to the public, on the subjects which divide Protestants from Roman Catholics. When you demand an apology, you forget the age and the land in which we live. My "apology" for writing and publishing my letter, so far as not already given, shall, with God's help, be seen in a public vindication of divine truth, and of the rights of man, against a system, which, in my humble judgment, is at war with both.

I remain your obedient servant,
JOHN BRECKENRIDGE.

Philadelphia, Dec. 4th, 1832.

To the Rev. John Breckenridge.

Sir,—The object of the present letter is to intimate before you commence the publication of our correspondence, that *I agree to the proposals you have made, for the purpose of bringing the disputed ground of controversy between Catholics and Presbyterians fairly before the public.*

In your letter of yesterday, you allude to the offer you had made of the columns of "The Presbyterian," and to my having declined it, in a tone of triumph, which my *reasons* for declining were somewhat calculated to subdue. However, you are pleased to overlook those reasons; and since you decline every mode suggested by *me*, I will even meet you in your own proposals—and hereby signify my acceptance of the same.

Of course "The Presbyterian" will continue to publish until one or the other of us think proper to decline the contest. I, on my part, shall have the whole republished in one of *our* papers, so that Catholics may receive the enlightenment of your arguments.

I must, however, enter my protest against your rejection of the 2d rule, as explained in my last letter. The "mens conscia recti" has nothing to dread from its operation.

Now, sir, you may proceed with the publication of our correspondence; and as soon as it shall have appeared, I will open the controversy, by addressing a letter to you through the columns of "The Presbyterian," on the "Rule of Faith," as already agreed upon.

Yours, very respectfully,
JOHN HUGHES.

PRELIMINARY CORRESPONDENCE.

Philadelphia, Dec. 6, 1832.

To the Rev. John Hughes.

Sir,—I am truly gratified that we can so far agree, at last, as to have the prospect of beginning promptly the proposed discussion. In my last letter, I suggested a personal interview, in order to settle some of the details of the controversy—such as the question to be investigated--the order—the quantity of matter from week to week, &c. &c. It is understood, of course, that the particular paper furnished on your part is regularly pledged to reciprocate the arrangement made by "The Presbyterian," in a weekly republication. My determination to publish our correspondence was suspended upon the event of your declining the terms offered to you in my last letter. I am pleased, however, that you consent to the publication—as the letters themselves will best explain the nature and origin of the pending controversy.

I propose in fine an interview to-morrow morning, in the presence of two mutual friends, if you please, at such time as may be most convenient to yourself.

I am your obedient servant,
JOHN BRECKENRIDGE.

To the Rev. John Breckenridge.

Rev. Sir,—I regret that it was not in my power to see you, on the day proposed in your last letter, for the purpose of arranging those particulars to which you very properly allude.

If it meet your views, I shall be very happy to see you, on Monday at 10 o'clock, A. M., with any gentleman you may think proper to bring, at my dwelling adjoining St. John's church. If the hour or place be inconvenient, you may mention any other, and I shall make it convenient to attend. But sometime on Monday will suit me best, as I shall be obliged to go out of town next week, and shall start probably on Tuesday morning.

Yours, very respectfully,
JOHN HUGHES.

Dec. 8th, 1832.

The proposed meeting took place, when the following agreement was made between the parties.

The undersigned, agreeing to have an amicable discussion of the great points of religious controversy between Protestants and Roman Catholics, do hereby bind themselves to the observance of the following rules:

1. The parties shall write and publish alternately, in the weekly religious papers called "The Presbyterian," and a Roman Catholic paper to be furnished by the first of January. it being understood that the communications shall be published after the following plan. One party opening, the first week; the other party replying the next

week: and every piece to be republished in the immediately succeed ing number of the Roman Catholic paper. The communications not to exceed four columns of "The Presbyterian," nor to continue beyond six months, without consent of parties.

2. The parties agree that there is an infallible rule of faith, established by Christ, to guide us in matters of religion, for the purpose of determining disputes in the Church of Christ.

3. They moreover agree that after giving their views of the rule of faith, they will proceed to discuss the question, "Is the Protestant religion the religion of Christ?"

4. The parties agree respectively to adhere strictly to the subject of discussion, for the time being; and to admit no second question until the first shall have been exhausted. Each party shall be the judge when he is done with a subject, and shall be at liberty to occupy his time with a second subject, when he is done with the first; leaving to the other party the liberty of continuing to review the abandoned topic, as long as he shall choose; subject, however, to be answered if he introduce new matter.

5. Mr. Hughes to open the discussion, and Mr. Breckenridge to follow, according to the dictates of his own judgment.

JOHN HUGHES.
JOHN BRECKENRIDGE.

Dec. 14th, 1832.

Philadelphia, Dec. 26th, 1832.

The Rev. John Breckenridge.

Dear Sir,—In the correspondence that has taken place between us, you must have perceived that I left several topics unanswered, inasmuch as they had no immediate bearing on the arrangements of the rules by which the controversy was to be conducted. On those topics I will now make a few observations.

In your letter of the third inst. you give a statement of the facts connected with the origin of this discussion, which I am not disposed to call into question, because, even admitting them, they do not sustain the conclusion which you have endeavoured to build upon them. Now the only portion of the statement, with which I am concerned, is the fact that in the "Christian Advocate," for August and September of this year, you published a letter headed "Roman Catholic Controversy," which on perusal I found to contain charges, which if they were true, would render our religion an object of horror to all good men.—For example, you stated on the authority of Usher and St. Thomas Aquinas, that according to our brief, *images* representing Christ are to be adored as Christ himself. After having made this statement and given those names to support it, you ask, "What is this? Is it not divine worship of idols or images—i. e. *idolatry* sanctioned by standing authors, and ordered by the great accredited council of Trent?"

Who this Usher is, from whom you quote, I am at a loss to conjecture. There is an author of that name, but he does not possess much authority with Catholics, for the reason that he happens to have been a *Protestant* Archbishop. But no matter for this testimony: the main point is that you, with your proper signature, charge upon Catholics that they are idolaters, by doctrine and authority.

You next charge upon them what you call "legalized immoralities," and designate the doctrine of indulgences as "a bundle of licenses to sin, and making merchandise of souls." You even go into the detail of this traffic, and tell us the scale of prices on which crime was graduated—"for a layman murdering a layman, *about* 7s. 6d; for killing a father, mother, wife or sister, 10s. 6d." &c. p. 392.

Now, dear sir, I would appeal to yourself, and ask whether it was well possible for us, desirous to share in the good opinion of our fellow citizens, to let such charges, sanctioned by your name, go forth on the wings of the press to every village and hamlet in the land, without claiming a hearing for our defence. It is true, that the charges are, in themselves, too gross and absurd to be believed by men of enlightened and educated minds. But when published with your name, when published in this city, when published with a direct, express, and positive call on the "Priests and Bishops" of the church to meet you in the broad field of this important and vital discussion—then the case is changed; and there is no alternative left, except either to obey your summons to the field of controversy, or allow the opposite course to be construed into a tacit admission of the charges thus boldly preferred. Persons were already begining to ask the question—"If these accusations were unfounded, why do not some of the Catholic clergy deny them, or meet Mr. B. in the field of controversy to which he has invited them? If they are silent, when such charges, sustained by a respectable name, are brought against their religion, what are we to infer from their silence?"

It was in this stage of the question, that your letter was brought under my notice, and the *circumstances* seemed to leave no room for hesitation as to the course to be pursued. The charges against the Catholic religion, and the challenge addressed to its ministers, were clear and unequivocal. Our readers, then, will pronounce whether any Catholic priest or bishop has been the *assailant* in this controversy, or whether I, among the least competent of them to undertake it, should not be considered as the party standing in the attitude of defence.

It is true, you qualify these facts and conclusions by reverting to a private controversy between a Catholic layman and a member of your congregation in Baltimore; but this is an incident of ordinary occurrence, and has no necessary relation except to the parties immediately concerned. Your challenge—for I must use that term in the absence of a more dignified one—was the same when addressed to the young lady in Baltimore that it now is—except that the Priests and Bishops of the Catholic church whom it *summoned* to the discussion, were entirely ignorant of its existence. But when you spread out before the American public the elaborate impeachment of their doctrine and morals which your letter contains, then it was that the document was served on the parties whom it arraigned, and the public duly advised of the proceeding. Do not suppose that I am now complaining of your proceedings in this matter. My object is different; it is merely to show, by a statement of the facts, that view it on what side you will, every aspect determines clearly our relative positions; yours as the assailant, and mine as the assailed. You speak of my letter addressed to the editor of the Philadelphian during the prevalence of the Cholera, as one of the immediate reasons for the publication of yours, but even then I was only repelling an unprovoked attack upon the moral character of the Catholic clergy.

I am well pleased to have this opportunity of stating to the public the grounds on which I utterly disclaim having provoked this controversy; and the more so, because there are many persons who deprecate such discussions: some, regarding the truth of religion with as much dread or indifference as Pilate; others, from the admixture of personal invective and even scurrility which has sometimes characterized controversy. Of this latter, however, I trust nothing shall appear in our correspondence. I cannot conceive that a strict adherence to the established laws of literary decorum and propriety imposes any restraint on the freedom of debate, or forbids the thorough dissection of an adverse argument.

There is only one other topic connected with our correspondence, to which I shall, at this time, call attention. You have frequently expressed your surprise that I did not take up your letter as I found it in the "Christian Advocate," and answer it, instead of adopting the present course. You have even intimated that it is beyond the reach of refutation. I assure you, dear sir, that it never so appeared to me, and that my motive for adopting this plan was entirely different. There are first principles at the bottom of every subject, the application of which never fails to throw light on questions in detail springing out of such subject. I saw in your letter that you had entirely overlooked those first principles of Christianity by the application of which truth may be distinguished from error. I saw our doctrines incorrectly stated, arraigned, tried, and triumphantly condemned—but then you were conducting these proceedings in the absence of every tribunal except that of your own opinion, and the opinion of those who might happen to agree with you.

But knowing that Christ, in the constitution of his church, has provided a tribunal expressly for the purpose of determining such disputes as those agitated in your letter, I chose to appeal to the legitimate umpire. I am happy that you have also recognised the existence and competency of this divinely appointed tribunal, and although our controversy is to commence with an investigation of *what it is*, still the fact of its existence is a point on which there is no dispute between us. This starting from a common principle should indicate that *truth*, and not personal triumph, is the object we have mutually in view:— and proceeding under the guidance of the rules agreed upon, I hope and trust that the discussion will lead to consequences neither unpleasant nor unprofitable to our readers or ourselves. In this way questions will succeed each other in the rational order both of time and place—and it now remains for me to open the correspondence with that great question, viz. " What is that infallible means which Christ has appointed for determining disputes in his church?"

Yours, very respectfully,

JOHN HUGHES.

New York, January 5th, 1833.

To the Rev. John Hughes.

Sir,—I had hoped that our prolonged correspondence would cease with the adoption of the rules, and give place to the expected discussion. You have felt it necessary, however, to write again on preliminary subjects, and your letter calls for some notice by me on several accounts.

In reference to the origin of the controversy which is about to be undertaken, I now in conclusion lay before you the passages which relate to it in the published letter. They are taken in part from the beginning, and in part from the close of that communication.

" Baltimore, 25th July, 1831.

" My dear Madam,—When you first put into my hands ' Father Clement,' with the strictures of an anonymous writer, I cursorily looked at his remarks, and sent you, in reply, a work called the ' Protestant,' originally published in Edinburgh, as containing a full and satisfactory refutation of those strictures."

" You have since informed me that a *written* answer would be more satisfactory—nay more, that it was in some sort triumphantly demanded as impossible."

" You are fully aware, that the points at issue between Protestants and Papists are numerous and vital, and that it would require far more leisure than I ever can command, and far more talent than I possess, to do justice to this discussion."

" Nor is the writer to whom I am requested to reply, in the proper sense, a responsible one. His name was for some time withheld, and when at my request it was given, the author, though highly respectable and intelligent, did not appear to me an *accredited* defender of his principles; though in all likelihood as wise as his teachers. He may not be acknowledged as authority by those whom he here represents."

" Notwithstanding these things, however, I feel your call to be imperative. As your pastor, it is my duty and my privilege to do all in my power to aid you in arriving at a knowledge of the truth, and in repelling attacks on our precious faith. And when to this is added the declaration that we *do not* reply to such things because we *cannot;* when our delay, arising from pressing avocations, from dislike of controversy, or from a delicate regard to what is proper, in the mode and spirit of conducting it, are triumphantly appealed to as evidences of the conceded weakness of our cause, it appears indeed our duty to take up the challenge." [Christian Advocate, August, 1832, p. 347.]

" In pressing these questions, we intend to be respectful, though plain—and as we have been called on for a defence of our views, so we feel it a duty to reply."

" Finally, we expect a reply to these various objections and inquiries, and we ask one from some *accredited respondent*, not from one whose defence may be disclaimed, after the trouble of an extended discussion has been gone into. There are priests and bishops, &c. We are willing to meet any of them on the broad field of this important and vital discussion; and hereby make this disposition known."

"Though removed from Baltimore, I shall be near at hand [in the city of Philadelphia], and by God's grace, prepared for any respectful and intelligent communication of responsible character, on this subject."

In these passages you have the history of the discussion, prior to your taking it up. Let it speak for itself. I have already given you some of my reasons for its publication, and need not here repeat them. I freely own that the publication of my letter gave notoriety and intensity to the call for a reply. But it did not *begin* the controversy—nor did it first *publish*, though it first printed it; for the whole matter had become a subject of conversation in Baltimore, and the manuscripts severally written, were so far read, as to constitute a publicly known issue. It is also a little remarkable, that the reasoning which you adopt, as to the Roman Catholic community, applied strictly to the congregation of which I was then pastor. It was known to many that I had been addressed; that an answer was demanded of me; that I had at first declined to give one, sending only a *book* on the controversy, and that a *written reply from me* was then, with some triumph, insisted on. And it was not until nearly a whole year had passed, and many of my friends thought my own character, and even the cause of truth suffering from my silence, that I took up my pen. There is another fact which may cast some light on this subject In due time, a manuscript *attempt* at a reply to my letter was sent after me to Philadelphia. My alternative then became as follows, that is, according to your reasoning—I must reply to the Baltimore layman, or be silent. The former, I had pledged myself not to do; the latter would have been by construction, and almost by confession, a surrender of my principles, as incapable of defence. What then could I do? Honour forbade me to *publish* his communications; consistency and common sense forbade me to reply to them.—The only course which remained for me therefore, was to publish my own letter, and thus transfer the discussion to a responsible author, if any such should choose to take it up. Yet when I do this, you claim the public sympathy as an injured defender of your faith, against the unprovoked attacks of a presuming Protestant! But sometimes an objector's consistency is best discovered by comparing him with himself. I have heretofore barely alluded to your publication, last autumn, in the U. S. Gazette. Before you saw what you term my challenge, you took occasion in reply to an article from the editor of the Philadelphian to speak in the following terms of Protestant ministers. "And what can they [the Roman Catholic Priests,] what can the public think, when they see the shepherds, who are all remarkable for their pastoral solicitude, so long as the flock is healthy, the pastures pleasant, and the fleece luxuriant, abandoning their post, when disease begins to spread desolation in the fold?" And again, "How comes it then, that these objects [cholera patients] have been so generally forsaken by the Protestant clergy? It is not long since I read an account of eight missionaries, that is two missionaries [the rest being wives and children], embarking for the conversion of the distant heathen. The conversion of a single Gentoo is blazoned over the land, as a triumph of Christianity, and a victory above all value of money and labour; and how comes it that the Protestant of Philadelphia, **less fortunate** than the Gentoo of Hindostan, cannot find a clergyman of his own persuasion, who would whisper to him words of hope, through the redemption of Jesus Christ, from the moment that the fatal disease has seized upon him. I do not say that this was the case with *all* the Protestant clergy; but I do say it of some."

You will not understand me as intending at all to defend the article to which you reply, or to find fault with you for answering it. But I present to you for your consideration, your most ungenerous, and unjust, and injurious aspersions of Protestant ministers. And is it true, then, that the body of Protestant ministers, Episcopal, Baptist, Methodist Episcopal, Presbyterian, Congregational, &c. "*generally*" "*though not all,*" forsook the dying sufferers, after having lived on the fat of the land, and the sweat of the people's faces, when in prosperity and health? And is it true that these Protestants with all their missionary efforts are so base, so hypocritical as this? If you can prove your charges, then we deserve your most faithful exposure, with all the reprehension and infamy which your statements, if well founded, are fitted to produce. But my principal object in this reference is, to show what liberties you take with Protestants, in contrast with your strictures on and complaints of my letter, published in the Christian Advocate; I need not add that the very framework of your periodical publications involves the scheme of aggression on the religion of Protestants: that if we enter your places of public worship we are continually liable to meet with the denunciations applied to heretics alone;—and that between propagandism and intolerance, in all countries where your worship is established by law, Protestants have no enviable lot. Let not the odium then attendant on *unprovoked* attacks be levelled at me; and if at the proper time, I sustain with suitable evidence, the statements made in the Christian Advocate, may I not claim the universal privilege of pleading justification in the proof of the facts? You will scarcely look for me to enter on this proof now.

As to archbishop Usher, however, you can hardly imagine that I wished to adduce *his* opinion of your doctrine as *authority* in your church. You know, however, that he has written on this subject, and stands high with *Protestants*. It was his quotations from the catechism of the council of Trent, &c. [having the originals before him, which I had not at the time,] which I intended to refer to as *authority* in your church. But by some strange error, a prince among Protestants was made a Romanist, a mistake which corrects itself, and does him only injustice. It is to the catechism we wished to refer—quoted by him. You mistake me when you suppose, that the reason of my insisting on an answer to my published letter, was my impression that it was so very conclusive as to preclude reply. I thought that the candid, natural, honourable course, for a scholar, a gentleman, and a Christian to pursue, and having heard of you as one of the most distinguished ministers of your church, supposed you the more likely to concur in so obvious a suggestion. It is also at a great sacrifice on my part, that I now conform to your wishes, and enter on the present mode of controversy. A *connected* discussion either oral, or from the press, would have been more convenient to me, on all accounts. Yet I have waived my rights; I have in chief part adopted your rules; I have conceded to you the choice of questions, in the two general propositions suggested as the basis of investigation: and you are to commence the discussion, and I am to *defend* the Protestant faith, though you call yourself the challenged person; and while mine is the life of a traveller, yours is one of sanctuary, quietude, and literary leisure. Yet still I meet you with hearty satisfaction, having it as my chief source of regret, that whilst American Protestant Christians present a galaxy of great and good men, abundantly qualified to defend our precious faith, this momentous controversy has fallen into such poor hands as mine.

I fully reciprocate the wish that we may be enabled to pursue our investigation in the right spirit and to the best ends. I shall affect no false charity; I pray that the God of truth and love may imbue us with that which is true.

I have only to add, that I admit no infallible rule of faith, or judge of controversy, but the revealed will of God. What that revealed will is, according to previous arrangement between us, is the question with which you are now to open the controversy. The delayed receipt of your last letter, it having reached me only the evening before I left Philadelphia for this city, is my apology for a corresponding delay in sending this.

I remain yours, respectfully,
JOHN BRECKENRIDGE.

P. S. In the event of inevitable interruptions, I shall claim the indulgence mentioned in a former letter, of a temporary suspension of the discussion.

CONTROVERSY

RULES.

THE undersigned agreeing to have an amicable discussion of the great points of religious controversy, between Protestants and Roman Catholics, do hereby bind themselves to the observance of the following rules:

1. The parties shall write and publish, alternately, in the weekly religious papers, called the Presbyterian, and a Roman Catholic paper, to be furnished by the first of January. It being understood that the communications shall be published after the following plan:—One party opening the first week, the other party replying the next week, and every piece to be republished in the immediately succeeding number of the Roman Catholic paper. The communications not to exceed four columns of the Presbyterian, nor to continue beyond six months, without consent of parties.

2. The parties agree that there is an infallible Rule of Faith established by Christ to guide us in matters of Religion, for the purpose of determining disputes in the Church of Christ.

3. They moreover agree, that after giving their views of the Rule of Faith, they shall proceed to discuss the question, "Is the Protestant religion, the religion of Christ?"

4. The parties agree respectively, to adhere strictly to the subject of discussion, for the time being, and to admit no second question, until the first shall have been exhausted. Each party shall be the judge when he is done with a subject, and shall be at liberty to occupy his time with a second topic, when he is done with the first, leaving to the other party the liberty of continuing to review the abandoned topic, as long as he shall choose; subject, however, to be answered, if he introduce new matter.

5. Mr. Hughes to open the discussion, and Mr. Breckinridge to follow, according to the dictates of his own judgment.

JOHN BRECKINRIDGE,
JNO. HUGHES.

Philadelphia, December 14th, 1832.

RULE OF FAITH.

January 21, 1833.

TO THE REV. JOHN BRECKINRIDGE,

Rev. Sir,—I am extremely happy to have this opportunity, not of my own seeking, to submit to your consideration and that of our readers, the reasons which prove the truth of the Catholic Religion, and the tendency of every other system to weaken the principles and sap the foundation of Christianity itself. In doing this, however, I shall be careful to abstain from the use of gross or insulting epithets I shall make no appeal to prejudice or passion—but availing myself of those advantages which are peculiar to the cause of truth—I shall address your reason, through the medium of rational argument found ed upon solid principles and indisputable facts. I shall merely premise in addition to what I have stated, that I discriminate between the false doctrines of modern sects and the individuals whose misfortune it is to have been educated in the belief of them, without a knowledge, and sometimes without even a suspicion of their erroneousness. Ignorance of truth is criminal, only when it is voluntary, and when men, through party attachments, prejudice, or human respect, dread the consequences of investigation. But even then, God alone is the judge, before whose tribunal they shall stand or fall. I judge no man —be the sect or denomination to which he belongs what it may.

When we reflect that there was a time when the multitude of believers had but one heart and one soul, and contrast that period with the conflict of opinions, and the rivalship of creeds which have produced the present distracted condition of the Christian family, the lover of truth may find enough to make him weep for charity. Then, there was one Lord, one faith, one baptism; constituting the unity of spirit in the bond of peace. Now, the baptism, the faith, and the Lord himself are become so many topics of dispute, watch-words of division, and signals of contradiction. Men, under pretence of reforming his church, have tampered with the integrity of Christian belief, and either blind or desperately indifferent to the *consequences*, have burst the ligament which bound the doctrines of Christianity together, and left them defenceless against the invading spirit of infidelity. The ancient land-marks of the Christian's belief have been removed—the works of the citadel have been broken down, and the breach once made, Religion has been robbed, as far as it was in the power of man's perverted ingenuity to rob her, of the very privilege and principle of self-preservation.

What is the cause of this unhappy state of things? What is the prolific principle that has produced such a harvest of creeds, in which the wheat of sound doctrines is scarcely perceptible amidst the tares and cockle of delusion? That principle, Rev. Sir, is *private interpretation.*—The Presbyterian Church, like every other church that has adopted it, is too weak to sustain its pressure, and is consequently falling apart, under its operation. That principle, or as it is regarded among Protestants, that privilege, is destructive of unity, by making doctrine, like matter, infinitely divisible. Let a sect be composed of only three individuals, and, if private interpretation be adopted as the cement of religious union, they will not long cling together. But the confessions of faith by which Protestants endeavour to preserve the unity of spirit in the bond of peace, is a practical proof that they themselves do not regard private interpretation as conservative of truth. Let it not be said that these remarks warrant the charge that the Catholic Religion is hostile to the dissemination and perusal of the Holy Scriptures. I protest against such an inference; all that I want to establish is contained in the spirit and letter of St. Peter's declaration, that "no prophecy of Scripture is of any private interpretation."

Now the Protestant "rule of faith" utterly reverses this declaration, and makes *all* Scripture of *every* private interpretation. The Protestant rule of faith is, if I am not mistaken (and if I be, I will thank you for correction) *the Bible alone.*

"The Bible alone," then, is, you suppose, "that infallible rule of faith established by Christ, to guide us in matters of religion, for the purpose of determining disputes in the church of Christ," to the existence of which we have both subscribed our names. Allow me, Rev. Sir, here to remark, that whether you chose to recognise, or to deny the existence of an "infallible rule of faith," was to me, a matter of utter indifference. The cause of truth would have been vindicated as much by the denial, as it can be by the admission. In the former case you would have reduced the religion of Christ to a matter of opinion, and this is precisely what you do, not by admitting its existence, for in this you were right, but by restricting it as Protestants are obliged to do, to the *Bible* alone.

You have sufficiently defined the rule of faith by telling us that it was established by Christ, "for the purpose of guiding us in matters of religion, and of determining disputes in his church." Now it is altogether inconsistent with our belief of the personal character and attributes of Jesus Christ, to suppose that he would have established this "rule of faith," as a *means*, without having rendered it *competent* to the *end* for which it was established. As a rule, therefore, it must be *practically* as well as *theoretically* infallible.—Otherwise it would be incompetent to the end for which it was established, and could neither "guide us in matters of religion, nor determine our disputes." It would be a mockery; more worthy of the Arabian impostor, than of the Son of God. The "infallible rule of faith," then, which you have admitted in our regulations for this controversy, must be infallible not only in itself, but in its *application* to the purpose of its establishment, so as to give those who abide by its decision an infallible certainty that they abide in the doctrines of Christ.

Let us now examine whether the Protestant rule of faith—the Bible alone—is competent by practical application, to the end for which such a guide was established by the Saviour of men. In other words, let us see whether your definition of that rule, as a Protestant, does not conflict with your admission of its existence as a Christian. I shall conduct the examination on the principles already laid down, which you are at liberty to refute if you can; but which, if you do not refute, shall be looked upon as conceded;—for I wish you to be advised, that in the whole controversy, every inch of ground which is not disputed by you, shall be looked upon as *so much* given up to the cause of Catholicity and truth. And at the same time, I have to request of you, as an honourable adversary, that in attempting a refutation, you will take up my arguments in *my own words*—and according to their context and meaning.

The question then is this: Is the *Bible alone*, that practical rule of faith, established by Christ, to guide us in matters of religion, and to determine disputes in his Church?

If it is not, then it will follow, that the whole Protestant system that is, the system of all who adopt the Bible alone to "guide them in matters of religion," hinges on a principle which is vicious and defective. I will now proceed to state the reasons which should make it manifest to every unprejudiced mind, that the *Bible alone*, is not, and cannot be the infallible rule established by Christ for the purpose of determining disputes in his Church. These reasons I will lay down in distinct paragraphs in order to make them convenient for the purposes of reference, and to bring them more within the reach of refutation, number for number.

I. The Rule of Faith adopted by Protestants, is the *Bible alone*—and that rule, you admit, was established by Christ, and infallible. The Bible includes all the books of the Old and New Testament, acknowledged by the Protestant canon of Scripture. Now if Christ established the rule of faith, it certainly was not the Bible; for it is an historical fact, that no part of the New Testament was written for several years, and some of it, not until more than half a century after Christ's ascension into heaven. How could the Bible alone, then, be a rule of faith to those Christians who lived, and believed, and died in the first century, *before the Bible was written?* Had they no infallible rule of faith—for they had not the Bible? Or did Christ establish *two* rules, one for them and another for us? And if he did, show us the evidence of the fact, from the Bible alone.

II. The belief that the Bible alone is the infallible rule of faith, is not only an article, but a *fundamental* article of Protestantism. Now as it is the peculiar boast of Protestants that *they* believe nothing but what is contained in the Bible, I ask you to point the chapter and verse which says, that the "*Bible alone* is the infallible rule of faith established by Christ to guide us in matters of religion, and to determine disputes." If there is no such text, then it follows that the Protestant rule is a mere gratuitous assumption, unauthorized by the very document from which they profess to derive all their doctrine. This assumption is the pedestal on which their system stands, and I ask *what* supports the *pedestal itself?* You will tell me that "Scripture is profitable, for reproof," &c. I admit it, but between that and its being the only rule of faith there is a wide difference. You will tell me that the Jews were recommended by our Saviour, and the Bereans by his apostle to read the Scriptures; I admit it, but all that goes no farther than to prove that they are profitable, &c. St. Paul commends his disciple for having been acquainted with the Scripture from his childhood; I admit it, but St. Peter tells us that there are persons who wrest the Scriptures *to their own destruction*. Where then, I repeat the question, is the scriptural warrant, for making the "Bible alone" our rule of faith?

III. What do you mean by the Bible *alone?* Is it the Bible on the shelf of your library? Or is it the Bible as you peruse it? The former cannot be your rule of faith, and the latter is not the Bible alone, but you and the Bible together. Do you then, Rev. Sir, look upon yourself and the Bible together as constituting that infallible rule established by Christ?

IV. The Bible alone cannot be our rule of faith, because we are bound as Christians to believe that the Bible is an *authentic* and *inspired book*, and this I defy any one to prove *from the Bible alone*.

V. The Redeemer of the world never intended that the Bible alone should be the rule of faith—because, it was not universally known until the end of the fifth century, what books were to be regarded as inspired scripture—consequently the Christians of the preceding ages were destitute of that infallible rule which you admit was established by Christ; or if they possessed a rule at all, it certainly was not the Bible alone. Besides, consider the millions who believed in Christ and could not read, or could not possess themselves of a Bible, before printing was invented and since, were they on this account—are Protestants now who cannot read, destitute of a rule of faith?

VI. The Protestant rule of faith is not the infallible rule established by Christ—for, the object and end of that rule, was to " determine disputes in his church:" and it is an undeniable fact, that whilst this false rule has given rise to interminable controversy among the sects that have adopted it;—since the origin of Christianity, not so much as one single " dispute" has been *determined* by the Bible alone!

VII. The Bible alone, or the Bible operated upon by private interpretation, has given rise to all the heresies that exist. The Socinian, the Universalist, the Swedenborgian, have as good a right to understand its meaning as you. They protest against the doctrines of the Catholic church as you do: they have the same rule of faith, the Bible alone; and is theirs the infallible guide appointed by Christ? *His rule*, you admit was infallible; can you say as much of theirs? His rule was conservative of unity in his doctrine; is yours?

VIII. Do you not admit that in holding the Presbyterian doctrine you *may be* in error? If so, then you must admit the possibility of the Socinian's being right—especially as he follows the principle which you recommend to all, as the infallible rule of faith, established by Christ to guide us in matters of religion—the *Bible alone.* Now I ask, is it consistent for you to exclude the Socinian from the pale of Christianity, whilst *you are compelled to admit by your own rule*, that your belief *may* be false, and his *may* be true! I say you are compelled as a consistent Protestant, to make this admission—and I am prepared to prove it.

IX. If the Bible alone be the rule of faith, it must be the Bible according to each one's interpretation. Now, Rev. Sir, let me suppose a case to illustrate my meaning. I will imagine four Presbyterian clergymen reading the Bible—yourself being included in the number. The one becomes *persuaded* that Unitarianism is the doctrine of the Bible. The other that it is universal salvation;—the third that the doctrine of Swedenborg, is the true doctrine, according to Scripture,—I ask you whether these brethren would not be bound before God, as *honest men*, to quit your church and embrace respectively these different systems, which according to the Protestant rule of faith are found (*relatively to them*) in the Bible? I say they would—and I call on you for the proof of the contrary. But this is not all. What if a ray of divine light should break in upon your own mind—what if the scales of prejudice should fall from your eyes in the perusal of the sacred page, and you should see, or imagine you saw, the evidence that Christ established a church to which he communicated the attribute of infallibility, and that this church can be no other than,—shall I say it?—the Roman Catholic church—I ask again, under such a persuasion would you not yourself be bound *before God*, to embrace the doctrines of that church—even at the risk of being *called* an idolator. I say you would. I mention these various operations of *your rule* of

1*

faith, to show that the Redeemer never did establish—"to guide us in matters of religion and determine disputes in his church"—a principle which in application, is found to *work the destruction*, instead of the accomplishment of the ends for which it was instituted. For these reasons, then, I say it is impossible that the "infallible rule of faith" established by Christ should be the Bible alone. And consequently that the Protestant rule is false.

X. The doctrines of Christ were delivered to mankind, and believed as positive *truths*, or *facts*, about which there could be no ground for disputation. Now the object for which an "infallible rule of faith was established, by our Saviour, was to *guard these* eternal and unchangeable truths, or facts, from being confounded with, or lost in the erring speculations of men, who, he foresaw, would endeavour to supplant him, by substituting their *opinions* for his *doctrine*, and teaching error in his name. And this being the case, is it not as clear as noon-day, that the Protestant rule is not the rule established by Christ. Why? Because instead of teaching the doctrines of Christ as *positive truths, facts*, it merely submits them to its votaries as *opinions*, held by the *preacher*, agreed to by those who drew up the confession of faith, and *supposed to be contained in the Bible*. But supposed by whom? by the members of the sect. And supposed how long? just until a change comes over the spirit of private interpretation. Sir, the most vital tenet of Christianity, the divinity of Jesus Christ, if brought in *contact* with the Protestant rule of faith, will be dissolved by the very touch, into a matter of speculation and mere human opinion, whereas Jesus Christ never inculcated the belief of *an opinion*. Therefore, the Protestant rule of faith so far from being the fountain of infallible assurance as to what doctrines we should believe, is, on the contrary, the very parent of *uncertainty*, and cannot consequently be that "infallible rule established by Christ to *guide us* in matters of religion, and to determine disputes in his church."

I might still multiply these arguments, but it is unnecessary. The conclusions are fairly drawn, and I hold myself prepared to prove the premises and vindicate the reasoning whenever they are called in dispute. The question is not how many great and good men have been involved in the same delusion as yourself with regard to the rule of faith. The question is not how many brilliant minds have been warped, and turned aside from rectitude of judgment on the subject of religion, by adopting or inheriting from birth and education, a principle of guidance in religion, which principle, when *examined*, is found to be in itself repugnant to reason, unauthorized by Revelation, and in its practical consequences utterly subversive of the doctrines of Christianity, by reducing them to the uncertainty of mere opinion. But the question is, what is "that infallible rule established by Christ to guide us in matters of religion, for the purpose of determining disputes in the church of Christ,"—whose existence you have recognized?

The cause of truth requires that you should meet my arguments and refute them, article for article. What course you will adopt to accomplish this, it is difficult for me to conceive. But I am satisfied that our readers will not be contented with that sliding system of controversial tactics by which the opponents of the true religion, are accustomed to "slur the notes" of an argument, which they *cannot answer.* One part of this system is, to draw consequences from our language which we never intended, and then refute *their own* deductions, instead of taking up the *real* difficulty, and grappling with the reasons by which it is sustained. Another is, to appeal to *party feelings,* and touch the string of prejudice against the Catholic religion. I know that there are individuals, in every Protestant denomination, who are not to be operated on by any or all the resources of evasion. There are men of every denomination, who with a candid, honest, and impartial mind, will judge our arguments according to their intrinsic evidence—I ask no more.

The importance of determining the question of the rule of faith must be manifest to all who have reflected on the subject. In controversy, it is like the standard of weights and measures used in the disposal of merchandise; whenever the merchant uses *false standards,* he is certain to cheat his customers or himself. It is then, Rev. Sir, useless for you to condemn the doctrines of the Catholic church, until you shall have proved that the rule by which you judge them is the infallible rule. The doctrines of Christianity have been regarded by the Catholic church from the beginning, as fixed stars in the firmament of Revelation. She ascertained and certified their existence by the same infallible rule, (or if I be allowed to continue the figure,) the same telescope which she received from Jesus Christ himself, as the true, and only true medium of observation. By this means she knew them from the commencement, by this means she defined more clearly in her general councils, their existence, relative position, and influence, as occasion required,—and by this means also, she was enabled to detect the "new lights," which men in every age attempted to plant in her firmament. Thus it was, that amidst the contending elements of heresy, on the right hand and on the left, she has pursued the even tenour of her way, imparting to all nations, and to all generations, as she passed, the knowledge of the doctrines which her founder, Christ, commanded her to teach and preach to every creature. Some fifteen hundred years after her establishment, a few individuals rise up in the might of *private opinion,* and assert that the church had fallen into error, begin to teach new doctrines, and reject others which had always been believed. This act is what is called in history by the specious name of Reformation. At first they professed their willingness to abide by the decision of the church, touching their opinions, but as soon as the church, by applying the proper medium of infallible discernment, had pronounced their opinions to be contrary to the doctrines of Christ, as soon as she had refused to raise their "new lights" to the dignity of fixed stars in the heavens of belief—from that moment, it was determined that they should declare themselves independent of the church, and that they should fabricate a "telescope" of their own. They have done so, but neither could this determine what were the fixed and immutable doctrines of Christianity. The German Reformer wished all men to see as he saw—but the medium of observation which was correct at

Wirtemberg, was found to be deceitful at Geneva, and thus every man who felt himself called upon to labour in the Reformation, began by making his own telescope. And not only this; every individual is furnished with a pocket spy-glass—by which he has a right to judge the doctrine of his minister, and see whether it is conformable to the discoveries of the great telescope, contained in the "Confession of Faith"—to judge of the confession itself, whether it is conformable to the Bible—and to judge of the Bible, and see whether it is conformable to his—spy-glass—that is, *private interpretation.*

Thus, Rev. Sir, thus it was that you judged of the Catholic doctrines of Christianity in your letter which gave occasion to this controversy. You say it is our faith that is contrary to the doctrines of Christ: I say it is not our faith, but your spy-glass; and I protest against your mensuration of either Catholic or Protestant doctrine, until you shall have proved that your *instrument* of measurement is the "infallible rule of faith established by Christ," as expressed in our articles of agreement. Now the Westminster Confession of Faith, to which, some will contend that you pay greater deference than to the Bible itself, declares that "the infallible rule of interpretation of Scripture is the Scripture itself." But be it remembered that this is the enactment not of the Bible, but of a number of men, assembled at Westminster, Anno Domini 1647, by order of Parliament, *to make a religion* for the united kingdoms of Great Britain and Ireland. And I leave it to any man of common sense, if this rule of interpretation, which they call infallible, is not a mere sophism—seeing that the Scripture to be interpreted, and the Scripture *by which* it is to be interpreted, are both *equally* subjected to the pocket-glass of the reader's private interpretation. Would it not be absurd to say that the laws of this commonwealth expound their own meaning, without a judge? The same Confession of Faith says, that "the supreme judge by which all controversies of religion are to be determined, can be no other but the Holy Spirit speaking in the Scriptures." But this is only begging the question, and does not reach the difficulty:—Seeing that the subject of dispute turns precisely on this question, *what does the Holy Spirit say?*—"speaking in the Scriptures."

You will observe, Rev. Sir, that I have said nothing on the subject of the Catholic rule of faith—which, however, cannot but be considerably, though indirectly strengthened, if my arguments against the Protestant principle cannot be met by evidences stronger on the other side, than those I have put forth. It only remains for you to show that the Protestant rule of faith, is that "infallible rule established by Christ to guide us in matters of religion, and to *determine disputes* in his church."

The Scriptures are indeed the inspired word of God; as such they have been guarded and vindicated by the church. God forbid that I should ascribe to *them*, the errors of those who claim to walk under their guidance. The only object I have had in view, is to show that the rule of faith adopted by Protestants, is a rule which will lead infallibly to the abuse of the Scriptures, and to the destruction of the revealed doctrines of Christianity. The Bible alone; in other words, private interpretation may serve the purpose of the Presbyterian against the Catholic, but it will equally serve the purpose of the Socinian against both.

In the course of this letter I have spoken with entire freedom of the principles of Protestant doctrine. If any one should be offended at this, I beg such a person to remember that you invited me to the discussion; and that, having accepted the invitation, it would not be generous to find fault with me for speaking the truth, and the whole truth, provided I give facts and reasoning to prove that I may speak *nothing but the truth.*

Yours, very respectfully,
Jno. Hughes.

P. S. In your last letter, published under the head of private correspondence, you introduced several topics which are certainly foreign to the occasion of this controversy. The first is, quotations from your letter in the Christian Advocate, to show that you were obliged to answer the difficulties presented to you in the Baltimore manuscript. Now, in reference to this, I have already stated that I professed to know nothing of the matter, until your letter published in August and September made it *public, that you had challenged,* "Priests and Bishops," to this discussion, the whole field of controversy.

The second is, that you represent me as having, in a letter addressed to the editor of the Philadelphian, arraigned the clergy of some half a dozen of protestant denominations for manifesting a spirit of retreat during the Cholera. This may, of course, enlist the feelings of those clergymen against me as a public accuser; but I appeal to the letter itself, and to the recollection of this community, to say whether I preferred any charge of my own against them. On the contrary, I took up the charges as they had been preferred, *by a correspondent of the Philadelphian, signed a "Presbyterian,"* against the Protestant clergy, for abandoning their posts at such a time. It was in the act of replying to these charges of his correspondent, by the editor, that the unfortunate insinuation was made against the moral purity of the Catholic clergy, which, after all, may have been a lapsus pennæ. This being the case, how could you represent me as the person framing accusations against the clergymen of all the denominations mentioned somewhat ostentatiously, in your last letter? Now, however, I assert, that the testimony of the physicians who attended in the Cholera hospitals, and who periled *their lives* in the duties of their profession, would go far to establish the charge as suggested by a "Presbyterian."

Lastly, you take great pains to show in all your letters how much you have to do, and how much leisure, "sanctuary quietude," remains on my hands, intimating thereby the advantages which my situation gives me over you in the conducting of this controversy. Be assured, Rev. Sir, that if I thought the public could be interested in the detail of my avocations, I also, could make out a tolerable list of duties; enough perhaps to turn the scales of comparison. But to make your mind easy on the subject of your official occupations, I beg to state that I am prepared, if God give me health, to sustain the Catholic

B

argument against any or all the clergymen of the Synod or General Assembly, provided he or they *write with your signature, and adhere to the rules*. I make this remark not by way of boasting, but because you allude to, and dwell, as I think, too emphatically on the multitude of your official duties. My confidence is not in my own abilities, that would be a poor and pitiful reliance, but it is in my cause—*truth*, and her eternal evidences.

JNO. HUGHES.

RULE OF FAITH.

New-York, February 2d, 1833.

To the Rev. John Hughes,

Sir,—It is one of my principles neither to seek nor to shun controversy. Of the origin of this discussion the public will judge; and I am willing to abide by its impartial decision. In the work of the ministry, it has been and still is my happiness, to enjoy the most peaceable and pleasant communion with my brethren of those denominations of Christians, whom Protestants are accustomed to call evangelical. As controversy is now clearly my duty, I think myself happy that it relates to a system, against which all such Protestants are united, and with whose rise or final overthrow, in the opinion of them all, the most precious hopes, and the highest interests of men and nations, as well as the supreme honour of Jesus Christ, are inseparably blended.

And now in the outset, I would inquire by what right you say, "In this whole controversy, every inch of ground which is not disputed by you shall be looked upon as so much given up to the cause of Catholicity and truth?" Is it then presupposed that you are the representative of the universal church in this matter? Is the *residuum* of truth with you?—But passing this, I only remark that, whatever you may arrogate, I shall confine myself as far as possible, to prominent points, and hope to show so clearly your fallacy in them, that what may be left, will not be worth contending for. I shall of course pursue my own order in replying to your strictures and queries. But where you repeat, I shall not be expected to answer twice the same thing, and where you confuse the question before us for want of order, you must not expect me to follow your example.

The first point for discussion is the Rule of Faith. It is agreed that "there is an infallible rule of faith established by Christ, to guide us in matters of religion, for the purpose of determining disputes in the church of Christ." I regret that you did not define your own rule of faith. Ours is "The Word of God as contained in the Scriptures of the Old and New Testaments." We own no judge of controversies but God. Your rule of faith is "the Old and New Testaments, with the books called Apocrypha, as contained in the old Vulgate Latin edition, and unwritten traditions interpreted by a visible, infallible judge of controversies, according to the unanimous consent of the fathers." (See Council of Trent, 4th Sess. Decree on Tradition and the Scriptures; and Creed of Pope Pius IV.)

You introduce your attack on our rule, by the broad assumption, that the principle of private interpretation has been the cause of all the divisions, heresies, and other evils, which distract and weaken the church of Christ. You bring against it 2 Pet. i. 20, "No prophecy of the Scripture is of any private interpretation," and you say, "Now the Protestant rule of faith utterly reverses this declaration, and makes *all* Scripture of *every* private interpretation." In this you follow your standards, certainly; for the Catechism of Pius IV. refers to the same passage of Scripture in answer to the question, "Why may not every particular Christian have liberty to interpret the Scripture according to his own private judgment?" &c. &c. The exposition given by the Pope is an *infallible* commentary on *Peter's* Epistle. But what says the passage. "Knowing this first that no prophecy of the Scripture is of any private interpretation. For the prophecy came not in old time by the will of man, but holy men of God spake as they were moved by the Holy Ghost."—(vs. 20, 21. English translation.) Here we remark, 1. That Peter tells the *people*, in a previous verse, that they do well to take heed unto the more sure word of prophecy. 2. It is important to be noticed by you that it is the *prophecy* of the Scripture, not *the Scripture*, that is obscure. 3. Should your interpretation be correct, the apostle is made to argue thus—"The Scriptures are infallibly revealed or inspired, and ye do well that ye take heed to them, therefore they are obscure, too obscure for private explanation." A strange inference, and one forcibly against yourself—for you contend for the *clearness* of your church's interpretations, because they are *infallibly guided by God*. 4. The vulgate is the only authorized version in your church. Yet you and the catechism of your church, follow here, our English translation! The reason is obvious. It *appears* to favour you. The vulgate is "Prophetia Scripturæ propria interpretatione, non fit." "The prophecy of Scripture is not made by a man's own interpretation;" or "no prophecy of Scripture is its own interpreter"—if you please. Here the interpretation refers to *prophecy*—and to the *prophets*, not to Scripture at large, nor to the *reader*, at all. As if he had said—Prophets do not prophecy their own inventions, nor are their predictions to be taken singly; or in an insulated way—but every prophecy is dictated by the Holy Ghost as a part of a whole, as a link in the great chain of prophecies. And yet an infallible judge, followed by a distinguished priest, would make this passage go against "private interpretation" of the Bible! It is almost as defective a use of Scripture as one once made, (he was a Protestant,) who was arrested in the act of striking another, by the timely recollection of Paul's injunction to Timothy, "*Lay hands suddenly on no man.*" It is here remarkable that the Apostle Peter, claimed by you as the I. Roman Pontiff, in his last epistle, bidding farewell to the church before his decease, and looking down with a shepherd's love, and a prophet's eye into future ages, while giving an infallible rule for determining the sense of prophecies, (See Horsely on this place) says not one word about an infallible judge. Yet surely had there been one, there could not have been so fit a man, or so fit a place to make it known.

In the course of your remarks, you seem to claim merit to your rule, from particular difficulties charged by you on the Protestant rule, yet yours may be chargeable with the same, or equal, or still greater difficulties. You profess to bring one of these formally to view in the 10th head; yet as this is a sort of subtle thread that runs through your argument, let us cut it here, and thus disentangle the subject from that error. Take then for example the charge of *uncertainty*, brought against us at the close of that 10th head, as follows, "The Protestant rule of faith, so far from being the fountain of infallible assurance, as to what doctrines we should believe, is on the contrary the very parent of *uncertainty*, and cannot consequently be that "infallible rule established by Christ, to *guide us* in matters of religion, and to determine disputes in his church."

Now let us look at your rule. If you have an infallible, visible udge of controversy, how do you get at the proof of his infallibility? Is he not appointed by Christ? You say he is.—Then you find the proof of it in the sacred Scriptures of course. How then do you interpret those Scriptures, in discovering that there is such a judge? Not infallibility, for the existence of any infallible judge is yet to be proved. And as regards his existence you are left, as you must admit, to decide from Scripture by your own unaided reason. Your judgment on the subject is formed upon the same principles as ours. Can you then claim any more certainty for your opinion than we for ours? If you can, show it, if not, your argument against our rule, if sound, destroys your own.

Again, when you are satisfied by private, fallible judgment, that there is an infallible judge, you must seek the true church, for in it alone is *he* to be found. Then how do you identify the true church? By the word of God, as you acknowledge. You find out the *notes* of the true church. Of these notes Bellarmine numbers fifteen.—These are all to be proved from Scripture. By whom? By fallible men, (for the infallible judge is yet to be found;) by private interpretation; for the public oracle is yet to be discovered after you have searched out from the word of God the notes of the true church, and applied them to find that oracle. Then having found him you go back to ask of him, what the word of God means.—Now is not this uncertain, and fallible? Yet this is the foundation on which your system of infallibility rests. It is more uncertain than our rule, by one remove. We go directly to the Bible for all our doctrines, and there stop. But you being fallible, take the Bible to find the infallible judge; and then return with him to learn what the Bible means. But when you have got the decrees, confessions, bulls, &c. of this infallible judge, are they better or more clear than our Bible? Can your judge be more lucid than our Lord and Saviour Jesus Christ? And after you have gotten these infallible judgments do not they also need an interpreter as much as the Bible? So palpable is the defect here, that your writers own that you have no infallibility but only strong probability, "PRUDENTIAL MOTIVES," and "MORAL CERTAINTY" in finding out the true church, and the infallible judge in her. The Rev. Mr. M'Guire in the "discussion," &c. page 134, owns "that the catholic has only to exercise his private judgment upon the Scripture-proofs of the authority of the church; that once established, the catholic is enabled to make an act of faith upon divine authority." Once established. But how establish it? Ah, here is the fatal gap! A house without a foundation! If "private judgment" must find out your infallible judge why may it not also find out, what we need to guide us to God? May we not as certainly determine the authority of the Bible and its true meaning, as you the notes of the church, and the infallible church? May we not be as certain of "the divinity of Jesus Christ" as you of the true church? May we not rest as securely on the infallibility of this great and only head of the church, and of his inspired apostles, as you on the infallibility of your judge of controversies? If, without infallibility, you can reach an infallibile judge, may we not without it also reach certainty and safety?

I. But though there are points of sophistry which I had wished to expose on the threshhold, I will, for want of space, pass to meet your objections. The first is " the *Bible* is the Protestant rule of faith. But the Bible was not written until more than half a century after Christ's death—therefore the Bible *alone* could not have been the only rule of faith established by Christ." (The reader is referred to the entire paragraph.) Do you mean then to say that the Bible was not written until fifty years after Christ's death? A *very small part* of the New Testament was not. But it is a strong figure of speech to say the Bible was not written. The Old Testament canon was sanctioned by Christ and his apostles. Before the New Testament was written, and during the continuance of Christ and his apostles on earth, the Old Testament with their inspired instructions, whether spoken or written, attested by miracles, was the infallible rule of faith. Before the death of the last Apostle, the entire New Testament was written. Now you will hardly say that the paper, ink, type, lids, &c. &c. of the Bible, *make* the Revelation, though they *record* it. If not, then all who had the Old Testament and the inspired instructions of Christ and his apostles, had (essentially) our rule of faith—and if you prove yourself inspired by the same miracles they gave, we will take you too for our infallible guides. But they were to have no such successors, and their writings were intended to preserve and perpetuate their infallible instructions.— Hence, either the Apostles did not *write* the same doctrines which Christ and they *spoke*, or else we have the same rule of faith with those who died before all the New Testament was written.

II. You call for the "Scriptural warrant for making the Bible alone the rule of faith" and require " chapter and verse." You concede that " the Scriptures are indeed the inspired word of God and as such have been guarded and vindicated by the Church." What then are the Scriptures? A revelation from God to man, written by inspired men—for the use of the race—containing infinitely important communications in which all are interested, addressed to the reason, conscience and affections of men—and as clearly intelligible (or will you dispute this?) as other books.

What then can these Scriptures be but our *rule of faith*, and, as they are inspired, an infallible rule? And if no specific statement to the contrary be found in them, they must of course be regarded as the *only* one. Here then I remark, 1. The presumption from the admitted fact of its being a revelation is, that the Bible is the only infallible rule of faith. 2. If it be not so, it is the duty of those who deny it to prove their statement. You claim a *prescriptive right*, to dictate to man what this revelation *means*, and what they shall *believe*. This is " a dominion over their faith" that Paul the inspired author of a large part of the New Testament, disclaims— (2 Cor. i. 24.) It is a claim abhorrent from reason, at war with the rights of conscience, and a usurpation of the prerogative of God.

If not, you ought in all propriety to prove it, being a most unusual claim. 3. The only adequate proof that can be given of it will be a miracle—convincing the very senses as well as reasons of men, that you have a power from God to rule our faith, and if it need be, *add new Scriptures* (see John iii. 3.)—I am happy to know that your church concedes this, by her *pretended miracles*, while her utter failure to work them explodes all claim to infallibility. Christ has thus attested his mission and his claims: so did his inspired apostles. You claim to succeed them in these respects. Then give the same proof of your claim. Until you do, the world cannot admit the pretension. It is absurd and most presumptuous. 4. But what proof have you from *the Bible*, " chapter and verse," of such a right, viz. " that your church has in her, a human infallible judge of controversies, that the books called Apocrypha are part of the word of God, that " unwritten traditions" are of equal authority with the Bible, and that all these, " interpreted according to the unanimous consent of the Fathers," make the true rule of faith ?—Produce it, " chapter and verse, or else your rule is a mere assumption."

Here we might safely rest this head, for you are bound up inextricably.—But 5. We have proof, " chapter and verse," of what you require, and though not *ipsissima verba*, the very words you prescribe, yet equivalent words. See then, Isaiah viii. 20.—" To the law and to the testimony, if they speak not according to them, it is because there is no light in them." 2 Tim. iii. 15—17. " And that from a child thou hast known the Holy Scriptures, which are able to make thee wise unto salvation, through faith which is in Jesus Christ. All Scripture is given by inspiration of God, and is profitable for doctrine, for reproof, for correction, for instruction in righteousness, that the man of God may be perfect, thoroughly furnished unto all good works."—You have given us a garbled extract from this passage, comprised in only *four words*. Here you have it in full. Here is 1. The Holy Scripture, all of which is inspired, and therefore infallible. 2. It is able to make wise to salvation—without any *human* judge or help, through faith in Christ Jesus. 3. It answers all the ends of a divine revelation, " is profitable," and adequate "for *doctrine*," " for reproof," or confutation as to all sin, error, &c. &c. " for correction," " for instruction in righteousness." Is any thing wanting here? 4. By it the minister of Christ, " the man of God," as well as the private Christian, " may be perfect," " THOROUGHLY FURNISHED" without any but the Holy Spirit's teaching, " unto all good works." 5. Timothy was *assured* of all this; and needing no *change*, " should *continue* in these things." If this does not constitute an infallible rule, for all uses, whether " determining disputes," or " guiding us in matters of religion," I am at a loss to imagine what does. Here then the word of God is the " very standard" which you justly say, it is so important to settle; and it is fully and infallibly sufficient as a rule of faith.

III. A rule of faith supposes a God to give and a mind to receive and use it. My God, my Bible, and my mind are therefore supposed, in my use of this rule. Now for your argument. It is profound indeed! It runs thus:—The Bible alone, " on the shelf," is *one.* A man reads it: that makes *two;* therefore the Bible *alone* is no rule of faith. And again :—The reader is fallible—the reader and the Bible make the rule of Protestants, therefore the rule is fallible! Such logic, dear Sir, will not soon assert your claim to infallibility.

IV. Under this head you say that the Bible alone cannot be the rule of faith, because we are all bound as Christians to believe that the Bible is an *authentic* and *inspired* book, and you defy any one to prove this from the Bible. So are we required to believe in the existence of a God, yet you do not go to the Bible for the proof of this great doctrine. It is *pre-supposed* from the very existence of things. Just so, the authenticity of the sacred volume is assumed at the outset, when it is admitted as a revelation and a rule of faith. And yet you demand a proof of its being authentic, &c. from itself, or deny its being the alone rule of faith! Suppose an infidel were to argue thus with you: " Your revelation demands of you a belief of a Deity, but by the Bible alone the fact of his existence cannot be proved, therefore your revelation is defective." You would laugh him to scorn. How then will Protestants regard your application of the same reasoning to overturn their rule of faith? Admitting it to be, as you do, a Revelation from God, you ask for that proof of its authenticity, &c. which is inseparably connected with and presupposed in the very existence of a revelation! Your latent meaning in all that paragraph is, that we need the church to tell us what is Bible and what is not. Thus, by the true church, you would prove the authenticity of the Bible. And how do you verify the true church? By the marks—by the Bible. You will prove the church by the Bible, and then the Bible by the church; and thus your argument will run in a constant circle, proving nothing but its own absurdity.

V. Here you argue, (see the head,) that it was not universally known, until the end of the fifth century, what books were to be regarded as inspired Scriptures,—therefore, before that time, there was no infallible rule, or if there was, it was not the Bible alone. I reply, if there had been an infallible living judge of controversy in the church at this time, who was authorized as you say your church is, to settle what books were "inspired Scripture," then how comes it that it was not universally known, which they were for five hundred years? But if there were no such infallible judge, what becomes of your rule of faith? You say in the 4th head, " we are bound as Christians to believe the Bible is authentic and inspired," and again, that " the doctrines of Christianity have been regarded by the Catholic Church, from the beginning, as fixed stars in the firmament of revelation." " She has ascertained and certified their existence, from the commencement," &c.; therefore it follows, that the church knew from the beginning which books were authentic, and taught (as one of her doctrines) which those books were. When you say then, they were not known, you contradict yourself. If you cover your retreat under the word " universally," then either the church concealed what she knew, or wherever the church was known, this was known. But I deny that there was this uncertainty about the canon of Scripture until the end of the fifth century. Some contend that it was settled by the apostle John. Origen, A. D. 210, Eusebius in 315, Athanasius in 315, Cyril, 340, Council of Laodicea, 364, &c. &c. give catalogues of the inspired books. Most of them give an exact catalogue of the New Testament. Some who were certain as to the rest, were doubtful only as to four of these many books. In the mean time, the churches had "all the books;" and these doubts of some, did not make it less truly the real and full rule. How strange, then, that you should speak of the Bible at large, as uncertain until near the end of the fifth century, when all the books of the Old, and all of the New Testament, except four, were certainly known before the death of the Apostle John. As to those who lived before the "art of printing was invented," and those who "cannot read," it is an unworthy quibble; for I suppose you will not deny, that in each case, they could as well understand the fallible interpretation of Scripture by a Protestant preacher, as the fallible interpretation of your decrees of councils, bulls, &c. by a Romanist?

VI. and VII. You say the Bible alone, or the Bible and private interpretation, have settled no disputes, but promoted them. They have also promoted heresy. But the infallible rule of faith is designed to settle disputes and promote unity. Therefore the Bible alone cannot be the infallible rule of faith. Poor Bible! what a transgressor thou hast been! How right was it for the Council of Trent to lay thee on the shelf! To all you say on this point, I answer, your rule has worked worse than ours, to say the least, for you have either to put an end to disputes by force, and so wanted not a rule but a ruler, or driven off church after church, and nation after nation from you. How did you *settle* the dispute with the Waldenses and Albigenses? How with the Greek Church, and how with the Reformers? Again, you argue from the *abuse* of a thing against its perfection: now when we say the Bible is an infallible rule of faith, and competent to settle disputes, we mean that it is a sufficient, not a compulsory means—nor do we say that it is incapable of abuse. Will you say this of your rule? Has it not been abused? When a rule is abused, it is the fault of men, not of the Bible. This you admit, when you say that an infallible rule must "give to those who abide by its decision an infallible certainty," &c. So we say.— But what if they will not abide? Is there any remedy? I know of none but the Inquisition, and the like. If you are willing to take this ground, you are welcome to it. Once more—your argument would lead to this, that as no rule which can be abused is infallible, and some men will abuse the best rules, therefore a rule cannot be infallible.

Your VIIIth and IXth heads are only changes hung on the same fallacious reasoning exposed above. (The reader will please examine them.) The sum of the argument is this—"Do you not admit, that in holding Presbyterian doctrine, you may be in error; if so, what confidence have you in the infallibility of your guides— then you are compelled to admit, by your own rule, that you may be wrong, and the Unitarian right." I answer, do you not admit that *you* may be wrong in *finding out* your infallible church? Then what certainty is there, and what confidence have you in the infallibility of your guides? Again—Joannah Southcoate claimed to be infallible—and so the Shakers: now, as they use your rule of faith no less than Unitarians ours, may they not be *right*, and you wrong? Yet on such logic hangs your argument.

In your IXth head you *apply* the above. You suppose four Presbyterian preachers, (and include me in the number,) *one* becomes Unitarian—another Swedenborgian—and I, happy honoured I, become a Papist, by light breaking in upon my dark soul. Now we must of course disperse, and join these various people. Hence, as under our rule we *may* do this, that rule "*works destruction*," and is not infallible. Let me consummate this felicitous illustration. We are told in Genebrard's Chronicles, A. D. 904, "that for 150 years, fifty Popes had been apostate, rather than apostolical." There is then no lack of subjects. For the first, take Pope Liberius, who became Arian; then Pope Honorius, a Heretic, who was condemned by a council; Pope Marcellinus, an Idolater. You, Sir, may be the fourth—with your faith unshaken, and on the high road to the Vatican and the Triple crown. Now ought not one of these to join the Arians; another the Swedenborgians; another the Gentile Idolaters; and would not this " work destruction?" Yet this is the operation of your rule, or at least it is in spite of your rule, which must therefore, on your own reasoning, be defective. I could apply your argument to your councils too; but I forbear.

X. The argument on certainty, I have answered in the introduction.

And now, Sir, having waded through the queries, which you have so magisterially propounded to me, I would propose to your consideration the following difficulties, to which I also expect a prompt reply.

1. You prove your church infallible as a judge of controversies, by true notes or marks which are very numerous. They embrace sanctity of doctrine, agreement in doctrine with the primitive church, &c. &c. It presupposes much knowledge of Scripture to find them out. Now you must find all these notes, to get at the true church; and *in her to find the infallible judge.* The question then is, are you infallible in finding out these notes? Is it not by private, or at least *fallible* judgment? Then as your infallibility is built on fallible judgment, is it not an empty name, and a presumptuous pretension?

2. As to the judge of controversies, you say in the eighth page, " would it not be absurd to say, that the laws of this commonwealth expound their own meaning, without a judge?" Now let us look at this illustration. The judge in the commonwealth must be of neither party. But your judge of controversies is always a party in the case, unless you contend with some, that he is *above law.* The civil judge binds not the conscience; for though he deprive me of my property, the law does not require me to *think* with him; but your judge *lords* it over the *conscience,* which none can rightly do but God. The civil judge is easily found out; but can you identify your infallible judge? Is it the Pope, or a general council, or both united, or the church at large? What would a civil judge be worth, whom nobody could find?

3. You say in your second page, that your church is "not hostile to the dissemination and perusal of the Holy Scriptures." Yet the 4th Rule of the "Expurgatory Index," under the authority of the Council of Trent, and the Pope, says in so many words, "Inasmuch as it is manifest from experience, that if the Holy Bible translated into the vulgar tongue, be indiscriminately allowed to every one, the temerity of men will cause more evil than good to arise from it"—and it goes on to say, that permission may be given in writing by bishops or inquisitors, to such as priests or confessors recommend, *to read the Bible*, if translated by Catholic (Roman) authors.—"*But if any one have the presumption to read or possess it, without such a written permission, he shall not receive absolution, until he has delivered up such Bible*," &c. Booksellers selling to men without a license were liable to penalties. *The liberty of the press* also is directly violated in that same document. Not only in Rome, but " in other places," the vicar or inquisitor or other authorised person must examine, approve, and permit a book to be published! Does this seem like friendship to the discussion of the Scriptures and of general knowledge?

4. Your living judge of controversies being infallible, your system ought to be uniform and unchangeable, admitting of no new doctrines and no contradictions—and this you allow. when you say, " Your doctrines have been from the beginning, as fixed stars in the firmaments of Revelation," and the church " knew them," by the infallible rule of judgment "*from the beginning.*" I give only a few examples of heresy and variation, and innovation in doctrine, to disprove this assertion.

In the fourth century, *Liberius*, the Pope, signed the Arian creed—and the great body of the clergy *became Arian*. Hilary called his confession the "Arian Perfidy." Arianism was sanctioned by the Papal Church, that is by the Pontiff, a general council, and the collective clergy. I need not refer to Honorius, who, in the seventh century, was an acknowledged and condemned heretic.

As to *the Pope's supremacy*, there are no less than three systems in your church. Some contend for a mere presidency; such are Du Pin, Rigathius, Filaster, Gibert, and Paolo. The councils of Pisa, Constance and Basil, sustained this view. Others make him an unlimited monarch, civil and ecclesiastical. This is the Italian school, and the Jesuits agree with them. The councils of Florence, Lateran, and Trent, patronized this system. Another system set him by the side of God. The canon law in the gloss, denominates the Pope, ' the Lord God.' Bellarmine says, [4. 5.] " Si papa erraret, præcipiendo vitia," &c. " If the Pope should err in commanding vices, and prohibiting virtues, the church would be bound to believe vices to be virtues, and virtues to be vices." These views were largely patronized.

As to *the seat of infallibility* in the church, there is neither union nor uniformity. There are no less than four systems on this subject, stoutly advocated in different ages, by writers, popes and councils; and your church is not now united upon it. One system places infallibility in the Pope; another in a general council; a third in the two united; and the fourth in the church collective.

You are not agreed among yourselves even *which are the general councils.* As to image worship, there are three parties. (Bellarmine 2. 20.) One party allows the use of them,—another the lower worship—a third, the real divine worship of them. The council of Nice, says Bellarmine, agreed with the second. The ups and downs of images in the church, for a whole century, I need not here detail.

As to *the valiauty of oaths.*—The third general council of the Lateran, 16th Canon, says, " An oath contrary to ecclesiastical utility is perjury—not an oath." Labb. 13. 426. The 4th Laterean, a general council, in A. D. 1215, 3d canon, " freed the subjects of such sovereigns as embraced heresy, from their fealty." Labb. 13. 934. The guilty celebrity of the Council of Constance, I need not dwell on.—Delahogue, Tract. de Euch. p. 214. art. 2, says, that *denying the cup to the laity* did not begin until the 12th century. *Now,* it is an approved doctrine of the Church of Rome.

Lastly—In the letter from Bononia, by the three bishops to Pope Julius the 3d., Sept. 20th, 1553, " on the way to establish the Church of Rome," are these confessions : " This is a downright Lutheran maxim, that it is not lawful to depart in the least degree from the things that were used among the Apostles. But who of us doth not every day often depart from them? Indeed in our churches we scarcely retain the least shadow of doctrine and discipline which flourished in the times of the Apostles ; but have brought in quite another of our own." (More of this hereafter.) See Preservative against Popery, vol. 1. p. 88.

Amidst such heresies, variations, corruptions, and novelties of doctrine and worship, where is your infallible judge of controversies?

5. Your rule of faith requires you, as your oath of office binds you, to interpret " unwritten traditions" and the Bible, according to the " unanimous consent of the fathers." Now, I ask, is there any such unanimous consent? If not, how can your rule be applied ? If there be, will you make it appear?

6. The Apocryphal books, as we call them, were excluded from the canon of the Jews. They were not recognised as canonical by Christ or his apostles ; nor by the *earliest* fathers. They do not claim to be inspired—they are unworthy of credit, except as ecclesiastical histories. Yet you introduce them into the canon ; what proof have you of their claim to this?

7. What right has the Church of Rome to make " unwritten traditions" a part of the rule of faith ? Why have they been left unwritten if they are known? Can she trace this mass of human inventions up to the teachings of the Lord and his inspired apostles ? If not, how can you require us to believe them ? Why not record them, that we may know them, and that they may be preserved ?

8. Your rule of faith usurps the prerogative of Jesus Christ, " sitting in the temple of God," " as God." For God alone can dictate what we are to believe. He tells us, " to call no *man* master." " If we *must* believe what the church believes," then we are no longer at liberty to inquire, and think, or even believe ; for belief is on *evidence,* not *dictation.*

9. Your judge has taught, as infallible doctrines, things which vio-

late the *natural senses*, and thus undermine the evidence from miracles in support of revelation itself—as for example—transubstantiation. It is also abhorrent to true religion not to say every reverent feeling, that a priest can make his God, then sacrifice him, then give him to the people, then worship him, and then eat him.

10. Finally, the system which includes an infallible living judge of controversies, to guide us in matters of religion, and to regulate not only faith, but worship and morals, ought not to be corrupt in its tendency or tolerate corruptions in morals and manners. Now if I can show this to be the tendency of your rule in operation, it must prove the rule not only vicious but ruinous, and therefore not infallible. I will refer you to a memorable letter written to Paul 3d, by nine distinguished prelates of Rome, England, Brechdusium, Verona, &c. &c., shortly before the Reformation, on the state of the Church and the need of Reformation. They mention abuses as follows—Ordaining uneducated youth, of evil manners—Simony, as being general—Pastors withdrawing from their flocks, which were intrusted to hirelings—Clergymen guilty of sins and then by exemption from penalty—The orders of the *Religious* so degenerate that monasteries ought to be abolished—Sacrileges committed with the nuns in most monasteries—Rome especially corrupt, though the "mother of the church, and the mistress of churches." "*In fine*," they say, "*The name* of Christ is forgotten by the nations, and by us the clergy, and the vengeance of God which we deserve is ready to fall on us!" I ask if this be the *fruit* of infallibility, or could be patronized by a living infallible judge?

Now, sir, if you will apply your telescope to the Roman heavens, and narrowly survey the permutations of the "stars" you boast of as fixed," you will find many a shifting planet, and many a star, which in apostolic days rose upon the church, quenched from your horizon.

And these are the things which led "those few individuals" as you call them, to assert that your church was corrupt and needed reform. And was there not a cause?

It sounds not a little strange, in the light of these facts, which mark the growing corruption and successive collapse of your *unchangeable* church to hear you talking of the "Presbyterian church falling apart, under the pressure of private interpretation!" Under what is yours falling?—We are willing to trust the Presbyterian church in the hands of Jesus Christ. Truth and liberty is her blessed banner.

Yours, respectfully,

JOHN BRECKINRIDGE

CONTROVERSY. No. III.

RULES.

The undersigned agreeing to have an amicable discussion of the great points of religious controversy, between Protestants and Roman Catholics, do hereby bind themselves to the observance of the following rules :

1. The parties shall write and publish, alternately, in the weekly religious papers called the Presbyterian, and a Roman Catholic paper, to be furnished by the first of January. It being understood that the communications shall be published after the following plan :—One party opening the first week, the other party replying the next week, and every piece to be republished in the immediately succeeding number of the Roman Catholic paper. The communications not to exceed four columns of the Presbyterian, nor to continue beyond six months, without consent of parties.

2. The parties agree that there is an infallible Rule of Faith established by Christ, to guide us in matters of religion, for the purpose of determining disputes in the Church of Christ.

3. They moreover agree, that after giving their views of the Rule of Faith, they shall proceed to discuss the question, "Is the Protestant religion, the religion of Christ ?"

4. The parties agree respectively, to adhere strictly to the subject of discussion, for the time being, and to admit no second question, until the first shall have been exhausted. Each party shall be the judge when he is done with a subject, and shall be at liberty to occupy his time with a second topic, when he is done with the first, leaving to the other party the liberty of continuing to review the abandoned topic, as long as he shall choose, subject, however, to be answered, if he introduce new matter.

5. Mr. Hughes to open the discussion, and Mr. Breckinridge to follow, according to the dictates of his own judgment.

JOHN BRECKINRIDGE,
JNO. HUGHES.

Philadelphia, December 14th, 1832.

RULE OF FAITH.

Philadelphia, February 14, 1833.

To the Rev. John Breckinridge,

Rev. Sir,—On the evening of the 9th instant, I had the pleasure of receiving your reply, after a lapse of eighteen days from that, on which I placed my first letter in the hands of the Editor, with a request that he would furnish you with a copy as soon as possible. Our readers were generally disappointed at your not answering in order, according to the time prescribed in our rules. It was admitted, however, that you had *reasons* for procrastinating : and many of those, who have never reflected on the difficulty of the task, accounted for the delay, by supposing that you meant to overwhelm your adversary in the energy of the onset—that you would throw the whole strength of your cause, and of your mind into your first paper, and thus ensure a prompt and triumphant vindication of the Protestant rule of faith—a vindication, which would not only refute, but exterminate, all the arguments that had been, or that might be raised against it. For my own part I had no such anticipations. But I must confess, that I did expect something more energetic and to the purpose. I have read your letter carefully; and although you attempt to neutralize my reasoning by recriminations and glosses, which are ingenious enough, still I am utterly unable to discover any thing, that reaches the difficulty, or approaches the character of manly argument. Before I proceed to review those portions of it which relate to the subject of discussion "for the time being," (see rules,) I shall make a few observations on certain passages, which are, in my opinion, objectionable, on other grounds, besides their being foreign to the present topic of controversy.

The first is your use of the words "Papist and Romanist." We learn from history, that the ancient Athenian laws specified neither prohibition, nor penalty, for the crime of *parricide:*—the legislator believing, that the commission of it was impossible. Influenced by a similar supposition, it never occurred to me, in fixing the laws of this controversy, to stipulate for the use of *courteous language.* Your official standing, the clerical character, and the courtesies of the age in which we live, were *pledges*, in my mind, that you would use no other. I had, however, in conversation, informed you, that the appellation by which we choose to be called, is Catholics, or Roman Catholics;—and I do not perceive what *good* feelings are to be gratified on your side, by *preferring* to either of these, an epithet known to be offensive, and which adds nothing, either to sense or argument. Besides, you should, in my opinion, recollect, that for nearly a hundred years past, the world has laughed at the ludicrous picture of Presbyterianism, drawn by the Protestant pencils of Dean Swift and the author of Hudibras. If I wished to employ unpalatable epithets, I have only to consult their pages. But they are useless to any cause, and I allude to the matter, merely to advise the reader, that I shall receive the appellation of " Papist, Romanist, &c." at your hand, with the express understanding, that they are *nicknames*.

The next passage, which I consider you to have treated in a manner unbecoming the pen of a clergyman, as well as the importance of the subject, is that in which you allude to transubstantiation. I do not mean *now* to violate the order of proceeding, by saying one word in proof of that doctrine. It is a doctrine, however, of great antiquity; admitted even by Protestant writers, to be older, by many hundred years, than the sect or denomination of which you are a minister: it is a doctrine, sacred with the vast majority of the Christian world at the present day, and which *they* believe to be as old as Christianity; —and I submit to your own reflection, and to that of our readers, whether such a doctrine was not entitled to a more grave and dignified notice, than that which you have been pleased to take of it—in telling us " that a priest can make his God, then sacrifice him, then given to the people, then worship him, and then eat him." There is a tripping levity of phrase in this passage, which your friends will regret for your own sake, quite as much as I can do for any other motive. Be assured, Rev. Sir, that Catholics, however incredible it may appear, claim the possession and exercise of reason, no less than Protestants. If we are in darkness, you may charitably undertake to enlighten us; but it must be by something more solid and permanent, than the flash of abortive wit and ridicule, with which you have thought proper to visit the doctrine of transubstantiation. Besides, I would not have the infidel, who regards Christianity, as you do the "real presence," to derive any accession of materials to his stock of sarcasm, from the pages of this controversy. Volney has an argument against Christianity, bearing so near a resemblance to yours, that did we not know the difference from other sources, it would be difficult to say, whether it is the infidel, that has imitated the Christian, or the Christian, that has borrowed from the infidel:—So much are they like children of the same family.

Volney is exposing the absurdity of belief in the trinity, the incarnation and divinity of Jesus Christ. Volney was an *infidel*, and we are not surprised to see him indulging a vein of humour.— "You make your God," says he, "the well-beloved Son, born without a mother; and then, as old as his father; and then the son of a woman, who is at once a virgin and a mother, and then you have him *killed*, for the benefit of mankind." I shall pass from this part of my subject, by asking you, whether Volney has not been quite as witty, pungent, and *conclusive* against Christ's divinity, as you have been against transubstantiation?

The proverb says that there is a *time* for all things; and our rules of controversy lay it down, as most conducive to *order*, to treat of but *one* thing at *one* time. We are now, Reverend Sir, discussing the "Rule of Faith," and "the parties agree respectively, to adhere strictly to the subject of discussion for the time being, and to admit *no second question, until the first shall have been exhausted.*" With the recollection of this rule fresh on my memory, judge of my surprise at beholding the host of "second questions," which you have contrived to marshal into the very van of the contest. "The Expurgatory Index,"—"Pope Liberius."—"The Arian heresy."— "The Pope's Supremacy."—"Seat of infallibility."—"General Councils."—"Validity of oaths."—"Letters from Bononia by three Bishops."—"Traditions."—"Apocryphal Books," &c.

———Stiphelumque, Bromumque
Antimachumque, Helimumque, Securiferumque
Pyracmon.

These subjects may be more serviceable in the rear as a body of reserve. You will thus have an opportunity of *reviewing*, and preparing them for action, when their turn shall have come. There is, however, one topic, which has a closer affinity to the subject now under consideration, and which demands a more proximate attention. It is your objections to the Catholic rule of faith. Now, the state of the question, as laid down in my first letter, required of you not to attack my rule, by *anticipation*, but to defend your own; which, by the laws of the controversy I was authorized to investigate. I had placed the result of that investigation before the public, in a few brief, plain, but solid and practical arguments, which, I was well aware, it would require something more than the female theology of "Father Clement," to shake from their foundations. But, before I proceed to review your attempt at a reply to them, I take occasion to assure you, that at *a proper time*, I shall defend the Catholic rule with positive arguments, quite as strong, as those already advanced in opposition to the Protestant principle.

In the mean time, the reader will please to bear in mind, that Protestants profess to be guided by *one* rule of faith, and that Catholics not only profess to be, but are in effect, guided by another. Now, as you have agreed with me, that Christ established *one*, and *only one*, rule of faith, " for the purpose of guiding us in matters of religion, and determining disputes in his church,"—it follows, as a necessary consequence, that either the Catholics or the Protestants have *forsaken* that true rule, and put themselves under the guidance of a false one, which Christ *did not establish*, and which is therefore, inadequate either to direct us in matters of religion or to determine our disputes. Deeming it more conducive to clearness and perspicuity, to give *either* rule a *separate* trial, I began by arraigning that principle which has been adopted by Protestants. I stated that the " Bible alone," as each individual understands it, is the Protestant rule of faith, and you have not disputed the correctness of the statement. Now if you prove that this rule was actually established by Christ—that it *guides* those who have adopted it in matters of religion—that it *determines* their disputes, you will thereby simplify the investigation, and your friends may congratulate you on an easy triumph when you come to examine the Catholic branch of the inquiry. But if, on the other hand, I prove by unanswerable argument, that the Protestant rule fails on all these heads, then it will follow, by the very tenor of our agreement, that the Catholic rule *must be* the true rule appointed by Christ. This, however, I pledge myself to prove by *positive* arguments, when the question shall have come fairly under discussion. At present, it is the duty of my position to urge those facts and arguments, which overthrow the Protestant rule of faith—of yours, *to answer them*. I wish it to be clearly understood, that I will not go aside of the question now under consideration, to answer any objection even against the Catholic rule of faith, until the present topic shall have been entirely disposed of.

The first sentence that arrests my attention in the foreground of your reply, is the startling declaration that you " own no judge of controversies but God." Do you not, Reverend Sir, perceive how flatly this proposition contradicts the admission of every rule of faith ? If Christ has established a rule of faith to " determine disputes,"—surely you will " own" *that rule* as a judge of controversy —unless you can discover a distinction between " judging controversies" and " determining disputes !"—for my part, I can see no distinction whatsoever. You admit, on the one hand, an infallible rule appointed for the express purpose of determining disputes ; and, on the other, almost in the same breath, you " disown" every judge of controversy but God ! Protestants *usually* profess to acknowledge the *word* of God as the judge of controversy ; and, as each minister possesses the right and the talent of making the word of God decide in favour of his own doctrines, the principle, I should think, allows ample latitude for the irresponsible rovings of private opinion. But for *you*, it seems, that even the *word* of God is too restrictive;—since you will "own no judge of controversies but God himself." It is true that he is the ultimate judge of all things, but to say that he is the immediate judge of controversy, by whom "disputes in the Church of Christ are to be determined;"—is an assertion that will be found *novel* in the annals of polemical disputation.

In my introduction, speaking in reference to private interpretation, I quoted the words of St. Peter, in which he says that "no prophecy of the Scripture is of any private interpretation," and contrasted them with the practice of Protestants, who, in fact, make *all* Scripture and prophecy of Scripture, of every private interpretation. By this remark, I intended simply to show, that, if St. Peter meant what his language so *obviously* expresses, *he* at least was not disposed to leave the Scripture, or the prophecy of Scripture, subject to the arbitrary or capricious interpretation of each private individual. But it seems I was mistaken;—and you, Reverend Sir, are kind enough to write nearly a whole column of explanation, to instruct me, and our readers generally, *how we are to understand the text.* That you felt the necessity of giving this explanation is a timely hint, that either the Scripture is not, after all, so plain as you are accustomed on other occasions to assert, or else (what amounts to the same) that we are not competent to understand its meaning. But unless you claim for yourself, either mental superiority, or some small portion of that infallibility which you deny to the whole church, I can see no reason why you should pretend to *understand* the passage better than myself, or than any of our readers. You say that "it is important to be noticed by me that it is the *prophecy* of Scripture, and not the *Scripture* that is obscure." Then, you admit that prophecy, at least, *is* obscure. This is indeed a concession. But pray is not "prophecy" a part of Scripture? and if it be, then we have your own authority for believing that some part of Scripture is obscure. You next urge that, by my interpretation the apostle is made to argue thus, "the Scriptures are infallibly revealed or inspired, and ye do well that ye take heed to them, therefore they are obscure, too obscure, for private explanation." The premises, dear Sir, are St. Peter's, but the conclusion is your own. "The voice, indeed, is the voice of Jacob, but the hands are the hands of Esau." I would find a better conclusion in the apostle's own words, "therefore, (as no prophecy of Scripture is of any private interpretation) you will not *wrest* it, as some do also the *other Scriptures*, to your own destruction." 2 Pet. iii. 16. I am not disposed to dwell longer on this subject, but I must remark that, to my mind, your explanation of the passage appears quite as *obscure* as the text itself.

As to the Latin quotation from the Vulgate, it means precisely what is expressed in the text as quoted above, and for which, I assure you, I am not at all indebted to what you call "our English translation."

As all the rest of your introduction consists of premature objections against a rule of faith, which is not yet under consideration, you will excuse me, if I pass them over, with a promise to refute them *in their proper place.* When we come to the Catholic rule, I shall show you how we *know* the true church, how the Scriptures *designate* her; how we solve the vicious circle; how the true church is distinguished by her divine characteristics from all would-be churches;—and a great many other things with which it is not wonderful to find Protestants rather unacquainted. At present you are called upon to vindicate the *Protestant* rule of faith; and instead of defending your own position, you attack ours. It seems to be the height of your ambition to show that the Catholic system involves as many difficulties as the Protestant system: but even if you succeeded, the only consequence that would follow is, that neither possesses the true rule.

Now for the arguments:—

I. My first argument against the Protestant rule of faith was, that *Christ never appointed it*. The reasons by which I supported this argument were simple *facts*. It is a *fact*, that the Bible alone, interpreted by each individual for himself, is the (nominal) rule of faith, adopted by Protestants. It is a fact, that Christ never appointed this rule;—because he never wrote any part of the Old or New Testament himself;—he never commanded any part to be written by his apostles. It is a *fact*, that what constitutes the Bible (according to the Protestant canon of Scripture) was not complete, until the close of the first century; and consequently, it is a *fact*, that the Protestant rule of faith did not exist *in the first century*, and is therefore not the rule which *Christ* established:—I call upon you to deny one single proposition here stated as a *fact*.

To supply this deficiency, you are pleased to assign an origin to the Protestant rule of faith, which, while it corresponds with these facts, relinquishes all pretensions to that rule's having been established by Christ. You assert that the "Old Testament," with the instructions of Christ and his Apostles, constitute the rule of faith, from the demise of the synagogue, until just before the death of the last Apostle, when the "entire New Testament was written;" and when, as you suppose, the Protestant rule of faith went into operation. Your clerical brethren will, no doubt, admire your candour in admitting that the Protestant rule of faith, so far from having been *established by Christ*, had not so much as an *existence* until the *close of the first century*; and the Jews will feel complimented, by the acknowledgment that the "Old Testament" was placed in the same chair of authority with Christ and his Apostles, for the purpose of *determining* the doctrines of Christianity, during the same period. Either admission, is a concession of my argument, that the Bible alone is not the rule of faith established by Christ.

II. My second argument was, that "as Protestants boast of believing nothing but what is contained in the Bible, they are bound to show *some texts of Scripture*, to prove the Bible alone is the rule of faith established by Christ." *This is the fundamental principle* of Protestantism. If *this* is not a divinely revealed tenet of religion, then it follows, that the Protestant rule of faith is precisely what I said of it, in my former letter, a mere 'assumption,'—a thing taken for granted, without proof or examination. It is easy to perceive in your answer, that you were not *insensible* to the strength of this position, nor to the feebleness of its opposite:—hence, instead of assailing it, with *that* superiority of evidence which Protestants associate with their belief, you go round it, asking yourself questions and answering them: "what then, you say, are the Scriptures?" Permit me again, Rev. Sir, to give the answer. They are the *written* word of God. Are they the *only rule of faith?* they themselves, from the beginning of Genesis to the end of Revelation do not say that they are. Why then do Protestants believe, that the Bible alone is *the rule of faith*, when the Bible itself does not say so? I leave you, Rev. Sir, to answer this *question*.

But in fact your language indicates an abandonment of the undertaking. You say ingeniously, that the "presumption from the admitted fact of the Bible's being a revelation is, that it is *the* rule of faith." Now I ask you, can that be the rule of faith appointed by Christ, which, according to your own acknowledgment, rests upon a mere "presumption?" A presumption is an *unequivocal basis* for the Protestant's belief in time, and his hope in eternity!!

As to your subdivisions under this head, they all belong to *another* part of the subject, and certainly do not prove, that the *Protestant* rule of faith is authorized by any single text of the sacred writing. It is true you attempt to strengthen the "presumption" by a text of Scripture;—not from the Gospel, but from the prophet Isaiah viii. 20. "To the law and to the testimony, if they speak not according to them, it is because there is no light in them." The prophet in this verse, was not pointing out a rule of faith, but reminding the people that it was forbidden in the land, (Deut. xviii. 10.) *to consult false oracles*, which was natural enough. But to infer that *this text* constitutes a divine warrant for the Protestant rule of faith, is indulging private interpretations, with a vengeance. The next passage that is brought forward, is that in which St. Paul approves Timothy, (2 Tim. iii. 15, 17.) for his knowledge of the Scripture. You first quote the passage entire—and then, as if conscious of its inconclusiveness as to the Protestant rule of faith, you take it apart, and weave, from the fragments, a chain of reasoning favourable to your "presumption," but in which, be it *noted*, that for every link furnished by the Apostle, two are added, of your *own* fabrication. Allow me to quote a specimen. "The Scriptures are able to make wise unto salvation," says the text; "without any *human* judge or help," adds Mr. Breckinridge. But, Sir, if this addition be true, what will become of the clergy, who live by judging "and helping" to explain the meaning of Scripture. Will they not say, in the words of another text, "a man's enemies are those of his household." But, so far as the *Scripture* is concerned, it is manifest that the "presumption," on which the Protestant rule of faith depends, must remain *what it is*.

III. My third argument was,—that the Bible *alone*, is a *misnomer* in theology,—in as much, as we can know nothing of it except through the medium of interpretation. And, as this medium is, in all cases, confessedly fallible, according to your rule of faith, it follows necessarily, that no Protestant can be certain, whether the doctrines which he believes, and on which he *grounds his hope* of salvation, are contained in the Bible. Be assured, Rev. Sir, that our readers will find something more "profound" in this argument than you have seen fit to acknowledge. You say "my God, my Bible, and my mind are supposed in *my* rule of faith :" precisely,—and for that reason it is, that the opinions and prejudices of your "*mind*," receive a fallacious authority with the people, by being put forth and accepted, as *emanating* from the pure word of God, *the Bible alone!* Has not the Episcopalian, the Baptist, the Methodist, the Moravian, the Swedenborgian, the Unitarian, the Arminian, and the Universalist, each "his God, his Bible, and his mind?"—and will you for a moment, pretend to say that *they* are guided by the rule of faith which you and they equally profess to follow, the Bible *alone ?* It is not the Bible *alone ;*—but the Bible, twisted into harmony with the Confession of Faith,—viewed through the Westminster Telescope,—which constitutes your rule of faith. As to the silly argument which you are pleased to ascribe to me, under this head, I must beg leave to disown it. It is the child of Presbyterian " logic," and is quite too *young* to sustain my " claim to infallibility."

IV. My fourth argument was, that the Protestant rule of faith actually undermines the authority of the Scriptures, by extinguishing the proofs of their *authenticity* and *inspiration*, and consequently terminates in moral suicide. Just imagine to yourself an ordinary will or testament, written but twenty years ago ;—purporting to be the last will and testament of a wealthy deceased relative, and designating you as *heir*, but without either signature or probate ;—and ask yourself what it would be worth? Could such a document establish its own authenticity? And yet, this is precisely the situation to which the Protestant rule of faith reduces the Scriptures, in rejecting the collateral testimony of the church, by which, and by which alone, their authenticity could have been established. St. Augustine, of whom Presbyterians are sometimes wont to speak with respect, declared that it was the testimony of the church which moved him to believe in the Scriptures. But *now*, the order of belief is " reformed." Men pick up (pardon the phrase) the sacred volume, as they find it, floating on the sea of two thousand years, and by one great, but *gratuitous*, act of belief, which flings all intermediate church authority and tradition to the winds, they say, " the Bible is the Bible, and we are its interpreters," every man for himself.

Is it not a fact, Rev. Sir, that Protestantism rejects tradition, and adopts the Bible *alone* as its rule of faith ? and if so, what other testimony is left in the universe to establish either the authenticity or inspiration of the Bible ? When you say, therefore, that my latent meaning in all this argument is, that we " need the church to tell us what is Bible and what is not," you express my meaning exactly, and it is " latent" no longer. It is now incumbent on you to show how a Protestant, by the Bible alone, can be assured that the Scriptures are *authentic* and *inspired*.

V. My fifth argument was, that Christ neither established nor intended the Bible alone to be the rule of faith, because it was not universally known until the end of the fifth century, *what* books were to be regarded as inspired Scripture. The argument which you here raise against the church, for not making known what books were Scripture, until the period referred to, I shall answer in its proper place. In the mean time, the *fact* is an everlasting proof, that the Bible alone was not the primitive rule of Christian faith. You have given authority indeed, to prove that some of the books of Scripture were certain; this I never denied; but you have admitted, that even as late as the Council of Laodicea, 364, *some* were doubtful, and this is quite sufficient for my argument. These *some* prove that the Protestant rule of faith was not complete, even " at the death of the last apostle," nor for 264 years afterwards, and consequently was not *established* by Christ: therefore it is a false rule.

But besides, the condition of the world at that period renders it absurd to suppose, that the Bible alone was even thought of as the rule of faith, 1st, Because of the multitude of languages into which it would have been necessary to translate the Bible: 2d, Because of the multitude of pens necessary to transcribe copies, so as to furnish believers with a rule of faith: 3d, Because of the multitude of schools and schoolmasters necessary to teach the people of every nation how to read. And this is the argument which you call a " quibble!"

VI. My sixth argument was, that as the true rule of faith was established "*to determine disputes in the church of Christ,*" it cannot be the Protestant rule, *because*, it is a *fact*, that, since the beginning of Christianity until the present hour, no dispute has ever been determined by that rule, the Bible alone. Are you then still prepared to say, that a rule which, in no single instance, *has accomplished the end of its institution*, is the rule appointed by Christ? Does the Bible " determine the dispute" between you and the Episcopalians on the institution of bishops—between you and the learned editor of the Christian Index, on the subject of Infant Baptism—between you and the Unitarian on the divinity of Jesus Christ—between you and your Rev. Brethren of the Second Presbytery in your own church.

VII. My seventh argument was, that the Protestant rule of faith, so far from "*determining any dispute,*" has given rise to all the heresies that exist. By that rule the Bible is made to prove the divinity of Christ in *one* pulpit, and to overthrow the belief of it in *another*;—to prove the eternity of torments, and the non-existence of hell. And can *that* be the rule appointed by Christ, which gives the same warrant of authority to him that " plants, and to him that plucks up that which had been planted?" Is there a more palpable proof of this argument, than the multitude of sects and the endless contradictions among Protestants, on the subjects of doctrine? After stating this argument, you turn round and exclaim, " Poor Bible, what a transgressor thou hast been!" and then avenge yourself on my reasoning, by saying that " our rule has worked worse than yours." *That is not now the question.* Neither do I charge the " transgression" on the Bible, as you insinuate. God forbid!—But I assert boldly, that it *is not the abuse*, but the *use* of the Protestant rule of faith, which has produced all the sects that claim to be guided by it. It is indeed the *abuse* of the Bible;—but the regular *use* of the *rule*.

VIII. My eighth argument was, that the Socinian has the same *persuasion* of being right in his belief, that you have in yours; and consequently, that you are *both* under the guidance of a principle, which can impart certainty to *neither*. But you yourself have admitted that the true rule of faith, "must give to those, who abide by its decisions an *infallible certainty:*" and therefore, *te judice, your* rule is not the true one: since, under its operation, the divinity of Jesus Christ, agitated between you and the Socinian, becomes a doubtful tenet, on which each of you may entertain or express his *opinions,* but nothing more. You have not even attempted to wrestle with this argument.

As to the assertion that "Joanna Southcote and the Shakers use *our rule* of faith;" it is a piece of information, with which, I believe, history was altogether unacquainted before. I deny the fact, however; and I should be sorry to see my "logic hanging" on any such admission.

IX. My ninth argument was, as you say, a practical illustration of the above. In order to make it clear, I supposed (by hypothesis) that the Presbyterian doctrine was the true doctrine of the Bible. I supposed four clergymen of that denomination, no matter who, in searching the Scriptures, to become persuaded that Unitarianism, Universalism, Swedenborgianism, or Catholicity is the religion of the Bible.

I ask you whether, in that case, they would not be bound before God, to quit the *true* religion of Christ, represented by the Presbyterian church, and embrace the *heresies ;*—and whether, in doing this, they would not act in *strict conformity* with the Protestant rule of faith? I say they would: and I submit to your own reason, and that of our readers, whether a rule, which would thus *drive* men from the true faith, and *compel* them to embrace heresy, is likely to be that infallible rule, " which Jesus Christ established to guide us in matter of religion, and to determine disputes in the church." Genebrard's "Chronicles" will not, I assure you, furnish you a solution of the difficulty.

X. My tenth argument was, that the doctrines of Christ were delivered to mankind as *positive truths, facts* about which there could be no grounds for disputation. That the object for which an infallible rule of faith was established, was *to guard those eternal* and *unchangeable truths* of God, from being lost or confounded with the opinions of men. From this I argued, that the Protestant rule of faith is not the rule which Christ appointed: *because* every doctrine which is tried by the Protestant rule, is *changed by the very test,* from a fact or positive truth, into a *mere opinion.* What is it that has so multiplied creeds among Protestants? What is it that has never ceased to evolve one sect out of another from the days of the " Reformation," so called? It is the Protestant rule of faith. Why. is it that Protestants are in everlasting controversies among themselves? It is because their rule of faith has *robbed them, all alike,* of *certainty,* as to the truth of their respective doctrines. What is the character of their warfare? It is the battle of *opinions,* about the meaning of the Bible, in which the privilege of private interpretation furnishes the Unitarian and the Universalist, with the same weapons which it bestows upon the Presbyterian and Baptist. Now, sir, I again assert, that Christ never inculcated the belief of an *opinion!* I assert, on the other hand, that the human mind, under the influence of the *Protestant rule of faith,* never has held, and never can hold, one single doctrine of Christianity, except by the dubious tenure of *opinion*—and *I challenge you* to disprove either of these assertions.

You say you have refuted this argument in your introduction, but I appeal even to our Protestant readers, whether, from the beginning to the end of your letter, they will not look in vain for a refutation. You have indeed, attempted to show that Catholics are equally destitute of certainty, but when we come to speak of the Catholic rule of faith, I shall show how easy it is to prove the contrary.

As the rest of your letter is "about every thing," you cannot expect me to notice it, since we are both equally forbidden by our rules to travel out of the subject "under discussion for the time being.' This is, perhaps, a circumstance which, on the whole, you ought not to regret; as it will give you an opportunity of *reviewing* your authorities. Remember that Archbishop Usher was a Protestant, and yet you once quoted him to prove that Catholics are idolaters:—and, added, addressing the young lady in Baltimore, "of Usher's authority among Romanists we need not speak." However, you have since explained it, as some strange mistake of printing. It was indeed very strange; and such mistakes ought to be guarded against in future, for your authorities, as well as arguments, are, henceforward, to be under the inspection of many a scrutinizing eye. But for the present, I shall not pluck out a single gem of authority, nor controvert a single proposition in the multifarious matter of your epistle. When the time shall have come, however, *I bind myself* to prove that several of the former are spurious, and several of the latter, false.

The actual question now under consideration is, THE PROTESTANT RULE OF FAITH. It cries out for a defender—for one, who will prove it to be "*infallible; established by Christ; competent to guide us in matters of religion; and to determine disputes in his Church.*" It demands to be vindicated by *its own evidences*, which cannot be wanting, if it was established by Christ—and it scorns to triumph by the hand, which, instead of protecting it with the shield of *its own evidences*, strikes at a defenceless rival. Think you, Reverend Sir, that I accepted this controversy, for the pleasure of playing a mere polemical chess-game with him who offered it? God forbid! I accepted it with a view to drive the ploughshare of reason, evidence, and argument, through the radical delusion, the "origo malorum," of Protestantism. I reflected, that possibly, in the inscrutable providence of God, the salvation of souls might depend on this controversy—and looking, I trust, with some portion of the charity of Christ, at the wanderings of my Protestant brethren, I determined to expose the fundamental delusion, by which, since the unhappy separation, they have followed their clergy, their parents, their prejudices;—whilst all three, perhaps, conspired to persuade them into the erroneous supposition, that they were following, forsooth, the "pure" word of God, the "Bible alone."

Now, sir, I again request you to "adhere strictly to the subject of discussion for the time being," as we have agreed in our rules;—to prove, if you can, the "Protestant rule of faith," and, by close, positive, and pertinent arguments, to overthrow, *article* for *article*, those which have been laid down against it, whilst I remain, very respectfully, &c

JNO. HUGHES.

RULE OF FAITH.

New York, February 18*th*, 1833.

To the Rev. John Hughes,

Sir,—It would appear from your exultation at the delay of my reply, that you were writing against time. I assure you that the force of your reasoning did not occasion that delay; as I think my answer sufficiently evinces. When you gravely attempt to turn such an event to your own advantage, it must convince the public of the weakness of your cause; and it will more fully explain to you the reason and propriety of my bringing so distinctly to view, in our preliminary correspondence, the nature of my occupation.—If I had been in Philadelphia *at the press*, my reply would have appeared in its proper order as to time. As, however, you seem to intimate that there is merit in despatch, let me inform you that I have to-day, [the 18th February,] received your letter, No. 3; and that the time allowed me for reply, extends only to Thursday the 21st, when the manuscript must be mailed, in order to be in season for the next paper.

In regard to the terms "Papist and Romanist," which you call "nicknames," it is proper here to remark, that *truth* requires their use. You assume the rank and name of "Catholic," that is, "the universal Church," and all who are not in communion with you are heretics, doomed to perdition by your anathema, now in full force, unless they repent and return. You beg the question, therefore, which is now in discussion, by the very name. Roman Catholic, in strict speech, is an absurdity, being equivalent, "particular universal." Protestants, as members of the universal Church, claim to be catholic; and it is as proper to call you "Papists," as us "Protestants."—The one name defines those who hold to the supremacy of the Pope; the other those who *protest* against that system. If you are Roman Catholics, we are Protestant Catholics. I regard names then as signs of things; and use them for truth, not reproach. I shall feel no pang if you call me heretic, "for after the way you call heresy, so worship I the God of my fathers;" and with this explanation, I will hereafter endeavour to oblige you in the use of names.

What you say of Volney is not even an illustration, much less an argument; for it is not true that the doctrine of the Saviour's divinity contradicts our senses, or that *He* was in any way made, or his divinity destroyed by man; all of which are true. The ribaldry of Volney is one thing, and the exposure of bad theology is another. I meant no reproaches in what I said. But it seems impossible to define this doctrine without offending those who hold it. Perhaps you are not aware that John Huss wrote against the following sentiment of a Bohemian Priest: "that a Priest before he says Mass is the Son of God, but afterwards he is the Father of God, and the creator of his body." I charge nothing evil to the intentions of those who hold this doctrine; I only show its inconsistencies and its tendencies.

But to proceed—The candid must be forcibly struck with the peculiar manner in which you pass by every argument brought by me against your rule of faith. Thus you say, "We are discussing the rule of faith; and the parties adhere strictly to the subject of discussion for the time being, and to admit of no second question until the first shall have been exhausted." And again you say, " Now the state of the question, as laid down in my first letter, required you not to attack my rule by *anticipation*, but to defend your own."—This indeed is strange reasoning. Is not the whole subject of the rule of faith before us? But the following paragraph explains your design in this course. " If I prove, by unanswerable argument, that the Protestant rule fails, in all these heads, then it will follow, by the very tenor of our agreement, that the Catholic rule *must* be the true rule appointed by Christ." This is saying, in other words, that your Church is the residuary legatee of truth. If the Samaritans are wrong, then *must* the Jews be right! It is like the claim once set up by a wily shepherd. All the flocks of the surrounding fields met at the brook on a summer's evening. The lambs were tender, and were not yet marked with the several shepherds' marks. When the flocks were separated, *he* claimed all the lambs. The others expostulated, one saying this is mine, and another, this is mine. But he replied, "each of you have a mark for your sheep; these lambs have no mark upon them, and cannot be yours; therefore, they are mine." In the spirit of this extraordinary plan of argument, you continue in this, as in your former letter, to keep your own rule wholly out of view; and you decline, in so many words, to answer my many objections to it. While you thus pass by all discussion of it, the inference is irresistible, that your hope of success rests upon the plan, of keeping out of view the defects of your system; and in seeking to perplex the general question before the public mind, by scholastic subtilties, when the subject calls for manly argument.

In view of these things, I feel myself called on to pursue, in the first place, the line of discussion with which I closed my former letter This course is on every account demanded; for your letter of the 14th inst. is only a second edition, head for head, of that already answered by me.

I. I have shown that your rule is not *infallible*. I will now prove that it is the parent of UNCERTAINTY.

1. The authorised version of the Bible is in Latin, as well as the prayers, &c. of the church service. The Vulgate, with all its errors, was adopted by the Council of Trent as authentic and correct; yet a *corrected* edition was ordered by the same council, and it was printed under the care of the Pope, and published with his Bull, prohibiting any alteration in it. But so many errors were detected in it, that the edition was suppressed! These are statements you will hardly deny. 2. The ponderous acts, decisions, &c. of the infallible church are deposited in the following works, and in an *unknown* tongue. Archbishop Manse's Councils, 31 vols. folio; Great Book of Bulls, 8 vols. folio; Acta Sanctorum, 51 vols. folio; Decretals, about 10 vols. folio; total 100 folio volumes, and then 35 folio volumes of the Fathers, whose *unanimous* consent is a part of the testimony. These are the *fountain*, but who of the people can get at it? What is drawn thence is transfused through the fallible and uncertain minds of innumerable priests, before it reaches the people. Yet these are the *helps to understand the Bible!* 3. The Church

of Rome is utterly *silent* about many doctrines; as whether the Virgin Mary was born sinless. There have been fierce contests about it in your communion. But the oracle is dumb. Every Protestant child can decide this question. As to the very seat of the boasted infallibility, she was silent at Trent, and is now divided and uncertain; and so of some other doctrines. 4. According to the doctrine of intention, [see Council of Trent, Sess. 7. Canon 11.] the efficacy of the sacraments depends on the *intention* of the officiating minister; some of these sacraments, of which you make *seven*, are *necessary* in order to salvation, and all of them necessary in their places, to certain states in life. Thus *marriage* is not valid, if performed without the intention of the priest. Baptism and penance are not valid without his intention; and on these depend salvation. But who can be CERTAIN of the *intention* of the Priest? If the Bishop who ordained that Priest, lacked intention in the act, then the ordination is invalid, and, of course, all that Priest's acts are invalid. But who can be certain that in this chain of ages some link is not wanting? *Who then can be certain of salvation in the Romish Church?* Yet the Duke of Brunswick, assigning his fifty reasons for becoming a Roman Catholic, says, "The Catholics, to whom I spoke concerning my conversion, assured me that if I were damned for embracing the Catholic faith they were ready to answer for me at the day of judgment, and to take my damnation upon themselves; an assurance I could never extort from the ministers of any other sect, in case I should live and die in their religion." While such daring impiety discovers the absence of all right feeling, it also evinces a desperation peculiar to a cause which needs propping at any price. Now if these statements be put together, they will show that your system is shrouded in *uncertainty*. But you contend in the first and second editions of your 10th head, "that a rule which is the parent of uncertainty, cannot be that infallible rule established by Christ, to guide us in matters of religion."

II. *The unwarrantable liberties of your church with the word of God, show her fallible to a deplorable degree.* 1st. We have seen on a former occasion the liberty taken by your church in *adding* to the word of God the Apocryphal books and unwritten traditions. 2d. We see how she *takes away* from the Bible by her treatment of the Decalogue. The catechism of the Council of Trent repeats only *four words* of the second commandment, and closes with an expressive *et cætera*. A strange way to give a divine law, especially to a people who are deprived by the church of the word of God! The version used in the Highlands of Scotland (by authority) mutilates it almost in the same way. The version used in Ireland entirely omits the second commandment! The Doway Catechism is wiser, as it was to circulate where the omission would not be borne; but it plainly perverts the commandment "thou shalt not adore nor worship images," whereas the true translation is "thou shalt not bow down thyself to them, nor serve them." The reason for the change is very plain. 3d. The evidence adduced in proof of the sacrament of extreme unction by the Council of Trent, is no less than a literary, or, if you please, a *pious fraud;* and I am prepared to prove it. The Rhenish and Bordeaux translations have been signalized by their numerous and glaring frauds. 4th. Your church has added to the word of God new articles of faith, and even new sacraments to the institutions of Jesus Christ. Leo X. condemned Luther for saying, *it is not in the power of the church or the Pope to constitute new articles of faith.* Divers writers, as the Abbot of Panormo, Ancona, &c., contend that the Pope is the measure and rule of faith, and can make new articles. The Bull of Pius IV. appended to the decrees of the Council of Trent, makes a new creed—including many new articles of faith, to be sworn to by all ecclesiastics; and all are cursed who reject them. Among these innovations, brought in at different times, was transubstantiation, as *young* as A. D. 1215—purgatory—depriving the people of the cup in the Eucharist—indulgencies—the worship of images—prayer in an unknown tongue. It is of this that some one has remarked that your faith like the new moon, is *crescent*, with this difference, however, (let me add,) that it is not like hers, the growth of *light*. Bellarmine we suppose means this, when he says of one article, "*ferde de fide*" (de concil. auth. l. 2. c. 17. s. 1.) "almost a matter of faith;" a probationer for a seat in the creed! If this be not " teaching for doctrines the commandments of men, and making void the law of God by your traditions," I know not what is. How true it is that " *Rome was not built in a day.*" Here then your church both innovates upon the doctrine, and usurps the rights of God; and by this, she proves herself both *fallible* and guilty before God.

III. *Your rule, if observed, requires implicit faith in the decretals and interpretations of fallible men, which is subversive of the very nature and end of religion in the soul.* Faith supposes knowledge, conviction on evidence, and trust in God, founded on a belief of divine truth. But your rule requires unconditional submission to the dicta of the church, in the lump. The " *Carbonaria fides*," or faith of the collier, is the very faith required. It is as follows; When asked, " What do you believe?" He answered, " I believe what the church believes." " What does the church believe?" Answer, " What *I* believe." " Then what do you and the church together believe?" Answer, " We both believe the same thing." This is the grand catholicon for believing every thing without knowing any thing. In this soil grew the maxim that " ignorance is the mother of devotion." It is believing by proxy, or rather not believing at all, in the true sense. Here is the secret of the unity of your church. That this is not my bare assertion may be seen in the creed of Pope Pius IV., when it is said, " I admit the Holy Scripture according to the sense which the Holy mother Church, (whose right it is to judge of the true meaning and interpretation of the sacred Scriptures,) hath held and doth hold." The catechism also declares, that we avoid the damnation of our souls, " by taking the meaning and interpretation of the Scriptures from the same hand, from which we received the book itself, that is the church." (Chap. 2. ques. 2.) Now I argue from these facts, that the operation of your rule is to annihilate inquiry, knowledge and faith, properly so called; and shows it to be a most vicious and fallible rule.

IV. *The means which have been resorted to by your church in support of her rule, most clearly show that she is fallible, and that your rule is utterly indefensible.* I mention only a few specimens. 1st. We have seen (in my IIId head, letter No. 2,) that by supreme, binding, infallible law, the circulation and perusal of the Scriptures are restricted as follows: No layman has a right to read the Bible without permission from a priest; and then, no Bible not translated by a Roman Catholic. The priest is the exclusive judge of the question, whether or not he is fit to read the Roman translation. Even if permitted to read it, he is by no means to think for himself, but as the church thinks. If he reads without license, he cannot get absolution of sin, until he delivers up his Bible—that is, for the time he is under the curse of unpardoned sin. And all this is on the assumed ground *that God's word will injure* the great mass of men if they read it. Again, all printers selling to those not *licensed* to read, are to lose the edition printed, and otherwise be dealt with;—and all this is now binding on all, as well American citizens, as others: and those who reject these laws are anathematised heretics. 2d. A permanent committee, styled the "Congregation of the Index," has charge, by authority, of the work of watching the press, and prohibiting the reading of any books they disapprove. "Their Index," which enrols these books, has swelled to a great volume. The American reader will be surprised to hear that Locke, Bacon, Sir Matthew Hale, Addison, Robertson, (Charles V.) Walton, (Polyglott) Saurin, Young, (Night Thoughts,) are *actually prohibited; some wholly; others in chief part!* (See the "Ten Rules of the Index," approved by Pope Pius IV.) 3d. Beside this, Pope Clement VIII. in the year 1595, published a decree that all Roman Catholic authors, written since 1515, (the era of the Reformation,) should be corrected, so as not merely to *blot out* doctrines not approved, but to *add* what was necessary. These are his very words: "In libris catholicorum recentiorum, qui post annum christianæ salutis 1515 conscriptisint, si id quod corrigendum occurrit, paucis demptis aut additis emendare posse videatur, id correctores faciendum curent; sin minus, omnino deleatur." And worse than all, the process of expurgation has reached even to the "Fathers." Johannes Pappus and Franciscus Junius published an edition of an Index Expurgatorius, prepared by the Inquisitors, under a commission from the king of Spain. From that it appears, that the works of Chrysostom, Ambrose, and Augustine, had passages purged from them, which were supposed to be unfriendly to the Roman Catholic faith. Such passages, for example, as these, are struck out; "there is no merit but what is given us by Christ." "God alone is to be worshipped," (see Bishop Taylor's dissuasive from Popery, chap. 1. for further reference.) Now we say, that by such a process, we may prove any thing we please. The church which restricts the use of the Scriptures; which sits enthroned upon the ruins of human liberty; which forbids men to read, to print, and even to think, except as she shall dictate; which amends, changes, and tortures the writings of the living and the dead. and in support of her system, ventures to approach with her reforming hand even the testimony of antiquity—has evinced to all men that she is not a safe depository of the truth; that she is utterly fallible; that she does by these acts confess and prove it; and however she may by such means transmute all things that she touches into her own image, the Lord of truth never appointed such a guide to his people's faith.

V. *Allow me next to say, that your rule, when in full and proper force, is incompatible with civil liberty and the rights of nations.* Your system, with the Pope at its head, is a species of universal monarchy, civil and religious, extending to the whole world. As the vicar of Christ, he claims to be head of the church and of the state, wherever there is either on earth. Now, for the proof: 1st. *This right has been distinctly claimed.* Pope Innocent III., says, "The church, my spouse, is not married to me without bringing me a dowry. She hath given me the mitre for the priesthood, and the crown for the kingdom—making me *Lieutenant* of him who hath written on his vesture and on his thigh, King of kings and Lord of lords. I enjoy the plenitude of power, that others may say of me next to God, *Out of his fulness we have received.*" (Itinerar. Ital. part 2. de coron. Rom. Pon.) I know no equal to this blasphemy but the ravings of a madman who once said, in my hearing, that he had been appointed by God *commander-in-chief of the celestial hosts!* The reader will please compare with the above, John i. 10. The Bull of Clement V. for crowning the Emperor Henry, contains the distinct assumption of universal temporal empire; so do also the twenty-seven sayings of Gregory VII.; Clement VI. claims the same; so does the canon law, the Gregorian Epistles, Martin V., Boniface VIII. &c.; not to mention Bellarmine, and a number of other writers in your church, who contend for the same rights. But not only have Roman Catholic writers and Popes contended for temporal jurisdiction over nations, but Councils and General Councils, whose authority you all acknowledge, have done the same; as I am abundantly prepared to prove if you deny it. 2d. This claim has been on divers occasions *carried into practical operation,* so as to leave no doubt as to what it means. The Popes have taxed nation after nation for the *spiritual treasury* at Rome, so that "Peter's pence" became a by-word to express the tyranny of Rome. They have deposed princes and set others up in their stead; they have cut asunder the very bonds of society by absolving subjects from the oath of allegiance to heretical princes; they have required princes to exterminate their subjects, and encouraged subjects to destroy their princes; and under this broad claim, they have even given away kingdoms to foreign princes, and have made crowns and nations their playthings and their toys. It is a curious fact to an American citizen, that Spain and Portugal have a universal grant from the Pope of the two Americas. 3d. *Institutions have been erected and encouraged throughout the world, wherever they would be tolerated, and systematic and legalized persecutions have from age to age been carried on, to sustain this system of universal empire.* At the very name of the Inquisition, some of the nations of Europe still tremble; and the heart of every civilized man is moved with mingled indignation and horror. This is a painful, but necessary topic. I will not here enlarge on it, but stand prepared with abundant facts to substantiate my statements, if you deny them. Now the reasoning from these facts against your rule is irresistible. God has made all men free and all nations are endowed with the inalienable rights of self-government; and He who has said, "My kingdom is not of this world," has also said, "Render unto Cæsar the things that are Cæsar's." The church, therefore, which claims these powers, is at war with the Bible; and he rule of faith under which she holds these doctrines, and practises these usurpations, must be, in the strongest sense, a *fallible and misguiding rule.* If Roman Catholics reject these principles, as every true American *must*, and as I doubt not multitudes of your people in this country and Great Britain *do*, then where is your infallibility? But you say the church is infallible, and her system unchangeably fixed. I call on you then for a defence.

Once more. *The effect of your rule of faith is to corrupt the worship of God, and to engender abundant superstitions.* Idolatry, (excuse the word,) is enthroned in the temple of God, by the bulls of Popes, and the decrees of Councils; and is practically illustrated every day in the worship of the church. The spirituality of religion is lost amidst a crowd of images and relics; of interceding saints, and human inventions: and ignorance perpetuates what your erring rule has legalized. Need I point you to exorcisms and incantations, to prayers to the saints, and worship of the Virgin Mary, to holy water, and the baptism of bells, to pilgrimages, and penances, and the crowd of superstitions which are encouraged in your church in confirmation of my statements? Who would believe it, if it had not been seen, that in the nineteenth century of the Christian era, there is a great anniversary day, set apart in "Rome. the mother and mistress of churches," for blessing all the horses and asses and other beasts of that great city, whilst the same pontiff who sanctions such a system, publicly denounces Bible Societies, as the organizations and servants of the devil? I ask if this is the product of infallible guidance; or if the rule which sanctions, teaches, and perpetuates such things, can have been given us by God to direct us in matters of religion?

I would superadd these heads to those contained in my former letter; and must wait in expectation of your redeeming the *pledge* to answer them hereafter. In the mean time, that you may have no ground of complaint, even in appearance, I will close by briefly noticing your second edition of the ten Heads against *our* rule of faith. As to all you say about my denying the *word* of God to be a judge of controversies, our readers will judge whether you have not attempted to blind them by sophistry, rather than convince them by argument. You knew that I spoke of God as the ruler, the Bible as the rule. God is the judge and the only judge, properly so called. The Bible contains the record of his infallible judgments. It is God speaking to man.—Again, you so evidently and consciously *labour* to disentangle yourself from my exposure of your use of 2 Peter i. 20, (on private interpretation,) that I am entirely willing to leave the subject to speak for itself, without another word.

Here allow me to remark, that in your two letters, *which two are one,* your current reasoning is this: *There are certain defects which no infallible rule can have, the Protestant rule has these; therefore it is not infallible.* Now I have shown, (so clearly that you pretend not to refute it,) that these defects are inherent in your rule; therefore, at every step, your own blows return upon your own cause. The force of this reasoning is irresistible, if you were honest in using it; for it is *your own reasoning*. Yet when the blow rebounds, you cry out, this logic was to destroy the Protestant rule, not mine. I was not talking of *my* rule! You press me to keep to the point. What is the point? The rule of faith. Only do not touch Mr. Hughes' rule of faith. But I not only thus exposed your rule of faith, I also defended our own rule from point to point. Let us summarily review these *old* acquaintances.

I. "Christ never appointed the Protestant rule." "Christ never wrote any part of the Old or New Testament, and never commanded any part to be written by his apostles." (1.) Let us apply this to your rule. Christ never wrote or commanded his apostles to write the Apocryphal books, or *unwritten* Traditions; therefore, Christ never appointed them as a part of the rule faith. (2.) Either the prophets and apostles were moved by inspiration when they wrote, or they were not. If they were, then they wrote by divine authority. But do you not deny that they were? Hence your statement is false, and if it proves any thing, it is that the Bible is not God's word. Your next proof is that the "Protestant rule of faith did not exist till the end of the first century." Now this is a mere play on words. I say that the *Divine Revelation* is our only rule of faith. The Bible contains that Revelation finally made out. The *precise equivalent* to this existed while Christ and his apostles were on earth, viz: the Old Testament and their infallible instructions. Before inspiration ceased, the Bible was completed. I will carry out your argument. The Bible is a *printed* book; but at the death of John, the art of printing being unknown, the word of God was *written with pens*, therefore the *Bible* is not God's word. In the latter part of this head, you virtually deny that the Old Testament is of equal authority with the New. Is this so?

II. You call for "*Scripture warrant*," that the Bible is the rule of faith. We reply as before, 1. *The presumption*, (prior to the proof,) always is, that the Bible *alone* is the rule of faith. I ask, will you join the Infidel and say, that the presumption is the other way? 2. If any thing else is to be added to the Bible, those who say so are bound to prove it. Hence the attack on the pretensions of *your* rule is the fair order of discussion. Feeling this to be a sore spot, you cover it up. 3. The only admissible proof, as God tells us, *is a miracle*. Well, therefore, may you shift and turn and be silent, to shun a call you cannot meet. The only reply you make to this reasoning, is to charge me with saying, that "the Protestant Rule is founded on presumption;" a misrepresentation so glaring, that unwilling to distrust your candour, I must charge it on your cause. 4. I then gave you Scripture warrant for our rule, which you cannot torture so as to weaken its direct proof. I will adduce more Scripture in connexion with which the reader will please to examine 2 Tim. iii. 14, 17, and Isaiah viii. 20. In John vii. 17, we are taught that obedience gives certainty to doctrinal knowledge.—From 1 Peter i. 23. 1 Thess. ii. 13. James i 18, that *the Bible* in the hands of the Holy Spirit, <u>is</u> the instrument of converting the soul. John xvii. 17. *The Bible* is the means of sanctification. Eph. vi. 17. Hebrews iv. 12. It is the great power of God. Gal. i. 8. It is the rule by which even Apostles are to be tested, (though the *Pope* refuses.) 1 John iv. 1—3. It is the *people's rule* to try the spirits; no infallible Judge is named. John xii. 48. It is the *rule of judgment* at the great day. John xx. 30—33. *One Gospel* is sufficient to give eternal life. Luke xvi. 29—31. Nothing, no, not a miracle, can convince those who reject it. Rev. xxii. 18. Awful judgments, (I beg you to look narrowly at this,) are denounced against those who tamper with even a *part* of the Bible. The church who would mend this rule, is entitled to the epitaph of him who was destroyed by the nostrums of quacks, and directed to be written on his tomb, "I was well—I wanted to be better—and here I am."

III. You argue "as the Bible is known through the medium of interpretation, and as the Protestant medium is fallible, therefore the rule is fallible." 1. I reply, until you *prove* your infallibility, which you have not yet done, you are in a much worse case than we, as your Apocrypha, unwritten Traditions, and one hundred folios, with "all the Fathers," exceed in number our Bible, since you have to interpret all these, to get at the true sense. 2. Your reasoning, reduced to form, is this; every rule, (say one for measuring distances) is handled by men; but men are fallible—therefore every rule is false—and cannot measure infallibly—or, in other words, none but an infallible man can use the Bible. Is not the following reasoning just as good? Either it rains, or it does not rain—if it rains, it does not rain—if it does not rain, it rains. Then does it rain, or not rain?

IV. You say the Bible cannot prove its own authenticity and inspiration; therefore, it alone cannot be the rule of faith. We reply, 1. The inspiration of Scripture may be proved from prophecy, from its contents, &c. 2. On the question, "are these the *authentic* or *genuine books* which they profess to be?" you confound the *proof* of a thing with the *matter* of it; as if you had said, a twelve inch rule is not a true rule, unless it can prove itself. This is absurd. Your illustration of the will is every how faulty. The testator is Christ—the Bible is the will—the church is the heir. Who is the court before whom the proof is to be laid? Why the church, you say. But who gave it authority? The church. No—the testator, for the church is *heir*. Who is the witness? The church again.—Yet with this *figure* you would prove your point! Now the case is this. Here is a *will*. We want *witnesses* to *prove* that the testator made the will—not to *give it authority:* that comes from the testator. So it is precisely with the Bible. The church does not give it authority; the Bible gives authority to the church. *The testimony* of those who lived in the Apostles' days is what we want. Jewish writers testify, Heathen writers testify, and Christian writers testify, that this is the Book of God. If you call this tradition, then it is the tradition of *written testimony;* it is the tradition of universal antiquity; it is such a tradition as falsifies your *unwritten traditions*, your apocryphal books, and your judge of controversies. If this be not so, will you tell me when and where the church authority settled the canon?—In a word, if the church of Rome had never existed, the proof would have been entire.

V. You are constrained to admit here that you made a misstatement in the former letter of *one entire century!* You also misinterpret my statement as to "sacred books" being doubtful. I said "some" (not books, but men) were doubtful, as to four of the many books. In the mean time the churches had "all the books," and these doubts of *some*, (men, not books,) did not make it less truly the real and full rule. Of course, besides. the distrust occasioned by such unfairness, your conclusion that the canon was so long uncertain, drawn from this perversion, falls to the ground. I also refer the reader under this head, to the contradiction I have there exposed, to which you render no reply. You assume that the church *knew;* and yet argue against our rule, that it was *not* known. Now which is true? If the former, your reasoning is false; if the latter, your rule is fallible.

VI. & VII. There are two methods of settling disputes; *reason* and *force.* You take the latter; we the former. There are two rules, the Bible and the church of Rome. You assert that the Bible has failed, and thus make your church better than Christ and his apostles. I call for your proof. As to heresy, Augustine, whom you claim and quote, mentions eighty-eight heresies, down to his time! I will in due season give you more of your own history on this topic.

VIII. & IX. You have "slurred the notes," to use your own expression, and made no reply to me. 1. I have proved (see introduction to former letter,) that by confession of Roman Catholics, they are as uncertain as Protestants. 2. I have proved in this letter, (see head on uncertainty,) that you are wholly uncertain:—and now, 3. You have at last to adopt our rule, or give up the question. For you get at the proof of your infallible rule by fallible men; and you get the proof entirely from the Bible. Is not this then making the Bible interpreted by fallible men, your rule of faith!

And now, Sir, in closing this letter, I wish you to know that I will not be *diverted* from the fair and full discussion of the whole subject, viz. the rule of faith. Common sense demands it; and the third and fifth articles in our agreement justify it. I wish you also to understand, that all I say is to be applied to your *system*, and not to your people. In this country especially, that Proteus-system conforms itself as much as possible to the advance of the age, and the genius of a free and thinking people. You must go to Spain, to South America, to Rome, to see your system. The people here know not the half. It is *in spite* of being Roman Catholics—not *in consequence* of it, that you number the good and wise among your people.

Your challenge to our whole church provokes a smile among us.— When I need any aid to meet your calls, I will tell you so. I am, I own, among the most insufficient of the sons of that venerated church to which I belong; but she feels as if no mighty shield were needed to quench your arrows, and cover her sacred bosom from your assaults.

--I remain, yours, &c.   JOHN BRECKINRIDGE.

CONTROVERSY. No. V.

RULES.

The undersigned agreeing to have an amicable discussion of the great points of religious controversy, between Protestants and Roman Catholics, do hereby bind themselves to the observance of the following rules :

1. The parties shall write and publish, alternately, in the weekly religious papers called the Presbyterian, and a Roman Catholic paper, to be furnished by the first of January. It being understood that the communications shall be published after the following plan :—One party opening the first week, the other party replying the next week, and every piece to be republished in the immediately succeeding number of the Roman Catholic paper. The communications not to exceed four columns of the Presbyterian, nor to continue beyond six months, without consent of parties.

2. The parties agree that there is an infallible Rule of Faith established by Christ, to guide us in matters of religion, for the purpose of determining disputes in the Church of Christ.

3. They moreover agree, that after giving their views of the Rule of Faith, they shall proceed to discuss the question, "Is the Protestant religion, the religion of Christ?"

4. The parties agree respectively, to adhere strictly to the subject of discussion, for the time being, and to admit no second question, until the first shall have been exhausted. Each party shall be the judge when he is done with a subject, and shall be at liberty to occupy his time with a second topic, when he is done with the first, leaving to the other party the liberty of continuing to review the abandoned topic, as long as he shall choose ; subject, however, to be answered, if he introduce new matter.

5. Mr. Hughes to open the discussion, and Mr. Breckinridge to follow, according to the dictates of his own judgment.

JOHN BRECKINRIDGE.
JNO. HUGHES.

Philadelphia, December 14th, 1832.

RULE OF FAITH.

February 28, 1833.

To the Rev. John Breckinridge,

Rev. Sir,—I am delighted to find that the pressure of your "official duties" has not prevented you, in this instance, from replying to my letter, within the time prescribed. But *writing* and *reasoning* are not the same thing ;—and if you had replied not merely to my *letter*, but to my *arguments* against the Protestant rule of faith, you would, in my humble opinion, have rendered a better service to the cause in which you are engaged, at the same expense of postage and of press-work. The rapidity of transportation, as well as of composition, has probably contributed its share to the confusion, in which the topic returns from New York. When I last had the pleasure of addressing you, I requested you, by the respect you entertain for your own *signature at the head of this letter, to confine yourself to the actual "subject of discussion for the time being, and to bring forward no second question, until the first shall have been exhausted.*" The reader, who will take the trouble to cast his eye over the first two or three pages of your reply, will perceive with what elaborate fidelity you have *violated your own regulation*. I can hardly think of a subject, that has been omitted in your enumeration ;—except original sin, the foreknowledge of God, and the covenant of election. It would seem, that you had *copied* the whole theological index—the entire table of contents. For my own part, I do not find the space allowed us, ample enough for the multiplied evidences, appertaining to the single question at issue between us. It is true the fifth rule allows you to "follow me according to the dictates of your own judgment." But the fifth rule cannot warrant the violation of those which precede it. Your judgment, in this case, seems to prefer the instinctive, but wily logic of the bird, which is observed to quit the *nest* at the first approach of the truant school-boy, and to flutter about in every other direction. For having adopted this course, I am willing to grant you the merit of *sagacity*. If the Protestant rule of faith is founded neither on reason, nor revelation, but a manifest delusion, which *prejudice* alone has consecrated, then you did well to abandon its defence. This will account for the impatience of your pen, and your premature attack on the Catholic rule, in which, by introducing the old catalogue of " questions," you seem determined to bear me down, if not by the *quality* of your *reasoning*, at least by the *quantity* and confusion of your *matter*.

You are, indeed, correct in saying, that *the* rule of faith is the subject of discussion. And although I asked you to meet me in the investigation of the Protestant principle *first*, as the natural order of proceedings : yet I am candid enough to admit your right to deny this request. The argument of comparison seems to be your favourite— and the *Panacea* of religion, which you have provided for the acknowledged infirmities of the Protestant rule of faith, is the everlasting assertion, that "our rule works worse than yours." Since, however, you insist upon it, that both shall be placed side by side, for simultaneous investigation and comparison, I shall proceed to comply with the requisition.

" The parties agree that *there is an infallible rule of faith, established by Christ, to guide us in matters of religion, and to determine disputes in his Church.*" This, Rev. Sir, is the standard, by which, according to your own agreement, the *true rule* of Christian belief is to be determined. Now the professed principle of Protestantism is " the Bible alone, interpreted by each individual for himself." (If I mistake the Protestant rule, I request you to correct me.) I have given under ten distinct heads, the reasons, which make it manifest to my mind, that the Protestant principle, though *specious* in its theory, and flattering to the self-sufficiency of the human mind, is found to be a *delusion in practice*, and does not correspond, in a *single property*, with the definition of the rule instituted by the Redeemer of men. The Protestant rule is flattering to human pride, by teaching the most unlearned individual, that God has given him a Bible and an understanding, and that, by the application of the *one* to the *other*, he cannot be deceived, since it is the Almighty himself that speaks in the text. But who speaks in the *understanding?*—By this principle, however, he is bound to *frame his own creed;* and though all Christendom should agree in pronouncing his belief a heresy, he is bound to hold that *all Christendom* is in error, and that he alone is right, since he follows the infallible word of God, the Bible alone! This principle is the more delusive and dangerous, because it carries with it a seeming air of respect and reverence for the inspired writings; whilst in fact there is not a text in the sacred volume, which it does not give up to be broken on the wheel of private interpretation. It entirely overlooks the distinction, that it is not the book, but the *true meaning of the* book, which constitutes the word of God. It is thus, that Protestants, by following *out their own rule of faith to its legitimate consequences*, have walked, under the pretended guidance of the Bible alone, into the doctrines of Socinianism. This has been called "the grand heresy of the Reformation;"—but how bitterly may its professors retort on their Protestant brethren of other denominations. "You have proclaimed," they may say, "that since the Reformation every man has the right to interpret the Scripture for himself, and when *we exercise this right*, you stigmatize us with the brand of heresy! You are truly consistent, gentlemen! You tell us to interpret the sacred record for ourselves, and *when we follow your advice*, we are heretics, forsooth." Can this then, Rev. Sir, be the RULE appointed by Christ? But you will ask me, as usual, in what is the Catholic principle better? And it is but reasonable that I should endeavour to satisfy your inquiry.

Our rule of faith is laid down in the apostles' creed. "I believe in the Holy Catholic Church." This rule, you perceive, does not exclude, but comprises the belief of the Holy Scriptures. By the Church, I understand, that visible society of Christians, composed of the people, who are taught, and the Pastors who *teach*, by virtue of a certain divine commission, recorded in the 28th chapter of Saint Matthew, addressed to the apostles and *their legitimate successors*, "until the end of the world." "Go ye, therefore, *teach all nations:* baptizing them in the name of the Father, and of the Son, and of the Holy Ghost; *Teaching them* to observe all things whatsoever I have commanded you: and, behold *I am with you all days, even to the consummation of the world.*" 19, 20. By consulting the pages of the New Testament, not as an inspired book, if you choose, but as an authentic historical document, in which sense it is admitted even by Deists, I find that Jesus Christ proved the divinity of his mission and of his doctrine by evidences which it required the *power of the Deity* to exhibit. After having thus proved *himself* to be infallible, he required that men should believe his doctrines *under pain of eternal ruin.* "He that believeth not shall be condemned." Mark xvi. 16. Now, you have agreed, that the rule, by which our *belief* is to be guided, was appointed by Christ himself, and is therefore infallible—since it would be blasphemy to say, that Christ has appointed a principle of guidance, capable of leading astray. In my first argument against the pretension of the Protestant rule of faith, I showed that *Christ did not establish it.* That *he did establish the Catholic rule*, is what I shall now proceed to demonstrate.

I. In the commission referred to above, *all nations* and *all days*, even to the end of the world, *are included.* Therefore, the fulfilment of the Saviour's injunction required that the apostles should have *successors* in the ministry of "teaching;" since the term of human life, which remained to them, bore no proportion of the *extent of the "commission,"* which was limited only by the boundaries of the *universe*—"all nations"—and of time—"all days, *even to the consummation of the world.*" I defy you, Rev. Sir, to detect *error*, either in the premises or conclusion of this reasoning. Since, then, Christ appointed a perpetual succession of pastors in his Church, for the purpose of "*teaching all nations,*" during "*all days,*" it is not by exercising an unfounded or arbitrary prerogative, but in simple *obedience to the injunction of Jesus Christ,* that Catholics hearken to the voice of the church, and the teaching of its pastors. I called on you in a former letter, to show that Christ established the *Protestant rule;* and those, who never before suspected the delusion of that principle, must have been disappointed, and pained at the lame manner, in which you endeavour to escape from the difficulty. They were obliged to *suppose,* that the "commission," instead of extending to "*all nations and all times,*" as *Christ had said,* EXPIRED with the apostles;—and to *suppose* that *every* believer had the inspired instructions of some one of the "twelve," and a copy of the Old Testament;—and *to suppose* that the latter, together with the last "apostle," (after the death of the others,) constituted what you call "the equivalent to the Protestant rule of faith," during the interval between the ascension of Christ and the death of St. John. And, finally, they were obliged to *suppose,* that from the moment of *his decease,* all living authority of "teaching" was supplanted, by placing the Bible alone in the hands of each individual; leaving him to infer, that the *dreams of private interpretation* constitute the rule of Christian belief, appointed by *the Saviour himself!!* And all this on your authority! —And all this, in opposition to testimony, which Protestants *profess* to respect. For, besides the "*commission to teach,*" the Son of God has declared to the same effect, "I will pray the Father, and he shall give you another comforter, that he may abide with you FOREVER, the Comforter which is the Holy Ghost, whom the Father will send in my name: He shall *teach you all things,* and bring all things to your remembrance, whatsoever I have said unto you." John xiv. 16, 26. "He, that heareth you, heareth me." Luke x. 16. In the same manner has he pledged *his veracity,* that "the gates of hell shall not prevail against his church"—that, "He himself will abide with it FOREVER"—and St. Paul tells us, that "faith comes by HEARING, and hearing by the word of God"—and that Christ has "given some apostles, and some prophets, and some evangelists, and some *pastors* and *teachers,* for the perfecting of the saints, for the work of the ministry." Eph. iv. 11. The same apostle elsewhere says of the church, that it is "the pillar and ground of truth." Will you, then, Rev. Sir, impugn the veracity of the Saviour, by asserting, that when, in these texts, he said "*forever,*" *he* MEANT only "till the death of the last apostle?" If you say so, the *Universalist* will comprehend the value of the *admission;* and he will borrow your key to explain *everlasting* punishment.

The question is not now, Rev. Sir, whether it is to the pastors of the Roman Catholic church, or to those of the Protestant churches, that belongs the inheritance of this divine commission and of these immortal promises. The question is not now, what are the marks of the *true* church;—but the question is *the true rule of faith.* The texts of Scripture adduced above, prove that the Catholic principle has the *first property of the true rule;* viz. "*it was established by Christ.*" But this is not all. To prove that, in the primitive church, these texts were understood in the sense in which I have used them, I will take the liberty of quoting briefly the testimony of two credible witnesses. St. Irenæus, the disciple of St. Polycarp, says: "supposing the *apostles had not left us the Scriptures,* ought we not, still to have followed the ordinance of *tradition,* which they consigned to those to whom they committed the churches? It is this ordinance of traditions, which *many nations of barbarians, believing in Christ, follow, without the use of letters or ink.*" Iren. adv. hæres. L. iv. C. 64. Tertullian, who lived two hundred years after Christ, says in his book of Prescription, pp. 36, 37: "*that* doctrine is evidently *true,* which was *first delivered;*—on the contrary, *that* is false, which is of a *later date.* This maxim stands immoveable against the attempts of all late heresies. Let such, then, produce the origin of their churches: let them show the succession of their bishops from the apostles or their disciples. If you live near Italy, you see before your eyes the Roman church. Happy church! to which the apostles left the inheritance of doctrines with their blood! Where Peter was crucified, like his master; where Paul was beheaded, like the Baptist. If this be so, it is plain, as we have said, that heretics are not to be allowed to appeal to the Scripture, since they have no claim to it." Similar to this is the testimony of St. Vincent, of Lerius, in the *fifth century.* "It *never was,*" says he, "or *is,* or *will be* lawful for Catholic Christians to *teach* any doctrine, except that which *they once received:* and it *ever was,* and *is,* and *will be* their duty, to condemn those who do so. Do the heretics, then, appeal to the Scriptures? Certainly they do, and this with the *utmost confidence.* You will see them running hastily through the different books of Holy Writ, those of Moses, Kings, the Psalms, the Gospels, &c. At home and abroad, in their discourses and in their writings, they hardly produce a sentence, which is not crowded with the words of Scripture.—Let us remember, however, that Satan transformed himself into an angel of light. If he could turn the Scriptures (referring to St. Matt. iv. 6.) *against the Lord of Majesty, what use may he not make of them, against us poor mortals.*—Finally," he continues, " the *divine text* is to be interpreted according to the *tradition* of the Catholic church." Now, let me inform you, that the word " *tradition,*" in all these passages, means simply, the *doctrines transmitted* from the apostles, in the ministry of *teaching* by the Pastors of the church.

The next evidence I shall produce in support of the Catholic rule of faith, and against the Protestant principle, is derived from a source, which I am sure you will respect. It is the doctrine and practice of your own church, laid down in the Westminster Confession.

The first is the *Baptism of* INFANTS, sanctioned by the "teaching" of the Pastors of the Church, but certainly not susceptible of proof by any text of sacred Scripture. (Page 159.) The second is the violation of the Sabbath, commanded by God to be sanctified, (Exodus xx. 8.) and the substitution of Sunday, (*without the* AUTHORITY *of any single text of Scripture;* but in accordance with the constant "*teaching*" of the Pastors of the Church. (Page 132.) The third is, in the mutual *promises* exacted both from the *minister* and the *congregation* in the ceremony of ordaining, when the former is *obliged* to promise "*submission* to the discipline of the church," and the latter, both "OBEDIENCE and *submission* unto the new minister, as having RULE OVER THEM *in the Lord.*" (Page 590.) Is there any Scriptural *evidence* to show that St. Paul required such promises, from either Titus or Timothy, previous to ordination? I use this reference not as an argument, but rather as a commentary; which, considering its *source*, is no small compliment to the Catholic rule of faith, at the expense of your own. I may add also, that in the year 1729, the Synod of Philadelphia passed an act, called the "adopting act," by which not only candidates, but professed ministers, were "*obliged*" to adopt the Westminster Confession, as *containing* the summary of the Scriptural doctrine,—by way, I suppose, of proving the *sufficiency* of the "Bible ALONE; interpreted by each individual for himself." (See Dr. Miller's 2d and 6th letters to Presbyterians.)

My first conclusion, then, is, that the Catholic rule of faith *was instituted by Christ;* that it is the rule, which prevailed, except among the deluded votaries of heresy, in all the former ages of the Christian Church—and finally, that it is the principle to which the Presbyterians are *obliged* to have recourse, on a variety of occasions. The reader of course, must judge, whether the facts and the reasoning authorize this first conclusion.

II. Is it infallible? If the foregoing conclusion be correct, it must be infallible, *according to your own definition*—since "it was established by Christ." At this stage of the comparison and investigation of the two rules, let us pause and compare notes. You say that the Scriptures are infallible: and I agree with you entirely in this belief.—But, then, you will agree with me, that the infallibility of the Scripture consists IN THE SENSE and not in the ink, binding, or paper of which the volume is composed. Itself declares that "the letter killeth, but the *spirit* giveth life." The Protestant principle, therefore, is not rational, for this reason, that, although the Book be in every case infallible, the private INTERPRETATION of the book is, in every case, confessedly *the reverse.* If you hear a Unitarian quote Scripture, *to prove* that Jesus Christ was a very good man, but *nothing more;*—a Swedenborgian, to prove that this "very good man" was *Jehovah the eternal God*, and that the idea of two other distinct *persons* in the Deity is an *error;*—if you hear the Episcopalian quoting it to establish the distinction between bishops and presbyters,—the Universalist,—indulging his charity, for the *honour* of the Almighty and the comfort of the human race,—quoting it, to *disprove* the existence of a devil or a hell, which he regards as superstitious, that not even the light of the reformation was capable of expelling—what do you say in all these cases? You say that the individual has, indeed, the ink, paper, book, and even the *words of Scripture*, but that the *sense* and *true meaning* are *wanting*. Then—EVERY THING IS WANTING. Where then, I would ask, is the *security* on which either *they* or *you* can depend, unless the *interpretation*, as well as the text, be infallible? But this you have given up—and methinks I hear you solving the difficulty by the all potent interrogatory—" in what is your rule better?"

It is better in this; that according to our rule, the Scripture, so far as *doctrine and morals* are concerned, has but *one sense* and *one meaning*, through *all the ages of the church, and all the nations of the earth*. With us, it is a principle of religion and of common sense, that the Holy Ghost does not contradict himself either in the Scripture, or in the interpretation of it; and consequently the *meaning* is the same *now*, that it was before the Reformation, and up to the days, when the church *received the Divine Book* from the hands of the inspired authors. But you will say we are forbidden to read the Scriptures. Indeed, Sir, we are not. But if they were liable to the *same* abuse, *by our rule*, as they are by *yours*, we should not only accept but even *solicit* the prohibition.

Here you will say, or rather you have said in your objections, that our rule is also fallible, " in as much as I can never be more certain, in learning the doctrines of the church, than you are in your interpretation of the Bible." To this I reply, that I can—and I will show you in what way. According to the Catholic rule of faith, the doctrines of Christianity are not *abstract speculations;* they are "*positive truths, facts*," unchanged and unchangeable, as they came from the lips of Jesus Christ and his inspired apostles. But, being *public truths, or facts*, they were taught by the pastors of the church, and believed by the people in all countries, and in every century since the *establishment* of the church. Consequently, I can verify them with the same *certainty*, which I have that such an event as the battle of Waterloo, the decapitation of Charles I., or the council of Nice, took place in the world. In neither case is a *divine* or *personal infallibility* necessary. When I say that 2 and 4 make 6;—that Charles X. was expelled from France;—that Luther had a *misunderstanding* with Leo X.;—that John Huss was burned to death at *Constance*, and Michael Servetus in *Geneva;*—I assert propositions which are infallibly true. But when I take up the words of Jesus Christ, "This is my body," and assert their *meaning* to be " this is *not* my body;" the case is entirely changed. And why? Because, in this I utter a *mere speculative proposition—an opinion*. Now, according to the Protestant rule of faith, every text of Scripture, *connected with doctrine*, must go through such an ordeal of SPECULATION: and is it to be wondered at, that, under the guidance of *such a principle*, men should be divided off into *parties* and *opinions; for*, and *against*, every doctrine;—from the " washing of feet," up to the Saviour's divinity? The situation of a Catholic is very different:—

when he is a child, he is instructed in the summary of the Christian doctrine, by his parents and his catechism. This is the order of nature as well as of religion. When he grows up, he finds his immediate pastor inculcating, and developing from the pulpit, the same dogmas of belief which were laid down in his catechism. He finds his pastor *teaching the same* DOCTRINES which are *taught* by all the other pastors, monks, friars, doctors, cardinals, bishops, including the Pope—and believed, by all the Catholic people and pastors in the whole universe! If he be a gentleman of leisure and fortune, and fond of travelling, he may visit France, Scotland, Germany, Greece, Spain, Egypt, Palestine, China, Italy, Ireland, Peru, Canada, and our own Republic—and in every island, and on every continent, in every country under heaven, he will find the pastors of the Catholic church *teaching*, and the people, with the pastors, *believing* identically the same DOCTRINES. If he be a scholar, the pages of universal history are before him. He may consult *antiquity*, and he will find that the DOCTRINES, which are *now taught* by the pastors, and believed by both pastors and people, were *taught* and believed by pastors and people in every age since the birth of Christianity. If he be a linguist and a biblical critic, he may consult the writings of the fathers, and the sacred volume, either in the original text, or as we have it, and he will find that Jesus Christ made *the promises* of infallibility to the succession of *teaching*, and, NOT to *writing, reading*, or *private interpretation*.

But what, you ask, if he be a "*collier?*" Why, in that case, his mother will have taught him the Lord's prayer; the angelical salutation, commonly called the " Hail Mary!"—and the Apostle's Creed, in which he says, "I believe in the Holy Catholic church"—a profession of faith, which includes every article, believed (with more *accuracy* of conception, indeed, and *distinctness* of definition) by the most learned doctor or bishop of the church. But besides, his mother will have taught him to make the sign of the cross, in the name of the Father, Son, and Holy Ghost, to signify, by this *sign*, his faith in the redemption of Christ on the cross; and by the *words*, his belief in the adorable Trinity—and now, I will send him down to the *mines*, at the age of ten years, furnished with a more *orthodox creed*, than some of your Protestant ministers profess, after having " worked" by the Protestant rule of faith for forty years. Neither God, nor common sense requires him to read the 101 folios, which you have been pleased to compile for his use.

But if he be a Protestant "collier," what then? He must *wait* until he is able to regulate his belief according to the " Bible alone." Of course, he must read *all*, to make the rule complete. But if some passages seem to contradict others? Why, then he has to *compare parallel passages, and explain one text by another*. But he cannot read. Then he must hear it read. The first chapter of the gospel of St. John, is not more than half finished, when he exclaims, " I am a poor uneducated man, and I really do not understand what you read. Just tell me, *in plain language*, what the book says." " It says, that Infant Baptism is sufficient," replies my learned opponent. —" No," retorts the Baptist, you must *believe* and be baptized, and that by immersion."- - 'The baptism of the spirit is sufficient," says the Quaker.—"Why, gentlemen," cries out the collier, "you startle me!" "You must repent and avoid hell," continues the Methodist. "There is no hell in the Bible," says the Universalist, "it is a bugbear invented by priestcraft."—"You must worship Christ," says the Lutheran. "If you do," says the Unitarian, "you will commit idolatry; for Christ is nothing more than a mere creature, *according to the Scriptures*—the Father *alone* is God." "Oh! how you blaspheme," exclaims the Swedenborgian, "The Son *alone* constitutes the Deity; 'The Father"—"Stop, gentlemen," interrupts the collier; "pray whence did you get this book?"—"From the Saviour of the world," answer all.—"And for what purpose?"—"Why, *as an infallible rule of faith*," says Mr. Breckinridge, "*to guide us in matters of religion, and to determine disputes in the Church of Christ.*" —"But by what rule do you interpret it?"—"We are Protestants," answer all, "and the Bible alone, interpreted by each individual 'for himself,' is *our* rule of faith."—' Well, gentlemen, I am, as you perceive, a plain, uneducated collier; but if God has given me an ounce of common understanding, whereby to form a judgment, my judgment, from what I have *seen and heard*, is *this*—either, that Jesus Christ was a *juggler;* or, that your rule of faith is *false;*—or, that I am DERANGED. You are all learned men—and you will select whichever of these three alternatives you may prefer. Farewell."

The case of the collier is one that has an *important bearing* on the general question, and I am glad you reminded me of it. It furnishes the illustration, and proves the truth of a remark I made at the commencement of my first letter—that the "*tendency* of the Protestant principle of private interpretation is to *sap the foundations* of the Christian religion." Will you, then, Rev. Sir, still say, that admitting your rule to work *badly*, "ours works worse?"

Having disposed of the collier, I must now proceed to answer the objections, so called, which you have brought forward against the Catholic rule of faith.—"Their name is Legion." If the foregoing *facts* and *reasoning* of this letter be correct, however, then the largest portion of the *brood* has already been "eaten up," in the arguments. The rest are founded on a *misconception* of the real state of the question, and disappear as soon as they are understood.

1st. Then, it is a principle of our belief, that the dogmas of our Church were originally *revealed by Christ, and taught by his apostles:* that these dogmas, or *articles of faith*, and morals, are the only objects for the definition and transmission of which, in the "teaching of the pastors," the divine promise of infallibility is recorded in the Scripture, claimed by the church, or necessary in the revelation of revealed truth. The *obstinate rejection* of one or more of these *articles of faith* —by following private opinion, in opposition to the teaching and belief of the whole church, is what constitutes the crime of heresy; and the man who acts thus, ceases to belong to our communion. But as the individual has no right to reject what has been always, and is everywhere *taught and believed*,—so neither does the church *claim*, nor has she *ever exercised the right* of *creating*, or *imposing on him* the belief of *new* articles of faith. You mistake, then, Rev Sir, the language of *definition* for *the words of creation*, whenever you say that any of our *doctrines began* in "such a year," or in "such a century:" until which time it had been, as you suppose, "a probationer for a seat in the creed." However, in thus confounding the *definition*, with the *creation* of doctrine, you only follow the example of a learned Protestant, and they say, a very benevolent and moral man—I mean Dr. Priestly. In his "History of Early Opinions," he argues, that the *Divinity of Christ*, never dreamt of, as he supposes, in the *life* of the apostles, "crept in," as an "opinion" a short time afterwards, spread silently, and *waxed strong*, until it was finally ENACTED *into an article of faith* in the council of Nice, A. D. 325.

2d. Besides *doctrines—articles of faith*——and morals—which are *immutable*, there is *discipline*, for which infallibility is neither claimed nor necessary. Discipline is *different* from doctrine; it may be adapted to the circumstances of different ages and countries. It is the mere *livery* of faith: and obvious as is the *distinction*, we have heard Protestant Doctors, if they can detect a single *button*, more or less in Spain or Italy, than they have been accustomed to see in our own country, exclaim, "Lo! what is become of the boasted infallibility?" Answer, It is watching, as a guardian angel, by the side of those "*positive truths*," "*facts*," "*doctrines*," which Jesus Christ revealed to his apostles, and commanded them *to teach* to "all nations," in "all days," even to the end of the world. Discipline may vary—doctrine is always the same—just as a man may change his garment, without *forfeiting* his personal identity.

3d. There are besides *doctrine* and *discipline, opinion*,—but they are not about the "Divinity of Christ," or the "real presence." They are on questions, concerning which no positive revelation has been given by the Saviour, or preached by the apostles. That these *opinions* have been *warmly* and *uselessly discussed* and agitated, is a fact that I am as willing to proclaim as you are. Catholics may hold *either* side in any of these opinions, without ceasing to be Catholics —precisely because they are *opinions*, and not *doctrines*. This distinction is not new. St. Augustine referred to it, when he said, "*In necessariis unitas; in non necessariis libertas; in omnibus, charitas.*"—"In matters of *faith, unity;* in matters *not of faith, liberty;* in *all matters, charity.*"

4th. There are besides these, *local* customs and habits peculiar to different countries and ages.

Now, Rev. Sir, I defy human ingenuity, to extract from all you have written, one single *genuine* argument against the *Catholic rule of faith*. You present, indeed, in each of your letters, a crowd of assertions against local customs and free opinions of Catholics: against the discipline or doctrines of the church, with which doctrine *alone* is the infallibility of the Catholic rule of faith connected; and condemning our doctrines by your confessedly fallible principle of guidance, you arrive at the easy conclusion, that our rule of faith is not the true rule! Have you attempted to show that it did correspond with *your own definition* of the true rule?—That it was not "established by Christ?"—That it is not competent "to guide us in matters of religion"—or "to determine disputes in the Church of Christ?" No!

And yet THIS DEFINITION is the *true standard*, by which we have both agreed to compare the Catholic and the Protestant rules; and to determine which of the two is the *false*, and which is the *true principle* of guidance, in ascertaining the doctrines of Christ, as distinguished from the opinions of men. This is the *standard* with which *I* compared the Protestant rule of faith—when I proved in my former letters, that *the one* has *not a single property*, in common with the other. This I proved in ten distinct propositions, supported by facts and arguments, to which, as laid down in my *last* letter, I beg leave to refer the reader. He will perceive that you never take up my argument, *as it has been arranged by myself*—but having *moulded* it into a *manageable shape*, you refute the *creature* of *distortion*, but leave the *difficulty*, unsolved. Allow me to give a specimen from your last epistle.

VI. VII. "There are two methods of settling disputes, *reason* and *force; you* take the latter; *we* the former. There are two rules, the Bible and the Church of Rome. *You assert that the Bible has failed, and thus make* YOUR CHURCH BETTER THAN CHRIST AND HIS APOSTLES." Indeed, Rev. Sir, I should be sorry to be *guilty* of either the argument, or the *blasphemy*. Let the reader compare this with my own argument, VI. and VII. and I have no doubt but he will acquit me of the charge. What opinion he may form of the cause which required it, or the individual by whom it is preferred, it is not for me to determine. The other weaknesses of your attempt to reply to those ten arguments I shall leave for the present unexposed. For I have not the talent of " adhering *strictly* to the question under discussion for the time being"—and yet broaching, in the same letter, every *question*, that has been agitated since the Reformation. These are contradictions, which your pen alone, it seems, can reconcile.

But a more painful task is imposed on me, in reference to two or three assertions of yours, in which there is an entire departure from the *truth of history and of facts*. You assert that *opinions pass into articles of faith, or doctrine in the Catholic Church;* and for this you quote the authority of Bellarmine, but I defy you to quote ten lines *before*, and ten lines *after* the words " fere de fide," without convicting yourself of what is not becoming a " minister of the Gospel." In the same manner you say, that Leo X. condemned Luther for saying : " *It is not in the power of the Church or the Pope to constitute new articles of faith. This is untrue*. Being a mere historical *fact*, if it is not untrue, you can easily prove the contrary." Another assertion which is *untrue*, is, that, " as to the Pope's supremacy, there are no less than *three* systems in our church." Now I defy you, or any one else, to name a single Catholic in the whole universe, that has publicly denied *the Pope's supremacy*, WITHOUT FORFEITING COMMUNION AND MEMBERSHIP, BY THE DENIAL. And if you cannot, what will Protestants think of your assertion, that there *are three systems* (of doctrine) in our church on that subject ?—and what will they think of a cause defended by such—*argument?* When we come to speak of the " Vulgate edition of the Scriptures;" " the Sacraments ;" " the doctrine of intentions ;" " the Apocryphal books," as you term them ; " the liberties, which you say (falsely, as I hold) the church has taken with the word of God ;" " the Writings of the

Fathers;" "Purgatory;" "depriving the people of the cup of the Eucharist;" "Indulgences;" "Prayer in an unknown tongue;" &c. &c. &c. &c. *I bind myself to prove,* that you have misrepresented these doctrines, and asserted what is not correct. In the mean time, the question is, the RULE OF FAITH. If it be true, as I have shown, and as you have admitted, that Protestants have nothing, and, by their *rule of private interpretation, can* have nothing, more certain, than their *speculative opinions,* even for the *most sacred* of their own doctrines; so, neither can they have any thing more for the *condemnation* of ours. You first condemn our doctrines by your own *opinions,* and then condemn our "rule of faith" by our doctrines! The rule of faith is to be judged and determined not *by your opinions* of either your own doctrine, or ours—but by the *definition.* Is *your rule true?* Is IT INFALLIBLE? "WAS IT ESTABLISHED BY CHRIST?" That is the real question. For if Christ revealed *doctrines,* and required of men to *believe* those doctrines, under pain of eternal condemnation (Mark xvi. 16.) and yet, appointed as a medium for ascertaining *what they are*—a *rule* by which, instead of being preserved *as doctrines,* they are *resolved into a mass of opinions,* as diversified and contradictory *as those which spring* from *private interpretation;*— then we need not inquire, who is *right* or who is *wrong.* Every man has a right to his "*opinion,*" whether he denies the *real presence* in the Eucharist, the necessity of *regeneration,* or the Divinity of Jesus Christ. In all revelation there is not an *opinion*—and in all Protestantism, there is nothing else but opinion;—you have not attempted to deny either of these propositions.

You have quoted the ambitious projects and pretensions of individual Popes. Among them there have been a few bad, out of a multitude of good, virtuous, and holy men. The fact, however, proves nothing more against *our rule of faith,* than the crime of Judas does against the infallibility of *Jesus Christ;* or the incarceration of a wretched Presbyterian clergyman in the State-prison of New York does against the orthodoxy of the "Westminster Confession." You know to whom I allude—and although *he* belonged to *your* communion, I would rather shed a tear over his misfortunes, than stop to glean arguments from the dark record of his crimes, conviction, and ruin. I should distrust my cause, if I thought it required them.

Your pretty little story about the "shepherds at the brook," would be admirable in *pastoral* compositions—it is so *simple.* But in *polemics* it is quite out of place. Would you know why? Because, *there* the *shepherds, sheep* and *lambs* were many;—*here,* the rule of faith, according to your own definition and agreement, is but ONE. And if I prove that it is *not that,* which Protestants profess to follow—the reader can easily draw the conclusion.

But then in Rome, there is one day in the year (not to speak of kissing the Pontifical slipper) for "blessing horses, asses, and other beasts!" In answer to this, I have only to say that on *no day* of the year, would a minister of the Gospel refuse, *if respectfully invited,* to perform a similar operation, over a piece of good beef, such as may always be found in our Philadelphia markets. I see no difference, except that in *this case* the "beast" happens to be dead; and that the maxim has it "nil nisi *bonum* de *mortuis*." But, Rev. Sir, the courtesies of society regard *us both* as *clergymen*, notwithstanding your mutilated exordium, "Sir"—and *as clergymen* it does not become us to treat so grave a subject, with levity or ridicule. Is the Protestant *principle* the true rule of Christian faith, or is it not the rule, exclusively of sectarian opinion? That is the real question—on the proper solution of which *may depend* the salvation of immortal souls, for whom Christ died. If there are under heaven, in the whole volume of reason and revelation, arguments to prove, that the "Bible alone, interpreted by each individual for himself," is "the *infallible rule of faith*"—that "the Bible alone, interpreted by each individual for himself," is "*the rule established by Christ*"—"*to guide us in matters of religion and to determine disputes in his church,*"—I again entreat you to furnish them. If *no such arguments* can be furnished, then is *your rule of faith* of *human* invention, and not of Christ's appointment. The "definition" constitutes the *mark* of the Divine "Shepherd" stamped upon the *true rule*, under the guidance of which, there is but "one sheepfold," his disciples being "one" in *doctrine*, as "He and the Father are one," in nature and purpose.—Yours, &c.

JNO. HUGHES.

RULE OF FAITH.

New York, 5th March, 1823.

To the Rev. John Hughes.

Rev. Sir,—You rise from your prostration with the air of victory. It is however, I think, a little abatement to your chivalry, that you should still *cry out* against my arguments, and yet meet them, in chief part, with reiterated complaints of my departure from " the Rules," and clamorous demands to keep to the question. When you proposed to undertake a discussion with me, I requested a reply to my first printed letter. You declined. I proposed a public, oral discussion. You declined. After much negotiation, the present channel was agreed on. The rules were, very much, of your own defining; you insisted that we should first discuss the rule of faith, and *you* must begin. I proposed that after examining the rule of faith, we should take this for the point of debate, " Is the religion of *Roman Catholics* the religion of Christ?" You still declined, and we must change it to this, " Is the religion of *Protestants* the religion of Christ?" And now, after all these concessions, you claim to *interpret* these rules, and even to *determine how I* shall conduct my argument; and while the nerves of your cause are cracking under the pressure of truth, gravely charge me with violating rules and passing by the question! I am weary of this unmanly strife of words, and " vain jangling" about modes and forms. Once for all therefore, let me settle this matter. If the reader will refer to " the rules," at the head of your letter, he will perceive that the 3d assigns the "*rule of faith*" as the first subject of discussion, and with the following amplitude, " *after giving their views of the rule of faith,*" &c. Does this not bring up the whole subject of the rule of faith? The 4th rule requires us, " *to adhere strictly to the subject of discussion for the time being—and to admit no second question,*" &c. &c. Now I ask, have I not discussed, throughout, one and the same question, viz: the rule of faith?—Both in my first and second letters, (Nos. 2 and 4.) I replied to all your objections. But I did not stop there. I went on to expose your rule. By a great number of yet unanswered arguments, I proved its utter fallibility. I have shown, by the confession of your own writers, that you are compelled to use *private interpretation*, by fallible men, in order to find out from the Bible your church and your rule: I have exposed your judge of controversies, as one whom you could not agree on among yourselves, and who could not possibly be a judge, from the nature of the case: I have shown that your church has varied in doctrine from age to age, and therefore has not an infallible judge in her, as she pretends to have: I have shown that the direct tendency of your system was to corrupt the morals of the people and the worship of God, and therefore your rule was entirely fallible, and even greatly evil: I have shown that your rule usurps the prerogative of God, and that it violates the testimony of the senses: that it was not only fallible, but entirely uncertain: that it requires ignorance and implicit faith at its foundation in the minds of men: that it is incompatible, not only with personal, but with civil liberty: that under the guidance of your rule, the Bible has been shut against mankind: that the commandments have been mutilated, additions made to the word of God, and that new articles, and new sacraments have been added, under the authority of your rule: that even "the Fathers," the professed fountain of evidence in your behalf, have been purged of matter which went against you: and that by the authority of the Pope, writers in your communion of a later day, have been abridged, enlarged, or changed, to fit them to be witnesses to the Roman Catholic rule. These things have been clearly shown, as may be seen by a reference to the letters themselves. I ask, do they not bear directly on the question? Your chief reply to them as yet, is, that they violate the rules! When you attempt a rejoinder, the public will judge both of their fitness and their force.

Before I enter on the examination of your reasoning, it is proper here to meet and repel a paragraph near the close of your letter, viz. "But a more painful task is imposed on me, in reference to two or three assertions of yours, in which there is an entire departure from the truth of history and of facts. You assert that opinions pass into articles of faith or doctrine in the Catholic Church, and for this you quote the authority of Bellarmine; but I defy you to quote ten lines *before* and ten lines *after*, the words ' fere de fide,' without convicting yourself of what is not becoming ' a minister of the Gospel.' " Now I had said in my letter, "your church has added to the word of God new articles of faith, and even new sacraments to the institutions of Jesus Christ." I appealed for proof to various writers, and to the Bull of Pope Pius IV. You say nothing of these proofs. I then added, "*Bellarmine, we suppose, means this*, when he says of one article, ' fere de fide,' almost a matter of faith." Now if, instead of "slurring the notes," you had quoted from Bellarmine ten lines " before and ten lines after" the offensive passage, it would have come with a better grace from a Parthian arrow shot while in flight. But you proceed to remark, " In the same manner you say that Leo X. condemned Luther for saying: *It is not in the power of the Church or the Pope to constitute new articles of faith.—This is untrue*. Being a mere historical *fact*, if it is not untrue, you can easily prove the contrary." This is strong language! Yet you put the subject to a fair issue; let us try it—it is done in few words.— The Bull of Leo X. dated June 15th, 1520, levelled at Luther by name, contains forty-one pretended heresies, which are extracted from his writings, and solemnly condemned—his books are doomed to the flames—and he allowed sixty days to recant, or meet the thunders of the Vatican. The 27th article, by which Luther is anathematized for holding, is as follows; " Certum est in manu Ecclesiæ aut Papæ *prorsus non esse statuere articulas fidei.*" Which is, word for word, what I said before, viz. " *It is certain it is not in the power of the Pope or church, to ordain, or decree articles of faith.*" He denounces this and the other forty articles as " pestiferous," " scandalous," " seductive errors."—And yet you assert that " *it is untrue!*"—My proof then, is fully fortified. I would willingly explain your mistake, by referring it to ignorance—and your being startled at the statement shows the monstrous nature of the doctrine. But how shall I account for your *indecorum;* especially after convicting you of such an error?

I must, however, go into the defence of yet another "assertion," as you style it. " Another assertion which is *not true* is that as to the Pope's supremacy—there are no less than three systems in our (the Roman Catholic) church." I gave you proof of this when it was stated; but I will subjoin more. The council of Basle, A. D. 1439 (see Caranza's Summa Conciliorum, 33d. sessions, page 645) decreed as follows: " *That according to the council of Constance, it is a true article of the Catholic faith, that a council is above a Pope, and that whoever pertinaciously rejects this truth, is to be condemned as a heretic.*" Here, besides its own testimony, that of the Council of Constance is likewise conveyed. *This is one system.* It gives to the Pope a rank not only unequal in *degree*, but dissimilar in *kind* from the *second* system, which is called *Italian*, from its being the prevailing one at Rome, as the former is called *Gallican*, from its prevalence in France. The Italian school or second system hold to the Pope's *unlimited sovereignty* over the church; and make him officially infallible, and virtually *the church*. The Council of Florence, 5th Lateran and Trent make the Pope superior to general Councils. This you will hardly deny; if so, I have proof at hand. Johannes Devotus (Vol. 1. Book 1. Tit. 3. sec. 1.) on the supremacy of the Pope, has this caption: " The power of the Pope is episcopal, metropolitan, patriarchal and temporal. His decisions *from the chair* are infallible." The *third* system *deifies the Pope*. According to Gregory II. " the whole Western nations reckoned Peter a terrestrial God." (Labb. 8. 666.) We are told that Marcellus, in the Lateran Council, called Julius " a God on earth," and without rebuke from the Council. Bellarmine on Authority of Councils, Book 2. c. 17—says; " all the names which are given in the Scriptures to Christ, even these same names are given to the Pope— whence it appears that he is superior to the church." In Gratian's Decretals, p. 1. Dis. 96. Pope Nicholas to Michael, 7th chap. the Pope says, *He is a God, and therefore men cannot judge him.* I might multiply these proofs at pleasure. Here then are the *said three systems* distinctly made out. How you can then so positively say it "*is not true*" our fellow-citizens must judge.

We are now come to quite an era in this discussion, viz: *the first defence of your rule of faith!* Though it be in the 6th letter of the controversy, and its appearance now is only a peep at us from behind the clouds, yet we welcome its approach. Our rule of faith, you say, is laid down in the Apostles' Creed. " *I believe in the Holy Catholic Church.* This rule, you perceive, does not exclude, but comprises the belief of the Holy Scriptures." It may be said to be in substance, *this, the Holy Catholic Church, is the living, infallible interpreter of Scripture.* Now it will be borne in mind, that before any church can *interpret*, she must know what is to *be interpreted*. What do you mean then by " *the Holy Scriptures?*" The Council of Trent has settled this question for you, infallibly (as you say,)

'ALL THE BOOKS CONTAINED IN THE OLD VULGATE LATIN EDITION ARE SACRED AND CANONICAL." (Decree of the Coun. Trent, 4 sess.) Then besides our Bible, the Roman Catholic Scriptures include a number of books, viz. 1 and 2 Esdras, Tobit, Judith, Wisdom, Ecclesiasticus, Baruch, and 1 and 2 Maccabees. These make a *large volume* of themselves. The Jews, our Lord Jesus, the Apostles and early Fathers, unite to *exclude* these from the canon. You ought then to have *proved* them canonical, or dropped them from the Scriptures, as a preliminary step. The former you do not attempt; the latter were *heresy* in you.— When you say then that the Holy Scriptures are comprised in your rule, you deceive the reader,—since by "Holy Scriptures" he means one thing, and you quite another thing. Again, in defining your rule, you omit two other very material features which are strongly brought to view by the Council of Trent, (4 Sess.) 1. They say divine truth is contained both in the written books and " IN UNWRITTEN TRADITION." 2. Every Roman Catholic of every grade, binds himself solemnly as follows, " I *will never take or interpret them*, (the sacred Scriptures,) *otherwise than according to the unanimous consent of the Fathers*." (See Creed of Pope Pius IV.) Now it is apparent from these facts, that what you can call divine truth is quite another thing from the Bible; and it is equally clear that your church is restricted by her own decrees, to *interpret* this compound of Bible, Apocrypha, and unwritten tradition, according to the unanimous consent of "the Fathers." At this point, we see then either that "the fathers" were infallible and also unanimous in their interpretations of Scripture, or else your church receives her creed from fallible men, and can have no uniformity in her doctrines. But "the Fathers," you will own, were *fallible;* and that they were far from *unanimous*, I will presently unite with your Bellarmine and others, to prove. Let me here say, that the Roman Catholic rule, though withheld by you, is spread at large upon the records of your church, and from it I draw these definitions. If I err in them, the task of confutation is easy.

Having laid down your rule of faith, you proceed to prove that it was established by Christ, by an appeal to the Apostolical commission given Matt. xxviii. 17—20. The reader will please refer to it. Allow me here to put by the side of this, those passages which, added to it, make out the commission in full. " And these signs shall follow them that believe; in my name shall they cast out devils; they shall speak with new tongues." " They shall take up serpents; and if they drink any deadly thing, it shall not hurt them; they shall lay hands on the sick, and they shall recover." Mark xvi. 17, 18. "And ye are witnesses of these things."—"And behold I send the promise of my Father upon you; but tarry ye in the city of Jerusalem until ye be endowed with power from on high." Luke xxiv. 48, 49. " But ye shall receive power after that the Holy Ghost is come upon you; and ye shall be witnesses unto me, both in Jerusalem, and in all Judea, and in Samaria, and unto the uttermost parts of the earth." Acts i. 8.

Now we freely grant that the above passages confer a commission on the Apostles; and that they were divinely endowed, for the discharge of the great work which was given them to do. But on these texts you found the following reasoning; "*In the commission referred to above, all nations and all days even to the end of the world are included. Therefore the fulfilment of the Saviour's injunction, required that the Apostles should have successors in the ministry of teaching.*" "*Then it is not by exercising an unfounded prerogative, but in simple obedience to the injunction of Jesus Christ, that Catholics hearken to the voice of the Church and the teaching of its Pastors.*" The sum of it is this: the Apostles had certain divine endowments for their work; Christ intended the Apostles to have successors to the end of time; therefore their successors must have the same endowments. Now what was it that constituted an Apostle? (1.) No man could be an Apostle who had not been "*an eye witness*" to Christ's person, and works. (See Luke i. 2. and 2 Peter i. 16.) Paul says, 1 Corinthians ix. 1, "*Am I not an Apostle?*" "*Have I not seen the Lord?*" (See Acts i. 21, 22, and x. 41.) (2.) An Apostle *must receive his mission directly from Christ*, not by any human ordination. For this reason, Christ appeared to Paul visibly on his way to Damascus, and called him to the work of an Apostle; and this is what Paul means when he says, "*Last of all he (Christ) was seen of me, as of one born out of due time.*" 1 Cor. xv. 8. (3.) Every Apostle had *miraculous* and *extraordinary endowments:* such as inspiration, making him *infallible;* the gift of tongues; power to work miracles, (Mark xvi. 17, 18.) and to impart that power to others. (2 Cor. xii. 12.) The Apostles were told, (Acts i. 8.) to wait at Jerusalem for these supernatural gifts; and on the day of Pentecost they were accordingly furnished from on high, by the miraculous and extraordinary effusions of the Holy Ghost. By these endowments, they were enabled to speak at once many languages; to write inspired books; to cast out devils; raise the dead, &c. (4.) Every Apostle, as the name (*one sent*) signifies, and as the terms of the commission plainly show, was to go all abroad, with plenary authority; not to be stationary; or make his permanent seat any where, exclusively. Now it is obvious that the Apostles had no successors in these respects. It was impossible *after* the generation, in which Christ lived, had passed away, that the Apostles could have *such* successors; for it was necessary to their office and work *to have seen the Lord.* But this the second generation could not have done. It is plain also that such a succession was never designed by our Lord, or attempted by the Christians of the next age. It is true that JUDAS had a successor; but it was before the Apostles were fully endued by the Spirit and sent forth. And if *any* were to have successors, why not *all*, as well as *one?* Why not James at Jerusalem, John at Ephesus, and Paul at Antioch, as well as Peter at Rome? Why *Rome* more than eleven other cities? Will not all the texts you have quoted, apply as well to James at Jerusalem as to Peter at Rome? Had he not the promise of the same *Holy Spirit* to guide him as Peter? Is not John called "a pillar," (Gal. ii. 9.) as well as Peter? Why do you single out *infallibility* for your succession, and leave out all *other* qualifications? It is curious to remark how you omit even a *reference* to Mark xvi. 17, 18, where the gift of miracles is so inseparably united to the office of an Apostle You must admit, then, that there *are some respects in which the* Apostles had no successors. But if *some things* are wanting, your argument is vain. If *some things* are wanting, may not one of them be infallibility? And if *all the other* superhuman endowments ceased, why should infallibility continue? The conclusion is irresistible, that the Apostles had no successors, endued with extraordinary powers of any kind; and therefore the Roman Catholic rule of faith was not established by Christ.

But yet we hold to a commission still standing and binding, which reaches to the close of time: we believe in a visible catholic (not Roman) church, to which appertain the ministry, the oracles, and ordinances of God; which is to continue to the end of the world—to which the Holy Spirit is promised as an abiding gift; against which the gates of hell shall not prevail; and which is at last to fill the world. Of this church, Jesus Christ is the only head; and the Holy Spirit speaking in the Bible, the only infallible rule of faith.

You next introduce some of " the Fathers," to prove that the texts quoted by you were understood in their days, as you interpret them. I would here say that " *The Fathers*" have a hard lot in your church. You treat them as some people do their " *children*," or as the Hindoos do their idol gods; they *honour* them when they serve their purpose; and *whip* them when they do not. I have already shown the corrections to which they have sometimes been subjected, to square them to the uses of the church. Now let me bring some proofs directly to our purpose. Chrysostom, (who lived A. D. 398,) says, " *the church is known, (tantummodo,) only by the Scriptures.*" (Homil. 49 in Matt.) Bellarmine, however, says of this passage, " *It is probable the author was a Catholic, but it seems to be none of Chrysostom's.*" (De Scriptis Ecc's. A. D. 398.) Augustine, who lived A. D. 395, says, " Thou art Peter, and upon the rock, which thou hast confessed, upon *this rock*, which thou hast known, saying, 'Thou art Christ, the Son of the living God, will I build my church; I will build thee upon me, not me upon thee." (De verb. Domin. Serm. 13.) Yet Stapleton says of it, " it was a human error caused by the diversity of the Greek and Latin tongue, which either he was ignorant of, or marked not." (Princip. doct. lib. 6. c. 3.) But I will pass to examine an authority quoted by yourself, from Tertullian, in his book of Prescriptions, &c. &c. From the manner in which you extract it, the author is made to testify, that Rome is the great centre and head, where the " SUCCESSION" from the Apostles has its seat; and where the " Happy Church," reigns in undisturbed supremacy. Your quotation runs thus : " If you live near Italy, you see before your eyes the Roman Church. Happy church! to which the Apostles left the inheritance of doctrines with their blood! where Peter was crucified like his master, where Paul was beheaded like the Baptist."—But let us see his entire, ungarbled statement: " Survey the apostolical churches, in which the very chairs of the Apostles still preside over their stations, in which their own letters are recited, uttering the voice and epresenting the presence of each of them. Is Achaia nearest to thee? Thou hast Corinth. If thou art not far from Macedonia, thou hast the Philippians and the Thessalonians. If thou canst go to As'a, thou hast Ephesus; but if thou art near Italy, thou hast Rome, whence to us also authority is near at hand." (Prescriptions against Heretics.) And now, how very different is the passage and the meaning! How directly against Peter's supremacy and the exclusive claims of Rome! How extraordinary the liberty which you take with the author and with historical evidence! It was thus a man once proved from the 14th Psalm that there is no God—" 'The fool hath said in his heart, there is no God," is the entire verse. But dropping the first part of the sentence, it runs thus, "There is no God."

You ask in the second place, "Is the rule infallible?" and infer that it is, since it is established by Christ. I grant you that a rule established by Christ, *is infallible*. But as I have proved that Christ did not establish your rule, your conclusion falls to the ground. But let us proceed. It is not self-evident that your church is infallible, or your rule the true one. By what process then do you apply these texts to the *proof* of your rule? The process, I answer, of *private interpretation*. Then I would ask, is your interpretation fallible or infallible? If fallible, where is the right or safety of your interpretation, especially when the point in question is no less than that on which all others depend, viz. *where shall we go for an infallible rule?* This is the more surprising, as you charge upon the use of private judgment all the evils of heresy and schism, which have in every age rent the church of Christ—perverted the word of God—and ruined the souls of men. Do you refer me to your infallible church? But we are inquiring after the *proofs* of her infallibility. Then does she refer me to Scripture passages for *proof?* But how can I be certain that her interpretation is correct? Her infallibility does not *assure* me, for she has not yet *proved* her infallibility; and if she can prove her infallibility in *this way*, then private judgment is sufficient to settle the undoubted meaning of a great body of Scripture-passages, and terminate the *grand controversy*, on which all others depend. And what then becomes of the church of Rome's complaint of the great obscurity of Scripture, which is affirmed to render her aid so indispensable? And what must we think of her outcries against the supposed arrogance of pretending to the exercise of free inquiry, and of judging of the Scriptures for ourselves, when, without such an exercise and such a power of judging, it is found impossible to obtain the least *proof* or presumption of her pretended infallibility? *Some parts* of Scripture then, the church of Rome herself must allow, are capable of being understood without her aid. Those declarations on which she rests her claim to implicit submission and obedience, she *must* allow to be sufficiently plain and intelligible to bind the conscience of every member of her communion, who is prepared to give a reason for his being a Catholic: and as an entire agreement with the dogmas of the church is all the faith which she requires, in order to the salvation of her members, *she* must acknowledge, as well as ourselves, that the Scripture contains a rule of faith sufficient for the purpose of salvation. The only difference is, that in our opinion, the Scriptures clearly unfold a system of saving truth; while in that of the (Roman) Catholics *they are obscure in every point, except the few passages which direct us to the church,* (the only authentic and immediate source of saving knowledge.) "Her treatment of Scripture, almost reminds us of the fabulous history of 'Jupiter, who ascended to supreme power by the mutilation and banishment of his father.' "—*Robert Hall.*

We see then that your rule utterly fails as to the *proof of itself. In the next place it wholly fails in its application.* For either the Pope is infallible; or the council; or both united; or the universal church. It seems not to be agreed among yourselves where infallibility is lodged, and therefore even at the threshold, a great difficulty arises. If the universal church be the seat, this is plainly useless, for you can never come at its decisions. If the Pope be so, the world must go to Rome; or die in darkness. If a Pope, and a general Council united make the infallible judge, (which is not self-evident, and must therefore be proved,) then as Roman Catholics commonly believe, you have the absurdity, that *two fallibles make an infallible.* Two negatives may make an affirmative in grammar; but it will not do so in religion—for if you add *fallible* to *fallible* forever, the *sum* is fallible still. But if the infallible judge, (which is your rule of faith,) be found in the Pope and Council united, still it is out of the reach of the people. Such a council has not been held for two hundred and seventy years! But to answer any end, it ought to hold a constant session.—And not only so, but it ought to be omnipresent—for otherwise the millions of the people, which you speak of, in "France, Scotland, Germany, Greece, Spain, Egypt, Palestine, China, Italy, Ireland, Peru, Canada, our own Republic, and in every island, and on every continent, and in every country under heaven"—cannot consult this *oracle. All these* millions are concerned to know its declarations; yet cannot; and ruin ensues. For there are only two possible ways to reach the mass of men, viz., either by *living-teachers*, or by the *decrees of councils.* But both these methods are *liable to error;* you are therefore without a rule. No teacher is infallible, as you allow; the decrees of the councils which few possess and fewer read, are at least as obscure as the Bible. The private interpretation of the Bible you call "*the grand heresy of the Reformation;*" surely *then the private interpretation of decrees,* is not *less* an evil! *It appears then, that your boasted infallible rule is utterly inapplicable;* and while you decry the Bible, in the hands of the people, as the rule of faith, you have no *substitute;* and your cause is ruined

I remark next, *that your reasoning as to an infallible rule of faith, if well founded, leads us to reject every system that does not make all men perfect.* For you agree that Christ has established an infallible rule to "*guide us in matters of religion,*" as well as "*settle disputes*" in his church. You argue that a rule which does not "settle disputes" *as to doctrine,* is fallible, and therefore not Christ's rule. Now by parity of reasoning, a rule that does not regulate *practice* so as to make an *end of sin*, and make *men perfect here*, must be a fallible rule. For faith is in order to holiness—and the rule of faith looks finally "*to the purifying of our souls even as Christ is pure.*" But your rule, I need hardly say, "*makes none of the comers thereunto perfect.*" On the contrary, one of your own distinguished advocates said that the generality of your writers on morals, seemed "*to have it as their great business, to teach how near a man might lawfully come, and yet not sin.*" (Sir Thomas More.) Surely then if you are consistent, you should reject your rule. I do not see how you can retain it, and yet argue against the Bible as a rule of faith, because it fails to make those infallible who adopt it as such.

You take peculiar pleasure in associating the Protestant name and cause with infidelity and extreme heresies. The names of " Volney and Priestly," of " Universalists," " Unitarians," &c. &c. seem to fluctuate through your fancy in close alliance with liberty of thought, with the use of the Bible, and the freedom of the press. Now it is very certain that the Bible never made a *Roman Catholic;* and the fear expressed by one of the defenders of your faith in former days, that its *free perusal made Protestants*, ever haunts your loyal breast. Let me here remind you that *Atheism* has always flourished most, by the side of the Roman shrine; and where the Bible has been opened on the human mind, there truth and order, like the sun, has arisen and shone upon the people. Compare Scotland with Spain; Holland with Italy; Prussia with Portugal; England with France; our own country with the Mexican or South American States. What has made the immense difference? *The Bible*, read without restraint, and multiplied without limit, and preached with boldness and fidelity to a thinking people. Having no space now for this topic, I promise, in future numbers, to give you ample proof of the intimate union between Romanism and infidelity, and Romanism and extreme heresy.

You slip the case of "the collier" with far nearer approaches to profanity than right reasoning. It is possible " your rule of faith may be fallible;" or your collier may be " deranged," when he begins to *inquire* and *think*, after the slumber of his faculties for some half a century, under the Roman anodyne of *implicit faith*. But surely it ought never to be made an alternative in a proposition, that "Jesus Christ was a Juggler!" Suppose, however, you apply the illustration to any other book, say the creed of Pius IV. or the " Book of Bulls," or " The Fathers." Has language not a fixed meaning? Are there not plain rules for its interpretation? Can we not understand a book because one man says it means this, and another *that*, and a third *something else?* And must we call the Bible a *fallible guide*, because some men may, and will, *wrest* it? Must we pin our faith to the Pope's sleeve, because *we* are liable to error? Yet this is all you have to say in defence of implicit faith. The sum of it is this—that the collier does (even as we have said,) *believe what he is told, and because he is told it; but it is better to do so, than worse; and he will do worse if he thinks for himself!*

You next attempt an oblique defence of your rule from the many objections which I have brought against it. In page 51, last paragraph, you say, " *articles of faith and morals are the only objects of definition and transmission; neither does the church claim, nor has she exercised the right of creating new articles of faith."* Now I ask, did not the Council of Trent make new articles of faith? Did she not order a new Creed, containing these 12 articles, and binding all her communion to hold them, under pain of spiritual death? And were there not even new sacraments among these articles? I referred you for proof to the *literary fraud* by which *"extreme unction"* was attempted to be made a sacrament, in your church standards. You are silent about it! What I have said above about Leo X's condemnation of Luther, plainly shows that you differ from him, and that he claimed the right not only to " *define,*" but " *create*" articles of faith, and "*impose them on men for their belief.*" Transubstantiation, indulgences, taking the cup from the laity in the Lord's Supper, and *five* of your *seven* sacraments are palpable innovations; are new articles of faith, brought in by your church from age to age, and gathered up, and put into the creed, by the Council of Trent.

In your second answer " *to objections,*" page 52, you pass by the questions by saying " *discipline* may vary." I suppose it is a point of discipline to forbid the use of the Scriptures; to restrict the freedom of the press; to claim the government of kingdoms; to establish the inquisition; to burn heretics; and encourage extended and bloody massacres; as of the Waldenses and Hugonots! Under this head too, I suppose you comprehend your apology for the " *ambitious projects*" of "*individual Popes.*" This is strange language! " Individual Popes!" And yet is this *all* you can reply to *all* I have rought from the Popes and from the councils, showing that your system is incompatible with personal and civil liberty? Your allusion to the Presbyterian minister now in the state prison of New York, is legitimate. We mourn over such men—we depose them from their office; for we do not think, with your church, that a man may, like Judas, be a *good Pope,* and yet a *bad man.* The history of your Popes is the blackest page of human story. The *moral* of " *bad man* and *good Pope*" reminds us of the Archbishop, (he was also a prince) who swore profanely in the presence of a peasant; the peasant exclaimed with surprise, " *Archbishop, do you swear?*" " *No,*" he replied, " *I swear as a prince.*" " *Then,*" said the peasant, " *When Satan comes for the prince, what will become of the archbishop?*"

I will refer to only one other evasion of yours. You answer my statement, that the Pope held a great anniversary at Rome, to bless all sorts of beasts (while he curses Bible societies) with an unworthy levity, about " *a similar operation over a good piece of beef.*" I have been accustomed to think that such a service was thanking God, *and asking his blessing on ourselves, not on the food we eat.* But the superstition and darkness of that Pontiff who can encourage such an anniversary, and the degraded condition of " the Mother and mistress of churches," who can uphold such a celebration, remain still unexplained. If, however, the blessings were confined to *dead* beasts, and the anathemas removed from *living men who circulate the Bible,* it might be pitied, if not defended.

Your objections on the points of infant baptism, the change of the Sabbath, and the practices of our church as to the pastoral relation.

surely have little to do with the rule of faith. The 1st and 2d come appropriately under the subject of tradition, on which you yet are silent. I will here only say that we find satisfactory proof for all the three practices in the word of God; or we would discard them. We reject not testimony which sustains our doctrines; (not opinions) but we look not to "*unwritten tradition*" for their support; and " if the candlestick of the Roman angel were removed to-morrow," we lose not a jot of *proof* on any subject, except that of the *depravity of man*. But more of this hereafter, when, Providence permitting, we hope to satisfy you in still further defending and illustrating the true rule of faith, i. e. the *Holy Spirit speaking in the Bible*.

I have been informed that Bishop Kenrick did, on the 17th of February last, in St. Mary's church, (Philadelphia) publicly warn the people against reading this controversy. I ask, is this true or not? If it be, it is not only a manifest interference, but a portentous intimation. I remain, Sir, yours, &c. JOHN BRECKINRIDGE.

CONTROVERSY. No. VII.

RULE OF FAITH.

Philadelphia, March 15, 1833.

To the Rev. John Breckinridge,

Rev. Sir,—The first paragraph of your last letter, purports to be an epitome of our preliminary arrangements, and of the victories you have gained since the campaign has been regularly opened. In reference to the former I *had* thought, that our readers must have been sufficiently punished by the publication of a correspondence which was as tedious as it was puerile. Ten minutes' frank conversation would have settled the rules of this discussion. The perusal of those letters, like Swift's meditation on a broomstick, showed how much could be made of a trifle. Finally, however, we reached the goal; the rules were arranged and signed by mutual agreement. If there is any thing more to be said on the subject, let it be reserved for the *Appendix*. But I cannot consent that these same rules *which cost us so much trouble*, should be construed into mere "modes and forms." You, indeed, have hitherto treated them *as such*, and thus compelled me to expose your violation of them. If I had compared the Protestant rule of faith, with Calvin's blasphemy, in asserting that God is the author of sin, and that Jesus Christ spoke *ironically*, when he directed the young man in the Gospel to keep the commandments, such reasoning would have been violating the rules. Because it would have been *taking for granted, what you deny;* but you, on the contrary, have assailed all those doctrines of our church *which Protestants have rejected;* and instead of comparing our rule of faith with your OWN DEFINITION of the TRUE PRINCIPLE, you appeal to the tribunal of prejudice where it had been already condemned! I say that the doctrines of the Catholic church are the true doctrines of Jesus Christ—and that Protestants, in rejecting them, have forsaken the fountains of living water, and digged to themselves *broken* cisterns. But I should be sorry to make this *assertion* the basis of an argument against your rule of faith. For you would very properly say, that I was begging the question by such a procedure. It seems, you find the strict principles of logic *irksome*, and all things considered, I am not surprised at it. Nevertheless, they are and *must continue to be* the polar star of this discussion.

But then your victories! "You have exposed our rule"—"you have proved its utter fallibility"—"you have shown that our church has varied in doctrine from age to age"—"you have shown that our rule is *not only entirely fallible, but greatly evil*," not only "greatly evil"—but it "*usurps the prerogatives of God*"—not only "it usurps the prerogatives of God," BUT IT "IS INCOMPATIBLE WITH PERSONAL OR CIVIL LIBERTY," &c. In short, one is at a loss to imagine what it 's, that you have *not* "shown." And what was my reply to all these "showings?" Chiefly that they violate the rules!!!

Among the ancient Romans, it was for the *senate* to vote the honours of a *triumph ;* and to you I need not hint, that the patience with which a Roman general, at the head of his *victorious* legions, *waited the decision of the senate,* furnishes a beautiful example of republican *modesty,*—and, conveys a *moral.* It was only in the degenerate times, when boys were emperors, and emperors were tyrants, that it became fashionable for a man to wreath *his own brows* with the laurel of victory—for having simply "marched an army up the hill, then marched them down again."

Still, on the subject of what you have " shown," and " proved," and accomplished, all our readers will form their own judgment.— That you *intended* to do all you have said, I make not the least doubt; but beware of the "doctrine of intentions." For be assured, that whatever opinion you may form of your own labours, the public begin to look upon your situation, (in reference to THE RULE OF FAITH at least,) as somewhat like that of Pyrrhus, when he exclaimed, on the battle field : "Give me another *victory like this*, and I am ruined."

In my last letter, I said that one or two of your assertions were "untrue." I expressed, at the same time, my regret that you had left it *in my power*, or rather *compelled* me, so to characterize them. For religion always suffers, when they, who profess to be her ministers, violate, even in the slightest degree, those sacred principles of moral integrity which constitute the bond of well-ordained society, and the foundation of honour ;—even as it is understood in the ordinary transactions and intercourse of men. It was on this ground, that I considered the "*task painful.*" I did not, nor do I now, make the slightest charge against you personally ; but I perceived that my suggestion to be cautious in quoting authorities, had been *slighted*. I perceived from your letter to the young lady in Baltimore, that you were ready to take up, as *weapons of destruction*, those *antiquated calumnies*, by which the "delusion" of Protestantism has sustained itself, against the apostolical evidences of the Catholic religion for the last three hundred years. And that, without intending it, perhaps, you would copy the falsehoods, which have been asserted one thousand times by your predecessors in controversy, and as often refuted by mine. I perceived that you had forgotten the philosophy of the Holy Scripture, which tells us " the Ethiopian cannot change the colour of his skin," nor " the leopard his spots,"—that the proposition, which was *false, when it was asserted for the first time, cannot become true,* by multitudinous repetition. All this I had perceived before we began this controversy. My experience since, has not disappointed my anticipations. I told you that *Usher*, was a *Protestant* Archbishop ; although you had placed him side by side with St. Thomas Aquinas as a *faithful expositor* of Catholic doctrine ;—you were *candid enough* since, to acknowledge that I was right ; and to plead that the error was to be ascribed to "some strange mistake of printing."—But how comes it that this "strange mistake" *has not been corrected ?* How comes it, that the sentence " of Usher's authority, among Romanists we need not speak"—is still going the rounds of the Protestant newspapers, for the edification of the illiterate and the amusement of the learned ?

In your last letter but one, you asserted that " Luther was condemned for saying ' it is not in the power of the church or the Pope to constitute (' NEW') articles of faith.' " I replied, that this assertion was " untrue ;" and if the word seem uncourteous, you must blame the poverty of the English language, which could not furnish me with any other to express my *exact meaning*. Luther's words are these—" Certum est in manu Ecclesiæ aut Papæ prorsus *non esses statuere articulos fidei*, imo nec leges morum, seu bonorum opertum." 27. The literal translation of which is this : " It is certain that it is not in the power of the church or the Pope to define or determine articles of faith, nor even laws of morals or good works." In your *first* translation you inserted the word ' NEW' before ' articles ;' in your second, you deem it more prudent *to leave it out*—and yet you have the courage to say, that your second version is " WORD FOR WORD WHAT YOU HAD SAID BEFORE !" Let the reader compare them. It was yourself, Rev. Sir, and not Luther, that spoke of *new* articles of faith. Here, then, is my first plea for having said the assertion was " untrue."

My second is, that Luther, thanks to his Catholic education, was too good a classical scholar to use the word " *statuere*" if he had meant exclusively " to create," or—according to the *liberal* translation which you first gave it, to " constitute *new articles* of faith."— Every one, the least acquainted with ecclesiastical language, knows that *statuere* is a kind of standing or *technical word*, to express the judgment of a council or other authoritative body, in *determining questions*, or deciding controversies. If this is not sufficient, let us recur back to the good old Latin terms, when Livy said, " Statuere terminos"—" to fix, settle, or determine the boundaries." Cicero, " Statuere, documentum"—" to deliver instruction." Plautus, " Statuere, navem"—" to bring the ship to anchor." This, according to your vocabulary, ought, I suppose, to be translated—" to constitute a *new* ship"—or " create a ship." And yet, you say, towards the close of your last letter, " What I have said above of Leo the tenth's condemnation of Luther, plainly shows that you (Mr. Hughes) differ from him, and that he *claimed the right* not only to ' define,' but to ' create' articles of faith, *and impose them on men for their belief !*"

My third plea is, that the Bull of Leo X. censured, *en masse*, all the forty-one propositions of Luther. One of which was, that the " Contrition which a man conceives from considering the multitude, grievousness and defilement of his sin ;—the loss of heaven, and exposure to hell ;—that this kind of contrition or repentance makes him a *hypocrite* and a *greater sinner*.* This was *one* of the propositions.

How then, Rev. Sir, came you to assert and repeat, that " Leo X. condemned Luther simply '*for saying*' (what in fact Luther never

---

* " Contrito quæ paratur per discussionem, collationem, et detestationem peccatorum, qua quis recogitet annos suos in amaritudine animæ suæ, ponderando peccatorum gravitatem, multitudinem, fœditatem, amissionem æternæ beatitudinis, ac æternæ damnationis acquisitionem, hæc contritio facit *hypocritam*, imo *magis peccatorem*." Luther's 6th proposition included in the Bull of Leo X.

meant to say) 'that it is not in the power of the church or the Pope to constitute NEW *articles of faith?*'" In reference to this matter therefore, without pretending to much knowledge, I must decline being protected by the shield of "ignorance," which you have charitably offered me. If you have no use for it, you might hang it up amidst the other trophies of your victory. *Thus it is*, that you are warranted in saying, that "the nerves of my cause are cracking under the pressure of *truth!*"

But, it is difficult to conceive, how you could have imagined that Bishop Kenrick ever dreamt of " publicly" (or even privately) " warning the people against reading this controversy." Be assured, Rev. Sir, that he regards, as too precious, this opportunity of letting the people *see what kind of weapons* are employed on your side, in assailing the everlasting foundations of their religion. They, certainly, invade no man's rights, when they claim the simple faculty of *knowing* what they believe;—and in the enjoyment of this faculty, they are highly amused at the successive *portraits* of their belief, which proceed from your pencil. The Pope, or a General Council, if any doctrinal controversy were to arise in the church, might determine what they *ought* to believe; but you go a little farther, and tell them exactly what they *do* believe. Bishop Kenrick has too great a zeal for the religion of Christ, not to allow the reading of this controversy: and if there were any doubts in the minds of Catholics as to the divine origin of their faith, the perusal of your letters would be quite as *effectual* in removing them, as that of mine. What will even Protestants conclude, when they perceive, that you labour to support your positions by assertions, which are *untrue?* Shall I quote another instance? In your letter, No. 4. of this controversy, you assert, that "the Catechism of the Council of Trent, repeats only four words of the second commandment, and *closes with an expressive "et cætera."* Now, every Catholic throughout the world, that ever read the Catechism of the Council of Trent, knows that this assertion is *untrue!** And still you begin your last letter with a flourish of trumpets to sound my defeat, and proclaim that " the nerves of my cause are *cracking* under the *pressure* of *truth.*" Protestants themselves will begin to learn the *real* state of the case;—and the *means*, by which their religious opinions are vindicated, will begin to have a *reflex operation* which you little suspect.

Will the public deem it *too much*, if I request you to *correct these assertions;*—and henceforward to *quote the entire passage* or text of our authors, on which you *build an argument?*

Since your allusion to Bishop Kenrick has led me, into this episode, I may as well close it with a little incident which occurred to myself last spring, and does not therefore depend on "information." I happened to go into the session-room of the " General Assembly," and found the "Bishops" engaged in settling a question, which I soon discovered to be *interesting*; viz. " Whether baptism, administered by a Catholic Priest, *is valid?*" A committee, it seems, had been appointed to draw up a report, which was being read when I entered.

---

* Pars III. deDecal. obser. De primo præcepto C. I. 16.

The committee had decided in the *negative,* and in support of this decision, reported a variety of reasons, with two of which I was particularly struck. One was, that they (Catholic Priests) baptize in *Latin ;* as if infants were not quite as well acquainted with *this language,* as with any other. The second was, that they (Catholic Priests) BAPTIZE WITH OIL—a discovery reported on the authority of a certain Doctor, I think, of Maryland. It was listened to with great, but *silent* solemnity—although there were at the moment *five baptismal founts,* in as many Catholic churches, within half a mile of where the Assembly was sitting:—and though it is known to all the world that the Catholic baptism is, and ever has been, with water I retired from the presence of these "Teachers in Israel," revolving in my mind, the words of our blessed Redeemer; "If, in the *green* wood they do these things, what shall be done in the *dry ?*"

But to return to your assertions. You stated that it is a principle of Catholics, " that if the Pope were to command vice and prohibit virtue, he is to be obeyed." Now it *is a fact,* that Bellarmine, to whom you refer,* used *these words,* to express the *absurd and impious* consequence, that would flow from the opinion which HE WAS THEN REFUTING! Just as I argued that the Protestant rule of faith, as exemplified in the case of the " collier," would lead to the *impious* alternative, that " Christ was a juggler." Will you have the *courage* to deny, that Bellarmine made the statement, to show the *absurd* and *immoral* consequence that would flow from the argument *he was refuting ?* What then will Protestants think of such *perversions ?*— Again, you refer to the 16th canon of the 3d Council of Lateran, on the " validity of oaths"—to show that, according to Catholic doctrine, " an oath, contrary to ecclesiastical utility, is *perjury,* not an oath !" (Mr. Breckinridge—conclusion of Letter No. 2.) Now what is the FACT ? That the Council was legislating on cases of ecclesiastical *elections,* where a *factious minority* pleaded the *obligation of a previous oath, to justify their dissent from the voice and vote of the majority.*† Just as if the Supreme Court were to say, that an oath, taken under the late " Ordinance" of South Carolina, is to be considered not an *oath,* but rather *perjury.* What will Protestants think, of *this perversion ?* or of the cause which required it ? Will you have the candour to publish the *errata ?*

If, instead of being the advocate of truth, I were merely the representative of a *party,* I might triumph in this *exposition,* which *I challenge you to contravene.* But *I* am not the person to enjoy such a triumph; and it would have been infinitely more grateful to *my feelings,* both as a Christian and as a man, if you had spared *me the necessity* of making this exposure.

---

* " Secundo, quia tunc necessario erraret, etiam circa fidem. Nam fides Catholica *docet omnem virtutem esse bonam, omne vitium esse malum :* Si autem Papa erraret, præcipiendo vitia, vel prohibendo virtutes, teneretur Ecclesia credere vitia esse bona et virtutes esse mala, nisi vellet contra conscientiam peccare." Bellarmine, Lib. iv. de Rom. Pont. C. V.

† Nec nostram constitutionem impediat, si forte aliquis ad conservandam Ecclesiæ suæ consuetudinem *juramento se dicat adstrictum :* non enim dicenda sunt juramenta, sed potius perjuria, quæ contra utilitatem Ecclesiasticam et sanctorum Patrum veniunt instituta." Con. Lat. C. xvi.

Another point, on which we are at issue, is the "Pope's supremacy." You had asserted, that on this subject "there are no less than three systems in our church. This assertion I pronounced to be, what it is, "untrue." I gave you the whole universe, and challenged you to name so much as one Catholic, who denied the Pope's supremacy! You have not been able to discover one. The *supremacy* of the *Pope* and the *infallibility* of the *church*, are articles of *Catholic faith and doctrine:*—and on no point of Catholic doctrine are there *three*, or even TWO systems, in *our* church. We have *one Lord*, *one faith*, and *one baptism*. You refer to the authority of the Council of Basle—but that Council became a spurious assembly, after the Pope's legates, and *greater part* of the Bishops, retired from it to Ferrara—and those, who remained, had about as much authority to *define a tenet of Catholic doctrine*, as Luther had to excommunicate the Pope, which he did right manfully, by way of returning a compliment, which his Holiness had recently paid him. 2dly. Even this spurious remnant of a Council did not pass any decree affecting the *dogma of the Pope's supremacy.* That which you have quoted, relates to a supposed case, in which an actual Pope and an actual Council, should be opposed to each other, and it was decided that in *such a case* the *preponderance* of authority should belong to the Council. This decision, though emanating from a spurious source, and founded on hypothesis, does not even *question the Pope's supremacy as an article of Catholic doctrine.* Devoti's testimony has reference, in the *very text*, to the Pope's *infallibility*, which is *not an article of faith*, but between which and *supremacy*, it seems you are unable, or unwilling to make a *distinction.* These, then, are your first two systems.—The third, you tell us, "*deifies the Pope*"—this acknowledges the very *plenitude* of supremacy. But how can you be serious, when you make this assertion? If some of our citizens were to theorize on the constitution of our government—one school teaching that Congress is *superior* to the President—another, that the President is *superior* to Congress—would *that* circumstance warrant an English traveller to publish to his countrymen, that the "Americans are divided into two systems" on the subject of the *President's supremacy as chief magistrate of the whole republic?* And if some orator, in the glow of patriotic reminiscence, which the fourth of July usually inspires, should happen to say, "the god-like Washington, the saviour of his country," would *that* prove that the "*Americans deify their Presidents?*" Here are "three systems," on which even Mrs. Trollope could build a fine tale, if she could only induce people to believe it. But, just lend me the "Protestant rule of faith" for a *few minutes*, and I will *prove from Scripture*, that it is right to call the Pope God. "You are Gods." Psalms lxxxi. 6.—"I have appointed thee God of Pharaoh." Exod. vii. 1. See also Exod. xxii. 28. John x. 34. Now, Rev. Sir, I return you *your rule of faith*, and hope you will be satisfied with my *proof*, since "I give you chapter and verse for it." But as to the "three systems" of doctrine in our church, on the subject of *the Pope's supremacy,*—you might as well look for "three suns" in the heavens. Throughout the whole universe there is but ONE system of doctrine among Catholics on this point. Every proposition asserting the contrary is "untrue." Name, if you can, a Catholic in the whole world, who has publicly denied that supremacy, without breaking the bond of communion and membership which united him to the church.

We have now arrived at your review of my arguments in favour of the Catholic rule of faith. In my last letter I gave the authority of Scripture to prove that Jesus Christ established a Church, by giving a *divine commission* to his apostles and their legitimate successors, *until the end of the world*—that this commission extended to the teaching of *all nations*—that to this commission he attached the attribute of his own infallibility. "As the Father hath sent me, so do I send you"—" He that hears you, *hear me;* and he that despises you, *despises me;* and he that despises me, despises him that sent me."

How did you, Rev. Sir, answer these arguments? Did you deny the authorities? Did you detect error in the reasoning? Did you accuse me of illogical deductions? Not at all. You have recourse to the old method of distortion; and tell us that my rule of faith is "*in substance this:*" "*the Holy Catholic Church is the living infallible interpreter of Scripture.*" And then you deduce your own consequence from your own distortion of my argument. "Now it will be borne in mind, that before any church can *interpret*, it must know what is to be *interpreted.*"—"What do you mean by the Holy Scriptures?"—"the Council of Trent has settled the question, &c."—And then having worked out the distortion to your own purposes, you tilt away at the Council of Trent, and affect to wonder that I did not begin by settling the canon of Scripture, instead of proving "the rule of faith!" The canon of Scripture held by the Council of Trent, is the same that was settled by the Council of Carthage in 397. And if John Calvin, in *the 16th century*, thought proper to become a Protestant against some books of that canon, *it is for his followers to look to it*. But when you say that the "Jews, our Lord Jesus, the apostles, and early fathers, *unite to* EXCLUDE them from the canon"—you make another of those assertions which might be indecorous to call by its proper appellation.

It does not appear that "our Lord Jesus" or "the apostles" ever determined or wrote upon the subject of such exclusion, which they certainly would have done, if the "Scripture alone" had been intended as the rule of Christian faith.

Your next alternative to evade the *consequences* flowing from the commission given to Jesus Christ to his apostles, is to collate with *it*, those texts which communicated the power of miracles. These certainly do not destroy the commission which extended to "all nations in all days, even to the consummation of the world." Now either the apostles *had successors*, for the *discharge* of the commission, or they had not. If they *had*, then your position is untenable. If they had *not*, then please to tell us, what Christ could have meant by *commanding the teaching of all nations during all days, even until the end of the world*. Was he speaking *ironically?* If they had not— what did St. Paul mean, by saying of the Christian ministry, no man taketh this honour to himself, but he who is called of God, as was Aaron? What did he mean, by *appointing* Titus and Timothy, and instructing them to *appoint other faithful men* for the discharge of the same commission?

The little sophism, about the meaning of the word apostle (one sent,) has not the merit of much ingenuity. However, according to your logic, in order to "be sent" one must have "seen the Lord," and as the second generation had not seen the Lord, therefore, the apostles had no successors!! But pray, did the *commission to teach all nations during all days*, extend only to *those* who had *seen the Lord?* Did *it* also expire with "the last apostle?" If it was discharged in the second generation, were not those *by whom* it was discharged, *in so much*, THE REGULAR SUCCESSORS of the apostles? This is what I contend for. Had General Washington no successors in the presidency of this Republic, for the very logical reason, that they succeeded him, and their appointment differed, in some *circumstances* from his? Jesus Christ gave a commission extending to all nations and all ages of the world. Mr. Breckinridge says that the commission ceased to be discharged *after the first generation*,—inasmuch as it was given to the twelve apostles, who lived but a few years *and* "*had no successors.*" Which shall we believe? Do not the society of "Friends" view *baptism*, and the Universalists, *everlasting* punishment, in the same arbitrary lights of analogy! And if *your* assertion on this subject be credited, will it not become natural, or rather unavoidable, for men to believe that Jesus Christ was merely sporting with human language, and immortal souls?

But how comes it, that even *Presbyterian clergymen* apply to themselves (when it *suits* them,) *every text*, by which the Son of God commissioned his apostles *to* "*teach all nations;*" to *preach* the gospel to every creature, and *to evangelize the world?* It is not a contradiction in terms for them to *claim the authority of a succession which they* DENY? It is no wonder that the ranks of infidelity should thicken around us. As long as the human mind is governed by the ordinary laws, men must and *will* look for *consistency somewhere:* either in the desperate alternative of *total scepticism*, or in the bosom of the Catholic church, from which their fathers separated. When we hear you asserting that the "apostles had no successors," would it not be proper that some one should move at the next General Assembly, that the following article *be expunged* from the "Westminster Confession of Faith."

"'To these (church officers) *the keys of the kingdom of heaven* are committed, by virtue whereof *they have power to retain and remit sins, to shut that kingdom against the impenitent.* both by the word and censure; and to *open* it unto penitent sinners by the ministry of the Gospel, and by *absolution* from censures, as occasion shall require." Chap. xxx. art. 11. page 166.

These are modest pretensions for gentlemen who assert that the Apostles had no successors. Now I had always thought that these same keys belonged to St. Peter and his successors. I know by whom and to whom they were originally given, and to whom they still belong, if *priority of title* and *possession* be admitted. But as Mr. Breckinridge had informed me, that the apostles had no successors, I was at a loss to imagine what had become of the "keys"—

until, peeping into the "Confession of Faith," I learned to my great edification, that they had been *miraculously* discovered at WESTMINSTER, *England,* in the year of our Lord, 1647, and graciously fastened, by act of Parliament, to the belt of the Presbyterian Church!

The whole of your strange position, against the institution of the "Catholic rule of faith," is founded on the assertion, that the "Apostles had no successors"—an assertion, which is inconsistent with the character and extent of the commission given by the Saviour. How could Christ impart such a commission *without* PROVIDING *for its fulfilment;* and how could *he provide for its fulfilment without* a SUCCESSION in the ministry of teaching? Therefore, unless you make it appear, that Christ *has deceived us,* it will follow as a necessary consequence, according to the proofs and reasoning of my last letter, that the promise of infallibility was made to the Apostles, and *the Pastors of the churches, their legitimate successors,* in the ministry of teaching *all nations,* during *all days,* even to the consummation of time:— and not to the *private interpretation of the Bible.* Consequently, that the *Catholic rule of faith* is the true rule, having been "established by the Son of God himself."

I said that this Catholic rule is *infallible,* and in your reply, you "grant that if it was established by Christ, *it is infallible.*" But then you say, that you have *proved that Christ did not establish our rule,* and my conclusion falls to the ground. Indeed, Rev. Sir, *the language of Christ, the language and practice of the Apostles, the practice of the Christian church for* 1800 *years, and your own Confession of Faith stand against you,* and show that you have proved no such thing. And if you had much confidence in either the *strength* or *evidence* of your "proofs," so called,—it would have been superfluous in you to attempt the *exposition of its fallibility.* You say, that "it is not selfevident that our church is infallible, or our rule the true one. By what process, then," you ask me, "do I apply these texts to the proof of my rule?" You answer the question yourself. "The process of *private interpretation.*" On this question and answer you build an argument, to show that I arrive at the proofs of the divine establishment of the Catholic rule, by *my own private interpretation of the Scriptures:*—and so, that I am *obliged* to have recourse to the Protestant principle in *the last resort.* I had answered this objection, before it was written, by showing, that in the Catholic church *every doctrine, and every proof of our doctrine, is reduced to a simple matter of fact:*—That these texts have been understood, as I have used them, in all countries and ages:—That their authority, merely AS HISTORICAL EVIDENCE, establishes the point, and shows that *Christ instituted* A MINISTRY OF TEACHING, to *transmit* to all nations the knowledge of the doctrines which he revealed:— That to *this ministry* he promised *his own perpetual presence*—all of which are FACTS, with which the principle of *private interpretation* has as little to do, as it has with ascertaining whether or not the city of Philadelphia was founded by William Penn. For the farther proof of this, I refer the reader to my *own* arguments in the last letter, which you took good care not to assail.

Your next position may be called the argument of confusion

"Either the Pope is infallible, or the Council: or both united: or the universal church. It seems not to be agreed among yourselves, where infallibility *is lodged*, and therefore even at the threshold a great difficulty arises." Christ, Rev. Sir, was not less the Son of God, because "he was a scandal to the Jews and a stumbling block to the Gentiles." The *distorted portraits* which Protestant writers have drawn of the *infallibility*, as well as of the other doctrines of the Catholic church, may, indeed, raise difficulties at the "threshold," and *prejudice* may regard them as insurmountable. *We* can see no difficulty whatever. *Every definition of doctrine and morals by a General Council is infallible.* It was of such definitions (according to Catholic interpretation) that Christ said: "He that *hears you hears me*," and "he that will not hear the church, let him be to thee as the heathen and the publican." *No Council is General or Œcumenical without the* POPE's *concurrence*. Consequently, the spiritual empire of Christ is not *divided* in the Catholic church. A man may be a very good Catholic, without inquiring, whether the Pope is officially infallible or not. He may even hold it as an opinion, *that he is not infallible*, and neither Priest, nor Bishop, nor Pope will frown upon him for *his opinion*. The Pastors of the church are not, like the Reformers of the sixteenth century, the *creators*, but they are merely the *guardians* and *expositors* of the doctrines, which they derived from Jesus Christ and his apostles. They are the WITNESSES OF TRUTH, and they are warranted by a sacred authority, to reject even " an angel from heaven," if that angel attempt to preach *another doctrine* besides that which they have received. *They all teach the same doctrines.* But let me show your argument in a light, which does not require the use of a "*sectarian telescope.*" All Americans agree that these United States are *independent*. Now would it be an argument against this independence, if any one should raise "difficulties," by asking where this independence "*is lodged*"—whether in the *President*—or in the Congress—or in *both* united—or in the whole Republic.

Is not the PROMISE OF JESUS CHRIST, that he would be *with the apostles and their successors* in the ministry of "teaching" until the end of the world, as good a *guarantee*, for the *infallibility of the Church*, as the immortal "declaration" is, for the *independence* of our country? Would Christ be with a ministry, which is supposed by Protestant *opinions*, to have been teaching error and idolatry for a thousand years before the "Reformation" was born, or for three hundred since. If he was *not*, what became *of his pledge and promises?* Do you not perceive, Rev. Sir, how *questionable* your assertions would render the VERACITY *of Christ?* And how they tend to shake the very foundations of Christianity? Do you imagine that the fulfilment of these promises, is to be overturned by a rule of grammar? —"Two negatives make an affirmative."

I must now show the reader, what a chemicological process the arguments of my last letter were doomed to undergo in New York. "I remark," says Mr. Breckinridge, "that your reasoning, as to an infallible 'rule of faith,' if well founded, leads us to reject every system, *that does not make all men perfect*. For you agree that

Christ has established an infallible rule to guide us in matters of religion, as well as to settle disputes in his church. You argue, that a rule, which does not settle disputes, as to doctrine, is fallible, and therefore, not Christ's rule. Now, by parity of reasoning, a rule that does not regulate *practice*, so as to make an END OF SIN, and make *men perfect* here, must be a fallible rule." This reasoning is your own, dear sir, and I would not spoil it by a single word of comment.

You next complain that I should have adduced the arguments of Volney, Priestly, and what you call "extreme heresies," to show the inconclusiveness of your reasoning, against the Catholic doctrines Unitarians, Universalists, &c. (whom, I suppose, you intend to designate by "extreme heresies") are the legitimate descendants of the Protestant rule of faith. And, if every man has a *right to interpret the meaning of the Bible for himself*, it becomes something like *nonsense* in the ear of reason, for *one* Protestant to call the opinions of *another* Protestant by the name of "heresy." What do they, but INQUIRE, THINK, and EXERCISE *the privilege* which you proclaim to be the right of all. Will you have them to *stop thinking* at the point where Presbyterians have *halted?* Will you say to the ocean of their thought; "*hitherto* thou shalt come, *but no farther?*" That ocean is too boundless to be hemmed in by the "Westminster Confession." Its course is onward—and the present condition of Protestants in Germany, *where infidelity is preached from the pulpit, and proved from the Bible*, by the Protestant rule of faith, shows how it can sweep away the feeble remnants of Christianity, that were spared by the *first* Reformation.

Your frequent charges against the Catholic church, for "restricting the freedom of the press;"—"claiming the government of kingdoms:"—"establishing the inquisition:"—"burning heretics:"— "encouraging extended and bloody massacres of the Waldenses and Huguenots," and a hundred other sins which she never committed, certainly do not prove the "Protestant rule of faith," *nor disprove* that which Christ established. Childhood, full grown ignorance, grey-haired prejudice, and last, though not least, ladies of *delicate nerves*, may be frightened by these tales of horror inconceivable! But to *these* their effect will be exclusively confined. I dislike recrimination, but you will not take it amiss, if I remind you, *inter nos*, that the standard of Presbyterianism in the United States of America, and in the nineteenth century, makes it a *sin* against the *second* commandment of God, "to TOLERATE *a false religion*." It is true the General Assembly have not as yet told us, what religions are to be regarded as "false." But I cannot well understand how the Presbyterian conscience can be at peace with itself, or "the Great Head of the church," as long as it is burthened with this *sin* of TOLERATION.

In my last letter, in order to exhibit the delusion of the Protestant rule of faith, I introduced an uneducated "collier," to whose experience and judgment I refer the reader. You pass by the argument contained in the paragraph, and seem to be shocked at the profanity of the poor man's language. But, Rev. Sir, these are times when men's *minds must be braced up*, so as not to be shocked at any consequence flowing from the common fountain of Protestant error, inconsistency and extravagance: I mean, the *pretended competency of private opinion to interpret the religion of Jesus Christ from the voiceless pages of the Bible*. I defy any man, reasoning from the same premises, to arrive at a conclusion *different* from that of the "collier." You have not condescended to show us how it is *even possible to escape* it. You represent me as calling the Bible a *fallible guide*, because, as you say, "men may and will *wrest* it." No, Sir; but I am arguing against the fallible and fallacious principle of *private interpretation*, by which the Bible is degraded into *a book of contradictions*, and made to decide for and against even the most sacred points of doctrine—Baptism, the Lord's supper, the order of Bishops, the existence of hell, the Divinity of Christ, and the Trinity of persons in the Godhead! All this was illustrated in the case of the collier. Now, although you admit that "men may and will *wrest it*," I do not see why *one* denomination of Protestants may not be *as sincere in its opinions* about the meaning of the Bible as another. And as " the Protestant rule of faith" is incapable of producing any thing but *opinions*, I do not see, by what *right you* are warranted in saying that *those, who differ from you* "*wrest the Scriptures ?*"—Albeit, the question, after three hundred years, remains still to be settled; but one thing is certain, that Jesus Christ never revealed an *opinion*—in the Bible, *or out of it*.

I have no farther explanation to give respecting the blessing of "beasts" in Rome or elsewhere—except that the inhabitants of the "seven hills," would, I suppose, be very much hurt, if they were to find out that you disapprove of it. But I would simply ask you to gratify the public with the document, in which you find that the Roman Pontiff has pronounced "ANATHEMAS *against living men who circulate the Bible.*"

You have a brief, but comprehensive reply to *the departure from* the Protestant Rule, which I pointed out in the " Confession of Faith," on the subject of *Infant Baptism*, the *Sabbath*, and *the Ordination of Ministers*. " You find satisfactory proof for all three in the word of God:" but you have prudently declined furnishing the public with a sight of it—not even a reference! This is a *summary* mode of conducting a controversy.

If I have succeeded in dissipating the vapors, which you have attempted to raise between the mind of the reader and the testimony of the *Holy Scriptures*, the "*fathers*," and permit me to use the expression, of *common sense*, in support of the "Catholic rule of faith" in my last letter, then your task of refutation is still unaccomplished. I do not accuse you of any intention to mystify the question; but really if there are any arguments in your whole letter against the Catholic rule of faith, *as I had laid it down and vindicated it*, they are so loosely jointed, that I could hardly compress them *into tangible form and consistency*. They are like spectres, which make a transient impression on the organ of vision, but elude the grasp, that would attempt to *seize or hold them responsible*. Perhaps others may see them differently. But if any man will assert, that you have *proved the Protestant rule of faith*, or *disproved the arguments adduced by me, in support of the Catholic principle*, I have only to say, that I do not envy the grade of his intellect, nor his powers of logical discrimination.

I only regret, that you do not grapple *closely* with the question—that you do not plant the fulcrum of your reasoning on some solid basis; that you do not say with that manly boldness, which the consciousness of a good cause usually inspires—Sir, the Catholic rule of faith is false:—which I prove *thus*, It is manifest, that when Christ said; " Go ye, *teach all nations*, and behold I am with you *all days*, even to the consummation of the world ;" his *meaning was*, that the apostles should die " without successors" in the ministry of *teaching*—that *all days*, and *forever*, signify till the "death of St. John"—that when the *first* creed says, " I believe in the Holy Catholic church," the *true meaning is*, I believe in every man's *private interpretation of the Bible*, but *chiefly in my own.*" Having thus proved the main position, that *Christ did not establish the Catholic rule of faith*, you could easily dispose of the minor difficulties. The moral phenomenon, by which it happens, that *all* Catholics in *all ages* and in *all nations* believe the *same identical doctrines*, is produced manifestly, not by the operation of their rule of faith, but by the *magic* of priestcraft, the *terrors* of the inquisition, and the *moderate tariff* on the *commission of sin*. " Seven shillings and sixpence for killing a father or mother !" Only think of it !! Is it any wonder that the hundreds of millions of souls that belong, or have belonged to *that church*, should be united *as one family*, in the belief of the same tenets of religion ?—as for the little differences of opinions, which grow up under the fostering protection of the " Protestant rule of faith," touching the *Divinity of the Messiah, &c.*, you might glorify them, by calling them beautiful evidences of Protestant *freedom*, as contrasted with Catholic subjugation to the " yoke of faith," which renders them so bigoted, that they *all think alike*.—" The liberty of the Gospel" would be a good name.

But I suppose you will take your own way, and in truth I do not claim any right of either dictation or direction in the matter. If you have nothing further to say against the *arguments* of my last letter, we may return to the unfinished condition in which we left the Protestant rule of faith; but this also shall be at your option, for I wish to be accommodating, whilst I remain, very respectfully,
—Yours, &c   Jno. Hughes.

MISTATEMENT CORRECTED

Perceiving in the letter of Rev. John Breckinridge (No. 6 of the Controversy) the following paragraph, I deem it due to the public, as well as to myself, to give it the earliest and most unequivocal contradiction.

" I have been informed that Bishop Kenrick did, on the 17th February last, in St. Mary's church (Philadelphia), publicly warn the people against reading this controversy "

Not having on that or any other occasion, made the remotest allusion to the pending controversy, and not having even in private given, to any individual whatever, any such warning, I declare the information to be utterly groundless. Given under my hand this 13th day of March, 1833.   † FRANCIS PATRICK KENRICK, Bp. &c.

N. B. Understanding that the above mistatement was contained in the letter, I sent the contradiction of it to the office of the *Presbyterian*, on Monday between 2 and 3 o'clock, that it might appear together with the letter then in press; but to my surprise, no notice is taken of it in that paper published this morning.

CONTROVERSY. No. VIII.

RULE OF FAITH.

New York, 21*st March*, 1833.

To the Rev. John Hughes,

Rev. Sir:—Your letter of March 15th, running far into the *seventh* column, reached me on the 18th inst. It is hard work, you find, to meet and parry stubborn facts, especially when your own authors and formularies are turned against you. No wonder your defence struggles in the greatness of the way,

"And like a wounded snake drags its slow length along."

I regret to see that you grow *less courteous*, as well as more feeble and prolix; and it would seem that these qualities keep pace with each other, in the progress of the discussion.

But let us address ourselves to the question, viz. *The claim you set up of infallible teachers as the successors of the apostles.* In my last letter, (and I think with some clearness,) I proved,

I. *That the apostles had in certain respects no successors.* Under this proposition, it was shown, (see letter, No. 6.) 1st. That no man could be an apostle who had not seen the Lord. 2d. That an apostle must have received his commission directly from Christ. 3d. Every apostle was endowed with the power to work miracles, with inspiration, (from which resulted infallibility) in *speaking* and *writing;* also with the gift of tongues, so as to speak, untaught by men, various languages; and even the power to enable others to work miracles, and the knowledge to discern spirits. 4th. The apostles were not to be stationary; but with plenary power, went from nation to nation, to set up the kingdom of the Lord. From these facts, supported by many clear Scripture proofs, it was shown that in these *extraordinary respects*, they had no successors; that Christ intended them to have none; and that it was impossible they should have any, from the very nature of the case. Wherefore, as your claim to infallibility rests on the notion of succession, it falls to the ground, and with it, your *rule of faith.*

Again, II. I showed that if the Apostles had successors, then they must *all* have had successors; and hence, if there be any Pope, there must be *twelve Popes;* and if *any* church has infallibility upon Apostolical succession, *many* must have it.

III. *If their successors had* any *of these miraculous powers, they must have had* all *of them;* for all are as necessary as *one.* The attempts in your church to work miracles, are an *acknowledgment* of this principle; while the *failure* proves that the *power* is wanting. To the last two arguments, in particular, I anxiously wait your reply. As yet I have not seen any thing like it.

Excuse me, when I say, there is a want of candour in your statement of this argument. You represent me as holding, "*that the Apostles had no successors.*" This, like your quotation from Tertullian, is *just one half.* I said, "*then the conclusion is irresistible, that the Apostles had no successors endued with extraordinary powers of any kind. But we hold to a commission still standing and binding, which reaches to the end of time!"* (See my last letter, No. 6, pages 61, 62.) I still say that the Apostles had no *infallible* successors—none *such* as you claim—nor have you met one single point of my whole argument on this subject. Your system, among other absurdities, leads to this, that there is a SUCCESSION OF FOUNDATIONS. For we are told (Ephes. ii. 20.) that the church "is *built upon the foundation of the Apostles and prophets, Jesus Christ himself being the chief corner stone,*" and thus "*the whole building is fitly framed together:*" and "*other foundation can no more lay, than that is laid, which is Jesus Christ.*" (1 Cor. iii. 11.) Here is the basis of truth; the *only foundation is inspired authority.* To this, the faith of every Christian must look. No *authority* or *succession* can come in between God's people and the Apostles, as the Pope attempts to do. The Apostles themselves still live in *this foundation*, that is, in their *infallible writings;* and they have no successors in an office, whose force never has ceased, and whose authority will never expire. It is therefore piling foundation on foundation, or defending the absurdity of a *succession of foundations*, when you claim to inherit their infallibility. But you ask, "pray did the commission to teach all nations, during all days, extend only to those who had seen the Lord? Did *it* also expire with the last Apostle? If it was discharged in the second generation, were not those by whom it was discharged, *in so much*, the regular successors of the Apostles?" I answer, *certainly*, the commission to "teach all nations," and "to baptize them in the name of the Father, the Son, and the Holy Ghost," runs to the last day and the last man; and the promise of the Divine Redeemer, "lo! I am with you always, even unto the end of the world"—is faithful and unfailing, and is perpetually realized in the experience of every true minister of the Gospel. And here is the very point of defect in your system. You *confound the standing ministry* with the apostolical office. The Apostles were invested with an extraordinary office, in which they were to have no successors. This I have clearly proved. They also transmitted an office, which is *standing* and *ministerial*. Of such were the *Elders* of *Ephesus*, (Acts xx. 17 and 28) to whom the apostle Paul said, "Take heed therefore unto yourselves, and unto the flock over which the Holy Ghost hath made you overseers, to feed the Church of God, which he hath purchased with his own blood." To this also allusion is made, in 2 Tim. ii. 2. "And the things that thou hast heard of me among many witnesses, the same commit thou to faithful men, who shall be able to teach others also." Here *three* links in the chain of this standing ministry are distinctly recognized. The office is ministerial and pastoral, not apostolical: and the work is to *publish* the Gospel—salvation, and to *feed* the flock of Christ. But you profess to find an insuperable difficulty in the *want of infallibility in these teachers;* and your grand corrective is, that as successors of the apostles, you secure this infallibility.— Now let us look at this point. On your plan, every preacher or teacher *must be infallible*. When Mr. Hughes, for example, ad-

L

dresses his flock, either he is *infallible*, or e.se he *may err;* for, if he be not *infallib'e*, when he interprets Scripture, why may he not err? Does he refer you to Rome and the Pope? But "it is not a doctrine" he tells us " of the church, that the *Pope* is infallible."— Does he refer you to the Pope and Council? They have not met for 270 years! And prior to that, for many centuries, their decrees, &c. fill *volumes*. Then Mr. Hughes in Philadelphia, and every priest in the whole world, is to interpret the Bible by these *voluminous written decrees*. Either then Mr. Hughes is *infallible*, (which he disclaims,) or else he *fallibly* interprets *these infallible interpretations* of the Bible! Now I ask any honest man to judge, if this be any improvement to the system? May not a Protestant minister as well go to the *written Bible*, where the Apostles speak infallibly to us, and directly expound the inspired word to the people, as Mr. Hughes and all other Roman Catholic priests to the Bible through volumes of decrees, bulls, &c., and then expound on private interpretation this same Bible at last? If the Protestant minister be fallible, so is Mr. Hughes, and every Roman Catholic priest; but the Protestant goes directly to *the Bible*, whereas Mr. Hughes wades to it through all the decrees of his councils, *fallible* as he is; and he has *first* to interpret these decrees, and *then* to interpret the Bible, *by them!* I proceed to remark that you virtually yield the point in discussion, by the following admissions: " According to the Catholic rule of faith, the doctrines of Christianity are not *abstract speculations*, they are *positive truths. facts*, unchanged, and unchangeable, as they came from the lips of Jesus Christ and his inspired Apostles. But, being public truths or facts, they were taught by the pastors of the church, and believed by the people in all countries, and in every century since the *establishment* of the church. Consequently, I can verify them with the same *certainty*, which I have that such an event as the battle of Waterloo, the decapitation of Charles I., or the Council of Nice, took place in the world. In neither case is a *divine* or *personal infallibility necessary*. When I say, that 2 and 4 make 6; that Charles X. was expelled from France; that Luther had a *misunderstanding* with Leo X.; that John Huss was burned to death *at Constance*, and Michael Servetus at *Geneva;* I assert propositions which are infallibly true." (See Mr. Hughes' letter, No. 5.) And again—" ALL OF WHICH, (that is, the doctrines of the Roman Catholic church) ARE FACTS, with which the principles of *private interpretation* have as little to do, as it has with ascertaining whether or not the city of Philadelphia was founded by William Penn," (see Mr. Hughes' letter, No. 7.) If *then* ALL YOUR DOCTRINES ARE POSITIVE TRUTHS, and PUBLIC FACTS, as certain as the burning of John Huss, or the occurrence of the Reformation, why is it said that the Scripture is an *obscure* book, in which, without an infallible guide every man must err? And if *some* of the statements in the Bible are facts, are not *all* so? Are those doctrines which serve your purpose *clear truths* and *stubborn facts*, and all the rest dark hieroglyphics, and floating phantoms? Is it not an historical fact that Christ appointed a ministry and promised to sustain it? Is it not also an historical fact that Christ died for sinners; that he taught the doctrine of regenera tion; the doctrine of man's depravity; the doctrine of the final destruction of the wicked; the doctrine that Christ is the only head of the Church; the doctrine that all sin is *mortal* if not repented of; the doctrine that *the Church of Rome should be broken off, if it became corrupt;* (Epistle to the *Romans*, chap. ii. 18—25 verses.) the doctrine, that it is a great sin to make and worship images; the doctrine, that none but God can pardon sin; the doctrine, that the *cup* as well as the *bread* is to be used in the sacrament of the Supper; the doctrine, that the Bible is a sufficient rule of faith; the doctrine, that *force* is never to be applied to compel conformity? I say are not ALL these PUBLIC TRUTHS, and POSITIVE FACTS? And if so, do we need an infallible guide to find them out, or understand them? If, as you say, "*a divine or personal infallibility is not necessary to verify them,*" any more than to verify "*the facts that* 2 *and* 4 *make* 6;" and if, like it, they are "*propositions which are infallibly true,*" why may we not give the Bible to the people as a sufficient *rule of faith?* And why should I go to Rome to catch light from the sickly taper of the Pope? And why should he sit in empty state crying out " the temple of the Lord—the temple of the Lord are we," and trim this dying taper, when the *Sun of Righteousness* has arisen upon the earth? *Surely this system* " *decayeth and waxeth old, and is ready to vanish away.*"

I have a single thought to add, to this part of the discussion. It is suggested by the following extract from the Catholic Herald of Feb. 28th, on " private interpretation of Scripture." " We will recommend them (the people) to *search the Scriptures,* for they bear testimony of Christ and his church. But when they have once come to the knowledge of Christ and his church, then they need inquire no further, with a view of making new discoveries in matters of faith, but should become *like little children,* and receive the word of truth in the humble simplicity of faith from those whom Christ commissioned to *teach,* and whom he commanded us to *hear and obey.* The words '*search the Scripture,*' ' *seek and ye shall find,*' do not apply to believing Christians!" I pass by the extraordinary position that *Christians need not search the Scripture.* It speaks for itself. But the writer concedes that the Scripture ought to be searched by men until they find out Christ and the true church. " *Here they need inquire no more.*" But I would ask, how are we guided in our search *until then?* By what aid do we find out the true church? The true church being unknown, is there any help to any man but *private interpretation?* So then every man must at least, if he joins any church, if he chooses any religion, do it by private interpretation. In a former number I presented this difficulty to you; you have not met it. Let me remind you of it in repeating the quotation from the Rev. Mr. M'Guire, Amicable Discussion, page 134. He owns, that " the Catholic has only to exercise his PRIVATE JUDGMENT upon the Scripture proofs of the authority of the church; that once established, the Catholic is enabled to make an act of faith upon divine authority." Others call it " PRUDENTIAL MOTIVES," " STRONG PROBABILITY," &c. Now to any impartial mind, I think this is a total surrender of your rule of faith. But I wish you explicitly to avow or disavow this position, and to explain to us this principle. In my next letter, if my life is spared, I design to enlarge upon the *Bible as the rule of faith*, and to meet your remaining "objections." I had wished to do this in the present number, but must pass, lastly, to mention some things of a miscellaneous character.

The first I notice, is your entire silence about the quotation from Tertullian, in which I convicted you, (excuse the word, for you force it upon me,) of *garbling* the passage, and leaving out one half, and making the other half prove the very *reverse* of what the father meant. Why are you silent? You are silent also about Bellarmine and "*fere de fide.*" In your previous letter you said, "*I defy you to quote ten lines before, and ten lines after it, without convicting yourself of what is not becoming a minister of the Gospel.*"—The reader will recollect that in my letter, (No. 4.) I had quoted a few words from Bellarmine, to illustrate other proofs, that your church claims and uses the right to make *new articles* of faith. Now let us for a moment return to this mooted question, especially as you informed me in Philadelphia that Bellarmine was a standard author in your church. *Three lines* above the quotation, *a new chapter* begins; *so that seven of the first ten lines* you call for, are on another subject; yet I will give *them*, if you wish it. It would seem then, that *you had not the book*, and *spoke at random, not knowing what was there, and what not there.* Here follow *ten lines below*, and *three above* the quotation—from the beginning of the chapter.

Bellarmine, chap. 17. lib. 2.

Tertia propositio: *summus pontifex, simpliciter, et absolute est supra ecclesiam universam, et supra concilium generale, ita ut nullum in terris supra se judicium, agnoscat.* Hæc etiam est FERE DE FIDE, et probatur primo et duabus præcedentibus: nam si Papa est caput ecclesiæ universæ, etiam simul congregatæ, et ecclesia universa simul congregata non habet ullam potestatem ratione suæ totalitatis: sequitur Papam supra concilium esse, et supra ecclesiam, non contra.

Secundo probatur ratitione, in scripturis fundata: nam omnia nomina, quæ in scripturis *tribuuntur Christo*, unde constat cum esse supra ecclesiam, *eadem omnia tribuuntur Pontifici:* ac primum, Christus est pater-familias in domo sua, quæ est ecclesia. Pontifex, in eadem, est summus œconomus, id est, pater-familias loco Christi.—Luc. xii. 42.

Prop. Third. The supreme Pontiff is simply and absolutely above the church universal, and above a general council, so that he acknowledges no jurisdiction on earth above himself. This is also ALL BUT AN ARTICLE OF FAITH, and is proved (1) from the two preceding: for if the Pope is the head of the church universal, even when met in assembly together, and if the church universal when thus assembled, has no power, on the ground (simply) of its totality; it follows that the Pope is above a council, and above the church and not contrary (to either.)

(2) It is proved by an argument founded in the Scriptures: for all the names, which in the Scriptures are applied to Christ, proving him to be above the church, are in like manner applied to the Pontiff as first, Christ is *Pater-familias*—*head of the family* in his own house, which is the church. The Pontiff is high steward in the same, that is, he is *Pater-familias* in the place of Christ.—Luke xii 42.

I here pass by his *profaneness* in saying, that all Christ's titles are applied in the Bible to the Pope; and also his *weakness* in quoting Luke xii. 42, as *proof*, when in Luke xii. 46—48. (*three verses below*,) his whole system is exploded.

But observe, (1.) The author expressly declares the opinion, that the *Pope is above a general council, and above the universal church*. (2.) He affirms that this opinion is ALMOST AN ARTICLE OF FAITH. (3.) In the same chapter, and on the same subject, he says, " Quod vero concilium hoc rem istam non definierit, proprie, ut decretum fide Catholica tenendum, *dubium est*, et ideo non sunt proprie heretici, qui contrarium sentiunt, sed a temeritate magna excusari non possunt." But whereas the Council did not strictly define this matter, as a decree to be held by the Catholic faith, it is subject to DOUBT, and therefore they are not properly heretics, who maintain a contrary opinion, yet they cannot be freed from the charge of great temerity.

Is it not plain then, that an opinion may be ALMOST AN ARTICLE OF FAITH; or DOUBTFUL, (*in your unchangeable, infallible church*,) and that it may GROW into an ARTICLE;—and be so NEAR an article that it be DOUBTFUL whether it be one or not; and be LIKE an article, that he who rejects it is ALMOST A HERETIC. And now, (begging you not to be silent about this in your next letter,) I ask you, if you *had not* Bellarmine in your possession, how could you deny so positively that the author bore such a testimony; and how could you venture to level such a charge at me while ignorant of *what* he said? But if you *had* his work before you, then you must not complain, if retorting *with proof* your groundless charge, I say, " *You are convicted of what is not becoming a minister of the Gospel*." *If you had* the work before you, how can these things be explained? I leave you to solve the problem, and shun, if you can, so peculiar a dilemma.

I would next recall you for a moment to the *injured* words *statuere articulos fidei*. I supposed myself addressing one sufficiently a scholar to *know* or to *search out* the real meaning of these words. I assure you the omission of the word " NEW" had no design in it. You know as well as I do, that " *to constitute new articles*," and " *to constitute articles*," convey essentially the same idea. Dr. Johnson defines " constitute" *to give formal existence, to make any thing what it is, to erect*, &c. And this is what I meant to say, that the Pope condemned Luther for denying, " *that the Pope or Council had a right to constitute*," (to give formal existence to, or erect) articles, or make new articles of faith. But it is in vain, by shallow and evasive criticism, to attempt to shun the force of the word " *statuere*." Bailey defines it, " *to set up; to raise; erect, appoint, ordain, decree*." The word, I am well aware, has various shades of meaning; but an *honest* critic, not to say a *learned* one, must see at a glance, when you translate it " *define articles of faith*," or " determine questions," that it is a mere evasion of the force of the phrase. Thus Cicero says, " Statui columellam," *I have erected*, (*defined*, you say) a little pillar. Virgil, " Ipse Pater statuit quid luna moneret." The eternal Father hath decreed the courses of the moon. Horace, " Qui *statuit* te, meo agro." Who *planted thee* (a tree, you would say *defined*) *in my soil?*

You next bring to view, *one* of a multitude of my "objections," (from letter 4) under the head of "*unwarrantable liberties, taken by the church of Rome, with the word of God*." In exposing the utter fallibility of your rule, I showed your *additions* to the word of God; you pass them by; I showed a *pious fraud* of your church; you pass it by: I referred to the *twelve new articles* of faith added by the Council of Trent; you pass them by: I referred to the astonishing *corruptions* and *perversions* of your *translations* of the Bible; you pass them by: but you faintly rally, with " a word of contradiction," as to the charge that you mutilate the second commandment. When I speak of the second commandment, I mean, that which forbids *images* and *idolatry*—and not the third, which your church makes the second. As you are silent about the various versions in which I stated that the second commandment was clipped or omitted, shall we infer that you admit it? And again as to "the Doway Catechism," and "the Poor Man's Catechism," what have you to say in defence of the mistranslation of the passage, "*thou shalt not* BOW DOWN *thyself to them,*" into this, "*thou shalt not* ADORE *or worship them?*" And now I ask, will you deny that the "catechismus ad Parochos" runs thus: "Primum præceptum Decalogi, &c. Non habebis Deos alienos coram me," (Here ends the *first* commandment.) 2d. *Non facies tibi sculptibile,* &c. &c.; and these four words are all that are quoted? The translations of the catechism into various languages carry out the same plan, in substance. The *Montpelier* catechism adds a few more words. The *Irish,* drops the whole. "The Christian doctrine," by the Rev. Father James Ledesma, published by permission of the "superiors," wholly omits the second, and for the fourth commandment, has this "*Remember to sanctify the Holy days.*" Please then excuse me from "*making corrections,*" —until your church corrects her treatment of the *word* and *law* of God.

Such is your *Diarrhœa verborum,* that I fear I shall weary the indulgent reader in the circuit of reply; but as we are upon *proofs* which you challenge, it must be done. Then as to Bellarmine, I still insist that he makes the Pope, living, infallible law; and *you,* not *I,* pervert his reasoning. He argues *that the Pope cannot err* in decretis fidei, *in decrees as to faith,* neque in præceptis morum, *nor in moral precepts.* His reasoning is this: The church is bound to submit to the Pope because he cannot err; and while he owns that in the judgment of the church virtue is good, and vice evil, yet whatever the Pope enjoins is law; and the subversion of moral principle would not be such an evil as the subversion of his infallibility. In other words, the Pope must be followed, right or wrong. But I would ask you in your next letter to explain what Pope Nicholas says to the Emperor Michael, (quoted in may last.) THE POPE IS A GOD, AND THEREFORE MEN CANNOT JUDGE HIM.

What will you say to the following? Immutat substantialem rei naturam, puta faciendo de illegitimo legitimum. Durand, 1, 50.— *He* (the Pope) *can change the very nature of a thing for example; he can make that lawful, which is unlawful.* Habet plenitudinem potestatis, et supra jus est. Gibert, 2. 103. *He possesses plenitude of power, and is above law.* He is then *above law,* can *change law,* and *transmute right into wrong,* and wrong into right; is in a word, "a God on earth," even "our Lord God, the Pope." It is indeed a desperate escape you make, from these profane authorities, to compare this deification of the Pope, with the amiable hyperbole of a grateful people, who sometimes in the fervour of their praise, may have said "the godlike Washington." Washington is called *godlike;* I will not defend it; the Pope is called *God.* Washington made no such pretensions; he bowed to the laws, which under God, his unparalleled courage and wisdom had done so much to establish. The Pope usurps the rights of the people, and the seat of the Saviour, and would sit enthroned on the riches of the commonwealth of Israel. In a word, your infallible church thus speaks of the Pope, and your infallible Pope loves to have it so. Never then join together again, names and pretensions so dissimilar, and so discordant.

We come next to the subject of the validity, or rather *invalidity* of oaths, in the Roman Church. By your own admission, then, "*Ecclesiastical utility makes it right to violate an oath.*" "*He that sweareth to his own hurt, and changeth not,*" is David's good man. But here is the old Popish maxim, that *the end justifies the means.* The interest of the church must be regarded, though a lawful oath lie in the way. You talk of the "*factious minority*" of an infallible Council, and of the Council of Basle as "*a spurious assembly.*" What will you say of the Council of the 4th Lateran decreeing, *that the subjects of heretical sovereigns were freed from their allegiance?* What of the Council of Constance declaring in solemn sessions, *that Emperors, &c. &c. are not bound to keep their promise of security made to heretics, or to persons accused of heresy.* Here observe that the heretic may be ever so innocent of any crime against the state—but his "heresy" in doctrine is enough, (as the case of John Huss,) to tear him from the *civil* power, to be *tried by the Church,* and then *handed back,* to be put to death by the same *civil* power.

And now let me gratify you, in the call for the document, "in which the Pope anathematizes the living men who circulate the Bible." In using the word "*anathema,*" it may be that, from want of familiarity with the weapon, I may have not applied it in its strictly *technical* meaning; but if the spirit of the following sentences is not that of an anathema, I should scarcely know whither to go in search of such a spirit. "The Pope's circular letter," May 3d, 1824. "It is no secret to you, venerable brethren, that a certain society, vulgarly called 'The Bible Society,' (*audaciter vagari*) is audaciously dispreading itself through the whole world. After despising the traditions of the Holy Fathers, and in opposition to the well known decree of the Council of Trent, (session the fourth, on the publication and use of the sacred books,) this society has collected all its forces, and directs every means to one object, to *the translation,* or rather to *the perversion* of The Bible into the vernacular languages of all nations! From this fact, there is strong ground of fear, lest, as in some instances already known, so likewise in the rest, through a perverse interpretation, there be framed out of the Gospel of Christ, a Gospel of man, or, what is worse, a Gospel of the Devil." (St. Jerome, chap. 1. Epis. ad Galat.)

Alexander, Emperor of Russia, having tried Bible Societies for a short time, found the spirit of liberty, and the power of light so great, that he must abolish them, or lose his crown. And he issued his royal ukase, putting them down in his empire. How expressive is this coincidence!

In China preachers of the cross are not tolerated. The Jesuits found their way by intrigue into the empire; but they aimed at the *throne* more than the *souls* of the people;—and still farther threw back the hopes of the empire. The illustrious Dr. Morrison has translated the *entire Bible* into that perplexing and interminable language. And they are a *reading* people; and in this way alone can they be now enlightened. Yet every Bible Society, and translation, and donor, is *cursed* for this labour of love. How well for China, and for us, that while the Pope *curses*, the Saviour *smiles* upon the heavenly work of giving the Bible to every creature.

Perhaps it may also "gratify" you to see some more recent news from Rome. It is found in the Pope's *Encyclical Letter*, lately sent forth. He tells his Bishops all over the world, "*that now is the hour and the power of darkness; yes, the earth is in sorrow and perishes; the chair of the blessed Peter in which we sit*, where Jesus Christ has laid the foundation of his church, is violently shaken, and the bonds of unity are weakened and broken every day." He calls it, "an absurd and dangerous maxim, or rather the raving of delirium, that it is proper to allow to every man liberty of conscience." He calls the liberty of the press, "*that fatal license of which we cannot entertain sufficient horror;*"—and brings against the license of unfettered printing, the Apostolical practice, of *publicly burning evil books!*—And such is the Head of the Universal Church—seated in his tottering chair, amidst the gathering ruins of his hierarchy; complaining of the freedom of the Press, and denouncing the spirit of the age! In vain does he murmur, and in vain denounce. The thunders of the Vatican no longer cause kings to tremble, and nations to bow down at the haughty Pontiff's feet. Like aged Priam, in the sacking of Troy, he grasps a useless sword:

"Urbis ubi captæ casum, convulsaque vidit
Limina tectorum, et medium in penetralibus hostem,
Arma di usenior desueta trementibus ævo
Circumdat nequidquam humeris, et inutile ferrumCingitur."

It is wholly new to me that "*the Presbyterian Church makes it a sin against the second commandment to tolerate a false religion.*" In your next letter please to mention where you find this passage. In the form of government, Book 1. Chap. 1. Sect. 1, you will find as follows: "*they are unanimously of opinion, that God alone is Lord of conscience,* and therefore they consider the *right of private judgment*, in all matters that respect religion, as *universal* and *unalienable*." Confession of Faith, chap. xxiii. sec. 3. "Civil magistrates may not in the *least* interfere with *matters of faith*—they should give no preference to any one denomination of Christians above the rest—and ecclesiastical persons should enjoy free, full, and unquestioned liberty."

In contrast with the above, let me point you to the following decrees of the great Lateran council, held by Pope Innocent III. A. D. 1215 at which were present, 2 Patriarchs, 70 Metropolitans, 400 Bishops, and 812 abbots, priors, &c. besides imperial ambassadors, &c.

In this *infallible general council,* it was decreed as follows : (I have the original before me, but for want of space give the translation.)

3d Chapter. " We excommunicate and anathematize every heresy extolling itself against this holy, orthodox, Catholic faith which we before expounded, condemning all heretics by what names soever called. And being condemned, let them be left to the *secular power,* or to their bailiffs, to be punished by due animadversion. And let the *secular powers* be *warned and induced,* and if need be *condemned* by ecclesiastical censure, what offices soever they are in, that as they desire to be reputed and taken for believers, so they publicly *take an oath* for the defence of the faith, that they will study in good earnest to *exterminate, to their utmost power, from the lands subject to their jurisdiction, all heretics denoted by the Church;* so that every one, that is henceforth taken into *any power, either spiritual or temporal,* shall be bound to confirm this chapter by his oath."
" But if the *temporal lord,* required and warned by the church, shall neglect to *purge his territory of this heretical filth,* let him by the Metropolitan and Comprovincial Bishops be tied by the bond of excommunication ; and if he scorn to satisfy within a year, let *that be signified to the Pope, that he may denounce-his vassals thenceforth absolved from his fidelity,* (or allegiance,) *and may expose his country to be seized on by Catholics, who, exterminating the heretics, may possess it without any contradiction,* and may keep it in the purity of faith, saving the right of the principal lord, so be it he himself put no obstacle hereto, nor oppose any impediment; the same law notwithstanding being kept about them that have no principal lords." " And the Catholics that *taking the badge of the cross shall gird themselves for the extermining of heretics,* shall enjoy that indulgence, and be fortified with that holy privilege which is granted to them that go the help of the holy land."—" And we decree to subject to excommunication the *believers and receivers, defenders and favourers of heretics,* firmly ordaining, that when any such person is noted by excommunication, if he disdain to satisfy within a year, let him be *ipso jure,* made infamous."

Finally—I find in an accredited Roman Catholic writer, the following sentence, which goes to show, that no means are spared in order to bring these heretics to *justice!* " Admittuntur ad accusandum, atque ad ferendum testimonium etiam infames;" that is, *even infamous persons, are to be admitted to accuse and bring testimony* (against heretics.)

With these facts submitted for your consideration, I for the present, bid you farewell. JOHN BRECKINRIDGE.

(POSTSCRIPT.)

I present through you to Bishop Kenrick the expression of my sincere regret that the mistake as to himself was ever made. A most respectable and responsible name was given me as authority; and it was not until I had repeated the inquiry, and been re-assured of the truth of the statement, that I asked you whether it were true or false. This gentleman still insists that such a warning *was* given on the day named, and in one of your churches in Philadelphia, by a Roman Catholic Priest.—Yours, &c. J. B.

CONTROVERSY. No. IX.

RULE OF FAITH.

Philadelphia, March, 26. 1833.

To the Rev. John Breckinridge,

Rev. Sir,—The precept of the Apostle, which forbids Christians to return "railing for railing," must be my apology for not noticing those parts of your last letter, which come under the head of personality. I engaged in this discussion, with a determination to use only the legitimate evidences of religious *truth*—such as are furnished by reason, revelation, and history—and I am not disposed, under any provocation, to alter my resolution.

But there are a few points, on which you and I are notoriously at issue; and it is necessary that these points should be settled, before we proceed to graver matters.

1. In your letter No. 4. you quoted three words from Bellarmine, to support your assertion, that *with us opinions pass into doctrines*. I said in answer to this, that Dr. Priestly attempts, in his history of early opinions, to disprove the *Divinity* of Christ, by similar assertions—and that you could not quote ten lines before, and ten lines after, the words "fere de fide," without convicting yourself of what is not becoming a minister of the Gospel. You have endeavoured in your last letter, to extricate yourself from this position:—but to my mind you have only confirmed it. If the reader will take the pains to examine the words of the author, as you have quoted them, he will see the *evidence*. Bellarmine takes up the matter, on which he is writing, as an *opinion;* he treats it as an *opinion;* and he leaves it as an *opinion*. What then have you done by the quotation? You have proved that Bellarmine had been *perverted*, when his words "fere de fide" were quoted, to show, that Catholic *faith is*, "*like the new moon, crescent,*" and that the topic on which he was speaking, was "a PROBATIONER FOR A SEAT IN THE CREED." Now, I would ask you, is it becoming a *minister of the Gospel* to pervert an author?—to assert that he said, what he never said?—or that *he meant*, what he *never meant?* This is precisely what the quotation establishes against you, and even less than "ten lines" completes the "conviction."

It was Cardinal Richelieu, I believe, who said, that if he had the privilege of selecting three lines *at his pleasure*, from an author's book, he could have him *hanged for treason*. And we all know, that if the infidel were allowed to select *three words* from the Psalms of David, as you had done from the writings of Bellarmine, he could make it appear, that "there is no God," and that the Royal Prophet was an *Atheist*. But in either case, "ten lines before, and ten lines after," would "convict" the offender of what might be tolerated in *politics*, or *scepticism*, but is, in my opinion, not becoming in the MINISTRY OF THE GOSPEL. You beg me in your last letter "not to be silent about this matter," and I have only one word more to say upon it. It is this: that I will *meet you with a copy of Bellarmine on any day you please to appoint;* and submit the passage to any sworn interpreter of languages, and let *him decide its meaning.* If he says that Bellarmine's meaning was *not* perverted, in your first use of the words "fere de fide," I *hereby* pledge myself to apologise publicly. But if the decision be against you, then you will be candid enough to *acknowledge the perversion,* and leave the public to judge of the cause *which required it.* The decision, however, shall be in writing, with the interpreter's signature, and given to the public.

You ask me, "if I had not Bellarmine in my possession, how could I deny so positively, that the author bore such a testimony; and how could I venture to level such a charge at you, while *ignorant of what he said?*" Answer. Because I was *not* ignorant "of what he said." 2. Because the "doctrines of the Catholic Church are *fixed stars* in the firmament of belief," and the transmutation of an *opinion into a doctrine,* (for proof of which *you referred to Bellarmine,*) would be the raising of a "new light," a species of religious reformation which Protestants have taken *into their own hands,* and for which Catholics have neither the talent, inclination, nor authority. So much, then, for this first point on which we are *at issue*

2. As to Luther's proposition—I showed that you had *interpolated it,* by inserting a word ("new,") which *is not in the original.* That subsequently, when you *gave the original,* you left the word "new" out of the translation; but supplied the place of it by an assertion which was unfounded in truth—viz. that your second version "was word for word what you had said before." In your last letter, you assure us that the *omission* of the word "new," (in the *second* version,) had no design in it. That is, you omit the *interpolation,* and yet take pains to assure our readers, that for this act of literary honesty, they are indebted to chance, and not to intention, since "the omission had no design in it?" But then you tell us that, "statuere arborem," means, according to Horace, "to plant a tree." Agreed. And that "statuere columellam," according to Cicero, means, "to erect a little pillar." Agreed, again. But what follows? Will you say that *therefore* in Luther's proposition, "statuere articulos fidei," means "to make *new* articles of faith?" And yet, on this pivot of *new* logic, turns the only defence, you have been able to set up against all the arguments of my last letter, touching the charges involved in the point at issue. It is not a tenet of Catholic belief, that either the Church or the Pope, or both together, have the power to *create,* or *reject* DOCTRINE: to *make,* or to *destroy* one single article of FAITH. Protestants alone, who are responsible to no rule of faith, except to their individual private opinion of the *meaning* of Scripture, may *plant* and *pluck up* doctrines at *their pleasure.* Again, therefore, I am constrained to say that your charge against the Catholic church, of "claiming the right to make new articles of faith," is *painfully* untrue.

3. You had said that the "Catechism of the Council of Trent gives only four words of the second commandment, and closes with an expressive *et cætera.*" This is "untrue." And, can you ima-

gine, that the *moral sense* of the community, Protestant as well as Catholic, does not *hunger* for an explanation of the motives which could induce a "minister of the Gospel," *thus* to bear false witness against his neighbour.

4. You had said, that in the Catholic church there are no less than three systems of doctrine, on the "Pope's supremacy." Now every Catholic in the whole world might be called as a witness, to prove that this assertion is "untrue." On every *article of faith*, the Catholics of the present, and of all past ages, are as *united in belief*, as if they all dwelt under the same roof. Is it not, therefore, humiliating to sincere Protestants to discover, that their ministers and their books are obliged to use *such* means, and to confound *all distinction* between doctrine, discipline, opinions, and local customs, in order to prove disunion of belief among the Catholics?

5. You had said, that it is a principle of Catholics, "that if the Pope were to command vice, and prohibit virtue, he is to be obeyed." For this assertion you referred to Bellarmine. In reply, I quoted the passage of Bellarmine, in my last letter, which shows that he stated it, *as the impious* and ABSURD *consequence*, which would flow from the opinion he was then refuting. You did not attempt to meet the quotation with any thing stronger than assertion. "I *still* insist," you say, "that he (Bellarmine) makes the Pope living *infallible* law; and *you*, not *I*, prevent his reasoning." Bellarmine maintained, as *a matter of opinion*, that the Pope, in his official character is infallible. Bossuet, *as a matter of opinion*, maintained the contrary; both were Catholics, and believed as a *matter of faith*, the Pope's *supremacy*, and the *infallibility* of the church. And here is the maxim of St. Augustine, exemplified " in *matter of faith*, UNITY; *in matters not of faith*, LIBERTY." But *I* insist upon it, that Bellarmine, so far from saying, that "the Pope can make virtue vice, and vice virtue," professes to prove the erroneousness of the opinion, which he was then refuting, by showing that *this* would be the impious consequence of its adoption. Thus then we both " insist." Who shall decide between us? I say, any sworn interpreter of languages, and (stipulating always, that the decision be published, with his signature and agreement) I CHALLENGE you to the *alternative*. How then can you "bear false witness against your neighbour," by saying that Bellarmine *taught*, and Catholics *believe*, what Bellarmine NEVER *taught*, and what Catholics *do not believe?*

6. You had stated, that according to the 16th canon of the 3d Council of Lateran, "an oath contrary to ecclesiastical utility, is perjury, not an oath." I answered that *this* had reference to *unlawful* oaths, which were sometimes pleaded by factious minorities, or individuals, to justify their rebellion *against the choice of the majority*, in certain cases of ecclesiastical elections. To these *cases exclusively*, was the decision of the Council limited. Yet, my Rev. opponent spreads it out into a *general proposition* of Catholic doctrine. Again, therefore, I challenge you to abide the decision of any sworn interpreter. Here, then, are six different heads, on each of which I am constrained to say with regret, that you have asserted what is "untrue." It is useless, therefore, for you to calculate on

the verdict of our readers in general, who are unacquainted, *as you know*, with the *language and the books*, to which you have referred, with such bold but deceitful confidence. You will please consequently *to clear up, as I give you an opportunity of doing*, these six topics, before you expect me to pay any attention to your silly references. Of these you have already made *too many*, for the honour of your fame, and the sanctity of your cause, as I shall have occasion to show the public, before the controversy shall have terminated.

Judging by what my own feelings should be, I fear that these remarks are calculated to give you pain; but remember that you have left me *no alternative;*—except to bring the matter fairly to issue, or *bow in acquiescence to charges, which are utterly "untrue."* My own principle is, never to assert, in argument, except what I am convinced is true. And as I admit the *possibility* of mistake, so, *in such a case,* do I hold myself ready to admit opposite evidence, and *correct cheerfully* any statement in which I may happen to have erred. A charge of this kind is brought against me in your last letter. "It is wholly new to me," you say, "that the Presbyterian church makes it a *sin against the second* commandment, to "tolerate a false religion." At this, Rev. Sir, I am "wholly" surprised. Being, like myself, something of a "high churchman," I did not suppose that *any thing* contained in the "Confession of Faith" would be "new" to you.

The "tolerating of a false religion" is laid down as a *sin against the second commandment* in "Larger Catechism," page 268, of the edition published by Towar & Hogan, in 1829. Perhaps it is also new to you—that in order to show how *great a sin it is*, reference is made, in the same page, to certain texts of Scripture, in one of which, DEATH is specified as the *penalty of teaching a false religion!* I shall here quote the text, "and it shall come to pass that if any one shall yet prophesy" (meaning falsely) "then his father and his mother that begat him, shall say unto him, *thou shalt not live; for thou speakest lies in the name of the Lord.*" Thus, it seems that, according to the Confession of Faith, and to the Scriptures, Presbyterians look upon it, as an *orthodox sin,* to "tolerate a false religion." The *constitution* of our country, however, has decided *otherwise.*

This same Confession of Faith teaches that even *good works*, done by "unregenerate men" are *sinful*. (Chap. xvi. page 100,) and (chap. xv. page 92) it tells us, "there is no sin *so small*, but *it deserves damnation*"—from whence it would follow, that if an "unregenerate man" give a dollar to a poor widow, to keep her from *perishing in the winter,* he commits a *sin,* and deserves to be damned for it! True, the text adds, that if *he does not do it*, he commits a "*greater sin;*" by which it appears, that he is to be damned *for doing it,* and damned for leaving it undone! And yet there is an *abundant* profanation of sacred texts, to *prove* all this, on the same page! You refer me to chapter xxiii. for the following quotation, in your last. "Civil magistrates may not in the least, interfere with *matters of faith,* they should give *no preference* to any denomination of Christians, above the rest—and ecclesiastical persons should enjoy free, full and unquestioned liberty." I have *not found* any such words, in the reference. But in the very same chapter and section, I find the following: "He (the civil magistrate) hath *authority*, and it is *his duty*, to take order, that unity and peace be preserved in the church, that the *truth of God be kept pure and entire*, that all *blasphemies* and HERESIES *be suppressed*, all corruptions and abuses in worship and discipline prevented or reformed, and all the ordinances of God duly settled, administered and *observed*. For the better effecting whereof, he hath *power to call Synods*, to be present at them. and *to provide that whatsoever is transacted in them*, BE ACCORDING TO THE MIND OF GOD." Westminster Confession, chap. xxiii. sec. 3. p. 141. Here the "mind of God" is made the *rule of just proceeding*, and the civil magistrate, is supposed to be on such *terms of familiarity and confidence with the Almighty*, that *he knows* what is the "mind of God," and is *bound* to see that matters shall be *regulated accordingly*. Still, there is a *powerful array of Scripture texts*, at the bottom of the page, to show that *all this* is right and true according to the Bible! *Your* quotation, and mine, founded on the *same reference*, differ very materially! Will you please to explain the disagreement?

I would now follow you through one or two of the heads of what I suppose you intended as an argument against the Catholic rule of faith. But really, there are so many contradictions under my eye, as I look upon the first part of your last epistle, that I am at a loss to understand whether you *admit* or *reject* the succession from the Apostles in the ministry of teaching. First, you say, that "as the claim" (of the Catholic Church) "to infallibility, rests on the notion of *succession*, it falls to the ground, and with it our *rule of faith*." Next, you say, that if the Apostles had successors, then *all* must have had them, and as there were twelve apostles, so there should be exactly twelve successors, every one of whom should be a Pope! Then, these successors, if there were any, must *be able to work miracles*. And then, finally, you say that I am *uncandid* for "representing you as holding *that the Apostles had no successors!*" And a little farther still, you tell us, that "you hold to a commission still standing and binding which reaches to the end of time." When you tell us clearly what you mean by all this, I shall be extremely happy to meet any arguments you may be disposed to put forward. In the mean time, it is manifest, that I cannot drive you from a position, until you signify exactly what ground you mean to assume.

The whole of your next position is one continuous train of misrepresentation. You begin by asserting that on my plan every preacher or teacher "*must be infallible!!*" And taking this assumption, unfounded though it be, for the ground work of your reasoning, you draw your own consequences. But as "my plan does *not* require every preacher or teacher to *be infallible*," so your deductions founded on this hypothesis are *gratuitous*, and are overturned by the simple denial of both the premises and the conclusion. "My plan," as you call it, is that Jesus Christ, after having proved, that he *was sent* by the Father, for the establishment of a divine religion, as well as for the redemption of the world, *instituted a ministry* of TEACHING in his church—that this ministry was to extend with the duration of time —that it was the *channel of communication*, by which the *knowledge of that divine religion* should be conveyed to *all nations,*—and that *to this ministry of teaching,* the Son of God actually promised the *Spirit of Truth* and his own *perpetual presence all days,* even till the consummation of the world. This is "my plan:" and if you feel yourself competent to overturn it, the first step is—*to state it correctly.* The next step is, to take up those passages of the *Scripture history,* by which it is proved that *this was* the means appointed by Christ, and show that, instead of proving the *ministry of teaching,* they prove, on the contrary, that all infallibility ceased with the death of the Apostles, except the infallibility of individual opinion, in the private interpretation of Scriptural doctrine. It would be the mere repetition of *unanswered* arguments; were I again to adduce the proofs and reasoning of my former letters on this subject. It is useless for me to publish the same proofs of the Catholic rule of faith in every letter. If you had taken up my arguments, stated them in my own words, suffered them to enjoy the meaning which they possessed, *as they went forth from my own pen,* refuted, or *attempted* honorably to refute them, then it might be necessary to review the testimonies adduced to show that Christ established the *immortal, uniform, Catholic teaching of his Church, as the only infallible rule of faith.* I refer the reader to a serious perusal of my letters on this subject, Nos. 5 and 7: and let him ask himself, as he is to answer at the last day, whether, according to the evidences furnished on either side, the testimonies of reason, revelation and history, by which the Catholic rule of faith is supported, are not infinitely stronger than any thing you have been able to produce in favour of *private* interpretation. I appeal to that reader to say, whether your letters, *thus far,* instead of presenting a clear chain of controversial reasoning on any *one* subject, are not an "olla-podrida" of crimination, scandalous anecdote, fierce assertion, and general evasion of the question on which we are disputing.

It may be useful to state again the subject now under discussion. That there is "an infallible rule of faith, *appointed by Christ,* to guide us in matters of religion, and to settle disputes in his Church" is agreed. Now the Catholic church, being a visible and perpetual society, and the *original inheritor* of the *doctrines, commissions and promises of Jesus Christ, leans,* as it were, on the arm of her Divine founder;—trusts in his *promises,* discharges his *commission,* and *testifies* to *all nations,* during all days, what are the true doctrines, of which it was said, "He, that believeth *not,* shall be condemned." Mark xvi. 16. *How shall we know what we must believe, in order to escape this condemnation?* That Jesus provided an *infallible means,* to arrive at this knowledge, is admitted by my Rev. opponent. Then it must be either the Catholic or the Protestant rule of faith. That it is *not* the Protestant principle, appears to me one of the clearest moral truths that ever presented itself to human understannding.

1. Because that principle stabs the authority of the sacred volume, which it professes to cherish. That principle makes the Bible, as efficient to *overthrow,* as to *uphold, any doctrine of Christianity.* According to *that* principle, no man can be certain *what doctrines* Jesus Christ revealed and required men to believe, at the risk of be-

ing condemned. Let the *sincere* Protestant reader ask himself, what is in *reality* his rule of faith. His ministers tell him—the Bible alone. Let him then take up the Bible and read these words of our blessed Redeemer—" the Father and I are one ;" turn, then, to the other words, " the Father is greater than I." That *one* of these passages, is to be explained by the *other*, is certain : but *which* shall take the preference of the other, *the sacred writings do not determine.* If he is a Unitarian he will come to the conclusion, that Christ is not God. If he is a Presbyterian, his *opinion* will be different. In the mean time, his belief, no matter to which side he belongs, is founded, not on the *Bible*, but on what *he* THINKS *to be the meaning of the Bible.* Now, Rev. Sir, I request you, *as a favour*, to take up these two texts, and show me and our readers, *how you can save the Divinity of Jesus Christ* from the *destructive operation* of the Protestant rule of faith, in the hands of the Unitarian. If you *can* and *will* do this, it will prove a service to religion, at which, although it by no means concerns me, I shall heartily rejoice. What is said here, in relation to this fundamental article, is equally true of *every other tenet of religious belief.* I defy any Protestant in the whole world, who is *consistent* with his own rule of faith, and rational in its application, if he will only take the pains to *analyze his belief*, to find it resting on any other foundation, save his own PRIVATE OPINION. For if his rule of faith be the Bible ALONE, then he must fling to the winds all *creeds, confessions, and teachings of men.* And when he *has* perused the Bible, if he is asked what doctrines it contains, he will be obliged to answer according to his OPINIONS of its meaning. *You* believe in predestination ;—another, reading the Bible with equal sincerity, disbelieves it :—a third reads the Bible and believes in everlasting punishment :—a fourth rejects that belief, &c. Are they all right ? Certainly not ; though they *may be all sincere.* Is it the Bible that deceives them ? Certainly it is not. But they are deceived *by the Protestant rule of faith*, which taught them, that in order to know *what doctrines had been revealed by the Saviour of men*, each individual must pass the Bible through the crucible of his own private judgment. And, though his mind should have undergone a thousand changes, as to the *meaning* of the inspired book, still the Protestant rule of faith has determined, with the hand of destiny, that he shall end where he began, and never arrive at any thing more certain than *opinion*.

Not so the Catholic. He may read the Scriptures, notwithstanding the calumnies that Protestantism has perpetuated against the church, from one generation to another, since the era of the " Reformation." But, on *points of doctrine*, he does not substitute his own *opinions*, by way of *inspiring the sacred text*. He takes it for granted, that the meaning was understood, before he came into existence. He inquires *what it is* of the church, which has been the *guardian* equally of the book, and of the doctrines it contains, since the day, when Jesus laid her foundations on the rock of eternal truth. Her pastors have *never ceased to teach* the things, which, according to *Revelation, we must* BELIEVE and PRACTICE, in order to be saved. By this rule of faith the whole Christian world was UNITED IN DOCTRINE, when the Father of Protestantism began to sound the trumpet of religious discord, and to preach *new opinions*, 1500 years after Christians had been *warned*, not to receive any *new* doctrines, even though they should be preached by an " angel from heaven."

2. The Protestant rule of faith *is that*, which was adopted by all the acknowledged heresies of antiquity. By this rule of private interpretation, the Sabellians denied the Trinity of persons in God, (S. August. lib. de hæres. cap. 41.)—the Arians, the Divinity of Christ —the Macedonians, the Divinity of the Holy Ghost. By this rule, the Manicheans rejected the Old Testament—the Pelagians denied Original Sin—and so, of all the others. Did Christ then appoint as the *infallible rule of faith* a principle of guidance, which, in its *legitimate use*, and *not by its abuse*, has given rise to *all the heresies of ancient and modern times ?*

In the Catholic Church, on the contrary, heresy has never found a resting place. The *truth of doctrine*, which *had always been taught* by the pastors, and believed by *all*, was *present* EVERY WHERE to convict the novelty of error. Protestants indeed, have asserted, that the church had *apostatized*, but none accuse her of heresy. Being herself the *oldest society of Christians*, there was no other from which she could have *separated*. We meet the charge of apostacy, by saying, that if she *did* apostatize, as they will have it, then " the gates of hell prevailed against her."—contrary to the Saviour's promise! Are they prepared for this ? But if the Saviour's promise did *not* fail, " then the gates of hell did *not prevail against her*, and Jesus Christ was *still* with her, when Martin Luther, John Calvin, and the King of England, took it into their heads to make *churches of their own*. Think you, Rev'd Sir, that the Redeemer *forgot* his promise, or forsook his spouse, by abandoning his own church : did Zion say, " our Lord hath forsaken me, and our Lord hath forgotten me ? Why ; can a *woman* forget *her infant*, that she will not have pity on the *son of her womb ?* And if she should forget, *yet will I not forget thee*. Behold I have written thee in my hands." Isaiah chap. xlix. 14.

3. In your last letter, you lay it down as an argument against the Catholic rule of faith, that the Apostles *alone* were inspired and infallible. And thus, in your thoughtless zeal, you strike a fatal blow, although I am sure you did not intend it, at a large portion of the New Testament. If the Apostles *alone* were inspired and infallible, as you assert, then what is to become of the two Gospels of St. Luke and St. Mark ? What is to become of the Acts of the Apostles ? It is well known that the authors of *these books* were not Apostles, " and had not seen the Lord." Will Protestants adopt your *ruinous* argument, I mean assertion, on this subject, which, if it were true, would blast the authority of so large a portion of the written word of God ? Will they not rather, in *this instance* at least, join with me, to shield the sacred writings from the destruction of your weapons ?

4. You have frequently in your letters appealed to the prejudices of our Protestant readers, on the subject of what you are pleased to call the Apocryphal Scriptures. But *how*, I would ask, are you enabled *by the Protestant rule of faith*, to determine, what books are canonical ? That this cannot be done by the Scripture itself, is palpa-

bly evident. You certainly cannot be ignorant, that several books, which in the *first ages* laid claim to inspired authority, are not in the canon. Of these I may name a few—the Gospel according to the Hebrews, or according to the Apostles—the memoirs of the Apostles—quoted frequently by Justin Martyr,—and different tracts under the names of Peter, Paul, Matthias, and other Apostles. (See Euseb. lib. iii. c. 3. 24.) Why, then, are *those* left out of the reformed canon of the *Protestant* Scriptures? On the other hand, the inspiration of the Epistle of St. James, the Epistle of St. Jude, the Epistle to the Hebrews, the second Epistle of St. Peter, the second and third of St. John, and the book of Revelations, was *controverted* in the same ages. And why, I would again ask, are these admitted into your reformed canon? Luther admitted the Epistle of St. James, in his edition of 1529 and 1534, but scornfully expelled it from those of 1535 and 1540. It continued to be excluded from the following Lutheran editions after his death; viz. that of 1548,—66,—72—75, —82,—89,—93,—99. So, also was the Epistle of St. Jude excluded from the edition published in 1619. The Apocalypse is excluded from the same editions, and that of 1609.

As to the Epistle to the Hebrews, the good " Reformer" did not know exactly what to think! After the two editions, of 1529 and 1534, it was agreed, that it should be retained, and tolerated as *apocryphal*, and *so* it continued in the Lutheran Bibles, until the time of the two Wallemburgs, say 1669. Now every Protestant has the *same right* to sport with the sacred books that Luther had. And since the Scriptures themselves, do not *determine* what books are canonical and what books are not, is it not something like arrogance for you or Mr. Martin Luther to mutilate the inspired volume, and lop off, at your pleasure, branches from the tree of life, by capriciously applying the pruning hook of *private, individual opinion*. By WHAT RULE, then, can you *prove* according to the Protestant principle of belief, that *these* books are canonical, and that *those* are *not* canonical? Let the General Assembly try their wisdom on the question.

5. The Protestant rule of faith supposes, that the Scriptures are *plain and obvious* in their meaning. And yet,—the *plea* for the Reformation, and the cry of the Reformers, was, that the *whole Catholic Church* had *been mistaken* as to the *true meaning* of this same book;—which was so plain withal, that *every* Protestant, who has been blessed with ten months' education, may take it up and "read as he runs!"—and that every such Protestant, is bound to believe, that *his crude conception of its meaning*, make him *wiser* and more *infallible*, than ALL the *councils*, FATHERS, TEACHERS, PASTORS and PEOPLE, of ALL the ages of the Christian church!!!

6. But even admitting the absurd supposition, that *such* a man is qualified to understand the meaning of what the book says, how does he know that the book is, *in all respects*, the same *now*, that it was, when it came from the hands of its inspired authors? Has it been *correctly* translated? Has it been *fairly copied*, from one manuscript to another, previous to printing? *These* are difficulties, for which his rule of faith furnishes no solution. And these difficulties are increased an hundred fold, when he remembers that the Scrip-

tures were in the keeping of the *Catholic Church*, which the *prejudices* of his education have taught him to look upon, as a *universal anti-Christian conspiracy;* and that the *work of transcribing the Bible,* generally devolved on those MONKS, whose name is synonymous, in his mind, with *ignorance, dishonesty, perfidiousness* and *cruelty.* " What!" he will ask with astonishment;—" is it from *such* a source, that we receive the written word of God?"—Yes,—gentle reader —do not be startled at the discovery. Before the squabble between Martin Luther and Leo X. in the sixteenth century, there was not a single Protestant in the whole universe, to take care of the Bible. Mr. Breckinridge may tell you, that God was pleased to reveal the *Protestant rule of faith* 1500 years after he *had* revealed the *Christian religion*—and that the Holy Bible was not in the least *tainted,* by the tide of corruption, on which it floated down. But, you may reply to him, in my name, that God *could have preserved the doctrines of the Church in the same way*—and that, if Martin Luther *believed her,* when she told him, that the Scriptures are *the* INSPIRED *written word of God;*—he *might* have believed her, when she told him, *what doctrines they contained*—especially, when it is remembered that it was HE, and *not* the Church, that undertook to give them a *new* meaning, with which Christianity, during the same space of 1500 years had been totally unacquainted. With this remark I leave my reader, and my Rev. opponent, to finish the dialogue. The latter will have an opportunity to speak for himself; and *the public will see* HOW *he* will meet *these difficulties.*

The Catholic believes the INFALLIBILITY of the church. The *grounds* of this belief, are briefly stated in my last two letters; particularly in No. 5. He knows that there has been no such thing as a *moral* DEATH, or CHASM, in the *teaching and belief* of those doctrines, which Christ revealed, and men are bound to receive, as they value their salvation. He knows, that in *this sense,* the church is a WITNESS to the universe; and, as he receives *her* testimony when she says, *that the Scriptures are the inspired word of God,*— that she *received and preserved them* AS SUCH : so *he* receives *her testimony,* when she says, that the *opinions* of heretics—no matter of what age or country, are *not the doctrines,* which *she received,* with the Scriptures, *from Jesus Christ* and his Apostles,—and he yields, but a "reasonable obedience," to *her* authority, when she admonishes him, not to follow the notions of *Martin Luther,* or any other individual.

Wishing to stand corrected, as to the *length* of my letter, by the gentle reproof of our publishers, and the *moral* of the "wounded snake," with which you begin your last epistle, I deem it prudent to hasten to a conclusion. There are one or two points, however, which you have protruded on the consideration of our readers with no other view that *I can perceive,* except to gratify prejudice, where it exists, and to divert general attention from your palpable abandonment of the rule of faith. To these I shall briefly advert,—although, until you have agreed to clear up the points, on which *we are at issue,* IN THE WAY *I have* proposed;—I feel that the moral sense of the community would sustain me in refusing to notice any reference of yours, in which the *whole passage is not quoted.*

In your last epistle you ask me, to "explain what Pope Nicholas meant, when he said to the Emperor Michael, " THE POPE IS A GOD AND THEREFORE MEN CANNOT JUDGE HIM." Now, as you have the modesty in *this* instance, to acknowledge that it is instruction you stand in need of, I should be sorry to refuse what you desire. Know then, and understand in the *first* place, that *Pope Nicholas never said,* "*the Pope is a God.*" Here I might stop :—but *secondly,* know and understand that the Emperor Michael, *had expelled Ignatius, Patriarch of Constantinople from his* SEE :—and that Pope Nicholas was expostulating with him, on the *unlawfulness* of disturbing the SPIRITUAL ORDER *of the church,* by the exercise of *secular* power. Among other things, he reminds the Emperor, that his *predecessor, Constantine the Great,* when called upon to sit in judgment on the bishops of the church, *refused to do so ;* and, addressing them in the figurative language of the Scripture, (Psalm lxxxi. 6.) said to them : " Vos dii estis, a VERO Deo constituti"—" Ye are Gods, *appointed* by the true God"—to show, that *he, Constantine,* regarded their *spiritual authority,* as an authority FROM GOD, and therefore TOO SACRED for the judgment of *temporal princes,* and the interference of *secular power.* Similar language was used, in similar circumstances, by *Theodosius the younger. And these are the examples,* which Pope Nicholas is holding up to the *memory* of the Emperor Michael, to induce him to desist, and to show him *how much* the Emperors, his *predecessors,* had respected the *authority of God,* in the persons of his ministers ;—and that, though he could command armies, and ravage provinces, yet he could neither *bestow,* nor *take away,* the spiritual authority of *a bishop,* in the church of Christ. Constantine used the words *in the sense I have mentioned.* Pope Nicholas did *not* use them *as his own ;* but *referred* to them in the sense, and for the purpose here stated. He speaks of himself, in the document, as the humble "*minister*" of Jesus Christ.

If, then, you had waited for this information; you would not have exposed yourself, nor deceived your readers, by building the following assertion on *the circumstance,* which I have just explained. Your words are evidence of zeal, which would better befit a *better* cause : but it is not "the zeal according to knowledge." "'The Pope *usurps* the rights of the people, and the SEAT *of the Saviour,* and would sit enthroned on the riches of the commonwealth of Israel. In a word your infallible CHURCH, *thus speaks of the Pope ;* and your *infallible* Pope *loves to have it so.*" On this whole concern, I have only to say, that if *I* were found as you are, in this matter, I feel that Catholics would blush for me :—and that heaven will *judge* the calumnies that have been heaped on the Catholic church and on her supreme *visible* head—the Bishop of Rome.

You make a long extract from the Council of Lateran :—on which I have two questions to ask you. First, do you give it as a *literal* and *continuous* translation ? Second, do you affirm that in the original it has the *same general meaning* that it *seems* to have in the quotation? As you say you have the "original before you," you can, of course, have no difficulty in giving a positive answer to these questions. In the mean time, a little information on the character of *that* quotation, or rather the circumstances to which it relates, may not be useless or uninteresting to the reader.

It is to be observed, in the first place, that this council was held at a time when the *feudal system* was in its full operation. A council was, as it were, the *general congress* of Christendom; in which, states and sovereigns were represented for the purpose of conferring together, on *such matters*, as concerned the general welfare. These *secular* representatives had nothing to do with the *definitions* of doctrines or morals;—and the *infallibility of the church* had *nothing to do* WITH ANY THING ELSE. Still, it was deemed the most *convenient time and place*, for sovereigns and statesmen, to adopt such means in *conjunction with the clergy*, as might protect the altar and the throne; or, as the *exigencies* of the period required. The social picture, mingled theocracy and civil policy, of the puritan settlements in New England, presents but a diminutive analogy, when the pilgrim fathers and their immediate successors, (not to speak of other things *far more serious*,) would hardly ring the town-house bell, unless they found a *text of Scripture for it*.

At the period of *this Council* the Albigenses were scattering the materials of civil and religious revolution, in the bosom of *peaceable* empires;—among nations, which acknowledged but *one God*, and knew but *one religion*, whereby he was to be worshipped. Sovereigns were obliged to *provide for their own safety*. They may have foreseen those *consequences* which *Mr. Breckinridge* proclaims would have resulted from the *toleration* of the Bible Society in Russia. They would have *been obliged* to abolish the institutions just as the Albigenses might think proper to direct, or "else lose their crown." *This* was the fate, we are told, which awaited the Russian autocrat *if he had not put down the Bible Society!!!* If *this* be so, as Mr. Breckinridge asserts, then there is *no man*, who, placed in the *same* situation, and foreseeing the consequences, would not have done the same thing as Alexander. So it was in the temporal regulations adopted by the commingled representatives of Church and States, at the general council of Lateran. Had they not the right, I would ask, *as the majority*, by a million to one, to take measures for the common welfare? The doctrine of Christ teaches submission to "the powers that be:" —Consequences, such as you predicted *of the Bible Society in Russia*, have *always* followed the footsteps of fanaticism. Had not, then, the Catholic kings, and Catholic barons, and Catholic vassals, and all the *orders of feudalism* in *Catholic Europe*, the right, by *virtue* of their majority, to take precautions *against* such consequences? No *Republican*, I should think, would deny it. You have said, indeed, that "you render unto Cæsar the things that are Cæsar's"—speaking, I presume, in the name of your Church. But your hypothetical *prediction*, in reference to "*Bible Society in Russia*," is rather *a strange* commentary on the text. And, by the bye, is it not a singular coincidence with your remark, that "Cæsar" *never was* in the power of your Church, but once; and that THEN the "tribute money" was paid with the *blood of a Protestant king!* Should you not, then, *delicately* touch the subject of persecution, until you can persuade yourself that history *has lost her* MEMORY? At a time when there were not, perhaps, a million of Presbyterians in the whole world, Mr. John Knox, the insular founder of Presbyterianism, laid it down as a *maxim*, that, " It is not only *lawful* to punish *unto the death*, such as labour to subvert the true religion ;—but the magistrates and people ARE BOUND *so to do*, unless they will provoke the wrath of God against themselves." (Appellation of John Knox annexed to his History of the Reformation, page 25.) Had not Catholic Europe as good a right *to take measures of safety*, against the *revolutionary* spirit, of a few religious innovators in the twelfth century;—as a few religious innovators had to " punish unto the death," all those who should *contradict* THEIR *religious opinions*, in the sixteenth century ? Now, I again submit to your cool reflection, whether it would not be as profitable to your fame, and to your cause, if you would condescend to redeem your *signature*, by " adhering *strictly* to the subject of discussion for the time being"—as it has been, to wander into the labyrinths of *irrelevant matter*, from which you do not seem to have well studied the faculties of retreat.

In conclusion, I would remark, that my charity for the mass of Protestants, has been infinitely enlarged, by my *experience* in this controversy. I would not dare to question the wisdom or the justice of that divine Being, who permits it to *be so :*—But when I consider the character of their *books*, and the weapons of their *theologians*, I can hardly imagine how it could *be otherwise*. They hate truth ; not because it *is* truth ; but *because* their ministers, and their books teach them to regard truth as *error*. And they are *confirmed* in their hatred, by the general " delusion" which teaches them to regard the *prejudices*, that have been *instilled* by their books, and education as the *testimony* of the *pure word of God*, THE BIBLE ALONE. How many of them, after having been " tossed to and fro," on the deluge of religious opinions, with which Protestantism has inundated the world, and not finding whereon to rest their foot, would *return*, like the weary *dove*, to the " ark," from which *their fathers*, in an hour of irritation and excitement, inconsiderately launched forth into *the great deep*. For myself, it has taught me to bless God with inexpressible gratitude, for having permitted to be *born* in the Catholic Church of Christ ; otherwise, I might have ranked among the fiercest of her *opponents*, and imagined that, in persecuting *her*, even with my pen, I was " doing God service." Thus, I may say with the poet, though not in the *literal* sense,

Haud *ignarus* mali, *miseris* succurrere disco.

Yours respectfully,
JOHN HUGHES.

P. S.—Bishop Kenrick is entirely satisfied with your explanation of the "mistake ;"—which, it seems, was *not* a mistake, after all ; since that " most respectable and responsible gentleman, on whose authority you relied, still insists that *such a warning*, (viz. a prohibition to read this controversy,) was given, *on the day named*, and in *one* of *our churches*, in *Philadelphia, by a Roman Catholic priest.*" Now, as this is a matter of some consequence to us, will you be pleased to request this " most respectable and responsible gentleman," to *tax his memory*, and try to recollect *in which* of our churches he was, *on that day*. Tell him, that there are only *five* Catholic churches in the city; and that he may leave *the two*, in which Bishop Kenrick and myself officiate, *out of the number*. I am really curious to know in which of *the other three* the warning was given; —and so *slyly*, it seems, that he was the *only* person that overheard it!! J. H.

CONTROVERSY. No. X.

RULE OF FAITH.

New York, 3d *April*, 1833.

To the Rev. John Hughes,—*Sir*,

      " No falsehood can endure
      Touch of *celestial temper*, but returns
      To its own likeness;—up it starts
      Discover'd and surprised."

There is a heavenly virtue in the sword of the Spirit, when faithfully wielded by the hand even of a frail man, which error cannot resist. The " atrocious crime" of having " told you the truth," as to your *system*, and your *authorities*, has, I regret to perceive, disturbed your temper not a little ; and led you to depart, not only from the dignity of a minister, but from the decencies of a gentleman. Though you begin your letter with professions of decorum, you charge me in less than two columns with *six deliberate falsehoods!* But I advise you to be *composed;* for the good people of this country do not think by *force*, nor believe upon *prescription*. I know it is natural for a system, which has rested for ages on *authority*, to be impatient of inquiry into its title to dominion. But the days of unquestioned lordship over men's consciences have gone by ; and as you stand the representative of a body, claiming *infallibility*, wisdom suggests that you should not stumble in *the example*, while you are pleading for *the doctrine!*

Now, even admitting that I am mistaken in the interpretation of Bellarmine, as to "*fere de fide*," &c. ; and of the Pope as to " *statuere articulos fidei*,"—must every such mistake be charged to a want of veracity? I put it to your Christian honour, I level it even to your common honesty—can you defend a course so much at war with candour, propriety and justice ? In these references, did I not meet your call, time after time, with quotations, translations, and expositions ? And, now, either by your extracts or mine, are not the facts on which a just judgment may be formed, fairly before the public ?

But so far from thinking or owning myself mistaken, every return of my attention to the subject, and every struggle you make to shield your cause, give me increased conviction that I am right. What surprises me exceedingly is, that you cavil at these points, and make these charges against me, when such a mass of unanswered matter, is left by you *entirely unnoticed;* and your strange liberties with ancient testimony left wholly unexplained. I will refer you for example once more, to the famous quotation from Tertullian, where you omitted half the passage, (as was shown by me in the next letter) and thus made the other half prove the very reverse of what the author intended. I have called again and again for your explanation, and you have given none !

I will here repeat the quotations side by side.

| Mr. Hughes' quotation, intended to show, that Rome was the seat of the true church, and the Pope the supreme head and successor of Peter. | The ungarbled passage. " *Survey* the Apostolical churches *in which the* very chairs of the Apostles still preside over *their stations*, |

"*If you live near Italy, you see before your eyes the Roman Church. Happy Church! to which the Apostles left the inheritance of doctrines w th their blood! where Peter was crucified l ke his Master; where John was beheaded like the Baptist.*"—(See letter of Mr. Hughes, No. 5.

in which their own letters are recited, uttering the VOICE, *and representing the* PRESENCE *of* EACH *of them.* Is Achaia nearest to thee? Thou hast CORINTH. If thou art not far from Macedonia, thou hast the PHILIPPIANS, and the THESSALONIANS. If thou canst go to Asia, thou hast EPHESUS; but if thou art near Italy thou hast ROME, WHENCE TO US ALSO AUTHORITY IS NEAR AT HAND."

And now we ask, is this not taking a very great liberty with the evidence of this father? Does he not put *all the Apostles,* and *all their seats and cities,* Achaia, Corinth, Philippi, Ephesus, &c., on the same footing of " authority," as *Peter* and *Rome?* Yet Mr. Hughes adduced a *part of this* to prove just the reverse!

I have still another illustration, if possible, more palpable than the last. It is your QUOTATION FROM STANDARDS NOT OUR OWN, to prove that the Presbyterians, united under " the General Assembly," in this country, " FORBID THE TOLERATION OF A FALSE RELIGION." You refer, with an air of great assurance, to the edition published by Towar & Hogan, in 1829. *There was no edition of our standards published by Towar & Hogan in* 1829. *And in the edition published by them in* 1827, *the phrase which you profess to cite is not found, either in the page to which you refer, or in any other part of the book!!* The public has already judged of this. In my last letter, I gave you references to our standards, repelling your unfounded and slanderous charge. You say you "*find no such reference.*" This fact ought to have led a candid man to suspect his mistake; and a just one to seek its correction. But you go on to give *more extracts;* and then call on me to account for the discrepance of our references. In responding, (1.) I assure you I hardly know *how to account for it as it respects yourself;* when on a former occasion, I referred a misrepresentation of yours to *ignorance,* you declined the apology which it furnished. *Where* to rest *this* mistake, I know not.—(2.) As to the *extract itself,* and *the source,* the only way in which I can account for your extraordinary misrepresentation is to suppose that you have availed yourself of a *reprint* of the Larger Catechism and Westminster Confession of Faith, as they originally appeared in Great Britain in 1647. To this you refer (in letter No. 1.) when you say with more flippancy than historic truth—" *a number of men appointed at Westminster, A. D.* 1647, *by order of Parliament to make a religion for the United Kingdom of Great Britain and Ireland.*" It was a glaring perversion to say that *their assembly* was convoked to " *make a religion.*" But now you assume this high prerogative for the Presbyterian church! Truly we are not yet prepared to take our seats by the side, or in the bosom of the church of Rome, as an *intolerant communion* and a *persecuting power,* however your hasty and self-convicted zeal may have indiscreetly caught at the doings of another age, and land, and people, and charged them upon us! Need I tell you at this late day, that some fifty years ago, when the basis was laid of the present union of the Presbyterian church in the United States in one General Assembly, and THE FORMULARIES of the church prepared, *all the offensive passages which you have quoted were solemnly rejected;* that the passages to which I have already referred you were *solemnly adopted;* that those you cite are not, and never were *a part of our standards* any more than the decrees of Trent; or the creed of Pius IV.; or the acts of the British Parliament? While the public mind alternates between surprise at your ignorance, and suspicion of your motives, the question must often be repeated, *how could he be ignorant? Yet if not, how could he have ventured on so extraordinary a misrepresentation?*

I give below, in *contrast*, the true extracts from our standards—and that which you have *transferred to us* from the Times and the Realms in which the church and the state were united, and intolerance inseparable from the very nature of that union.

Extracts from the Standards of the Presbyterian Church, on Toleration and the Civil Magistrate.

Form of Government, Book 1st, chap. 1st. sec. 1st page 343, Towar & Hogan's edition, 1827.—" They are unanimously of opinion, that God alone is Lord of the conscience, and therefore they consider the right of private judgment in all matters that respect religion as universal and unalienable."

Confession of Faith, 23d chapter, 3d and 4th sections.—" Civil magistrates may not in the least interfere with matters of faith—they should give no preference to any one denomination of Christians above the rest—and ecclesiastical persons should enjoy free, full, and unquestioned liberty;" &c. " It is the duty of the people to pray for the magistrates—and to be subject to their authority for conscience' sake—from which ecclesiastical persons are not exempted—much less hath THE POPE any power or jurisdiction over them in their dominions—and least of all to deprive them of their dominion or lives, if he shall judge them to be heretics.

Mr. Hughes' misrepresentation.

" The standard of Presbyterianism in the United States, and in the 19th century, makes it a sin against the second commandment of God to TOLERATE A FALSE RELIGION.—It is true the General Assembly have not yet told us what religions are to be regarded as 'false.' (Mr. H.'s Letter, No. 7.) But in the very same chapter and section, (23d chap. 3d sec.) I find the following: " He" (the civil magistrate) " hath authority, and it is his duty, to take order, that unity and peace be preserved in the church; that the truth of God be preserved pure and entire; that all blasphemies and heresies be suppressed; all corruptions and abuses in worship and discipline prevented or reformed; and all the ordinances of God duly settled, administered and observed. For the better effecting whereof, he hath power to call Synods, to be present at them, and to provide that whatsoever is transacted in them, be according to the mind of God." (Mr. H.'s Letter, No. 9.)

It seems peculiarly fit, in juxta-position with the above, to advert to the decrees of the Council of 4th Lateran, (extracted into my last letter,) for the *extermination of heretics.* You ask (1.) " *Do you give it as a literal and continuous translation?*" I answer, unhesitatingly—I do. It is as literal as the sense will bear. (2.) You ask, " do you affirm that in the original, it has the *same general meaning* that it *seems* to have in the quotation?" I answer, it is from your own " Caranza's summa conciliorum" that I quote. As I suppose you have the original, you can compare it with any extracts, and with my translation. I omitted the original for want of space alone. I consider the 2d question an indignity offered to the feelings of any honest man. Go to the original, and give us another translation, and if you can, prop a sinking cause with good sense; but do not think to turn the edge of these solid authorities by charging me again with falsehood! Your remarks on this decree against heretics are most peculiar. You say (1.) "*The council was held at a time when the feudal system was in full operation.*" You give no 2d, but go on to add, "A Council was, as it were, a *general congress of Christendom*, in which states and sovereigns were represented," &c. *Next*, "The *secular* representatives had nothing to do with the *definition of doctrines and morals,* "and *the infallibility of the church had nothing to do with any thing else.*" Next, "The sovereigns, in conjunction with the clergy, deemed it a convenient time and place, to adopt such measures as might protect the altar and the throne;" lastly, the Albigenses were endangering the universal state, the universal church, and "*the sovereigns (of Europe) were obliged to provide for their own safety.*"

(1.) Now this council is acknowledged by your church as a general council, lawfully convened.—The necessary result on your principles is, that its acts were *infallible*. But you are driven to defend *some* of its decrees by abandoning *others*. Yours is a strange *alembic*, by which you separate the *secular* from the *infallible decrees*. But did not this decree against the heretics directly concern "*faith and morals?*" Heresy is relative to *faith* as departed from, and the *murder* of heretics is a violation of the *moral law;* and the command to do it, supposes *obedience*, which is a *moral act*. The decree designates "EVERY HERESY EXTOLLING ITSELF AGAINST THIS HOLY, ORTHODOX, CATHOLIC FAITH, WHICH WE BEFORE EXPOUNDED." "Those who before expounded this faith" were of course not " *seculars,*" for you say " *they had nothing to do with the definition of doctrines and morals.*"—Therefore, according to your own admission, it was done *ecclesiastically*—and therefore infallibly. And what makes this certain is, that a little below it says, "ALL HERESIES, DENOTED BY THE CHURCH, MUST BE EXTERMINATED BY THE SECULAR POWER," &c. The decree, then, is all your own.

(2.) When you call this council, a "*congress* of *Christendom,*" you make the Pope by your own confession, the universal head of the state and the church. The Pope presided—it was an ecclesiastical general council—the states and sovereigns were represented in it—and the body passed decrees on the lives and property of subjects, on the crowns of princes; and on the allegiance of subjects, as well as on matters of faith and morals; and the ultimate, the supreme sanction for bringing kings to their orthodoxy, was this; " But if the temporal lord, required and warned by *the church*, shall neglect to purge his territory from this heretical filth, let him, by the Metropolitan and comprovincial Bishops, be tied by the bond of excommunication;"—" and if he scorn to satisfy within a year, let that be signified to the Pope, that he may thenceforth denounce his vassals absolved from their fidelity," (i. e. their allegiance to their prince) and *may expose*, (i. e. the Pope may expose,) his country to be seized on by Catholics, who, exterminating heretics, may possess it without any contradiction—and keep it in the purity of faith."

(3.) While crowns are thus put at the Pope's feet, and the lives of men are at his disposal, not a word is said " *about providing for the safety of the sovereigns,"* at *"this congress* of *Christendom."* No, their safety was in submission and silence;—and they felt themselves well off, if, after holding the Pope's stirrup, and kissing his feet, they could hold their crowns by doing homage for them, and their lives by his lordly grant.

(4.) And then to think of explaining this atrocious decree, which deluged Europe in blood, by referring to the poor Albigenses, as disturbing the peace of kingdoms, and "obliging sovereigns to provide for their own safety," by indiscriminate extermination of all *who did not think with them!* They were no more in strength and numbers, compared with all Europe, than a little flock of kids before a great army.

(5.) But the strangest of all your expositions is this—"had not then Catholic kings, and Catholic barons, and Catholic vassals, all the orders of feudalism in Catholic Europe, the right by virtue of their majority, to take precautions against such consequences? No republican, I should think, would deny it." *The argument is, that a majority have a right to exterminate the minority; for disagreeing with them in opinion.* Heresy was the sin for which all these bloody acts were passed. No sin against the state is mentioned; nothing that it concerns the civil power to punish; but just what the Protestants of this land are doing, protesting against the Papacy!— Yours is truly strange republicanism. How well for us, in view of old decrees and new arguments for them, that Protestants have yet the majority in our country!

But my heart grows sick at the recital. Indeed, sir, yours is a sad business, to defend or explain such enormities. But no skill can torture it into propriety. No Jesuit can cover, or excuse, or deny it.

I next pass to meet your demand, and sustain my statement, "that the Catechism of the Council of Trent gives only four words of the second commandment, and closes with an expressive et cetera." I find that you are accustomed to *make calls* on me, which from their wording, convey the impression to the public that I am wholly in error as to some authority or fact, and then, when I produce the proof, instead of owning it, you drop it in silence. So you did in reference to the Pope's anathematizing Bible Societies, so you did in reference to Bellarmine's "fere de fide." Before the proof was adduced, you brought a heavy charge against me. After it was produced, you do not say one word in the way of interpretation or argument, but pass the discussion with a petulant taunt. So as to the three systems in your church, as to the Pope s supremacy—viz : a presidency, an unlimited monarchy, and deification. Twice have I brought proof, you answer only by a denial.

And now as to the second commandment and the Council of Trent You say my statement is "untrue," and that it is "bearing false witness against my neighbour." Now for the proof.

Catechismus Concilii Tridenti Pii. V. pontif. max. *Jussu promulgatus. Primum Præcep'um Decalogi.*	Catechism of the Council of Trent published by order of Pope Pius V. 1st. Precept of the Decalogue.
Ego sum Dominus Deus tuus qui eduxi te de terra Egypti, de Domo ser-	I am the Lord thy God who led thee out of the land of Egypt and out of the

vitutis. Non habebis Deos alienos coram me. Non facies tibi sculptile, &c.
Secundum Decalogi Præceptum.
Non assumes nomen Domim Dei Tui in vanum.

house of bondage. Thou shalt have no other Gods before me. Thou shalt not make to thee a graven image, &c.
Second Precept of the Decalogue.
Thou shalt not take the name of the Lord thy God in vain.

Here then we see even as I have said, that four words only are given, viz., non facies tibi sculptile, thou shalt not make to thee a graven image, and then follows the expressive et cetera. It is true these four words are fastened to the end of the first commandment, and no doubt for the purpose of casting even them into the shade. But it is the real 2d commandment which begins with these four words. But however you *class* the long and expressive command against making and bowing down to, and worshipping images, where are all the other portions of it? Are they not dropped? And do we not clearly see why? Here then is on one hand the catechism word for word, and on the other, Mr. Hughes denying it, and charging me with falsehood for reporting it. Truly your denial will presently be to us, a stereotype proof of the truth of a proposition. What is thus so clearly proved from the catechism of the Council of Trent, the translations into various languages, copy in a greater or less degree *according to circumstances*. I have mentioned several instances of the kind in my last letter. You take no notice of them. There is now on my table an example, "The most Rev. Dr. J. Butler's Catechism, enlarged, improved and recommended by the four Roman Catholic Archbishops of Ireland, as a general catechism for the kingdom." Philadelphia, published by Eugene Cummiskey, 1827, lesson 14. 1st commandment, I am the Lord thy God, thou shalt not have strange gods before me, &c. 2d. Thou shalt not take the name of the Lord thy God in vain. 3d. Remember the Sabbath day to keep it holy, &c. &c. Here is not one single word about *graven images*. Have I not justly called this expressive silence?

Once more, your attempt at explaining Pope Nicholas' calling himself a god, is a veil too thin to cover the deformity and blasphemy of the assumption. It is true that he quotes from the Emperor Constantine; but he so quotes as to approve of what he had said. Upon your construction, there is no meaning or sense in the reasoning of the Pope. Whereas the Pope uses the reference to prove himself superior to all secular authority. In proof of this, see his words; Satis evidenter ostenditur a seculari potestate nec ligari prorsus, nec solvi posse pontificem quem constat a pio principe, Constantino (quod longe superius, memoravimus) Deum appellatum, nec posse Deum ab hominibus judicari manifestum est. It may very evidently be shown that the Pope, who as we have already related was called God by Prince Constantine, can neither be bound nor released by the secular authorities, for it is evident that *God* cannot be judged by *men*.

Your pompous challenge to a reference, with the reason assigned for it, viz., that *the language and the books about which we differ are unknown to the mass of our readers,* is curious enough; especially when we consider that your public prayers and standard Bible are both in *an unknown tongue.* I have uniformly studied to be simple, faithful, and full in my references. I now greet your arrival at the principle of *private interpretation.* If you will add to the points you mention, the question about the Catechism of the Council of Trent, and the other catechisms, and about the Pope calling himself God; also, the question of the true sense of my extract from the 4th Council of Lateran, and the interpretation of 2 Peter i. 20. then I will promptly agree to such a reference, it being understood that the parties shall be neither Roman Catholics nor Presbyterians.

But now let us return to the *line* of our argument. If I am not greatly deceived, your reasoning in behalf of your *rule of faith,* " in THE APOSTOLICAL SUCCESSION" has been fairly shown to be unscriptural and fallacious—I proceed to remark still farther.

I. One of your methods of defending your church's infallibility, is this, " if the church be not infallible, then the gates of hell have prevailed against it, and the Redeemer has forgotten his promise to his spouse." Now observe, (1.) The question in debate is whether this infallibility was ever promised; and whether the existence, security, and triumph of the church at all depend upon such infallibility. We say not all. The gates of hell shall never prevail against the church, because Christ her head is with her. By such an inference therefore, you *beg* the question, but do not prove it. (2.) In this way also you *assume without proof,* that yours is the true church, and then argue that she is infallible. But you must first prove yours the true church, and the only true church; or else on your own system your conclusion is worth nothing. You can only prove it by *private interpretation;*—you cannot prove it all. (3.) Supposing that Christ *did* promise (which we deny) *an infallible church on earth;* there is another conclusion far more obvious than that which you draw. It is this—*the church of Rome has proved herself fallible in doctrine and fallible in morals—therefore the gates of hell have prevailed against her;—and she cannot be the true church of Christ.* This is on your own principles, and you cannot consistently escape the conclusion.

II. *Allowing that Christ appointed an infallible tradition of doctrine, and a succession of infallible teachers, then the church which does not dispense his ordinances, and teach his doctrines, as he instituted, and taught, cannot be a* TRUE *church of Jesus Christ.* Now I will prove that your church has corrupted the ordinances of Christ, and the doctrines of Christ. If so, she is destitute, of the true rule of faith, on your own principles. I refer you for proof of this to the decree of the *Council of Trent,* 21 Sess. 1st. and 2d. chaps. I suppose you have the original, and can compare it with this translation —" Although Christ the Lord did in the last supper institute this venerable sacrament of the Eucharist, in the species of *bread* and *wine,* and *thus delivered it to the Apostles;*" " and though from the *beginning* of the Christian religion, the use of *both kinds,* was not unfrequent—yet when in *process of time,* that practice, was, for *weighty* and *just causes, changed, Holy Mother Church,* recognising her *acknowledged authority,* in the administration of the sacraments, approved the custom of communion in one kind, and *commanded* it to be observed as a *law.*" Chap. iv. Canon 1st. "Whosoever shall affirm that all and every one of Christ's faithful are bound by divine command to receive the most holy sacrament of the Eucharist in both kinds, as necessary to salvation, let him be accursed."

Here then is (1.) a confession that Christ *instituted* the sacrament of the supper in bread and wine. (2.) That *from the beginning* the use of both the bread and the wine was common (not unfrequent.) (3.) That there were *weighty and just causes* for CHANGING (mark it!) CHRIST'S LAW. (4.) *That the Roman Catholic church made the* CHANGE into a LAW. (5.) Whosoever finds fault with this dreadful innovation IS ACCURSED. (6.) Yet this is no less, than dividing in twain a solemn sacrament of Jesus Christ, and dropping one half of this sealing ordinance! How expressive is the prophecy. (Daniel vii. 25.) "And he shall speak great words against the Most High; and shall wear out the saints of the Most High, and *think to change times and laws.*"

To the *two sacraments* instituted by Christ, your church has *added* no less than *five new ones.* One of these, viz. *extreme unction*, is thus proved by the Council of Trent, Sess. 14. chap. 1. "Truly the Holy unction of the sick, was instituted *as it were*, truly and properly a sacrament of the New Testament, *hinted at* indeed, (insinuatum) by our Lord Christ in Mark, but recommended and preached to the faithful by James the Apostle and brother of our Lord." In the canon just below, it is said to have been "instituted by Jesus Christ our Lord," but there is no attempt at other or better proof than that quoted before. A sacrament resting on an "AS IT WERE," and a "HINTED AT" by CHRIST! And then the proof from James (5 chap. 14, 15, ver.) is perverted in the translation and use of it. "Anointing the sick," as mentioned by James, "raised him up," by miraculous power, to live again. The Lord who "raised him up," "forgave his sins."—But *extreme unction*, as the name imports, is a *last act;* and the translation from the Greek, in the decree of the Council, changes the meaning to this, "the Lord will ease him." But besides the fact that this institution is utterly an innovation, there is about it a most singular dilemma, which explains in part the *cautious* language of the decree. The Council had decreed (3d chap. of Sess. 14.) that "the proper ministers of this sacrament are either Bishops or Priests regularly ordained by them." The same Council decreed that "in the last supper, our Lord appointed his Apostles priests of the New Testament." (Sess. 22d. chap. 1st.) When the Apostles administered the unction to the sick, (Mark vi. 14.) they were then priests, or they were not priests. If they were priests then, they were not made priests at the last supper; and the Council in affirming they were, have erred: or if they were not priests then, or till the last supper, the unction, not being administered by priests, was no sacrament; and the Council in declaring it was a sacrament, has greatly erred. In either case, the Council has overthrown its own infallibility, and that of the church of Rome.—Space alone is wanting to apply the same train of reasoning with equal effect to show that your church has *corrupted the doctrines of Christ and his Apostles;* so that many of those which you hold to be *cardinal*, are *novelties* and *errors;* such are Transubstantiation, Purgatory, Indulgences, the Pope's supremacy, &c. which, if my life be spared, I hope in due time to make appear. *So that it is easier to show that our religion was before Luther, than yours before the Council of Trent.* The inference is most conclusive, that since the church of Rome has altered and added to the sacraments of Christ, and corrupted his doctrines, she is not *unchangeable,* that she has not been an "*infallible teacher,*" and of course *lacks that rule of faith,* which Mr. Hughes himself says the *true church must have!*

III. *The canon of Scripture, used by your church, is not the canon of the Christian church.* As to the canonicity of all the books of the true Bible, *you and we are agreed.* It is true you have often in this discussion taken common ground with the Infidel, and attempted to perplex the proof of the authenticity of the Bible, in order to carry your system. We *did not receive* the Bible *exclusively* through the church of Rome. But allowing that we did, so did you receive the Old Testament canon exclusively through the Jews. If then because we receive it from you, we ought to take your traditions with the text from you, so ought you, because you receive the Old Testament from the Jews, to take their traditions with the text from them. Again—though you get the Old Testament from the Jews, you *add many books to their canon,* which they rejected. Why have you done this? If you may add what the Jews rejected, and yet hold a part in common with them as you do, may not the Christian church reject what you add, and yet hold a part in common with you? This is what the Christian church has done. Now as to the Old Testament canon, it is conceded by your church that the Jews rejected, as not canonical, those books called "Apochryphal," which the Council of Trent decreed to be a part of the canon. Neither Christ nor his apostles ever found fault with the Jews for rejecting *true Scriptures from the canon, or adding false books to it;* though their false *glosses* and *traditions* were continually exposed by them. So far from this, Christ and his Apostles continually quoted from the present Old Testament; yet not a word from your *additional* books—Maccabees, Tobit, &c. &c. But they referred the Jews "to whom were committed the oracles of God," (Rom. iii. 2.) to their own Scriptures—"search the Scriptures, for in them ye think ye have eternal life—and they are they which testify of me." (John v. 39.) "As it is written," "that it might be fulfilled," &c. were the familiar and unqualified approbation of Jesus and his Apostles, to the Jewish Scriptures. And by comparing the 27th with the 44th verse of Luke's 24th chapter, you will find Christ saying that "*all the Scriptures*" were compromised in the "law of Moses, and the Prophets, and the Psalms." That was the common division of the whole Jewish Scriptures, *without* the Maccabees, Tobit, &c. &c.

Again—these Apocryphal books, (according to the present canon of the Protestant churches) are excluded from the true canon by the earliest Christian writers. Justin Martyr, (A. D. 150.) quotes not one word from these Apocryphal books. The first catalogue of the Old Testament Scriptures, which we have after the days of the Apostles, is that of MELITO, preserved by Eusebius. (Ecc. Hist.

Lib. v. c. 24.) This precisely accords with our canon, (excluding all the Apocryphal books,) except that after the "Proverbs of Solomon," he mentions "Wisdom," which Rupin and Pineda, a Romanist, say, means the same with Proverbs, i. e. "PROVERBS OR WISDOM."—Athanasius, in his synopsis, gives *our canon*. Hilary, who was contemporary with Athanasius, rejects the "Wisdom of Sirach," "Judith," "Tobit," &c. Augustine calls the Jews, the "LIBRARIANS" of the Christian church. The Council of Laodicea, (Can. 60th, See Labbæus and Cossarte on the sacred councils,) gives our canon and excludes the Apocrypha;—And so from age to age, down to Erasmus, we have a line of testimony against the canon decreed by the Council of Trent. It is true these Apocryphal books were considered by the early Christians as *ecclesiastical* histories, which might be read with profit, bating their errors and extravagancies; but not *inspired*, and therefore *not canonical;* and it was by unperceived degrees, and through a series of ages, that the way was prepared for CANONIZING them at Trent, in the 16*th century*. Your church therefore has not the pure word of God. Instead of handing down the truth, it has exceedingly corrupted it, and that at the fountain head. At this we need not be surprised, when we call to mind, that many of her doctrines rest for authority on these Apocryphal books.

By the same facts it appears that the Protestant canon is the true word of God, as held by his people from the beginning. When therefore you ask me how we know that such and such books are *canonical*, you may hereafter know that we do not learn it from the church of Rome, which has corrupted the canon. And when you say, at the 6th head of your last letter, "How does he, (the Protestant,) know that the Book, (the Bible,) is in *all respects now* the same that it was, when it came from the hands of its inspired authors? Has it been correctly translated? Has it been fairly copied, from one manuscript to another previous to printing?" I reply, full well we know, that if this matter had been left to those hands that added the Apocryphal books to the word of God—that forged decretals, and erased the testimony of the Fathers—we might have trembled for the ark, and despaired of the word of God. But a gracious Providence, before the canon was corrupted by your church, and before it was in its power to shut in the Bible, had caused it to be translated into many languages —published in many countries—and preserved and transmitted it by so many hands, and channels, that we need look not at all to the church of Rome for this precious treasure. I regret that room is wanting to extend the argument for the true rule of faith. But I must, before I close, notice your most wanton admission, as to the evidences of the Saviour's divinity in the sacred volume. In the 1st head of your letter, No. 9, you hold the following language: "Let him, (the Protestant reader,) take up the Bible, and read these words of our blessed Redeemer,—'the Father and I are one'—turn then to the other words—'the Father is greater than I.' That *one* passage is to be explained by the *other* is certain; but *which* shall take the preference of the other, the *sacred writings do not determine*." The obvious tendency of this statement is to sacrifice that eternal doctrine of the Christian scheme, or else arrive at it by the authority of your church.

Indeed in so many words you admit, that "*the sacred writings do not determine* WHICH *shall take the preference of the other.*"—And will you say then that the Bible contradicts itself, and that God cannot so speak to man in his word, that he shall not contradict himself? And that *men* are necessary to prevent God from contradicting himself in his Revelations? And is Bellarmine so lucid, and so plain, that you insult me for differing from you as to his meaning, and yet tell us that God cannot so speak as to be consistent or intelligent without the glosses of councils and the mediation of Popes? Does language lose its sense, or thought its lustre, and point in the hands of the Holy Spirit *alone?*—Truly I know not whether it be most *profane* or *puerile*—to speak as you have done! But there is this good from so great an evil, THAT ALL THE WORLD MAY IN THIS SEE HOW IT IS THAT ROME AND HER SONS LIGHT THEIR CANDLES TO HELP THE SUN TO SHINE. In fine, he who runs may reconcile the passages you cite, and so greatly slander. Without the full and proper meaning of *both*, Christ could not have been the Saviour of the world.

Yours, &c.

JOHN BRECKINRIDGE

CONTROVERSY. No. XI.

RULE OF FAITH.

Philadelphia, April 12, 1833.

To the Rev. John Breckinridge.

Rev. Sir,—The polite charge with which you begin your last letter, where you accuse me with having " departed from the dignity of a minister, and the decencies of a gentleman," is not in good keeping with that evangelical *meekness*, which is the loveliest, if not the most brilliant, ornament of the ministerial character. I had stated indeed, that several of your assertions were " untrue ;" but I did not charge *you* with either " *deliberate* falsehood" as you assert, or with a " want of veracity." On the contrary, I suggested that you had been deceived by following in the beaten path of calumny and misrepresentation, which has been trodden *with impunity*, by many of your predecessors in controversy. You seem to have imagined that I should receive your unfounded statements, *with the same implicit* confidence as the young lady in Baltimore, to whom you addressed the famous epistle published in the Christian Advocate of last August. But was this expectation reasonable ?

I engaged in the controversy, neither as the enemy of Protestants, nor as the echo of their prejudices; but as the advocate of TRUTH; and shall I not oppose assertions which are untrue, so often as you leave it in my power ? It is not my business to inquire who was guilty of the " deliberate falsehoods," and " want of veracity," which you are pleased to consider as charged upon yourself. It is enough for me, that on each of the six heads enumerated in my last letter, you have asserted what is " untrue." To the arguments of that letter on the whole question, I refer the reader, and I appeal with confidence to his candour, to say whether in it, I have departed from either the " dignity of a minister," or the " decencies of a gentleman." If I found in your letters, assertions which are untrue, had I not a right, nay, *was I not bound to expose them as such ?* Which of us offended—*you* in *making,*—or I in *detecting them ?* When you insisted, did I not propose that a sworn interpreter of languages should decide between us? Was *this* ungentlemanly ? If you were as convinced that those assertions are true, as I am that they are untrue, would you not have been glad of such an opportunity to have them cleared up ? Would not this course have been much more honourable to you and your cause, than that which you have adopted, by indulging a fretful pen, and imputing to me a " departure from the dignity of a minister, and the decencies of a gentleman." Did you dread the presence of a *sworn interpreter ?* Then, there must be cause for your timidity. This, I think, is the legitimate inference which your shrinking from so impartial a test, will warrant in the mind of the intelligent reader, no matter what may be his creed.

But you will say you have not shrunk from it—and refer to the following passage for the evidence : " If you will add to the points you mention, the question about the Catechism of the Council c Trent"—(certainly I will) "and the other catechisms" (there has been no dispute about them) "and about the Pope calling himself God;" (the Pope never called himself God,) also the question of the true sense of my extract from the Council of Lateran" (with great pleasure) "and the interpretation of 2 Peter i. 20.—" (What! abandon the Protestant rule of faith? A sworn interpreter to *decide the meaning of Scripture*—to "help the sun to shine!") "*then* I will promptly agree to such a reference, it being understood that the parties shall be neither Roman Catholics nor Presbyterians." The "party" may be a TURK, or a JEW;—provided he be a good Latin scholar, and an honest man. I am satisfied to leave the points on which we are at issue, to the decision of the Professor of languages in the University of Pennsylvania. Will you agree to this reference? If so, advise me of it in your next letter. He is a Protestant clergyman, but he is a scholar, and a gentleman of literary, as well as moral integrity, and I want no more.

With regard to the Westminster Confession of Faith from which I quoted, it is now on my table, and I invite any gentleman who may choose, to come and see, whether I have made *even a mistake*, in my quotation from it. It is the *original, genuine, Westminster Confession of Faith.*—And any other book, containing either *more* or *less*, is NOT the original, genuine Westminster Confession. I considered it as the standard of Presbyterianism on the *authority of Dr. Miller*, who tells us that, by the act of the Synod of Philadelphia in 1729, called the "Adopting Act," not only candidates but professed ministers were OBLIGED *to adopt it as such.* Now it did not occur to me, that a book, which in 1729, ministers were "OBLIGED" to adopt as the *summary of doctrines contained in the Scriptures*, could *so far* have degenerated, as to become a spurious authority in 1833. Have the *doctrines contained in the Scriptures* changed? If not, why was the *summary* of them changed? But without explaining this, you tell us, that some fifty years ago, the "offensive passages," which I have quoted, were "solemnly rejected." What! Part of the summary of the doctrines *contained in the Scriptures*, "solemnly rejected!" And rejected, why? because they were "offensive!" But may not the *same authority* adopt them *again*, as soon as political circumstances may make it *convenient* to do so? You say, "they are not, and NEVER WERE, a part of your standards." But Dr. Miller asserts positively, the contrary; and you are both Presbyterians, who can, no doubt, reconcile the contradiction without the intervention of an interpreter. You are both *teachers* in Israel, and it is not for me to say *which* of you has *stumbled* in the testimony.

That the Westminster Divines were "appointed by order of Parliament to make a religion for the united kingdoms of Great Britain and Ireland," is an historical fact, at which I am surprised you should take exception. The Act of Parliament by which they were "appointed," and the wages which they received from the public treasury, four shillings per diem, for their labour and expenses, *are on permanent record.* What, then, were they appointed and paid *for*, if it was not for "making a religion for the three kingdoms?"

So much then, for the Westminster Confession of Faith, and my quotations from it. As to your charge against me for having garbled Tertullian, I shall do full justice to it in the sequel of this letter. In the mean time permit me to say that you have entirely, (intentionally or otherwise) violated your engagement, in departing from the subject of discussion, which is the rule of faith. You had frequently informed me in our preliminary arrangements, that your object was the investigation of truth. If this then is your object, why do you shun that process *by which* truth and error may be distinguished? Why do you discuss *doctrines*, before you have determined, or at least examined, the *principle*, by which true doctrines are to be tested? The rule of faith, and not the prejudices of our readers, is the tribunal at which doctrines must stand or fall. The rule of faith is a *primary* question; on this depends the solution of every other. The Protestant rule of faith, stripped of its sophistry, is "every man's *opinion* of the Bible"—which is a very different thing from the Bible alone. Protestants, in following their own opinions, have taken it for granted, that they were following the "pure word of God," the "Bible alone"—and their education, books, parents, and ministers have all conspired to enbalm this delusion. In my last letter I exposed in six distinct arguments, the fallacy of the Protestant rule of faith, and instead of attempting to answer them, you indulge in a strain of invectives against the popes. They obliged kings to "hold their stirrup," and "kiss their feet." But every Protestant child knew this before. These are mere *nursery tales*—and to those who have been conversant with the most abusive productions against the Catholic religion, I am sure your letters do not convey a single new idea, much less an argument. And how will this meet the expectation of *intelligent Protestants?* They look for argument and reasoning—and you furnish them with the mere elements of prejudice. They ask for bread, and you give them a stone. What have you opposed to the arguments of my last letter? Nothing that I can perceive, except assertion, invective, and misrepresentation. Your first has reference to the Council of Lateran.

Catholics, as I have repeatedly stated, understand the distinction between doctrine, discipline, and ceremonies—and candid Protestants will not be at a loss to comprehend your reason for extending the infallibility of the church to *every* enactment recorded in her history. You have even coined infallibility for the 2d canon of the Council of Lateran, and put it into circulation in several paragraphs of your last letter—as genuine Catholic doctrine. It is however, decidedly spurious. I again repeat, that the infallibility secured to the church by the word and promise of Jesus Christ, is claimed for the *preservation* and *definition of those* DOCTRINES *of faith and principles of morality* of which Jesus Christ made the revelation to the world. But according to your misrepresentation, *every thing* done by a council or pope must be *infallible!* The explanation of this canon given in my last letter, will satisfy the *candid* reader, that it was an arrangement entered into, by the common consent of the church and states, for a *special* purpose, and a temporary duration. It had no relation to sovereigns, but only to lords of fees, who, according to the system which then prevailed, were the possessors of frank-allodial property. It enacted that "if the lord of a fee, patronise the Albigenses, he shall be excommunicated by the Metropolitan and the Bishops of the province; that if he does not amend within twelve months, his contumacy shall be denounced to the Pope who shall declare his vassals freed from their oaths of fealty, and shall expose his lands to be occupied by others." Now this decision was based on a principle which is universally recognized. The conditions of every engagement are reciprocal—and if the lord of the fee was the *first* to violate the conditions on which his vassals swore fealty, were they not virtually absolved by the very fact, from the obligation of their oaths? But it was, you tell us, persecution. Well, admitting that it was; is it for a disciple of John Knox, who held that it was not a *privilege*, but a DUTY to persecute "unto the death;" and of Beza, who wrote in *defence* of persecution; and of John Calvin, who *wrote* and *preached* and PRACTISED this doctrine; is it, I say, for the disciples of such men, to brand their neighbours with the charge of persecution? Why, Rev'd Sir, do you not give me *argument* to refute on the rule of faith, instead of brandishing weapons which, if they cut at all, inflict the deeper wound on him who is the first to wield them? Why not discuss the rule of faith, as your signature to our agreement *binds you to do?* If we were treating of persecution, I should find it as ready to enlighten the public mind, with a faggot snatched from the pile which consumed Servetus, as you can, by a reference to the "decree" of the Council of Lateran against "the little flock of kids," the Albigenses. But we should leave these criminations to the infidel, who makes them a *pretext* for sneering at your religion as well as mine—and for the bigot, who is ever ready to point at the mote in his brother's eye, but cannot see the beam in his own.

Before I pass to the review of your letter, I must notice the injustice of charges which have been insinuated by yourself, and formally urged in several Protestant papers, not excepting even the soberminded Church Register of this city. When I argue against the Protestant *rule of faith*, I am represented as arguing against the Bible! Is this just? Is it honourable? I defy the Church Register, and all the ministers in the United States, to point out one single passage that can even be tortured into an argument against the Bible, *as a book of divinely inspired authority*. When I point out and prove the destruction which the Protestant rule of faith, brings upon the Bible, I am represented as taking "common ground with the infidel," and as aiming a blow at the sacred volume itself! When I exposed bad logic, it appears I insult the Bible! No, sir; but I show that the Bible, under the Protestant rule of faith, is as defenceless as the desolate vine of Judah; the "bear from the woods," may ravage it. Is it not by that rule applied to the Bible, that some Protestants have robbed Jesus Christ of his Deity—that others, have annihilated by an *opposite error*, the two other persons of the Holy Trinity? Is it not by that rule of faith, that Calvin taught the blasphemous doctrine that God created some men under *an unavoidable necessity to be damned for his glory?* And when I prove that your rule of faith, *gives identically the same sanction* to *all* these doctrines—I am represented as arguing against the Bible! It is astonishing that pious and sincere Protestants do not shrink from the approbation of a principle, which makes it lawful for one sect of Protestants to teach from the Bible that Christ is a *mere creature ;* and for another to teach from the *same Bible*, that the Father and the Holy Spirit are only mere attributes of Christ, to express different operations. Now blend these two consequences of the Protestant rule of faith into one, and you see the belief of a supreme being, destroyed by the combination ;—and pure *atheism* extracted, not from the Bible, but from the Protestant mode of interpretation! According to one party, Christ is not God ; according to the other, if *Christ is not* God, there is no God ! But you will say they interpret erroneously. I answer that they interpret strictly according to the *rule of faith*, by which *you* interpret. You say that the Bible alone is your religion ; they say the same of theirs. You say that God speaks plainly in the Scriptures ; they say that God speaks plainly in the Scriptures—and that by the authority of the *Protestant rule of faith*, and your own acknowledgment, they have as good a right to understand what God says in the Scriptures, as you have. You may say they pervert the Scriptures, but they may retort the charge upon yourself. In a word, I defy you to use a single argument, which is not as good for them as it is for you. As a Catholic, I know, that the church never ceased *to teach*, since the days of Jesus Christ, the doctrines which both *you* and *they* have rejected—but for the rest I look upon them to be as sincere and as moral as Presbyterians are. They may have departed *further* from the doctrines of Christ ; but the difference is in the *degree* of error, and not in the *principle by which it was engendered.*

Just pause, then, I pray you, and survey with a cool mind and a dispassionate eye, the field of Protestant Christianity. Consider the diversities of doctrine, and the multitude of sects which it presents, and ask yourself whether it is possible that *this* is the " one sheepfold" of that church which Jesus Christ established on the earth. If your own brethren, who call themselves Presbyterians are charged with the impending crime of heresy, for a slight departure from your standards, how numerous must be the heresies of *other* denominations who condemn your standards and the doctrines contained in them. Heresy, as you know, is a crime, and every crime supposes moral culpability. But to what source will you trace the guilt of *Protestant* heresy, as *you* understand the word ? To the Bible ? That would be blasphemy. To wilful perversion ? That is uncharitable and presumptuous, since God alone can judge in the sanctuary of men's thoughts.

Where then, is the *error*, of those that err most ?—for you are among the first to proclaim that there is error of doctrine among Protestants, and consequently heresy, crime, and culpability. But does not the man of extreme heterodoxy do *all that is required by the Protestant rule of faith ?* And if he does, how, according to your own principles, *can he be guilty of heresy ?* The only heresy is, that his OPINION and your OPINION *about the meaning of the Bible*, are different, one from the other. And if this be heresy, the number of the elect will be small indeed. But you will remember that the

Protestant rule of faith destroys all possibility of determining who is *right* or who is *wrong*. Can this then be that "infallible rule," which Christ " established to guide us in matters of religion, and to determine disputes in his church?"

I mentioned in my last letter that Jesus Christ says of himself in one place, "the Father and I are one," in another, "the Father is greater than I"—and asked you as a favour, to show me how, in the comparison of these two passages, you could *save* the *divinity* of Jesus Christ from the destructive operation of *the Protestant rule of faith* in the hands of a Unitarian. This, you either could not, or would not undertake. But your mode of defending the Protestant rule of faith in presence of *this test*, is so curious that I cannot withhold it from the reader. I shall merely use a few parentheses as I proceed, which shall contain corrections of misrepresentation. My remark on the two passages above was, that one of them was to be explained by the other, but that the sacred writings do not determine which shall take the preference. Mr. Breckinridge clears up the difficulty in the following manner: " The obvious tendency of this statement is to sacrifice that eternal doctrine of the Christian scheme, (viz. the divinity of Christ,) or else arrive at it by the authority of your church. (The tendency, Rev. Sir, was to show the utter *fallacy* of the Protestant rule of faith.) Indeed in so many words you admit (I *proclaim*, rather) that the sacred writings do not determine WHICH shall take the preference of the other. And will you say then that the Bible contradicts itself, and that God cannot so speak to man in his word, that he shall not contradict himself. (I have not said any such thing.) And that men are necessary to prevent God from contradicting himself in his Revelations? (Not at all.) And is Bellarmine so lucid and so plain, that you insult me (I would not insult a child intentionally—but when you misquote authors, it is my duty to correct you,) for differing from you, as to his meaning, and yet *tell* us that God cannot so speak to be consistent or intelligent (intelligible) without the glosses of councils and the mediation of Popes? (I never told you so.) Does language lose its sense, or thought its lustre and point in the hands of the Holy Spirit *alone?* (I am arguing against the Protestant rule of faith, and *not* against the Holy Spirit.) Truly I know not whether it be most *profane* or *puerile*—to speak as you have done. (It would be both profane and puerile to speak as you have taken the liberty to misrepresent.) But there is this good from so great an evil, THAT ALL THE WORLD MAY IN THIS SEE HOW IT IS THAT ROME AND HER SONS LIGHT THEIR CANDLES TO HELP THE SUN TO SHINE. (And yet, Protestant ministers enjoy larger emoluments for *their* "lighted candles" than even the "sons of Rome.") In fine, he who runs may reconcile the passages you cite, and so greatly slander. (I cannot see how I slandered them.) Without the full and proper meaning of *both*, Christ could not have been the Saviour of the world." What a strange mode of getting clear of a difficulty!

After this *lucid exposition*, the *orthodox* reader will have no difficulty in saving the divinity of Jesus Christ, from the destructive operation of the Protestant rule of faith, in the hands of the Unitarian.

You give your opinion at large on the canon of Scripture—and although I should respect your opinion, I cannot consider it of equal authority with the fact, that the *Catholic canon* had been established and recognised by the whole church, for more than a thousand years before the pretended Reformation. Luther put the Epistle to the Hebrews among the *Apochryphal books*. Calvin conferred a *similar honour* on the Apocalypse; and you nor I have quite as good a right to strike a book from the canon, as either of them. The " canonizing" of what you call the Apochryphal books, you tell us, took place at the Council of Trent " in the 16th century." Here you have committed a slight anachronism of about 1150 years. This event took place in the 4th century, A. D. 397, in the Council of Carthage. However, this is a mere trifle, and you will never think of it again. You were pleased in a former letter to tell us that none but the Apostles were *inspired* or infallible; and consistently with this assertion the two Gospels, and the Apostles' Acts were uninspired!—Do you mean then, that these books shall be considered as Apochryphal? If not, why do you not recall the *assertion* alluded to, by which you sapped with all the influence of your signature, the foundation of their *inspired authority?* What will Protestants think of their champion, who denies the inspiration of St. Mark and St. Luke, *by the unqualified assertion, that none but the Apostles were inspired?* I respectfully asked an explanation of this on a former occasion, but like the affair of " Usher's authority among Romanists," you forgot it. It seems you have adopted the memorable words of a Roman governor —" what I have written, I have written." Thus you publish on the authority, as you say, of a " most respectable and responsible gentleman," that one of the Priests of this city, on a particular day, warned the people against reading this controversy. Now this statement is *untrue.* Will you then give the name of your author? Will you mention the church in which he was *on that day?* Will you do any thing to explain this strange affair? Will not the public consider yourself as the author of the statement, as long as you do not choose to say who the author is? And how can you leave yourself exposed in this manner?

Again, you insist that the Pope *anathematized* the Bible Society. This is untrue. You attempted on a former occasion to *prove it*, but your authority, as the reader may perceive by a reference to it, *proved only that the Pope warned the faithful against your Bibles, and Bible Societies,* just as *you* warn the people against the *Unitarian Bible!* The motives assigned in the document, are such as every man of *good sense* will approve. How then, Rev. Sir, can you have the courage to repeat this unfounded assertion, when the document *adduced by yourself*, supplies, not the proof, but the refutation! Truly the Protestant rule of faith must be a magnificent cause, when *these* are the means by which you are obliged to support it. These things may do very well in Protestant pulpits; they may excite prejudice and uncharitableness towards the Catholics and their religion; but *in a public discussion*, when BOTH SIDES have an equal hearing, you should be cautious in having recourse to them.

The manner in which you refute my argument on the rule of faith is truly curious. I will give the heads of your *demonstrations*.

I. " One of your methods of defending your church's infallibility, is this, *if the church be infallible, then the gates of hell have prevailed against them, and the Redeemer has forgotten his promise to his spouse.*" This argument you placed between inverted commas, to show that you had taken it from my letter. It is *not* mine, however; —and its want of *sense* renders it very easy of refutation. My argument was, that Christ promised that " the gates of hell should not prevail against his church"—and that the infallibility of *this promise*, clearly proves the delusion of Protestantism, since the Reformation *was founded* on a supposition which *clashes* with the *promise of Christ*, viz. the supposition that the gates of hell *had* prevailed against the Church ;—and that her doctrines required to be " reformed ;" that is, thrown back into the Bible, in order that all future generations might enjoy the glorious uncertainty of private interpretation. My argument is this—if Christ did *not* fulfil his promise, what is to become of his *infallibility ?* But if he did fulfil it, then he *was still with the Church, redeeming his promise*, when Martin Luther, John Calvin, Henry VII. and Socinus undertook to make *experiments in her doctrine*, and to dignify the battle of their various and *conflicting opinions*, with the general name of " Reformation."

II. "Allowing that Christ appointed an infallible tradition of doctrine and a succession of infallible teachers, then the church that does not dispense his ordinances, and teach his doctrines, as he instituted and taught, cannot be a *true* church of Jesus Christ." Agreed. " Now I will prove that your church has corrupted the ordinances of Christ, and the doctrines of Christ." And how, Rev'd. Sir, do you prove this? By taking it for granted that the doctrines which *Protestants have rejected*, are *errors?* But since the Church had the *promise that Jesus Christ would be with her " all days,"* how could she continue to teach these errors, unless Christ *had abandoned her*, and violated his promise? And if you prefer to say that the promise was made to *the Protestant Church, or churches*, how comes it, that these churches were born after a mysterious gestation of some 1500 years from the *period when Christ made these promises*—which were to be fulfilled in ALL DAYS, *even to the consummation of the world ?* If Protestantism be the *Church* of Christ, where was the Church of Christ before Martin Luther?

III. " The canon of Scripture," you say, " used by your church, is not the canon of the Christian Church." Why, yes, it is the canon of what was the Christian church from the days of Christ, until the time when the gentlemen mentioned above, undertook to make Christian churches of their own. I defy you to show that the Christian church, previous to Luther, ever held a *different canon.* Your arguments are generally very unfortunate, for the reason that they are generally in direct opposition to facts, and without facts, in a discussion of this kind, zeal, learning, and even logic, are absolutely useless.

The question is the " rule of faith." In other words, the question is, how shall we know the doctrines, of which Jesus Christ said, "he that believeth *not* shall be CONDEMNED." Now the *Protestant* rule of faith reduces the doctrines of Jesus Christ to the sincere *opi-*

nion of each individual in reading or hearing the Bible. If I have misrepresented the Protestant principle, I request you to give me the true practical definition. I think that every *Christian* who *can* and *will* reason consistently, will conclude with me, that Christ never did appoint so doubtful and precarious a principle of guidance. For the proof of this position, I refer the reader to the *unanswered* arguments of my last letter on this branch of the subject.

Reason tells us that since Christ made the belief of his doctrines necessary for salvation, he must have provided some *infallible means for ascertaining* what those doctrines are. This, my Rev. opponent has admitted. And yet, he does not attempt to show that the Bible, *interpreted by each individual for himself*, constitutes *that infallible means*. Why? Because his arguments would be as good for the Unitarian, as for the Presbyterian,—as good for the Universalist, as for the Methodist, Baptist, or Episcopalian. If the Protestant rule of faith is right, then are ALL right. If it is wrong, they are all equally bound, before their conscience and their God, to abandon it—for truth, next to God, is greater than all.

Reason tells us, moreover, that no society *can* subsist; and history assures us, that no society ever *did* subsist, without the right of *judgment*, and the supreme *power of decision*, in cases of controversy among its members. Even in this country, where freedom is supposed to be unbounded, the laws are not left to the arbitrary interpretation of each private individual. Is it consistent then, with reason to suppose, as the Protestant rule of faith *teaches*, that the Son of God revealed a religion,—made the belief of it necessary to salvation, and yet left it at the discretion of every individual *who can read*, to determine, with all the certainty of opinion, what it is? So far reason and history are directly against the Protestant rule of faith. But what says the written word of God? I will merely state its *historical* testimony.

How were controversies decided under the Jewish dispensation? Not by the private interpretation of the Bible? Read "Parlip. ch. xix. v. 10 and 11. Every cause that shall come to you of your brethren, that dwell in their cities, between kindred and kindred, wheresoever there is question concerning *the law, the commandment*, the *ceremonies*, the *justifications*, SHOW IT TO THEM, that they may not sin against the Lord, and that wrath may not come upon you and your brethren, and in so doing you shall not sin. And Amarias, the priest, your high priest, shall be *chief in the things which regard God*." This is the principle appointed by God, in the old law. Why should it be different in the new? Josephus testifies in like manner (lib. 2. contra Apionem) that the "High Priest sacrifices to God before the other Priests, guards the laws, and *determines controversies*." And even Herod, though a Jew, instead of interpreting the Scriptures as Protestants do, *by private opinion*,—"assembling together all the chief priests and scribes of the people, *inquired* of them where Christ should be born." Matt. xi. 4.

Did the Saviour of men appoint a different principle whereby to "determine disputes in his church?" Did he not say, "Hear the church; he that will not hear the church, let him be to thee, as a heathen and a publican?" But how can we *obey Jesus Christ*, if instead of "hearing the church," we make our private explanation or opinion of the Bible, our rule of faith? Christ would not, could not enjoin on us to hear the church, under such a penalty, *if the church were not an infallible authority.* That it is an infallible authority, I have already proved in my fifth letter, to which I refer the reader. Again, look at the *usage and practice of the church from the earliest days of her history.* Look at the decision of the Apostles, in the first council of Jerusalem. (Acts xv. 28.) "It hath seemed good to the Holy Ghost and *to us,*" &c. See again, (Euseb. lib. 5 cap. 23. et sequent) the controversy about the time of celebrating Easter, settled finally by the decision of Pope Victor, A. D. 198.

In 255, Novatian was condemned *by the Roman Council under Pope Cornelius,* for teaching that sinners who had relapsed after baptism, could not be reconciled to God on their repentance, by the absolution of the church. (See Baronius on this year.)

Sabellius was condemned in the Council of Alexandria, under Pope Sylvester, in the year 319, for teaching that there is but *one* person in God. Of the Council of Nice, held a few years afterwards, it is unnecessary for me to speak.

Thus, then, it appears, that the Catholic rule of faith is found to be consistent with the light of reason and philosophy, with the experience of history, with the testimonies of Revelation, with the practice of the Jewish and Christian Church;—whilst the Protestant principle is *contradicted by them all.* But why should I not refute that delusive principle, by a reference to the practice of Protestants themselves. If God speaks so plainly in the Scripture that *every man* can understand what he says—why, I should like to know, do you, ministers, intrude yourselves between God and the people to help the Almighty to speak, and your hearers to understand? With us a ministry is *consistent*—with you it is a palpable contradiction. Why your Confessions of Faith and Articles? But so it is, that those who depart from the rules of religion instituted by Christ,—those who quit the rock of truth, to build upon the quicksands of opinion, will ever be involved in the labyrinths of self-contradiction and inconsistency.

I shall now conclude by giving the passage from Tertullian, which you accuse me of having garbled. But first I must correct your *misstatement* of my argument, in support of which, it was introduced. You say, it was "intended to show that Rome was the seat of the true church, and the Pope the supreme head and successor of St. Peter." It was not, I assure you, Rev. Sir, intended for any such purpose; although it is, *even for that,* a very appropriate testimony. It was intended to show, that in Tertullian's time, heretics *alone* had recourse to the rule of faith which Protestants now profess to follow;—and that the Catholic Church possessed by prescription, in *the succession of teaching and belief,* the doctrines which were received from the Apostles. Tertullian was showing where the *true* doctrines of Christ existed, and *how* they could be distinguished from the errors, which private interpretation pretended to discover in the pure word of God, the Bible alone. Let me then give what you have quoted as the "ungarbled passage," and see whether it does not bear me out MORE STRONGLY than the briefer extract which I had furnished. "Survey the Apostolic churches in which the very chairs of the Apostle still preside over the stations, in which their own letters are recited, uttering the voice, and representing the presence of each of them. Is Achaia nearest thee? Thou hast seen Corinth. If thou art not far from Macedonia, thou hast the Philippians and Thessalonians. If thou canst go to Asia, thou hast Ephesus; but if thou art near Italy, thou hast Rome, whence to us also authority is near at hand." Now, if this does not prove against the Protestant rule of faith, I am at a loss to understand what proof is. How does he refute the heretics? By the Bible alone? Not at all—but by comparing their doctrines with *those held* by the succession of teaching in the Apostolic churches—which were numerous in his time. He refutes heresy by the argument of *prescription*—by showing that in the Christian Church, *truth existed* before the heresy was broached, and that the *first* or *oldest* doctrines are the *true doctrines*. In reference to the Church of Rome, read the conclusion of the chapter from which you have quoted—Let Protestants reflect upon it: "heresies were not *of that church;* because they went out from her, *and have since their apostacy turned all the malice of their united efforts against her.*" One would suppose that in this short sentence, Tertullian was the historian, or prophet of the calumnies that have been heaped on the church of Rome, for the last three hundred years. But no: he was the historian of his own times, for the adversaries of the church have *always* been distinguished by the same characteristics.

Let me entreat you, in conclusion, not to consider me as intending to insult you, whenever I find it necessary to correct the unfounded statements of your letters; and to name, or authorize your friend to agree with me on the selection of a sworn interpreter, to decide the questions on which we are at issue, as I wish the decision to be published before the meeting of the General Assembly. Yours, very respectfully, JNO. HUGHES.

CONTROVERSY. No. XII.

RULE OF FAITH.

Philadelphia, April 18, 1833.

To the Rev. John Hughes.

Sir,—It is difficult for me to express to you my surprise at the pertinacity with which you reiterate the charge of "intolerance" against the Presbyterian church. After the statement of facts made in my last letter, ignorance can no longer be your apology and the plea of inadvertence, which we were ready to make for you in our minds, is silenced by your assurance, that "you have not made even a mistake in quoting." You insist that it is the original, genuine Westminster Confession of Faith, and any other book, containing either more or less, is not the original, genuine Westminster Confession." But the question, was whether this was the Confession of Faith of the Presbyterian Church under the care of the General Assembly? Mr. Hughes had said, (Letter 7th,) "The *standard of Presbyterianism* in the United States of America, and in the 19th *century*, makes it a sin against the second commandment to tolerate a false religion;" and he had identified it with our church, by a direct reference to its supreme judicatory, viz: "It is true the General Assembly has not told us what religion it regards as false." And to show us that he did not quote from an antiquated copy, or a foreign edition, (which *might* have been the standard of the *Scotch* church, or of *some other* church) he informed us that it was published by Towar & Hogan, in this city, in 1829!

In vain do we tell him that our church does not adopt the Westminster Confession on the subject of "Intolerance;" that Towar & Hogan printed no edition of our standards in 1829; that the Synod of 1729 was not the "General Assembly of the Presbyterian Church," and that the very *union* which incorporated that and other parts of our church into one body was based upon the principles of equal rights and *universal toleration*. Having then so grossly misrepresented the public standards of the Presbyterian Church; having asserted that something is found in her accredited book, not one word of which, as every well-informed person knows, is contained in it; and having been convicted of this misrepresentation, you have the hardihood to deny that you have done our church the smallest injustice! I had really expected from you a different course: if not from a love of justice and truth, at least from a regard to your own reputation! Dr. Miller's repose will hardly be disturbed by your efforts to put his "Letters to Presbyterians" at issue with our standards. You have certainly been in good company while writing at his side, and as his friend, I feel quite willing to leave his defence to be gathered from the expressive contrast between your letters and his, as they have simultaneously appeared in the columns of the *Presbyterian*. I close my notice of this subject, by noting it as one of the items of the proposed reference.

I have been much struck (and not I alone) with your *summary* method of replying to my arguments. You called with great confidence for proof, that the Catechism of the Council of Trent "took liberties" with the commandment touching the making and worshipping of images. When I adduced the proof, *you drop the subject.* You called on me to vouch for the faithfulness of the translation and the continuity of the sense of the long extract from the Council of 4th Lateran, about burning heretics. I met your call; and exposed your "feudal" defence of that atrocious act—*you drop the subject.*

Again, in reply to a whole series of facts and reasonings on subject after subject in dispute, you say "I REFER THE READER TO MY FIFTH LETTER," or some other letter: and when we turn to your fifth letter, lo! there is no answer there! Your letters aid each other in this respect, like the *idle* boys who combined to deceive their master: "Jack," said he to one of them, "what are you doing?" "I am helping Dick, Sir. "Dick, what are you doing?" "*Nothing, Sir.*" Such defence is almost as easy and as victorious as the colloquies got up in Kentucky by the Bishop of Bairdstown, in which two strolling priests, in Thespian style, personated the Romanist and the Protestant. The Protestant fought long, and died hard; but was *always beaten!*

I had at least supposed that you would defend the *sacraments* of your church. But in reply to what has been said as to her *abuse* of the eucharist, and her *promotion* of extreme unction into a sacrament, you say not one word. I have called until I am weary for your reply, as to the admission of the Rev. Mr. M'Guire. As the whole controversy turns on this point, I will present it once more; and your silence, if persisted in, must be *construed,* even by your friends, into a confession that you cannot meet it. The admission is this, "THAT THE CATHOLIC HAS ONLY TO EXERCISE HIS PRIVATE JUDGMENT UPON THE SCRIPTURE PROOFS OF THE AUTHORITY OF THE CHURCH: THAT ONCE ESTABLISHED, THE CATHOLIC IS ENABLED TO MAKE AN ACT OF FAITH UPON DIVINE AUTHORITY." *Now is this so, or is it not?*

I have still further to say, that in all this discussion, the *obligation of proof* is on your side. *Your church claims to be the only true church, and asserts that out of her there is no salvation.* Here is an exclusiveness so great and so peculiar, and so unlike to all other churches, that the whole world has a right to claim the *proof,* or the *surrender* of it. Your *rule of faith,* contrary to all other churches, claims the authority to decide, 1. *What is Scripture?* 2. *What that Scripture means?*" This is a most unusual, a super-human claim; especially by one who is a *party* in all these questions. If you have these awful trusts committed to you, surely you ought to make out your title to them very clearly, before we can commit our consciences implicitly to your lordly sway; and if you have these powers from God, the proof is very clear. Moses and Aaron, the ancient Prophets, the Apostles, and the Lord of all, made out their commissions very clearly, by such proofs as appealed to the outer senses as well as to the reason and conscience of men.

It is for this reason, you ought to have begun with your own *rule of faith.* But claiming to be Apostolical, you come to us, and say,

I am of the only true church; your church is false, prove that yours *is not false.* We answer, *prove* to us that you are what you say, and we will believe you. But you decline. Suppose Jesus had said to the Jews, "*I am the true Messiah; prove to me that I am not.*" Did he not proceed to prove it by such evidence as no man could honestly resist? As you come in his name, and to the exclusion of all others, call yourselves the successors of his Apostles, why do you not follow his example? And when we say we will prove you *false,* while you cannot prove yourselves *true,* you cry out, that we ought to defend our own rule! Surely, then, until your rule is proved, and your claims are fortified by proper evidence, *our rule,* the usual, universal, good old rule, stands, and withstands, and will still stand.

Your last letter is so jejune, that I really see scarcely a thought in the shape of an argument, which is not a "familiar acquaintance," that has appeared and re-appeared, until it has at least this claim to *antiquity,* that it has lost all *novelty.* Allow me, then, to pass to some additional considerations.

You have, with great frequency and confidence, charged the Protestant rule of faith, i. e., "The Holy Ghost, speaking in the Bible," with producing Unitarianism and every species of heresy. Even as recently as the close of your letter, No. 9, you venture to assert that no one can, without your infallible church's guidance, decide whether Jesus Christ was equal to God the Father or not.

I. *For the reviving of your own recollection, let me give you the following coincidences,* Rev'd Mr. Hughes' Letter No. 9. "Let him, (the Protestant reader,) take up the Bible and read these words of our blessed Redeemer, '*the Father and I are one*'—turn then to the other words—'*the Father is greater than I.*' That one passage is to be explained by the *other* is certain; but *which* shall take the preference of the other, *the sacred writings do not determine.*" Unitarians are more consistent than yourself, for they admit that the word of God (*as well as Bellarmine*) has *some* meaning, and is not dependent on the Roman Church to preserve it from contradiction and absurdity. But you agree with them in this respect, that you say Christ's divinity cannot be proved from the Bible, *without* infallible interpretation; and they say it cannot be *proved at all.* It is true you would, by *authority,* make the Bible mean what you say its obvious sense does not teach. But who ever heard of *authority* giving to words a sense contrary to their true meaning. It is absurd: therefore if you are right, so are they, by your own concession; and in the end you reach the same fearful issue with them. It is a cardinal point with Unitarians that "*The doctrine of a Trinity in the Godhead is not taught in the word of God.*" Bale, a Roman Catholic writer, asks (see Protestant, Vol. 4. page 258.) "where is it plainly written, that there are three persons in the Trinity?" Tract 1. ques. 9. Here both parties agree that the unaided Bible does not prove the doctrine of the Trinity. The Unitarian asks for a new *revelation* before he will believe it. The Romanist asks for a new and superadded authority before he will receive it. But as for the *Bible alone* they agree that the *doctrine* is not to be looked for *in it.*

Rev'd Mr. Hughes' Letter No. 3. "*It is a fact, that Christ never appointed this rule;—because he never wrote any part of the Old or New Testament himself;—he never commanded any part to be written by his Apostles."*

UNITARIANS take precisely the same ground; they contend that the sacred penmen were credible historians, who wrote as circumstances required, and according to the dictates of their own judgment, but not under the impulse of inspiration. *Their* object is to prove, that the word of God is not an infallible book. The object of *Mr. Hughes* is to show, that it is not *sufficient of i'self.* UNITARIANS make inspiration *unnecessary.* MR. HUGHES makes it *useless and even injurious,* without the aid of the Church of Rome. They agree wonderfully in this, that they dishonour and degrade the inspired word of God.

Bellarmine, and indeed Romanists at large, are accustomed to affirm that many of the canonical books have perished. Bellarmine says expressly, (book the 4th, chap. 4. on the unwritten word of God,) " Many books truly sacred and canonical have perished." " Multi libri vere sacri et canonici, perierunt." Socinus, Valkelius and others affirm the same, viz. *" It is understood that many of the books of the Old Testament have perished."* The ROMANIST would drive you in this way to the traditions and teaching of his infallible church. The UNITARIAN would reduce you by the irreparable defect of the canon to natural religion, and uninspired records. But is it not a fact which stares us in the face, that they entirely agreed to cripple and lay in the dust the *Bible alone as a sufficient rule of faith?*

In fine, when Dr. Priestly says the Apostles reasoned *" inconclusively,"* and that Moses gives *"a lame account of the creation,"* wherein does he differ from the Rev. Mr. Hughes, who says, letter No. 3. 6th head, " DOES THE BIBLE DETERMINE THE DISPUTE BETWEEN YOU AND THE UNITARIAN ON THE DIVINITY OF JESUS CHRIST? SINCE THE BEGINNING OF CHRISTIANITY *until the present hour no dispute has been determined by that rule,—the Bible alone?"* I hope, therefore, that your empty clamour about the tendency of the Protestant rule of faith to make Unitarians will cease until you have satisfied the public on the above evidences; and that henceforth you will bear in mind, that because Unitarians and we *use the same Bible we do not hold the same doctrines.* Our rule, like the sun of our system, is common property. It is your rule, if you will use it. It is our rule, it is the universal and only rule, of all men, and you had as well attempt to put your feeble shoulder to the burning orbit of the luminary in the heavens, and heave it back into the night, as to stop the freedom of inquiry, or arrest the " free course of the word of God."

II. Much has been said during this discussion on the subject of the true canon. In my first letter, I called upon you to defend the unheard of violence done to the word of God by your church, in " adding" to it a large volume of spurious books called " Apochryphal." In my last letter this difficulty was pressed upon you at some length. It was shown that the Jews, the Lord Jesus and his Apostles, the early Fathers, the Council of Laodicea, and the ancient church at large, rejected these books—and that our present canon coincides with that of Christian antiquity. You have not attempted to account for

R

the absence of these spurious books from the canon for so many ages, nor to meet the objections made in my letter No. 1, 6th head.

While you thus elude the force of truth and fact, as to the Old Testament, you have striven repeatedly to perplex the question about the genuineness and authenticity of the New Testament. The arguments which you urge against Protestants are in singular resemblance to those used by infidels against Christianity itself; and you seem to have proceeded upon the plan of making Romanists if you *can*, or infidels if you *must*. Thus in the 9th letter, 4th head, you say "*you cannot be ignorant* that several books, which in the *first ages* laid claim to inspired authority, are not in the canon. Of these I may name a few—the Gospel according to the Hebrews, or according to the Apostles—the memoirs of the Apostles—quoted frequently by Justin Martyr, and different tracts under the names of Peter, Paul, Matthias and other Apostles." And in the same letter, 6th head, you write as follows: "How does he (the Protestant) know, that the book, (the Bible,) is in *all respects now* the same that it was when it came from the hands of its inspired authors? Has it been correctly translated? Has it been fairly copied, from one manuscript to another previous to printing?"

I have often been curious to know how you would meet an Infidel or a Pagan on this question. Bellarmine was rightly compared by the writer of a former day, to the amphibious bird in the fable, which was sometimes a bird and sometimes a fish. He was a *bird* when the king of fishes exacted a tribute; and a *fish* when the king of birds exacted it. Bellarmine speaks like a *Protestant* when he reasons for the Bible as the word of God against the Libertines, and others. He refers, in proof, to such evidence as this: "At sacris Scripturis, quæ Propheticis et Apostolicis literis continentur, nihil est notius, nihil certius, ut stultissimum esse necesse sit, qui illis fidem esse habendam neget. Notissimas enim esse testis est orbis Christianus, et consensio omnium gentium, apud quas multis jam seculis summam semper auctoritatem obtinuerunt: certissimas autem atque verissimas esse, nec humana inventa, sed oracula divina continere." Bellarm. De Verbo Dei, lib. I. cap. II.

"Nothing is better known, nothing more certain than the sacred Scriptures which are contained in the Prophetical and Apostolical writings,—insomuch that he who refuses to believe in them is to be esteemed a fool. For the whole Christian world bears testimony to their notoriety, as well as the consent of all the nations among whom for so many ages their supreme authority has been acknowledged; and they are most certain and true, comprising no human inventions, but the oracles of God."

He proceeds to deduce proof. 1. From the truth of Prophecy. 2. From the wonderful divine harmony of the sacred writers, though of so many different ages, places, occasions, languages, &c. 3. From the interposition of divine Providence for the preservation of the Scriptures. 4. From the book itself; which claims *inspiratio*. 5. From the testimony of miracles.

Now will this reasoning lose any of its force when turned against yourself? If not, admit it, or else answer it. But let me go on to say to you once more, that we do not, and never did, depend on the Church of Rome for the proof, or the preservation of the word of God; and while you drop apologies to the Infidel, remember that there is a high road of evidence through which the Bible has passed unhurt, from God to the present generation, amidst the assaults of open enemies and pretended friends.

It would require a volume, (while I have room only for a few paragraphs,) to do justice to this subject. But let me refer the reader to Paley, and a crowd of other writers, who have reduced to order and fortified with unrivalled power the evidence of the genuineness and authenticity of our Bible, against the assaults of infidelity, and the Church of Rome. In the mean time, let me say a few words, that there is no evidence, that any of the spurious books you name existed in the first century of the Christian era: that they were excluded from the churches, and from the catalogues of the canonical books: were not noticed by friends or foes in discussions about Christian doctrines: and besides the *silence* of the *early* ages, they were rejected and " reprobated with a consent nearly universal by the writers of succeeding ages." You will hardly deny *these* facts; or that the *converse* of all this is true of our present canon. And finally, for all this proof, we make no more reference to the *authority* of the Church of Rome, than we do to the *authority* of the Cæsars or of the great Mogul. It is such proof as does not depend upon her testimony as a church, or her authority as a judge of controversies. Indeed it is a very singular fact, that the church of Rome, as late as the fourth century, rejected Paul's Epistle to the Hebrews! "Apud Romanos usque hodie, quasi Pauli Apostoli non habetur—Jerome (A. D. 345 to 420 De viris. Illus.) *Among the Romans, even at this day, it is not held to be the apostle Paul's.*" If this mean the church of Rome *locally*, then where is her *supremacy?* If *universally*, then where is her *infallibility?* one must fall.

III. *I come next to your argument in defence of your church as a judge of controversies.* Here as usual, you make no attempt to prove that the church of Rome is the true church of Jesus Christ. This you take for *granted.* But passing this in silence, you ask, " *How were controversies decided under the Jewish dispensation?*"

This is a very important question, and, as will appear below, of most unhappy omen to the church of Rome. You cite (Paralipomena) 2 Chron. chap. 19 verses 9, 10. You omit the 8th, which is as follows, " Moreover, did Jehoshaphat set for judgment, &c."— Observe then, that this was a *court* of the *king's* ordering.

You also omit the latter part of the 11th verse, viz.—" *And also Zebediah the son of Ishmael shall be chief in the things which regard the King.*" (I quote as you have done from the Vulgate.)— This verse shows that there were *two Presidents* of this court,—one for the ecclesiastical causes, " *the things which regard God,*" the other for the civil, " for all the things *regarding the King.*" But we suppose the resemblance is near enough, especially as you have sometimes had *three* Popes;—and as the councils were sometimes convoked by the *Emperors.*

And now as to the argument. You say, " *This is the principle* appointed by God in the old law; why should it be different n. the new?" "Even Herod, though a Jew, instead of interpreting the Scripture as Protestants do, *by private opinion*—assembling together all the chief priests and scribes of the people, *inquired* of them where Christ should be born." Matth. xi. 4. Your reasoning, then, is this, that the high priest and the sanhedrim were the judges of controversy under the old law;—and of course by the same principle, the Pope and council are the judges of controversy under the new. This you assert when you ask, "did the Saviour of men APPOINT A DIFFERENT PRINCIPLE *whereby to determine disputes in his church?*" And again, this judge of controversy was ultimate and infallible. For Josephus as quoted by you, tells us, *"the High Priest* guards the law and determines controversies." The High Priest, then, and the Council were the judges of controversy, and from their decision, which was final and infallible, there was no appeal. Let us apply the reasoning to the condemnation of Jesus Christ.

1. Jesus was arrested by order of the "high priests, scribes, and elders." Mark xiv. 43: "And immediately, while he yet spake, cometh Judas, one of the twelve, and with him a great multitude, with swords and staves, from the chief priests, and the scribes, and the elders."

2. When arrested he was brought directly before the regular tribunal. Mark xiv. 53: "And they led Jesus away to the high priest: and with him were assembled all the chief priests, and the elders, and the scribes."

3. They proceeded to try him, and condemn him for pretended "Heresy"—"as Judges of Controversy," and they charged him "with blasphemy," and condemned him to die! Mark xiv. 60—64: "And the high priest stood up in the midst, and asked Jesus, saying, Answerest thou nothing? what *is it which* these witness against thee? But he held his peace, and answered nothing. Again the high priest asked him, and said unto him, Art thou the Christ, the Son of the Blessed? And Jesus said, I am: and ye shall see the Son of man sitting on the right hand of power, and coming in the clouds of heaven. Then the high priest rent his clothes and saith, What need we any further witnesses? Ye have heard the blasphemy: what think ye? And they all condemned him to be guilty of death."

4. They then handed him over to the civil power. Mark xv. 1: "And straightway in the morning the chief priests held a consultation with the elders and scribes, and the whole council, and bound Jesus, and carried *him* away, and delivered *him* to Pilate."

5. And the civil power ordered him to be crucified, and Pilate executed their will though he pronounced Jesus an innocent man; and he died for *his doctrines*. No other charge was brought against him. Matt. xxvii. 24—26: "When Pilate saw that he could prevail nothing, but that rather a tumult was made, he took water, and washed *his* hands before the multitude, saying, I am innocent of the blood of this just person: see ye *to it*. Then answered all the people, and said, His blood *be* on us, and on our children. Then released he Barabbas unto them; and when he had scourged Jesus, he delivered *him* to be crucified."

Never did the universe witness so bloody a drama! Never did a council commit a deed so atrocious! But here was the "judge of controversies," the high priest, the Pope's original,—here the regular council, and sitting in judgment " *on doctrine,*" not as a " feudal," or civil, but "ecclesiastical court." Then were they fallible or in fallible? Did they decide right or wrong? Such is your reasoning, that you are bound by consistency to defend their acts,—or by candour, to say that a council though regularly convened, and general, with the Pope presiding, *may err,* in matters of doctrine and morals!

IV. *The Scripture, according to the ancient Fathers, is the sole judge of controversies and interpreter of itself.*

It was Augustin who laid down this great radical principle, "*there a man is said to be judge where he has power and authority to correct.*" On this principle your church has actually proceeded, in assuming to be *judge* of controversies, for she has *added* a large volume to the word of God, (as we proved in letter No. IX.;) and though a party in the controversy, she assumes to *judge* with authority in her own cause.

Optatus, A. D. 370, held the following language: " You say it is lawful, we say it is not lawful; the people's souls do doubt and waver, let none believe you nor us, we are all contending parties, judges must be sought for: if Christians, they cannot be given on both sides, (for truth is hindered by affections.) A judge without must be sought for; if a Pagan, he cannot know the Christian mysteries; if a Jew, he is an enemy to Christian Baptism: no judgment therefore of this matter can be found on *earth; a Judge in heaven must be sought for. But why knock we at heaven, when we have the Testament of Christ in the Gospel.*" (De cœlo quærendus est Judex, sed at quid pulsamus ad cœlum habemus in Evangelio Testamentum. Opt. lib. 5 contr. Parmen. Donat.) The above is on the question of re-baptizing, in his discussion with " Heretics."

Chrysostom, who was ordained Bishop of Constantinople, A. D. 398, makes the following very striking and appropriate comments upon the subject at issue: " Let us follow the scope of the Holy Scripture in interpreting itself: when it teaches some hard thing, it expoundeth itself, and suffereth not the hearer to err. Let us not fear, therefore, to put ourselves with full sail into the sea of 'Scriptures,' because we shall be sure to find the word of God for our pilot, (Chrys. Hom. 13, in Gen. Chrys. in 1 Thes. Hom. 7.) The same author prompts a Gentile to the use of the word of God in the following language: " When thou buyest a garment, though thou have no skill in weaving, yet thou sayest not I cannot buy it, they will deceive me: but dost use all means to learn how to know it: do, therefore, those things which are to be done, seek all those things of God, and He altogether will reveal it unto thee." (Idem. Homit. 33. in Act.)

Athanasius, who flourished about the year 335, speaking of the Bible, says: " For the holy and divinely inspired Scriptures are of themselves sufficient for the discovery of the truth." (Speech against the Gentiles.) It is very important here to observe, that this Father in his catalogue of the books of Scripture, gives precisely our canon., excluding from the inspired word the Wisdom of Solomon, Judith, Tobias, &c. &c. From this it appears, 1. That ours is the true canon, while Roman Catholics have corrupted the Word of God, by the addition of writings called by Athanasius " NOT CANONICAL." 2. That this our very canon is a *sufficient* rule for the *discovery of divine truth.*

I might cite many other testimonies from the Fathers: but these may serve as specimens in proof of the fact, that they held the Protestant rule of faith. It is true "The Fathers" were not unanimous, neither were they inerrable. The Roman Catholic rule of faith, as we have elsewhere shown, binds its followers " *never to take or interpret them* (the sacred Scriptures) *otherwise than according to the unanimous consent of the Fathers.*" The defect of such unanimity utterly explodes the rule which rests upon it. But that the Protestant rule was known, owned, practised from the earliest ages, is sufficiently evident from the quotations already adduced ; and as the pruning-knife of Papal expurgation has been applied even to these Fathers, we may well suppose that what is left in the form of proof for our own rule is indisputable authority with Roman Catholics. In a word, it appears according to testimony which you have admitted to be authentic, that the word of God is the sole Judge of controversy, and its own interpreter.

As to the famous passage from Tertullian, I would ask you, with all due respect and candour, why did you not cite the passage in the first instance, as you have cited it at last ? You charge me with injustice as to the passage from Bellarmine on the power of the Pope. But here the whole sense of the passage is altered, and the very shape of it is changed. Yet even upon your own admission, Tertullian makes *many apostolical churches* and *many apostolical chairs.* And these churches and these chairs were of *equal authority*, one with another ; and to be consulted indifferently according to their vicinity to the inquirer. And also, " the letters of the apostles, uttering their voice and representing the presence of each of them, are recited" as *supreme* authority. Then, on your own reasoning, Philippi, Thessalonica, Ephesus, and Corinth, as well as Rome, were apostolical seats And " the writings of the apostles," and not a living infallible judge " *was the infallible rule of faith established by Christ to guide us in matters of religion for the purpose of determining disputes in the Church of Christ.*"

Your attempt to pervert my argument, on the apostolical succession, shows the desperation of a defence, which was feeling for a foundation, and could find none. You say, in letter No. 9, " If the Apostles *alone* were inspired and infallible, as you assert, then what is to become of the two Gospels of St. Luke and St. Mark, what is to become of the Acts of the Apostles ? It is well known that the authors of these books were not Apostles, and had not seen the Lord." Here you but resort to the old practice of injuring the *canon*, rather than spare the *Protestant.* It is known to yourself, that Mark's writings received the sanction of Peter, and Luke's of Paul. The Apostle Paul says, in his Epistles, " Paul an Apostle of Jesus Christ and Timotheus our brother."—" Paul called to be an Apostle and

Sosthenes our brother." The writings were theirs, whether penned by themselves, or others under their eye."

And now as to the reference to a sworn interpreter, you contradict yourself and misrepresent me in two successive paragraphs, by saying in the first, "You shrink from so impartial a test." "Did you dread the presence of a sworn interpreter?" and then own that, in my last letter, I agree to such a reference.

On this whole subject I would say, 1. By this very proposal you abandon the principle on which you heretofore proceeded; which is, that a *fallible interpreter cannot be authority*. 2. While the opinions of learned and good men, shall always have great weight with me, yet my principles forbid me to commit the last decision to any human tribunal. 3. We are at issue about *translations*, and about *facts*. For example, you deny that your church forbids the reading of the Scriptures. I affirm it. So of several other facts, some clothed in a dead language, and some not. In the reference proposed, I wish to settle each class of questions so far as a reference can do it. 4. I wish the fair *translation* of several passages of Scripture, particularly that mentioned in my last letter, that the same may be spread out before the public. 5. With these statements, I do most cordially agree to the reference itself, and to the Rev. Dr. Wylie, the respected Professor of Languages, named by you as our referee; and I agree to make him a standing referee, so that whenever you please, he may be called on for this purpose. As soon as convenient, I am prepared through a friend to proceed in this reference.

A gentleman, who knew the feelings of a gentleman, should have understood, without explanation, the delicate nature of my situation in regard to the name of my informant, as to "*the warning against reading the controversy.*" I did not proceed in this matter without a responsible name; and even then, knowing *the defects of tradition*, I asked it of you as a question, whether my informant was mistaken, and left it open for correction. I have now the name before me, and the permission to make it public, if requested by the Bishop. If he demand it, therefore, it shall be given.

I wish to say, in conclusion, that our rules, which you profess greatly to respect, require us to pass, at *some time*, and I think the public expect us to pass, *soon*, to other topics. I give you notice, therefore, that I shall avail myself very soon, if my life is spared, of this privilege, reserving the right to respond to your arguments if you choose to linger on the threshold. Yours, &c.

JOHN BRECKINRIDGE.

CONTROVERSY. No. XIII.

RULE OF FAITH.

Philadelphia, April 26, 1833.

To the Rev. John Breckinridge.

Rev. Sir,—As my reference to the Westminster Confession of Faith, touching the power and duty of magistrates, seems to have given you some pain, I shall commence by saying all I have to say on that subject. This is the more necessary, as you recall the plea of "*ignorance* and inadvertence," which you had hitherto mercifully extended.

It is a *fact* that Towar & Hogan published the Westminster Confession in 1829. It is a *fact* that it contains the passages I quoted, as to intolerance and the magistrate's duty in matters of religion—and it is a *fact*, which rests on the authority of Dr. Miller, that ministers and candidates were "*obliged*" to adopt this Confession as the "standard of Presbyterianism," exactly one hundred years before. Consequently, it is a fact, that if this be not *now* your standard, it is because *you have departed*, in so much, at least, from the faith once delivered to the "*saints.*" The passages which you call "*offensive*," were supported by seven or eight different texts of Scripture; and I thought that these texts might, possibly, have the same meaning *now*, that they had in 1729. Indeed, until you advised me of it, I did not conceive how these scriptural authorities could have become so "offensive" in the interval, that they deserved to be "*solemnly rejected.*" The doctrines, which they were intended to support, are as true (though perhaps not so *palatable*) since the revolution, as they had been before. If, in the *first* instance, they were false, it was injurious to the written Word of God to employ *it* so profusely for their support—and it was tyrannical to "oblige" either "professed ministers" or candidates to *adopt them*. If, on the other hand, they were *true*, I do not see why they have been "solemnly rejected." The doctrines of Christ do not change with the shiftings of every political gale. And though the British Lion gave place to the Eagle of Independence, "some fifty years ago," yet, I find it difficult to discover, by what mysterious process *this* event could have *nullified the scriptural doctrines of your standards*, or converted them into "offensive passages." Albeit, it seems that the work of "Reformation" in the doctrines of Christ, is not the *peculiar* privilege of any age—that the children are not satisfied with what their fathers have done in this behalf—and that I was led astray by taking it for granted that the "Standard of Presbyterianism" in the 19th century was the same, that ministers had been "obliged to adopt" in the 18th. What it will be, in fifty years more, is not known to any man living. One thing is certain, that the melody of Calvin and the chorus of the Westminster divines, have been enriched with *variations* in every key. I suppose, however, that in reference to your standards, I might venture (with safety) to go as far back, as the year 1821. In the "amended" edition of that year, although the civil magistrates are shorn of the prerogatives, with which the Westminster divines and the "Adopting Act" of 1729 had invested them, *as to the words*, yet they are clothed with *undefined* attributes, in which a keen eye may discover the lurking *essence* of the very passages which are so offensive. In page 105 they (civil magistrates) are honoured with an office full of tenderness and parental affection. "As NURSING FATHERS, it is their duty to *protect* the church of our common Lord, without giving the preference to any denomination of Christians above the rest," &c. The latter clause might seem to have been added, to prevent the passage from being "offensive." But as soon as it will be convenient for the Assembly to tell us, *what* is the "church of our common Lord," may not one half of the Christian denominations, who enjoy the equal protection of the Constitution, be astonished to find themselves excluded from the pale—and regarded by the "nursing fathers" of the other half, as step-children—or worse? And again, if the babe should languish, would it not be natural for the General Assembly, as the physician, to prescribe a little of that *political nutriment*, by which it waxed strong in Geneva, Scotland, and England itself, when the magistrates were, in very deed, its "nursing fathers?" I will pursue this topic no farther—except to say that, in my humble opinion, the magistrates of this Republic are well employed, if they study the laws and administer them with justice and impartiality—and that it is an insult to the spirit and language of the Constitution, to invoke them as "nursing fathers," to what the General Assembly may think proper to call the "church of our common Lord."

The other paragraphs of your first column contain two pretty little stories—one about "Dick doing nothing and Jack helping him,"—the other about the two "strolling priests in Kentucky"—one of whom, it seems, personated the Protestant, and evidently *understood* his part, since he "fought long, died hard, but was *always beaten*." This was genuine acting, so much like the reality—for

> Halting on crutches of unequal size,
> One leg by truth supported, one by (flies,)
> They sidle to the goal with awkward pace
> Secure of nothing but to *lose the race*.

So it was with the antagonist of the Rev. Mr. Maguire, whom you have introduced. Mr. Pope, the king of Protestant controversy in Ireland, had the courage to enter the lists with him, where he fought long, and though I will not say he was beaten, lest I should offend you, yet it is certain that from *that* day to *this*, he has carefully shunned every thing like controversy with a Catholic priest. He did not possess that happy talent for which Goldsmith immortalized the village schoolmaster. So it was with the celebrated Claude, whose glory it was, says Eustace, to have fallen by the hand of the illustrious Bossuet. So it was with the Pope of Calvinism in France, Du Plessis, in the discussion held at Fontainbleau, in the presence of Henry IV. in the year 1600. (See Sully's Memoirs, vol. 2, page 354.) This case is so illustrative of the manner in which

Protestant controversialists assail the Catholic religion, that I will give a brief sketch of it.

Du Plessis had written a book, *not to prove his own religion*, but to refute the Catholic doctrine of the Eucharist and the Mass. The Catholics were startled, as usual, with the number of falsehoods it contained, and spoke so freely of them, that the author in his rashness challenged any one to point out a single false quotation in the whole book. M. Du Perron, then Bishop of Evreux, and afterwards Cardinal, undertook to show as many as FIVE HUNDRED AND FIFTY. The parties met before the king. Judges were appointed by him, some of whom were Catholics and some Calvinists. Fifty passages were to be examined every day; but after the examination of nine of them, in which he was *unanimously convicted*, Du Plessis *became sick at the stomach*, and the investigation proceeded no farther. "Every one knows," says Sully, (a Protestant,) "how the dispute was terminated. Du Plessis' defence was weak, and ended in *his disgrace*." One of the commissioners, Fresne-Canaye, a Calvinist, and Sainte Marie Du Mont, another eminent Protestant, were roused from the "delusion" of Protestantism, by the *issue* of this controversy, and soon after embraced the divine, but *calumniated* religion of the Catholics.

Having disposed of your anecdotes in reference to the priests in Kentucky, with the citation of a few instances, in which Protestant disputants had the privilege of *speaking for themselves*,—in which they "fought long, died hard, and were always (*substantially*) beaten," I shall now proceed to follow you through the heterogeneous materials of which your letter is composed.

"You have called until you are weary for my reply to the admission of the Rev. Mr. Maguire." But pray by what right do you call on me to adopt the language used by Mr. Maguire? Supposing I were to call on you to adopt and defend the language of some Presbyterian brother, would you, on that account, feel yourself bound to answer? Not that I mean to decline answering your call, but to intimate that I am able to meet you in *my own words*, without having recourse to those even of Rev. Mr. Maguire. The sum of the quotation is this:—"You (Mr. Hughes) prove the authenticity and inspiration of the Holy Scriptures by the testimony of the church." But *how do you prove* the authority of the church? Mr. Maguire says, it is "by your private judgment on the Scripture proofs." And therefore you (Mr. Hughes) are obliged to have recourse for the proof of the church to the principle of "private interpretation." Is not this what you mean?

Answer 1st. Protestants *admit* the testimony of Scripture, and on this account I quote it to prove the authority of the church. 2. I quote it, not as an inspired book, if you prefer to take the ground of a *Deist*, but I quote it, *in that case*, as historical evidence of the fact, in which sense you will be obliged, even as a Deist, to admit its testimony. 3. The history of Christianity proves the authority of the church. From the days of the Apostles, the church *proscribed heresies*,—*preached the doctrines of Christ* to all nations,—*determined*. by a final decision, all controversies,—and in *all matters of religion* ex-e *cised* SUPREME *authority.* So that the authority of the church is proved with, or without, the Scripture. It seems that you cannot comprehend the distinction between a fact and an *opinion.* When I quote Scripture to show that Christ appointed a ministry in his church, or that he was crucified, I merely furnish historical evidence bearing on a *fact,* with which private interpretation has nothing to do. But when Protestants quote Scripture to support their private *opinions,* which *they call their doctrines,* then it is that they use it, not to establish *facts,* but to support *speculations,* and thus *degrade* the written word of God, by making it a book of contradictions, as various as their minds, or their sectarian prejudices. This is manifest, from the multitude of your sects, and your endless disputations among yourselves about the *meaning of the Bible.*

But I should have proved, you say, my own rule of faith. I answer that I have done so, and as long as you are pleased to shun a struggle with the reasoning and facts of my letters, I need not repeat what has already been said. You complain of my monotonous reference to them; but you should remember, that although you have catered industriously for the prejudices of Protestant readers, by indulging in the antiquated calumnies of your predecessors against the Catholic Church and the Bishops of Rome, you have not had the courage TO CLOSE WITH ME in a single argument. Even in your last epistle, although our discussion professes to be on the *rule of faith,* you tell us with great self-complacency, that "you had supposed at least that *I would defend the* SACRAMENTS *of our church*"—and with the happiest versatility of talent, you wind up by expressing a desire to pass to "other topics,"—as if you had not confused your letters on the "rule of faith," by the introduction, pell-mell, of every topic that has been discussed since the days of Martin Luther.

In my last I took occasion to protest against the injustice of those who represent me as arguing against the Bible: and instead of admitting my protest, you return to the charge, and employ nearly the whole of your second column to show that my arguments and those of Unitarians coincide in our estimate of the Bible! Whether or not you have done justice to *their* doctrines, it is not for me to determine. My reference to them was not for the purpose of canvassing their doctrines, but merely to show that they and you are children of the same parentage—*your rule of faith is the same*—not the Bible, but your own respective *opinions* as to the meaning of the sacred book: to show farther, that, under the guidance of this fallacious principle of private opinion, *they* have the same right to hold their doctrines that *you* have for yours. I have multiplied arguments to show that Protestant Christianity, whether it be Presbyterian or Unitarian, rests *not* on the Bible, but on *opinion,* as its basis, and that every article *in* the superstructure of belief shares the uncertainty of the foundation. What is heresy among Protestants? Opinion. What is orthodoxy among Protestants? Opinion. Every thing is opinion; and yet it is certain that opinion formed no part of the Revelation of Jesus Christ, and that there is not a single opinion in the whole Bible!!— Now, if this be so, is not the Protestant rule of faith a *mere prelude* to infidelity? Does it not destroy the *certainty* of Revelation, and the sacred character of the divine volume, which, with insidious embrace, it affects to cherish? But if it is *not* so, why do you not deny it, and show your Protestant readers, how they may have, by your rule, a better foundation for their religious belief, than they have for their politics, viz : opinion. To illustrate the truth of these observations, I will insert a " few facts" taken from an article in the Vermont Chronicle, the production, evidently, of a Protestant pen. 1. " Out of about one hundred and eighty Unitarian Societies in England, about one hundred and seventy are orthodox Presbyterian Societies revolutionized. 2. In Ireland a large number of Presbyterian ministers and churches have become Arian. 3. A large proportion of the Unitarian Societies in Scotland were once Presbyterians. 4. The Presbyterian churches in Geneva and in Switzerland generally have gone over in a body to Unitarianism, or to something equally hostile to vital piety." One thing more I have to say, that *you* will do well never to engage in a controversy with an educated Unitarian, unless it be for the improvement of your logic. Not that I would side with him against you on doctrine, but because it is the *inevitable* misfortune of all those who adopt the Protestant rule of faith to have no better foundation for *true doctrines, even Christ's Divinity*, than their brethren have for the contrary *opinion*.

Now for your remarks on the canon of Scripture, in which you are as unfortunate as before. You say, " it was shown that the Jews, the Lord Jesus and his apostles, the early fathers, the Council of Laodicea, and the ancient church at large, rejected these books"— (meaning what Protestants call Apocryphal books.) Now I reply boldly, that you cannot furnish *proof* of what you have asserted.— That there is not a single evidence on record, that they were " rejected" either by our Saviour, or his apostles ; and if you assert thus inconsiderately what is untrue, can you blame me for reminding you of it ? With regard to the " fathers," " councils," and " church at large," when you appeal to *them* to determine what books are canonical, and what books are not, you act as a rational man ; and I take your invocation of *their* testimony on the matter as a tribute paid to the Catholic principle of belief. If, therefore, their authority moves you in your selection of Scriptural books, then I hail you as the child of *tradition*, no less than myself. But, then, what becomes of your rule of faith ? The Scripture *alone* does not determine the canonical books. Our Lord and the apostles are silent on the subject, notwithstanding your assertion to the contrary. And lo! you are constrained to invoke the aid of " fathers" and " councils" to tell you what is Scripture and what is not. But what say you of the later " fathers ?"—of Father Luther, for instance, for having rejected the *Epistles of St. James*, and St. Jude, and that of St. Paul to the Hebrews ? What say you of Father Calvin, for having expunged the Apocalypse from the canon ? Were *these* apocryphal ? If not, why did these " fathers" reject them ? And the two Gospels and Acts, written by St. Luke and St. Mark—were *they* apocryphal ? Their authors were *not* apostles, and you have told us, that none but the apostles were inspired. I had pressed this difficulty before, and instead of meeting it, you accuse me of a disposition " rather to *injure* the cause than *spare* the Protestant." You certainly injure my intentions in this charge, whilst you indirectly invoke my forbearance. Still, you try to extricate yourself. "Mark's writings received," you say, "the sanction of Peter, and Luke's of Paul." So did those of Barnabas and Clement. But what then? Again, the Apostle Paul says in his epistles, "Timotheus our brother." But what then? and "Sosthenes our brother." What then? I really cannot imagine *what you mean by all this.* But to come to the point—were St. Mark and St. Luke inspired to write, or were they not? If they were then you were wrong in saying, *that none but the apostles were inspired: and for the sake of the Gospel of Christ, you should not leave your testimony to that effect on record.*

In reference to what you call apocryphal Scriptures, which, you say, have been added by our church, I have to reply again, that your accusation is a manifest acknowledgment of the *necessity* of ecclesiastical infallibility. You pretend that the Bible *alone* is your rule of faith—and yet it is by *tradition* that you attempt to show " what is Bible and *what is not.*" Catholics possess that canon of Scripture which has been recognised by the Christian church since the beginning. *Some* of the early fathers hesitated about the canonicity of certain books, but during the same period, the same doubts were entertained respecting several books in *the Protestant canon;* and the fact would go to exclude the Epistle to the Hebrews, the Apocalypse, and several other books of the New Testament. Calvin on this account rejected the revelations of St. John. Why then will you not be *consistent* and reject *all,* or receive *all?* The Syriac version, so much praised by Protestant critics, and which, they say, dates from about the time of the Apostles, contains OUR canon. The council of Carthage in 397, composed of 127 Bishops, gives OUR canon, expressly naming every book, and adds, that these had been received from the fathers as divine and canonical—" A Patribus ista accepimus in ecclesia legenda." Innocent I. in his letter to Exsuperius in 405, makes the *same* enumeration. So does the Roman Council under Gelasius I, in 494. Melito, to whose catalogue you refer, was only an individual.* He mentioned the books of the Old Testament which were *then* recognised every where, but did not say that the others were *uncanonical.* And he omits the book of Esther, which I find in your Confession of Faith of 1821. The synopsis, attributed to Athanasius, is considered by critics as the production of the 6th century. The Council of Laodicea in 375 was composed of only 22 Bishops, and if you had taken the pains to be informed on the subject, you would not have exposed yourself, by saying on its testimo-

* When, therefore, I went to the East, and came as far as the place, where these things were proclaimed and done, I accurately ascertained the books of the Old Testament, and send them thee here below. The names are as follows. Of Moses five books, *Genes's, Exodus, Leviticus, Numbers, Deuteronomy.—Jesus, Nave Judges, Ruth. Four of Kings. Two of Paralipomena, (Chronicles,) Psalms of David, Proverbs of Solomon,* which is also called WISDOM, *Ecclesiastes, Song of Songs, Job.* Of Prophets, *Isaiah, Jeremiah.* Of the twelve prophets one book—*Daniel, Ezekiel, Esdras.* From these, I have, therefore, made the selection, which I have divided into six books, (Melito according to Cruse's Euseb p. 164.)

ny, that " your present Protestant canon coincides with that of Christian antiquity." First, 22 Bishops did not represent " Christian Antiquity :" and secondly, they made no mention of the Apocalypse. So that the "coincidence" is destroyed, except in your own imagination. One of the most ancient catalogues, cited by Beveridge, gives the *Catholic* canon. Eusebius (lib. 3. c. 3. x. 25) says, that some rejected the Epistle to the Hebrews, and regarded as doubtful that of St. James, St. Jude, the 2d and 3d of St. John, and the Revelation. Are these *therefore* Apocryphal? Is not one part of the inference as well deduced as the other? As to the books of the Old Testament, the *Catholic* canon corresponds with the Greek version, which was used in the synagogue of Alexandria, and by the Jews in Asia Minor, Africa, and generally wherever the Greek language prevailed. Some of them were written, *after* the canon of Esdras had been formed—and this, I trust, will account for their not being *there enumerated.* Origen, in his letter to Julius Africanus, speaks of them, as having been in use *from the commencement of the church.* And St. Augustine, writing against the semi-Pelagians, who denied the canonicity of some of these books, as *you* do, appeals to the authority of *preceding ages* in their support,—" tam longa annositate"—and if their antiquity was an argument *in the 4th century* against the semi-Pelagians, I do not see why it should not be as good, against Protestants *in the 19th century.* Our canon is that held by the Christians of Syria to this day, whether Maronites or Catholics, Jacobites, or Eutychians. It is used by the Cophts of Egypt, by the Ethiopians, and the Nestorians, separated as they have been from the church, for more than 1200 years, (see Perpet. de la Foi. t. 5. l. 7. also Biblioth. Orient. t. 3 and 4.) The Greek schismatics, in their Synod held in Jerusalem in 1672, under the Patriarch Dositheus, give the *Catholic* canon, and add, " these books we hold to be canonical, and confess them to be *sacred Scripture*, since they have been handed down to us as such by *ancient usage*, or rather by the Catholic church." Shall we then turn aside from this mass of authority and hearken to the ipse dixit of Martin Luther, John Calvin, or the Rev. John Breckinridge, about Apocryphal books? Did not the two former gentlemen expel books even from the Protestant canon, in the most arbitrary and capricious manner? Read over, I pray you, these testimonies, and reflect how *imprudent* you were, in a former letter, when you asserted that *our canon* of scripture was framed only " in the sixteenth century by the Council of Trent." And hereafter, if you should feel disposed to challenge " Priests and Bishops to the field of controversy," remember that there are *other books* to be consulted, besides " Taylor's Dissuasive from Popery."

In the Jewish dispensation controversies were decided by the judgment of the High Priest and Sanhedrim—in reference to which you make me say, that "of course by the same principle the Pope and Councils are the judges of controversies under the new law." You will observe, Rev. Sir, that I did not institute any such direct comparison. I spoke of the PRINCIPLE being the same under both dispensations. I must again refer the reader to the proofs contained in letter No. 5, to show that it is not by any feeble analogy, but by the

POSITIVE INSTITUTION OF JESUS CHRIST, that the ministry of his church are clothed with power to preach the Gospel, administer his sacraments, and proscribe the heresies of *innovaters* in religion. They have exercised this prerogative from the beginning of Christianity. And it would have been iniquitous so to have exercised it, if the Son of God had appointed the *Bible alone* according to private interpretation, as the infallible rule of faith.

But the reference to the condemnation of Christ, in which the High Priest erred, is no argument on the subject. Jesus Christ the Sun of Righteousness, had already *manifested* himself to the world, by his miracles and doctrines, and thus superseded the authority of the Synagogue. Previous to this manifestation by *miracles*, the decision of the Jewish Council, as to the birth-place of Christ, was true. And even in the conspiracy against his life, when Caiaphas declared it expedient that one man should die for the people, the evangelist adds, that " this he spoke *not* of himself; but being *the High Priest of that year*, he prophesied that Jesus should die for the nation." John xi. 15. You ask me then was the tribunal, appointed by Almighty God in the old law, " fallible or infallible ?" Answer, it was infallible, until it was superseded by *Him*, to whom " was given all power in heaven and earth." " Did they decide right or wrong ?" Answer, they decided wrong—because Christ had already *proved to them*, that He was the Messiah, and they shut their eyes against the *evidence of truth*. The term of their commissions had virtually *expired*. It was known to themselves that their authority would be superseded by the coming of the Holy One—and consequently their defection *after* His coming is no argument against their infallibility before—much less is it an argument against the infallibility of the church, secured in the commission given by Christ to her pastors, when he said : " Go, TEACH all nations....and lo I am with you ALL *days*, even to the consummation of the world."

" The Scripture," you say, " according to the ancient fathers, is the sole judge of controversies and interpreter of itself." Here again you appeal to the fathers, and give up the Bible alone. That the ancient fathers spoke in the most eloquent language in the Scriptures, is certain. That all Catholic theologians so speak of them, is equally certain. That they quoted them against heretics, who *affected to admit no other testimony*, is indubitable. But to say that they regarded the *Scripture alone*, as the rule of faith or the judge of controversies, is an unfounded assertion. I defy you to show one single instance of it in all ecclesiastical history, in which heresy was condemned by the testimony of Scripture alone. The Church was in *possession* of the *true doctrines* of Christ—and heresy *began*, in every age, by some individual *pretending* to have discovered in the Bible, tenets, with which the *church* had never been acquainted. This was *novelty;* and until a new revelation be made, *novelty* of doctrine and ERROR are, and will be, the *same thing*. Is not this the principle even of Presbyterianism itself? When you argue against Catholics you accuse them of denying the sufficiency of the Scriptures *alone*, as a rule of faith ; whereas *they* contend that God never appointed them as an *exclusive* rule. But when you argue against your brethren of the low church party, you drop the boasted sufficiency of the Scriptures as a proof rule, *unless your standards be superadded!!* Your standards, as "amended" by the General Assembly of 1821, have attained the venerable antiquity of twelve years: and yet you talk of "*new lights!!*" Heresy has always appealed to the Bible alone, for the purpose of *secession* from truth; but so soon as it had seceded, it never failed to give up the sufficiency of the Bible, and to fence itself around with arbitrary Creeds, Articles of belief and Confessions of Faith.

You ask me, why I did not cite the passage from Tertullian *at first*, as I did *at last*. Answer: I did not wish to make the quotation too long. But *you* are at liberty to cite the whole chapter, or the whole book, and you will find that every sentence, taken one with another, will be a dagger of testimony against the principle of Protestantism, on the rule of faith. You pretend to have won a great concession, when you say, that "even on my own admission, Tertullian makes many *Apostolical churches, and Apostolical chairs*." Answer. There were many churches, *but only* ONE DOCTRINE. And you assert what is utterly unfounded in fact, when you say, on Tertullian's authority, that the "writings of the Apostles" constituted the infallible rule of faith: in this you are as unjust towards your author, as you had been in other instances; and yet you allude to *this case* as an offset to your affair of Bellarmine, in which you say, "I charge you with injustice to the passage." My charge was much *stronger* than this. I charged upon you, that in six distinct instances you had quoted authorities, and that in reference to each of these six authorities, your assertions were *untrue*. I challenged you to meet me before a sworn interpreter, or even Dr. Wylie, and you shrink from this alternative. I now challenge you for the third time: and I trust that, without clogging the proposal with irrelevant conditions, you will either meet me, or give up your pretensions. Certainly you will *understand* this language.

With regard to "the warning against reading this controversy," I *insist upon an explanation*. In the *first* instance, it was Bishop Kenrick, who gave the warning. He denied—you apologized—and he was satisfied. But still, the "most respectable and responsible gentleman INSISTED that such a warning was given in one of our churches on the day named." And in your last letter, you soften it down into a mere *question* "left open for correction!" But how could that be, since the gentleman still "insisted," *even after the correction was given?* The information was *false:* and now I require of you, in the name of the clergymen, who officiate in the *other churches*, to give the name of your informant. Shall you give circulation to *false* testimony, PERSIST IN MAINTAINING IT, and yet plead "the delicate nature of your situation" for concealing the name of its author? Even public morals will not tolerate such trifling. We require then that the charge be *proved*, or *retracted*, or else the *name of the author given*.

And now with reference to Dr. Miller, I have not a word to say against the encomiums you have passed upon him. I know him only by his writings, of which I may be permitted to speak, since they are public property. He seems to be one of those happy mortals, who, if I may judge from his last letter, are perfectly acquainted with the Catholic religion, without ever having taken the trouble to study it. On that subject he can instruct others, without having learned himself. He has put forth in his last letter to Presbyterians, for Catholic doctrines, assertions, for which he cannot find *authority in any Catholic approved writer in the whole universe.* If he can, I pledge myself to give $500 to the Bible Society, provided he, or any other Presbyterian will give me the same sum for the Orphans, in *case he cannot.* The Doctor's other writings have been made sufficiently free with, by Protestant adversaries; and though I have never seen a criticism on his style, yet I have been often compelled to laugh at the expense of his logic. You have no doubt seen the treatise of Dr. Cook of Kentucky, in which the author has the advantage of being able to use Catholic arguments, in support of Episcopacy.—For our friend of Princeton has wielded his pen against his Episcopal brethren, no less than against Catholics. And as his testimony will no doubt be dear to you, I will give you a specimen of his language, touching the Bible alone. His first position was against Episcopalians. "The sufficiency," says he, "and the infallibility of the Scriptures ALONE, as a rule of faith and practice was *assumed* as the grand principle of the Reformation from Popery, and is acknowledged to be the foundation of the Protestant cause." (Dr. Miller, Vol. 1. p. 26.) A Presbyterian clergyman in Baltimore, Rev. Mr. Duncan, happening to understand the Doctor *literally*, concluded, that of course, the Confession of Faith was *superfluous*, since the Bible *alone* was *sufficient;* and proceeded accordingly to dispense with the standards of the church. Whereupon the wisdom of the Catholic principle, in reference to the rule of faith, broke in upon the Doctor, and he wrote as follows:—"How is she (the church) to ascertain the character of her candidates for the holy ministry, when according to the brother, whom I am constrained to oppose, she is forbidden to employ any *other* test than that, (the Bible,) which the most CORRUPT AND UNQUALIFIED WILL BEAR just as well as the most excellent: and which is *of course, in reference to the point to be decided*, NO TEST AT ALL." (Letter to a Gentleman in Baltimore, page 24.)

Now, pray, what more have I said touching the Bible, as a test of doctrines than that it is a test, which the "most corrupt" as well as the "most excellent will bear;" and that, in the Professor's own language, "in reference to the point to be decided, it is NO TEST AT ALL." And if it is "*no test at all,*" then it is not "sufficient" as the *only* rule of faith and practice. Here then is the testimony, even of Dr. Miller coming to support my argument, which is strong enough without it.

As you seem to be anxious to quit the rule of faith, which, by the way, you had quit from the beginning, I need not remind you, that according to our agreement the next question will be—"Is the Protestant religion the religion of Christ?" Now I hope that you will not undertake to prove the Protestant, *by assailing the Catholic religion*. I do not say that I will follow you immediately: but in the mean time be pleased to let me know what I am to understand by the "Protestant religion?" Give me your own definition and I will respect it. Above all, let us have the *six passages* on which we are at issue decided by Dr. Wylie, or any other interpreter of languages. I shall be ready on the 6th of May, next Monday, if it meet your convenience. Please also to favour us with the name of the gentleman who abused your confidence, by asserting and " *insisting*" that the people were warned by one of the Catholic Priests in this city, against reading his controversy.—Yours, &c JNO. HUGHES.

CONTROVERSY. No. XIV.

RULE OF FAITH.

Philadelphia, May 2d, 1833.

To the Rev. John Hughes.

Sir,—At an early day in the present controversy, "with all the pomp and circumstance of war," you announced to the American public your confident determination "TO DRIVE THE PLOUGHSHARE OF REASON, EVIDENCE, AND ARGUMENT, THROUGH THE RADICAL DELUSION OF PROTESTANTISM." It now becomes that candid public, rather than myself, to judge whether you have redeemed a pledge so self-confident and presuming. The smile which was provoked by the perusal of these lofty pretensions, was probably succeeded in many a Protestant's breast, as well as in mine, by the recollection of Ahab's admonition to Benhadad, "*Let not him that girdeth on his harness boast himself as he that putteth it off.*" Sounding epithets, your readers find, are not synonymous with solid arguments; and the skill of the Jesuits, and the mad zeal of the Crusaders, with all the enginery of Rome, must ever prove themselves impotent against "the truth as it is in Jesus."

Nothing can more strongly evince the weakness of your cause, and your own consciousness of it, than your repeated efforts to divert me from the course of the discussion, by the introduction of various and irrelative details. As to the Rev. Dr. Miller, whom you so feebly assail, and so indelicately introduce, it is superfluous for me to say to you, or to the country, that he stands in no need of defence from me. Your notice of his triumphant exposure of the devices and errors of your church (in a late letter addressed to Presbyterians) is good proof of the efficacy of that appeal. As it regards your proffered bet of $500, you may not be aware that Protestants are not accustomed to gamble; and if, as I *suspect*, he should not close in with the wager you have laid, you must attribute his declining it to our principles, and not to our fear of defeat. I am pleased to find Dr. Miller, in one of his works published more than twenty years ago, distinctly avowing that "*the Bible is the only infallible and the sufficient rule of faith and practice:*" and you will excuse me for expressing my utter amazement, that any one who claims a character for either candour or common sense, should see any contradiction between this proposition and another, which maintains *that the church is bound to be careful, that those whom she receives interpret this rule as she thinks right, before she agrees to walk with them in ecclesiastical communion.* Does it imply any contradiction to the principle that the rule is infallible and sufficient, that a body of Christians refuse to receive any but those whom they consider as interpreting this rule in a Scriptural and correct manner? And, besides, does not every Confession of Faith profess to found itself *solely on the Scriptures;* to receive nothing but what the Scriptures teach; and to receive it simply and solely, because it is found there? It is, therefore, a definitive evidence of what a church *does* believe, not an authoritative rule by which *to* believe; and of what the Bible *does* say, not what it *should* say.

In reference to the extract from the Vermont Chronicle, true or false, we freely allow that Presbyterian churches *may* become Unitarian, and that at different times certain congregations *have* become so. But if there be weight in the fact, where does its pressure lie?—Thousands of congregations, millions of individuals, yea, nations, in chief part, and they the most enlightened, free, and virtuous, of the ages in which they lived, once Roman Catholics, and who under that denomination never read the Bible, have at different times become evangelical Protestants, and from that hour have been diligent, devout, and affectionate students of the Bible. Does this prove that their former profession and creed were erroneous? It must be so, according to your argument.

And now a final word in regard to your slander of our Confession of Faith. And it is simply this, that your misstatements, so pertinaciously repeated, though greatly to your own detriment, are its best defence.

I. Your vain struggle to extricate yourself from the difficulties of your argument on the Jewish Sanhedrim as an infallible judge of controversy, moves one's compassion. Having been driven to the alternative (on your own principles) of justifying the crucifixion of our blessed Lord, or of rejecting the doctrine of Infallibility, you say "even in the conspiracy against his life, when Caiaphas declared it expedient that one man should die for the people," the Evangelist adds, that " this he spoke *not* of himself; but being *the High Priest of that year*, he prophesied that Jesus should die for the nation." John xi. 15. Then you plainly mean to say that as Caiaphas delivered a true prophecy as High Priest, he was infallible in doctrine. Now in the same council, by the advice of the same High Priest, it was determined that Christ should die; and we are told that (John xi. 53.) "*from that day forth they took council together to put Him* (Christ) *to death.*" Either then, (by your argument,) the High Priest was infallible in *the prophecy*, and *fallible in the decree*, that is, fallible and infallible at the same time; or else Christ was righteously condemned.

You proceed thus: "You ask me then, was the tribunal appointed by Almighty God in the old law, fallible or infallible? Answer; It was infallible, until it was superseded by *Him*, to whom " was given all power in heaven and earth." Did they decide wrong?—Answer; They decided wrong, because Christ had already *proved to them, that* he was the Messiah, and they shut their eyes against the *evidence of truth*. The term of their commission had virtually *expired*." Here then, you admit "*that this tribunal was infallible until it was superseded.*" When was it superseded? Was it superseded *before the death of Christ?* Was it not *after* this decree, that Christ died, and in the act of breathing out his soul unto death, said " IT IS FINISHED?" Was it not *after* this that he arose from the dead, instituted Christian Baptism, and commissioned the Apostles " to go into all the world, and preach the Gospel to every creature?" Then, was this tribunal superseded at the time of that decree? On what a precipice's brow do you stand, rather than give up your fatal system!

Probably, afraid of this dreadful dilemma, you attempt to explain by adding—"*the term of their commission had* VIRTUALLY *expired!*" But what do you mean by *virtually* expired? Either it had, or had not, expired. If it had *actually* expired, why do you say *virtually*— only? If it had not actually expired, it was still existing, and hence by your reasoning, infallible; and therefore we are again brought to the horrible conclusion, that Christ was righteously put to death.

You admit that "a tribunal" (for example the Church of Rome or its Pope and Council) "may be *superseded when it is proved to them that they shut their eyes against the evidence of the truth;*" consequently your church may be superseded, and of course lose its infallibility. How striking in this connexion does the Apostle Paul's warning to the *Roman Church* appear, especially as he by divine inspiration was comparing the *Jewish* with the *Roman Church.* "And if some of the branches be broken off, and thou, being a wild-olive tree, wert graffed in among them, and with them partakest of the root and fatness of the olive tree; boast not against the branches.— But if thou boast, thou bearest not the root, but the root thee. Thou wilt say then, the branches were broken off, that I might be graffed in. Well; because of unbelief they were broken off, and thou standest by faith. Be not high minded, but fear: for if God spared not the natural branches, *take heed* lest he also spare not thee." Rom. 11. chapter.

This passage proves, without a question, that the Church of Rome *may* be cast off, like the Jewish Church. And here we see the presumption of your church, in first calling herself supreme and universal, and then contending that if *she* fails, *the universal Church fails!* The universal, the true Church of Christ cannot fail; and the only way to prove that it can, is to prove that the Church of Rome means the only true and universal Church.

II. You have not even attempted to answer the body of my arguments on the "Apocryphal Books." For example, why did the Jews reject them? especially as they had (you say) "an infallible tribunal until superseded by the coming of Christ!" Why did our Lord and his apostles sanction their rejection of them? Why, for several centuries after the death of Christ, are ancient writers, and the earliest catalogues silent about them? Why do some of these catalogues explicitly exclude them from the canon? *It is a fact that the oldest Syriac version does not contain these books.* I assert also the following propositions concerning these books, and shall prove them, if you dispute them.

1st. They possess no authority whatever, either external or internal, to procure them admission into the canon of Scripture.

2d. They contain many things which are fabulous, contradictory, and directly at variance with the canonical Scriptures.

3d. They contain passages, which are in themselves false, absurd, and incredible.

4th. They do not even claim to be inspired. And yet they are made by your "infallible church" a part of the Holy Word of God!

III. You seem to be utterly unwilling to meet the question which was put to you in the words of the Rev. Mr. M'Guire. He allowed " THAT THE CATHOLIC HAS TO EXERCISE HIS PRIVATE JUDGMENT UPON

THE SCRIPTURE PROOFS OF THE AUTHORITY OF THE CHURCH." Dr. Milner says in his " End of Controversy," chapter 13, " Hence it is as clear as noon-day light, that by solving this one question, *which is the true Church?* you will at once solve every question of religious controversy that ever has, or that ever can be agitated." " It is agreed upon then, that all we have to do, by way of discovering the true church, is to find out which of the rival churches, or communions, is peculiarly One, Holy, Catholic, and Apostolic." " Yes, my dear sir, these marks of the true church are so plain in themselves, and so evidently point it out, *that fools cannot err*, as the Prophet foretold, Isa. xxxv. 8, in their road to it. They are the *flaming beacons*, which for ever shine on *the mountain at the top of the mountains of the Lord's house, Isai. 22.*"

Bellarmine also thus writes:

"Dicimus ergo, notas Ecclesiæ, quast adferemus, non facere evidentiam veritatis simpliciter, quia alioqui non esset articulus fidei, hanc ecclesiam esse veram ecclesiam; neque ulli invenirentur qui id negarent, sicut nemo invenitur, qui neget sententias, quas Mathematici demonstrant, sed tamen efficiunt evidentiam credibilitatis, juxta illud, Psalm 92.— "Testimonia tua credibilia facta sunt nimis." Apud eos autem, qui admittunt Scripturas divinas, et historias, ac Patrum veterum scripta, faciunt etiam evidentiam veritatis. Tametsi enim articulorum fidei veritas non potest nobis esse evidens absolute, tamen potest esse evidens ex hypothesi, id est, supposita veritate Scripturarum; quod enim a scriptura evidenter deducitur, est evidenter verum, suppositis Scripturis.

We say, therefore, that the marks of the church which we shall adduce do not plainly (or of themselves) constitute the evidence of truth, because otherwise it would not be an article of faith *that such a church is the true church*, nor could any persons be found who would deny that article, just as no person can be found who will deny the points which the mathematicians demonstrate. Yet they (the marks of the church) constitute the *evidence of credibility* according to the 92d Psalm. "*Thy testimonies are very credible.*" But among those who admit the divine Scriptures and histories, and the writings of the ancient Fathers, they constitute the evidence of truth. For although the truth of the articles of faith is not *absolutely* evident, yet it is evident *by hypothesis*, that is, the truth of the Scriptures being admitted; for *whatever is evidently deduced from the Scriptures*, is evidently true, the Scriptures being admitted. Chap. 3. Book 4. concerning the marks of the church.

Such are the admissions of your standard writers. Then it is acknowledged, that the marks of the true church are not self-evident, but that the proofs of them must be *deduced from the sacred Scriptures*. It is also acknowledged that there is *one subject* on which *private judgment* must be exercised, viz. *In finding out from the word of God, the marks of the true church. All the passages* of the word of God, then, that go to show which is the true church, are to be judged of by private judgment. There are fifteen marks of a true church mentioned by Bellarmine, viz. 1. "*The name Catholic.* 2. *Antiquity.* 3. *Duration.* 4. *Amplitude of Believers.* 5. *The succession of Bishops.* 6. *Agreement in doctrine with the primitive church.* 7. *Union of the members among themselves and with the Head.* 8. *Sanctity of doctrine.* 9. *Efficacy of the doctrine.* 10. *Holiness of life.* 11. *The glory of miracles.* 12. *The light of*

Prophecy. 13. *Confession of adversaries*. 14. *The unhappy end of the church's enemies*. 15. *Temporal felicity*." These marks must be found out, before you know whether the Greek, or Episcopal, or Roman, or Presbyterian, or any other church, be the true church. But a very large amount of Scripture is to be interpreted in order *to find* the true church. For example, to make out the 6th mark, a man must know what the doctrines of the Primitive church were, (in a word must know the whole word of God) before he can compare its doctrines with those of the churches now existing.

So, too, in finding the 8th mark, " sanctity of doctrine." Bellarmine tells us, " The church is said to be holy, because its profession contains nothing false as to doctrine of faith, nothing unjust as to doctrine of morals." It is true Dr. Milner says (as quoted above) "*these marks of the church are so plain in themselves, and so evidently pointed out, that fools cannot err in their road to it.*" But when you come to examine the proofs which are brought from the Scripture, they will be found as a whole to be less clear than the body of Scripture is, and far less so than those portions of the word of God on which fundamental doctrines and practical duties rest.

If *private interpretation* is ruinous in the use of all other Scripture, why is it not ruinous here? If *private interpretation* is sufficient to explore the whole word of God, in order to find out the true Church, why is it not sufficient for the rest? And if truth stands out as clear as the mountain tops, so that the fool cannot err, in whatever relates to the church, how does it become suddenly and impenetrably dark in all things relating to Jesus and salvation, to sin, and holiness, to all doctrine, and all duty? If *private interpretation* may, with moral certainty, and indisputable credibility, lay the foundation of your whole system, why may it not avail for the whole volume of truth, and the whole catalogue of doctrine? Here, then, by the admission of your own writers, *private interpretation* is the only guide in a search after salvation, and all the articles of faith; for you say, there is no salvation out of the true Church, and the true Church alone teaches infallibly the articles of faith; and private interpretation must find out the true Church! Is not this, then, a ruinous chasm; a palpable contradiction; a most disingenuous and deceitful argument?

It may simplify and enforce the above remarks to give the following dialogue between a Romanist and a Protestant, extracted from an able work on the subject of infallibility.

Papist. I pity your condition, Sir, to see you live at such uncertainties for your religion, and obstinately refuse to consult that living oracle and infallible judge, whom God hath placed in his church, to decide all controversies in faith and worship.

Protestant. Sir, I thank you for your charity; and though I do not find myself so uncertain as I perceive you think I am, yet I should be glad of such an infallible guide as you talk of, if I knew where to find him.

Papist. He is to be found in the church of Rome; for that is the church which is the pillar and ground of the truth; there is St. Peter's chair, whom Christ made the supreme governor of his church.

whom he commanded to feed his lambs and his sheep; that rock on whom Christ promised to build His church, and that the gates of Hell should not prevail against it; and, therefore, in communion with this church, and in obedience to the supreme pastor of it, you cannot err.

Protestant. But pray how shall I be sure of this?

Papist. Do you ask that now, when I have referred you to such plain texts of Scripture for the proof of it?

Protestant. Will you allow me then, to interpret these texts according to my own private judgment? And why then may I not use my judgment in other matters? for I think all the articles of my creed are as plain in Scripture, as that the Pope or church of Rome is the supreme infallible judge; and, indeed, if I must stand to my own judgment in this matter, I can find no such thing in these texts as you have alleged.

Papist. Your own judgment! No, by no means; this causes all the heresies in the world, that men will presume to judge for themselves.

Protestant. What course must I take then?

Papist. You must stand to the judgment of the church, which cannot err; and whatever heretics say, she will tell you, that these texts prove the church's infallibility.

Protestant. Hold, Sir, what is it we are to prove?

Papist. That the church is infallible.

Protestant. And this I must prove from Scripture?

Papist. Yes.

Protestant. And must not rely on *my own judgment* for the sense of Scripture, but on the interpretation of the church?

Papist. Right, this is the true Catholic way.

Protestant. That is, I must take the church's word that she is infallible?

Papist. No, you must believe the Scriptures, which say so.

Protestant. But I must believe the Scripture, not because I understand this to be the sense of it, but because the church so expounds it?

Papist. Right, for heretics expound it otherwise.

Protestant. And what is it *then but to take the church's word for her own infallibility; to believe it because she says it herself,* or *to believe it because she makes the Scripture say it? And so then you can never be infallibly certain of your church's infallibility; —and of course you can never be infallibly certain that its teaching is true.* Then as to any doctrine, *say the divinity of Christ,* Protestants believe it, because the inspired word of God in its plain and obvious sense clearly teaches it. Papists believe it because the church says so—and they believe the church to be infallible because they think the plain and obvious sense of Scripture teaches it. In a word the faith of the Protestant is resolved into the infallibility of Christ and his Apostles;—whereas the faith of Papists is resolved into the infallibility of Popes and councils. " Whether it be right in the sight of God to hearken unto you more than unto God, judge thou!" Peter, Acts iv. 19.

IV. *It is agreed between us, that one great end of the infallible rule of faith established by Christ, was to determine disputes in his church.* (See rule 2d.) One of the artifices of your reasoning upon the rule of faith, is to insist that no rule is infallible which does not finally settle all disputes, and since the Bible fails to settle all disputes it cannot be, (you say) an infallible rule of faith. Now all that you can say of your boasted rule of faith (unless you resort to fraud or force) is, that it settles disputes among all who will submit to it. The same in the strictest sense is true also of the Bible. But if men will not submit to the Bible, then disputes cannot be determined by the Bible. If men will resist its authority, and pervert its true meaning, then we say there is no remedy on earth. You, on the contrary insist that there is. We say if the Bible is not sufficient, nothing is, and they who go beyond it and resort to other means, are guilty of fraud, usurpation, and rebellion against God. In a word,—I shall prove that the *method of determining disputes in the church of Rome, is anti-scriptural, and anti-Christian, and, therefore not that infallible rule established by Christ.*

1st. In order to secure a pretended and apparent union, you draw a distinction between DOCTRINES and OPINIONS. All those points upon which the church is divided, however important, are called *opinions;* and those are called *doctrines* upon which you are agreed. Of course, you are always *agreed* upon doctrines or points of faith. Thus, for example, it is a cardinal doctrine with you, that your church is infallible. But where this infallibility is located, is a matter of *opinion,* or in other words, it is a thing about which you are not *agreed.* The least observation will convince any one, that infallibility is useless, unless you can locate it. Suppose, for example, I wish to bring a suit before the Supreme Court of the United States. When I ask, " who compose this court," and " where this court holds its sessions," I seek for information which it is indispensable for me to possess, in order to secure a decision. Now what if it should be replied, " there is a Supreme Court appointed by the President of the United States, with the approval of the Senate, which is supreme judge in certain controversies; but who compose this court, and where it holds its sessions, is a matter of *opinion.*" " It is not *agreed who they* are, or *where* they meet; but this court, and this alone, takes cognizance of such cases!" Is it not equally absurd to say that there is a living infallible judge of controversies in the church of Rome; but *who* he *is,* or *where* he has his *seat,* we are not *agreed;* it is a matter of *opinion;* we cannot tell? It seems to be the *opinion* of Mr. Hughes, that the Pope and the council united are infallible; a host of writers are of *opinion* that infallibility is seated in the Pope; and another host commit it to the church universal. But it is not a *doctrine* in any case; it is only a matter of *opinion.* Again the church of Rome has for ages been divided upon the question, " whether the Virgin Mary was conceived in the womb of her mother, with the same purity that is attributed to Christ's conception in *her* womb." Multitudes contend for both sides of the question. If it be true that she was thus conceived that is, *immaculately,* then the Bible account on the whole subject of sin is utterly false. It is

U

therefore a question of immense importance. Yet even the Council of Trent were divided on this question, and the heated disputants were finally left unsatisfied, and the question unsettled; and finding it could not be made a *doctrine* without a schism, they finally agreed to decline any interference with the point in dispute, and leave it *undecided and free.* Now by such a procedure your church holds out a show of union, when in fact evangelical Protestants do really agree more in doctrines that are essential to salvation, than the members of the church of Rome. As to agreement in " doctrines that are damnable," we confess we covet it not; and in this respect, yield to you the unenviable distinction of such a concert.

Here let me add, that this is a very curious process for an infallible church. Why leave some points untouched? Why ignorant; or if *informed* about them, why *silent*, on some points, and infallibly certain and fiercely zealous about others? Does the Holy Ghost enlighten only the "hemisphere" of truth to the eye of Rome? Do "light and darkness thus dwell together" in the Roman Councils? Why, for example, are you so infallibly certain that *infants cannot be saved without the baptism of a Priest, and that his baptism is null without his intention in administering it,* and yet not be able to say whether *all* the race were conceived in sin? Why hold one part as *opinions* and another part as *doctrines?* Have you not said (see letter 3d, tenth head) "*that Christ never inculcated the belief of an opinion?*" Why then as *all are doctrines,* do you not *teach* all? If you are *ignorant of some*, then how are you infallible? If you *withhold* your decisions for fear of schisms, is not your union a fiction or a fraud?

2d. *But when this passive way of settling disputes fails, you have a more vigorous method,* at which we have before hinted. It is worthy of a more distinct and ample exhibition. And here I refer to your own Bellarmine, who (as you informed me) is a standard writer with you, who was the nephew of a Pope (Marcellus the 2d;) was a cardinal in the church; and, above all, whose works received the sanction of the Pope. I extract parts of the 21st and 22d chapters of his 3d book on the laity.

Posse hæreticos ab ecclesia damnatos temporalibus pœnis etiam morte mulctari.

Nos igitur breviter ostendemus hæreticos incorrigibiles ac præsertim relapsos, posse ac debere ab ecclesia rejici, et a secularibus potestatibus temporalibus pœnis atque ipsa etiam morte mulctari.

Primo probatur scripturis. Probatur secundo sententiis et legibus imperatorum, quas ecclesia semper probavit. Probatur tertio legibus ecclesiæ. Probatur quarto testimoniis Patrum. Probatur ultimo ratione naturali. Primo hæretici excommunicari jure possunt, ut omnes fatentur, ergo et occidi. Probatur consequentia quia excommunicatio est major pœna, quam mors temporalis.

CHAPTER 21st.

That heretics condemned by the church may be punished with temporal penalties, and even with death. We will briefly show that the church has the *power, and it is her duty,* to cast off incorrigible heretics, especially those who have relapsed, and that the secular power ought to inflict on such temporal punishments, and even death itself. 1st. This may be proved from the Scriptures. 2d. It is proved from the opinions and laws of the Emperors, *which the church has always approved.* 3d. *It is proved by the laws of the church.* 4th. It is proved by the testimony of the fathers. Lastly. It is proved from natural reason. For *first :* It is owned by all, that heretics, may of

Secundo experientia docet non esse aliud remedium, nam ecclesia paulatim progressa est et omnia remedia experta; primo solum excommunicabat deinde addidit mulctam pecuniariam; tam exilium, ultimo coacta est ad mortem venire: mittere illos in locum suum. *Tertio*, falsarii omnium judicio merentur mortem; at hæretici falsarii sunt verbi Dei. *Quarto*, gravius est non servare fidem hominem Deo, quam feminam viro; sed hoc morte punitur, cur non illud : *Quinto*, tres causæ sunt propter quas ratio docet homines occidendos esse ; prima causa est ne mali bonis noceant; secunda est, ut paucorum supplicio multi corrigantur. *Multi enim quos impunitas faciebat torpentes supplicia proposita excitant; et nos quotidie idem videmus fieri in locis ubi viget Inquisitio.* Denique hæreticis obstinatis beneficium est quod de hac vita tollantur; nam quo diutius vivunt eo plures errores excogitant, plures pervertunt, et majorem sibi damnationem acquirunt.

right be excommunicated—of course they may be put to death. This consequence is proved because excommunication is a greater punishment than temporal death. *Secondly. Experience proves that there is no other remedy ;* for the church has step by step tried all remedies —first,—excommunication alone ; then pecuniary penalties; afterward banishment; *and lastly has been forced to put them to death; to send them to their own place.* *Thirdly*. All allow that forgery deserves death; but heretics are guilty of forgery of the word of God. *Fourthly*. A breach of faith by man toward God, is a greater sin, than of a wife with her husband. But a woman's unfaithfulness is punished with death; why not a heretic's! *Fifthly*. There are three grounds on which reason shows that heretics should be put to death: the 1st is, lest the wicked should injure the righteous—2d, that by the punishment of a *few, many* may be reformed. FOR MANY WHO WERE MADE TORPID BY IMPUNITY, ARE ROUSED BY THE FEAR OF PUNISHMENT; AND THIS WE DAILY SEE IS THE RESULT WHERE THE INQUISITION FLOURISHES. *Finally*, It is a benefit to obstinate heretics to remove them from this life ; for the longer they live the more errors they invent, the more persons they mislead : and the greater damnation do they treasure up to themselves.

CAPUT 22d.
Solvuntur objectiones.

Superest argumenta Lutheri atque aliorum hæreticorum diluere. Argument, primum, ab experientia totius ecclesiæ: *Ecclesia* inquit Lutherus *ab initio sui usque huc nullum cambussit hæreticum* ergo non videtur esse voluntas Spiritus ut comburantur.

Respondeo, argumentum hoc optimè probat, non sententiam, sed imperitiam, vel impudentiam Lutheri : nam cum infiniti propemodum, vel combusti, vel aliter necati fuerint, aut id ignoravit Lutherus, et tunc imperitus est, aut non ignoravit, et impudens, ac mendax esse convincitur : nam quod hæretici sint saepe ab ecclesia combusti, ostendi potest, si adducamus pauca exempla de multis.

Argumentum secundum ; experientia testatur non profici terroribus. Respondeo, experientia est in contrarium ; nam Donatistae, Manichaei, et Albigenses armis profligati, et extincti sunt.

CHAPTER 22d.
Objections Answered.

It remains to answer the objections of Luther and other heretics. Argument 1st. *From* the history of the church at large. *The church*, says Luther, *from the beginning, even to this time, has never burned a heretic.* Therefore it does not seem to be the mind of the Holy Spirit, that they should be burned! I reply, this argument admirably proves not the sentiment, but the ignorance, or impudence of Luther ; FOR AS ALMOST AN INFINITE NUMBER WERE EITHER BURNED! OR OTHERWISE PUT TO DEATH, Luther either did not know it, and was therefore *ignorant ;* or if he knew it, he is convicted of impudence and falsehood—for *that heretics were often burned by the church may be proved by adducing a few from many examples.*

Argument 2d. *Experience shows that terror is not useful* (in such cases.) I reply, EXPERIENCE PROVES THE CONTRA-

Argumentum decimum tertium: Dominus attribuit ecclesiæ gladium spiritus, quod est verbum dei, non autem gladium ferri; immo Petro volenti gladio ferreo ipsum defendere, ait: *Mitte gladium tuum in vag'nam.* Joan 18. Respondeo, ecclesia sicut habet Principes Ecclesiasticos, et seculares, qui sunt quasi duo ecclesiæ brachia, ita duos habet gladios, spiritualem, et materialem, et ideo, quando manus dextera glaudio spirituali non potuit hæreticum convertere, invocat auxilium brachii sinistri, ut gladio ferreo hæreticos coerceat.

Argumentum decimum octavum: Numquam Apostoli brachium seculare contra hæreticos invocaverunt. Respondet S. Augustinus in epist. 50 et alibi, Apostolos id non fecisse, quia nullus tunc erat Christianus Princeps, quem invocarent. At postquam tempore Constantini........Ecclesia auxilium secularis brachii imploravit.

BY—FOR THE DONATISTS, MANICHEANS, AND ALBIGENSES WERE ROUTED, AND ANNIHILATED BY ARMS.

Argument 13th. The Lord attributes to the church "*the sword of the Spirit, which is the word of God;*" bu. not the material sword, nay, He said to Peter, who wished to defend him with a material sword, "*put up thy sword into the scabbard.*" John 18th. I answer; *As the church has ecclesiastical and secular princes, who are her two arms; so she has two swords, the spiritual and material; and therefore when her right hand is unable to convert a heretic with the sword of the Spirit, she invokes the aid of the left hand, and coerces heretics with the material sword.*

Argument 18th. The Apostles never invoked the secular arm against heretics. Answer, (according to St. Augustine, in letter 50 and elsewhere) *The Apostles did it not, because there was no Christian Prince whom they could call on for aid. But afterwards in Constantine's time,.........the church called in the aid of the secular arm.*

The mere translation of these infamous passages, discloses the very "mystery of iniquity" which for ages has been working in the church of Rome. Here we have the extraordinary fact, that the Old Testament and the New, the laws of the Church, the testimony of the Fathers, the history of the Church, reason, the good of *other* men, and even *mercy* towards the unhappy victims, are all adduced in one cumulative argument to prove that the church of Rome *has the authority, and that it is her duty to put to death men who differ incorrigibly from her in their doctrines!* You will hardly say, *these are opinions;* for here, we find, that he adduces, 1st. *ecclesiastical law!* Now can you say that the church did not burn these heretics, but that the civil power did it, for we see, 2d. that "*the civil power* (as stated above,) *is one of the arms of the church, and its sword,* one *of the swords of the church;*" and *that* " *the church has always approved*" the edicts and acts of emperors in this way—and "*that heretics were often burned by the church!*" Perhaps you have read the life of George Wishart, who was martyred by your Cardinal Beaton, of bloody memory. In it, you will find that when the cardinal failed to secure from the Regent the condemnation of Wishart for heresy, without a fair trial, he returned for answer, that he had sufficient authority to condemn heretics without the interposition of the civil power; and accordingly he actually tried, condemned, and burned Wishart, in despite of the distinct prohibition of the Regent of the country. 3d. This, your standard author, calls Luther a fool or a knave, for denying that the church had burned heretics. He says, "*almost an infinite number of heretics were burned by the church, and instances the Donatists, Manicheans, and Albigenses* '

4th. He tells us that the only reason why the church did not burn heretics before Constantine, was that *there was no prince who would do it ;*—but as soon as she could have it done, she did it. Query. Why is it not done in the United States? It is done in Spain! I beg Mr. Hughes to tell us why! 5th. And this is the *unchangeable church!* Of course, she is the same *now* that she was *then*,—and would, if she could, do the same now she ever did. She does not lack the *will*, but the *power;* and wo to this land if that power be ever acquired! 6th. This passage may be compared with the long extract which I gave in letter No. 8. from the Great Lateran Council decreeing the destruction of heretics, which you so strangely passed, on a former occasion.

Illustration from History—Massacre of St. Bartholomew.

Mezerai's History of France, fol. vol. 2. p. 1098. (Paris 1646.) During two months, this horrible and cruel tempest overspread France, in some places more, and in some less, and destroyed not less than 25,000 persons. Davila, page 275, says, 'The report constantly prevailed, that in the course of a few days not fewer than 40,000 of the Huguenots had perished.

The holy father and all his court displayed a great rejoicing, and went in solemn procession to the church of St. Louis, to render thanks to God for so happy a success.

The following extracts from the letter of Pope Pius V. book 3. let. 45. incontestably proves that the massacre of St. Bartholomew owes its origin to the vindictive councils of the Popes. " To our most Dear Son in Christ, Charles, the most Christian King of the French. The public joy of this city has very much augmented our pleasure, which at the first certain intelligence of so great a victory, rejoiced and does rejoice. The fruit of this victory consists in this, that by a just animadversion, the wicked heretics, the common enemies being removed out of the way, its former peace and tranquillity may be restored to that kingdom." Thuanus in his History, book 53, tells us, that " on the news of this massacre being received at Rome, it was instantly resolved that the Pope with the Cardinals should straightway go to the church of St. Mark, and should solemnly return thanks to the Lord for so great a blessing conferred upon the Roman See and the Christian world, that thence a jubilee should be published in the whole Christian world. Its causes were declared to be, that they should return thanks to God for the destruction of the enemies of the truth and of the church in France," &c. &c.

Finally, Fleuri in his Ecclesiastical History, vol. 23. book 173. p. 557. tells us, Gregory the XIII., only regarding the good which he thought likely to result from this, to the Catholic religion in France, ordered a procession, in which he himself joined, from the church of St. Peter's to the church of St. Louis, to return thanks to God for so happy a result; and to perpetuate the memory of this event, he caused several medals to be struck, wherein he himself is represented on the one side, and on the other side an angel carrying a cross in one hand, and a sword in the other, exterminating the heretics.

Allow me to add one item more to this delectable catalogue.—

Among the extracts from Bellarmine given above, there is this distinct approval of the inquisition: "WE DAILY SEE THE SAME RESULTS (viz. the good done in putting an end to heresy) IN PLACES WHERE THE INQUISITION FLOURISHES." You are not a stranger, I suppose, to Joannes Devotus. His INSTITUTIONS have the highest sanctions of your Church at Rome itself, *as containing nothing contrary to faith or good morals.* Of course, his authority will not be questioned; and as his writings are of comparatively recent date, (1793) they give us glances at the Roman Church in our own times. I omit the original, because so much has been already introduced. But it is open to your inspection, if you have it not in your possession, vol. 4th, tit. 8th, page 101—118, under the head, " *Inquisitors of Heretical pravity,*" he gives the following statements. "The cause of instituting the tribunal, called the Inquisition, was this. At first every Bishop in his own diocese, or a number of Bishops assembled in a Provincial Council, made inquisition of those errors which arose in the diocese or Province; but the more weighty matters were *always referred* to the Apostolical seat (Rome;) and thus every Bishop or Provincial Council took care to bring to its proper issue whatever was decreed by the Apostolical See. But in process of time, when greater evils pressed, it became necessary for the Pope to send legates into those regions in which heresy had long and widely spread, that they might assist the Bishops in restraining the audacity of abandoned men, and in deterring Christians from foreign and depraved doctrines. But when new errors daily sprung up, and the number of heretics was greatly increased—seeing that the legates could not always be at hand, nor apply the proper remedy, it was determined to INSTITUTE A STANDING TRIBUNAL, that should always be present, *and at all times, and in every country,* should devote their minds to preserving the soundness of the faith, and to restraining and expelling heresies as they arose. Thus it was, that the *Inquisitors were first appointed to perform the office of Vicars to the Holy See.* But as in a matter so weighty as the preservation of the purity of the faith *the Inquisitors* needed that close union of mind, and sentiment, which is proper to the Apostolical See, as the centre of unity, *there was instituted, at Rome by the Popes an assembly or congregation of Cardinals in which the Pope presides. This congregation is the head of all Inquisitors, over the whole world; to it they all refer their more difficult matters; and its authority and judgment are final.* It is rightly and wisely ordered that the Pope's office and power should sustain this institution. For he is the centre of unity and head of the church: and to him Christ has committed plenary power to feed, teach, rule, and govern all Christians." Now from this it appears, 1. That according to the government adopted at Rome, the Inquisition is a constituent part of their system;—and that it is established wherever they have such a foot-hold as to make it possible. Buchanan found one even at Goa, in the East Indies Whether there be one in this country, is a *matter* of *opinion.* But it is *sound doctrine* to have it if possible. 2. The Pope is the head of the Inquisition over the whole world—and the congregation of the cardinals at Rome is the supreme court of the Inquisition; of course it is to the Pope, and his cardinals, we are to look as the authors, originally, of the unparalleled enormities which have characterized this bloodiest institution in the history of the world.

Let me here give another word of history.

A critical History of the Spanish Inquisition, by D. J. A. Llorente, formerly Secretary of the Inquisition, &c. &c., translated from the Spanish manuscript in the presence of the author, by Alexis Pellier. 2d edit. (Paris 1818.)

It is the Inquisition which has ruled in Spain from the year 1481 to the present day, of which I undertake to write the history, *Tom.* 1. p. 140.

Recapitulation of all the victims condemned and burnt,	31,912
Burned in effigy,	17,695
Placed in a state of penance with rigorous punishments	291,450
Total,	341,057

Tom. 4. p. 271.

When the French obtained possession of Spain, under Joseph Bonaparte, Llorente obtained permission to examine all the archives of the Inquisition. His work, therefore, is the most authentic that is extant. When we come to speak of these subjects as principal, and not illustrative topics, we design, Providence permitting, to make such disclosures of its history as truth demands. But now let it suffice to say that this is the institution which Bellarmine praises, as a fine method of settling disputes! On this plan we grant you that it is easy to "*determine disputes*" by putting an end to all the disputants on one side of the question. And now Sir, having at some length stated the methods used by the church of Rome, I ask if the inference is not irresistible, that yours is a rule of fraud, and of force; abhorrent to right reason, mercy and truth; and as such, that it is an insult to our holy religion to say it was instituted by Jesus Christ, or that yours is an infallible rule?

In regard to "the reference," I shall be prepared to meet you, Providence permitting, on Friday the 10th of May. On Monday the 6th, and until the evening of the 9th, I expect to be absent from the city.

Your call for the name of my informant is not candid. I am authorized to give it (as I have already informed you,) whenever the Bishop shall ask it. I now inquire, does he or does he not demand it?

Your attempt to pervert my statements on this subject, is unworthy of the character you profess to bear. From first to last, it was stated by me in the form of a question; and the confidence expressed in the truth of the testimony was not mine, but that of my worthy informant.

It is my purpose, in the next letter, to meet your call for a definition of the Protestant religion, and to proceed to the discussion of other topics connected with the controversy; holding myself in readiness at the same time, to meet with promptness whatever you may say in addition, on the rule of faith. Yours, &c.

JOHN BRECKINRIDGE.

P. S. I owe an apology to the Editor of the paper for the length of the present number, it will be apparent however, to the reader, that a large amount of space is occupied by the Latin extracts which have been introduced. J. B

CONTROVERSY. No. XV.

RULE OF FAITH.

Philadelphia, May 10, 1833.

To the Rev. John Breckinridge.

Rev. Sir,—If there was any thing wanting to show the weakness of the Protestant principle in reference to the rule of faith, it is found in your attempt to supply the absence of argument, by the introduction of reproach. I wished to spare the feelings of our readers, in regard to the crimes which history has ascribed to Catholics and to Protestants on the subject of religious persecution. Men of education, on both sides, have long since come to the conclusion, that although persecution forms no part of the religion of Jesus Christ, yet, unhappily, there are few denominations that have *not* persecuted *when they had the power*. But all are agreed, that *this charge* comes with a peculiarly bad grace from either John Calvin or any of his disciples. There is blood upon his memory; and it looks doubly dark and deep when associated with the recollections that he set up to be A MAN OF GOD, and a REFORMER of the church of Christ. Bellarmine, indeed, sanctioned the right of Catholic princes to wield the sword of civil power against persons condemned by the church of heresy;—but so far as he is concerned, the fact exhibits only the *theory* of persecution and the sanction of his pen. Calvin's was the sanction of the pen and faggot, the theory and the *practice*. The example of the master has been faithfully imitated by his followers. And, appealing to the decision of impartial history, I defy you to show a single state in Europe or America, in which Calvinists or Presbyterians conceded free *toleration* from the moment they possessed civil power, whether derived by grant from the crown, as in New England, or acquired, as in Europe, by rebellion and usurpation!

If then, history does not contain one single exception, on this head, I would leave it to the good sense of our readers, whether it is wise, whether it is modest in you to charge Catholics with persecution, and that too, in the name of a sect which has stained the soil of every country in which it ruled, with the blood of the Protestant, as well as Catholic, victims of its bigotry and intolerance! It would seem that it is a crime for any *other* denomination to do what Presbyterians have never failed of doing *when they had the power*. I do not perceive by what *divine right* Presbyterians claim the MONOPOLY of persecution. If it be a privilege at all, which I deny, *Catholics* possessed the priority of title. *They* did not spring up in the 16th century of the Christian church, to dispute the faith of Protestants. But on the contrary, the Protestants then came into existence to dispute with them, for something more than " the kingdom which is not of this world ;"—viz. for their churches, their castles, their towns, and their kingdoms. It is a fact, that at the rise of the Reformation so called, Catholics possessed every thing; and that Protestants *as such* possessed nothing, save their private individual estates. How came they then to possess themselves of public power and property which did not belong to them? Did they give any equivalent? They had none to give. Did the Catholics resign them *voluntarily?* No, certainly:—if they had, they would have escaped the charge of *persecution*. They were in possession—*defence* was their *natural* privilege. Kingdoms were tranquil and united in the profession of the same religion, whenever the heresy began, and the question was, whether it was the right of nations to extinguish the *spark*, or allow their institutions, civil and religious, to be consumed in the political conflagration which it never failed to excite. It was to illustrate this question, that Bellarmine embarked on the sea of political casuistry. He contended that the civil magistrates were, in the language of your standard of 1821, " nursing fathers of the church"—and it is a remarkable coincidence that he attempts to prove his position by reference to the *same texts* of Scripture by which the WESTMINSTER DIVINES, and the " adopting act of 1729," made it a *sin* for Presbyterians to " tolerate a false religion."

Bellarmine himself must be responsible for his opinions on this subject, which do not at all belong to the faith of the Catholic religion. He is a " standard writer," in treating of Catholic *doctrines*—of questions " de fide." But on points of political economy, or civil government, as they are not even " fere de fide," his pen was at liberty to ramble as well as that of any other individual. His reasoning on the question, appears to me as extravagant as it can be to you—and I am just as ready to reject it. For, you will observe that Catholics, as such, are responsible only for the *doctrines* of the CHURCH, and not for the private opinions of her members. Show me then the decree of any Council, or the bull of any Pope, proposing persecution as a part of *our religion*—and let *that document* be the proof of your charge.

Neither does the inquisition of Spain constitute any part of our religion. Of course you are at liberty to make it the theme of declamation as long as you please. If, however, you were questioned as to what the inquisition really is, I doubt much whether your information would not be found very defective. It would probably correspond with your knowledge of indulgences—" a bundle of licenses to commit sin."

With regard to the " Massacre of St. Bartholomew," I condemn it as much as you. It was a deed of blood and horror. But let the blame attach to *its authors*, Charles IX. and Catherine of Medicis, who favoured the Huguenots and Catholics, alternately, as their interests seemed to require. But to form a correct judgment of this sanguinary event, it is necessary to consider it in connexion with the events by which it was preceded. The Huguenots of France had committed many similar acts of barbarity. Davila relates that upon the death of Francis II. when *liberty of conscience was granted them*, besides burning churches and monasteries, they massacred people in the very streets of Paris. Heylin, a Protestant, relates that in time of a profound peace, they fell upon and MURDERED *the whole clergy* who composed the procession of Corpus Christi in the city of Pamiers; and afterwards committed similar outrages at Montauban, Rodez, Valence, &c. (Hist. Presb. l. ii.) It is known by the proclamation of Charles immediately after the massacre, that it was not on account of their religion, but to anticipate the conspiracy of Coligni and his associates—"*non religionis odia*, sed utne fariæ Coliniiet sociorum conjurationi obviam iret." ('Thuan. lib. lii.)

The Huguenots constituted a kind of independent party in the heart of the nation. They had their own treasury to support themselves in their wars *against their sovereigns*. And Admiral Coligni went so far, as to propose furnishing ten thousand Huguenots for the army —and declared that *he and they would be obliged to take up arms against the king himself*, if he declined this offer, and refused to aid the Protestants of Flanders !! (See Walsingham's Despatches quoted by Digges. 226.) Was it from St. Paul, that this chieftain of the Protestant party in France, learned to hold *this language* towards his sovereign? Here was a subject *dictating* to his king. Still, all this does not justify the horrible measure by which *that* king rid himself of *that* subject and his party. It furnishes, however, a different range of motives, besides those to which Protestants usually ascribe the massacre.

It is also certain that the king took infinite pains to make his subjects and foreign princes, especially the Pope, believe that in killing the Huguenots, he had only taken the necessary measures of self-defence to preserve his own life, together with the constitution and religion of his kingdom. (Thuan. l. ii. Maimb. l. vi.) And the Biographer of Gregory XIII. clearly shows that the deliverance of the French king from this *pretended* conspiracy, was the event for which public thanks were offered at Rome, and not for the massacre itself, as you have stated. (Pagi vol. vi. p. 729.) Again, in reference to the *number* of the slain, it is evident that your information has not kept pace with your zeal. Among the Huguenot writers, Perrifix reckons 100,000, Sully 70,000, Thuanus 30,000, La Popelirine 20,000, the Reformed Martyrologist 15,000, and you 40,000, "according to the *report* which prevailed." But the Martyrologist, wishing to be more *correctly* informed, procured from the ministers in the different towns where massacres had taken place, the names of those who had perished or were *supposed* to have perished ;—he published the result in 1582: and in all France he could discover the names of no more than 786 persons. (Caveirac, Dissertation xxxviii.)

It would be well, also, for you to understand that the Catholic clergy were the most active in protecting the Huguenots from the vengeance of popular fury. And that among other instances, the Bishop of Lisieux, a Dominican Friar, opposed the execution of the orders given in the name of the king—declaring "it is the duty of the good shepherd to lay down *his* life for the sheep, not to let *them* be slaughtered before his face. These (the Huguenots of his diocese) are my sheep, though they have gone astray, and I am resolved to run all hazards in protecting them." (Maimb.) But, Rev. Sir, are you not driven to great straits, when you give a dissertation on the horrors of the inquisition, the massacre of St. Bartholomew, &c. instead of *arguments* on the rule of faith ? These are stale topics. Your introduction of them was utterly uncalled for by the question, under discussion ; and it can have no other effect ; except to mislead ignorance, confirm prejudice, and inspire hatred. To do this is not a comely or benevolent office for a minister of the Gospel, which breathes but peace and charity.

If, however, Protestants were *immaculate* on the subject of persecution, you might have put forward this charge with some degree of consistency. But all the reformers persecuted when they had the power, and sanctioned it, when they had not. If, therefore, I give a few quotations and facts to prove this assertion, I hope that neither you nor our readers will be offended at an exposure to which your eyes are accustomed, but which you have made necessary. I do it not to increase the separation between Catholics and Protestants, which is already too great;—not in a spirit of bad feeling or retaliation, but simply to show that Protestants, if they are to be accountable for the deeds of *their* ancestors (and if *they* are not, I do not see why *we* should be) have no reason to boast of superiority on the subject of liberality and religious toleration. But, Rev. Sir, if your forefathers and mine have done those things *in the name* of religion, which religion *does not sanction*, I would rather have joined you in walking backwards, to cover their deeds with the mantle of oblivion, than be obliged to join you in exposing them. Still, painful as the task is, you have made it necessary, and it must be accomplished.

It is but right that I should begin with the Reformer of Geneva, Calvin himself. "Servetus," says he, "was cast into prison, whence he escaped, I know not how, and was wandering through Italy for about four months. At length, having, under evil auspices, come hither, he was arrested, AT MY INSTIGATION, by one of our Syndicts," (Calvini, Epist. et Respons. p. 294.) Again, (p. 290.) "The author (Servetus) is held in prison by our magistrates, and soon, I HOPE, to *suffer his punishment*."

In his letter to M. Du. Poët, he says, of those who differed from him in the interpretation of the Bible, "Pareils monstres doivent etre etouffes, comme fis ICI en l'execution de Michel Servet, Espagnol." That is, "they ought to be strangled, as was done HERE with the Spaniard, Michael Servetus."

This gentle Reformer would have strangled (etouffes) Gentilis, Okin, Blaudrat, and others, if they had not either *fled* or *retracted;* which they were *obliged* to do—to save their lives. Melancthon, Bullinger, and the Protestant clergy of Switzerland generally, and in *solemn session, approved of the faggot*, which consumed Servetus. Bucer declared that he should have been "torn limb from limb!"

John Knox, was ready to prove, "by the Prophets and plain Scriptures of God, what trees and generation they (the Catholics) be, to wit, unfruitful and rotten; APT FOR NOTHING BUT TO BE CAST INTO HELL FIRE." (Appellation, p. 30.)

Even the meek John Wesley as late as the year 1780, proclaimed that "they (Catholics) ought not to be tolerated, by any government, PROTESTANT, MAHOMETAN, or PAGAN."

Let us now look for the mild, tolerant, evangelical language of Luther: "If," says he, in his book against Sylvester Prieras, "we dispatch thieves by the *gallows*, highwaymen by the *sword*, HERETICS by *fire;* why do we not rather attack with ALL KINDS OF ARMS, these monsters of perdition, these Cardinals, these Popes, and all this sink of the Romish Sodom, which corrupts without ceasing, the church of God, and WASH OUR HANDS IN THEIR BLOOD."

In England the history of Protestant *toleration* has been written in statutes of similar tint. Protestants were burned alive for *heresy*, and Catholics " hanged, embowelled and quartered," because they would not become Protestants. To deny the supremacy of Henry VIII., or of his daughter, when she became head of the church, was quite enough to entitle any one to all the privileges of *martyrdom*.

Your old friend, Archbishop Usher, by way of showing his " authority among Romanists," entered a Catholic chapel with armed soldiers, seized the Priest in his vestments, and hewed down the crucifix. He and eleven other Protestant bishops, solemnly decided that " to give them (Catholics) a toleration, or to consent that they may freely exercise their religion, IS A GRIEVOUS SIN." (Plowden, vol. 1. c. 4.) In 1642, the same Usher extorted a promise from Charles I., *never to connive at Popery*—and *on this intolerant pledge*, administered to him the Sacrament. (Birch, p. 278-9.) Poor Charles little imagined that his Presbyterian subjects would entitle *himself* to a place in the martyrology of Protestant persecution.

But Presbyterians have persecuted greater men than *mere* kings. The learned Protestant, Grotius, in his dungeon, is an instance of it—in the Low Countries—where the Presbyterian Gomarists persecuted the Presbyterian Armenians with the most *deliberate* and unrelenting fury. If we turn our eyes to the Cromwellian ascendancy in Great Britain and Ireland, we shall see *what kind* of toleration Presbyterians practised. Dr. Taylor, (a Protestant, A. B. of Trinity College,) tells us, " that they (Puritans) employed BLOOD-HOUNDS to track the haunts of these devoted men (Catholic priests.) And that " during the latter part of the 17th and beginning of the 18th century, ' *Priest hunting*' was a favourite field sport in Ireland." (See Hist. Ireland, vol. 2. p. 52., Harper's Family Library.)

The Presbyterians, indeed, were themselves persecuted. But nothing could teach them mercy. The " Pilgrim fathers," fleeing from intolerance across the ocean, had scarcely landed on the rock of Plymouth, till they began to persecute each other. They put the Quakers to death without pity, " as pestilent heretics." (Hist. of Bapt. in New England, vol. 1. p. 329.) " Whipping," " branding," and " cutting off the right ear," were mitigated forms of punishment for the crime of heresy—that is, for *interpreting the Bible for themselves*. In a word, *show, in all history*, a *single instance*, in which Presbyterians possessed civil jurisdiction over ten square miles of the surface of this earth, without practising intolerance and persecution, within the limits of their territory!

If, on the other hand, Catholics had been as persecuting as you pretend, could they not have rid the world of the first Reformers, as Calvin rid Geneva of the Spaniard? I will take but one or two cases in point. The same Dr. Taylor already quoted, says, " It is but justice to this maligned body (the Catholics—he might well say, ' *maligned*,') to add, that on the three occasions of their obtaining the upper hand, (in Ireland) *they never injured a single person in life or limb, for professing a different religion from their own.*"— And Thomas Campbell, the Poet, (Morning Chronicle, London, February 11, 1833,) says, the toleration practised by the Catholics of Poland, "ought to make *Protestants* blush."

Again, the Catholic colony of Maryland unfurled the first banner of religious freedom that ever floated on the breeze of Heaven. The charitable Dr. Miller, however, denies them even the merit of good *motives* in this. He seems to have had *access to their intentions*, and tells us accordingly, that they did it " from *policy.*" But their " policy" in this regard availed them little,—and the following testimony from Jefferson's notes on Virginia, shows how *unkind* it was in a descendant of "the Puritans," such as Dr. Miller, to have made the remark: "'The *persecuting laws* which were passed by the Virginians soon after this period against THE PURITANS, made the latter emigrate in considerable numbers, to Maryland, that they *might enjoy,* under a POPISH PROPRIETARY, that *liberty of conscience,* of which they were *deprived* by their FELLOW PROTESTANTS." (Jeff. Query XVII.) What was the consequence? Puritanical gratitude, of course.

" When, upon the Revolution, power changed hands, the *new-men* (Ah! Doctor!) made but an *indifferent requital* for the liberties and indulgence they had enjoyed under the old administration. They not *only deprived the harmless Catholics of all share in the government, but* THEY EVEN ADOPTED THE WHOLE BODY OF THE PENAL LAWS OF ENGLAND AGAINST THEM." (Wyne's Hist. of British Empire in America, London, 1770, vol. I. p. 239.)

Need I inform you that to *this day* the laws of Protestant *intolerance* are unrepealed in New Jersey and North Carolina; so that for exercising *the freedom of conscience,* a Catholic in those States is disqualified from holding the office even of constable!

Now let Protestants see whether it is *becoming* in them to charge us with persecution. At the time of the Reformation, the faith, the ecclesiastical jurisdiction, the civil power, the churches, the fortresses, the cities, the kingdoms, the crowns, in a word, every thing, belonged to Catholics. They could plead for their title the *prescription* of a thousand years. Supposing, then, we grant that in defending themselves in any, or all of these possessions, they were guilty of excesses, by how many considerations may these excesses be extenuated? But where shall we find the plea for *Protestant* intolerance? All their possessions, whether belonging to this world, or the world to come, were of recent origin, and acquired by the title of usurpation. Yesterday, they claimed *freedom of conscience;* and to-day, having THE POWER TO REFUSE IT, they " hang," " embowel," and " quarter," or burn to death, the wretch, who acts upon their own principles!! If God has appointed, as the RULE OF FAITH, that every man shall understand the Scriptures for himself, then Servetus was as *justifiable* as Calvin in their interpretation. Why then did Calvin BURN Servetus? On *that* principle, Servetus would have had quite as good a right to burn Calvin. Why did Henry VIII., the father of the Reformation in England, burn every body that stood in opposition to *his* religious *opinions,*—if the freedom of opinion be the right of all? Why did his Protestant daughter, Queen Elizabeth the third head of the English church, why did *she* burn, and hang and embowel, and quarter, those who differed from *her opinions?*

Why did the Rev. Mr. Wesley proclaim, in his writings, that not even "Turks or Pagans" were justified "in tolerating Roman Catholics?" Why did John Knox preach that Roman Catholics were "apt only for hell fire:" and proclaim that it was the duty of the magistrates and people to put them to death? Why did Presbyterians put their fellow-protestants to death in Geneva, England, and America? And these are the people who reproach Catholics with what does not belong either to the spirit or the letter of their religion, viz: the massacre of St. Bartholomew and the Inquisition!!

Let honest and impartial Protestants, therefore, place these accounts side by side, and strike the balance between their ancestors and ours. Are you not, consequently, as unfortunate in appealing to *this* test, in favour of the Protestant rule of faith as you have been in every other? But pray, Rev. Sir, what have *these matters* to do with that principle, which the Son of God established, "to guide us" in our discrimination between truth and error? The other portions of your letter shall now be attended to.

1st. I trust it will not be considered extravagant in me, to insinuate that the ploughshare has actually passed through the radical delusion of Protestantism, on the rule of faith: when the reader will recollect, that you have not dared to grapple with a single argument of reason, fact, or history, that I have adduced, to show its absurdity. You have, indeed, presented yourself as the advocate of the Bible, and the defender of the Holy Ghost, as if my arguments against the Protestant, or in support of the Catholic rule of faith, were directed against the sacred volume, or the Divine Spirit!!! You have made quotations, which are found to have been falsified, in every instance *that I have had time to examine.* You have, by *adding* and *omitting* words, *changing* punctuation, &c. made the *champions* of the Catholic church to speak the language of the "Protestant delusion," which they never uttered. You have brought forth Luther *acquitting*, and Bellarmine accusing the church of persecution! You have made me a fellow conspirator with the Jews in condemning the Son of God; and with the Unitarians in condemning the Bible. In a word, our candid readers will perceive with astonishment, that you are obliged to distort my position by *misrepresentation*, before you are able to bring your feeble artillery to bear against it.

2. Doctor Miller has said, that the Bible alone is the "only and sufficient rule of faith and practice;"—he has said also, that in reference to the points to be decided, the Bible "IS NO TEST AT ALL." And you accused me of wanting "candour and common sense" for believing that *these two propositions* are contradictory to each other!! Does the reader imagine that he will save his character for "candour and common sense," by subscribing the paradox with you, that the Bible which is "NO TEST AT ALL," *is*, at the same time, the *exclusive* and "*sufficient* rule of faith and practice?" Doctor Miller has subscribed *both* propositions, and you are pleased to endorse them. Now I would sooner forego your opinion of my "candour

and common sense," than believe that they mean exactly the same thing. In proposing to convict the Doctor of ignorance or misrepresentation, of the Catholic doctrine, under the penalty of five hundred dollars, I did not imagine that there was any gambling. The Doctor ought not to *impute false doctrine* to his Catholic fellow citizens—he ought not to *coin* a religion, and say it is theirs; when in fact they abhor and disclaim it.

3. With regard to the manner by which Catholics arrive at the knowledge of the church, I have twice proved that it is not by private interpretation. Even in my last letter, I showed that the authority of the church is a fact that can be established *with* or *without* the Scripture; and you do not pretend to dispute my reasoning, but return to the charge *as if it were original!!*

4. You are strangely at a loss to distinguish between a *doctrine* of the church, and an *opinion* of schoolmen—although the distinction is obvious.

5. As to the boast you make of the advantages which Protestant countries possess in consequence of reading the Bible, I regret as much as you can, that they are only the offspring of a fruitful imagination. Germany, Geneva, England, the Reformed churches in France and Holland, exhibit the *necessary consequences* of the Protestant rule of faith. In most of these countries, infidelity is preached from the pulpit, and from the Bible itself. The principle of *that* rule has a *silent*, but progressive, and certain tendency towards infidelity. Nightingale, a Protestant, admits this—and adds, "that there is no way to prevent it," as long as you admit the principle of private interpretation. In Germany, says the Scottish Episcopal Magazine for 1822, "many of the CLERGY....consider Christianity as a *vulgar superstition*, which may be taught while the popular mind requires it, THOUGH IT IS NO LONGER BELIEVED BY HIM WHO TEACHES IT."— Here then, is one of your "evangelical" nations. The Rev. Mr. Rose, a Protestant, in his sermon before the University of Cambridge, ascribes the state of religion to the right of *private interpretation*, and urges "the wisdom and necessity of restraining it." He says, that "among the German *Divines* it is a favourite doctrine, that it is impossible there could have been a miracle!" Such are the blessings resulting from the Protestant rule of faith! When Jesus cured the man with the withered hand, he merely, says the Protestant Professor Paulus, "pulled it into joint." This is the glorious consequence of Protestant freethinking! And Professor Shultness explains the cure of the paralytic in the Gospel in the following manner. "He was," says the Professor, "an idle fellow, who for thirty years had moved neither hand nor foot. Christ asked him *ironically*, 'perhaps thou wouldst be made whole?' This irony stirred him up; he forgot his hypocricy." This is the privilege of Protestantism. He judges for himself.

Mr. Jacob, a Protestant, in his Tour, tells us, that "even our avowed *Socinians* would be considered by the *Lutheran* and *Calvinistic* clergy of Germany, as *equally credulous* with the orthodox!"

Mr. Robert Haldane (second Reveiw of the British and Foreign Bible Society) says—"On the whole, the greatest number of Pators and PROFESSORS in the north west and middle parts of Germany, are Rational Naturalists; in other words, decided DEISTS." "They (Protestant Christians) are very little better than the *heathens*, either in refined scepticism or gross superstition." Still they work by the Protestant rule of faith, and profess to follow "the Bible alone."— "The Protestant ministers in France, (says the same author,) are *Arians, Socinians, Neologists*, and of no *fixed opinion* whatever, as respects the Gospel." So much for the Protestant rule of faith!— *They* do not violate. The use of the rule warrants them in the blasphemous *abuse* of the Scriptures. If, then, these be the consequences of the Protestant rule of faith, think you that the principle of private interpretation is that which the Son of God appointed "to guide us in matters of religion, and to determine disputes in his church?" Reason and experience prove it impossible. It is the "delusion" of Protestantism; and its votaries—become its *victims*. It breaks down the barriers of faith, leaves the doctrines of Jesus Christ at the mercy of every Christian infidel, or dreaming interpreter of the Bible; and thus prepares the way for that infidelity, which has already inundated Germany, and even in our country, has seduced many an orthodox congregation from the Presbyterian church. It caused all the heresies of ancient and modern times—and yet you pretend that it is the infallible rule of faith, appointed by the Son of God! Now I beg of you, do not, in your answer, pervert all these testimonies and this reasoning into an argument used by Mr. Hughes, "*against the Bible.*" It is against the "delusion" of Protestantism, by which every individual is authorised to make the Bible *say just whatever he pleases*, that Mr. Hughes is arguing.

How different is the Catholic rule, by which the Pastors of the church in every country beneath the sun, teach the *same identical doctrines!* This *alone, considered with due reflection*, is enough to show that it is not a human, but a divine rule. It is the *opposite* of the principle which has divided Protestants into such a multitude of sects and schisms, from the high church Episcopalians, down through all the moods and tenses of sectarian guess-work, at the meaning of the Bible, until they arrive at the condition of Protestant Germany, where they *teach Deism* from its pages, and this (let it be particularly *remembered)* without *violating* one iota of *the Protestant rule of faith.*

You may say that infidelity has made ravages also in Catholic countries; but you will observe that in doing so, its advocates throw off the mask, *rebel against their rule of faith*, do not preach *Deism* in the *name of Jesus Christ himself.* In Catholic countries, infidels pride themselves on being the children of Philosophy; in Protestant nations, as Germany, Geneva, Scotland, and elsewhere, they are the legitimate descendants of the Protestant rule of faith. You tell them that the Bible, interpreted by each individual for himself, is the ONLY rule. They interpret the Bible, therefore, and discover, or imagine they discover, that the Bible teaches neither mystery nor miracle, and that the divinity of our Lord Jesus Christ is not a doctrine of that book. Then you call them *infidels*, for denying that divinity, whilst they charge you with superstition and idolatry for admitting it.

Who shall decide between you? Appeal to the *public teaching and belief*,—the tradition of the church? But this neither of you admit. You judge for *yourselves*. How then will you be able to save this fundamental doctrine of Christianity? But you have said in your letter that "if men will pervert the *true meaning* of the Bible, there is no remedy on earth." Now if private interpretation be the right of all, who is to determine what is the "true meaning" of the Bible? Your Presbyterian forefathers interpreted the Bible differently from you, so that it was found necessary, some fifty years ago, as you tell us, that certain "offensive passages," should be "solemnly rejected" from the standards. They had mistaken the "true meaning," it seems. All other denominations differ from you in their intrepretation of the Bible. Then according to you, they have "perverted the *true* meaning." But pray are all denominations except yourselves dishonest and insincere? O what an unhappy state of contradictions and inconsistencies must Protestants find themselves in?

If the Bible ALONE be the rule of faith—and every *sincere* man is *capable of understanding it*—away with your HUMAN TEACHINGS, your CREEDS, ARTICLES, COMMENTARIES ON THE SCRIPTURES, CATECHISMS, SERMONS,—extinguish "your tapers" since they cannot "help the sun to shine." God speaks infallibly and plainly, you say, in the Scriptures. Why then do Protestant ministers receive large salaries for telling the people what God says? On what title can those salaries *be received?*—where is the *equivalent?* If the Bible is *plain* and *obvious* in *its meaning*, as you pretend, then furnish them with Bibles, and teach them to read. But do not interpose with your *fallible* human teachings between their minds and the INFALLIBLE TEACHINGS of the Holy Spirit in the Scriptures.

But, Rev. Sir, Protestants themselves furnish evidence on every side that their rule of faith is a "delusion." I need not remind you of Dr. Miller's unguarded testimony, in the case of Mr. Duncan, quoted in my last letter. The Rt. Rev. Dr. Marsh, a Protestant, says, (Inquiry p. 4.) "the poor who constitute the bulk of mankind, *cannot*, WITHOUT ASSISTANCE, *understand the Scripture.*" Dr. Balguy, a Protestant, (Discourses, page 257,) tells us, that we might as well expect them "to enter into the depths of criticism, of logic, of scholastic divinity.....to compute an eclipse, or decide between the Cartessian and Newtonian Philosophy." Burk, a Protestant, says, (Vol. 10. p. 2. Lond. Edit. 1818.) "The Scripture is no *one summary* of doctrines regularly digested, in which a man could not mistake his way; it is a most venerable, but a most multifarious collection of the records of the divine economy; a collection of an infinite variety of cosmogony, theology, history, prophecy, psalmody, morality, apologue, allegory, legislation, ethics, carried through different books of different authors, at different times, for different ends and purposes." Paley, a Protestant, says, (Philos. p. 40. Lond. Edit. 1819,) speaking of the Scriptures, "it is evident they *cannot be understood* without study and preparation. The *language* must be learned, the various writings which these volumes contain, must be carefully compared with one another, and with themselves. The qualifications *necessary* for such researches, demand, it is confessed a degree of leisure, and a kind of education *inconsistent* with the exercise of any other profession." And yet, according to Mr. Breckinridge, and the Protestant rule of faith, the fisherman of Cape May, and the inhabitants of the Jersey Pines, are perfectly "qualified" to understand them!! But still they will do well to have a minister if they can pay him, who will treat them every Sabbath to an essay of *human* teaching, and *fallible* interpretation. And no matter *what* SECT he may belong to, the poor people are astonished to find, that he and the Bible speak exactly the same doctrine—even *they* will hug the Protestant "delusion," and imagine that they follow the pure word of God, the Bible ALONE.

What surprises me, however, is, that you attempt to make the fathers of the Catholic church speak as *advocates* of the Protestant principle of belief. When they recommend the perusal of the Scriptures, it is to be understood that they recommend it *according to the interpretation of the Church*. But I defy you, in a single instance, to show that they held the Scripture ALONE, *as " a rule of faith."* Whenever, therefore, you quote the word "alone," as the expression of the fathers, look, I pray you, at the text, and see whether they used it. In this way you will find your mistake, or the mistake of those from whom you copy. The Protestant rule of faith was the principle of the heretics, in the time of the fathers;—but they themselves followed the rule of the Catholic church. St. Augustine says, " the church, (speaking of baptism) the *divine authority* commends, and, as *it cannot deceive us,* he, who fears to be imposed on under the obscurity, of the present question *will consult the church*." (Contra. Cresc. L. 1. T. vii. p. 168.) " Do thou run to the tabernacle of God; *hold fast to the Catholic church;* do not depart from the *rule of truth*, and thou shalt be protected in the tabernacle from the contradiction of tongues." (Enar. iii. in Psal. 30. T. viii. p. 74.)

St. Jerome. "The church, to which you should adhere, is that, which, having been founded by the Apostles, continues to the present day." (Adver. Lucif. T. 1. p. 627.)

St. Epiphan. "There is a royal way which is THE CHURCH, and the road of truth. But each of these heresies, *deserting* the royal way, turning to the right and to the left, trusting to error, is carried away, so as to keep within no bounds. Therefore, ye servants of God, and *children of the church,* who follow a SURE RULE OF FAITH, and walk in the way of truth, take care that you be not *deceived by inconsistent discourses of lying sects*." (Hær. xlix. t. 1. p. 504.)

St. Athanasius. "Let us again consider, from the earliest period, the tradition, the doctrine, and faith of the CATHOLIC CHURCH, which God first delivered, the Apostles proclaimed, and the succeeding Fathers fostered and preserved. On *these authorities the church* is founded; and whoever falls from her communion, neither is, nor can be, called a Christian." (Epist. ad. serap. T. 1. parte 2. p. 676.) And yet you quoted him in favor of the Protestant rule!!

Origen. "As there are many who *think* they believe what Christ taught; and some of these differ from others, it becomes necessary that *all* should profess *that* doctrine which *come down from the Apostles*, and now *continues in* THE CHURCH. That ALONE is truth which in nothing differs from what is thus delivered." (Præf. lib. 1. Periach. T. 1. p. 47.) I could fill a volume, Rev. Sir, with *similar testimonies* from the Fathers of the first five centuries:—and yet you take up an expression of theirs, commendatory of the Scriptures, tack the work " ALONE" to it, and thus pretend that they were advocates of the Protestant rule of faith!

Does not their language and practice, living so soon after the times of Christ and his Apostles, form the best interpretation of the meaning of the sacred text itself? Does it not correspond with the words of St. Paul, calling the church " the pillar and ground of the truth." (1 Tim. iii. 14, 15.) " Now I beseech you, brethren, to mark them that *cause dissentions* and offences contrary to the doctrine *which you have learned*, and to avoid them." (Rom. xvi. 17.) And again, " other sheep I have, that are not of this fold; them also *I must bring*, and they shall hear my voice, and there shall be ONE FOLD, and one shepherd." (John x. 16.) " Now, I beseech you, brethren, that you speak the SAME THING, and that there be no *schisms* among you." (1 Cor. i. 10.) Again, " He that heareth you heareth me." (Luke x. 16.) " *Faith* then (mark this) cometh by HEARING, and hearing by the word of Christ"—(i. e. *preaching* the Gospel.) (Rom. x. 17.) "He that knoweth God, *heareth us;* he that is not of God, heareth us not;—by *this* we know the spirit of *truth*, and the spirit of *error*." (1 John iv. 6.) Finally, " Go ye, therefore," said Jesus Christ himself, " TEACH ALL NATIONS.....and lo, I am with you *all days*, even till the end of the world." (Matt. xxviii. 19.)

It is thus, Rev. Sir, that the " ploughshare of *reason, evidence,* and argument, drives through the radical 'delusion' of Protestantism ;" which *because it is* a 'delusion,' you are unable to defend. " Reason !" She pronouncing it a supreme absurdity to say that *every man* is able to interpret a book such as Burk rightly describes the Bible to be. And the blasphemies which the Protestant rule of faith has extracted from the sacred volume, confirm the judgment of reason on the matter. " Evidence !" Look at your unhappy divisions on the *most fundamental doctrines !* " Argument !" Like the lever of Archimedes, you cannot get a place to rest it on ! If you look to antiquity for your " rule of faith," you will, indeed, find it— among the Manachæans, Pelagians, Eutychians, Arians, &c. But not among the Fathers of the Catholic church. As to Scripture, although by the Protestant principle, you can explain the miracle of the withered arm, by calling it the mere " jerking into place," of a dislocated limb, as they do in Germany ; still you will hardly find in *it* a warrant for the principle of its own destruction, viz.: the Protestant rule of faith.

As you appeal to Bishop Kenrick's mercy, on the " warning against reading this controversy"—I shall allow him to have mercy on you, and shall pursue the matter no farther. The public are pretty well satisfied as to the real state of the case. The charge was from first to last a silly fabrication, although I do not suppose that you were its author. It would have been honourable for you, however, to have retracted, or explained it, as soon as you discovered the mistake.

Yours, &c.   JOHN HUGHES.

Philadelphia, May 10th, 1833.

Rev. Messrs. Hughes and Breckinridge,

Gentlemen,—I had the pleasure, this morning, of receiving a note from each of you, intimating your intention to call on me this evening, touching your reference to me of certain points mentioned in your published letters. I beg leave to make the following reply:

Gentlemen: While I duly appreciate the honour conferred on me by your concurrent selection of me as umpire in some points of interpretation at issue between you, I very respectfully beg leave to decline the acceptance of the office.

1. Because, I feel entirely indisposed to interfere in any shape whatever, in the pending controversy.

2. I am already, by profession, a party—a protestant Presbyterian. Of course, it is not for a moment to be expected, that the public could or would recognise me as a disinterested and unbiassed judge. Then, as to my decision, *cui bono?*

3. Any decision of mine would only itself become a new subject of controversy, and thus be calculated rather to divert attention from the main point, than induce both the disputants themselves and the public to concentrate their force and regard on the grand question in debate. This would have a tendency to dilate and protract, instead of invigorating the discussion, and accelerating a profitable termination.

4. The literary public who feel an interest in such learned and elaborate investigations, as the present controversy so abundantly furnishes, will no doubt decide correctly. The *right* to decide is theirs. Their decision alone, *can*, and *will* be *ultimate*.

For these reasons, Gentlemen, and others unnecessary to mention, with great respect, I decline the honour you have had the goodness to confer upon me.

Gentlemen, with sentiments of high consideration, I am your obedient servant,

S. B. WYLIE

CONTROVERSY. No. XVI.

RULE OF FAITH.

Philadelphia, May 17th, 1833.

To the Rev. John Hughes.

Sir,—One of the ends of the infallible rule of faith, which, (as we have agreed,) was established by Christ, is "*to determine disputes in His church.*" In my last letter, among other arguments, I dwelt at large upon this, *that the method of determining disputes in the church of Rome is anti-Scriptural and anti-Christian, and therefore, not the infallible rule of faith established by Christ.* In support of this proposition, the bloody persecutions of your church became a subject of legitimate inquiry and of direct proof. The force of the proof against your rule, consisted in the fact, that these nefarious persecutions and massacres were *legalized* by the church of Rome. It was shown from your own standard writers, who had received the sanction of the Popes themselves, that the *burning of heretics*, that public persecutions, and the indiscriminate massacre of heretics was held to be, not only the right, but the duty of the church : that the Inquisition was established by the Pope ; that he was its centre and head for the whole world, and that the Inquisitors were no more than his vicars. And now, Sir, how do you meet these overwhelming facts ? By the comprehensive and magical reply, that these standard authors (and of course the Popes who approved what they said) were entirely mistaken—that it was a *mere matter of opinion* with them, not at all a *doctrine*, and that they, not Mr. Hughes and his HOLY church, "must be responsible for their opinions." Thus, with David Hume, the stubborn existence of matter itself was a mere *idea* when it stood in the way of his system. The world was only a *circular* idea; man only a *walking* and *garrulous* idea; and so the laws of your church, by which "Infallible Councils" decreed the destruction of innumerable heretics, was only an *ecclesiastical* idea, and the blood which flowed in torrents under her maternal tenderness and tutelary care, was only a *rubicund* idea! It seems, however, that history, faithful, tell-tale history, extorts from you the confession, that Roman Catholics have been guilty of *some* of the blood which I have charged upon them. But then, you reply, *Protestants have persecuted too*, and in proof of it, you give us several columns of farrago on the persecutions of High-Churchmen and Presbyterians, Lutherans, Huguenots, &c. &c., and present to us, in bold relief, a distorted history of Luther, and Calvin, and Knox, and Wesley, &c. The amount then, of your defence is simply this, *if Roman Catholics have erred and sinned in this way, Protestants have done the same.* I reply, we admit that in a comparatively small measure, Protestants have done the same ; and we condemn it, we renounce it, we mourn over it, we pronounce every such act criminal, every doctrine defending it false, and every council, or ecclesiastical body of men, decreeing such doctrines or acts fallible, and so far guilty too. And if you, Sir, would be candid and consistent, and would allow the same of your Councils and your Popes, truth would be the result. But never, no never! for what then would become of your boasted infallibility !—

But you have put it in my power to bring this question to a speedy and final issue. You say in the first column of your last letter, "For you will observe that Catholics, as such, are responsible only for the *doctrines* of the CHURCH, and not for the private opinion of her members. Show me then the decree of any Council, or the bull of any Pope, proposing persecution as a part of *our religion*, and let that document be the proof of your charge." And now for the "*documents.*" "Bull of Pope Innocent VIII., for the extirpation of the Vaudois, given to Albert de Capitaneis, his Legate and Commissary General for that expedition in 1477." (The original of this bull, with several others, is kept in the library of the University of Cambridge.)

"Innocent the Bishop, servant of the servants of God, to our well beloved son Albertus de Capitaneis......we have thought fit to appoint you by these presents, our Nuncio and commissary of the Apostolic See, for this cause of God and of the faith, in the dominions of our dear son, Charles, Duke of Savoy, &c., to the intent that you may cause the said Inquisitor (Blasius de Mont-Royal) to be received and admitted to the free exercise of his office—and we by these presents, grant you a full and entire license and authority, to *call and instantly to require by yourself, or by any other person or persons, all the Archbishops and Bishops* in the Duchy of Dauphiny, and the parts adjacent, and *to command them*, in *virtue of holy obedience*, together with the venerable brethren our ordinaries, or their vicars, or the officials general, in the cities and diocesses, wherein you may see meet, to *proceed to the premises*, and execute the office which we have enjoined you, and with the aforesaid Inquisitor, that they be assisting to you in the things mentioned, and with one consent proceed along with you to the execution of them : *that they take arms against the said Waldenses and other Heretics, and with common councils and measures crush and tread them as venemous serpents.*

"And if you think it expedient that *all the Faithful* in those places should carry the salutary cross on their hearts and their garments, to *animate them to fight resolutely against these heretics,—to cause to preach and publish the crusade by the proper preachers of the word of God*, and to grant unto those who take the cross and fight against these heretics, or who contribute thereunto, the PRIVILEGE OF GAINING A PLENARY INDULGENCE, AND THE REMISSION OF ALL THEIR SINS ONCE IN THEIR LIFE, AND LIKEWISE AT THE POINT OF DEATH, BY VIRTUE OF THE COMMISSION GIVEN YOU ABOVE—and likewise to dispense with them, as to any irregularity they may be chargeable with in *divine things*, or by *any apostacy*, and to agree and compound with them as to *goods which they may have clandestinely or by stealth acquired*, or which they dishonestly or doubtfully possess, applying them only for the support of the expedition for exterminating heretics ;.....in the mean time to choose, appoint and confirm *in our name, and in the name of the Romish church*, one or more captains or leaders of the war, over the CROSSED soldiers....to grant further to every one of them a permission to seize and freely possess the goods of the heretics whether moveable or immoveable—moreover, to *deprive all those who do not obey your admonitions* and mandates, of whatever dignity, state, degree, order, or pre-eminence they be, ecclesiastics of their dignities, offices, and benefices, *and secular persons of their honours, titles, fiefs, and privileges*, if they persist in their disobedience and rebellion—and to fulminate all sorts of censures according as justice, rebellion, or disobedience shall appear to you to require."

Given at Rome, at St. Peter's, in the year of the incarnation of our Lord 1477, the 5th of the Kal. of May, in the third year of our pontificate.

Here then is "the Bull of a Pope" *in the name of the church of Rome* as well as in his "*own name*," legalizing a ferocious war of extermination; calling "*Archbishops and Bishops*," &c. &c., "*in virtue of holy obedience*," and "*all the faithful to exterminate heretics by arms*," "and the proper preachers of the word of God," to preach this crusade, and excite the people to destroy heretics; and here with the keys of heaven in his hand is the Pope "*giving a plenary indulgence and the remission of all their sins for one year, and at death*," as the reward of their crimes in shedding the blood of innumerable men, women, and children, because they did not *think* with them! Is this too "a *feudal*" bull? Is this too "an *opinion*" only, of the Pope? And now have you not some subtle evasion by which the school of Loyola has taught you to slip the toils of truth?

But we will pass from the Bulls of Popes, to the "*Decrees of Councils*." Bellarmine, (as quoted in my last letter, under the head that "*it was the duty of the church to burn heretics*, book 3. c. 21. of the Laity) proves it, "3dly, *by the laws of the church*." He refers us to divers chapters, as that "on excommunication," "on heretics," &c. &c. where "the *church decrees that incorrigible heretics should be delivered to the civil power that merited punishment may be inflicted on them*." He proceeds—"*the Council of Constance also condemned the sentiments of John Huss, and handed over the said John, with Jerome of Prague, to the civil power, and they were both burned to death*." This author then expressly tells us that "the *laws of the church*" direct the destruction of heretics. Is it not then a *doctrine* that the church has a right to make and inflict such laws? He appeals also to the infallible Council of Constance and instances their decrees, in the case of John Huss, and Jerome of Prague. Here then is *one* Council. Again, the decrees of the 4th Lateran Council, which was extracted at large, into my letter (No. 8,) is a living monument to this doctrine of your church. In your letter (No. 9,) you tried to explain that fearful decree into a "feudal" act, *not* relating *to doctrines* at all. But in letter (No. 10,) I showed that it *did* relate to *doctrine* by the very words of the decree. You made no reply,—you gave up the defence, and there it lies staring you in the face, and the voice of blood cries to you from the ground!

Once more.—The Council of the 3d Lateran, a general Council held at Rome, under Pope Alexander the 3d in the year 1179—27th Canon, decreed as follows: " As the blessed Leo says, although ecclesiastical discipline, content with sacerdotal judgment, does not exact bloody vengeance; yet is it *assisted* by the constitution of the Catholic princes, in order that men while they *fear that corporal punishment* may be inflicted upon them, may often seek a *salutary remedy*. On this account because in Gascony, Albi, in the parts of Toulouse, and in other regions, the accursed perverseness of heretics, variously denominated *Cathari* or *Patarenæs* or *Publicans*, or distinguished by sundry other names, has so prevailed that they now no longer exercise their wickedness in private, but publicly manifest their error, and seduce into their communion the simple and infirm. We therefore *subject to a curse* both themselves and their defenders, and their harbourers; and, under a curse, we prohibit all persons from admitting them into their houses, or receiving them upon their lands, or cherishing them, or exercising any trade with them. Moreover we *enjoin all the faithful, for the remission of their sins*, that they manfully oppose themselves to such calamities, and that they *defend* the Christian people against them by *arms*. And let their goods be confiscated, and LET IT BE FREELY PERMITTED TO PRINCES, TO REDUCE MEN OF SUCH A STAMP TO SLAVERY. We likewise, from the *mercy* of God, and relying upon the authority of the blessed Apostles, Peter and Paul, *relax two years of enjoined penance to those* faithful Christians, who, by the council of the Bishops or other prelates, *shall take up arms to subdue them by fighting against them;* or, if such Christians shall spend a longer time in the business, we leave it to the discretion of the Bishops to grant them a longer indulgence. As for those, who shall *fail* to obey the admonition of the Bishop to this effect, *we inhibit them from a participation of the body and blood of the Lord*. Meanwhile, those, who in the ardour of faith shall undertake the just labour of subduing them, we receive into the protection of the church; granting to them the same privileges of security in property and in person, as are granted to those who visit the holy sepulchre." Labb. Concil. Sacrosan, Vol. 10. p. 1522, 1523.

Here, then, is a third instance of an INFALLIBLE COUNCIL decreeing *the persecution and destruction of heretics*. And more than this, we see, 1st, that "THE REMISSION OF SINS" is promised to the act; and 2d, on the other hand, those WHO FAIL TO OBEY THE ADMONITION (*to take up arms against them,*) ARE INHIBITED FROM A PARTICIPATION OF THE BODY AND BLOOD OF THE LORD! Did not this decree relate to *morals*, to *duty*, to *doctrine?* Was it not by an "*infallible council?*" How then can you shun the irresistible conclusion, that your church, on principle, by standing law, decrees the destruction of heretics? Either then, give up infallibility, or candidly own that *your rule of faith* carries force, persecution, and death itself, as one of its engines to *settle disputes in the church of Christ*.

But this question is decided and sealed up by the creed of Pius the IV. which binds the whole communion of the church of Rome. In it, it is expressly declared, " I promise and swear true obedience to the Roman Bishop, the successor of St. Peter, the prince of the Apostles, and vicar of Jesus Christ."

" I also profess, and undoubtedly receive, all other things delivered, defined, and declared by the sacred canons, and general councils, and particularly by the Holy Council of Trent; and likewise, I also condemn, reject, and anathematize all things contrary thereto, and all heresies whatsoever, condemned, rejected, and anathematized by the church."

" This true Catholic faith, out of which none can be saved, which I now freely profess, and truly hold. I promise, vow, and swear most constantly, to hold and profess the same whole and entire, with God's assistance to the end of my life."

Then every Roman Catholic receives *all the things, delivered, defined, and declared by the sacred canons and General Councils, and condemns,* rejects, and anathematizes all things contrary thereto. The decrees I have recited are part of your faith! And all these canons, and decrees of councils, taken collectively, make the " *true Catholic faith, out of which none can be saved.*" How then can a true Catholic *reject* these decrees? Will you, Sir, say they *were not infallible?* Can you deny that they are part of the *received faith* and doctrine of the church of Rome? Will you say you are not bound by them?

In fine, Bishop Walmesley, (Gen. Hist. of the Ch. chap. 9. pp. 224,) thus speaks: " When a dogmatical point is to be determined, the Catholic church speaks but once; and *her decree is irrevocable,* the solemn determinations of general councils have remained *unalterable* and *will ever be so.*" Thus also the Bishop of Aire (Dicuss. Amic. vol. 2. pp. 324) declares that " the principles of the Catholic church, once defined, are *irrevocable.* She herself is *immutably* chained by bonds which at *no* future period can she *ever* rend asunder."

I do not wonder then, though I much regret it, that you lose your temper and sense of propriety with your cause. You had been taught to believe by the submissive adulation of a few partial and ignorant devotees, that the Protestant religion was a system of frailty and error through which your mighty " plough-share" could drive perdition at will; and like the unthinking Phæton, you sprang with unhappy ardour into a seat which you could neither fill nor guide. While you share the fate, you shall inherit the fame of Phæton.

>Hic situs est Phæton, currûs auriga paterni
>Quem si non tenuit, magnis tamen excidit ausis.

Shall I be esteemed speaking too strongly, when I confirm these remarks by a return to your sad dilemma, in the case of the Jewish Sanhedrim. You had appealed, in letter No. 11, to the method of deciding controversies under the Jewish dispensation, as an illustration and defence of your own rule. From Josephus, as well as from the Old Testament, you adduce " the High Priest as guarding the laws and determining controversies;" and holding to view, the high Priest and his Sanhedrim as a model of the Pope and Council, you asked with much confidence, " *Did the Saviour of men appoint a different principle whereby to determine disputes in his church ?*" " *This is the principle appointed by God in the* OLD *law ; why should it be different in the new?*" In letter No. 12, to which I refer the reader, it was most palpably proved, by your admission, that " the Judge of controversy," to whom you alluded, was *fallible,* or else, *that Jesus Christ was justly crucified.* Seeing the precipice to which you had brought your infallible rule, you are driven to the absurdity of admitting, that *one* infallible tribunal was superseded before *an other* was established; and thus to save your cause you make a fatal *chasm* in the Church of God, between the two dispensations. You were also driven to admit that in "allible tribunals "*may be superseded when it is proved to them that they shut their eyes against the evidence of the truth;*" consequently your Church *may* be superseded. And farther, it was shown that what *your admissions* established, the Apostle Paul in his Epistle to the Roman church, 11th chap. distinctly declares, viz. that if the Roman church continue not faithful. "*she shall be cut off.*" In your last letter, you abandon the defence of this whole ground with the following sentence, "*you have made me a fellow conspirator with the Jews in condemning the Son of God.*" And it is, most truly, just as you have said. But then, sir, it was your argument, your principle, which led you to so disastrous a result! and yet strange as it may seem, you make not a single attempt at the support of your cause, from this destructive consequence, in a letter covering one page of a newspaper. And can it be that such a defender of his faith still talks of "*the plough-share of destruction,*" and has time and heart to fill up column after column with scandal and misrepresentation? Can you be believed or vindicated by any honest mind, when, instead of grappling with an argument you dare to say that I have "*added*" and "*omitted words,*" "*changed punctuation,*" &c. and by so doing "*made the champions of the Catholic church speak the language of Protestant delusion, which they never uttered? And that in every instance in which you have had time to examine,*" "*the quotations*" *I have made,* "*have been found to be falsified?*" Where are the quotations on burning heretics? where the Pope's attack on the *freedom* of the press? Where the crowd of *unnoticed* evidences I have adduced? And why have you not *had time* to examine one of all these? You have descended in the use of such language to a level, from which I hope Christian principle, self-respect, and a decent regard to the opinion of others will always preserve me. But I feel called in duty, publicly to charge you with injurious misrepresentations, and to challenge from you, proof of your statements, or an apology for your insolence.

Let us now summarily review your arguments for the infallibility of your church. The ground taken by Mr. Hughes is, that "*the Bible alone,*" cannot be the true rule of faith; but that it must have "an infallible interpreter;" "that the church of Rome, is that Infallible Interpreter of Scripture," and "that private interpretation is the radical delusion of Protestantism, from which all heretics have sprung." Of course before you can interpret or understand the Bible, you must go with it to the *infallible church.* But the question arises, which is the infallible church? For there are many churches. And is there any infallible church? for it is denied that there is any such thing. How then shall we know? Mr. Hughes says, "I prove it *with the Scripture.*" (See letter 15, 3d head, and other letters!) But it is replied, we cannot prove any thing from the Scripture, without the help of this very church we are hunting for. Here then at the threshold we are undone on Mr. Hughes' plan; for we dare not interpret the Bible without *the true church;* and we know not which is the true church *until* we *interpret* the Bible and find it out. Here Mr.

M'Guire fell. Here Bellarmine and Dr. Milner find, and leave an irreparable breach. In this "slough of despond" Mr. Hughes began to sink and he fled back, and never, for three months, have we been able to recall him to the discussion of this radical, and with him ruinous, question.

The obvious result is, that infallibility is a figment, except as found in the Bible itself, as its own interpreter; and we must resort to private interpretation, or shut the Bible, and never find the church!

2d. But Mr. Hughes rallies on new ground and says, "*The authority of the church is a fact that can be established without the Scripture.*" "Even in my last letter I showed that the authority of the church is a fact that can be established *with, or without* the Scripture."—Again, "2d. I quote it, not as an inspired book, if you prefer to take the ground of a *Deist*, but I quote it, *in that case*, as historical evidence of the fact, in which sense you will be obliged, even as a Deist, to admit its testimony. 3. The history of Christianity proves the authority of the church. From the days of the Apostles, the church *proscribed heresies,—preached the doctrines of Christ* to all nations,—*determined*, by a final decision, all controversies,—and in *all matters of religion*, exercised SUPREME *authority*. So that the authority of the church is proved with, or WITHOUT the Scripture." (See Letter XV. 3d Head; and Letter XIII. Ans. 2d and 3d.)

The amount of the argument is, that the church of Rome has always exercised this authority, of an infallible teacher, therefore she is an infallible teacher! If this be not what you mean, I know not what it is; for without this it is nonsense. If this be your meaning, it is the same as saying, if you will admit her infallibility, then I will *prove* it! But I deny it. Again, if you prove to a Deist from the Bible as from any other document that the church has always exercised authority—what then? The argument is this and no more: The church has exercised authority, therefore she has exercised it. Does her exercise of authority, prove her infallible? By no means. You will say it would be vain and nugatory to exercise such authority without infallibility, therefore she was infallible. But, Sir, you beg the question again, for the very matter in dispute is, whether she was infallible! In a word, you presuppose her infallible, in order to prove her so! For it is only on the supposition that this infallibility exists that the practice of the church (in the exercise of her authority) can be alleged to prove it. Behold then your irresistible logic, your endless circle,—the church has exercised authority to decide matters of faith, therefore she is infallible,—the church is infallible, therefore she has a right to decide matters of faith!

3d. There is still another circle, endless, and hopeless as the last. It is this: that we must look to the church to tell us what is Bible and what is not Bible; that is, the authority of the church must determine what is the word of God. This you declare with sufficient explicitness in the following passage (and elsewhere) in the 3d letter, 4th head, "When you say, therefore, that my latent meaning in all this argument is, that we need *the church to tell us what is Bible and what is not*, you express my meaning exactly, and it is 'latent' no longer." Of course we must know which is the true church, before we can know from her what is, and what is not Bible. But we are dependent upon the Bible for the knowledge of the true church. From it alone, can we learn whether the Jewish, the Roman, Greek, or Protestant Church, be the true church.

When we call on you for the proof that yours is the true church, you point us to the Bible for authority. When we appeal to the Bible, you say, I defy you to prove the Bible to be the word of God without the authority of the true church. So you prove the church by the Bible, and the Bible by the church. *Both* cannot *be first, and both last;* and yet they must be so, or your system is destroyed. Here then is the circulating syllogism in which the argument for infallibility runs its endless round.

"Labitur et labetur in omne volubilis ævum."

We see, then, how you precipitate the revelation of God into the vortex of hopeless Deism, by resting its evidence on ground so absurd and untenable. And these are the empty sounds which you have for months been ringing and repeating upon your interminable circle, and from which, (if you have nothing more and better to say,) mercy to our readers as well as to your cause, cries out for us to pass to our topics.

One very striking fact in your discussions, from first to last, is the *studious care with which you have withheld from view the true and real Roman Catholic rule of faith.* You have made many objections to *the Bible as the only rule,* which have been promptly met as they appeared; and when the pressure of accumulating difficulties forced you to defend *your rule of faith,* you avowed it in this timid, cautious, and partial form—"*I believe (in) the Holy Catholic Church.*" On it you founded a single argument from the apostolical succession, which even your friends and admirers must consider you as having entirely abandoned, after a very oblique effort at its defence. Let me not here repeat, but refer the reader to the examination of this subject contained in letters No. 6 and 8. But the excerpt from the creed "*I believe (in) the Holy Catholic Church,*" was surely a very sidewise announcement of your rule of faith. In my first letter, fourteen weeks ago, I stated your rule, and our's side by side, your's being extracted from the decrees, &c. of the Council of Trent; and I then called on you for a defence of its various and radical defects which were there summarily stated. Whatever may have been your promises and the demands of your cause to the contrary, you have to this hour almost left them out of view.

For example. In the Decree of the Council of Trent, 4th Session, "on the Canon of Scripture" among "the Sacred Books" are placed, "1st and 2d Esdras, Tobit, Judith, Wisdom of Solomon, Ecclesiasticus, Baruch, 1st and 2d Maccabees," making with the supplement to Esther, more than one hundred and sixty-five chapters, and it is added " *whosoever shall not receive as sacred and canonical all these books, and every part of them, as they are commonly read in the Catholic Church, and are contained in the old Latin vulgate edition, let him be accursed!*" Against these books I have made the most serious charges, and am prepared to substantiate them; and I have distinctly called you to defend their claims and character, and your church for bringing them into the canon. But you are pleased to pass by these charges and calls, and with some remarks and authorities on their canonicity (not reaching within several hundred years of the apostles,) you pass the whole subject by, and talk about "prejudices" against these books. This large, this neglected, and important part of your rule of faith, has called aloud for a defender, but you have not regarded the call.

2d. Again in the same decree it is said, "*that truth and discipline are contained both in written books and unwritten traditions which have come down to us.*" It is added that the Council "doth receive and reverence with equal piety and veneration (as the written books) "*the aforesaid traditions ;*" and finally "*whosoever shall knowingly and deliberately despise the aforesaid traditions, let him be accursed.*"

Here then, is another multifarious indefinable, and undefined, yet obligatory part of your rule of faith. In *my first* letter I also assailed these. Will you abandon them as the forlorn baggage of the camp? Shall your silence be considered conscious safety, conscious victory, or conscious indefensibility?

3d. In the creed of Pius the IV., which condenses into a symbol, the decrees of the Council of Trent, and is binding on every Roman Catholic, this restrictive oath is taken, "NOR WILL I EVER TAKE OR INTERPRET IT, (the sacred Scripture) OTHERWISE THAN ACCORDING TO THE UNANIMOUS CONSENT OF THE FATHERS."

Nec eam unquam, nisi jaxta un animem consensum patrum accipiam, et interpretabor. Thus, with all your imaginary infallibility, a body of fallible men, who did not unite as Councils, or Popes, but as private men,—who *have no unanimous consent ;* who *contradict* each *other*, and *you* abundantly ; and who, the higher you rise in antiquity, the more they condemn you—these men are assumed as your *guides*. *All* never *agree ;* if they did they are *fallible interpreters* of the word of God. If you follow *some*, you are sure to contradict others ; and many of them are now excepted to, and condemned by your standard writers ; and yet without their "*unanimous consent*" your rule is null and void. Such a rule you can never apply,— you constantly violate, yea, and you do not attempt to defend.

You have very often, had the hardihood to say, that the Bible alone as the rule of faith, has caused all the heresies—and that it was not the *abuse*, but the *legitimate use* of the Protestant rule which did this evil. For so sweeping and adventurous a charge, it is reasonable to expect some proof. And as you state these propositions with so much self-confidence, will not your readers, after so long a time, look for some evidence? I put you therefore on your *proof*, or on your *character*—and call on you to sustain these profane declarations—or else own yourself a defamer of God's holy word, and a compeer of those who denounce the Bible. For however you attempt to palliate such remarks, it must be apparent that they put you in the ranks of the Deist and the scoffer.

Your statements on the *religious degeneracy* of Protestants in Germany if we take them without qualification, (as I regret to say, can seldom be done with your statements,) certainly show that Germany needs *another* Reformation. But, you give us not one word of proof that the *free and self-interpreting use of the Bible* has done this evil.

If there be force in such references, how will you account for the present state of Spain, of Portugal, and of Rome herself, where yours has not only been the supreme, but the exclusive religion? There for ages no *rival* has existed, and no rule but yours has worked! How do these countries come out from the hands of the Papacy? Let us see: "The Inquisition was restored with its ancient plenitude of authority" (from 1814 to 1820) "and among its first acts were a publication of a long list of prohibited books, and a decree that all prints and pictures, as well as books, should be subjected to its previous censorship."—Brewster's Encyclopedia, Art. Spain. Again. "The sale of the bulls of Papal pardon and indulgence produces an immense revenue in Spain. That the *Spaniards* as a people are ignorant, *supremely ignorant*, it is impossible to dissemble; but this comes from the control of education being altogether in the hands of the clergy, who exert themselves to maintain that ignorance to which they are indebted for their power."—A Year in Spain, vol. 2. pp. 327, 360.

The Ecclesiastical establishment of Portugal is the *moral blight* and overwhelming curse of the country, from north to south, and from east to west. A *crafty priesthood* intentionally keep the lowest orders of the people under a *degraded superstition*." Portugal in 1828, by William Young, Esq. p. 38. "The re-institution of the Inquisition, of the Jesuits, and of Monastic orders in the 19th century is a retrograde step in the progress of society."—Rome in the 19th century, vol. 3. pp. 174.

"In a long succession of ages they (the people of Rome) have been the successive sport of Roman, Barbarian, Goth, Vandal, POPE and Gaul. But *freedom* has revisited the *seven hills* no more, and glory and honor and virtue, and propriety, one by one have followed in her train. Long annals of tyranny, of unexampled vice, of misery, and of increasing crime, polluted with still increasing luxury and moral turpitude, record the rapid progress of *Rome's debasement*."— Rome in the 19th century, vol. 1. p. 268.

"Superstition prevails not only in Rome but in all the states of the church. A government wholly pacific like that of Rome, might console itself for political nullity by encouraging and protecting letters; but an intellectual deadness seems to pervade the Roman States."— Malte Brun's Geography, vol. 7. p. 678, 679.

"There has actually been in Rome a grave and formal trial for witchcraft in the 19th century! I begin to think I must be mistaken, and that the world has been pushed back about 300 years! But it is even so. I understand that *not one miracle happened during the whole reign of the French*, and that it was not until the streets were purified with *lustrations* of holy water, *on the return of the Pontiff*, that they began to operate again. But with the Pontiff, darkness returned, and the age of Popish miracles revived, within this little month, (31st Ap. 1817,) three *great* miracles have happened in Rome. The last took place yesterday, when *all Rome crowded* to the capitol to see an *image of the virgin* opening her eyes.— When I behold crowds flocking to *kneel* before these talking and winking Madonnas, I cannot help asking myself if this is really the 19th century?"—Rome in the 19th century.

The practical effects of Romanism in producing and extending infidelity, as a matter of history is worthy of an extended notice—and we shall not forget it. But now let me ask whose *rule of faith* it was that wrought all this mischief? In Spain, in Portugal, in Rome, there is no religion but your own. Especially in Rome " our Lord the Pope" has all to himself, coffers, letters, (if any,) religion, both swords, and all the people. As "*ignorance is the mother of devotion*," they surely are too " devout" to " think?" and it would seem, that amongst all their miracles, a holy and enlightened man is the greatest!

If assertion without proof, can produce conviction, and a confident air in the worst circumstances can recommend a cause, you are surely the most happy and triumphant of all polemics. How must it have grieved your Christian readers, and made your office frown to see you sporting as you have done with the Redeemer's divinity. You had said that the authority of the church could clearly be proved from the Bible alone, and yet that *the cardinal doctrine of Christ's Deity*, was wholly inapplicable of proof from the same source! Now I would here give you the occasion of a fair trial of these positions. I will turn aside with you for a season from the subject we are now discussing, to examine before the public, the testimony of the Bible on this subject. Then we shall put your assertions to the test. But if you think it prudent to decline, I hope that henceforth literary consistency, if not reverence for your Master, will restrain the expression of such unhallowed and unfounded opinions.

I regret that room is wanting to recapitulate the various arguments which you have left unnoticed " in the rear" against your rule of faith. I still more regret that my letter has already overrun its assigned limits, without enabling me to pass as I had designed, into the *interior* of the Vatican. But I am not unwilling, for a season, to await your pleasure in these matters, if you have any thing more to say, which may justly claim a review.

As Bishop Kenrick in our late interview called for the name which had so long disturbed you, I now redeem my pledge and give it up to you. It will be found attached to a communication which follows this letter. You mistake me wholly when you proffer to me the " mercy of the Bishop;" and it seems you have mistaken *him* too! I did not ask " mercy" for myself or for my esteemed friend: faithful history has taught us what are the " *tender mercies*" of the Mother Church. *The Bishop* had a right to call for this name—you had not, unless future disclosures show that you have had a more immediate connexion with this whole matter, than now appears. And now that you have been gratified with the name of my author, I have these questions to ask—

1. Is it not esteemed and treated as a sin, (and made matter for confession) by your clergy to hear a Protestant minister preach?

2. Is not the reading of such Protestant works as Luther, Calvin, Lord Bacon, Claude, Sir Matthew Hale, Grotius, Locke, Milton, Robinson, Saurin, Jeremy Taylor, Young, &c. &c. *prohibited* to Roman Catholics?

3. Is not a license requisite in order to read them? Does not a man in reading them without a license, break standing regulations and laws of the church of Rome? Are not "*books of controversy between Roman Catholics and heretics*" "*subject to certain regulations,*" and "*forbidden to be indiscriminately read?*"

Is not the *indiscriminate* circulation of *the Holy Bible in the vulgar tongue* (*i. e.* not in the Latin) declared by the authority of your church productive of *more evil than good?* Is it not required, (when you enforce these laws,) that *written permission be gotten* before a layman can read it? *I ask an explicit answer to these questions.*

If upon examination these things be found to be so, then it will appear that even a *little credulity,* on our part was not a "*mortal sin;*" and that to encourage free inquiry on religious subjects, is a virtual renunciation of some of the principles of your "unchangeable church." Yours, &c.

JOHN BRECKINRIDGE.

TO THE EDITOR OF THE PRESBYTERIAN.

Philadelphia, 28th March, 1833.

Dear Sir,—As I am upon the eve of leaving the city, and as I perceive the Rev. J. Breckinridge, in a postscript to his last letter, refers to me in such a manner as may perhaps render it necessary for him to give my name to his opponent; I deem it proper to leave this in your hands, for the purpose of meeting the probable exigency, should it occur, in such a way as to relieve Mr. B. from all responsibility, and at the same time, secure justice to myself.

Some weeks ago, I casually mentioned in conversation, a report which I heard, that the Roman Catholic Bishop had, on a certain day, forbidden his audience to read the controversy now in progress between the Rev. Messrs. Breckinridge and Hughes. I was requested to communicate this to Mr. B., who was then in New York. I was willing that he should hear it, and it was communicated by a mutual friend. Mr. B. wrote back for confirmation. I stated, not to him, but to a friend, the evidence upon which I believed it to be true: and indeed, taking the testimony which I had, in connexion with a pretty general rumour that the Bishop did not cordially approve of the controversy, I could not well doubt it. Two friends of the most unquestionable honour and veracity, informed me that they had been told by one who was present when the prohibition was published from the pulpit, whose ears heard it, and who was thus for the first time, made acquainted with the existence of the controversy, and had applied to them for more definite information respecting it. In these circumstances, how could I doubt the truth of the report? I stated my impression, and the reasons of it, which, I *suppose*—for I have never inquired—were communicated to Mr. B., who felt himself authorized —not to *assert* it as a fact, that the Bishop had done so and so—but to put the question, whether the report which he had heard, was true, or not? To believe a report on apparently good evidence, and to ask a question of one who could with certainty answer it, are surely no great crimes. And these form the whole of the charge which can justly rest upon Mr. B. or myself.

When, however, the Bishop and Mr. H. replied to Mr. B.'s question in the negative, I was convinced that there must be some mistake in the business, and I took pains to discover how it had been made. The result of my inquiries follows:

The person with whom the report originated, whom for convenience sake, I shall call M——, has not been a great while in this city, has been educated among Roman Catholics, and although not a member, favours them. M——, as a stranger, was therefore liable to be deceived as to *names* of persons and places; but had no temptation from prejudice, or from any other cause, to fabricate a syllable that would operate to the disadvantage of the Catholics. M—— had never heard of the existing controversy before that day, when, as *she* understood the preacher, the audience were advised against reading it. It appears that M——, on the said day, (as far as she recollects the precise day,) attended service in St. John's chapel. The Rev. Mr. Hughes did not occupy the desk, but one whom M—— did not know, and was said to be a *bishop* by those of the audience of whom she made inquiry. I have since learned that it was a young priest from some part of the Connecticut valley, who might be of opinion that the question between the conflicting parties could be brought to a satisfactory issue, without the laity concerning themselves about it. That he, in some way or other, referred to the controversy now in progress, I think there can be little doubt; for M——, as I have observed, had not before heard of it, and could not be supposed to have *imagined* it. After the conclusion of the service, she herself made inquiry, and heard others inquiring, what controversy was meant. Not satisfied with the account which she then received of it, M—— inquired more particularly into the nature of it, of those persons from whom I first received my information; and it was only with the view of obtaining a definite knowledge of the nature of the controversy, and in *that* connexion, and she mentioned the admonition of the preacher, whom, from her faulty information, she took to be a bishop. If the Rev. Mr. Hughes deny that any such admonition was given to the people by the Connecticut valley Priest, then I shall feel bound by the respect which is due to him as a gentleman, to believe that M—— has been guilty of a misrepresentation. Of more than this, she cannot possibly be accused; for it is evident from the statements which I have made, that she had no temptation, and could have no motive to make a wilful misrepresentation. I will not take it upon me to say, that she could not, or did not mistake. Yet in so plain a matter, I should think a misapprehension rather improbable. If, however, after all, it should turn out to be a misapprehension, I would quote it as an instance of the uncertainty of all oral tradition.

In making my statement, I have purposely kept back the names of the parties from whom my information, or *mis-information*, as the case may be, was obtained. I have always acted upon the principle, that it is dishonourable to make aught that occurs, in private, friendly intercourse, an occasion of dragging the names of my friends before the public. There is an implied confidence mutually exercised in our fireside colloquies, which I would no more think of betraying, by exposing, without permission, to the public eye, what was said by this or that particular person, than I would think of pocketing the table-plate of my hostess, or appropriating the hats and great coats of my guests. I have freely shown what part I have had in the affair; and if I am blame-worthy for that part, then let me be blamed. I bow to the judgment of the impartial. Yours, respectfully,

JOHN BURTT.

CONTROVERSY. No. XVII.

RULE OF FAITH.

Philadelphia, May 22, 1833.

To the Rev. John Breckinridge.

Rev. Sir,—Apart from its own divine evidences, there is nothing that so much tends to confirm the Catholic in the belief of his religion, as the fact that its *opponents* are obliged either to *misrepresent* the doctrines they assail;—or else to *pervert* the testimonies, by which they attempt to combat them. This fact is attested by the history of almost every controversy that has taken place since the commencement of Protestantism, in the 16th century, not excepting the one in which we are now engaged. It was well, and candidly observed, by the Rev. Mr. Nightingale, a Protestant clergyman, that " from diligent inquiry *it has been ascertained*, that *party spirit* and *prejudice*, have thrown the most *undeserved* obloquy upon the religion and practices of the Roman Catholics;—in *scarcely a single instance* has a case concerning them been *fairly stated*, on the channels of history not *grossly*, not to say WICKEDLY, *corrupted*." (All Religions, page 65.)

If then, as this Protestant writer testifies, the channels of Protestant history have been " grossly, not to say *wickedly*, corrupted," it is easy to account for the blundering ignorance with which Protestant controversialists, generally, approach the discussion of Catholic doctrine. They will not read *our own* books—but they derive their impressions of our belief, from the distorted portraits which its *enemies have drawn*. The conversion of many Protestants to the church, has been the frequent consequence when they detected this original dishonesty and subsequent deception. The discovery of the misrepresentations and falsehoods contained in the writings of Bishop Jewel, produced this effect in several distinguished instances. One was Sir Thomas Copley—another was the Bishop's own Secretary or Chaplain, who " espied certain false allegations in his master's book whilst it was under the print in London, whereof advertising him by letter, the other (Jewel) *commanded*, notwithstanding, the print to go forward." That is, commanded these " false allegations," to be *published*, even AFTER they had been *pointed out to him!*—The third was W. Rainold " a professor and preacher of the Protestant religion ;"—who " fell to read over Mr. Jewel's book, and did translate some part of it into Latin, but before he had passed half over, he found *such stuff*, as made him greatly mislike of the whole religion; and so he, leaving his hopes and commodities in England, went over the sea," &c. (Athenæ Oxon. Vol. I. No. 174, 273.)

It is true that on *his death bed*, Jewel directed his chaplain, John Garbrand, " to publish to the world, that what he had written he had done against his OWN KNOWLEDGE AND CONSCIENCE, only to comply with the State, and that religion, which *it* had set up. Albeit, Garbrand did not, *for fear*, publish this so openly *as he was charged*, yet did he avouch it to many in Oxford." (Dr. Richard Smith's Prudential Balance of Religion, published in 1609, page 54.)

But why restrict myself to a single testimony—even the illiberal

Mr. Wix says, that the Catholic religion is "CALUMNIATED CRUELLY." —"It is," says Dr. Parr, "*insulted barbarously.*" "No religion," says Nightingale, "is treated *so unjustly.*" And Hume declares, that "the Protestants seem to have thought that NO TRUTH *should be told of the Papists.*" The learned Grotius reproaching the Protestant ministers on this head, received for reply "that they found it necessary for the public good of the Reformed religion." (Letters to Vossius.) And Vossius himself in the same correspondence writes, that when he reproached the ministers of Amsterdam, they admitted the iniquity of the proceeding, "but, added they, if we leave off such language, our people will soon leave us."

Now, however inexplicable these proceedings may appear to the honest but unreflecting minds of many Protestants, to me they present an obvious solution. The Reformers, as they are called, could *coin* new religions, according to the caprice of the times, and the circumstances in which they found themselves. But as they could not coin or create *truth* with the same facility; consequently, they were obliged to *counterfeit evidence*, to sustain the "delusion" which they had published, and which the strength of their neck, and the weakness of their heads, would not allow them to disown or abandon. The mass of Protestants are led to suppose that the Bible gave rise to the Reformation. But alas! how abundantly is this supposition refuted, by the testimony of their *own* writers. Grey, himself a Protestant, hits off the history of the English Reformation, in a single line—"The Gospel light first beamed from Bullen's eyes." It is a wicked line I must confess;—and if its author had been a Catholic, I should not have quoted it. Frederick the Great of Prussia says, in one of his letters, "If you reduce the *causes* of the Reformation to their *simple principles*, you will find that in Germany, it was the work of interest; in England, ——, and in France, the effect of novelty." And Baron Starke says, "These are facts completely conformable to history. The Reformation owed its success to a variety of passions," &c.

From what source, I would ask you, could *genuine* arguments be derived, to support such a religion as this—being indebted to a "variety of passions" for its origin, existence, and success? From the Bible? But the religion of the Bible and of Christ had been preached, promulgated, believed, and transmitted together with the Bible itself, during 1500 years before the Reformation;—and consequently this Bible could not belie in its old age, the testimony it had borne to the Christian world up to that hour. It could not forsake the Catholic church, to take sides with Martin Luther, to hear him through a quarrel originating in the passion of interest, and ending in the scandal of schism. Luther, indeed, *said* that he had discovered a new religion in the old Bible—But Calvin said that Luther's discovery was a cheat; that he himself had discovered the true religion of the Bible;—Whilst Socinus contended that the Bible condemned them both, in as much as they still retained the divinity of Christ among the "unreformed" doctrines! Thus by the *Protestant rule faith, they* were authorised to treat the Bible, as an *accommoda-oracle*; and as each individual by that rule, has the same right to ascend the tripod of interpretation; so, necessarily had each one the right to deceive the people in his own way by giving out the word of Christ, and proclaiming as loudly as he might " such saith the oracle." But the contradictions which were proclaimed from the tripod, gave ample proof that it was the PRIEST that spoke, *and not the oracle.* How then do Protestant controversialists confute the doctrines of the Catholic church, *by Scripture?* They have two ways. One is to blacken our doctrines with misrepresentation; as when you said that indulgences are " a bundle of licenses to commit sin"—and then, of course, the Scripture will condemn them.— The other, to quote Scripture against our *real* tenets; and whenever they do this it will be found that they give an *interpretation* to the text which it never had, except among heretics, until Luther raised the standard of revolt against the Christian church, about three hundred years ago. But if Protestantism were not a " delusion" would it require *either* of these expedients to sustain it? The religion of Christ would blush to acknowledge support from such artifices. And yet, I could crowd the page with additional names of Protestant writers who testify that such have been the artifices of Protestantism; and your letters, Rev. Sir, furnish painful evidence that Protestantism still preserves this peculiar feature of its identity.

The next testimony by which Protestantism could sustain itself would be Ecclesiastical History. But how could ecclesiastical history furnish evidence in favour of a religion *which did not exist?*— History has, indeed, transmitted to us the account of all the sects, that have sprung up, flourished and decayed, since the foundation of the church:—but Protestantism does not profess to derive *its origin* from any of them. It began with Martin Luther, and this fact is sufficent to show that history, previous to the 16th century, is *necessarily* silent, on the subject of Protestantism. Prophecy speaks of the future—history, of the past—and, as Protestantism *was not*, it was impossible for *history* to bear any testimony in its favour. And yet you talked of the fathers, who were all Catholics, and the champions of the Catholic rule of faith, with as much confidence as if they had been staunch Calvinists! What have Protestants to do with the Fathers? The Bible *alone,* as every one interprets it for himself, is *their* principle. How then, the reader will ask, can Protestant writers quote Catholic authorities to support their system? I answer, that, like Mr. Breckinridge, they " add" and " omit" words, change " the punctuation," &c.—You seem, Rev. Sir, to be greatly offended at my having made this charge against you. But whatever impunity you may expect from unsuspecting Protestants, it is too much to suppose that I should connive at the falsification of authorities with which your letters abound. You wish me to apologise for my " insolence." Here then is my apology. I WILL MEET YOU BEFORE THE GENERAL ASSEMBLY, OR IN ANY PUBLIC HALL IN THE CITY, ON ANY DAY YOU THINK PROPER TO NAME, AND CONVICT YOUR LETTERS OF HAVING " ADDED" AND " OMITTED" WORDS, " CHANGED THE PUNCTUATION," AND SO FALSIFIED THE AUTHORITIES—IN PRESENCE OF ANY NUMBER OF GENTLEMEN AND LADIES WHO MAY THINK PROPER TO ATTEND. I hope this alternative will be a sufficient atonement for what you are pleased to call my "insolence."

In our late interview I compelled you to acknowledge that you had garbled the extract from the 4th Council of Lateran *by leaving out whole sentences;* although, in your printed letter at the time, you proclaimed in a tone of indignant triumph, in answer to my question, that you quoted from Caranza, and that it was continuous as well as literal. Now if you quote as you say, "from our own Caranza," you must have known that it was *not* continuous; and with this knowledge, how could you answer " unhesitatingly" that it was ! It looks strange, but I make no comment.

In your last letter, you give an extract from a Bull of Innocent VIII., published in 1477. The original of this Bull, you tell us, is preserved in the University of Cambridge. But it is unnecessary for me to go to Cambridge in order to *convict* you of a misstatement in reference to it. Pope Innocent VIII. was elected in the year 1484—and it is not usual with our Popes, to issue Bulls seven years *before* their election; such Bulls come from another quarter. But, Rev. Sir, I cannot pass from one quotation to another of your letters, without being *pained* at the necessity you impose on me, of exposing either your ignorance of the authors you cite, or your dishonesty in quoting them. Even in your last letter, whilst you affect to be greatly incensed at my charges on this head, and require me to apologise for my " insolence," you are detected in new falsifications. But unfortunately for you, the original document is not so remote as " the University of Cambridge."

I shall cite the canon of the 3d Council of Lateran, just as you have done, except that I shall supply in italics, the passages which you have found it convenient to *suppress*. These passages I shall place in the context, that the reader may perceive how much the whole is falsified by you—and judge accordingly.

" As the blessed Leo says, although ecclesiastical *discipline*, content with sacerdotal judgment, *does not exact bloody vengeance;*—yet, it is assisted by the constitution of Catholic princes, in order that men, while they fear that corporal punishment may be inflicted on them, may often seek a salutary remedy. On this account because in Gascony, Albi, in the parts of Toulouse, and in other regions, the accursed perverseness, of the heretics variously denominated Cathari, or Patarenas, or Publicans, or distinguished by sundry names, has so prevailed, that they now no longer exercise their wickedness in private, but publicly manifest their errors, and seduce into their communion the simple and infirm. We therefore *subject to a curse*, (badly translated of course, but no matter) both themselves and their defenders and harbourers; and, under a curse, we prohibit all persons from admitting them into their houses, or receiving them upon their lands, or cherishing them, or exercising any trade with them." *But if they die in their sin, let them not receive Christian burial, under pretence of any privilege granted by us, or any other pretext whatever; and let no offering be made for them.*

As to the Brabantians, Navarii, Basculi, Coterelli and Triaverdinii who exercise such cruelty towards the Christians, that they pay no respect to churches or monasteries, spare neither widows, nor virgins, neither old nor young, neither sex nor age, but after the manner of the Pagans destroy and desolate every thing, we in like manner, decree that such persons as shall protect, or retain or encourage them in districts in which they commit these excesses, be publicly denounced in the churches on Sundays and festival days, and that they be considered as bound by the same censure and penalty as the aforesaid heretics, and be excluded from the communion of the church, until they shall have abjured that pestiferous consociation and heresy. But let all persons who are implicated with them in any crime (alluding to their vassals) *know that they are released from the obligation of fealty, homage, and subjection to them, so long as they continue in so great iniquity.*" "Moreover we enjoin (on these, and) all the faithful, for the remission of their sins, that they manfully oppose themselves to such "*calamities*" (no, Mr. Breckinridge,—look in your Dictionary :—"Cladibus" means more —the crimes alluded to in the passage which you "*omitted*," falsifying thereby the whole) and that they DEFEND (bless me what persecution ! ! !) the Christian people by arms. And let their goods be confiscated, and let it be freely permitted to princes to reduce men of SUCH A STAMP to slavery," &c.

The rest of the quotation the reader may refer to in your own letter. I wonder whether " men of such a stamp," would not be reduced to the *penitentiary*, if they committed such crimes in our day and in our country? Let Protestants read this as it is in the original, and then excluding the passages marked in italics, and *suppressed* by their champion! See the *means* by which their cause is defended! Would a good cause require *such* support? Will not honourable Protestants reject it with indignation? And yet *you*, Rev. Sir, have politely charged me with "insolence," for "daring" to question the character of your quotations. It was to save myself the painful necessity of these exposures that I long since, cautioned you to beware of your authorities,—knowing, that it is by such means, that the delusion of Protestantism has for the most part, sustained until this hour. It is a hard case indeed, that your falsifications of Catholic testimonies (with which the people are unacquainted in general) are now more numerous than your letters, which I pledge myself to prove, publicly, as soon as you please. It seems you cannot give even the title of a chapter in a book, without falsifying it. Bellarmine's Chapter is headed " Posse Hæreticos ab ecclesia damnatos, temporalibus pœnis, et etiam morte mulctari." Now every schoolboy knows that this merely states, that " Heretics, condemned by the church, *may be* punished with temporal penalties, and even death." And yet your version of it in your last letter placed in italics, and between inverted commas, is, that " it was the DUTY OF THE CHURCH TO BURN heretics." Book 3. c. 21. of the Laity—directing us to the very line, and page, which, if you ever saw it, you must have known would convict you of falsifying! These transgressions have been, Rev. Sir, so frequent and so flagrant, that were I so disposed, I might hold you as unworthy of *literary* intercourse, until you shall have cleared them up. When I accepted your challenge addressed to

"Priests and Bishops," I did not anticipate that I should have to suspect your references at every step of your progress. You have, indeed, *accused* me of misrepresentation; but you have not pointed out the passage in my letters that contains it. It is true that I have shown that all the Reformers, so called, were persecutors; but I quoted their conduct and language in support of the charge, and if you show me that I have made even a *mistake*, I will cheerfully correct it. In fact, it was impossible for me to "misrepresent," when I only repeated their own words.

Now for the subject of persecution. I proved in my last letter that the founders of Presbyterianism were men of blood, both in principle and practice. I challenged you to show in the history of the world, an instance in which Presbyterians had the political ascendancy, without using it *for the purposes of persecution*. And although, in reply, you "admit that in a comparatively small measure Protestants have done the same;" and although "you condemn it, you renounce it, you *mourn over it*," &c., yet it is extremely questionable whether Presbyterians are completely emancipated from the intolerant genius of their doctrines, and the perverse propensities of their forefathers. If there is no single instance in *all history* in which Presbyterians did *not* persecute, when they had the power, both Catholics and Protestants—then, I know not on what ground you can expect us to believe that they *would not* do the same again. Even now according to your standard of 1821, the magistrates are "NURSING FATHERS to the church of our common Lord."

Catholics on the contrary can point with pride to many countries, in which the Protestants are not one to twenty of the population, and yet are secured in the enjoyment of *equal rights*. The cases to which you refer, were such as involved many considerations, besides the mere rights of conscience. They involved the rights of property, power, and public order. It was not so much the preaching of doctrine, as the preaching of *anarchy in the name of doctrine*, that was guarded against. Civil war, bloodshed, and desolation followed in the footsteps of those fanatics who rose in Catholic countries to disturb the *established order* of society. This presents a case very different from any thing recorded in the crimson annals of Protestant persecution—where the *only* offence was the exercise of the rights of conscience. But, after the proofs contained in my last letter on the general subject, and considering that you are compelled to admit every testimony therein recorded, your returning to the topic of persecution is rather unaccountable. You insinuate that it is a part of Catholic doctrine; whilst the very documents adduced by yourself, all garbled as they are, prove the contrary. The canon of Lateran begins, "as the blessed Leo saith, although *ecclesiastical* DISCIPLINE, *content with sacerdotal judgment*, does not exact the punishment of blood"—or of death, &c. "Discipline' is not doctrine—and "sacerdotal judgment," condemns only the *doctrine of heresy*, leaving the heretic himself to the laws of the state which he disturbs. The quakers of New England who were hanged by the Presbyterians, were guilty of no such offences. The Priests of Ireland who were hunted down with Presbyterian bloodhounds, as Dr. Taylor relates, were not even charged with any other crime, except that of being priests. The fugitive of Geneva, whom Calvin had burned to death, was guilty of no crime, except that of *following the Protestant rule of faith by interpreting the Scripture for himself.* Luther wished the blood of all bishops, cardinals, popes, &c., that he might " wash his hands in it." Knox was for exterminating all Catholics. Henry the 8th, Elizabeth, and Edward VI. persecuted to death for the crime of exercising liberty of conscience. The Episcopalians of Virginia persecuted the Presbyterians ;—the Catholics of Maryland protected them, in the enjoyment of all their religious rights, and admitted them to *equal privileges with themselves in the civil administration of the colony.* The gratitude of the Presbyterians was the gratitude of the serpent that stings the bosom which has fostered it. They put down and persecuted these very Catholics as soon as it was in their power. They did the same in England, towards the Episcopalians themselves. John Wesley taught that not only Protestants, but *even Mahomedans* and *Pagans* are bound to *persecute Roman Catholics.* And yet *these* are the men who proclaimed that every one had the right to read the Bible and judge for himself! These are the *saints*, the *fathers*, the *apostles* of Protestantism! It was by these means that they propagated the radical delusion of their system, for which it would have been hard, if they could not invent, at least a *good name;* which they did, by calling it the religion of the " Bible ALONE." You did well, then, to say that you "condemn" all this, that " you renounce it," that " you mourn over it:"—but until your tears shall have washed it all away, you do wrong to charge any denomination with the crime of persecution. The imputation, therefore, of having recourse to *physical force,* in order to " determine disputes in the church," is one in which Protestants are more implicated than Catholics. With us, it was adopted as an antidote to *prevent* the rise of heresy, and its concomitant civil disorders, in Catholic states. With you, it was the torture applied as a *remedy,* to compel heretics to embrace the opinions of the *predominant party,* in the state for the time being. With you, it was the *nominal* right of every man to read the Scripture, and judge for himself—but woe to that man who dared to *exercise* this right, when *Presbyterians* had the political ascendancy in any country. In Ireland, he was given up to bloodhounds, in England to the scaffold, in Holland to the dungeon, in Geneva to the stake and faggot, and in Boston to the gallows. All this was done by Presbyterians and their founder—and yet, you, a Presbyterian, talk of persecution!! But it seems that Presbyterians have become quite meek and tolerant, since the rod of political power has been wrested from their hands, and we have Mr. Breckinridge making acts of contrition for the use made of it—" he condemns it, he renounces it, he mourns over it." It is wisdom, says the proverb, to make a virtue of necessity.

Now let us try to return to the rule of faith, which, if I may judge by your efforts to evade it, you seem to dread as cordially as you do persecution itself.—You would wish me even to deny the divinity of Christ, in order that you might have an opportunity of proving it from the Scripture alone. But I cannot gratify you, by acceding to this strange proposal. You may break a lance with any of your Unitarian or Universalist brethren, on this awful question; and the more so, as *they* and *you* have the same *rule of faith;* viz. your right of private judgment as to the meaning of the Bible. But beware of the consequences—for I can assure you that the Unitarian will bear you down by the logical consequences of your *own rule of faith*—and this alone ought to make Protestants see the " radical delusion" of their system.

The question between us, is touching that " infallible rule of faith which *Christ established*, to guide us in matters of religion, and to determine disputes in his church." Is it the Bible alone, interpreted by each individual for himself? If it is *not*, then it follows that the Protestant principle is fallacious. And *that* it is not, I think has been abundantly established in the progress of these letters. 1st. Because the Bible was not *completely* written, until after many years from the ascension of Christ into heaven—and consequently was not established by *him*, as the *only* rule of faith. 2d. Several books of the Bible were not *universally* received, as authentic and inspired, for some centuries after, and therefore the Bible was not, and could not be, the ONLY rule of faith by which the *first Christians were guided*. 3d. The sects, who, in those ages, adopted the Bible ALONE for their rule of faith, were heretics, *acknowledged* and *condemned as such by Protestants themselves*. 4th. Because the testimony by which we know the Bible to be what it is, must be *something different from the book itself*. Hence, the first act of a Protestant's *faith*, (which includes every thing else,) is founded on *that testimony;* and consequently is not founded on the Bible ALONE. 5th. Because even after we are convinced by this testimony, the Bible, all inspired as it is, cannot be a rule of faith, *except in as much as our minds are successful in evolving its true sense*. 6th. And as the Protestant is obliged to adopt *the opinion*, which grows up in his mind, *as to the sense*, when he reads the Bible or hears it read,—it consequently follows that this *opinion in point of fact*, is the Protestant rule of faith—and not the Bible ALONE. 7th. Because the Bible contains *mysteries* for the exercise of *faith*, to be believed *as facts divinely revealed*—but when reduced to the judgment of private opinion, they cease to be objects of *faith*, and become matters of speculation.

These are the conclusions which reason must draw from the facts and circumstances of the case. To these rational evidences may be added, that neither Christ nor his Apostles say, in any part of the sacred writings, that the Bible ALONE is the rule of faith. On the contrary, they command *us to be guided by the church*—" if any one will not hear the church let him be to thee as a heathen and a publican." The fathers all agree in this testimony, as I have showed in a variety of quotations from their writings. And it is an historical fact, beyond the reach of refutation, that no Christians ever professed to be guided by the Scripture ALONE, as their ONLY rule of faith, except *the Protestants who began in the* 16*th century, and the heretics of antiquity.*

What has been the character of your answers to all these arguments of reason revelation, and history? Why, that the written word of

God was completed before the death of the *last Apostle*—as if St. John banished to the Isle of Patmos, or dwelling in Ephesus, could be a *rule of faith* for all the provinces of the empire! And then, why did not the "infallible" church determine the canon of Scripture sooner than the year 397? As if the Scripture ALONE had been the rule of faith *even in the church!* And then, garbled or irrelevant extracts from the fathers—and then the "vicious circle" which I have solved at least twice, although once should have been enough. And then the Pope calling himself God—which he never did. And then the blessing of asses in Rome. And then the Inquisition; the massacre of St. Bartholomew; Taylor's dissuasive from Popery; Rome in the 19th century, &c. &c. Do you imagine, Rev'd Sir, that the sincere Protestant will be satisfied with these criminations, which, whether true or false, *have nothing to do with the main question?* Do you suppose, that even admitting the whole premises, he will conclude that therefore, the Bible ALONE, or to speak more correctly, the *opinion* which *he* may happen to form as to the *meaning of the Bible*, is that "INFALLIBLE rule of faith established by Christ to guide us in matters of religion, and to determine disputes in his church?" If you do, you pay but a poor compliment to his understanding. Do you suppose that a principle which *gave rise to all the disputes that exist* among Protestants is that "INFALLIBLE PRINCIPLE" appointed by Christ for the purpose of "determining disputes?" Will he be convinced that the principle by which Calvin and Luther rejected several *books of the New Testament*—as well as transubstantiation—by which Socinus, *rejected the Trinity*, by which the Protestants of France, Germany, and Geneva, are *Christian infidels*, denying the divinity of the Saviour who redeemed them—by which *you* are a Presbyterian, another a Universalist, a third a Quaker, a fourth a Swedenborgian, a fifth an Episcopalian, a sixth a Lutheran, &c., will he be convinced, I say, by all you have *charged upon Catholics*, that *such* a principle, is the INFALLIBLE RULE OF FAITH appointed by the Son of God? But no matter, the delusion goes on. The Bible is made the repository of all the contradictory doctrines of Protestantism.—It is *reported to be as* plain as the Holy Spirit could make it—and the ministers receive large salaries and comfortable livings for making it plainer still.

You seem to be frightened at the condition of Protestant Germany—and call upon me to show that the "free and self-interpreting use of the Bible has done all this evil." It is not the *use* of the Bible, but *the use of the Protestant rule of faith*, that has done all this evil. It is the *abuse of the Bible*.

I have repeatedly protested against the disingenuousness of your statements in which I am constantly represented as arguing against the Bible—or the "*use* of the Bible." The use of the Bible is in the Catholic church as I contend, and the abuse of it in the Protestant denominations. But I am surprised that you should require proof of a matter that is so plain and obvious. The Germans were told by Luther to read the Scriptures and judge for themselves. They have done so, and *ceased to be Christians!* Was it simply by reading the Scriptures that this occurred? No, certainly. But because reading the Scriptures *according to the Protestant rule of faith*, they were obliged to make *their* PRIVATE REASON the standard and measure of their belief in the doctrines contained in the Bible. As you require proof, however, I will give it you. Robison in his " Proofs of a Conspiracy" tells us, speaking of the Lutherans and Calvinists of Germany,—" The Scriptures, the foundation of our faith, were examined by clergymen of very different capacities, dispositions, and views, till by *explaining, correcting, allegorising*, and otherwise TWISTING THE BIBLE, men's minds had hardly any thing to rest on as doctrine of revealed religion. THIS ENCOURAGED others to go *further*, and to say *that revelation was a solecism*, as plainly perceived by the irreconcilable differences among those enlighteners of the public, and that man had nothing to trust to but the dictates of natural religion." (p. 64.) These "enlighteners" are *following the Protestant rule of faith every where;* and every where, the *same causes necessarily existing*, will be succeeded by the same effects as in Germany. Look at the congregations that have gone over to Unitarianism in New England at the beck of the "enlighteners." And all this by the use—not of the Bible—but of *your rule of faith*.

In the Catholic church, notwithstanding all that Protestants say to the contrary, we read the Scripture as the inspired written word of God—we exercise our judgment,—and arrive by a rational process of investigation, at the proofs of our doctrine. But we do not, like the Protestant readers, take upon us to become " enlighteners of the public, by *explaining, correcting, allegorising*, and *otherwise twisting the Bible*," according to the measure of *individual* capacity and *private opinion*. We hold that the Bible means *now*, what it meant 1500 years ago—and on points of *doctrine*, we interpret it according to the perpetual, unbroken, Catholic public teaching of the church. The consequence is, that we do not *change our creed*, to suit the genius of any country, or to keep pace with the improvements of any age. It is for those who acknowledge their religion to be of *human origin*, to improve their doctrines—and deny their tenets, as often as they shall have become ' offensive,' but we hold our *doctrines* to be divine, and consequently, beyond the reach of man's improvement.

Hence our doctrines are identically *the same* all over the world—and what they were when first preached to the world—that they are now, and that they will be until the consummation of time. The question, therefore, is not to be decided according to the arrangement of terms laid down in a recent charge, " The rule of faith,"—which, without *professing to be*, is generally regarded as a prop to the weakness of your arguments, in opposition to my reasoning, on the same subject. This being the case, I shall take the liberty of reviewing it, apart from this controversy, in a separate publication, in the course of a few days.

In the mean time before I close, I must allude to the train of little questions which are found in the conclusion of your last letter. But I have not space to answer them—for with all the indulgence of the editors, I should *trespass* were I to attempt to furnish you with instruction as well as argument. The "question" you asked in reference to Bishop Kenrick's warning " against reading the controversy," ought to have convinced you that even interrogatories are sometimes dangerous. But as the restrictions of Catholic states, on the liberty of the press, and prohibited books, seems to be a great hobby in all your letters;—it may be proper for me to say, that Catholic states, like Protestant states, manage their national affairs pretty much as they please.—When Presbyterians, however, sat at the helm of civil government, they did not do much better. In those days it was a *sin to print or even* READ *the Episcopal Book of Common Prayer.* By an ordinance of the Presbyterian Parliament, dated August 23d, 1645, "Any person using the book of Common Prayer, forfeited, for the first *offence*, five pounds; for the second, ten; and for the third, SUFFERED IMPRISONMENT. All Common Prayer books in churches or chapels were ordered to be brought to the committee within a month, under the forfeit of *forty shillings for each book*." (Rushworth, p. 207.) By another ordinance, passed August 29, 1654, for the ejection of scandalous, ignorant and inefficient ministers and schoolmasters, it is enacted "that such ministers and schoolmasters shall be accounted *scandalous*, as have *publicly* and *frequently read the common prayer book*," the reading of which was judged by this ordinance as great an offence as DRUNKENNESS, FORNICATION, ADULTERY, PERJURY, or BLASPHEMY.

   Yours, very respectfully,   JNO. HUGHES.

P. S. In your letter dated April, 1833, you say in reference to *the warning against reading this controversy*—"I did not proceed in this matter without a *responsible name;* and even then, knowing the defects of tradition, I asked it as a question, whether my informant was mistaken, and left it open for correction. I have now the name before me, and the permission to make it public, if *required by the Bishop.* If *he* demand it, therefore, IT SHALL BE GIVEN." Now, Rev. Sir, I call on you to *redeem your promise*, thus PUBLICLY MADE. The Bishop *has* "demanded it," and it has *not* been "given;"—John Burtt, whose name is appended to nearly half a column of special pleading on the subject, positively asserts, that he is not your "informant," and consequently I call upon you to redeem your public pledge—provided always, it is not a lady, "whom, for *convenience sake*, you might call M——." Poor M——! She could not distinguish between St. Mary's and St. John's, the one in 4th street, the other in 13th! She could not distinguish between the dress of a Bishop and that of a Priest, although Mr. Burtt tells us she "had been educated among Roman Catholics." She could not distinguish between some other day, and the 17th of February, the day on which your informant "INSISTED" that the "warning was given"—and on which it so happens that Mr. Hughes did occupy the desk of St. John's, and not the "Connecticut Valley Priest," whom M—— supposed to be *a* bishop! It seems the Catholics in educating M—— did not furnish her with the attributes of a good memory.

And poor Mr. Burtt! He heard it from "two friends," who had been told by "*one*, who was present, whose EARS heard it," (never!) and *he* told it to—a "mutual friend," and he *supposes*, for "*he ne-*

ver inquired," that it was "communicated to Mr. B." Mr. Burtt, therefore, Rev. Sir, is not your "informant"—and consequently your pledge to give the name, if the Bishop demanded it—as he has—is still unredeemed. Let this point of (Protestant) "oral tradition," as Mr. Burtt terms it, be cleared up. Is *this* Mr. Burtt the same who was formerly editor of the Presbyterian? Heu! Quantum mutatus ab illo! Were it not for his signature I never should suspect *him* of being the author of *such* a letter. But it is the name of your "informant," or the retractation of the charge, that is required.

J. H

COMMUNICATED.

To the Rev. John Hughes—

Rev. and dear Sir—As I am the only "Young Priest of the Connecticut Valley" who has visited Philadelphia during the current year, I consider myself justified in calling upon Mr. Burtt for an explanation of the very mysterious statement relating to me, which appeared over his signature in the Catholic Herald of the 23d inst.

Referring to the 11th No. of "The Herald," I find that the Rev. Mr. Breckinridge holds the following language—"I have been informed that Bishop Kenrick did, on the 17th of February last, in St. Mary's church (Philadelphia) publicly warn the people against reading the controversy." This misstatement having been corrected by the Rt. Rev. Dr. Kenrick, was acknowledged by the Rev. Mr. Breckinridge in the 13th No. of the Herald, though he insisted, upon the authority of a respectable *gentleman*, that the warning was given on "the day named" by a Roman Catholic Priest. The very respectable informant of this mysterious affair is now reduced to a Miss M——, who, though educated among Catholics, mistook the "*young* Priest of the Connecticut Valley" for a *Bishop*, being informed he was such by "the audience of whom she made inquiry." So says the article of the 23d inst. Let me now, for the edification of the Rev. Mr. B. and for the information of Mr. Burtt and Lady M—— observe, that there was NO "Connecticut Valley Priest" in Philadelphia on the 17th February. I, on that day, was in the city of Washington, and offered up the Holy Sacrifice of the Mass in St. Patrick's church, at half past eight o'clock, A. M. and preached to a highly respectable audience under the pastoral care of the very Rev. Mr. Matthews, in the afternoon of the same day. If this proves not the entire tale to be a forgery, it certainly reduces it to a paradox.

I remain respectfully yours, &c.   JAMES FITTON.
Hartford, (Conn.) May 27, 1833.

P. S. If Mr. Burtt's letter was published in the Presbyterian, the editor will please publish the above, as an act of justice due to one who has been reported of having "warned the people against reading this controversy."

J. F.

CONTROVERSY. No. XVIII.

RULE OF FAITH.

Philadelphia, May 30*th,* 1833.

To the Rev. John Hughes.

Rev. Sir,—It was remarked by the great Robert Hall (whose works I hope you will get a license from the Committee at Rome to read) "That one of the severest trials of human virtue is, the trial of controversy." At the commencement of our correspondence, refinement, Christian propriety, and official dignity, were pledged as the graces which should guide your pen and adorn your pages; and even in a recent communication, you have told me that you could not render "railing for railing." In your last letter, if never before, you throw aside all *reserve*, and give specimens, to the life, of a spirit and temper which fairly identify you with the renowned Ecclesiastical bullies of New York, who are now expending their coarse and vulgar railleries, against the Bible, and the friends of Christ: " who are edifying us much without intending it; and have the effect which the great critic of antiquity assigns to the atage, that of "*purifying the heart by pity and terror.*" In this service I must yield the palm to the models and representatives of the "Infallible church;" and concede to you, without reserve, every advantage which such superiority can confer. The application of these remarks will be promptly made even by the most cursory reader of your last letter.

Your "mock heroic" proposal to "*meet me before the General Assembly*" is unfortunately too late, since that body adjourned on the 27th inst. What effect the expectation of meeting the distinguished Secretary, who lately announced to us "the plenary indulgence of the Pope," might have had in delaying their adjournment, I cannot say. Your courage was not equal to a public meeting six months ago, or the whole ground of controversy might long since have been traversed; and if the meaning of the latter member of the sentence be that you will so meet me now, I am still prepared to pursue the discussion in that way. If not, then I add your pledge " to convict my letters of having added, and omitted words, changed punctuation, falsified authorities, &c." to the list of *things which we have referred*, and defy you to verify your slander, or to vindicate yourself by one single proof, for the " insolence" which has uttered them.

This may be as proper as any other place to expose by way of contrast, *some specimens* of your many misrepresentations.

1st. That which relates to our Confession, being on *file*, may repose until we can give the decision of the referees whom you have proposed.

2d. You say in your last letter, " the Catholics of Maryland protected them (Presbyterians) in the enjoyment of all their religious rights; and admitted them to *equal privileges with themselves in the civil administration of the colony*. The gratitude of the Presbyterians was the gratitude of the serpent that stings the bosom which has fostered it. They put down and persecuted these very Catholics, as soon as it was in their power." Now will you do us the favour to show when and where " the Presby terians put down and persecuted these very Catholics as soon as it was in their power?" I pronounce it an utter fabrication. There is not even the semblance of *fact* or truth in the statement. And let me ask, was it in the *power* of the Catholics of Maryland, according to the terms of the original charter, to exterminate or persecute Protestants, *if they had desired it?* The *fact* of their having *tolerated* Protestants stands forth indeed like a solitary green spot in that great wilderness over which the Papacy has spread its desolations, and I would not willingly pluck the only jewel from the bloody brow of your church. But it has yet to be shown that they had the *power* to persecute. What if Mr. Hughes should boast that he allows Mr. Breckinridge freely to publish his views, and though a "heretic," to "live and move, and have his being" in this country? Shall we thank *him* for *that?*

Poor Bellarmine, whom you have dismissed with your magic wand to the Limbo of "OPINIONS," because he was too honest for our latitude, gives us a very candid account of this matter. He says (Book 3. chap. 23 of Laics,) "But when in reference to heretics, thieves and other wicked men, there arises this question in particular, "SHALL THEY BE EXTERMINATED?" it is to be considered according to the meaning of our Lord whether that can be done without injury to the good; and if that be possible, they are without doubt to be *extirpated*; (sunt procul dubio extirpandi) but if that be not possible, either because they are not sufficiently known, and then there would be danger of punishing the innocent instead of the guilty; or because they are stronger than ourselves, and there be danger lest if we make a war upon them, more of our people than of theirs should be slain, then we must keep quiet (tunc quiescendum est.)

3d. You say "the Quakers of New England were hanged by the Presbyterians." This also, is, without qualification, a misstatement. There was a time when Congregationalists in some parts of New England *did* persecute that now amiable people. But I would ask, upon what authority you have ventured to utter so unfounded a charge against us; and since you will not permit me to excuse your misrepresentations on the ground of ignorance, to *what* account shall the public set down *this* misstatement?

4th. In two successive letters you have attacked the character of the celebrated John Wesley. In the first you say (Letter No. 15.) "Even the meek John Wesley, as late as the year 1780, proclaimed that they (the Catholics) ought not to be tolerated by any government, Protestant, Mohammedan, or Pagan." You repeat this charge in your last letter. While I leave to others, better acquainted with his history and opinions than myself, such a defence as may be thought necessary, I feel it to be my duty here briefly to expose a flagrant example of that unworthy garbling with which, in another case, you have ventured to charge me. In the very letter, and partly in the very paragraph from which you take the above sentence, there is a distinct disclaimer of the spirit of persecution. Let us quote it: "With persecu tion I have nothing to do; I persecute no man for his religious principles. Let there be as boundless a freedom in religion as any man can conceive. But this does not touch the point; I will set religion true or false out of the question. Yet I insist upon it that no government not Roman Catholic ought to tolerate men of the Roman Catholic persuasion. I prove this by a plain argument, let him answer it that can: that no Roman Catholic does, or can give security for his allegiance or peaceable behaviour I prove thus: It is a Roman Catholic maxim established not by *private* men, but by a *public council*, that '*no faith is to be kept with heretics.*' This has been *openly avowed* by the Council of Constance; but it never was *openly disclaimed.* Whether private persons avow or disavow it, it is a fixed maxim of the church of Rome. But as long as it is so, nothing can be more plain than that the members of that church, can give no reasonable security to any government, for their allegiance or peaceable behaviour. (Here follow the words quoted by Mr. Hughes.) *Therefore they ought not to be tolerated by any government, Protestant, Mahometan, or Pagan.* (The author proceeds.) You may say, 'nay, but they will take an oath of allegiance.' True, five hundred oaths; but the maxim, 'no faith is to be kept with heretics' sweeps them all away as a spider's web. So that still, no governors, that are not Roman Catholics, can have any security of their allegiance. The power of granting pardons for all sins, past, present and to come, is, and has been for many centuries, one branch of his (the Pope's) spiritual power. But those who acknowledged him to have this spiritual power, can give no security for their allegiance, since they believe the Pope can pardon rebellions, high-treasons, and all other sins whatever. The power of dispensing with any promise, oath, or vow, is another branch of the spiritual power of the Pope. All who acknowledge his spiritual power must acknowledge this. But whoever acknowledges the dispensing power of the Pope, can give no security for his allegiance to any government. Nay, not only the Pope, but even a Priest has the power to pardon sins. This is an essential doctrine of the church of Rome, but they that acknowledge this cannot possibly give any security for their allegiance to any government. Oaths are no security at all, for the Priest can pardon both perjury and high-treason. Setting, then, religion aside, it is plain that upon principles of reason, no government ought to tolerate men who cannot give any security to that government for their allegiance and peaceable behaviour.... Would I wish, then, the Roman Catholics to be persecuted? I never said or hinted any such thing. I abhor the thought; it is foreign from all I have preached and wrote these fifty years. But I would wish the Romanists in England, (I had no others in view) to be treated with the same lenity that they have been these sixty years; to be allowed both civil and religious liberty; but not permitted to undermine ours." (See Wesley's works, vol. 5. p. 817, 813. 826.)

From these extracts it is palpable to every honest mind, that gross injustice has been done to Mr. Wesley. While he disclaims persecution on the one hand, he proves on the other, that no *Roman Catholic, if consistent, can give reasonable security to any governor or government, not Roman Catholic, of his allegiance and peaceable behaviour!* And now if, instead of *scandalizing* his *memory*, you will answer his *argument,* you will do a good service to "your lord the Pope."

5th. You say "In our late interview I compelled you to acknowledge that you had *garbled* the extract from the 4th Council of Lateran, by leaving out whole sentences." I am constrained to say that it is absolutely and wholly a gratuitous misrepresentation—and I appeal in proof to the gentlemen who were present. I told you, as is the fact, that I gave an *abstract* or *continued sense of the whole* passage; that it was simply for want of room I gave no more; that what was omitted made nothing *for* you, nor *against* me. And now I challenge you to take up that passage, and show that I have left out one *line* or one *word* which will at all affect the sense of the decree. And I farther challenge you to defend that passage—*which by the authority of a general Council dooms heretics to destruction—rewards those who aid in their extermination—excommunicates those who received, defended, or favoured them—orders the princes and rulers of the nations to purge their land of heretical filth—absolves their subjects* (here see the force of Wesley's argument) *from their allegiance of the princes refuse; and gives the lands of the heretics to the pious papists who slaughtered or expelled them!* And yet, gentle reader, this is the Priest, who says this was only a "*feudal*" council :—and this the man who from several letters and many pages of Wesley's writings, *took out of its connexion one sentence,* omitting the disclaimers and explanations which looked him directly in the face!

6th. You charge me as follows: "It seems you cannot give even the title of a chapter in a book, without falsifying it. Bellarmine's chapter is headed—Posse hæreticos ab ecclesia damnatos, temporalibus pœnis, et etiam morte mulctari. Now every schoolboy knows that this merely states, that heretics condemned by the church, *may be* punished with temporal penalties, and even death. And yet your version of it in your last letter placing it in italics, and between inverted commas, is, that 'it was the duty of the church to burn heretics.'" And is it possible that you can so presume upon the ignorance of your readers when the very first sentence in the chapter (already cited at large by me in letter No. 14) thus begins: Nos igitur breviter ostendemus hæreticos incorrigibiles ac præsertim relapsos, *posse ac debere* ab ecclesia rejici et a secularibus potestatibus, temporalibus pœnis atque ipsa etiam morte mulctari. "We will briefly show that the church has the *power, and it is her duty,* to cast off incorrigible heretics, especially those who have relapsed, and that the secular power ought to inflict on such, temporal punishments, and even death itself." Here is both "posse" and "debere :" will you say that "debere" means only "*may be?*" Does it not convey the full force of the word DUTY or "OUGHT TO BE?" Really such disingenuous cavils would be beneath the simple dignity of a manly 'schoolboy!'

7. In your letter No. 15, you had evaded the force of many extracts from your standard writers by the sweeping specific that they expressed only their "*opinions*," and you called for Ecclesiastical authority. I proceeded accordingly to produce several specimens. For example, I adduced Bellarmine's reference to the Council of Constance: (Mark it,) not his *opinion*, but a *fact;* viz. he says that "*the Council of Constance condemned the sentiments of John Huss and Jerome of Prague, and handed them over to the civil power; and they were burned.*" As you say not one word in reply, are we to hold you as acknowledging *this fact?* If not, what is your reply? Again, the same author says, "*that the laws of the Church decree that incorrigible heretics should thus be dealt with, and that an almost infinite number of heretics were burned by the Church, as the Donatists, the Manicheans, and Albigenses.*" Do you deny it? And if you did, shall we believe *him* or *you?* I spread out to your view also the famous Bull of Innocent the 8th against the poor peeled and butchered Waldenses. And how do you meet it? Do you deny it? No, you *dare* not! Do you attempt to explain it? No, you *cannot!* What then is your answer? " Pope Innocent VIII. was elected in the year 1484—and it is not usual with our Popes to issue bulls seven years *before* their election; such bulls come from another quarter." That is, there is a mistake of *ten years* in stating the date of the bull! But will you deny that there was such a bull? That it was issued in 1487 instead of 1477; that it enjoined in the *name of the Pope, and the name of the Church, on all the Archbishops and Bishops—and all the faithful, in virtue of holy obedience—to exterminate heretics by arms—and that it gave to the crusaders a plenary indulgence, and the remission of all their sins once in their lives and at death?* Will you deny this? Can you explain it? Is it not according to your call, just such " a document in proof of my charge" as you have defied me to " show" you?—If you have any *doubts* on this subject, I refer you to Baronii Annales, Vol. XIX. page 386. section 25th.

To these authorities I subjoined an extract from the decree of the 3d Lateran Council, which in the most ample and awful form confirms the proofs that heretics without number have been exterminated by the authority of General Councils. You attempt no reply to the stubborn facts adduced, for you well know that none could be given; but as usual you descend to the Jesuit's last resort, *personal abuse.* You charge me with *suppressing a part* of this decree which materially affects the sense of the *whole.* This I am constrained, in self-defence, to say is wholly false. It would fill a folio volume to publish *at large,* the multifarious and abominable documents from which the Protestant is called to draw the evidences of your church's corruption and guilt. Covered up as they are in an unknown tongue, and carefully withheld in musty tomes and hidden recesses from the public eye, they must be dragged, like malefactors, to the light; and they come forth muttering anathemas, and giving out strange sounds of wrath. When I adduce them in evidence, it is always in reference to some leading topic; and it is my constant study in every case to give the true sense, and *connected* meaning of the passage in hand.

Of this every reader must be sensible, who has impartially and intelligently examined my letters. My object *in this case*, was to prove that *General Councils decreed the destruction of heretics;* and the extracts which I furnished, proved this without changing the meaning, or weakening the force of *a single word* of the passage. Faber quotes just as I have done; Baronius your great annalist himself does not give the decrees in continuity; Caranza with *filial care* omits the *whole;* and even Mr. Hughes leaves out *several sentences towards the close*, which go to strengthen my statement. For examples this: it is *enjoined that if any should presume to molest the crusaders they should be excommunicated; and if Bishops or priests refuse to oppose themselves decidedly to the heretics, they should be deprived of their offices.*

But in the next place I ask what do the omitted passages prove?— The first is this, "*But if they die in this sin let them not receive Christian burial, and let no offering be made for them under pretence of any privilege granted by us, or any other pretext whatever.*"— How, I ask, does this passage *help your* cause? Is it not a still farther *illustration* of the fact I am proving? Does it not show that the HOLY *Council* would not let the poor heretics *rest* even in the grave, where the most relentless laws of human *warfare* cease to *persecute?* Does it not further show that the HOLY Council superadded the pains of Hell, to murder, and to the refusal of "Christian burial?" "*Let no offering be made for them.*" That is, let the pains of Hell press them; let no sacrifice be made for them; no *oblation!*

The other passage with whose exclusion you find fault, is as follows: "As to the Brabantians, Navarrii, Rasculii, Cotcrelli, and Iriaverdinii, who exercise such cruelty towards the Christians, that they pay no respect to churches or monasteries, spare neither widows, nor virgins, neither old nor young, neither sex nor age, but after the manner of the Pagans destroy and desolate every thing, we, in like manner, *decree* that such persons as shall protect, or retain, or encourage them, in districts in which they commit these excesses, be publicly denounced in the churches on Sundays and festival days, and that they be considered as bound by the same censure and penalty as the *aforesaid heretics*, and be excluded from the communion of the church, until they shall have abjured that pestiferous consociation and heresy. But let all persons who are implicated with them in any crime, (alluding to their vassals) know that they are released from the obligation of fealty, homage, and subjection to them, so long as they continue in so great iniquity." Now this passage introduces *another people besides* those mentioned *above*, and *charges* them with *other crimes;* and yet *all* are comprehended in the same sweeping dispensation of death. Does this make for your cause?

The grave Council were not very specially scrupulous about *verity*, though "infallible." But suppose it all true, to what does it amount? Why to this, THESE HERETICS WERE A VERY WICKED MURDEROUS PEOPLE; THEREFORE THE COUNCIL HAD A RIGHT TO EXTERMINATE THEM! That this is what you mean is evident, because you immediately add, "I wonder whether men of such a stamp would not be reduced to the *penitentiary*, if they committed such crimes in our day and in our country?" But *who* shall *reduce* them to the *penitentiary?* Mr. Hughes owned that the Council decreed their destruction, and pleads that they *deserved* to die! Then Mr. Hughes, while trying to "*correct me,*" acknowledges that where men *deserve* "to be reduced to the penitentiary," the *church may do it!* From his own showing, therefore, and by the "*omitted*" passages, it is avowed that the church of Rome has the right in *certain cases to destroy heretics!* Again, Mr. Hughes shows by the "omitted" passage that in certain cases *vassals may be released, by the church, from their obligation of fealty, homage, and subjection,* to their rulers. (See again Wesley's argument in this connexion.) Besides in the passages *not disputed*, this said *Council*, (not the civil power but the church of Rome in Council) decreed these Heretics to "slavery." Tell me then, Mr. Hughes, "ARE LIFE, LIBERTY, AND THE PURSUIT OF HAPPINESS UNALIENABLE RIGHTS?" So says our memorable Declaration of Independence. Again, this decree *inhibits all who will not take up arms against said heretics from the body and blood of Christ.* Now what has the church of Christ to do with *making war and causing men to take up arms?* Will you tell me? Again; this decree of the church of Rome "*promises remission of sins*" for taking up *arms.* Strange wages for the soldier, even the price of blood! Will you then give up the whole matter, or else explain these decrees, and bulls? How long shall an astonished community wait, and for arguments receive scandal; for reasoning, passion; for facts, charges of falsehood? Is it any answer to arguments from the bull of Innocent 8th, to say *it was issued* in 1487, and not in 1477? Is it any explanation of the decrees ordering the murder of millions of heretics, to say they *deserved* to be destroyed, and that Mr. Breckinridge *omitted* the passages which *proved* that they deserved it? Tell me then, has the *church* the right to command or cause *any man*, however *wicked*, to be put to death? This is the question. I have proved from bulls and decrees that she has commanded and caused millions to be put to death (and most of them innocent.) Now why did she do it? Can you defend it? Can you explain it? Can you shun it? Can you meet it? *Yet this is your infallible rule of faith; and this your way to save the world!*

The result of all our inquiries is this, that the church of Rome is upon a *principle, avowedly* in her standards, a persecuting church. If Mr. Hughes denies it, he contradicts public documents; if he disclaims, and denounces it, *he gives up the infallibility of his church.* Protestants have persecuted also; but with this difference: 1. It has been in the ratio of a thousand to one. 2. They did it in *spite* of their *system*, not *according* to it, and as a part of it; and they neither deny it or defend it. Having disposed of these indefensible Bulls, Decrees, &c., let us see for a moment what you have done, or *rather omitted* in your last letter on *the rule of faith*, which of late days you scarcely touch. 1. What have you said to explain your dilemma, which makes you justify Christ's crucifixion, or give up infallibility? Not a word. 2. What have you said in answer to my threefold exposure of the doctrine of infallibility, in my last letter? Not a word. You seem afraid to touch again even the rim of one of your circulating syllogisms. 3. What have you said of " the Apocryphal Books?" Not a word. 4. What have you said of "Unwritten Traditions?" Not a word, except you allude to the powerful essay of Bishop Onderdonk. On this topic your reserve, though often called on by me, has left for his able pen an ample field. Your "*answer*" *to his* "*charge on the rule of faith,*" (like those gigantic arguments pledged in your letter No. 2 against me) is, no doubt, destined to live and die, in *the land of promise*. 5. " *The unanimous consent of the Fathers.* Where is it? It is a part of your rule of faith! But where is it? In vain have I proved it an impossibility, an absurdity, &c. Not a word from you on this subject, except that when I quote the " Fathers" *against* you, you say, I have left the *Scriptures* as a rule of faith, and appeal to the Fathers! 6. I offered to discuss with you, the evidence of the Divinity of our Lord, from the word of God. Though you had said this doctrine could not be proved from the Bible alone; yet you entirely decline to meet me on this subject. 7. I put *four questions* to you drawn from the " documents" of your church! You call them " little questions :" yet small as they are you do not attempt an answer. Why silent? Is it so then, that your people are prohibited from *hearing Protestants preach?* Why then such outcry about the warning against the *reading of the controversy?* Is it so, that your people are prohibited the perusal of Grotius, Locke, Milton, Saurin, Young, &c.! Where then, are the rights of conscience? Is not this despotism? Does it not show Rome an enemy to knowledge? Is not a *license* necessary to read them, and to read all " *controversies*" with heretics? And is this the reason that you help out in the *pulpit* the imbecilities of your appeals from the *press*, and give the *substance* of the *Protestant's* arguments on the *Sabbath* to those who may not without *license* dare *to read them* in the *week?* And is it true that the Bible is chained to the altar, and *none can, without permission, read it?* And does your rule of faith teach that *God's* word will *injure* and mislead his creatures?

8. Long, long ago, I brought to view the fact that the Pope had ordered *Catholic books to be altered*, and amended; and that even the Fathers had been by *authority* " expurgated" to make them speak the language of the church. Have you denied it? Have you explained it?

9. I proved from the Pope's Encyclical letter, lately issued, that he had pronounced *the liberty of the press* " THAT FATAL LICENSE OF WHICH WE CANNOT ENTERTAIN TOO MUCH HORROR :" and that he called " LIBERTY OF CONSCIENCE, AN ABSURD AND DANGEROUS MAXIM, OR RATHER THE RAVING OF DELIRIUM." You say in your last letter, as to restrictions on the press, and on books, " Catholic States, like Protestant States, manage their own affairs pretty much as they please." But the Pope's letter, as the name imports, is not for Italy or Spain, *but for the whole church every where,—for* the secretary who announced the Pope's jubilee; and *from* the head of the church! Does the *secretary* adopt the Pope's principles? or are these only " *opinions*" of the Pope? Do you think with a western Prelate of the church of Rome, that " as long as *the Republican Government*

(in this country) *shall subsist*," the labours of the missionaries among the western tribes of Indians are almost fruitless? Or do you think with Bishop England, who said " *The Americans* are loud in their reprobation of your servile aristocracy (in Ireland) who would degrade religion by placing its concerns under the controul of a king's minister; and could your aristocrats and place-hunters view the state of *Catholicity* here, they would inveigh against the *Democrats* who would degrade *religion by placing its concerns under the controul of a mob ; and I am perfectly convinced both are right. In both cases the principle is exactly the same—the mode of carrying it into operation is different*."

10. The 3d edition, (in rather an emaciated condition) o your TEN HEADS, though twice replied to, appears in your last letter. All I have to say now is this,—that, throughout your attempts at discussion, you have called "*private interpretation*" our rule of faith. *The Bible is our infallible rule of faith. The Bible is the rule;* interpretation is the *use* of the rule. If men pervert it, that is not the rule of faith. If men abuse the light of the *sun* to evil deeds, still it is the *sun*. If one takes a *true rule* and gives a *false* measure, is it the fault of the *rule.?*—While *the Bible* is *our* rule, I have shown that your rule is (1.) *the Bible*, (2.) the Apocrypha, (3.) "Unwritten Traditions," (4.) the unanimous consent of the Fathers, (5.) interpreted by an infallible judge, who has not spoken for near three hundred years; and whose writings and interpretations make a *library in a dead language*. And now when Mr. Hughes ascends the desk with these ponderous tomes, he has our *Bible, to interpret privately,* that is, to do it *himself*—and all the difficulties of the Protestants attend *him* too—for he is fallible: and he has also the Apocrypha, "unwriten traditions," (if he can find them) " the unanimous consent of the Fathers," and the immense volumes of decrees, canons, bulls, the missal and breviary, to *interpret* and *preach*. This Mr. Hughes owns in his last letter, where he says " *we exercise our judgment, and arrive by a rational process of investigation at the proof of our doctrines.*" And now when Dr. White, or Dr. Brantley, or Dr. Miller ascends the pulpit with the pure unincumbered Bible, are they not as likely to get at the truth as Mr. Hughes?— Either Mr. Hughes is *infallible*, which I think, *now,* no body will imagine, or else these Protestant preachers are, *to say the least*, as likely as he, to be safe instructors of the people. In a word, there is unanswerable proof that if your church has infallibility it is perfectly useless; and cannot be applied, *unless every priest and every prelate be personally infallible*. But your infallibility is a figment; and your rule of faith was never established by the Lord Jesus Christ.

But before I close this letter, I wish in preparation for the discussion of other topics, briefly to show *the necessity of a reformation in the Church of Rome at the time when Luther appeared, as well as for ages before.*

As my remaining space is small, and the sources of information are almost without limit, I will here confine myself to one or two authorities. Take for example, the letter written by four Cardinals and four other Prelates, to *the Pope*, by *his order* on the subject of reform in the church. (As this letter extends to many pages, you will not charge me with *garbling* if I give only extracts. The Catholic Herald, however, may have the *whole* of it for publication.) They tell his Holiness "*of abuses and most grievous distempers*, wherewith the *church of God*, and especially the court of Rome, has for a long time been affected; whereby it had come to pass, that these pestilent diseases growing to their height by little and little, the *church as we see is upon the very brink of ruin.*" "Your holiness very well understands the *original* of these mischiefs: that some Popes your predecessors, having *itching ears*, as says the Apostle Paul, heaped up teachers after their own lusts, not to learn from them what they ought to do, but that they should take pains and employ their wit to find out ways how it might be *lawful* for them to do *what they pleased*. Hence it is come to pass that there have been Doctors ever ready to maintain that all *benefices* being the Pope's, and the Lord having a *right to sell what is his own*, it must necessarily follow that the Pope is not capable of the guilt of *Simony*; in so much that the Pope's *will* and *pleasure*, whatever it be, must needs be the *rule* of all that he does; which doubtless would end in believing every thing *lawful that he had a mind to do*. From this source, as from the Trojan horse, so many abuses, and such mortal diseases have broken forth into the church of God, which have reduced her as we see almost to a state of desperation; the fame of these things having come to the ears even of *Infidels*, (let your holiness believe us speaking what we know) who deride Christianity more for this than for any thing else; so that through ourselves, we must needs say, *through ourselves*, the name of Christ is blasphemed among the nations." They proceed to say, "we will touch upon the matters only that belong to the office of *universal pastor*, some also that are proper to the *Roman Bishop*." They dwell with peculiar emphasis upon the point "that it is not lawful for the Pope who is Christ's Vicar, to make any *gain to* himself of the use of the keys." Another abuse is, "that in the ordination of Priests no manner of care and diligence is used; the most uneducated youths of evil manners, are admitted to holy orders; from hence grow innumerable scandals; and the reverence of God's worship is well nigh extinguished." "Another abuse is the changing of benefices upon contracts that are all of them *simonical*, and in which *no regard* is had to any thing but *gain*." "Almost all the Pastors are withdrawn from their flocks which are almost every where entrusted with *hirelings*." "In the orders of the religious, many of them are so degenerate that they are grown scandalous." "Another abuse is, that with Nuns under the care of conventual Friars, in most Monasteries, *public sacrileges are committed*, to the intolerable scandal of the citizens!" "The collectors for the Holy Ghost, St. Anthony, and others of this kind, put cheats upon rustics, and simple people; and entangle them in a *world of superstition*." "Another abuse is the absolution of a simonical person—this plague reigns in the church—they *buy* their absolution, and so they keep the benefice they bought before." "This city of Rome is both the mother of the church and mistress of other churches, wherefore the worship of God and purity of manners should flourish there most of all. But yet, holy father, all strangers are scandalized when they go into St. Peter's church, and see what slovenly, ignorant priests say mass there." " Nay in this city ****** walk about as if they were goodly matrons, and are at noon-day followed up and down by men of the best account in the *families of Cardinals*, and by *clergymen*." "We hope that you are chosen to *restore the name of Christ forgotten by the nations* and even by *us the clergy*, that hereafter it may live in our hearts, and appear in our actions; to heal our diseases, to reduce the flock of Christ into one sheepfold, to remove from us that indignation and vengeance of God, *which we deserve*, which is now ready to fall upon us, which now hangs over our heads!" This portentous letter was addressed to Paul the 3d. One of its authors was afterwards a pope himself. The picture it gives of the state of the church, leaves room for no comment. I only add, that LONG BEFORE THIS, COUNCIL AFTER COUNCIL HAD DECREED A REFORMATION TO BE INDESPENSABLE;—POPE AFTER POPE HAD OWNED THAT IT WAS NEEDED—AND EUROPE RESOUNDED WITH THE CALL FOR REFORMATION.   I am yours, &c.

JOHN BRECKINRIDGE.

P. S. I cannot stoop to notice any farther your impertinent calls for a *name*. Mr. Burtt was the original, responsible informant. In him my information terminates. He informed the person who wrote to me. His name you have: and can claim no more.   J. B.

CONTROVERSY. No. X

RULE OF FAITH.

Philadelphia, June 6th, 1833.

To the Rev. John Breckinridge

Rev. Sir,—I pay no attention to the charges of "insolence," "impertinence," "temper," &c., which you are politely pleased to make against me. If these traits were so manifest in my letters, it would have been quite unnecessary for you to apprise the public of the fact. On these matters, as well as all the rest, the public will form its own judgment without the aid of direction from either of us.

You say that my proposal to meet you before the General Assembly, for the purpose of exposing the falsified quotations in your letters, " is unfortunately too late." I regret this very much. * But you are aware that the Bishops continued in session, long enough, *after you had received my last* letter, for you to have the matter decided before them. If you have *not* done so, and will not expose yourself to the consequences of having the questions *of fact*, touching your quotations, decided by an impartial umpire, then I can only surmise that you have your *reasons* for your present course. *Prudence*, we are told, is the better part of valour. Experience has taught us both that no Presbyterian, who has the reputation of a scholar to lose, is willing to *risk it* on the decision of your case. If you would only reciprocate my courtesy, and choose a *Catholic* umpire, *he* would soon decide. None of those motives of delicacy, which influenced Doctor Wylie, would occur to him. But the public may expect to see the extent of your falsifications of authorities, in the shape of an appendix to this Controversy. The original text and context, placed in juxta-position with the garblings contained in your letters, will make the matter *plain* to all.

I was quite at a loss to know how you would exculpate yourself, for having *suppressed the passages* which I quoted in my last letter. But the moment I saw your reply, the whole difficulty vanished.—It seems that in your quotations, you are scrupulous only about *the sense*. And as the author did not understand what he was writing, you merely " add" or " omit" such words and sentences as may be necessary to make him express the meaning which you intend to convey. It is a pity that this Presbyterian *license* is not conceded to the members of the Bar. Then we should see the authorities of Blackstone, and Littleton, quoted to defend the guilty culprit, and screen him from the operations of justice. But the advocate who should be detected, suppressing a sentence in the middle of a citation, and thus perverting the meaning, of such authority, would, I believe, get permission to quit the court-house. But ministers of the *Gospel*, it seems, may do such things with impunity.

In fact, so far from being abashed by the exposure, you seem to derive new courage from it. One of the suppressed passages was as follows :—The Council decreed that those who died in the crime and guilt of heresy, should not receive the rites of " Christian burial." *This shows*, says Mr. Breckinridge, " that the Holy Council would not let the poor heretics *rest* even in the grave." No, Rev. Sir,—for the " poor heretics" were not *dead* yet. It merely shows that *when they should die,* they were not to receive the rites of burial, after the manner of the Christians from whom they had separated themselves by heresy. " No offering is to be made for them," says the council. *This shows,* says Mr. Breckinridge, " that the HOLY COUNCIL SUPERADDED THE PAINS OF HELL, TO MURDER, AND THE REFUSAL OF CHRISTIAN BURIAL." Why, sir, with the aid of your pen, "this" may "show" any thing—and to those who are *willing* to see, *it shows a great deal.* Comment is unnecessary.

But why should you not in your turn *accuse me* also of misrepresentation? And especially as you never attempt to prove what you assert, in making such charges. I find myself consequently arraigned on seven different counts. To wit, 1st. The Confession of Faith. 2. The persecution of the Catholics of Maryland by the Puritans.— 3. The hanging of the Quakers in New England by the same sect. 4. The principle laid down by John Wesley, on the subject of tolerating Catholics. 5. The reference to your acknowledgement at our late interview, of having garbled the extract from the 4th council of Lateran. 6. My charge against you, of having falsified the words of Bellarmine. To all of which I plead not guilty, for the following reasons, in order.

1. As to the Confession of Faith, I quoted the *words,* referred to the *page,*—specified the *Publisher* and the *date of publication.* I could not be more scrupulously exact in my reference. Did I say any thing that *I did not prove?* You have not been able to point it out. It is true there is a "reformed" edition of the confession, exactly twelve years old, from which it seems the "offensive passages have been solemnly rejected." But I quoted from the Confession, which, *according to Dr. Miller,* both Ministers and candidates, had been "obliged" to adopt, *as the summary of the Bible,* in the year 1729. How then am I guilty of misrepresentation? Was I deceived by Dr. Miller's authority?

2. In my letter No. 15, I quoted *from Jefferson's Notes on Virginia.* He testifies that the Puritans, persecuted by the Episcopalians of Virginia, emigrated in considerable numbers to Maryland, to enjoy under a Popish Proprietary that *liberty of conscience* which had been denied them, by their fellow Protestants. I quoted also Wynne's Hist. of Brit. Empire in America, for proof that they dispossessed the Catholics, who had thus received them, of *civil power* as soon as they were able. And that, on the Revolution in England, they adopted the *whole penal code* of persecution against them.— Consequently, there is neither *mistake* nor *misrepresentation in this.* I merely gave the testimony, not of Catholic, but of Protestant historians. If then all this is, as the *word* of Mr. Breckinridge assures us, "AN UTTER FABRICATION," then the issue is between him and the Protestant writers whom I quoted at the time.

3. As to the persecution and hanging of the Quakers in New England, I gave also Protestant authority, History of Baptists in New England, vol. 1. p. 390—where, besides others, whose names are given, there is an account of a *female,* named Mary Dyer, having been hanged for the crime of Quakerism on the 1st of June, 1660.— Consequently, there is no mistake, in this statement. You call the

authors of these persecutions "unto the death," "Congregationalists." But the distinction between them, and Presbyterians, is too fine for modern powers of discrimination. As I gave my authority *for the fact*, at the time, I am the more surprised at your asking, " UPON WHAT AUTHORITY *I have ventured to utter so* UNFOUNDED a charge ?" Unfounded !

The next case has reference to my remarks on the general proposition laid down by John Wesley, and if that be incorrect, again, let Wesley's own words be responsible. Two respectable gentlemen, of the Methodist persuasion, called on me the other day, to say, that, in their opinion, I had been unjust towards him, by the isolated manner in which his sentiment was introduced. I felt obliged to them for their politeness, in advising me of what *they* conceived to be my mistake, and what they regarded at the same time as an injury to one, for whose memory, it is but natural that they should entertain respect. Accordingly I shall, as agreed upon, submit that portion of the context, which *they* think necessary to elucidate the meaning of the passage already quoted......" That no Roman Catholic does or can give security for his allegiance or peaceable behaviour, I prove thus : It is a Roman Catholic maxim, established, not by private men, but, by a public Council (so said Mr. Wesley) that, ' no faith can be kept with heretics.' This has been openly avowed by the Council of Constance, but it never was openly disclaimed. Whether private persons avow or disavow it, it is a *fixed maxim* of the church of Rome : but as long as it is so, nothing can be more plain, than that the members of that church can give no reasonable security to any government of their allegiance or peaceable behaviour; therefore, *they ought not to be tolerated by any government, Protestant, Mahometan, or Pagan.*"

The words marked in italics are those which I quoted, to show Mr. Wesley's sentiments on the subject of tolerance and persecution. It is not an *accidental* phrase, snatched from the middle of a paragraph. But it is a cool deliberate conclusion, evolved with syllogistic precision from a train of artificial reasoning, and apparently sober reflection. But *could not*, and *did not*, every persecutor justify his cruelty by reasons which were satisfactory to *his own mind ?*—But reasons, of the justice of which, he never could convince the VICTIM of his intolerance.

The decision of the Council of Constance, referred to by Mr. Wesley, had its meaning qualified by the very circumstances in which it originated—which I shall briefly state. John Huss, a Priest of Bohemia, was cited before the Council ;—he recognized the tribunal ;—and obeyed the citation. His doctrines were condemned *as heretical*, and on his refusing to retract them, he was given over to the civil laws of that city, which was *free and independent*. According to these laws, *death* was the penalty of the crime, of which Huss had been convicted ; and accordingly, *like Michael Servetus in Geneva*, he was burned to death.

But then, the " faith" on which Wesley built his syllogism, had been *pledged* to John Huss, by the Emperor Sigismund in the form of a safe conduct, or passport going to, and returning from the Council. Now this "faith" had not been kept *with the heretic*, since he was not *allowed* to return; but was *executed*—whilst the Council decided, that the party who had pledged this "faith," was not bound by its obligation, for the following reasons: 1st. Because the safe conduct granted by the Emperor could not deprive the Council of its spiritual rights to determine whether the *doctrines* of Huss were heresies, or not. 2. Because it could not controul the administration of the civil laws of an *independent* state, (as Constance was) in which the Emperor *had no authority*. 3. Because Huss had attempted to escape, and *thereby* forfeited the protection of his passport, *even if it could have protected him*. 4. Because, it was understood between the Emperor and Huss, in their interview at Prague, that if the council should condemn his doctrines, he (Huss) would *retract them;*—the Emperor telling him, *notwithstanding the passport*, that if he did *not retract*, in such a case, he, himself, would *light the pile to consume Huss*. These are the facts of the case, and the decree simply declares that, as the Emperor had done "*what was in his power*,"—having *no power* over the *doctrinal decisions of the Council;* nor yet over the *magistrates of Constance;* there was *no violation* of the "faith" he had *pledged by his passport*. Here are the whole *extent, origin*, and *circumstances* of that famous decree, for which the Catholics of the British Empire have been persecuted for the last three hundred years. This decision, thus *truly* explained, is what Mr. Wesley perverts into a "*Roman Catholic maxim*," and from which he concludes, "therefore, Catholics *ought not to be tolerated* BY ANY GOVERNMENT, *Protestant, Mahometan*, or *Pagan*." It never *was* a Roman Catholic maxim, except when Protestant CALUMNY made it so.

But the occasion on which Mr. Wesley gave publicity to this un christian and intolerant sentiment, shows to what an extent his judgment, or his feelings had been perverted. It was at a time when the friends of civil and *religious freedom* in Great Britain, were struggling for the repeal of some of the most *unnatural* laws that ever were framed by the ingenious *cruelty* of man. The worst of them had been in operation against the Catholics for nearly one hundred years, having been enacted in 1699. It was for the purpose of *preventing* the repeal of these *persecuting laws* that the sanguinary mob, of which Lord George Gordon was the *prime spirit*, had formed itself into what was called the "Protestant association." Under the guidance of this fanatic, *first* a Protestant and then a *Jew*, the Catholics of London were sought for to be massacred;—their houses and chapels burned to the ground; and their clergy and themselves hunted into holes and corners. The Hon. Edmund Burke a Protestant, says, in reference to these Protestant barbarities so well calculated to stir the blood of men, that, on the *part of the Catholics*, "not a hand was moved to retaliate, or even to defend. Had the conflict once begun" says he, "the rage of *their persecutors* would have redoubled. Thus fury increasing by the reverberation of outrages, house being fired for house, and church for chapel, I am convinced that no power under Heaven could have prevented a general conflagration; and at *this day* London would have been a tale." (Speech at Bristol vol. 2. Bost. ed. page 261.)

Mr. Wesley was no stranger to their principles, and we may infer the character of his own from the fact, that in *his old age* he stood forth with all the influence of his reputed sanctity as the *public defender* of this " Protestant association ;" and attempted to prove by a syllogism, that " *Catholics ought not to be tolerated by any Government, Protestant, Mohammedan, or Pagan.*" A more savage theorem never proceeded from a Christian pen. Still Mr. Wesley *said* he would not persecute any man for his religion. But the Apostle tells us, " to love, not in *word* and in *tongue*, but in truth and in deed." Now I submit to the gentlemen themselves who called on me, to say, in candor, whether I had been unjust towards the memory of Mr. Wesley in my former remark.

5. You deny that, in our " late interview," you had acknowledged having garbled the extract from the 4th Council of Lateran, by " leaving out whole sentences." And characterise my assertion to that effect as a " GRATUITOUS MISREPRESENTATION." Let us see. In reference to this extract, in responding at the time, to my question— " Do you give it as *continuous* and literal ?" Your reply was, " I answer unhesitatingly—I do." In our interview you acknowledged that you *had omitted whole sentences* " in the extract." How then, could you have said, that it was " *continuous ?*" In your last letter you admit, that the *extract* was not " *continuous*," by telling us that you " gave an *abstract or continued* SENSE of the whole passage." How then, can you say, that it is " *gratuitous misrepresentation*" to have given you credit *for this acknowledgment ?* Let the public judge by the facts.

6. You were detected in representing a chapter of Bellarmine that, " it was the *duty of the Church* to BURN *heretics.*" Bellarmine never said so. But it was the ' sense' you will contend. No, Rev. Sir, it was not the sense; and even if it were, it was literary forgery, to place it between *inverted commas*, as it were *the very words of the author*. Now, however, you give a *new* quotation, and transfer it to the " very FIRST sentence in the chapter." It would be, the " first" sentence, *were it not that there are in the chapter two paragraphs going before it*. Bellarmine contended that the church " *may* and *ought*," to cast off heretics, from her communion. *This is* Presbyterian, as well as Catholic doctrine. Bellarmine contended that heretics, *so cast off*, " *may* and *ought*" to be punished " by the civil power, with temporal penalties and even death itself," as the case may require. This *is* not, never *was*, never *will* be, any part or portion of Catholic doctrine. And in the paragraph immediately *preceding* that which you call, " the *very first* sentence of the chapter, Bellarmine quotes Calvin, Beza, and other " Reformers," to show that *they all* held the principle which he was about to lay down. It is singular enough that whenever he wished to establish the *principle of persecution*, he invariably quoted the authority and practice of John Calvin. How much could he have strengthened the argument of intolerance, if, living at this day, he might appeal to

facts and show, as I can, that *persecution* even unto blood, has, *in every country*, attended the political ascendency of Calvinism!

7. The "*fact*" on which you lay such emphasis, touching the case of "John Huss and Jerome of Prague," has been sufficiently disposed of under the head of Mr. Wesley's case. Protestants look upon these heretics as "*Reformers*"—but they were such "Reformers," as would have been consigned to the gallows, if they had preached their doctrines in Boston, in the year 1660.

The remainder of your letter is miscellaneous. With regard to the Bull of Innocent VIII., the original of which is "in the University of Cambridge," (as you tell us) it appears you made a "mistake" of ten years as to its date. But such "mistakes" seem to be the very source and secret of your *prowess*. Accordingly gathering strength from exposure, and having an eye to the susceptibilities of human sympathy, you tell us quite pathetically :—" I spread out to your view also the infamous Bull of Pope Innocent VIII. against the poor peeled and butchered Waldenses." If they were "peeled and *butchered*," it was wasting parchment to make *any* decree against them. Parsons, it seems, can issue Bulls as well as Popes. You ask me how " I meet it?" I answer, so long as it is in the "University of Cambridge," *and nowhere else*, I am not disposed to meet it at all. You ask me, "Do I deny it?" And without waiting for my answer, you reply that " I *dare* not." Now I reply, that I "*dare*," and *do*, deny it, flatly. We have advanced *too far in the discussion*, for me or the public to receive your assertion, as authority for its existence in "Cambridge."—And there is no such document found in the Bullarium of Innocent VIII. which I have examined. Besides, the very history of it *given by you*, carries with it, to those who are acquainted with the subject, prima facie evidence of fabrication Lawyers, cunning rogues, have a way of sifting and exposing *false testimony*, which the witness himself never suspected.

But the 3d Council of Lateran, after having directed with great cruelty, that when the "poor heretics" died, " they should not receive the rites of Christian burial" in their interment ;—and that " no oblation should be made for them ;"—decreed also that it was lawful for princes to reduce those other " poor heretics" (whose history you thought proper to suppress) to SLAVERY; for no crime in the world! except " *destroying churches and monasteries, sparing neither widows nor virgins, neither old nor young, neither sex nor age, but desolating every thing, after the manner of pagans !!!* On this my Rev. opponent, says, " Tell me then, Mr. Hughes, " *are life, liberty, and the pursuit of happiness, unalienable rights?* So says our memorable Declaration of Independence." I will tell you then, as you do not seem to be aware of the fact, that Pope Alexander III., under whom this Council was held, did more for the extinction of slavery than *all* the Congresses and all the societies that ever existed in America. He abolished it as far as he could, and in allowing these " poor heretics," who committed such crimes against society to be reduced to slavery, he only made an exception to his own *laws*. But when you wished to pay a *compliment* to " our memorable Declaration of Independence, were you not rather unfortunate in coupling it with an allusion to the question of *slavery?* Was the allusion made *ironically?* It reminds me of the negro slave, who, on his way to Georgia through Washington, shook his manacled hands *at the Capitol*, and began to sing, "Hail Columbia, happy land."

Then follows the usual train of "little questions." 1. "What have you said to explain your dilemma, which makes you justify the crucifixion of Christ or give up your infallibility? Not a word." There was no dilemma in the case. The infallibility of the Synagogue ceased from the moment that Christ made the revelation of his doctrines. *This I had* "said." 2. "What have you said in answer to my threefold exposure of the doctrine of infallibility, in my last letter? Not a word." The only "exposure" I could discover in your last letter, was the exposure of yourself. And on this I said what I was compelled to say in truth; to the which, you reply with the argument of epithets "insolence," "slander," "bully," "impertinent," and other graceful expressions. 3. "What have you said of the Apocryphal books? Not a word." Why yes, I said and proved that the Reformers turned those books out of the canon;—that Calvin cut off the Apocalypse, Luther the Epistle to the Hebrews, St. James and St. Jude; and I showed that Protestants have the same authority for the books which they *regard* as apocryphal, which they have for any of those which are called deutero-canonical. Do you not recollect the letter in which I convicted you of having made a little *mistake* of about eleven hundred years, in reference to the formation of the canon? 4. "What have you said of unwritten traditions? Not a word." The same answer suits all questions. 5. "The unanimous consent of the Fathers. Where is it?" It is in every *doctrine* of the Catholic church—in *all* those dogmas which are held by Catholic *faith*—and rejected by Protestant *opinions*. 6. "I offered to discuss with you the evidence of the Divinity of our Lord, from the word of God." You did; and I referred you to the *Universalist with whom you agree*, as to the rule of faith. 7. "I put four questions to you—and yet small as they are, you do not attempt to answer them." The reader will observe that it was in answer to these questions, that I gave an extract from Rushworth, showing that the Episcopal prayer book was put on the *Presbyterian Index Expurgatorious*, as a *prohibited book*. The reading of it, was, for the first "*offence*," five pounds *fine;* the second, ten; and the third, "*imprisonment*."

As to "Grotius, Locke, Milton, Saurin, and Young"—ask the first *educated* Catholic you meet, and perhaps, notwithstanding the pretended *prohibition*, he will convince you that he is better acquainted with those authors, than some Protestant ministers. Even your letters are read; and Catholics, in the perusal, are comforted with the recollection of the divine words, "Blessed are you when men shall say all manner of evil against you *falsely*, for my sake."

Your reference to Bellarmine ("Book 3. chap. 23 of Laics") is attended with the usual fatality. There is *no* 23d chapter in the book. Bellarmine in the 22d and *last* chapter, speaking of the circumstances in which " heretics, thieves, and other wicked men, are to be rooted out," lays down the rule nearly as quoted. But the scrap of Latin which you have cited, in parenthesis, though consisting of three words only, is falsified. " Sunt procul extirpandi" are the words of your letter, "Sunt procul dubio extirpandi," are those of the *author*. But, as usual, you will say that you give the sense! and ask with increasing energy, what difference is caused, in the *meaning*, by the suppression! You might also have told your readers, that Bellarmine in the remarks referred to, gave them *as the sentiments of St. Augustine*, who is rather a favourite with Presbyterians. He gives the book and chapter of that Father's works where the sentiments may be found.

Having been *pressed* at an early stage of the controversy by arguments on the rule of faith, you seem to have thought that a topic which would be more in accordance with the *prejudices of Protestants*, would suit better. Persecution was a favourite theme. It was most likely to catch the eye of popular feeling. But the tables have been turned against you. It has been shown on the testimony of Protestant writers, that all the Reformers were persecutors—whilst the Presbyterians, when they had political power, sacrificed a greater number of human victims to the demon of intolerance than any other denomination. There is no country, no colony in which Presbyterians wielded the sword of civil power, without dying it, in the blood of persecution. What advantage, then, Rev. Sir, have you derived from the discussion of this unpleasant topic, which, considering the sect whose name you bear, *you* should have been the last to introduce. The religion of Christ does not authorise persecution —and yet Protestants have persecuted quite as fiercely as Catholics. This is the amount of it.

But then the rule of faith—to which you promised " *strict* adherence." What has become of it? Your last letter, brief as the allusion is to that question, gives us a *new* view of the subject. Here are your words, " all I have to say *now* is this, that throughout your attempts at discussion you have called private interpretation our rule of faith. The Bible is the infallible rule of faith. The Bible *is the rule*, interpretation is the *use* of the rule. If men pervert it, that is not the rule of faith." In this declaration, the " radical delusion" of Protestantism stands confessed. Is it not by " private interpretation" that Protestants are directed to understand the Bible? It certainly is. And here is the advocate of that principle declaring that " private interpretation is not the rule of faith !"

But the real question is, *how can a Protestant know what are the doctrines* of Jesus Christ? From the Bible. The Bible on the *shelf?* No. Then it must be the Bible *as he understands it*. No; that would be " private interpretation." And Mr. Breckinridge has just told him that ' *this* is not his rule of faith.' Here then is the acknowledgment of all that my argument required. Protestants have " perverted" that sacred book to the support of their own heretical opinions—and yet they charge upon the teaching of the Bible the impieties of their contradictory doctrines. The doctrines contained in the Bible are the doctrines of Christ, but " if men pervert them," by "private interpretation," then "they are *not* the doctrines of Christ."

Where, then, is that "infallible Rule of Faith established by Christ to guide us in matters of Religion, and to determine disputes in his Church?" Let Protestants look to it. "He that believeth not," says the Son of God, "shall be condemned." Christ would not have made this declaration, without providing some means by which Christians could find out, what they are to believe—whilst Mr. Breckinridge is compelled finally to admit, that no such means exist among Protestants. "Private interpretation," he says, "is not the Rule of Faith."

The reader who will take the pains to look back, to my arguments on the Catholic Rule of belief, as laid down in letters No. 5. 7. 9. will perceive the solidity of the basis, on which our principle is established. He will perceive that it is founded on the words of Christ and his apostles, sustained by the testimony of ecclesiastical history, and in perfect accordance with the light of reason itself. Let him compare letter with letter, and decide whether there has been, amidst all the assertion, crimination, garbled authorities and abuse with which the Catholic church has been assailed, one *genuine* proof adduced against the Catholic Rule of Faith, or in support of the Protestant principle. On the other hand let him decide whether it has not been proved by facts, undisputed and indisputable, that the Protestant principle of religious guidance, is that which was adopted by all the heretics of ancient and modern times, which has conducted the Protestants on the continent of Europe into the *substance of infidelity*, and which is bringing about the same state of things in our own country. Tracts, Bible classes, Sunday Schools, Camp-meetings, Revivals, and the general machinery of Protestantism, of which the most important part, are the ministers themselves, may arrest the progress of infidelity for a while; but the physical excitation produced by these irregular and artificial means cannot last. The principle on which the whole system rests, is *intrinsically* fallacious.

Perceiving, Rev. Sir, that you are anxious to pass to the second topic of discussion, I am now prepared to indulge you in your desire. The next question is this:—"Whether the Protestant Religion is the Religion of Christ?" Six months ago I requested you to furnish me with the *definition* of the "Protestant Religion." You promised, but you have not performed. Be pleased then, in your next letter to tell me *what the "Protestant Religion" is*. I wish to take your own definition, so that there may be no mistake on either side. It is unnecessary to add any thing more to this communication, since the subject is fairly exhausted by your unexpected declaration that "private interpretation is not the Protestant rule of faith." The Bible, *without this*, it CANNOT be.

Yours, JNO. HUGHES.

P. S. In the postscript to your last letter, you say as follows: "I cannot stoop to notice any farther your IMPERTINENT (O fie!) calls for a name. Mr. Burtt was the *original, responsible* informant."— Then, Rev. Sir, the Rev. Mr. Burtt shall be held to his responsibility. The charge was a gratuitous FALSEHOOD and CALUMNY. And as Mr. Burtt is "responsible," let him see to it.

CONTROVERSY. No. XX.

RULE OF FAITH.

Philadelphia, June 13*th.* 1833.

To the Rev. John Hughes.

Sir,—The celebrated Pascal, himself a Romanist, has said in his Provincial Letters, against the jesuits, that they publicly maintained this opinion, viz : *it is only a venal sin to calumniate and ruin the credit of such as speak evil of you, by accusing them of false crimes.* To what *other* school of morals shall I trace the unblushing and false charges with which your recent letter abounds. Your current argument which stands as the solitary reply to decrees of Councils, and Bulls of Popes, to authenticate public records, and undisputable facts, is this—" it is false," " you have garbled."

Your Bible, your public Prayers, your Breviary, and Mass-book, your Catechism, decrees of Councils, and Bulls of Popes, being in *a dead language*, the only way to examine your system is to bring them to public view by translations. My letters (as you know) have abounded with such matter, drawn from the *originals*—and very often the barbarous Latin has been given side by side with the *translations*. Finding these authorities too *stubborn to be tortured from their plain and terrible sense*, you have set yourself to *defame the witness*, and thus destroy the *testimony*. With ignorant or prejudiced persons, your *strong assertions* may have some weight. But every scholar must see that you assail my character in vain ; that these authorities have been honestly adduced ; that they expose your church ; and that you do not even *attempt* an answer to the body of them. Thus, for example, your answer to the Bull of Innocent the 8th was, that no such Bull was issued in 1477, and you intimated that *a mistake* in the *date* was a proof of forgery. " *Such bulls* (you say) *come from another quarter.*" When pressed by the question, was not such a Bull published in 1487, you have actually the unthinking hardihood to deny that there ever was such a bull. " I do deny it flatly." Now for the proof. In Baronius's Annals, 19th vol. page 386, section 25, we are told that the sprouts of the Waldensian heresy re-appearing, according to custom, an Inquisitor was appointed ; but these Heretics arose in arms, and slew his servant.

Qua indignitate permotus, Innocentus, Gallos, Sabaudos, ac Germanos, in quorum limitibus, impietas defixa hærebat, ad hæreticos delendos expedire arma jussit ; et gravibus pœnis, hæreticorum fautores perculit; tum Albertum de Capitanies Archidiaconon Cremonensem, amplissimis instructum mandatis decrevit ut religiosam crucis militiam ad Waldenses exscindendos promulgaret, ac principes, et Episcopos in eosdem concitaret—quibus literis hæc temporis nota adjecta est. Dat. Romæ. apud S. Petrum. anno incarnationis Dominicæ 1487. V. Kal. Maii. Pontificatus nostri anno iii.

By which indignity Innocent, much excited, ordered the Gauls, Savoyese, and Germans, within whose territories the impiety still remained firmly rooted, to take up arms for the destruction of the Heretics; and he smote the *favourers* of the Heretics with heavy punishments : at the same time he commissioned Albert de Capitanies, Archdeacon of Cremona, with ample powers to publish a crusade for the extermination of the Waldenses, and to stir up Princes and Bishops against them.—The date of this document is as follows : Given at Rome, at St. Peter's, in the year of our Lord's incarnation, 1487, 5th of Kalends of May, and of our Pontificate the 3d.

Here, then, we have the testimony of your own great annalist.—How you will settle the matter with him, I know not. Perhaps this is only his *opinion*—surely it is not a *Protestant* fabrication. But here is the Bull, Brief, or whatever you please to call it, *the public decree of the Pope, ordering three States to take up arms for the extermination of heretics; and in the name of God, commissioning Princes and Bishops to destroy them!* Whether, then, we regard the detestable act of the Pope, or your " flat denial" of it, the reader must alike be assured of the guilt of your church, and the *shifts* of her defender!

1. In your letter (No. 17,) you said " the Episcopalians of Maryland persecuted the PRESBYTERIANS; the CATHOLICS of Maryland protected them. *The gratitude of the Presbyterians* was the gratitude of the serpent, that stings the bosom which fostered it. They put down, and persecuted these very Catholics as soon as it was in their power." In letter (No. 18,) I told you it was " AN UTTER FABRICATION." In your last letter you reply, " *He* (Mr. Jefferson) testifies that *the* PURITANS (mark, reader, not *Presbyterians*, Puritans,) *persecuted by the Episcopalians of Virginia, emigrated in considerable numbers to Maryland*," &c. &c. And is this the only defence for the unfounded charge? Are the Puritans and Presbyterians the same people in history? Does not your defence confess that it was a fabrication? I would gladly attribute this to *ignorance*.

2. You are equally unfortunate in the case of the Quakers. Having said " *The Quakers of New England were hanged by the Presbyterians.*" I denied it, and called on you for proof. And what is your *proof?* You call the authors of this persecution unto death, 'Congregationalists.' "But the distinction between them and Presbyterians, is too fine for modern powers of discrimination." A man who writes with your *freedom*, should have a good *memory*. You can see *no* distinction between Presbyterians and Congregationalists, where it is convenient to make the terms convertible! Remember this when you speak of the *divisions* of Protestants!

3. Your *defence* of the proceedings against John Huss, is certainly *candid and ominious*. It is however a misrepresentation of the case in many of the most important particulars. Lenfant tells us that Huss said, in presence of the Council, *I came to this city relying on the public faith of the Emperor, who is now present.* He then looked him in the face; and *Sigismond blushed for his own baseness, feeling the truth of the reproach.* When the Diet of Worms plead this example of the Council of Constance, and of Sigismond, in order to induce Charles V. to betray Luther, he replied, " *I am resolved not to blush with my predecessor.*" And ought not you, Sir, to blush for defending such a deed? Dupin (your own historian) says, "The Council of Constance being now appointed, the Pope and Emperor invited John Huss to come thither, and give an account of his doctrine—and that he might do it with *all freedom*, the Emperor gave him a *safe conduct, whereby he gave him leave to come freely to the Council and return again.*" But more of this hereafter; I only add now, that we may see something of the spirit of this Council, which thus disposed of Huss's departing soul " WE DEVOTE YOUR SOUL TO

INFERNAL DEVILS." (Tuam animam devovemus diabolis infernis :) and, as Dupin informs us, the Bishops who were appointed by the Council to degrade him, and prepare him for the civil arm, put on his head a mitre of paper on which *devils were painted.*

4. The endless iteration of trifles is beneath the dignity of inquiry after truth. Yet they say, "straws show the way the wind blows." You charge me with suppressing *a single word*, as follows : " The scrap of Latin which you have cited in parenthesis, though consisting of three words only, is *falsified.* Sunt procul extirpandi, are the words of your letter—sunt procul *dubio* extirpandi, are the words of the author." Even had there been accidentally such an omission, the *full translation of the absent word*, looked you in the face, in the same sentence. But your readers must smile, if a more serious feeling be not produced, to see the *entire sentence* in all the papers, the Presbyterian, the Catholic Herald, &c. &c. How could you permit yourself to make such a mistake? Does it not prove beyond a doubt that you feel your difficulties, and are at a loss for a refuge from them? I do from my heart pity you.

5. As to the notorious decree which it seems you will *make* me confess that I did garble, I wish you would produce the whole passage. The parts left out did not "garble" the passage; but were all to my purpose; and I regretted to lose them. But I had cited a page or two, and had not room for more. Why do you not produce and contrast them with what I published, if I have altered the meaning of the decree? It was of the *translation* you spoke in your former letter. You asked, " *do you give it us a literal and continuous translation ?*" I replied, " unhesitatingly I do. It is as *literal* as the sense will bear." My *abstract* gave the *unbroken* meaning of the decree; repeated inverted commas marked the transition in the sentences; and what I omitted was all, *all* in my favour; and I cannot think one reader will believe you, until you adduce the omitted sentences, and show that they affect the meaning of my quotations. Such charges come with poor grace from *you*, after the memorable cases of Tertullian and Wesley.

6. Your *attempt* at a reply to Bishop Onderdonk's charge on the rule of faith, is not only meagre to the last degree, but manifests a spirit unworthy of a Christian or a man. Not content with vilifying me in the pages of your controversial letters, you have carried your assaults into the preface of the review. The following is a sample; after speaking of me in terms of coarse disrespect, you proceed to say : " But for some months back there has been a considerable undertone of dissatisfaction among the better informed Protestants generally, not excepting Presbyterians themselves." " Even some of the Protestant clergy did not hesitate to say that Mr. Breckinridge was not 'the man' that should have been selected." And again, " His (the Bishop's) charge has been received as a supplement, if not a substitute, to the attempts of Mr. Breckinridge." In your letter No. 17, you have also said : " ——— a recent charge, 'the rule of faith,' which without *professing to be*, IS GENERALLY REGARDED as a prop to the weakness of your arguments, in opposition to my reasoning on the same subject."

Now, Sir, I have long since frankly owned to you, that in the evangelical Protestant churches there are many men who are far better fitted than myself, by learning, talents, age, piety, and pursuits, to meet you in this discussion. But do you reflect that every effort to disparage *my* qualifications, still farther degrades *yourself?* If a youth, who spends half his life in the stage coach, and who holds so humble a rank amidst the constellation of Protestant ministers, finds it no hard task to expose and confound the fashionable, learned, and powerful Mr. Hughes, then either the cause of Catholicity is so desperate that the best powers of its priesthood cannot sustain it against the feeblest essays of Protestants, or else the hero of their cause is only a garrulous Daw, and has been renowned like Goliah, only for want of a *trial.*

May I here ask of you *evidence* of so *"considerable an undertone* of dissatisfaction among better informed Protestants, *generally,* and even among *Presbyterians,* and some of the *Protestant clergy?"* Will you favour me with one respectable name, from all these classes? For every such I will return testimonies the most ample and multifarious, and bring the highest authority directly falsifying all these unworthy insinuations. Besides, can you honestly say that the Bishop's charge is GENERALLY REGARDED AS A PROP to the weakness of my arguments? Have you gathered the public mind so largely? Does the public *generally* call my arguments weak?— Have you learned in *four weeks,* (the age of the charge) what the *community* think of the *reason* for delivering it? Must not every one see with what unpardonable laxity you venture to speak? Your little *world* of satellites may tell *you* so! But St. John's is not our country. I could give you *another public* sentiment, but I will not imitate your vain boasting. You shall hear it for yourself, as it gathers in a returning tide from the limits of the land. In the mean time be admonished that there is no collusion between the Bishop and myself. I have not the honour even of a personal acquaintance with him. Nor must you think that the nation will hold its breath, and the Protestant press stand still, while you swagger through the pompous rounds of arrogant and empty essays on the rule of faith.— Again, the Catholic press in this country teems with parallel discussions of the controversy now in progress. I have been personally attacked by one of your papers; and the Catholic Herald itself is continually publishing something intended to bear upon our controversy. In a word, a new era has come in our country. The American people will promptly see, "who the serpent is (to use your own illustration) that stings the bosom that warms it." They will henceforth know *where* to send their children for education, and *when to contribute* in generous and abused confidence, to build the schools, and convents, and chapels, that are to train the children to call their parents *heretics ;* and are arising to re-establish a religion which never did, never will, and never can, permit a free-government, or religious toleration. The people are awake or awaking; and you must change your system, or lose your prize.

7. As to WESLEY, your defence so sadly labours, that comment

seems unnecessary. Your explanation has turned *states-evidence* against you.

If space were not wanting, much powerful matter might be adduced in exposure of your treatment of him. Mr. Hughes says, Wesley was the public defender of "the Protestant Association." Wesley says, "*I have not one line* in defence of the association, either in London, or elsewhere." Mr. Hughes says, "It never was a Roman Catholic maxim, (that no faith is to be kept with heretics) except when Protestant calumny made it so." Wesley says, "the last volume (of Labbe's Book of Councils) contains a particular account of the Council of Constance, one of whose decrees, p. 169, is, " that heretics ought to be put to death, notwithstanding the public faith engaged to them in the most solemn manner. (Non obstantibus salvis conductibus Imperatoris, Regum, &c.) Whosoever, therefore, would remark upon it (his late letter,) to any purpose, must prove three things: (1.) That the decree of the Council of Constance *publicly made*, has been publicly disclaimed. (2.) That the Pope has not power to pardon sins, or to dispense with oaths, vows, and promises. And (3,) that no priest has power to pardon sins." These you never can *prove;* yet until you do, you have left an unanswered argument, which will last as long as the writings and memory of Wesley.

8. As to your allusion to our domestic slavery, I fully accord with you in the sentiment, that it is a great national crime, and a great national calamity. But then the question for you to answer is this: The Pope's Bull consigned heretics to *slavery*, in the name of God and the Church. Had he the *right* to do this? If the State sins in allowing slavery, may the Roman church encourage and incite to it, and be *guiltless?* Is such a church infallible? This is the question.

9. As to the rule of faith, you say "the subject is fairly exhausted, by your unexpected declaration, that private interpretation is not the Protestant rule of faith." *Unexpected!* Strange language at the *close* of a discussion, when in the *first* column of my first letter, five months since, I gave this definition of our rule of faith, viz:

"The word of God as contained in the Scriptures of the Old and New Testaments." It is to this definition I have adhered. By your own *admission*, then, you have evaded the real Protestant rule of faith, and argued *against* its *abuses* alone! And strange to tell, you have never to this day given a definition of your rule of faith: and the story of the Shepherds, and the *rogue's mark*, applies to it as directly this day, as it did three months ago.

At the close of my last letter I introduced many extracts from the famous letter of the cardinals to Pope Paul the 3d, *showing the necessity of a reformation in the Church of Rome.* Let us proceed to other testimonies. The next I cite is also on Romish authority—being the famous letter of the three bishops at Bononia, written to the Pope (at his request, and containing counsel for the establishment of the church,) after the Reformation had begun. This letter covers nearly six folio pages, and you will scarcely expect its entire publication. The Bishops say, " *The Lutherans receive and confess*

All the articles of the Athanasian, Nicene, and Apostles' creed." " And these Lutherans refuse to admit any doctrine but that alone which hath the Prophets, Christ and his Apostles for its authors, and wish that all men would be content with those few things that were observed in the Apostles' times, or immediately after; and would imitate the ancient churches, and not think of receiving any traditions, which it is not as apparent as the light were delivered and instituted by our Lord Jesus Christ and his Apostles." " In the days of the Apostles (to tell you the truth, but you must be silent) and for several years after them there was no mention made of either pope or cardinal—there was none of these large revenues belonging to the bishops and priests, no sumptuous Temples were raised; there were no monasteries, priors, or abbots, much less any of these doctrines, these laws, these constitutions, nor this sovereignty, which we now exercise over people and nations." " And here you must awake and exert all your force to hinder as much as you can, the Gospel from being read (especially in the vulgar tongue,) in all the cities which are under your dominion. Let that little of it which they have in the mass serve their turn, nor suffer any mortal to read any thing more; for so long as men were content with that little, things went to your mind, but grew worse and worse from that time, that they commonly read more. *This, in short, is the book,* that has beyond all others, raised those storms and tempests, in which we are almost driven to destruction. And really whoever shall diligently weigh the Scripture, and then consider all the things that are usually done in our churches, will find there is great difference betwixt them—and that this doctrine of ours is very unlike, and in many things quite repugnant to it." *This letter* is furnished by Verjerius, and Wolfius, and is translated at large by Dr. Claggett of Gray's Inn.

Many years before this, the 1st Council of Pisa had decreed a Reformation. The Council of Constance resolved that a reformation was necessary, and enumerated nearly twenty items, one on Simony, and another on Indulgences, &c. &c. in which it was called for. The Council of Basil, and the 2d Pisan Council also decreed a reformation necessary. *One* of these at least is conceded to be a general council, confirmed by a Pope. Now if the decrees of a general Council, confirmed by a Pope (as you say) be *infallible,* then a reformation was *infallibly* necessary; and if such a decree be an *article of faith,* then it is an *article of faith* that a reformation was necessary.

To these testimonies I might add almost innumerable authorities from the prelates and other writers of the church of Rome. Having not room for this, I refer you in fine to the " CENTUM GRAVAMINA, or HUNDRED GRIEVANCES, OF GERMANY," presented in a memorial to the Pope, by the diet of Nuremberg in 1523, the very era of the Reformation. Many years before, the Emperor of Germany joining the King of France in calling for reformation, drew up TEN GRIEVANCES, the 8th of which was, that " *new indulgences had been granted, and old ones revoked and suspended, merely to squeeze out money.*" About this time, (as Dupin, a Roman Catholic historian says) " *Pope Alexander VI. died August 17th,* 1503, *by the poison which he had prepared for another, loaded with the iniquities of himself, and* HIS NATURAL SON *Cæsar Borgia.*" But by 1522, the *ten* grievances had grown to *one hundred.* Some of these were as follows: (see Dupin on this subject:)

1*st. Too many human constitutions which they* (*the Papacy*) *dispensed with for money*

2d. *Indulgences were become an insupportable yoke, by which much money was squeezed out of the Germans, piety destroyed, and a door set open to all sorts of crimes—because by that means men are freed from punishment, for money; that the sums gathered by these indulgences, was consumed by the Popes in maintaining the luxury of their relations and family; that the stations and indulgences granted to certain churches were not less scandalous, nor did less injury to the poor.*"

10th. The encroachments of the ecclesiastical Judges in LAY (mark it) lay causes, and their malversations.

11th. *Exactions of the clergy* for sacraments, burials, masses, &c., and *even for licenses to keep concubines.*

These may serve as specimens of the *whole hundred.* Observe, these were complaints by a Roman Catholic Emperor, Charles V.; and a Roman Catholic Diet; and the account is taken from a Roman Catholic historian. These testimonies added to those given at the close of my last letter, plainly show that a *Reformation was necessary.* We shall prove still further hereafter, God willing, that this Reformation was needed in FAITH, as well as MORALS; in the WORSHIP of the church, in its HEAD, and in its MEMBERS.

Now the history of the church plainly shows, that the Popes and Councils did not, and would not, attempt the necessary reform. The very assumption of *Infallibility,* while persisted in, renders all essential reform inconsistentent and absurd; unnecessary and impossible. Hence the corruptions of the church of Rome, in doctrine, morals, and essential worship, have been perpetuated from age to age. Hence when you call yourselves *unchangeable,* you, by confession, and as an article of faith, declare against all reformation: and hence, though like the cameleon, you take the lights and shades of the objects around you, in different countries, still you are in essence the same church, UNREFORMED AND UNREFORMABLE, BOTH NOW AND FOR EVER. Wherefore the voice of God, speaking in his providence, in your history, and HIS HOLY WORD, called upon every lover of truth and holiness to fly from your communion, saying, COME OUT OF HER MY PEOPLE, THAT YE BE NOT PARTAKERS OF HER SINS, AND THAT YE RECEIVE NOT OF HER PLAGUES; FOR HER SINS HAVE REACHED UNTO HEAVEN, AND GOD HATH REMEMBERED HER INIQUITIES. (Rev. xviii. 4, 5.)

It was in obedience to this divine call that the illustrious, and ever memorable " Reformation," as it is emphatically styled, was at first effected. This Reformation was not the introduction of a *new* religion; but the restoration of the *old,* as found in the word of God, as preached by Christ, and his Apostles; as held by the *earliest* writers, and professed in the *creed called the Apostles,* that primitive Christianity, which was gradually and greatly perverted, and corrupted by the rise and establishment of the Papacy, and was more and more abused by the church of Rome until the 16th century.

To the question often put to Protestants, "*Where was your religion before Luther?*" we may answer with a youthful reformer, "*Where was your face before it was washed?*" or if you prefer this, "*Where was your religion before the Council of Nice?*" and where was it, when the Pope of Rome *signed* the Arian creed, and the chief part of the church *adopted* it? Protestantism is a *new name* for the *Catholicism* of antiquity; in contrast with *Romanism*, or the absurd term *Roman Catholicism*. This name was given to the Reformers, who PROTESTED in 1529 against the unjust decisions of the Diet of Spires. *Protestants*, properly so called, are Reformers, as their Lord was of the corruptions of the Jews; and are *heretics* as Paul and Peter were, in coming out from that *ancient* but *erring* people.

That Protestants are not INNOVATORS is virtually confessed by Romanists, and appears from this, that we hold to *the Bible* as the only rule of faith; whereas *they add* to it many things, as Traditions, Apocrypha, and the *interpretations* of their Councils. *We* hold to Christ's headship over the church; *they* add to it the *headship* of the Pope. *We* hold to *two* sacraments; they *add* five more. *We* hold to the *alone* merits of *Christ's* death, and the *one* only sacrifice of Christ; *they* add other, and *human* merits to Christ's merits, and profanely pretend to sacrifice him *anew* every day in the *Mass*. *We* hold to *confession* to God; *they* add *auricular confession*. *We* hold that Christ's church cannot *fail*; they add that *they*, as the church, are *infallible*. In a word, not to mention many such distinctions, their system is like a great wen on a man's head, which has appeared upon the church; and though growing out of, and cleaving to the true church, is not the true church; but a corrupt and vicious excrescence which has encumbered it for ages, and will at last be *cut off!*

Protestantism is not a NOVELTY, but became another name for Christianity in western Europe, marking an era when religion and learning and liberty revived. Romanism *is* a novelty; the parent of ignorance, corruption of truth, and oppression. There are no less than twelve new articles of faith in the creed of Pius IV. manufactured or adopted by the Council of Trent in the 16th century of the Christian era; and ascending from age to age, you may distinctly note when Purgatory, Transubstantiation, Indulgences, &c. &c. were firs broached and legalized. And while the Protestants *recalled* primeval Christianity, in Europe, there were churches scattered over large regions of Asia, and Africa, some of which were *never subject* to the church of Rome, as the Syrian Christians, and others *protested* against many of the false doctrines, and repelled the despotism of the Roman Hierarchy, as the Armenians in central Asia, and, in a greater or less degree, the Greek church at large. Add to this, that the Albigenses and Waldenses did for ages, and, in the very heart of Europe, like the *burning bush* which Moses saw, survive your fiery persecutions, and *protest* almost *in our language*, against the papal errors. These people may be traced up for many ages before the days of Luther; indeed Rhinerius, a Roman Inquisitor, tells us, that some have carried them up to the Apostles' times.

Roman Catholics profess to be the only true church, and that *Protestants* are *schismatics*. But is it not notorious, that in your church, there was a great schism in the 14th century, so that, for the space of fifty years, there were sometimes *two*, and sometimes *three Popes;* and scenes were acted out by their *Holinesses*, the continued occurrence of which rent the church and agitated Europe; and the very recital is enough to make one shudder. And where was the Greek church? Did it not break off from you, and *protest* against *many* of the very *errors* and *corruptions* which we reject? And with her did not whole nations irreparably forsake the church of Rome? Why did not your infallible rule of faith " *settle these disputes*" which rent your church so often and so long; which tore from you so much of Asia and eastern Europe on the one hand, and half western Europe by the Reformation on the other? And did not the President of the Council of Trent say, *that the depravation and corruption of discipline and morals in the church of Rome, was in a great measure the cause and original of all those schisms and heresies which then troubled the church?*

When, therefore, you call for a definition of "THE PROTESTANT RELIGION," (as the time to give it has now arrived,) I reply, it is the Religion of the Reformation, in contradistinction from the Roman Catholic Religion, as it concerns doctrine, and morality; government, discipline, and worship. It is the religion which is exclusively derived from, and consistent with, the HOLY SCRIPTURES, AS THE ONLY INFALLIBLE RULE OF FAITH AND PRACTICE; and which *protests* against the errors and corruptions of the church of Rome. To be more particular, we *protest* against the universal supremacy of the Pope; against infallibility, purgatory, and indulgences; against transubstantiation, the sacrifice of the Mass, and communion in one kind;—against the satisfaction and merit of creatures, not duly honouring the atonement and righteousness of our divine Saviour; against penance, auricular confession, absolution, and extreme unction; against the substitution of external services and rites for the work of the Spirit, and the religion of the heart; against worshipping the host, images, relics, saints, and angels; against prohibiting the Bible to the people, prayers and other worship in an *unknown* tongue, the doctrine of intention, innovations on the sacraments as to number and administration, the celibacy of the clergy and monasticism; against the manifold superstitions, and immoralities of the church; against sanctuary for crimes, exemption of subjects from allegiance, and priests from obedience to magistrates; against the oppression, persecution, and exclusive salvation of the church of Rome. These are the leading errors and evils against which we PROTEST; and I am, by the grace of God, prepared to prove that the PROTESTANT RELIGION (in contradistinction from the religion holding, teaching, and practising these things,) IS THE RELIGION OF CHRIST.

Especially do I stand ready to show, that the supremacy of the Pope is a usurpation, not founded in Scripture, oppressive to man, and injurious to Christ, the only head of the church; that Purgatory is a fiction, and ruinous to the souls of men; that Indulgences are " a bundle of licenses to commit sin," and the true *moral* of Purgatory; that Transubstantiation is a novelty, an impossibility, and an absurdity; that the sacrifice of the Mass is an impiety, and the worship of the host idolatrous; and so in order, if you can venture to meet me. And as you charge me so pertinaciously with being the *assailant*, I will now claim the privilege which you thus force upon me; especially as heretofore you have chosen your own ground, and called on me to *follow* where you led in the discussion. This is the more reasonable, since you profess to belong to the *true* and the *only* true church; and thus coming with exclusive salvation, and prescriptive claims, make all other forms of religion void; and present the alternative of *Catholicism*, or *no religion*. I shall therefore with great freedom examine these high pretensions. This is the proper and natural order of discussion. In this way our reasons for *protesting* will be fully brought to view; and the two systems presented in continued contrast. Yours, &c. &c.

JOHN BRECKINRIDGE.

P. S. I regret that in attempting to injure Mr. Burtt you should expose yourself.—" But he is of age; and shall speak for himself." As to the *reference*, delicacy, and justice, ought to have prevented you from speaking as you have of Dr. Wylie's *reason* for declining. Did not a sense of propriety hinder me, I also could make inferences from his dignified, and honourable letter. I do heartily wish that he would yet consent to give his decision on the score of referred topics. J. B.

CONTROVERSY. No. XXI.

RULE OF FAITH.

Philadelphia, June 21st, 1833.

To the Rev. John Breckinridge.

Rev. Sir,—I have read your last letter with all attention, and shall now proceed to notice such parts of it as require to be answered. It begins thus, "The celebrated Pascal, himself a Romanist." Pascal, Rev. Sir, was a *Jansenist*, and as such, was *not* a "Romanist," nor even a Catholic. This mistake of yours is common among Protestants, even those who ought to be acquainted with the difference. As to his Provincial Letters, critics of all parties are agreed that they were written in a spirit of satirical enmity towards the Jesuits. Racine says they are nothing but a "comedy," the characters of which were selected from Convents and the Sarbonne. Voltaire, who was certainly no friend to the Jesuits, says, that the whole work is a misrepresentation, in consequence of the author's attributing "artfully (adroitement) to the *whole Society*, the extravagant opinions set forth by a few of its members in Spain and Flanders." (Volt. Siecle de Louis XIV.) So much for your first sentence.

2. If I have charged you with "garbling authorities," and making assertions which are "untrue," I always supported the charge with *proofs*, which remain unanswered. The first sentence of the 2d paragraph is equally unfounded in the truth. It is as follows, "your Bible, your public Prayers, your Breviary and Mass book, your Catechism, decrees of Councils, and Bulls of Popes, *being in a dead language*." Now, our Bibles are in English, our public prayers are in English, our Catechisms are in English, our Mass book is in English; and how can you say that they are in a "dead language"—when any one may call at the Catholic bookstore of Mr. Cummiskey of this city, and purchase the very books you mention, all in English? If by such assertions your "credit suffers," as you say, do not, I pray you, throw the blame on me. Catholics have published more editions of the Scriptures in English, within the last thirty years, than any other denomination of Christians in the United States. This fact proves how far you are from being correct, when you assert that our "Bibles," are "in a dead language." It proves also how far Protestants are deceived by their blind credulity, and their prejudices, when they say that Catholics are not allowed to read the Scriptures. The *first edition* would be still on the booksellers' shelves, if there existed *such a prohibition*—since Protestants never purchase our Bibles.

3. The Bull of Innocent VIII. In your letter No. 16, you stated that it was in the University of Cambridge; and repeated *twice* that it was issued in 1477. You subsequently admitted your mistake of *ten years*, as to the time; but, nothing daunted, you "dared me to deny it." I did deny it. Then you proceed to the "*show of proof*," and quote the annals of Baronius. Does he say that such a Bull exists? No. The quotation merely testifies, that Albertus Cataneius was commissioned to preach a crusade against the Waldenses; who, as you yourself *acknowledge*, had already "*taken up arms and* MURDERED those who had been sent among them—or as you

express it, "slew his servant." This does not prove *the existence of the Bull in the University of Cambridge.* And after having made the assertion, and "*dared me to deny it,*" is it not strange that you should adduce such a vague citation, and then say—"here is the Bull, Brief, or whatever I please to call it?" Besides, the annals of Baronius, come down only to the year 1198; and yet you quote his authority for a fact which should have taken place in 1487!!! How is this?

4. I must give you great credit for the ingenious manner in which you get over the persecution of the Catholics of Maryland, by the Presbyterians. The persecutors were Puritans. ("Mark, reader, not Presbyterians, Puritans.") This important distinction is to show, I suppose, that the persecutors of Geneva were *Calvinists;* those of Holland, *Gomarists;* those of New England, *Congregationlists;* and those of Scotland and England, in the time of Charles the first, as well as their brethren of Maryland, *Puritans.* But pray, where were the Presbyterians, *all this time?* When children disown their parentage, it is a sign they are ashamed of it.

5. As to the case of John Huss, the authority of Lenfant is no better than that of Mr. Wesley or your own. He was the son of a Calvinistic minister, and was brought up to be a Calvinistic minister himself. In 1727, he published what he called a history of the Council of Constance, held one hundred years before the Reformation. And it was *such a production,* as might have been expected from the author of the "history of Pope Joan," which he published in 1694. But he lived long enough to be *ashamed* of having treated with grave authorship, so absurd and calumnious a fable. These few remarks are sufficient, Rev. Sir, to show your readers, that your own authority would be quite as unimpeachable against the Council of Constance, as that of Lenfant. He was a bitter enemy of the Catholic church. As to the safe-conduct given by the Emperor, I have already, in my last letter, established its *character, conditions,* and *circumstances.* With reference to the unfortunate Huss himself, the Council condemned his doctrine; and degraded him as an obstinate heretic, from his rank of Priesthood. But having done this, it declared that its powers as a spiritual tribunal extended no farther.—The civil laws of the age and of the city of Constance did the rest. I have the acts of that Council now before me, and I defy *enmity itself* to make any thing more out of them. As to the "devils painted on his paper mitre," it is one of those little tales by which Protestant children are frightened into hatred against Catholics;—the germ of prejudice is planted in their minds;—so that when they have grown up, they are the *unconscious* victims of the "radical delusion" of Protestantism, and imagine that their religious opinions, *no matter what,* are taken from the pure word of God—the Bible alone.

6. In paragraph 4th of your letter, you quote the words of Bellarmine "sunt procul *dubio* extirpandi" to show that they were not "falsified," as I had stated. But you know that we both write from the corrected *proof* of each other's letters; which is furnished several days before the paper is regularly issued. You know further that in the *proof* the passage was as I stated—and *candor* should have in-

tant religion, which I shall examine presently, is a description of abuses, and of the low state of public morals at, and previous to the pretended "Reformation." That there were abuses, and that there still may be abuses, is what no man of sense and education will deny. But it will be perceived, that Catholics themselves were crying out for the *correction* of these abuses. They demanded a reformation— but they did not conceive that in order to effect it, it would be necessary to deny the existence of FREE WILL in man, as a *moral agent*, with Luther;—they did not conceive it necessary to make God the author of sin, and the slave of his own *foreknowledge*, with Calvin; they did not conceive it necessary, to deny the Divinity of Christ, and destroy the belief of redemption through the merits of his blood, with Socinus:—and so of the other "Reformers." This was not the *kind* of Reformation that they anticipated. They desired that men would *reform their lives*, according to the religion of Jesus Christ;—but the Protestant Reformers *changed* the religion of Christ, and yet testified, as I shall prove in its place, from their own writing, that their followers became *less* moral and *more depraved* than they had been before the change. As for your authorities on those abuses, be pleased to let me know where I shall find them.— For example, the reference to the "letter of the three Bishops at Bononia," is too vague. Again, the testimony of "Dr. Clagget of Gray's Inn," is no better than yours or that of Mr. M·Gavin. He, a Protestant, quotes from Wolfius, another Protestant; and both together with Lenfant, Robert Hall, and John Wesley may be placed in the same rank of testimony with archbishop "Usher."

Altogether, you will be pleased to quote the *original* authorities, and I will do the same, as I have done from the commencement. Such authorities as those just referred to, are not a whit better than your own assertion.

Before we pass to another topic, it may be proper for me to take a retrospective view of the question which has been under discussion, viz. the Rule of Faith. We started on the principle, that the Son of God having made a revelation of divine truths, and having required the belief of them as one of the *conditions of our salvation*, appointed at the same time, an "infallible" means to arrive at the knowledge of what those divine truths are. To accomplish this, the Catholic church has preserved from the days of the Apostles until this hour, the same uniform principle of religious guidance. For the proof that the Catholic church in holding to this principle, has followed the rule appointed by the Divine Author of Christianity, I refer the candid reader to the evidences adduced in my letters No. 5, 7, and 9—from Scripture, history, Apostolical and primitive usage in the Christian church, and from the very necessities of the case. Let him also see whether in any or all the letters of my opponent, these evidences, arguments, and authorities, have been refuted.

On the other hand Protestants have adopted from their *origin* in the 16th century, as the "infallible" means of arriving at the knowledge of those divine truths, which Christ revealed, the sacred writings, exclusively, of the Old and New Testament, as *each understands them for himself*. This principle secures to each minister the right to propagate his own conceits, as DIVINE TRUTHS contained in the Bible—and consequently has given rise to heresy of every description, until it has thrown Protestant Christianity into a scene of confusion, contradiction, inconsistency, doubt, indifference and infidelity, in which no man can say who is right, or who is wrong. Is this principle of religious guidance, "infallible?" And if not, who will say that it was established by Christ?

In my first letter I laid down certain arguments to prove that this principle is neither infallible nor competent to the *end* for which a rule of faith was instituted by the Divine Redeemer. These arguments it will be admitted by the candid reader, have not to this day been refuted. The first was, that the Bible was not complete until about the beginning of the second century—and therefore, could not be *the* rule of faith previous to its completion. The 2d was, that the Bible *no where* speaks of itself as *the* exclusive rule of faith—and that, therefore, Protestants have no divine authority for this assumption. The 3d was, that the Bible "*alone*," is the Bible on " the shelf"—in which sense it is absurd to speak of it, as a rule of faith. Now the public will be surprised to perceive that you have given up the Protestant rule of faith, in your last letter, except in *this identical and absurd sense of the Bible on " the shelf.*" In your epistle No. 18, you frankly gave up " private interpretation," as not being " the Protestant rule of faith." In your last you tell me, that in arguing against " private interpretation," I have argued " not against the *real* Protestant rule of faith, *but against its abuses alone !*" You affect to be surprised that I was not aware of this sooner. But I believe, Rev. Sir, that you are the first Protestant writer that has recognised " private interpretation" as an " abuse." The real rule of Protestants is, you tell us, " The word of God as contained in the Scriptures of the Old and New Testaments." This is the real *rule*, but if men try to understand these " Scriptures," it must be by "*private interpretation,*" and this, you tell us, is the " ABUSE," against which you say I have been arguing. Now you will not be offended, I trust, at learning that so far as this admission goes, *you are a Catholic*. The church has always held your declaration on this point—and she has ever taught, that " private interpretation," as it is among Protestants, is an " abuse."

My 4th argument was, that the Bible alone cannot attest either its *authenticity, inspiration,* or *meaning*—which is proved by the contradictions which Protestants profess to derive from it;—and therefore is *not* the only rule of faith.

The 5th was, that during the first four hundred years of Christianity the Bible was not, and could not be, the only rule of faith—and the proof is, that during that interval the Canon of Scripture was not universally settled in the church; and even if it had been, copies of the sacred book could not be multiplied for the general wants.

The 6th was, that since the beginning of the world. no controversy was ever decided by the *Bible alone*. 7th. That the Bible PERVERTED by " private interpretation," in other words, the Protestant rule of faith—has given rise to all the heresies that ever did, or do exist.

8th. That in consequence of its "ABUSE," by private interpretation, it makes for the Socinian, as well as for the Calvinist. 9th. That by the same "abuse," it compels a man who is an *orthodox* Protestant to become heterodox, if he *thinks* that he was *wrong*, and *wishes* to be *right*. 10th. That it reduces orthodoxy and heterodoxy to the same quagmire of *uncertainty*, in which neither can find any thing more solid, as a foundation, than *mere private opinion*.

Thus it is, that Protestants by adopting a *false principle* of religious guidance, have unhinged Christianity, and left infidelity to reap the fruits of their rashness. Now, Rev. Sir, I contend that these plain, common sense arguments against the Protestant rule of faith, *have not been refuted in all you have written*. They have, indeed, been met with cavil and objection; but if cavil and objection are to be received as *proof*, then the Atheist may triumph. We all admit, Catholics and Protestants, the Bible to be the inspired word of God, but at the commencement of the controversy I assailed "private interpretation," as the "radical delusion of Protestantism," and I am happy to perceive that in your last letter you also denounce it as "abuse." Here then we may take leave of the rule of faith, and proceed to the second topic of discussion, which professes to be this:

"IS THE PROTESTANT RELIGION THE RELIGION OF CHRIST?"

To this question I answer with a full sense of my responsibility both to God and my fellow men, *that it is not*. And I am persuaded that all men who are candid, and competent to give due consideration to the reasons I shall adduce, will arrive at the same conclusion.

1. The Protestant religion is only three hundred years old,—whereas "the religion of Christ" is eighteen hundred years—therefore they are not the same. In proof of the premises of this argument, I challenge you to name on the face of the globe, or in the history of the whole human race, any society of Christians, *agreeing in doctrines* with the authors of the pretended Reformation, or with any sect that has grown out of it. Consequently *either* the religion of Christ was not professed by any society of Christians, until the days of Luther;—*or else*, the Protestant religion is not the religion of Christ. This is a dilemma from which escape is impossible. Is it not then, Rev. Sir, *strange* to hear you answering the question, "where was your religion before Luther?" by asking another, "where was your face before it was washed?"

2. Whenever God communicated any *revelation* or *new doctrine* to mankind, he invariably gave to the organ of *that* new doctrine, a *divine commission* to speak in his name; and the power of miracles to prove that God *had so commissioned him to speak*. This was the case with Moses; this was the case with Jesus Christ himself, during his life, and with his apostles, after his ascension into heaven. But the Protestant religion was a *new religion*, since no society of Christians had professed its doctrines *previous* to Luther, and yet its founders had *no divine commission*, and no power of working miracles to show that God had sent them, for this *new work:*—Therefore the Protestant religion is not the religion of Christ.

3. The religion of Christ consists of doctrines which have been revealed, taught, and believed as *positive truths;* whereas the Pro-

testant religion consists of doctrines which are *variable, unsettled*, and which are submitted and believed not as *positive truths*, but as *mere opinions;* therefore the Protestant religion is not the religion of Christ.

4. The Apostles of Christianity, besides their power of working miracles in proof of their having *been sent,* preached the same divine faith every where, without the least variation or disagreement; whereas the Apostles of the Protestant religion, Luther, Zuinglius, Henry VIII., Socinus, Calvin, &c., not only disagreed in their doctrines, but denounced each other in the most solemn manner, as *Heretics and deceivers of souls.* Therefore the Protestant religion is not the religion of Christ; even according to the testimony of its founders.

Here, Rev'd Sir, are four brief and distinct arguments, which I defy all the powers of human ingenuity to refute:—not because they are of my construction, but because they are *true,* in all their parts. Nothing can overturn truth. You may excite the passions of men to hate it, you may succeed to envelope it in the mists of prejudice, but still it is *truth,* and because it *is* truth, it cannot be altered or destroyed. Permit me then to invite your attention to these four arguments, examine them *joint by joint,* and if they are true, then admit *for the sake of truth,* that " the Protestant religion is not the religion of Christ."

Your definition of the Protestant religion, might have been much shorter and equally to the purpose. You might have said, at once, and in a few words, " The Protestant religion is *not* the Catholic religion." Now this is no definition. You tell me what the Protestant religion is *not;* whereas I require to know what *it is*. In order to a definition, you must describe a thing by *its own* properties, its own *distinctive characteristics.* " The Protestant religion, you say, is the religion of the Reformation." This is no definition; until you have fixed the positive *meaning* of the word Reformation. That word has a great variety of meanings, among Protestants; it gave birth to a numerous offspring of religions, and I should be glad to know whether you intend to bear a shield broad enough to cover and protect them all. In my arguments above, I disregarded all definition of the Protestant religion; because those arguments are equally strong, no matter *what it is.* But a definition is absolutely necessary, and as yours is the business of defence, it is your duty to furnish it. You have attempted another definition, and told us that the Protestant religion " is the religion which is exclusively derived from, and consistent with, the HOLY SCRIPTURES, AS THE ONLY INFALLIBLE RULE OF FAITH AND PRACTICE." This, Rev'd Sir, is precisely the definition, which the Unitarians, Swedenborgians, and Universalists, give of *their religion.* Do you purpose then, to prove that *their* religion, is the religion of Christ? But as I do not wish to misrepresent the Protestant religion, I desire that you tell me whether *these* denominations are included in it, or not; they are certainly included in *your definition.*

If I were allowed to define the Protestant religion, I should call it " the religion of free-thinking about the meaning of the Bible. The religion in which every man has a right to judge for himself;

and to make the sacred text of Scripture speak *in accordance with his judgment*. The religion, in which there is neither schism, nor heresy, neither faith nor heterodoxy, because being a religion of *individual speculation*, and *private opinion*, these things are necessarily rendered impossible. I should say, that it is the religion which *cannot recover*, from the moral shock of its own first principles. The religion which, if considered in the *aggregate* of its sects, allows its ministers to teach the people that the Bible contradicts itself ten times in one page. The religion, in fine, which occupies the *intermediate space*, between *ancient Christianity*, and *modern Deism*, combining certain elements of *both ;* and cherishing enmity towards *both*, (especially the former,) and unable to defend itself against either."

Such is, in my opinion, the *true definition* of the Protestant religion. Such are its own inherent properties and characteristics. But still as you have undertaken to prove that it is the " religion of Christ," you have a right to define it *as you please*, provided you will only tell me what it is, instead of amplifying its *negative* qualities, by telling me what *it is not*.

Before I conclude this letter, I must call your attention and that of our readers, to a passage of your last epistle, which, if I understand it, proves that the leaven of *intolerance* is still working in the bosom of Presbyterianism. It is not, indeed, the declaration of the General Assembly; and therefore I am inclined to impute it rather to the irritation of *your* pen, than to the body of Calvinists at large, among whom, I have no doubt there are many who will disapprove of its spirit and bearing as much as I do. It runs as follows :

" In a word, a new era has come in our country. The American people will promptly see, ' who the serpent is (to use your own illustration,) that stings the bosom which warms it.' They will henceforth know where to send their children for education, and when to contribute in generous and abused confidence, to build the Schools, and Convents, and Chapels, that are to train the children to call their parents *heretics ;* and are arising to re-establish a religion which never did, never will, and never can, permit a free government or religious toleration. The people are awake or awaking; and you must change your system or lose your prize."

This language, Rev. Sir, will be read not indeed, with astonishment, (considering its source) but with *indignation* by every true hearted American citizen. Is it then a crime in the " American people," that they do not exclude Catholics from the privileges which the constitution secures to ALL ? Is the demon of sectarian hatred, ill-will among men, and intolerance to be again invoked ;—are the penal laws to be again enacted ;—the fires of persecution to be again lighted up, as the nostrum of political salvation for these United States ; merely because Mr. Breckinridge is, or affects to be, frightened at the progress of Catholicity ? What are the crimes imputed to Catholics ? Why, that they establish houses of " education," and that Protestants have been generous enough to contribute to their erection. Now if they have founded such institutions, it is a sign that they are not those *votaries of ignorance*, which you yourself have elsewhere represented them. And if Protestants have " contributed," to aid them in this work (of which you furnish no evidence) it is a sign that these Protestants *approved* of the undertaking, and exercised the privilege of dominion over *their own property*, without consulting their ministers. Farther, Catholic literary Institutions have never cost the public one cent for their maintenance, whereas those under the management of Protestant professors, besides their primitive endowment, have obtained vast sums of the public money. Not to go out of our own State, look at the Dickinson *Presbyterian College of Carlisle, which never flourished except when it was allowed to *feed at the public treasury of the State;* and after having received a number of legislative grants, as if it were an alms-house instead of a College, it has finally transferred itself to the Methodists, who, I trust, will make a better use of it.

The Catholic colleges, and houses of education, never beg at the doors of government for any such aid. They hold that the institution which, in this country, is not able to support itself by its own intrinsic merit, ought not to exist. They are patronised by Protestants, and I regret that you should have betrayed your mortification at this circumstance. Protestants begin to understand their own interest in this matter. They wish to place their sons in those institutions where there are found good discipline, conscientious tutors, vigilant attention to health and morals, competent and zealous professors, and all the means of a sound, radical, and thorough education;—and if, in their judgment, all these advantages are found in Catholic colleges and seminaries, why should you blame them for not sending their children to Princeton and Carlisle? As for the charge of teaching them to call their parents " *Heretics*," it is a calumny too silly to deserve refutation. Their own interest would forbid them, even if they were inclined. But I appeal to all the Protestant parents that ever patronised those institutions, to say whether their children did not return to them as *obedient*, as *respectful*, as *affectionate* as before they went; and with a more *delicate* and *conscientious apprehension* of their *filial, social*, and *moral duties*. Why then should you blame them for their preference?

As to Catholics being a " serpent warmed in the bosom of the American people," it is language, which, as I said before, no *true* son of the Constitution will understand, except to execrate the spirit

---

* Grants by Legislature to Dickinson College:

1786, April 7, 500*l.* and 10,000 acres of land, exchanged afterwards for $6000, say	$7335 00
1788, Oct. 4, a lot of ground in the borough of Carlisle.	
1791, Sept. 30, 1500*l.* say	4000 00
1795, April 11, $5000.	5000 00
1806, Feb. 24, $8400 on mortgage free of interest for five years; but 1819, the trustees discharged from the payment,	8400 00
1821, Feb. 20, $2000 annually for five years,	10,000 00
1826, Feb. 13, $3000 annually for seven years,	21,000 00
	$55,735 00

Making in all fifty-five thousand seven hundred and thirty-five dollars of the public money given to the Presbyterian Dickinson College of Carlisle!

which it *seems* to breathe. The "American people," *as a people*, knows no distinction of creeds; and yet you speak as if the government were already *chained to the car of the General Assembly!* The Catholics, as citizens, are part and portion of that "people," being as peaceable in their demeanor, as upright in their dealings, as industrious in their avocations, and as ardent in their attachment to *civil* and *religious* liberty, as any other denomination. When the tree of American liberty was planted, was it not watered with Catholic blood? When the instrument of American independence was drawn up, was it not signed with Catholic ink? When the provinces on our borders were to be conciliated, was not the commission intrusted to a Catholic Senator, and a Catholic Priest; afterwards Archbishop Carroll? When the battle was won, was not the glory of the victory divided with the Catholic soldiers, of a Catholic king? And yet, you speak of Catholics as if they live and breathe the free air, by the *criminal* connivance of "the American people." But you, forsooth, are about to rouse that "people," from its apathy to teach them, that in allowing the Catholics to share the benefits of the constitution—for I know of no other privilege that they enjoy—they are "cherishing a serpent that will sting the bosom which warms it."

But this, you say, was my "own illustration," applied to Presbyterians. Yes, Rev. Sir, but applied on the *faith of history;* to the Puritans, who, when they were persecuted in Virginia, fled to the Catholic colony of Maryland, and in return for the hospitality they received, turned round at the first opportunity, and *persecuted those who had exercised it towards them.* Read M'Mahon's History of Maryland. This was *the* case, which was illustrated by the simile of the serpent; and if history testifies that Catholics have at any time, ever been guilty of *such* base ingratitude, I have no objection that you should borrow and apply "my illustration." Your application of it to Catholics, as *distinguished from* "the American people," borders too much on the ludicrous, and shows that you were straitened for matter wherewithal to excite prejudice against Catholics, when you quit the testimony of *past events*, and appeal to the visions of futurity. But I fear that your *fallibility* as an *historian*, will have impaired your credit as a *prophet.*—Since it is much easier to be acquainted with what *has taken place in the world*, than to thread with prophetic accuracy the labyrinth of future contingencies.

"Chi offende, non pardona," says the proverb. And it would be one happy result of this controversy, if you could only turn against the Catholics that current of jealous apprehension, which for some time past has been setting in, against the Presbyterians themselves in reference to their ambitious projects and political aspirations. It would be well, if the "American people," could be induced to cast their eyes in another direction. But, Rev. Sir, *I* shall not be the accuser of Presbyterians, as to any *ulterior* political designs. I have marked their movements; their professions of zeal for the glory of God; their *plans* for accomplishing it; their schemes of sectarian *quackery*, by which it would appear that *they* are accountable for the religious, and moral well-being not only of the "American people," but of the whole human race;—their wish to have "Christian parties" in politics, and Christian magistrates, whose duty it is, says their STANDARD, to be "nursing fathers of the church;"—their enumeration of *Presbyterian* votes on the day of election; their attempts to have the mail stopped on Sunday—in a word, their gigantic schemes for the reformation of the world, according to their ideas of perfection;—all conspire to produce the apprehension, not that they will seize the civil government, (the American people will take *care of that)* but that in their zeal for the sanctification of *others*, they may neglect the sanctification of themselves. This is *all* the evil that I apprehend from the intermeddling and pragmatic spirit, which seems to animate the zealous members of Presbyterianism, from the Moderator in General Assembly, down to those well meaning children who cherish large notions about curing the moral distempers of a whole neighbourhood, by thrusting tracts into every house, whether the family desires them or not. But as to the "American people," they have nothing to dread on either side,—they will take care of the *State*, if clergymen will only take care of the *Church*—the denomination, however, that *first attempts* to bring about a *union* of these two, makes preparations for tragic nuptials.

In your postscript you charge me with attempting to injure the Rev. Mr. Burtt. I really cannot suffer such a charge to pass unnoticed. How does the case stand? You stated that you had been informed, that Bishop Kenrick had warned the people against reading this controversy. You subsequently apologized to *him;* but transferred the charge to *some other* of the Catholic clergy in this city. The charge itself was a "GRATUITOUS FALSEHOOD," because there was not the *shadow of foundation for it*. This was manifest. from the ludicrous texture of that ludicrous composition, signed John Burtt—and more so still, from the letter of the Rev. Mr. Fitton, of the "Connecticut Valley," who proves it a *falsehood*, by showing that he was in Washington city, on the very day on which he is charged with having issued the "prohibition," in St. John's church, Philadelphia. It was a "CALUMNY," because it insinuated dishonesty of purpose on the part of the Catholic clergy, in forbidding the people to behold the light of *truth* which your pen was shedding, around the topic of controversy. This was the state of the case independent of any man's authorship. And when I held Rev. John Burtt as *accountable for it;* you should remember that I did so, on your own specific testimony, for in your last letter but one you stated positively, that Mr. Burtt was "THE ORIGINAL, AND RESPONSIBLE INFORMANT." If that gentleman is injured, therefore, let him charge the injury upon *you*, or upon *himself*, or on *both together;* but not upon Yours, &c. JNO. HUGHES.

CONTROVERSY. No. XXII.

Philadelphia, June 27th, 1833.

To the Rev. John Hughes.

Sir,—The great question now before us, is this: *Is the Protestant religion the religion of Christ?* The order of debate as agreed on between us, entitles me to introduce this topic. Hence you have called on me for a definition of "the Protestant religion," and pledged yourself to respect it. The terms of the question make it general—not *Presbyterian,* but *Protestant;* they also refer us to a *fact* out of which the name grew, viz: that a *protest* had been entered: and they point us *to the church and system against which we protest.*—The very first step, therefore, in the order of discussion, is to show *against what* we protest. *After* this, or if you please, in *contrast* with it, it will be proper to examine *that which* the Protestants propose, as true and good, *in opposition* to the errors and evils of the church of Rome. I have on this plan given you a definition of the Protestant religion. It is a *positive* definition, viz. a religion *exclusively derived from, and consistent with, the Holy Scriptures, as the only infallible rule of faith and practice*—and I referred for illustration of it to the *earliest creed* and the *earliest Christian writers,* as well as those who have been emphatically called *The Reformers* of the 16th century. It is also *negative* in contradistinction from the Roman Catholic religion as to doctrine, morality, government, discipline and worship, and as *protesting* against the errors and corruptions of the church of Rome. If I am then to show *why* I protest, I must exhibit *what* I protest against; else the *correlative* term *Protestant,* has no meaning. And if, as you say, I am the original *assailant,* why do you tell me that mine "*is the business of defence?*" And if, of two leading questions, (viz. "The rule of faith," and this) the first is given to you, and the last to me, shall I be required to *defend* under the *first,* and also under the *last?* Are you then *afraid* to follow me in the steps of my discussion, while I compare our respective religions with each other, and with the religion of Christ? If so, you concede the weakness of your cause. If not, then follow me.

I have already proved (in my letters No. 18 and 20,) on the authority of Roman Catholic writers, and Roman Catholic councils, that a Reformation was necessary—and that it *was an article of faith* that a Reformation was necessary—not only in the days of Luther, but for ages before: that a Reformation was needed, in the *head and in the members:* that the name of Christ had been forgotten by the nations, and even by the clergy; that Rome herself, the avowed mother and mistress of churches, was the very place where Christ's religion was scandalized and his worship corrupted: that simony and sacrilege with nuns, clerical debauchery, "a world of superstitions," and the most shocking corruptions abounded and reigned in the church; and in a word, that an ignorant and corrupt priesthood were bringing *ruin* on the church. Pope Adrian the 6th said, " the whole world groaned after a reformation:" the Suffragan Bishop of Saltsburgh (onus ecclesiæ) declared " it is vehemently to be presumed, and cautiously to be feared, that the ruin of the Latin (Roman) church, as to its ecclesiastical dignity, is near;" and the 2d Pisan council (sess. 3d apud. Richerium, b. 4. pt. 1st) decreed " that the universal church needed reformation in *faith* and *manners*, in the *head* and *members*."

And yet it has also been proved that the church of Rome *would* not be reformed; that it *was not* reformed; and that on the ground of its pretended infallibility, it never *could* be reformed. Such confessedly was the deplorable condition of the church of Rome when " the Reformation" began, and its authors received the name of *Protestants*. Treading in their footsteps, we PROTEST against her corruption of the religion of Christ.

1. She has corrupted this religion at the fountain-head, by making another Bible, adding to it " the Apochryphal Books," which I have already proved were rejected for many centuries by the Christian church, which contain fables, lies, false doctrines, and contradictions; and in which alone are found some of those very *errors* that are held by the church of Rome. She has also given to corrupt and unwritten traditions the same authority with God's own word; and thus at her will brought from this *forge* any doctrine that the times and ends called for. From these topics, while on the *rule of faith*, you uniformly shrunk, thus confessing that they could not be defended.

2. *The Supremacy of the Pope*, is a radical error in the church of Rome, is a wicked and anti-christian usurpation, which by a lawless monarchy oppresses men, and rebels against God.

In the famous creed of Pius IV., which every Roman Catholic is bound without qualification, to believe, is this oath : " I promise and swear true obedience to the Roman Bishop; the successor of St. Peter, the prince of the Apostles, and vicar of Jesus Christ." Boniface VIII. in a decree extant in the canon-law, pronounces it " necessary to salvation for every human being to be subject to the Roman Pontiff." Bellarmine says, (chap. 17. b. 2.) " All the names, which in Scripture are applied to *Christ*, proving him to be *above* the church, are in *like* manner applied to the *Pope*." Is not this profane? The Pope is also styled " Head of the church"—" Lord of lords"—" Father of fathers"—" our Lord God the Pope," and the like. As the *vicar* of Christ, the Pope is blasphemously set up to take his place on earth. Thus he is the *Prophet, Priest, and King*, of *the church on earth*. He is a *Prophet;* for no council is valid, unless *called* and *approved* by him; and from this infallible source we are to learn, (1.) What *is* the word of God and what not; and (2.) without daring to think for ourselves, we are to learn what it *means*, and what not. As a *Priest*, he professes to offer up continually *the true Christ* in the mass as a sacrifice to God; and as a *king*, he is a *monarch*, is Head of the church and the state, is King of kings; has both swords, and can make laws to bind the consciences of men, can depose kings, dissolve oaths, allegiance, &c. This can all be clearly made out on indisputable evidence. This is blasphemy. Is Christ *absent* from the world that he needs a substitute? " All power is given unto me on earth and in heaven, and lo I am with you always, even to the end of the world." (Matth. xxviii. 18-20.) Is he impotent? Is he neglectful of his kingdom? Does not the Scripture say, "There is one Lord," (Ephes. iv. 5.) *one head as well as one body: that Christ is the only potentate, the King of kings, and Lord of lords.* (1 Tim. vi. 15;) and *the only lawgiver.* (James iv. 12?) And did not Christ say to *Peter* and the other Apostles, " Be ye not called Rabbi, *(master)* for *one* is your master, even *Christ*, and *all* ye are *brethren;* neither be ye called masters, for *one* is your master, even Christ; but he that is *greatest* among you shall be your *servant*." (Matt. chap. xxiii. 8.) Does not Paul say, (2 Cor. i. 24.) " We have *not dominion* over your *faith:* (yet Paul was *equal* to Peter) but we are *helpers* of your joy: by *faith* ye stand," (Titus iii. 1.) " Put them in mind to be *subject* to principalities and powers, to obey magistrates." (Matth. xx. 25, 26.) Jesus said, " Ye know that the princes of the Gentiles exercise dominion over them, and they that are great, exercise authority upon them, *but it shall not be so among you.*" This was a rebuke to apostles, who were asking for *supremacy!* So palpable is the sacrilegious arrogance of the titles and authority of the Pope, that Pope Gregory I. said, (though many centuries ago) "I confidently say that whosoever doth *call himself universal Bishop*, or desireth to be so called, doth in his election *become the forerunner of anti-Christ*, because in *his pride he doth set himself before all others,*" and he calls that title, (which is *less* presumptuous than others since assumed,) " foolish," " proud," " profane," " wicked ;" and refers the man who aspired to it, to the example of *Lucifer* for *illustration*, and to the judgment of the great day for *retribution.* How fitting is the prophecy of Paul's,—than which a truer likeness was never drawn, and which God's people have been accustomed for many ages, *(uniting* with Pope Gregory) to apply to his *successors* at Rome! "And that man of sin be revealed, the son of perdition who opposeth, and exalteth himself above all that is called God, or that is worshipped; so that he as God, sitteth in the temple of God, showing himself that he is God. (2 Thess. ii. 3, 4.)

Add to all this what Genebard (chron. ad Ann. 901.) says : " For almost one hundred and fifty years, about fifty popes, having departed from the virtue of their predecessors, were *apostate*, rather than apostolical; at which times they entered in (to office) not *by the door*, but by a *back-door*, that is to say, by the power of the Emperors." Baronius too (vol. x. A. D. 908.) thus writes : " Hast thou heard of the most deplorable state of things at this time when Theodora the elder, a strumpet of noble family, obtained supreme controul (monarchism) if I may so say, in the city of Rome. She prostituted her daughters to the popes, the invaders of the Apostolic seat, and to the marquisses of Tuscany; by which means, the dominion of such wicked women became so absolute, that *they* removed at pleasure the lawfully created popes, and having expelled them, *introduced violent and most wicked men in their places.*" Such things are almost too bad to relate—how much *worse* to be *done* in the *infallible seat* by the *Vicar of Jesus*, and the universal head of the church ! Yet the same author informs us that these *monsters* were received by the church with the reverence due to the successor of Peter ! (eundem ut Petrum cole rent.) Now from such a church, is it schism to *come out?* Against such corruptions in doctrine and radical morals, is it heresy to *protest?*

3. As you have several times alluded to my statement, " that indulgences were a bundle of licenses to commit sin," I will next present that doctrine. The wanton and unprincipled *traffic* of Tetzel in indulgences, under the sanction of the Pope, may be considered the *salient* point of the Reformation. This, as you, know was Pope Leo Xth's way of paying for the *immense Apostolical* edifice of St. Peters, which is estimated to have cost $60,000,000. He published Indulgences and plenary remission of sins, to all such as should contribute money towards it. The *form* of these indulgences, drawn by the authority of the Pope, *shows* their *nature.* "May our Lord Jesus Christ have mercy upon thee, and absolve thee by the merits of his most holy Passion. And I, by his authority, that of his blessed Apostles, Peter and Paul, and that of the most holy Pope, granted and committed to me in these parts, do absolve thee, first from all ecclesiastical censure, in whatever manner they have been incurred, then from all thy sins, transgressions, and excesses, how enormous soever they may be ; even from such as are reserved for the cognizance of the Holy See, and as far as the keys of the Holy Church extend. I remit to you all punishment which you deserve in purgatory on their account ; and I restore you to the holy sacraments of the Church, to the unity of the faithful, and to that innocence and purity which you possessed at baptism : so that when you die, the gates of punishment shall be shut, and the gates of the paradise of delight shall be opened ; and if you shall not die at present, this grace shall remain in full force, when you are at the point of death. In the name of the Father, the Son, and the Holy Ghost." It was in the use of this daring and scandalous commission that Tetzel set up heaven for sale ; and it was in resisting this infamous traffic that Luther began the work of reformation. The Council of Trent teaches that " whoever shall affirm that when the grace of justification is received, the offence of the penitent sinner is so forgiven, and the sentence of eternal punishment so reversed, that there remains no temporal punishment to be endured, before his entrance into the kingdom of heaven, either in this world, or in the future state in purgatory : let him be accursed." It is also an article of faith in the creed of Pius IV. "that the power of indulgences was left by Christ to his church, and that the use of them is very helpful to Christian people." Bellarmine's second and third chapters of book 1. on Indulgences, are headed : " That there exists a certain treasury in the church, which is the foundation of indulgences ; that the church has the power of applying this treasury of satisfactions, and thus of granting indulgences." And he proceeds to tell us that this *treasury* is made up of the *merits of Christ* and of *the Saints.* The merits of the Saints are called *works of supererogation*, or what a man does beyond his duty. As lately as the year 1825, the Pope of Rome in publishing a jubilee, uses the following language : " the authority divinely committed to us (the Pope,) to open as widely as possible that heavenly treasury, which, being purchased by the merits, passions, and virtues of our Lord Christ, of his virgin mother,

and of all the saints, the author of human salvation has entrusted the distribution of it to us," &c.

In fine, that there may be no doubt of the fact, that the church of Rome still holds this article of faith in all its force, we point our readers to the *plenary indulgence*, published in the Catholic Herald, on the 2d of May, 1833, on the authority of his present Holiness, Gregory the XVI. and signed JOHN HUGHES, SECRETARY. This document we shall examine at large hereafter. The above history and extracts from the standards of the church, might suffice without further proof or comment, to show the anti-christian character of this doctrine.

(1.) Here we see that the Pope, a finite and sinful creature, *usurps* the power to forgive sins. But the word of God (in Mark ii. 7—13. Luke v. 21—26. Isaiah xliii. 25; xliv. 22. Acts x. 42., and a crowd of other passages,) teaches us, that it *is the prerogative of Infinite and Almighty God alone to forgive sins*.

(2.) This doctrine teaches that there is need of *adding merit to the merit of Christ*, viz: that of the *Saints*. But the Scriptures teach us that Christ's merits are *infinite*; that his righteousness is perfect; that he who believeth on Him is justified from all things; that Christ's *satisfaction* is a *perfect satisfaction*; and that he that believeth on *Him* has passed from death unto life: " that there is no other name under heaven, given among men whereby we must be saved, but the name of Jesus, neither is there salvation in any other." (See 1 John i. 6—10. Acts xiii. 39. Acts iv. 12. Ephes. ii. 8. 2 Cor. v. 21. Rom. iii. 23—29. Rom. viii. 2—4., &c. &c.) Away then with the wretched impiety of attempting to add to this divine and perfect satisfaction!

(3.) The doctrine of Indulgences supposes that a creature, and he a *fallen* one, can *do more* than his duty; and have works of supererogations for others. But what saith the Scriptures, (I quote from our version.) " Be ye therefore stedfast, immovable, always abounding in the work of the Lord." (1 Cor. xv. 58.) Is there any *room* left beyond " abounding;" or any *time* beyond " always?" " So, likewise ye, when ye have done *all* these things which are commanded you, say we are *unprofitable* servants; we have done that which was our *duty* to do." (Luke xvii. 10.) " Thou shalt love the Lord thy God with *all* thy heart, and with all thy soul, and with all thy mind, and with all thy *strength*; and thou shalt love thy neighbour as *thyself!*" Mark xii. 30, 31. Is there any place here, to render satisfaction for another, even if we had any merits of our own? But in this fallen world no man ever yet rendered any *meritorious* satisfaction for *himself*, much less for *another*.

(4.) This doctrine supposes money may buy pardon, and remission of sins. Hence the abundant sale of indulgences; and the moneys still paid for souls in purgatory! If this doctrine has antiquity on its side, it looks for parentage to Simon Magus;—and surely *Peter*, your first Pope (as you say) was against it; for it is written (Acts viii. 18—20.) When Simon (Magus) saw that through laying on of the Apostle's hands, the Holy Ghost was given, he offered them money, saying, give me also this power that on whomsoever I lay my hands he may receive the Holy Ghost. But Peter said unto him, thy *money* perish with thee, because thou hast thought that the *gift of God* may be *purchased with money!*"*

Room is wanting to add to these particulars. We hope hereafter to pursue the *proof* thus begun. In the mean time, the following contrast may show the difference between your religion and the religion of Christ.

Protestant Church. *The Gospel Preached.*	Church of Rome. *Another Gospel.*
The word of God says, "Thou shalt not make a graven image, or bow down to it."	The Church of Rome says, "We may have images to kiss them, and uncover our heads, and prostrate our bodies before them."
The Gospel of Christ says, "There is one Mediator between God and man, the man Christ Jesus."	The Church of Rome says, "The Virgin Mary is also a Mediator, and she worships her as such in her offices."
The Gospel of Christ says, "Christ was ONCE offered to bear the sins of many."	In the Church of Rome Christ is DAILY offered in the sacrifice of the Mass.
The Gospel of Christ says, "Other foundation can no man lay than *that* is laid, which is Christ Jesus."	The Church of Rome says, "The true foundation is St. Peter."
The Gospel of Christ says, "The heavens must receive Christ until the restitution of all things."	The Church of Rome says, "The body of Christ is every day substantially in the hands of the Priest."
The Gospel of Christ says, "It is a mark of apostacy to forbid to marry, for marriage is honourable in all."	The Church of Rome says, "Marriage is not holy or honourable to the clergy."
The Gospel of Christ says, "We should not pray in an unknown tongue, we should pray with the understanding."	The Church of Rome recites many of her public prayers and offices in Latin, which is an unknown tongue to most, and few can understand it.
The Gospel of Christ says, "Blessed are the dead who die in the Lord, for they *rest* from their labours."	The Church of Rome says, "Many of those who die in the Lord, go into purgatory, where there is no rest."

The Gospel of Christ says, " though we or an angel from heaven preach any other Gospel unto you, than that which we have preached unto you, let *him* be accursed."

I have now shown, as far as the space allowed me would admit, the anti-christian character of several of your leading doctrines.

---

* The following statement which was stuck up a few years ago in the churches of Madrid, may serve as a practical illustration of this subject:

"The sacred and royal bank of piety has relieved from purgatory from its establishment in 1721 to Nov. 1826,
   1,030,395 souls at an expense of £1,720,437 sterling.
   11,402 { do. from Nov. 1826 to Nov. 1827. } 11,276
   ―――――   ―――――
   1,041,797   1,734,703

"The number of masses calculated to accomplish this pious work was 558,921; consequently each soul cost about half a mass, or thirty-three shillings and four pence."

So true is it that the real character of Romanism is but half disclosed in this country.

Here observe, that *infallibility* is *lost*, if but *one* error is detected. But I have brought proof of *many*.

II. Having thus shown that several of the leading doctrines of the church of Rome are anti-christian, I proceed next to prove that they are *novel doctrines also*. Your church lays great stress on her *antiquity;* and you say in your 1st objection, "that the Protestant religion is only 300 years old." But, Sir, it is as old as the religion of Christ. I proved in my last letter that divers churches besides those called Protestant, had dissented from many of the cardinal doctrines of the Roman Catholic church; and pointed you to the Syrian church which had never been subject to her. You choose, however, for good reasons, not to notice these facts. I will now point out the *novelty* of some of those doctrines which you call apostolical, and prove them innovations.

1. The very *canon* of your church is an *innovation;* for you include in it many books that were for centuries rejected by the ancient Christian church, as I have heretofore proved. Cardinal Cajetan called "an oracle" in your church, thus writes, in his *Commentaries, &c.* (composed at Rome,) on the Bible. "That what books were canonical or not canonical to St. Jerome, the same ought either way to be so with us." "And that the whole Latin church is hereby very much obliged to St. Jerome, who by severing the canonical books of Scripture from those that are not canonical, hath freed us from the reproach of the Hebrews, who otherwise might say, that we had forged a new canon for ourselves, or parts of books, which they never had." "For this reason he excluded from his volume, all those which Jerome counted Apochryphal." "For Judith, Tobit, and the Maccabees, are placed *out of the canon*, and are placed among the Apocrypha, with the books of Wisdom and Ecclesiasticus, by the blessed Jerome." "These books are not canonical, that is, are not according to rule, for establishing the faith; (Non sunt hi libri canonici, hoc est, non sunt regulares ad firmandum ea quæ sunt fidei,) but yet they may be *called* canonical, that is, they are according to rule, for the edification of the faithful." "Neither *be disturbed by the novelty*, if at any time you should find these books numbered among the canonical, either in the Councils or sacred Doctors:" and he adds "that Augustine and the Council of Carthage are to be reconciled with Jerome, and the Council of Laodicea, by *this distinction*." (1 Cap. Epis. Heb.; and Epis. ded. ad Pap. ante com. in Lib. V. T.) This is most decisive. Erasmus is still more strong. And I could bring fifty testimonies, in the different ages, to prove that *your canon is a corrupted and new canon*.

2. The claim of the Pope to be universal Bishop and Vicar of Christ—is a *novelty*. The title of universal Bishop was not conferred on, or claimed by the Bishop of Rome till the 7th century. *Phocas* (not Christ) who murdered his predecessor, and who waded to the throne through his blood, conferred this title on Boniface the 3d in the year 606, after a criminal collusion between them on the subject. We have seen above, that Gregory, Bishop of Rome, had resisted the bestowing of this blasphemous title on the Bishop of Constantinople—as the *forerunner of Anti-Christ*. This very fact shows

that HE had no such *title*, and claimed no such *headship*. And it is notorious that the Bishops of Constantinople and Rome long contended for the supremacy; that it was first tendered to the Bishop of Constantinople; and taken from him to be given to the Bishop of Rome. The present Pope of Rome is as unlike the first Bishop, as a common justice of the peace is unlike an emperor. The Apostle John survived Peter, the pretended 1st Pope, some forty years. Either then there was no pope in the world for forty years, or else an apostle of Christ was subject to him! *Pope* is a name synonimous with father—and was given to *all* bishops until the time of Gregory the VII. Even the succession of the Bishops of Rome, on Papal principles, cannot be made out. If it could, they were like *other* Bishops—and most unlike the present Pope: they had nothing above other Bishops: they were wholly inferior to all the apostles: Peter was never Bishop of Rome: and the church of Rome instead of being the *oldest* church, was established *long after* the church at Jerusalem, Antioch, &c. So clear is it that the supremacy of the Pope is a *novelty* and an innovation.

3. *Transubstantiation* is an utter *novelty*. This doctrine was so far from being held by the Primitive church, that we know its date and age. It is an absurdity so great that it required *implicit* faith to believe it, and " is incapable of proof, by sense or reason, Scripture, miracles, antiquity, or by any testimony whatever." That it is a *novelty* is clear from this, that the famous Roman Catholic Scotus affirms *that it was not an article of faith before the Lateran council* (A. D. 1215) and *that it cannot be proved from the Sacred Scriptures.* Bellarmine owns (book 3 chap. 23, on the Eucharist,) that Scotus says so, and he admits " though the Scripture quoted by us above seems clear to us, and ought to convince any man who is not froward; yet it may justly be doubted whether it be so (*i. e.* proved by Scripture) *when the most learned and acute men, such as Scotus in particular hold a contrary opinion.*" Ocham, Biel, Bishop Fisher, cardinal Cajetan, and Melchior Cane hold the same belief. Now if it be not taught in Scripture, surely it is *not* an *ancient doctrine;* and if it be *doubtful*, then it " was not one of those *fixed* stars in the firmament of revelation" of which you speak, or a *positive fact or truth,* such as you contend every Roman Catholic doctrine is. Yet the Council of Trent decreed in all the fierce spirit of fanatical zeal, " Whosoever shall deny that in the most holy sacrament of the Eucharist, there are truly, really, and substantially contained *the body and blood of our Lord Jesus Christ, together with his soul and divinity, and consequently Christ entire,* but shall affirm that he is present therein only in a sign, or figure, or by his power, *let him be accursed.*" Here then, on the one hand, is history, and the testimony of your own chosen writers, proving the *novelty* of this doctrine, and a grave Council cursing and damning all who say it is not the very truth of Christianity, on the other.

4. It is an *antichristian novelty* to *deny the cup* to the people, in the eucharist. The canon of Trent says, " whosoever shall affirm that the Holy Catholic church has not just grounds for restricting the laity and non-officiating clergy to communion in the species of

bread only, or that she hath erred therein, let him be accursed." This is awful language when levelled directly at the Lord Jesus: for "He took the cup, and gave thanks, and *gave it to them*, saying, *drink ye all of it*"—"*and they all drank of it*"—"for as often as ye eat this bread and *drink this cup*, ye do show his death till he come." (See Math. xxvi. 1 Cor. xi. &c.)

Here then is annulling a law of Christ, and violating a sacrament of his appointing! And what makes the *impiety* as well as the novelty of this article of your faith apparent, is that the Councils of Constance and Trent, acknowledge it as an *alteration,* and vindicate the change. The Council of Constance, session 13, says: "that although this sacrament was received by the faithful under both kinds in the Primitive church, it was afterwards received under both kinds by the officiating priests, and by the people, under the species of bread alone . . . . this therefore being approved, *it is now made a law.*" And the holy synod ordered that all transgressors of this decree "be effectually punished." The Trentine decree is, if possible, still more outrageous. Here then, out of her *own mouth* your church is convicted of the most glaring innovations. And I need not quote Justin Martyr, Cyprian, Ambrose, Chrysostom, Pope Gelasius, Gratian, Aquinas, &c., to show that this flagrant change, is a *novelty* which none can deny, an *outrage* which none can defend.

The above specimens of the *novelty* and *innovations* of *your doctrines,* fully meet your first objection, and prove that your religion is not the religion of Christ, since as you say, "the religion of Christ is 1800 years old."

Your second objection has no application, except to your own religion, for we profess no *new* religion. Ours is as old as the Bible. Yours, I have proved above, is characterised by *novelty.* We pretend to no miracles, but those that established the religion of Christ. Whereas your *pretensions* to them indicate that your church feels the need of new seals to a *new* religion. And yet the utter failure of her attempts to work miracles, proves that she innovates without divine right, or being sent of God.

Your third objection is only a repetition of what has again and again been answered by me; and appears, with the *fourth* edition of your *ten* heads on the rule of faith, like the books of the sybil which were offered to Tarquin, growing less and less, and yet setting up the same claims time after time.

Your fourth objection will be easily exposed, and turned directly *against* you, when we come to show the *variations of Romanism;* and in its proper place, if Providence permit, we shall bring up in parallel with it, the Protestant Religion.

Before I close this letter, it is necessary to notice briefly what, for the sake of distinction, we will call MULTIFARIOUS MATTERS.

1. You tell us that "*Pascal was a Jansenist, and as such was not a Romanist nor even a Catholic.*" I am pleased to find that you *admit* the distinction between *Romanist,* and *Catholic.* It is from confounding these very dissimilar characteristics, that many of the errors of your church have arisen. The history of Jansenism most clearly proves that your communion has been no stranger to

sects: and its condemnation by the *Pope,* is one of the most remarkable evidences of the fact that the church of Rome is an *enemy to evangelical truth.* This is apparent as the light of day from the Bull of Pope Clement XI. issued in 1713, with advice of *a congregation* of Cardinals, against " Father Quesnel's moral reflections upon the New Testament." We are by no means disposed to defend his doctrines in the gross. But will not *Christians* of every name look with amazement at the head of " the infallible church" denouncing such propositions as the following.—We select them from 101 which was specified and condemned in the Bull, viz:

" No. 26. No graces are given except by faith. 66. He who would draw near to God, must neither come to Him with brutal passions, nor be led as beasts are by natural instincts, or by fear, but by faith and by love. 80. The reading of the Holy Scripture is for every body. 94. Nothing gives the enemies of the church a worse opinion concerning the church, than to see therein an ABSOLUTE DOMINION EXERCISED OVER THE FAITH OF BELIEVERS, AND DIVISIONS FOMENTED on account of such things as are prejudicial, NEITHER TO THE FAITH NOR MORALS. 100. That it is a deplorable time when God is thought to be honoured by persecuting the truth, and the disciples thereof. THIS TIME IS COME......We often think we sacrifice to God a wicked person, and *we sacrifice to the Devil a servant of God."*—These are some of the doctrines which the Bull " condemns and rejects as false, captious, shocking, offensive to pious ears, scandalous, pernicious, rash, injurious to the church and her practice."—How remarkably this Bull confirms a multitude of my former reasonings! How true is it that Romanism is not Jansenism, nor Christianity. And now as to *the Jesuits,* whom by *implication* you approve, and who were the *victorious* opponents of Jansenism at the court of Rome, the very name, though bespeaking a follower of *Jesus,* conveys an association so offensive that I will not define it, lest I should appear to be *personal.* But how strange is it that they were expelled in a former age from so many countries, and their order abolished by *one Pope,* and in *latter days revived* by another.—Each Pope gives potent reasons for the act. Both could not be *infallible.* Yet both seem to have been approved by the suffrages of the church. How do you explain it?

2. You say, "our Bibles are in English." Answer. Is your *English* version *authorized* by the *church?* You say, " *The first edition would be still on the bookseller's shelves, if there existed such a prohibition."* Answer. Has the following law of your church been repealed? If not, what does it mean? " *In as much as it is manifest from experience that if the Holy Bible translated into the vulgar tongue,* (for example into English) *be indiscriminately allowed to every one, the temerity of men will cause more evil than good to arise from it, it is on this point referred to the judgment of Bishops or Inquisitors,* WHO MAY BY THE ADVICE OF THE PRIEST OR CONFESSOR PERMIT THE READING OF THE BIBLE......*and this permission they must have in writing. But if any one shall have the presumption to read or possess it without such written permission, he shall not receive absolution until he have first delivered*

up such Bible to the ordinary." And even "Booksellers" (I hope Mr. Cummiskey will look well to the written permission) "*shall forfeit the value of the books*" (is not this church and state?) " to be applied by the Bishop to some *pious use,* and be subjected by the *Bishop* to such other penalties as the Bishop shall judge proper." Many of your readers, who wonder at your former silence on this subject, would esteem it a favour if you will *now* explain this contradiction. And as to your Breviary, your Mass-book in *full*, your book of Councils, and book of Bulls, do you say *they* are in English?

3. You shun the Bull of Innocent VIII., in a way that is most peculiar. In the first instance you evaded its bloody contents by the argument that a mistake of ten years had been made in its date by me. Next you defend it by saying that the Waldenses " slew the servant" (for these are the words of the annalist) of the Inquisitor! But what right had the Inquisitor to arrest and destroy the Waldenses? And if the Waldenses *did* slay his servant, what had the *Pope* to do with that? Where was the civil government? If a Protestant should wickedly slay a Roman Catholic in London, or in Edinburgh, has the Pope a *right to order his Inquisitor to slay him and all others who think with him?* Yes, surely, according to your reasoning! and the civil government is only the Pope's creature. Lastly, when I adduce your own historian in proof of the Bull, or Brief of the Pope, you say " the annals of Baronius come down only to the year 1198, and yet you quote his authority for a fact which should have taken place in 1487. How is this?" And is it then possible that this is designed for a serious and candid answer to the authority of the historian? Can you be ignorant of the fact that Raynald is the continuator of the annals of Baronius; that he brought them down to the year 1534, and that his continuation is published with the permission and approval of the highest authority at Rome? And can you mean to argue *that as it is the continuator only who says there was such a Bull, therefore there was no such a Bull?* I have not words to express to you my surprise at the impolicy of your defence, not to name its want of candour. The fact then still returns upon you with augmenting force, that the said *Bull, ordering heretics to be butchered, or made slaves, if not exterminated,* was indeed issued by the Pope, and executed by his minions in the name of the God of mercy!

4. It is true that Presbyterians were once in a generic term, classed with other protestants under the title of *Puritans:* and it is also true that Congregationalists, Independents, Presbyterians, and Puritans, as a body were and are, in their fundamental doctrines, one people. But you stated on the authority, as you say, of Thomas Jefferson, that *Presbyterians* persecuted Roman Catholics in Maryland, after having been protected by them: and then you *change* the *term* into *Puritans,* as if we were convertible with it, and say the Presbyterians persecuted them. Whereas the fact is, *there were no Presbyterians in Maryland at that time;* and by the *change* of words in your *two* successive letters, you first *misrepresent* the facts, and then seek to *conceal* that misrepresentation.

5. As for the authority of Lenfant, in the case of the martyr Huss, it is in vain you seek to destroy his authority in this matter. The treachery of the Council of Constance is too palpable to be denied by you, much less defended. But the rebound of your defence acts on your own cause alone. It were easy, by a number of Roman Catholic writers, to show that with more candour, they admit and justify the broad principle, "that no faith is to be kept with heretics." Simancha, (Cath. Inst. Tit. 46.) "Faith is not to be kept with heretics, as neither with tyrants, pirates, nor public robbers...... Certain heretics were, therefore, justly burned by the solemn judgment of the Council of Constance, although promise of security had been given them. For if faith be not kept with tyrants, pirates, and other robbers, who kill the body, much less with heretics who destroy souls." This writer was a Bishop, a Canonist, and a Civilian; and was surely of a very "different opinion" from you as to the Council of Constance. He also cites Salamonius, and Placa, as holding the same doctrine. And not only so, but *Popes* in great numbers, have in word and deed maintained the same general principle. Gregory IX., Urban VI., Paul V., Innocent X., Honorious, Eugenius IV., &c. avowed this infamous principle. And worse than all, *Councils* have done the same. The 3d and 4th Councils of Lateran, the Council of Lyons, and Pisa, as well as the Councils of Constance, held the same shocking doctrine. Why, therefore, should we stop to contend for *one* case, when it has been the common doctrine and practice of the church of Rome *to keep no faith with heretics?*

6. You strangely expose yourself in the alleged omission of the word "*dubio.*" That *word* was in my manuscript when it went to the press; it was corrected by me in the proof-sheet, on Saturday; it was in the revised proof, which I corrected on Monday; it was in the Presbyterian, and Herald, of Wednesday and Thursday; and I did not see your strange critique on its *absence* until the *next* Saturday! Charge me not then with want of candour; while you "strain at gnats, and swallow camels." I cannot consent to cover your blunders and cavils, at the price of owning what I never did.

7. After the above statement, the charge of "garbling" will be interpreted, without the need of my disproving it a third time.

8. "The considerable undertone" of Protestant and Presbyterian dissatisfaction dies away before my call for proof; and "the general" *impression* that the Bishop's charge was intended as a prop to my weak arguments, shrinks into " let me suppose that I was mistaken." But you are assuredly very much mistaken when you think that the Protestant press is receding from the publication of your letters. I am acquainted with almost *twenty* Protestant papers that publish this controversy. If then your reasoning is just in explaining thei. *pretended suppression of it* into a token of defeat, what conclusion must we draw from this redundant and undaunted republication? Not surely that Protestants despair of the truth, or shrink from free inquiry.

9. You seem much disturbed by my retorting your figure of the

serpent stinging the bosom that nurtured it. I assure you I meant neither to stir the American people to disturb the equal rights of our Roman Catholic citizens, nor to charge those citizens with being designing or ungrateful; and no ingenuity can pervert my language so as to convey this meaning. It was not to the people, but to the *priesthood* I referred, when retorting your charge against Presbyterians. I informed you that the nation was awaking to a proper discovery of *their* influence and designs. No man can be a *consistent* Roman Catholic Priest under such bonds and vows to a foreign prince, and spiritual dictator, without being of necessity exclusive, and an eager proselyter of all men to his peculiar system. The history of the Jesuits, (who have been called, by a strange union of discordant terms and dissimilar beings, "*the militia of Jesus*") is ample evidence of the truth of my assertion.

As to the sum which you say has been expended on Dickinson College, Carlisle, I take it on your word to be so. If Presbyterians (as formerly at Carlisle,) are selected by our public institutions to aid in their instruction, I leave you to determine whether it be their crime, their calamity, or their honour and duty to serve them: and if the Legislature of this State choose, in its bounty, to assist these institutions, whether you will condemn them for it? You should have known the history of Dickinson College better, however, than to call it a "Presbyterian College." I would remind you also, that Papal money is poured into this country from year to year for the very purpose of *proselyting us heretics*, and building up institutions for the establishment of Popery among us. In the year 1828, 120,000 francs were *confessedly* (I know not how much more in reality) sent from Rome to sustain your cause in this country! You compel me reluctantly to dwell on these topics. I hope in your next to see manly arguments in a Christian spirit, and a cessation of that low and vulgar warfare which must speedily weary the patient and kind readers of our letters.

  Yours, &c.   JOHN BRECKINRIDGE.

CONTROVERSY. No. XXIII.

IS THE PROTESTANT RELIGION THE RELIGION OF CHRIST?

Philadelphia, July 3, 1833.

To the Rev. John Breckinridge.

Rev. Sir,—In your letter No. XX. when we were discussing the previous question, you gave, as the definition of the Protestant Rule of Faith, "The word of God as contained in the Scriptures of the Old and New Testament;" and because I did not attack the "word of God," you charge me with having *evaded* "the *real* Protestant Rule of Faith, and argued against its *abuses* alone!" If you had thus candidly, given up *private interpretation as an "abuse" at the commencement of the discussion*, we might have saved much time and labour. But I am surprised and indeed gratified, to perceive that good sense, and the pressing necessities of the case, urged you, finally, to yield, however reluctantly, so precious a tribute to the majesty of Truth. It certainly did not occur to you that by *this* admission, you sapped the very foundations of the Protestant religion, since it is known to all men that this very "abuse" is the parent of the Reformation.

When I ask you to define the Protestant religion, you tell me, that it is "*a religion which protests against the (supposed) errors of the Catholic church*," (in *so much* the definition applies to Deism as well as Protestantism, since *both protest* against the *same* doctrines,) "and which is *derived* exclusively from, and consistent with the Holy Scriptures as the only infallible rule of faith and practice." This is your definition. But how is the Protestant religion "derived" from the Scriptures? Is it not by *private interpretation?* Now, Rev. Sir, will you "derive your religion through a medium which you, yourself, have *denounced* as an "*abuse?*"

Again, the Protestant religion is "a religion *consistent* with the Holy Scriptures." But who is to be the judge of this? Or how is it to be determined whether any particular doctrine of Protestantism is "consistent" with the Holy Scriptures or not? Does not *this* position again, betray the "radical delusion" of the whole system? Every sect considers that its own notions are "*derived* from, and *consistent* with, the Holy Scriptures." And pray, do the Holy Scriptures contain, in reality, the notions of every sect of Protestants? If we admit the principle of your definition *at all*, it will be as favourable to the Protestant who denies the Trinity of persons in God, as to him who admits it;—to the one who holds that there is *no sacrament*, as to the other who maintains that there are, at least, two, Baptism and the Lord's Supper. Every sect maintains that its own peculiar *prejudices* are "derived from and consistent with the Holy Scriptures," and how am I to know which are the doctrines that are *really, and truly, derived from the sacred volume?*

You make the following statement, in the first paragraph of your last letter.—"If, as you say, I am the *original assailant*, why do you tell me that mine is the business of defence?" Answer. Because, when I held you responsible as the original assailant, it was as the challenger "of priests and bishops" to the field of controversy;

but it was *agreed*, that we should *commence* by the rule of faith.—Those who have read your letters through, to the final and very memorable concession, by which you recognise " private interpretation" as an " abuse," will be able to appreciate the merits of your " defence" of the Protestant rule of faith. The second question to be examined, according to mutual agreement, was, whether " the Protestant religion be the religion of Christ." Now I undertake, as the very question supposes, to prove that it *is not :* and I should suppose that yours was the opposite side of the case, which I intimated by saying that yours is the " business of defence." This is the position selected by yourself, as may be seen by referring to your last letter in the preliminary correspondence, where you say, " I am to *defend the Protestant faith."* The sincere inquirer, who looked to your *last letter,* for this *promised* " defence" of the Protestant religion, must have found himself mortifyingly disappointed.

In my last letter I reduced the question to the simplicity of a dilemma, from which I defy you to escape. It is this: Either the Protestant religion is a religion *differing* from the religion of Christ; —and by this admission you give up the question ;—or else, the religion of Christ was NOT *professed by any society of Christians, previous to the time of Luther.* And in that case, the religion of Christ is only three hundred years old ! ! To which of these alternatives do you choose to cling ? for, one of them is *inevitable.* To this argument, you oppose the " defence" of—silence. Not a word of authority ; not a word of reasoning ! Silence only, *prudent* silence.

My second argumant grew out of the first: It was this, that whenever God gave *new doctrines,* such as the Protestant religion was, when Luther and the rest *began* to preach it ; he always gave, at the same time, to the preachers of such doctrines, the gift of miracles, to show that they were not *impostors ;* this gift, however, was denied to the authors of the Protestant religion, and therefore the inference is, that God never deputed them. To this argument the only answer given is, that " we (Protestants) profess no *new* religion." That you *say* so, I admit. But in order to show this, you were bound to prove that your religion *had been professed by some society,* in *some part* of the world, in *some age,* between the preaching of Christ, and the preaching of Luther. But there was *no such* society and therefore your gratuitous assertion of the Protestant religion's not being a *"new* religion," must go for nothing. We require *proof.*

My third argument was, that the Protestant religion being a religion of *opinions,* is not the religion of Christ, which was a religion of *positive truths.* Consequently that they are not the same. To this you give no reply, except *that I had introduced it before ! ! !* —But it has never been answered ; nor has even an attempt been made at a refutation of it. The one was a religion of *certainty,* the other is a religion of *chance.* Can you deny this ?

My fourth argument was, that the Reformers themselves denounced each other as *heretics and deceivers of souls.* And to this argument you reply that it " will be easily exposed and turned directly against me." As if this invalidated the inference which it furnishes against *the religion*, of which *these Reformers were the authors!* These few remarks of yours, are the only testimony contained in the whole of your last letter, to show the reader that " the Protestant religion, is the religion of Christ."

As to your objections against the doctrines of the Catholic church, even if they were well founded, they *do not appertain to the present subject;* and you will recollect that one of our rules binds us to " adhere strictly to the subject of debate *for the time being*, and to admit no second topic until the first shall have been exhausted." In obedience to this regulation, *I shall pay no attention to any thing you may have to say against the Catholic doctrine, until we shall have discussed the present question*, viz. " whether the Protestant religion is the religion of Christ." But *that* question once disposed of, I shall allow you " to take up any doctrine of the church, and I shall hold myself prepared to refute all the arguments you may bring against it."

The candid reader, who wishes to investigate the grounds of his religion with a view of arriving at the truth, should reject from his mind every preconceived opinion, which, on examination, he does not find to have been established on the basis of *facts*. The supposition which Protestantism holds forth to its votaries, is, that the religion of Christ, established in its purity, by the Apostles, gradually, and, what is rather strange, *imperceptibly*, became corrupted, and was finally restored to its primitive purity, in *the 16th century of the church*, by the event which is called the " Reformation." Now, Rev. Sir, to save you the trouble, at this moment, of *straying from the question*, to prove that this *was* the case, let us suppose for *sake of argument* that it was. Let us suppose that Christ after having promised to be with his church, in the teaching of " all nations, till the end of time," violated his promise; and that, in fact, all Christendom was buried, as the English Homily book has it, " in damnable idolatry for the space of eight hundred years and more"—and starting even from this extravagant supposition, you will find it a difficult task to prove that " the Protestant religion is the religion of Christ." And why?

1. Because no man can tell what *the* Protestant religion is. We know it as a compound of heterogeneous *opinions* about the meaning of the Bible. As you have *defined it*, you have bound yourself to prove that Quakerism, Episcopalianism, Baptistism, Methodism, Presbyterianism, Universalism, Arminianism, Unitarianism, Swedenborgianism, *are all* " the religion of Christ;" since the *mercy* of your definition graciously embraces them all! Each of them is " a religion, exclusively derived from, and consistent with the Holy Scriptures as the only infallible rule of faith and practice." Now, Rev. Sir, permit me to ask you, did you seriously intend to distribute, as your definition imports, the religion of Christ *equally* among all these sects? Do you mean to defend the doctrines of all these denominations? For all these according to your definition, constitute the Protestant religion; and *this* you have undertaken to vindicate, as " the religion of Christ." How much wiser would it have been in you, to have borrowed the language of the celebrated Bishop

Watson, of the church of England, and told us that the Protestant religion is that system of Christian *liberty*, in which "a man believes what he *pleases;* and *professes* what he believes." Sentire quæ velit, et quæe sentit, loqui.

2. But by another definition you have said that the Protestant religion is "the religion of the Reformation." Now the only way to ascertain the religion of the Reformation is, by bringing to view the doctrines of the Reformers as stated by themselves. To begin then with the father of that revolution, he tells us that "*God works the evil in us,* as well as the good."........Is this "the religion of Christ?" And that " by his own will, he (God) *necessarily* RENDERS *us worthy* of damnation, so as to seem to take pleasure in the torments of the miserable." (Luth. Opera, ed. Wittemb. Tom. ii. p. 437.) Is this "the religion of Christ?" Again. "If God foresaw, says he, that Judas would be a traitor, Judas was compelled to be a *traitor;* nor *was it in his power* to be otherwise." (Luth. de Servo. Arbit. fol. 460.) Is *this* the religion of Christ?" " Man's *will* is, (says the same Reformer,) like a horse : if God sit upon it, it goes as God would have it; if the Devil ride it, it goes as the *Devil would* have it : nor can the WILL choose its rider, but each of them (viz. God and the Devil) *strives* which shall get possession of it." (Ibid. vol. ii.) Is this "*the* religion of Christ?" " Let this be your rule," (continues the same father,) " in interpreting the Scriptures; whenever they command a good work, do you *understand* that they FORBID it." (Ibid. Tom. iii. p. 171.) Is this, Rev. Sir, "the religion of Christ?" O what a task you have undertaken!

And now let us see what Calvin, your own Calvin, puts forth as "the religion of the Reformation," *which, you say is, the religion of Christ.* " God requires, says he, nothing of us but faith; he asks nothing of us but that we believe." (Calv. Inst. L. iii. c. 23.) " It is plainly wrong to seek for any other *cause* of damnation, than the HIDDEN COUNSELS OF GOD.".... " Men, by the free will of God, without any demerit of their own, are predestined to eternal death." (Ibid.) Is this " the religion of Christ?" The whole operation of this doctrine is to produce fanaticism in belief, and quietude of conscience in the midst of immorality. This same impious doctrine of Calvin, is well approved, in the Presbyterian Confession of faith as *amended* in the year 1821.

" By the *decree* of God, for the manifestation of his glory, some men and angels are predestinated unto everlasting life, and others *fore-ordained* to everlasting death."

These angels and men, thus predestinated and fore-ordained, are *particularly* and UNCHANGEABLY DESIGNED; and their number is so certain and definite, that it cannot be either *increased* or *diminished.* (Presbyterian Confession of Faith, p. 16, 17.) Now what else is this, but saying, with Calvin, that " the hidden counsel of God, is the *sole cause* of damnation ?"

There are few persons who will not acknowledge the justice of the following commentary, on this doctrine of Calvin, by a Protestant companion of his own. " He is a false God," says this author, " who (according to Calvin's showing) is so slow to mercy, so quick to wrath, who has created the greatest part of mankind *to destroy them*, and has not only predestined them to damnation, but even to the *cause* of their damnation. This God, then, must have determined from all eternity, and he now actually wishes and causes that we be *necessitated to sin;* so that thefts, adulteries and murders, are never committed *but at his impulse;* for he suggests to men perverse and shameful affections ; he hardens them not merely by simple permission, but *actually and efficaciously*, so that the wicked man accomplishes the work of God and not his own, and it is no longer Satan, but CALVIN's GOD, who is really the father of lies. (Castel. in lib de Prædest ad Calvin.) Is this, Rev. Sir, " the religion of Christ ?"

This, however, was the religion of the Reformation :—of Luther, who maintained that the *will of man* is a *horse*, alternately bestridden, by God and the Devil, whichever succeeds to mount first, and is always obedient to its rider, *for the time being*. This was the religion of Geneva, as we have seen. This was the religion of England itself, as some of its most eminent divines admit and *deplore*, as for instance, Bishop Bancroft. (A survey of the pretended holy discipline, p. 44.) But we have nearer testimony than that of an English Bishop. Doctor Samuel Miller of Princeton, tells us, in his Introductory Lectures on " creeds and confessions," that " the *Calvinistic articles* of the church of England were the means of keeping her doctrinally *pure*, to a very *remarkable degree*, for the greater part of a hundred years ! In the reign of James the 1st, says the Doctor, very few opponents of Calvinism DARED to avow their opinions ; and of those who did avow them, numbers were *severely disciplined*, and others saved themselves from *similar treatment by subsequent silence and discretion*." (p. 60.) Those must have been glorious days for England, when, for *nearly* a hundred years, her church was *almost* pure, thanks, not to the Bible, but to her " Calvinistic articles," against which no one " dared" to say a word.

Here, then, is only one of the doctrines of the Reformation, by which we see *free will* extinguished ;—and man degraded from his station as a *moral* and *responsible agent*, to a mere machine, operated on for *evil* as well as good, by a *predestinating* influence, over which he has no control. On the other hand we see God himself, represented as punishing, with eternal damnation, his creatures for having done, what they *could not avoid*, by complying with those *inevitable decrees*, which had been framed in the solitude of eternity past. Is this " the religion of Christ ?"

5. But supposing, as Protestants do, that the *true* religion, contrary to the promise of the Saviour, had disappeared from the world ; —were the Reformers, I ask, such men as God would have employed to restore it ? I am aware that under the influence of those strong feelings with which that turbulent epoch abounded, their *opponents* may have done injustice to their character. On this account, I shall not give one line on the testimony of their Catholic cotemporaries. Such testimony would naturally be received with suspicion by my Protestant readers. In justice to all parties, then, I shall give the fathers of the Protestant religion as they describe themselves, and

as they describe each other. But first let me state who were the principal personages, by whom this great work was accomplished.

Luther, an Augustinian friar. Œcolampadius, a monk, Melanchton, a professor of Greek. Zuinglius, a curè in Switzerland. Bucer, a Dominican friar. Calvin, a French ecclesiastic. Ochin, a Capuchin friar. Henry the 8th in England. And in Scotland, John Knox, a priest, whom Dr. Samuel Johnson describes as " the ruffian of the Reformation."

Luther says of himself, that " while a Catholic he passed his life in austerities, in watchings, in fasts and praying, in poverty, chastity and obedience." (Tom. v. In cap. 1. ad Gal. v. 14.) But hear what he says of himself, *after* his "reformation." " As it does not depend on me not to be a man, so neither does it depend on me to be without a woman." (Ibid. Serm. de Matrim. p. 119.)

Melanchton, who was his very Boswell, testifies that he received blows from him, " ab ipso colaphos accepi." (Lett. to Theodore) " I tremble, says he, (writing to the same friend) when I think of the *passions* of Luther; they yield not *in violence* to the passions of Hercules."

Hospinian, another reformer, says, speaking of Luther, " This man is absolutely mad. He never ceases to combat truth against all justice, even against the cry of his own conscience."

Œcolampadius said of him, " He is puffed up with pride and arrogance, and seduced by Satan." And Zuinglius corroborates this testimony. " Yes," says he " the Devil has made himself master of Luther."

After the death of Zuinglius, however, Luther pronounced on him the following panegyric in return " Zuinglius, is dead and damned, having desired like a thief and a rebel, to compel others, to follow his error. (Tom. 11. p. 36. in Florim.)

The whole church of Zurick (against Luther's Confession, page 61,) writes as follows : " Luther treats us as an execrable and condemned sect, but let him take care lest he condemn himself as an arch-heretic, from the sole fact, that he will not and cannot associate with those *who confess Christ*. But how strangely does this fellow allow himself to be carried away by his devils. How disgusting is his language, and how full are his words of the Devil of Hell ! He says that the devils dwell *now* and *forever* in the *bodies of the Zuinglians*........He wrote his works by the impulse and the dictation of the Devil, with whom he had dealings, and who in the struggle seemed to have thrown him by victorious arguments." (Ibid.)

" In very truth," said Calvin, " Luther is extremely corrupt. . . . (cited by C. Schlusomberg,) would to God that he had been attentive to discover his vices." (Theol. Calv. L. 11. fol. 126.) Calvin elsewhere speaks very contemptuously of the Lutheran Church ; (in his *reply to Westphal*) he says, " Thy school is nothing but a stinking pig-stye ; dost thou hear me, thou dog ? dost thou hear me, thou mad-man ? dost thou hear me, thou huge beast ?"

Of Carlosladius, Melanchton says, that " he was a brutal fellow, without wit or learning, or any light of common sense ; who, far from having any mark of the Spirit of God, never either knew or practised any of the duties of civilized life." To Calvin himself, however, the testimony of his brother reformers, is certainly not very favourable.

"Calvin," said Bucer, "is a true mad dog. The man is wicked and he judges of people according as he loves or hates them." Boudoin could not bear him, because as he says, he found him to be vindictive and blood thirsty, " propter nemiam vindictæ et sanguinis sitim." This was the reason alleged by him for renouncing Calvin's doctrine.

Stancharus, one of the Reformers, addressing his brother of Geneva, writes " what demon has urged thee, O Calvin! to declaim with the Arians against the Son of God?......It is that antichrist of the north that thou hast the imprudence to adore, that grammarian, Melanchton." (de Mediat in Calv. instit. No. 4.) " Beware, Christian readers, (he continues,) above all, ye ministers of the word, beware of the books of Calvin. They contain an impious doctrine, the blasphemies of Arianism, as if the spirit of Michael Servetus had escaped from the executioner, and according to the system of Plato, had *transmigrated whole and entire into Calvin.*" (Ibid No. 3.)

Now, Rev. Sir, if Catholics had written these things of the Reformers, I should not have troubled you with a single quotation. But these are the *Reformers themselves*, speaking of each other: and of each other, in the exclusive *capacity* of Reformers! Their *private* character affords matter for quite as painful a chapter. But the question will naturally force itself on every reflecting mind, " if the promise of Jesus Christ *failed*, in *preserving the purity* of the doctrine which he brought from heaven, is it likely that *these* are the men whom God would have appointed to *reform his church?* *If they spoke the truth* of *each other,* then it is evident that they were lost to all principle of *religious rectitude:* but if they *calumniated each other*, it is clear that they were utter strangers to truth, and moral integrity." In *either* case their testimony proves, that both themselves and their doctrines stood quite as much in need of being *reformed*, after the " Reformation" as before.

But were the morals of their followers *improved*, by joining in that ecclesiastical insurrection of which they were the prime agitators?— And through which they pressed onward, in the spirit of *unanimous discord.* Let us hear their own testimony on the subject.

"The world," says Luther, (Serm. in Postil. Evang. i. adv.) "grows every day worse and worse. It is plain that men are much more *covetous, malicious*, and resentful; much more *unruly, shameless*, and *full of vice,* THAN THEY WERE IN THE TIME OF POPERY." " Formerly," says he, (Serm. Dom. 26 post Trin.) " when we were seduced by the Pope, men willingly followed good works, but now all their study is to get every thing to themselves, by *exactions, pillage, theft, lying, usury.*" The writings of this prime Reformer, abound with similar testimonies, which proves that as *regarded morals at least*, the Reformation was all in the *inverse* ratio. Aurifaber, Luther's biographer, reports him to have declared that " since the appearance of Gospel" (meaning his own separation from all the *religions in the world as well as the Catholic church*) *virtue* seems to be utterly extinct, and *piety driven from the earth.*"

But however the Reformers may have quarrelled about their *doctrines,* they are *unanimous* in their testimony, as to the retrograde movement of public and private morals, immediately subsequent to what they called the " preaching of the Gospel." Bucer's evidence accords exactly with that of Luther. "'The greater part of the people," says he, " seem only to have embraced the Gospel, in order to shake off the yoke of discipline, and the obligation of fasting, penance, &c., which lay upon them in the time of Popery ; and to live at their pleasure, *enjoying their lust, and lawless appetites without control.* They *therefore* lend a willing ear to the doctrine that we are justified by faith *alone*, and not by good works, having no relish for them." (Bucer de regn. Christ. L. i. c. 4.) Calvin's testimony is to the same effect. " Of so many thousands," says he, " seemingly eager in embracing the Gospel, *how few have since amended their lives?* Nay, to what else does the greater part pretend, except by shaking off the heavy yoke of superstition, to launch out more freely, into every kind of lasciviousness." (Calv. l. vi. de scand.)

These testimonies, Rev. Sir, coming from such witnesses, will convince you that the morals of the people, (the low condition of which you have set forth as a plea for the insubordination of those spiritual chieftains,) instead of being improved, became absolutely deteriorated by their walking in the footsteps of the change ;—and that the effect of the Reformation, was as Dr. Chalmers declares, " to reform men into vice."

Returning then, to the extravagant supposition, which for the present I shall not dispute with you, viz: that the gates of hell had prevailed against the church of Christ, *contrary to his promise :*—that she had ceased to be " the pillar and ground of the truth," as described by St. Paul ;—and viewing the impiety of the Reformers' doctrine, on the uselessness of good works ; the absence of free will in man,—the fatalism in all things, by predestination :—viewing the character which they themselves give of each other,—the bitterness of their language,—the coarseness of their mutual denunciations ;—the crimes and corruptions of the doctrines of Christ, *reciprocally* imputed ;—viewing, in a word, the concordance of their testimony, as to the increasing depravity of morals which distinguished those who followed in the wake of the " Gospel ;" ask yourself whether the religion of that *undefinable compound* called the " Reformation," can be the religion of Christ. Is there any resemblance between the *doctrines* of the one, and the *blasphemies* of the other ? Between the *Apostles* of the one, and the *inventors* or *revivers* of the other ? Between the *moral effects* of the one, and the *progressive immorality* of the other ? Reflect, I pray you, on all this, and remembering that an *infallible judge* will review all *our* judgments, ask yourself, whether *such* doctrines, originated by *such* men, and followed by *such* consequences, are " the religion of Jesus Christ."

" 'The religion of the Reformation" teaches that there are two sacraments, according to the Calvinists; and it teaches also, that there are *no sacraments,* according to the Quakers. It teaches that infant baptism is sufficient, according to the Presbyterians ; and that infant baptism is *not sufficient,* according to the Baptists—"He that *believeth,* and is baptized shall be saved." It teaches that there is a *real distinction* between Bishops and Presbyters, according to the Episcopalians ; it teaches that there is *no such* distinction, according to the Westminster Confession of Faith. It teaches that there is a hell for the wicked, according to the Methodists ; it teaches that there is *no hell* according to the Universalist. It teaches that Christ is corporeally present in the Eucharist, according to Luther ; it teaches that there is no such *presence,* according to Calvin ; whilst, to the believers in the thirty-nine articles and the book of Common Prayer, it teaches that Christ is, at the *same time, both absent,* and *present.* Christ is " verily and indeed" received in the communion ; although the communion is, " verily and indeed," nothing but bread and wine! It teaches that Christ is God, according to the Episcopalians ; it teaches that Christ is *not* God, according to the Socinians. It teaches that there are a trinity of persons in the Godhead, according to the Baptists ; it teaches that there is *no trinity* of persons in the God-head, according to the Universalists. It teaches that the father alone is God, according to the Unitarians ; it teaches that the father is *not God,* according to the Swedenborgians ; that the *Son alone,* Christ, is God. ALL THIS " the religion of the Reformation" *teaches ;* and you have unwittingly pledged yourself to the public, to prove that " the religion of the Reformation," is, "the Protestant religion," and that " the Protestant religion" is " the religion of Christ." Now, Rev. Sir, will you not find it rather difficult to prove that " the religion of Christ," teaches all this ?

It is mere sophistry, to assert that the Protestant religion " is as old as the Bible." The Turk may say, with equal propriety, that *his* religion is as old as God himself. But the main question is, did the Protestant religion exist before Luther ? If you say it *did,* then please to inform us of the time *when,* of the village *where ;* and the name of at least *one individual, by whom* it was PROFESSED. This is the *touchstone of truth,* which will test your assertion. I bespeak the attention of our readers to the ANSWER which you will give to this question. In the meantime I venture to predict that you *will evade it ;* but let us not anticipate.

Again, it is well known, that the doctrine of Jesus Christ inculcates subordination to authority. This doctrine is eloquently put forth by Presbyterians themselves, whenever they wish to tame a disorderly brother in their own communion. And whenever he refuses submission, this authority strips him of all the *ministerial* and *pastoral power* with which it had invested him. Thus it is with the Rev. Mr. Irvine of London, at this moment ; because forsooth, like a consistent Protestant, he wished to take his religion from " the Bible alone." Thus Luther had received his mission and ordination from the Catholic church, on the understanding that he should exercise his pastorship in *communion with the church, and according to her doctrines.* If the pastors of the Catholic church then, were not true pastors, it follows that the Christian ministry was extinct. Are you prepared for this alternative? But if they were the true and legitimate pastors, then Luther in the first instance presented himself as a rebel against the injunction of Christ, and a disturber of that spiritual *order*, which Christ had established. He trampled on the vows of his ordination—violated the solemnity of his promise—he became an apostate and a traitor. If Luther's case were true of a Presbyterian parson, instead of a Catholic monk, how well the General Assembly, "that highest judicatory of the church," would know how to pass a *just decision* upon it.

But Luther was, at the period of his revolt, *like Irvine, stript of all the spiritual authority* he had received from the Catholic church. Now will you please to tell us, from *what source, he derived those spiritual powers, by virtue of which he undertook to reform the church, which had excommunicated him?* How came he to arrogate to himself, the title of "the *Ecclesiasties* of Wittemburg?" Whence did he derive his *new* authority after his excommunication? Was it from the Land-grave of Hesse, to whom he granted the privilege of having *two wives* at once, whereas he himself was satisfied with only one? Was it from Melanchton, the Professor of Greek? Or from the populace, whom his gross invective, and fiery declamation roused into madness and fury against the whole church? In a word, from *whom* did he receive his authority? And if he received no authority, by what right did he put forth his sacrilegious hand, to stay the ark of the living God, with which Jesus Christ promised, himself, to abide, "all days even to the end of time?" Whence did he receive his *new* authority? From a *new* Revelation?—So, indeed, he asserts. But, at the same time, he informs us that the angel of this Revelation was no other than the devil himself, with whom he frequently disputed, and whom he describes as a first-rate logican and an *elegant Latin scholar*. But the question still returns, from whom did Luther derive his authority? He had been unfrocked by the Catholic church, from whom, I repeat, did he derive the *new* garment of authority? Will you have the goodness, Rev. Sir, to ANSWER this question. When Moses revealed the Jewish religion, he showed his *authority*. —When Christ revealed the Christian religion he showed *his* authority. But when Luther revealed *the Protestant* religion he showed NO *authority;* judging probably with Mahomet, that the world was no longer *worthy* of miracles. The ways of God, Rev. Sir, and the conduct of men are almost equally mysterious. The people were incredulous both in reference to Moses and to Christ, with all their miraculous proof of divine authority; and they hearkened to Luther and his reforming followers, without requiring that even a particle of primitive or subsequent authority should be exhibited! It is true, indeed, that to *be saved by faith* ALONE, was a reformation of religion, well calculated to make converts. The soul could rise to heaven, much more rapidly, when borne on the wings of faith ALONE, than when its flight, (as before the Reformation,) was wont to be retarded by the superstition of good works. But the question is, whence did Luther derive his authority? Until you are pleased, Rev. Sir, to answer this all important interrogatory, I feel warranted in maintaining, that Luther and Calvin, and their associates, during that epoch of ecclesiastical anarchy, and religious phrenzy, which has been mantled into a decent appearance at least by the word " Reformation," had not a particle of authority either from God or men. They were mere laymen *in this respect ;* and their successors in the ministry, are not, and cannot be substantially any thing more. Still I am not bigotted in this ; I will give it up, if you can show that Luther, or Calvin, or Socinus, or any of the others, received any subsequent authority, to supply the absence of that which they forfeited in their excommunication from the Catholic church. The *proof of this authority* is all I require.

But even then, how will you account for their denouncing each other as *corruptors of the doctrine of Christ ?* Their doctrines, *if they told the truth,* were all " exclusively derived from and consistent with the Scriptures of the Old and New Testament, as the only infallible rule of faith and practice;" and this, according to your definition, proves them to have been the doctrines of Christ. Then, why did they denounce each other? Why did they each deny the doctrines of the other, as the doctrines, not of Christ, but of the devil?

Nor is even this all. How did they derive those doctrines? It certainly was not by the Catholic rule of faith, which, for certain causes, known to themselves, *they had renounced.* Neither was it by the *Protestant rule of faith;* for this, you yourself, Rev. Sir, have recently told us, " is the word of God, contained IN the Bible;" of which, private interpretation, you also assure us, constitutes " the ABUSES ALONE." Now, the religion of the Reformation was derived from the Bible, or it was not. If it was not ; then, according to Protestants, it must be false. But if it was, then, according to your *own showing,* you are indebted for your religion to " the ABUSE *of the Bible."* And is it this monstrous offspring of " *abuse,"* which you say is the religion of Christ? Your own words, Rev. Sir, contend against you, and hem you in a difficulty, from which you cannot escape, until you deny, or disown them.

Again, touching what are called " orthodox" tenets among Protestants, I have to observe that they are all found in the Catholic church. These doctrines always existed in the church, and the Reformers in going out from the church carried them forth, although, on subsequent examination, as it appears, many of them cannot be discovered in the Bible, and they have consequently been *protested against,* as the *remnants of Catholic superstition.* The doctrine of the Trinity, of the Incarnation and Divinity of the Son of God ; the doctrine of Original Sin, and the Atonement through the death of Christ; these were, and are the doctrines of the Catholic church. But the DENIAL and REJECTION of these dogmas was " *the religion of the Reformation."* It is the *Protestant* religion which has discarded them, and you must vindicate the *rejection* of them, in order to prove that " *the Protestant religion"* is " *the religion of Christ."*

You perceive, Rev. Sir, that I allow you in this argument all the advantages you can desire ; the whole benefit of the Protestant hypothesis, viz. that Christ was unfaithful to his promises, and allowed the church to fall into the errors against which the children of the Reformation have protested. This will save you the trouble of proving any thing against the church, by allowing you to take the conclusion, for granted. And now to simplify the matter, let me put the arguments of this letter, in the form of a few questions bearing directly on the subject.

1st Question. Did there ever exist a society of Christians (previous to the Reformation,) agreeing *in doctrines* with any sect of Protestants? In other words, *were there* Lutherans before Luther? Socinians before Socinus? Calvinists before Calvin? or Episcopalians (in the Protestant sense) before Henry VIII? Yes, or no.

2d Question. Take the Reformers as they have been described by themselves, *is it clear* that *they* were the men, whom God would have selected to purify his church? Yes, or no.

3d Question. Does the "religion of Christ" teach *the doctrines* of Protestantism, from the highest point of Episcopalianism, down the descending scale to the farthest verge of Unitarianism?—if not, the Protestant religion, is not the religion of Christ. Yes, or no.

4th Question. Had Luther, Calvin, Socinus, and their associates in reforming the church, and re-establishing the supposed religion of Christ, *any lawful ministerial authority—derived in any regular way from either God, or men?* Yes, or no.

5th Question. If *they* had not, was it in their power to impart any ministerial authority to their successors—the present clergy (so called) of the Protestant religion? Yes, or no.

Now, Rev. Sir, if you believe the Protestant religion to be the religion of Christ, you will give me a *plain, categorical answer to these five questions.* Come up to them boldly;—answer them candidly, "Yes, or no;" and then support your answer by such authority, evidence, and argument, as *truth* can always command. In supporting whatever answer you may give successively to each of them, you will have opportunity of reviewing all the preceding arguments and authorities of this letter. What I have said of the Reformers, I have said on their *own proper testimony,* and I premise this observation, least you should charge me with a wish to calumniate them. I have no such a wish towards any man, living or dead.

The closing words of your last are these: "I hope in your next to see *manly arguments* in a *Christian spirit,* and a cessation of that *low and vulgar* warfare which must speedily weary the patient and kind readers of our letters." The advice, Rev. Sir, is a good one; but whether the rebuke was merited by myself, or *expected from you,* I shall not presume to say. I have tried in this letter to furnish you with *solid* and *substantial* " arguments;" and to show you that I am not disposed to be " unchristian," " low," or " vulgar," I shall conclude this letter by a quotation which breathes the soul of Christian charity, and which you will not prize the less, because it is the chastened and beautiful production of a female pen. It is taken from the letter of Miss Pitt, (relative of the English minister,) upon her conversion to Catholicity. " As to the Protestants, who may obtain information of it, I do not consider myself calculated to instruct them, much less to convert them; but I conjure them, as my brethren, whose salvation is most dear to me, to follow one piece of advice; which is, not to reject, without the most serious examination, the doubts which must be originated in their minds, if they think deliberately upon it; by the novelty of their belief, and its variations since the Reformation, compared with the antiquity and unity of the Catholic doctrine; for the true faith must be one; and must necessarily be traced to the Apostles and to Jesus Christ. May it please God to enlighten them, as he has deigned to enlighten me, in order to draw me from the errors in which my birth and education had unfortunately engaged me."

Yours, &c. JOHN HUGHES.

CONTROVERSY. No. XXIV.

IS THE PROTESTANT RELIGION THE RELIGION OF CHRIST!

Philadelphia, July 11*th*, 1833.

To the Rev. John Hughes.

Sir,—Whatever, in your fond fancy, or more honest fears, has been gained or lost, in the present controversy, one thing is certain, *that the Bible does not teach the religion of Rome*. With a redundant frequency and zeal you have told us that the Bible may be made to teach Unitarianism, while we cannot prove the Trinity from it; that Universalism, and Swedenborgianism, and in fact, any and every system may be supported by the Bible. In order to teach Popery, however, you own that you are compelled to resort to *authoritative interpretation*, which shall require all to think alike, right or wrong. This is Deism; barefaced Deism. It abandons the BIBLE, as not being a sufficient and infallible revelation of divine truth; and it proceeds upon the plan of forcing a meaning to an unmeaning book, and then of *enforcing* that meaning on an unthinking multitude. If the Bible however, in the hands of men, teaches any thing but your system, why then your cause is given up by you. Well did Eckius tell the Elector of Bavaria that the doctrines of the Roman church *could be proved from the Fathers, but not from the Bible!* This was honest and true. Protestants on the other hand hold that the Bible has a fixed meaning; that no *authority* can alter that meaning; that it is absurd to say that authority can give it a sense, which, otherwise it has not; and that it is an insult to its author, to say that he has so revealed himself, and his will, that his word may mean any thing, and every thing, unless interpreted by the church of Rome. As I have often told you, the Bible is the Protestant Rule of Faith; and honest, common-sense interpretation the way to ascertain the true sense of that rule. If men misinterpret it, as you do, and as many calling themselves Protestants do, this is the *abuse* of the rule, and of reason; it is not the rule, or the defect of the rule; but of those who abuse the rule. This is the definition given, and advocated by me from the first; and having failed to defend your rule, or disprove in the least degree the divine character of the true rule, you finally charge the defects of your arguments, on alleged changes in my definition. By so doing you virtually abandon your previous positions; and to this I trace your sudden consent to pass from the question without ever bringing your rule of faith to view; though we were discussing the general subject for five months. I hope therefore the intelligent reader will observe that as Mr. Hughes has not yet either produced, or defended when I have produced, several of the leading features of *his* rule of faith, (as the Apochryphal books, the unanimous consent of the fathers, and unwritten traditions,) he is hardly a fit person to define *our* rule. And I am perfectly willing to leave his suppression of his own rule, and his charge of change on mine, as proof and even confession, that his cannot be defended, nor ours weakened by him.

The expressive silence which you observe in your last letter tells but too plainly both your policy and your straits. On the first question, viz: the Rule of Faith, you pursued the same course. In your second letter you said, "at a proper time, I shall defend the Catholic rule with positive arguments;" and again, in the same letter, "when the time shall come, however, I bind myself to prove that several of the former (my authorities) are spurious, and several of the latter (my propositions) are false." But let any reader refer to the long list of these propositions, spread out at large in my first letter, and see whether this pledge has ever been redeemed. You flew at the authorities, and cried out for references: but after all your struggles the *authorities* still stand. As to the *propositions*, the 2d, 3d, 4th, 5th, 6th, 7th, 9th, and 10th, stand untouched; and the promised "strong arguments," linger like Sisera, "when his mother looked out at a window, and cried through the lattice, why is his chariot so long in coming?" (Judges v. 28.)

And now on the 2d great question, your plan is still the same.— For the chief part of three letters, I have advanced upon this question —your reply is *silence*, as to all that I have said, with the good old promise, to save us from despair, viz. "That question being disposed of, I shall allow you to take up any doctrine of the church, and I shall hold myself prepared to refute all the arguments you shall bring against it!" And so after going over the ground of Protestantism in perfect silence, and leaving the Papacy reposing in security and state, some three or four years hence, (not sooner, if you spend the proportion of time on each topic as on the rule of faith) you will answer my arguments against "*the doctrines of the church!*" But, Sir, the country has never fully seen the mysteries of your system; and are curious to behold them; and I design with the help of God *now* to do my part towards bringing them to view. As you say, so it is admitted, that "*I am to defend the Protestant faith:*" and as this is the true and natural, as well as the just order of discussion, I will proceed as I have begun, promising, like yourself, but in much shorter time, to meet all your objections and attacks. If this line of argument displeases, you have the option of a connected and more enlarged discussion of the whole subject, or of a public oral discussion by which in a few successive days the entire ground may be traversed. Each has often been tendered to you. The latter you have *prudently* declined. The former I am now preparing for the press as opportunity is allowed me.

To proceed, then. In my last three letters I have proved, on Roman Catholic authority, viz. of *prelates*, *popes*, and *councils*, that a reformation in morals, worship and doctrine was necessary before, and at the time of Luther's appearing.

I have also showed (upon testimony which you have wisely left untouched) that your canon of Scripture corrupted the religion of Christ at the fountain head: that the *doctrine of the Pope's supremacy* is a wicked, and anti-christian usurpation, oppressing men, and rebelling against God, by a lawless monarchy; and that the doctrine of Indulgences, against the express testimony of the Bible, gives to Popes and others the power to pardon sin, adds creature-merits to the infinite merits of Jesus Christ, and assumes the impious right to sell for money, the gifts and grace of God.

I also proved that the canon of Scripture used by the church of Rome, the Pope's supremacy, Transubstantiation, and depriving the Laity of the cup in the Lord's Supper, were innovations unknown for ages after the resurrection of Christ. Of course it follows that the church guilty of these anti-christian innovations, has *so far*, corrupted the religion of Christ.

1. In prosecution of this plan thus begun, I pass to expose the doctrine of TRANSUBSTANTIATION. In my last letter I proved that it was not promoted into a doctrine, as your Scotus affirms, until A. D. 1215! Surely then it is not an *ancient* doctrine; yet is it taught in your church "that *novelties* are subversive of Christianity, and that those who teach them must fall under the divine anathema, and are of the school of Satan!"

The doctrine according to the Council of Trent is this: "That by the *consecration* of the bread and wine there is effected a conversion of the whole substance, the bread into the substance of the body of Christ our Lord, and of the whole substance of the wine into the substance of his blood. Which conversion is fitly and properly termed by the Holy Catholic church, TRANSUBSTANTIATION." Sess. 13. C. 3. and Can. 1. "If any one shall deny that in the most holy sacrament of the Eucharist, there are contained, truly, really, and substantially, the body and blood, together with the soul and divinity of our Lord Jesus Christ; or say that he is in it only as a sign or figure, or by his influence, let him be accursed."

The following shocking and humiliating extract from the Missal, which is the authorized book of the church for the celebration of masses, will show how the consecrated bread is regarded. It is one of many such things. "If the priest vomit the Eucharist and the species appear entire, they must reverently be swallowed again, unless nausia prevent it; if so let the consecrated species be cautiously separated, and put in some holy place, until they be corrupted, and then let them be cast into holy ground; but if the species do not appear, the vomit must be burned, and the ashes thrown into holy ground." (Missale De. Def. in cel. Mass. occ.)

Now can any one in his senses need proof that this doctrine and this illustration, are contrary to the word of God? You say it is deduced from the institution of the supper, where our Lord said of the bread, "*this is my body*." But so it is said "*that rock was Christ*." 1 Cor. x. 4. Is this literal? John x. 9. and xv. 1. Christ says, "*I am the door*," "*I am the* TRUE *vine*." Heb. xii. 29. "*Our God* is a consuming fire." Num. xiv. 9. The spies said on their return to the camp "the people of the land are *bread* for us." Is this all figure? or all fact? for they stand or fall together. Isaiah xl. 6. says, "all flesh *is grass*." Peter explains this, 1 Peter i. 24. "All flesh is AS GRASS." Indeed I remember that you said in letter No. 7, "Just lend me the Protestant rule of faith for a few minutes, and I will prove from Scripture that it is right to call the Pope God "*You are gods. I have appointed thee god of Pharaoh.*" P. 71. 6. Exodus vii. 1. Such was your language when *figure* was conveni ent. To see the unscriptural character of this doctrine, you have only to look at 1 Cor. x. 16. and also xi. 26—29. where the element of bread is called bread *after* consecration, " As oft as you eat this bread," &c. ; and where by another figure the *cup* is put for the *wine*, " as oft as ye drink this cup;" and according to your doctrine the wine which was first made the *real* blood of Christ, is then transmuted into a real *cup;* and then *this cup* is changed into the New Testament! We are referred for proof of Transubstantiation to John vi. 53, " Except ye eat the flesh of the Son of man, and drink his blood, you have no life in you." But it is most clear that this cannot mean transubstantiation. 1. For in verses 32-3, he tells us *this bread* came *down from heaven;* but his natural body was born on earth. 2. Whoever eats *this bread* has eternal life. But do *all* that take the Eucharist, have eternal life ? 3. Whoever eats not this *living bread* (verse 53,) is forever lost—but surely *some* are saved who never received the sacrament. 4. As you deprive the people of the cup, so if this means the Eucharist and Transubstantiation, you destroy all their souls, for it says, " except ye drink his blood ye have no life in you." 5. To drink the blood of Christ at that time or at the institution was impossible—for it was *not then shed;* and if it be as you say, then Christ drank his *own* blood, and eat his *own* flesh! 6. In this same chapter Christ tells us that it is a figure, and has a spiritual meaning ; v. 63. " The words that I speak unto you they are *spirit*, and they are life."

I have already produced the admission of Bellarmine and the testimony of Scotus (see last letter) against this doctrine. Cardinal Cajetan (Notes on Aquinas, p. 3. q. 75. Art. 1. &c.) says, " The other point which the gospel has not expounded expressly, that is, the change of the bread into the body of Christ, *we have received from the church.*" Here is the church *against* the gospel ! Again : " There appears nothing in the gospel to compel any man to understand these words, *this is my body*, in a proper sense. Nay, that PRESENCE (of Christ) which the church holdeth, *cannot be proved*, unless the declaration of the church be added." Bishop Fisher, also Vasquez, Alphonsus de Castro, Erasmus, Durand, Melchoir, Cane, &c. &c. all of your church, not to mention others, bear the same testimony. By order of Pope Pius V. the above concession of Cajetan was expunged from the Roman edition of his works! Such is the testimony of Scripture and your own writers, against a doctrine which we are *cursed by your church* for rejecting.

But this doctrine invades the testimony of the senses. If it be true, that the bread by consecration becomes "substantially the body and blood together with the soul and divinity of our Lord Jesus Christ," and yet *appears* bread, and retains all the qualities of bread, then am I ever to believe my senses again ? I see, and handle, and eat the *bread*—a little piece of *wafer*, and yet you tell us that a few words by a priest have made it *the body, soul, and divinity of Christ?* If the properties of one substance may become those of another, an utterly different substance, and yet those properties remain, then I can be certain of no substance; nor of any thing I see, feel, taste, or touch. If transubstantiation is true, Christianity may be false— for the evidence of miracle appeals to, and rests on the testimony of the senses. As for example, after Christ rose from the dead, he said to his disciples, (Luke xxiv. 39,) "Handle me and see, for a spirit hath not flesh and bones, as ye see me have." Now this was appealing to their senses, that he was not a disembodied "spirit," (as they feared) but had a *real* body. Here the proof rested on the testimony of the *senses*. But the senses tell us the bread is bread, blessed or not blessed. But if it be the *real* body of Christ, then they deceive us in this important case, and they may have deceived the disciples in the Lord's resurrection: and then all miracles are vain, and Christianity which rests on them is vain; and David Hume is right in resolving all religion and all nature into illusions and ideas. And is there any thing more abhorrent than to suppose that a priest *can make his God*, by uttering a few *words?* And when he has thus made a wafer of senseless matter into the soul and divinity, as well as body of Jesus Christ, what becomes of them after the wafer is eaten? Does the wafer become our creator, possessed of the attributes, and capable of the acts of God? And does that wafer ever cease to be God after once becoming so? No doctrine of your church is more strenuously and exclusively pressed; none with less evidence, or greater absurdity; and nothing has more contributed to degrade the Christian religion, and make men infidels. There was more of wisdom than of Christian honesty in the confession of Mr. Cressy, when he said, "I have not learned to answer such arguments, but to despise them." Cicero says, "When we call the *fruits* of the earth Ceres, and the *wine* Bacchus, we use but the common language—but do you think any man so *mad* as to believe that which he *eats* to be God?" (De nat. Deornum b. 3.) Yet in that very Rome, where a wise heathen thus spoke, the infallible head of the church does this very thing. Amazing indeed!

Averroes, an Arabian philosopher, who lived after this doctrine was invented, says: "I have travelled over the world, and have found divers sects—but so sottish a sect, or law, I never found as is the sect of the Christians; because with their own teeth they devour the God whom they worship."

Such is the testimony of Scripture, and of your own writers, of reason, and of the senses, against this *cardinal doctrine of the church of Rome*. Is it not then a glaring novelty? Is it not most corrupt and anti-christian?

2. This doctrine leads directly to another equally novel, and corrupt, (for errors come in a chain, one drawing after it another,) viz: *the sacrifice of the Mass.* In chap. I. of the Council of Trent, on the institution of the sacrifice of Mass, we are told that "our Lord, in the last supper on the night in which he was betrayed, declared himself to be constituted a priest forever after the order of Melchisedek—offered his blood and body to God the Father, under the species of bread and wine, and by these symbols delivered the same to be received by his Apostles whom he then appointed priests of the New Testament, and commanded them and their successors in the Priesthood to offer the same, saying, "this do in commemoration of me," Luke xxii. 19. Chap. 2. "And since the *same Christ* who once offered himself by his *blood*, on the altar of the *cross*, is contained in *this divine sacrifice* which is celebrated in the Mass and

offered without blood, the holy Council teaches that this is *really propitiatory*, and *made by Christ himself*."

" We therefore confess that the *sacrifice* of the Mass is *one and the same* sacrifice, with that of the cross ; the *victim* is one and the same Christ Jesus..........and the oblation of the cross is daily renewed in the Eucharistic sacrifice........'The priest also is the same Christ our Lord." (Catechism, Coun. Trent, on the Eucharist.)

Such are the infallible decrees, &c., on this awful profanation, for I cannot truly call it by a better name. The substance is this, that every priest has power to turn bread and wine, by uttering a few words, into the real Lord Jesus, the Son of Mary, and the Son of God, who is now enthroned in heaven ; and that having thus made his Maker, he offers him up to God as an atoning sacrifice for the living and the dead, who are in purgatory !

Now *is this less than crucifying to themselves the Son of God afresh*, which Paul tells us, (Heb. vi. 6.) *is putting Him to an open shame ?* Is it not written (Heb. ix. 24—28.) expressly, " that Christ did not *offer* himself *often*, as the High Priest entereth into the holy place every year, with blood of others, for then must He *often* have *suffered* since the foundation of the world ; but now *once* in the end of the world hath He appeared to put away sin by the sacrifice of himself; and as it is appointed unto men *once* to die, but after that the judgment, so Christ was *once* offered to bear the sins of many." " For such a high priest became us, who is holy, harmless, undefiled, separate from sinners, and made higher than the heavens ; who needeth not daily, as those high priests, to offer up sacrifice, first for his own sins, and then for the people's : for this he did *once*, when *he* offered up *himself*." (Heb. vii. 26, 27.) " And every priest standeth daily ministering, and offering oftentimes the same sacrifices, which can never take away sins : but this man, after he had offered *one* sacrifice for sins, *forever sat down* on the right hand of God ; from henceforth *expecting* till his enemies be made his footstool." (Hebrews x. 11—13.) The repetition then of the sacrifice, if it were possible, by the priest's hands, would be antichristian and absurd. Is not this most express ; that *daily sacrifices* were not needed or designed ; that this was to be done *but once ;* and that *He* was to *do it ;* not *frail priests ?* And having done it once, He *forever sat down* at God's right hand, to die no more.

Again, (in Hebrews chap. ix. verse 22,) it is expressly said " without shedding of blood is no remission." But Christ *had not* shed his blood, at the last supper ; and " the vain oblation" of the Mass, is called a *bloodless* sacrifice ; yet in the extracts given above, your church says the Mass is a *real propitiatory sacrifice*. Query. Does Christ *now* suffer when he is sacrificed in the Mass ? It is said, " that it is the *same Christ*, who is the victim, in the oblation of the Mass, as in the oblation on the cross." If he suffer *not*, he is not a victim ; to say he suffers now is *blasphemy*. Let any man compare the Epistle to the Hebrews, especially the ten first chapters, with the decrees of the Council of Trent, and he will see at every step, the Gospel tortured ; the order of things turned backward ; the Pope and his priesthood caricatured into a Levitical household ; Christ degraded; his death dishonoured, his worship polluted, men exalted to gods, and God reduced to the creature of men's hands, and then alternately worshipped, offered up, and consumed by those who made him.

One dreadful feature in this system is the profane power it puts into the Priest's hands. The transubstantiation depends on the consecration of the Priest; and if " his *intention*" be wanting, then there is no real sacrament, and the poor people are all deceived, they idolatrously worship the bread and wine, and the sacrifice is lost. But supposing the true intention and proper forms, the priest offers up the *Christ* he has made, " as a true propitiatory sacrifice for the living and the dead." He does all that Christ need do for the poor sinner. To him he confesses his sins, from him he receives absolution, and he offers up the victim even Christ, and by his sacrificing act, the pardon of the sinner is secured. Hence masses abound. Hence preaching, pastoral visitation, studying the Bible, all things are secondary to the Mass, and to celebrate it, (as a *certain* distinguished priest recently told an astonished friend of mine) is the *chief business* of the priest.

Add to this that these masses are sold for money. I gave a specimen from the churches in Madrid in my last. " In the Laity's Directory," 1830, p. 22. 31. Those who contribute to the erection of a chapel are assured " that every Sunday, prayers shall be offered up for them publicly, and that a mass will be said every year within the octave of saints for the repose of their souls after death:" and " four masses in each month are regularly offered for the benefactors (subscribers for a particular fund) living and dead:" *i. e.* Christ is sacrificed thirty-six times annually in these masses, in return for their money! I have before me at this moment, the form of constitution of a " PURGATORIAL SOCIETY" in Dublin, A. D. 1815. The 22d rule is as follows: " Every person wishing to contribute to the relief of the suffering souls in purgatory shall pay one penny per week, which shall be appropriated towards PROCURING MASSES, to be offered for the *repose* of the *souls* of the parents and relations of THE SUBSCRIBERS to the institution, and all the faithful departed in general."

The 3d chap. of Dec. Coun. Trent is headed, " *Of Masses in honour of the Saints.*" That is, Christ is offered up, in honour of his sinful creatures! Thus the Missal (the Roman Directory containing masses for the various days and occasions, and sanctioned by Popes and used every where) under the title of " the feast of St. Peter's chair in which he first sat at Rome," has these prayers: " May the intercesssion of thy blessed Apostle PETER, we beseech thee, O Lord, render the prayers and oblations of thy church acceptable to thee, that what we celebrate (the masses) for his glory (pro illius gloria) may prevail for the pardon of our sins." Again, " Sanctify, O Lord, the offerings of thy people by the prayers of thy Apostle Paul, that what is acceptable to Thee, because by Thee instituted, *may become still more acceptable by his intercession.*" Here is the authorized Directory for your church worship; and the prayer it prescribes is, that " the offerings of the people," that is, *Christ sacrificed in the mass*, offered up in honour of Peter, and Paul, may be made MORE ACCEPTABLE, by the prayers of these creatures! Is this Christianity? Is it less than blasphemy? Yet this is authorised infallible Popery. Is it wrong then to *protest* against it? Was not silence a sinful connivance, protestation a public duty, reformation a universal right? It is a remarkable fact that the Council of Trent, as if conscious of its anti-christian character, does not attempt to found this doctrine on the word of God, but rests it on *the authority* of the church!

3. The *worship of the host* (which arises out of the former errors) is *unscriptural, and grossly idolatrous.*

The decree of the Council of Trent (Session 13. 5, and canon 6. are to the following effect, viz: " There is therefore no *room to doubt*, but that the faithful of Christ should *adore* his most holy sacrament with that highest worship due to the true God, according to the constant usage in the Catholic Church. Nor is it the less to be adored, that it was instituted by Christ our Lord as has been stated," (that is, to be eaten.)

Again, " whoever shall affirm, that Christ the only begotten Son of God, is not to be adored in the holy eucharist with the external signs of that worship which is due to God ; and therefore that the eucharist is not to be honoured with extraordinary festive celebration, nor solemnly carried about in procession, according to the laudable and universal rites and customs of the Holy Church, nor publicly presented to the people for their ADORATION ; and that those who worship the same are idolaters; let him be accursed." It is well for Protestants, that this *curse* is harmless, for that it is idolatry, the very language of the decree directly evinces. In our own country there is too much light to bear the public elevation, and ampulatory show of the Host. It is confined to the altars and ailes of the church.— But in Italy, and in Spain " this tremendous mystery," as some Romanist calls it, is often carried in *public processions*, and every man must *kneel* or be knocked down, as the Host moves by. In the above quotation the authority and practice of the church are again (as usual) substituted for the word of God, and the law of Christ.— As to the " *usage of the church*" what have we to do with that, when it practices gross idolatry? Besides, this usage is of comparatively modern date. The doctrine of Transubstantiation was not made (as we have said) an article of faith until the year 1215—so say Scotus, Tonstal, and others ; and of course before that the bread was not *worshipped*. And in the Roman Canon Law it is written that Pope Honorius III. in the following year directed that the priests, at a certain part of the service, *should elevate the host*, and cause the people to prostrate themselves and adore. Soon after this, he directed the words " *His Deum adora*"—*here adore God*,—to be inscribed on the doors of those places in which the host was reserved for the sick.

As to *other* charges of idolatry, some denial or explanation is entered up. But here it is avowed, and a curse levelled at those who decline it, or condemn it. If the bread be not God, *then* it is confessedly idolatry. But the Council of Trent decreed (Sess. 7. can. 11.) *that the intention of the priest is necessary to a true sacrament, and the Missal* says, "*if a priest should not intend to consecrate, but to deceive, there is no sacrament.*" But it is certain that in the innumerable millions of masses said, priests often *lack* the *intention*. Then in such a case there is gross idolatry; for as it is owned that in such case the bread remains unchanged, so those who worship it are idolaters. But who can be *certain* of the intention of a priest, especially when so many of them have been, and are among the most abandoned, and irreligious of men? Bellarmine (if he has not lost his *orthodoxy* with you) tells us " no man can be *certain* with the *certainty of faith that* he receives a *true sacrament ;* because it depends on the minister's *intention* to consecrate it: and none can *see another's intention.*" (Book 3. chap. 8. on Justification.)

The missal mentions no less than *ten heads*, and under those no less than *fifty* particulars, in which *defects* may occur. But whenever such defect occurs, (and who can be certain it does not on any given occasion?) the worship of the bread is confessedly *idolatry !* As for Scripture authority for this worship, there is not one *word*. But the church is residuary legatee of all power, and settles all questions at Rome now, as the sword of Brennus did in a former age. Vasquez (on 1 Cor. 28,) says, " the power of the Apostles to give commandments, has not been greater than that of the church and the Popes." Gabriel Biel (Can. Mass.) " Priests have great power over the one, and the other body of Christ......He who made me has, if I may say it, given me *power* to *create* him; and he that *made me* is made *by* my *means.*" And sec. 4th. " Christ is incarnate and made flesh, in the hands of Priests, as in the Virgin's womb......Priests do create their creator and have power over the body of Christ." I will not, as I might, multiply these shocking profanities. But here is the seat of the power, to make the bread divine, and of the authority to require it to be adored. And now is it anti-christian to protest against such abominations?

4. *Purgatory is a fiction of the Church of Rome, having no foundation in the word of God, and ruinous to the souls of men.*

In the decree of the Council of Trent on Purgatory (sess. 25,) it is written—" That there is a purgatory; and that the souls detained there are assisted by the suffrages of the faithful, but especially by the acceptable sacrifice of the mass; this holy council *commands* all bishops diligently to endeavour that the wholesome doctrine of purgatory, delivered to us by venerable fathers and holy councils, be believed and held by Christ's faithful, and every where taught and preached." The creed also contains the following article : " I constantly hold that there is a purgatory, and that the souls detained therein are *helped* by the suffrages of the faithful." The Catechism of the Council of Trent also teaches, (Part 1st. ch. 6.) " That the souls of the pious, who have departed this life, not fully cleansed, and having somewhat yet to pay, make *full satisfaction* through the fire of Purgatory."

Bellarmine heads this third general controversy with this extraordinary title :—" OF THE CHURCH WHICH IS IN PURGATORY!!!" In his first book, 1st chapter, on the same subject he says. " Purgatory is a certain place in which, as in a *prison*, after this life, the souls which have not been fully cleansed on earth, are *purified;* so that thus they may be certainly prepared for heaven, where nothing that defiles shall enter." Such is the summary of a doctrine so *profitable* to the *priests,* and so *ruinous* to the *people !* Bishop Foster of your church says, (In Confut. Luth. Art. 18.) " Many are tempted now-a-days, not to rely much on *Indulgences:* for this consideration, that the use of them appears *to be new and very lately known* among Christians: To which I answer, It is not very certain who was the first author of them; the doctrine of Purgatory was a long time unknown, was rarely if at all heard of among the ancients, and to *this day the Greeks* believe it not; nor was the belief of either Purgatory, or Indulgences, so necessary in the Primitive church, as it is *now;* so long as men were unconcerned about Purgatory, nobody inquired after Indulgences." The Greeks, to whom the above extract refers, says in their apology to the Council of Basil, (De Igne Purgatorio,) " we own no Purgatory-fire: we have received no such thing; nor doth our Eastern church confess it." And again : " For these causes, the doctrine proposed, of a Purgatory-fire, is to be rejected and cast out of the church, as that which tends to *slacken* the endeavours of the diligent, and which hinders them from doing their utmost to be *purged in this life,* since *another Purgatory* is expected after it." Otho Frising, an old Roman Catholic Bishop and historian, cotemporary with St. Bernard, tells us, " the doctrine of Purgatory was first built upon the credit of those fabulous dialogues, attributed to Gregory 1st, about the year 600." Roffensis, and Pollidore Virgil, inform us, that this doctrine was not believed by the early Greek Fathers, and that it was but lately known by the church as a doctrine. The earliest Latin Fathers also, were strangers to this innovation; and it may with confidence be asserted, that *for* 500 *years after the death of Christ not one of them can be named, who held, throughout, this article of faith, as now professed by the church of Rome.* This doctrine, besides being a novelty, is directly contradictory to the word of God. It supposes that the satisfaction of Jesus Christ does not procure a full remission of sins, either before we die, or perhaps long after: it supposes that a creature, and he *sinful,* can make a meritorious satisfaction to God for his sins *by suffering,* and thus *mend* the *imperfect* satisfaction of Christ: it supposes that God pardons men, and yet punishes them afterwards: it holds that God punishes the same sins twice, viz: in the death of his Son and then in Purgatory: that He applies pardon by punishment, and *remits* our debts by making us *pay* them: that there is a distinction between sins *venial* and sins *mortal,* i. e. that some sins are *trivial,* and *only some* deserve eternal punishment: it supposes that God forgives our *greater* sins freely, and yet punishes us for our *lesser :* it relies also upon this, that " God requires of us a full exchange of penances and satisfactions, which must regularly be paid here or hereafter, even by those who are *pardoned* here, which if it be true, we are all undone :" it admits that a priest's mass on earth will relieve a soul from purgatory, when Christ's intercession in heaven will not: it supposes ages perhaps of sufferings after death, by those who are the *children* of God, and not *guilty* in his sight: in a word, it is the parent of indulgences, makes the church a mart where sin, and heaven, and hell, the blood of Jesus, and the souls of men are suspended on the will of a priest, and commuted for money, so that the principal calamity, and crime, *is to be poor.*— Now, not one of these suppositions is accordant with the word of God; but all are directly opposed to it, as the following Scriptures sufficiently show. Rom. viii. 1. "'There is therefore, now *no* condemnation to them which are in Christ Jesus." 1 John i. 7. 9. "The *blood* of Jesus Christ His Son *cleanseth* us from *all* sin."...... "If we confess our sins He is faithful and just to *forgive* us our sins, and to *cleanse* us from *all* unrighteousness." Rev. xiv. 13. "I heard a voice from *heaven* saying write, blessed are the dead that die in the Lord from henceforth, yea saith the Spirit that they may *rest* from their labours." Picherellus, one of your doctors of the Sorbonne, confesses that " St. John, by this last mentioned Scripture, hath put out for ever the fire of Purgatory." And again, "There is no *fuel* in *Scripture*, either to kindle or maintain the fire of Purgatory."— (In Massa.) Matthew v. 22. "Whosoever shall *say* unto his brother, *thou fool*, shall be in danger of *hell fire*." There is no such thing as a little sin mentioned in all the word of God! See also Heb. i. 3. Matt. x. 8. Rom. iii. 24, and viii. 32. Colos. ii. 13. 2 Cor. v. 1. 8. Isaiah lvii. 1. Luke xvi. 22.—Jesus said, even to the thief upon the cross, "*this day* shalt thou be with me in paradise;" and he says to all men every where, (John v. 24.) " He that believeth my word and believeth on him that sent me, hath everlasting life and shall not come into *judgment*, but hath *passed from death unto life.*" On the other hand he hath also said, (John viii. 21.) "I go my way and ye shall seek me, and shall die in your sins; whither I go ye cannot come." As to the passage in Matthew xii. 32. Bellarmine owns that " Purgatory cannot by any rule of logic be proved from it, as the sin there mentioned was never to be purged, being damnable." Maldonat acknowledges that "Purgatory cannot be proved from Matt. v. 25, 26., as the prison there spoken of is *Hell* and not Purgatory." Peter de Soto allows, "it cannot be proved from 1 Cor. iii. 15. as it is not *persons* but *vain doctrines* called wood, hay, stubble, which some well meaning but mistaken teachers add to the true, that shall in the day of judgment be tried by fire and be burned, and *themselves* shall hardly escape, even as one escapeth out of the fire." This novel and unchristian doctrine, as the Greek *Protestants* quoted above, justly intimate, relaxes the efforts of men in fleeing from the wrath to come, and criminally holds forth the vain hope that their future sufferings will have an end. You have often alluded in your letters to the doctrine of the Universalists; and I agree with you in thinking them unscriptural, and destructive. But for all practical purposes, in deluding and destroying men's souls, the doctrine of Purgatory is equally efficacious; it is even *less* consistent; and from the extent of your communion (though a *profitable* fable to the priesthood in *this* world,) it spreads a far wider ruin than the other doctrine. Against this dreadful doctrine, enthroned as it is in the standards of your church, and hedged about with terrible anathemas, we protest, and pronounce it incapable of defence.

Here then are *four* other cardinal doctrines of the church of Rome, which, *if the Bible contains the Christian religion*, are as unlike to Christianity as they are to the Koran, and are far more like the religion of heathen Rome than that of Jesus Christ.

My two previous letters remain unanswered, and very much unnoticed by you. This of course is the 3d in the series. By this time it must be seen by all, that you feel the safety of Romanism to lie in its seclusion from the public eye. If after attacking the Protestant rule of faith, and withholding your own, you can manage to attack the Protestant *religion* also, so as to withhold your own, we must concede to you the palm of adroitness at least, especially when you also manage to *appear* the person standing on the defensive against the *attacks* of a disputant who has *challenged you*. Honesty however is the best policy, and as I met your attack on our rule of faith, so will I even in anticipation of the time, meet your attacks on the Protestant religion; for I plainly perceive that you are not disposed to meet me in discussing the peculiarities of Romanism. The following passage, which you *tell* us incloses a grand dilemma, is noticed chiefly to gratify yourself.—"In my last letter I reduced the question to the simplicity of a dilemma, from which I defy you to escape. It is this: Either the Protestant religion is a religion *differing* from the religion of Christ; and by this admission you give up the question; or else, the religion of Christ was NOT *professed by any society of Christians previous to the time of Luther*. And in that case the religion of Christ is only three hundred years old ! ! To which of these alternatives do you wish to cling? for one of them is *enevitable*. To this argument you oppose the 'defence' of silence. Not a word of authority, not a word of reasoning ! Silence only, *prudent silence*." Now I must beg pardon for passing it by before ; but like the "*pathetic part*" of the young advocate's speech, of which he gave the jury notice, when coming to it, I should never have known it, if you had not *told* me that it was a *dilemma*. Our religion existed so long before the days of Luther as the Bible existed. It is distinctly taught by the early Christians, Martyrs, and Confessors of the first three centuries; it is recorded clearly in the earliest creeds down to the days of Athanasius; it was taught and defended in the earliest councils; it was established in the first ages in Jerusalem and other parts of Palestine, in Asia, Greece, Egypt, and Rome herself; it was afterwards corrupted by that same church of Rome ; and we have "left the *rust* and kept the *metal*." The Reformation is of the *errors*, not the *true religion*. *You* have left Christ, not *we*. We have been driven from and left *you*, not *Christ* : the Reformation is *subsequent* to the errors it reforms, otherwise it were not a reformation but an unchristian change. Sound Christianity was primitive : to *it* we return. If any honest inquirer taking the natural sense of language (and can your *authority* justly give any other sense?)—will examine the word of God, and all these various early documents to which we refer, and compare them with the Protestant religion properly so called, he will find it in all its simplicity and fullness therein recorded. But if on the other hand, you choose to *ascend*, we can show you our religion " professed by societies of Christians" long before the days of Luther. The Magdeburg Centuriators, Vol. 3. Cent. 12. chap. 8. tells us of A PEOPLE whom your church in vain sought to destroy, professing such articles of faith as these. "The Sacraments of the church of Christ are two, Baptism, and the Supper of the Lord: Masses are impious, and it is madness to say them for the dead: Purgatory is an invention of men: the invocation and worshipping of dead saints is idolatry: the Pope has not the primacy over all the churches of Christ, neither has he the power of both the swords: Vows of celibacy are inventions of men, and occasions of Sodomy: the marriage of Priests is both lawful and necessary: the reading and knowledge of the holy Scriptures is open to all: commemorations of the dead, pilgrimages, &c., are diabolical inventions." See also two "confessions of their faith" furnished by John Paul Perrin; see also Reinerius Sacco, and Æneus Sylvius, Claudius Siesselius, all Papal writers, in proof of the *Protestant* doctrines of the WALDENSES, ages before Luther. Reinerius thus writes: " Among the sects (he says) which still are, or have been, there is not any more pernicious to the church, than that of the Leonists (Waldenses;) and this for three reasons, the first is, because their opposition has been of *very long continuance.* Add to which that this sect has become very general, for there is scarcely a country to be found in which this heresy is not planted. And, in the third place, because while all other sects beget in people a dread and horror of them on account of their blasphemies against God, this, on the contrary, hath a great appearance of godliness; for they live righteously before men, believe rightly concerning God in *every particular*, holding all the articles contained in the (Apostles') creed, but hating and reviling the church of Rome, and on this subject they are readily believed by the people." (Reinerius contra Waldenses in Perrin, b. 2. ch. 1.) Thuanus the historian, book 6, bears the same testimony to the *Protestant* doctrines of the Waldenses. So also Mazery says of these heretics, " avoient apeu pres mesmes opiniones que ceux qu' on nomme au jourd' huy Calvinistes." " 'They had almost the same opinions as those who are now called *Calvinists.*" Let it be remembered that these are *Roman Catholic Historians*. Again, the Greek church which you own to be an ancient church, also *protests* against your half-communion, Purgatory, merits (human,) supererogation, worship of images, concealing the Scripture in an unknown tongue, extreme unction, sale of masses, and infallibility. The ancient Arminian church rejects the Supremacy of the Pope, Transubstantiation, and Purgatory, and excommunicates those who worship images. The Jacobites, the Syrian, the Egyptian, and Abyssinian Christians also reject nearly all the Romish errors against which we protest.

How plain it is then from these testimonies, that the Protestant religion was professed, not only ages before the days of Luther, but existed from the beginning, and descended for centuries even in your own church, until she corrupted it and made it an anti-christian Papacy. The dilemma then reverts to you, and that on your own principles. Either the Roman Catholic religion differs from the religion of Christ (and by this admission you give up the question) or else the religion of Christ did not exist for many centuries after the death of its author.

So much for your dilemma. Now the posture of the question between us is this. Here is the Bible; you and I differ as to the best mode of finding out what it means; but we both agree that its meaning, when gotten at, is God's will and truth, and therefore consonant to the religion of Christ. We have for some time been *discussing* the best means for finding out its contents; but surely it is easy to say what are the doctrines which we actually have deduced from that book. This discussion relates to *those doctrines.* Now the Church of Rome deduces certain doctrines; Protestants also, certain doctrines; the question is not *how,* but *what* are they? In *some* points we *agree.* This you admit in your last letter when you say " touching what are called 'orthodox' tenets among Protestants, I have to observe that they are all found in the Catholic church. These doctrines always existed in the church, and the Reformers in going out from the church, carried them forth, etc." Then it follows that they are our doctrines and yours, and as to them there is no dispute. So far therefore as the *agreed* points go, if your church is the church of Christ, so is the Protestant church

Now as to *disputed* points against which we protest, you hold that *they* also are a part of the religion of Christ. These disputed tenets, I stated at large in my definition of the Protestant religion; and I have exposed many of them in this and in former letters.— Since then you hold these disputed points to be *part* of the religion of Christ, it is your business to prove that they are so. If I have not stated them to suit you, tell us what they are, and having stated, prove them. This you entirely decline to do, and shrinking from it, undertake to *prove a negative,* viz. that the Protestant religion is *not* the religion of Christ. While you cling to this absurdity, and shrink from the fair and manly meeting of the question, your cause is abandoned.

Again, according to the state of the question, you must go further, and show that these disputed tenets are such *essential* parts of the religion of Christ, that not to hold them is to unchurch us. Until you have done this, no reason appears why we may not hold the religion of Christ, and yet *reject them.* This is so incumbent upon you in the discussion of this question, that until you have done it, you may abuse the Reformers and laud the Papacy without measure, and yet no demonstration is given that the Protestant religion is not the religion of Christ.

Still further, if these disputed points are so essential, that if true we must hold them before we can be a church of Christ, (or our religion be His religion;) then, on the other hand, it follows, that if *false*, they are so essential that all who hold them are truly unchurched, and their religion is *not* the religion of Christ. This reasoning is not only conclusive, but it is so by your own showing. It follows, therefore, not only that ours is a true church and our religion the religion of Christ, but (Mr. Hughes being judge) ours is the only true church and religion, *unless you can prove these exclusive points.* How strangely then must you appear to the community of readers, when time after time you refuse to touch these disputed points, and leaving the only ground upon which the question can be settled, rove through declamatory pages, and garbled extracts from the writings of the Reformers, in order to prove a negative. Let me still further illustrate this subject. Take the doctrine of human merits, or the worship of the Host, or the doctrine of purgatory, or any of the leading points upon which we differ. These points are so *fundamental*, that you denounce us as heretics for rejecting them ; and we protest against you as anti-christian for holding them. In so far as we agree with you, ours is the religion of Christ if yours is, by our holding the agreed points ; but if your church be *wrong* in those fundamental points which we *reject*, then ours is a *true* church, and yours is not ; whereas if we are *right* in holding what *your* church *rejects*, then still ours is a true church and yours is not. If, therefore, you will not come up to the discussion of the points on which we differ, and on which the question turns, I must pursue the line of my argument as already begun, and the tenets in which you are interested, must be considered incapable of defence.

Your first question, viz. "Did there ever exist a society of Christians (previous to the Reformation,) agreeing *in doctrines* with any sect of Protestants ?" has been answered at large, in this letter, in my exposure of your fanciful dilemma. As you ask, however, "a categorical answer," to your dogmatic questions, I answer without hesitation, Yes. When, however, you include Socinus among Protestants, I refer you for answer to Simon Magus, the father of Papal Simony and Indulgences. His system revived in your church, was one of the articles for reformation. For the parentage of celibacy, I refer you to the Manichees : for the worship of the Virgin Mary, I remind you of the Collyridian idolators from whom (see Epiphanius) it is derived by your church.

"2d Question. Take the Reformers as they have been described by themselves, *is it clear* that *they* were the men whom God would have selected to purify his church ?"

Answer. From the caricature which you have given, in clipped extracts, of their character and doctrines, no just conception can be formed of the one or the other. This shall be shown to your own confusion, and in part even in the present letter. But allowing them to have been all that your injustice has ascribed to them, I ask, if they were unfit men to *reform*, what were the Popes to *sustain* a religion ? Let us take a glance at the *thirteenth* schism which disgraced the Papacy in the days of Formosus and Sergius. Formosus, A. D. 890, gained the Pontificate by bribery. Sergius his rival was expelled by royal power. Stephen the successor of Formosus, unearthed the dead body of Formosus, had a mock trial of him, and having cut off his head and fingers threw his body into the Tyber, and declared all his acts and *ordinations* invalid. The Romans soon after expelled Stephen from the Hierarchy : Baronius tells us that he entered like a thief, and died by the rope. Bruys says he was as ignorant as he was wicked. In the *nineteenth* schism Benedict, Sylvester, and John, reigned in one filthy triumvirate at the same time, (who then was Pope ?) They occupied in Rome St. Mary's, the Vatican, and the Lateran. Binius VII. 221, and Labbeus II., 1180, called them "a three headed monster rising from the gates of Hell, infesting in a most woful manner the most Holy chair of Peter." Triceps bestia ab inferorum portis emergens sanctissimam Petr Cathedram miserime infestavit. A clever link, this, in the sacred and unbroken chain of Pontifical succession! The great western, or *twenty-ninth* schism, which lasted for *fifty* years, broke to atoms the Pontifical succession, and exhibited to an astonished world, a HOLY war for half a century, amidst a band of ruffians, calling themselves the vicegerents of the Prince of *Peace*. I need not dwell here, nor point you again to the *fifty* Popes called by your historian "*apostate* rather than *apostolical*." But this brief sketch may suffice to show that the Reformers, however bad, were at least as well fitted *to reform*, as such Popes to *head* and *sustain* a religion.

Again, we never set up these Reformers as the vicegerents of God, but only as leaders in Reform to which every Christian is in his measure not only competent, but also bound by his duty to God and to the church. For such a work miracles are not required. Such a work was often accomplished in the Old Testament church, of which it is written, "now for a long season Israel hath been without the true God, and without a teaching Priest, and without law." 2 Chron. xv. 3.

"Question 3d. Does the religion of Christ teach *the doctrines* of Protestantism, from the highest point of Episcopalianism, down the descending scale to the farthest verge of Unitarianism? if not, the Protestant religion is not the religion of Christ."

Answer. You have unwittingly, but satisfactorily, answered this question for me, when you say in your last letter, "touching what are called *orthodox tenets among Protestants*, I have to observe, that they are all found in the Catholic church." Unitarianism, Universalism, &c., are not found in the Bible, and therefore make no part of the Protestant religion, "which is exclusively derived from, and consistent with, the word of God." Ours is not a religion of "opinions," as you mean by the word, (which, however, is an absurd and unphilosophical use of it,) but of evangelical doctrine. Our Bible does not teach any thing, and every thing, though you say it does *out of your hands;* and those who unite with you in saying that it does, are with you, defamers of the Bible, and as to truth, heretics. You are hardly a stranger to the innumerable sects which have arisen up in your church. The Pope once signed the Arian Creed, and the body of the church followed him. There is not a heresy of modern times that did not exist *before* the Reformation; in the days of Epiphanius they had increased to eighty, and in the time of Philaster to one hundred and fifty. Flagellism, Convulsonianism, and the Festival of the Ass, I must hereafter introduce to your notice. I now assert, and shall hereafter prove, *that no church on earth has had so many variations in doctrine, and so many heresies in its bosom, as the church of Rome.*

Your 4th question regards the Reformers' ministerial authority, and your 5th the transmission of that authority. I here answer in a word, that whatever authority your church possessed in this way was imparted to them; so that theirs is the same: and their abundant reasons for reform, and for separating from your church, when she *refused* a Reformation, fully justify them in disregarding her deposition; and render their "unfrocking" (as you are pleased to call it,) as vain as the authors of it were corrupt.

I close the present letter (too long already,) by exposing as a *specimen* of your quotations, the very adventurous and self-convicting way in which you have tortured the writings of Luther. Your first and second citations do not appear, after some search, in the places to which you refer. (I hope for your own sake you have not depended upon some of the slanderous excerpts of the Jesuits.) The third you thus give: "*Let this be your rule in interpreting the Scriptures; whenever they command a good work, do you understand that they forbid it;*"—and you say, "is this the religion of Christ? Oh, what a task you have undertaken!" In the previous paragraphs, Luther had been *recommending* the performance of good works, without relying on the merit of them, with great zeal, clearness and force, as the fruit of faith, and to the glory of God; and says, they should be gratuitous, abundant and spontaneous. He next proceeds to show what good works truly are. That I may do you no injustice, I will give the original Latin and the translation in parallel columns, and show in italics how your garbled extract comes in.

"*Opera vere bona.*"

Qui isto modo bona operantur, non sibi, sed Deo, tanquam instrumentum Dei, operantur, nihil in his sibi arrogant, solo Dei contenti, in quo sperant; qui non sic operatur, simiæ sunt sanctorum *virorum*. Adeo necesse est superstitionem fieri ex omnium sanctorum vita, nisi Patrem cœlestem in his didicerint glorificare. Recte ergo dicitur. "Universæ viæ Domini misericordia et veretas;" id est, tunc opera fieri bona, quando Ipse solus totus ac totaliter ea facit in nobis, ut operis nulla pars ad nos pertineat. *Quare hic tibi sit canon, ubi scriptura præcebit bonum opus fieri, sic intelligas, quod prohibeat te facere bonum opus*, cum id non possis sed, ut Sabbatum, Deo sanctifices, mortuus sit et sepultus, sinasque Deum in te operare. At hoc autem non pervenies unquam, nisi per fidem, spem et caritatem, id est per tui mortificationem et omnium operum tuorem. *Operatio in Psalmum V. Opera. Zom. III. fol.* 171.

"*Works truly good.*"

Those who perform good works in this manner work not to themselves, but to God, and as instruments of God, not arrogating any thing to themselves, but ascribing all to God, in whom they trust. Those who do not perform good works in this manner, are but the apes of holy men: so that the unavoidable consequence is, that superstition will be produced in the lives of holy men, unless they in these things glorify their Father in heaven. It is therefore rightly said, "all the ways of the Lord are mercy and truth;" that is, good works may then be said to be performed, when He alone, totally and entirely works them in us, so that no part of the work belongs to ourselves. *Wherefore let this be your rule, when the Scripture commands a good work to be done, you are to understand it as prohibiting* you *from doing the good work*, since you are not ABLE to perform it, but that you sanctify a rest to God, and become as dead and buried, and permit God to work in you. But to this you will never come unless by faith, hope and charity—that is by the mortification of self, and of all your *own* works.

I suppose you remember my allusion (on the extract you made from Tertullian in this same style) to the man who proved from the Bible *that there was no God*, by dropping half the verse! So here the half verse makes Luther talk like a libertine as to *morals*, and a fool as to *interpretation*, while the whole passage is designed to recommend good works, to purify them by grace, to derive them from God, to destroy self, and glorify God by active obedience, and mortification! strange! strange liberties! With such a pair of scales we can weigh the characters given to the Reformers by you: and see how much they gain when as you *say*, you *give their opinions in their own words*. Yours, &c.

JOHN BRECKINRIDGE

CONTROVERSY. No. XXV.

IS THE PROTESTANT RELIGION THE RELIGION OF CHRIST?

Philadelphia, July 19, 1833.

To the Rev. John Breckinridge.

Rev. Sir,—The question is about "the Protestant religion," and not about Transubstantiation or Purgatory. But I foresaw, and even predicted, that you would *evade* the subject at issue. You had repeatedly told us, that you had demolished the doctrines of the Eucharist, Purgatory, Indulgences, &c. &c. &c., and if so, why did you waste *five columns* of your last letter in doing what you had so frequently and so effectually done before? If *you* betray such want of confidence in *your own assertions*, you must not be surprised at the jocund incredulity with which they are received by your readers.

In my last letter I gave you what you had previously called for—"manly arguments;" couched in genteel language, except perhaps the quotations from the writings of "the Reformers," for which I must decline all responsibility. How have you met these arguments? You have not met them at all. No man, Catholic or Protestant, liberal or even bigoted, will say that your last letter is, or deserves to be called, *an answer to mine*. You had undertaken to prove that "the Protestant religion is *the religion of Christ;*" and, knowing that you would respect the *witnesses*, I gave you the testimony of the Reformers themselves, to prove that it is not. I gave their *doctrines*, by which they set forth that man has *not free will*, but is a mere machine; and that God is an omnipotent tyrant, condemning his creatures for violating precepts, which *he knew* in imposing them could not be accomplished! And all this, as they taught, according to the Bible! I gave you their characters, as *drawn by themselves*, and if they spoke the truth, it would be difficult to find materials for a darker picture. I gave *in their own words*, the *immoral effects* of the Reformation; and to all these things there is no reply. I confronted the *defender* of the Reformation, with its authors; and apparently surprised that *such* evidence should have been derived from *such* a quarter, the confessions of the clients seem to have chained the tongue of the advocate. Still he has written a letter, called it No. XXIV., and under the heading of the " Protestant Religion," he has given, at considerable length, *his* " views," on the Catholic doctrines of the Eucharist, and Purgatory!! He had disproved these doctrines several times, if he can believe himself; and in order to strengthen his faith, I had even indulged him with the concession for arguments' sake, that so it was: but it seems he would believe neither of us; and behold, he is demolishing transubstantiation again!—Who will say after this, that Protestants do not believe in works of supererogation? And then the conclusiveness of his logic! "Transubstantiation," says he, "is as young as 1215, therefore the religion of the Reformation, (viz: all the sects of Protestantism) is the Religion of Christ." Mahomedism is wrong, *therefore*, according to this species of logic, Presbyterianism is right.

But pray, Rev. Sir, did you place so low an estimate on the intelligence of our Protestant readers, as to suppose that the dullest vision would not see through all this? Do you imagine that their confidence in the divinity of your religion will stand unshaken, when they see their minister—after having bound himself by a *written agreement*, to show " that the Protestant Religion *is* the Religion of Christ,"—flinching from the task he had assumed, and returning to nis " labour of love," in aspersing doctrines which do *not belong to the Protestant Religion?* You could not, nor can you now, give me a definition of the Protestant Religion. But after having taken six months for reflection, you come out with the discovery that it is " the Religion of the Reformation!!" As I had promised to " respect" your definition, I proceeded to the fountain head; and detailed the result of the investigation in my last letter. It seems to have taken you by surprise; and your silence as to the *facts* and *authorities*, sufficiently indicates that even *you* were unacquainted with the *whole truth*, as respects the doctrines and authors of the Religion of the Reformation. They agreed in rebellion, but in *nothing else*. Each accused the other of receiving his doctrines by the inspiration of the Devil. Luther acknowledges that from *this* tutor, he first learned the arguments for the overthrow of the sacrifice of Mass.— But still he admitted the real presence of Christ in the Eucharist; *this* Calvin denied; wielding against the Eucharist those arguments and objections, of which your last letter is but the feeble echo!— Calvin's successors found, that by applying the same kind of interpretation, they could get rid of all the *other mysteries* of Revelation, and for the credit of their philosophy, the children have completed the work of desolation which the father had begun.

In the commencement of your letter you charge me with having maintained, in this discussion, principles injurious to the holy Scriptures. And after having *invented* for me a set of consequences which I disclaim, you go so far as to say, " this is Deism, barefaced Deism." I am certain there is not another man in the community, besides yourself, that can discover Deism in the principles which I have supported during this controversy. I have indeed, shown that Deism necessarily flows from the principles of Protestantism. The very *last* definition you give of the Protestant rule of faith, is pregnant with that consequence. You say " the Bible is the rule; and common-sense interpretation the way to find the sense of the rule."— *Your* " common sense interpretation," tells you, that transubstantiation is absurd and impossible—another's " common-sense interpretation" tells him that the incarnation and the deity of Christ are absurd and impossible—a third man's " common-sense interpretation" tells him that the book itself is a book of contradiction, as plainly appears by the contradictory " common-sense interpretations" which Protestants give of it, and that therefore, *revelation* is absurd and impossible. Thus it is, that starting from a *false* FIRST *principle*, reason evolves consequences, one from another, until having begun with " the Protestant rule of faith," it terminates with " DEISM, barefaced DEISM." I merely pointed out these consequences by showing that Protestantism is essentially inconsistent in itself, and with all the principles which usually govern the human mind.

You deny that you had changed your definition of the Protestant rule of faith. Did you not say in our agreement that it was " *in-*

fallible? Did you not in your very first letter DEFEND "private interpretation" as a part of "this infallible" *rule?* Did you not in letter No. 18, give it up, as an "ABUSE?" Did I not congratulate you on this *sensible* but "*unexpected*" concession? And in letter No. 20, did you not take up the word with a note of admiration "Unexpected! Strange language at the close of a discussion, when in the first column of my first letter five months ago, I gave this definition of our rule of faith, viz. *The word of God as contained in the Scriptures of the Old and New Testaments.*" You then charge me with having "evaded" the REAL Protestant rule, and "argued against its ABUSES alone." What are these "abuses," but *private interpretation?* And yet, it is the very key you put into the hands of every man, woman and child, whereby to unlock the meaning of the Scriptures—"honest common-sense interpretation is, you tell us, the way to ascertain the *true sense* of the rule." It seems that Unitarians, and Universalists, and Swedenborgians are not *Protestants*. And why? Because, says Mr. Breckinridge, although they have the "REAL Protestant rule," yet they have not "honesty and common-sense," to make the right use of it. Then, Rev. Sir, what will you say of the "honesty and common-sense" of the Quakers, Baptists, Methodists, Episcopalians, and Shakers of Lebanon, &c. &c.? You are ALL provided with the "*real* Protestant rule of faith." But WHICH of these denominations is so happy as to possess "honesty and common-sense" for the right interpretation of the *real* rule.

The mysteries of revelation have always been subjects of scoffing to the sceptic. If the real presence of Jesus Christ in the eucharist were the *only* mystery, then, indeed, Mr. Breckinridge might do the wish of the infidel, by arraigning it at the tribunal of "common-sense." The language of your first notice of this doctrine, Rev. Sir, brought you, as you may recollect, into such sympathetic harmony of reasoning with the infidel Volney, that one would suppose you had both studied theology in the same school. But since then, it seems you have discovered a secret, which proves that, in *philosophy* at least, you have a decided superiority over the author of "Ruins." The old puzzle about "the *essence of matter*," is solved at last. Formerly, it was considered that the senses judge only of *appearances*, and accordingly it was believed, that *by the* POWER OF GOD, the body and blood of Christ might exist under the *appearances* of bread and wine. *You*, however, have found out that the properties and appearances of a thing, and the *substance* of which it is composed, are the same, and that the senses determine both. Of course you do not believe that the "tongues of fire" which rested on the apostles were *any thing more* than tongues of fire. You do not believe that the "dove" which descended on the Redeemer at his baptism in the Jordan could be any thing more than a dove, which happened to be passing that way. It seems that *rationalism* is not confined to the ministers of Germany and of Geneva. The Unitarians and Deists, Rev. Sir, will make a whip of your logic.

Speaking of the mode in which certain Protestant controversialists treat the doctrine of the "real presence," Mr. Stanley Faber, author of the "Difficulties of Romanism," remarks, " While arguing on this subject, *some persons*, I regret to say, have been far too copious in the use of those unseemingly terms, impossibility and absurdity. To such language, says he, the least objection is its *reprehensible want of good manners*. The doctrine of transubstantiation, *like the doctrine of the trinity*, is, I contend, a question *not* of abstract reasoning, but of *pure evidence*."

It was on the supposed overthrow of the eucharist, that Socinus calculated on the destruction of the Trinity. Having shown, *like you*, Rev. Sir, that the doctrine of the eucharist is the grossest idolatry, he goes on to say, " So also we hope that the SHOCKING FICTIONS concerning God and his Christ, which at present are supposed to be sacred and worthy of the deepest reverence, and to constitute the principal mysteries of our religion, will, with God's permission, be so laid open and treated with such SCORN that every one will be ashamed to embrace them or even pay any attention to them."—(Tom. 1.)

There is *another* book, which I shall not mention, in which *your* arguments or rather cavils against the mystery of the eucharist, are brought out in still bolder relief, as APPLIED TO THE TRINITY. " But when, (says the impious author,) according to the Christian trinitarian scheme one part of God is represented *by a dying man*, and another part called the Holy Ghost, *by a flying pigeon*, it is impossible that belief can attach to such wild conceits." Such are the consequences of your unhappy reasoning.

Thus, Rev. Sir, you perceive that the *weapons* with which Calvin and his associates combatted the real presence of Christ, in the *mystery of the eucharist*, have passed from hand to hand until they are now wielded by the Deist, against the mystery of the Holy Trinity itself. Now please, in mercy to that *Christianity*, of which you profess to be a minister, review your argument drawn from reason and the " testimony of the senses ;" and instead of borrowing wisdom from PAGANS, for the explanation of the *Christian mysteries*, ask your *own* reflection whether the objection is not equally strong against the " real presence" of the Holy Ghost under the " appearance" of a Dove, or of " fiery tongues ?" Infidelity, be assured, is already making rapid strides, and you should leave to hands *less sacred* than your own, the task of *furnishing her* with implements of destruction against Christianity. The doctrine of the eucharist, believed by the vast majority of Christians, at the present day ; believed by all the generations of the church previous to Luther, and so frequently inculcated in the Holy Scriptures of the New Testament, is entitled to, at least, *reverential* notice. Your manifest ignorance of the doctrine and of its evidences, I shall expose in due season.

When you charitably insinuate, that masses are sustained by the love of money in the Priesthood, you certainly cannot expect to obtain credit for the sincerity of your charge. If we were wicked enough to have our consciences for sale, we are at least learned enough, to know that a higher price may be obtained in *the Protestant market*. We would embrace the Reformation, share in the spoils of the Bible and other societies, and stand our chance for " a call," *to two thousand a year*, as well as the best of you. It is true we are priests and " we have an *altar*, whereof they have no power to eat who serve the tabernacle," or belong to the Reformation; and it is true that " to offer sacrifice," is the chief official business of the priest. But still he does not neglect the other pastoral duties. He preaches, exhorts, encourages, consoles the distressed, and whenever he has money or bread, he divides with the orphan who has neither. He instructs the children in their religious and moral duties, he attends at the bedside of the sick and the dying, and inhales the corrupted atmosphere of pestilence, whilst his happier brethren of the Reformation are enjoying the bliss of domestic and connubial felicity, and laughing at his round of popish superstition. Still, it is true as your " astonished friend" has informed you, that the celebration of the sacrifice of mass is the *chief* business of the Priest.

Might I be permitted to ask who this " friend" is? Is Mr. Burtt at work again? Surely it cannot be the Presbyterian clergyman who has recently honoured me with an occasional visit. The allusion, indeed, reminds me of a conversation with him; but still I cannot imagine that he would descend to such a course as you intimate, of tale-bearing, or that, if he had, you would be imprudent enough to expose him by publishing his " reports." I believe I always treated him politely, because I thought him not unworthy of it. But your allusion seems to shed a little light on the *object*, or at least the use he made of his visits. Be pleased then to let us have a little more, just enough to clear away, or confirm the suspicion which you have awakened.

Now for " the QUESTION." You say the Protestant religion existed before Luther. But *where* did it exist? " In the Bible," you reply. But how comes it that for 1500 years, no one had been able to discover it in the Bible, which, as you say, is so easily understood. In answer to this you tell me after the Magdeburg Centuriators, that " A PEOPLE" had discarded several doctrines of the church, previous to the reformation; leaving me to guess who this " A PEOPLE" were.

But hold; the " Waldenses" are mentioned. The Protestants in claiming the " Waldenses" for their religious progenitors, are able to climb the tree of antiquity, only as high as the year 1160. This alone is fatal to the doctrine of *both*. But were the doctrines of both the same? So you admit and assert. But where is the proof? Did the Waldenses deny *free will*, with the Reformers? Did they hold that God by his hidden counsels *is the author of sin?* I say they did not. But this is not the only difference. The Reformers in trying to strengthen their party by the accession of the Waldenses, stipulated for certain *changes* in the doctrine and practice of the latter, which shows the difference between them. " They were required to assist *no longer at mass*, to abstain from all the papal superstitions, and to reject the ministry of the Catholic clergy." (Hist. des Egl. Ref. de Pierre Gilles, c. v.) It seems that your Protestant ancestors, therefore, before the Reformation, were in the habit of attending at mass! But besides, they believed in the sacraments, auricular confession, absolution, in the real presence, and even, horrible to relate, transubstantiation itself!—except when the priest happened to be in *mortal sin,* and then, they kindly allowed any layman in the state of grace, to *pronounce the words of consecration.* When the Reformers, Bucer and Œcolampadius, undertook to make *Protestants* of the Waldenses, the latter, by the proposed terms of union, were *required* to believe, " 1. That a Christian may lawfully give evidence on oath. 2. That auricular confession is not *commanded*. 3. That a Christian even among Christians may lawfully exercise the office of magistrate. 4. That a minister may lawfully be possessed of property sufficient to support his family. 5. That Jesus Christ has ordained only two sacraments, Baptism and the Eucharist." (Idem. ibid.)

These testimonies, Rev. Sir, show that when you wished to search for the genealogy of Protestantism beyond Luther, you have missed your way, in tracing it to the Waldenses. But they *protested* against some of the doctrines of the Church of Rome. Yes; and so did the Arians, Nestorians, Eutychians, Pelagians, Montanists, Manichæans, and their spiritual descendants—the Albigenses—not to name the 1001 other sects who *protested* in the same manner. Here, then, you are fast—and from the dilemma not all the ingenuity of man can extricate you. " Either the Protestant religion is a religion *differing* from the religion of Christ, or else the religion of Christ was *not professed by any society of Christians, previous to the time of Luther.* To which of these alternatives will you cling ? one of them is *inevitable.*" Will any Protestant, then, having the least concern for his soul's salvation, *risk his eternity,* on the chance of a religion which " no society of Christians, (either orthodox or heterodox) have ever *professed,* from the days of Jesus Christ till the coming of Martin Luther and John Calvin ? I say boldly, that in that whole interval, there never existed *such a society,* and I CHALLENGE you to name it, if there did. Therefore the Protestant religion is only three hundred years old, and consequently cannot be the religion of Jesus Christ. Now, Rev. Sir, meet this argument if you can. As a clergyman you are supposed to be acquainted with ecclesiastical history —and if you can name any society of Christians professing the doctrines held by any sect of the Reformation, I hereby pledge myself, either to prove that you are *mistaken,* or else give up the contest. But if you *cannot,* then, from a principle of conscience, you, and all Protestant ministers, should cease to delude yourselves and the people, by *pretending* that there were persons, who held your doctrines before the Reformation. Never ; in the whole universe !

But, then, says my Rev. opponent, " the Greek church which you own to be an ancient church, also *protests.*" This is nothing to the purpose—I make you a present of the various "*protests*" of all the heretics and schismatics of antiquity, beginning with Ebion and Cerinthus, and ending with Jerome of Prague—and even this cannot extricate your proposition from its difficulties. Do the Protestants, or any sect of Protestants, agree in doctrines with any society of Christians previous to the Reformation ? This is the question. This is the *knotty* point. Let us see, then, whether your appeal to the Greek church can aid you. The Greeks believe in seven sacraments, in the real presence, in transubstantiation, the sacrifice of mass, prayers for the departed, and even the invocation of saints. *These* are Mr. Breckinridge's Protestants previous to the Reformation—and no sooner has he named them, than he exclaims, " how plain it is then, that the Protestant religion *was professed* ages before Luther." It is not so plain, especially when we recollect that the Greek church anathematised the heresy of Protestantism as decidedly as the Council of Trent. When the patriarch, Cyril Lupar, was detected holding correspondence with the leaders of the Reformation in Germany and Holland, and it was ascertained that he had imbibed a *partiality for their novelties*, the consequence was, that for this he was *deposed and disgraced.* His successor summoned a council of twenty-three bishops, including the patriarchs of Jerusalem and Alexandria, in which Cyril and his *Protestant doctrines* were condemned, in language as vigorous as that of Leo X. The same took place in a subsequent council of twenty-five bishops, including the Metropolitan of Russia. Again, in 1672, Dositheus, patriarch of Jerusalem, held a third council at Bethlehem, which expressly condemned the doctrine of Cyril Lupar and the Protestants. (See Perpet. de la Foi, vol. 4. liv. 8.)

Thus, it is manifest, that whilst you acknowledge the *necessity* of finding the Protestant religion SOMEWHERE, previous to Luther, you fail in every attempt. But really it is too amusing to see a Protestant clergyman point to the Greek church, and exclaim—look there— " How *plain it is* that the Protestant religion existed before Luther!" —and then with great complacency—" so much for your dilemma." *Was the Protestant religion professed by any society of Christians before Luther?* If it was, give me the *name* of that society—the *name* of that PRECIOUS society; when did it exist? where did it dwell? who speaks of it? the name and the proof are all I require. But if you will do neither, then the matter is *ended*—and Martin Luther and John Calvin have the glory of being the first men that ever *professed* the religion of Christ. Can you meet this argument?

I cannot stop, Rev. Sir, to expose in detail, the twisting efforts of your letter to *evade* " the question," by embroiling it with doctrines which belong exclusively to the Catholic Church. But the spirit of your writings may be represented in a little dialogue between us, in which justice shall be done to your *defence* of the Protestant religion

Catholic. Good morning, Mr. B. How do you do?

Presbyterian. Good morning, Sir;—a little fatigued, from riding in the stage-coach, but still able, by the grace of God, to defend the Bible and the Protestant religion.

C. O dear! who has ventured to attack the Bible?

P. Why you, Sir; you would have all to think alike in religion, and " this is DEISM, bare-faced DEISM." (See commencement of Mr. B.'s last letter.)

C. But let me explain, did not Christ in making a revelation require that men should *believe it?*

P. Certainly; but look at your doctrine of Purgatory!

C. But that is not the question, if Christ required men to *believe*

his revelation, did he not require them ipso facto, to *think alike in religion?* And is this Deism?

P. In vain have I exposed your doctrine of Purgatory, I can get no reply.

C. I will reply, I assure you, when we shall have settled the present question. But pray have I written against the Bible?

P. You have written against the Protestant religion, which is the same thing. We take the Bible alone. Surely God can speak plainly in his written word. And then, transubstantiation is as young as the year 1215. Indulgences are a bundle of licences to sin. (See Doctor Claggot.)

C. But if the Bible alone be the rule of faith, and God speak plainly in his word, *how is it* that Protestants are divided into as many systems as there are sects; and opinions, as there are heads?

P. So then, you would have all men to think alike! " Deism, barefaced Deism." And then, look at your persecutions of heretics, by the infallible Popes, and the doctrine of human merits derogatory to the merits of Christ; and the church setting herself up above the word of God.

C. All this is irrelevant, it seems to me, and does not belong to the question. Why are Protestants so divided if they are taught by the Bible? besides the Bible *alone*, is the Bible on the shelf.

P. Profound logic! My God, my Bible, and my own mind are supposed in *my* rule of faith.

C. But according to this, the *mind* is the instrument of interpretation, acting on the Bible, and, as every man's mind is different from that of his neighbour, so there must be those different interpretations by which Protestantism is divided. Does the Bible contain them *all?*

P. Will you say, then, that the Holy Spirit cannot speak plainly in the written word of God? "Poor Bible, what a transgressor thou hast been!" And look at your own rule of faith, Decrees of Councils, Bulls of Popes, Apocryphal Books, Consent of the Fathers, through all those immense folios you have to wade before you can tell what is your rule of faith.

C. Excuse me, Sir; my rule is much more simple. 'I believe in the Holy Catholic Church." This is my rule. I agree in belief, *by this rule*, with all the millions of Catholics that live, or have lived, from the days of Christ; and am separated *by it* from all the heresies of modern as well as ancient times. Whereas your Protestant rule introduces heresies, as for example, Universalism, and Unitarianism, and leaves you *unable to refute them.* What do you say to this?

P. In vain have I called on you to defend your doctrines. I have proved that Transubstantiation is as young as 1215, that Purgatory is an invention of men, and that Masses are a way for Priests to get money. (See Epiphanius) To all these proofs, not a word. But you charge on the Protestant rule, the errors of *extreme* heresies. The Bible is the rule. Interpretation is the use of the rule. If men "ABUSE IT," that is not the rule. Are we ever to pass from this question?

C. I am happy, my dear Sir, to perceive that at length you have acknowledged private interpretation, as an "ABUSE." You are almost—on this point, *altogether*—a Catholic. We may now pass to the second topic, having closed this one, by your *unexpected* declaration.

P. "Unexpected!" Strange language this! After five months discussion, you admit then, that you have evaded the REAL PROTESTANT RULE, the Bible, and argued against its "ABUSES ALONE." And to this day you have not told us what your own "rule of faith" is. But I shall proceed to the second question. From the language of Romanists themselves, it is clear that a great many immoralities and iniquities were committed, and this among the clergy as well as laity of the church. (See letter from the three Bishops at Bononia.) Therefore a Reformation was necessary.

C. As you have confirmed your *first* admission, of private interpretation's being the "ABUSE" of the Bible; I now follow you to to second question. The Catholics, indeed, desired a reformation; but it was of *morals*, and not of *doctrine*. They held that the doctrine of the church was pure and holy, but that men had departed from its sanctity by the wickedness of their lives But pray what is "the Protestant Religion?"

P. "The Religion of the Reformation." And here I stand ready to prove that it is the religion of Christ.

C. Of course then, it comprises the *whole family of sects*, of which the Reformation was the parent? Are they ALL the religion of Christ?

P. You have not answered my arguments against transubstantiation and the other doctrines of your system. And now I shall show, by the grace of God, that your doctrine of transubstantiation is not in the Bible, and that if it be true, Christianity may be false, since it invades the testimony of our senses. (See Scotus and Bellarmine.)

C. But stay, my dear friend, the question is of *another subject*. And in order that we may reach it at once, let us *admit* that *every doctrine rejected by the Reformers* was erroneous. Let that be considered as granted, and now show me that "the Protestant religion is the religion of Christ."

P. Ah! Sir, I see through your Jesuit policy. You wish me to show that the Protestant religion is the religion of Christ. But as I have begun, so I shall continue to *expose your system*. And as in my last I showed that transubstantiation was promoted into a doctrine, A. D. 1215; so, now I shall prove that it is absurd to say that a priest can make his God and eat him. (See Cicero, and Averoes the Arabian philosopher.) Besides the doctrine of intentions, and masses in honour of the saints.

C. But this is not the question. Was there ever any society previous to Luther professing the doctrines of any sect of Protestantism?

P. Yes: the Centuriators of Magdeburg, *speak* of "A PEOPLE," who did not agree with the Catholic Church. And again look at the Waldenses and the Greek church, which you admit to be an ancient church.

C. And as to the Reformers, *is it clear*, that *they* were the men whom God would have selected to reform his church?

P. Why have you clipped their doctrine and character by your broken extracts. But look at your Popes, Sergius and Formosus, were they *better* than the Reformers?

C. Indeed it seems not. But the Reformers were *religion-makers*, by profession, whereas the Popes could change nothing of Catholic doctrine; however much they might degrade their station by personal vices. And besides, if you meant to compliment the Reformers, the *worst* of our Popes should not have been selected for the comparison.

P. But look at the Popes, called by your own historian apostate rather than apostolical......And then your doctrines of intentions, &c.

It is useless, Rev. Sir, to prosecute the dialogue. It shows the *spirit* and the *manner of your pen*. You have confused the questions, by the introduction of *extraneous* matter, as if the hope of your cause, depended on the jumble of topics and the mystification of argument. In all this, however, there is no merit of originality. It has been the custom of *all your predecessors*.

Zanchius, one of the REFORMERS, describes the controversial spirit of his reforming colleagues, in the following *candid language*. "I am indignant," says he, "when I consider the *manner* in which most of us defend our cause. The true *state of the question* we often, *on set purpose*, involve in darkness, that it may not be understood: we have the impudence to deny things the most evident: we assert what is visibly false: the most impious doctrines we force on the people as the first principles of faith, and orthodox opinions we condemn as heretical: we torture the Scriptures till they agree with our own fancies; and boast of being the disciples of the fathers, while we refuse to follow their doctrines: to *deceive*, to *calumniate*, to *abuse*, is our familiar practice: nor do we care for any thing, provided we can defend our cause, *good* or *bad*, *right* or *wrong*. O! what times, what manners." (Zanch. Ad. Storm. T. vii. Col. 828.) But if possible, let us come again to the point. Answer me the following questions, and they will decide the matter. They are supported by the reasoning and authorities of my last letter, to which I refer the reader.

1st. Question. Did there exist previous to the Reformation, a society of Christians, in any part of the world, professing the doctrines of any sect of Protestantism? Prove that there did and I give up the argument. But if there did not, then, Protestantism is any thing but the religion of Christ. Solve this, will you?

2d Question. Reviewing the doctrines and character of the Reformers, as stated in my last letter, from their own writings; viewing the consequences of the Reformation on the morals of the people; is there *any*, the smallest evidence that the *Spirit of God*, had aught to do with it? If it had, then please to account for the manner in which they spoke and wrote of each other.

3d. "Does the Religion of Christ teach the doctrines of Protestantism, from the highest point of Episcopalianism, down the descending scale to the farthest verge of Unitarianism? If not, the Protestant religion is not the religion of Christ." For all these belong to Protestantism.

But in answer to this it seems that "Unitarians, Universalists," &c

are not Protestants. But why not? Have they not their "God, their Bible, and their mind," as well as Presbyterians? Have they not " honesty and common sense" to interpret the Scriptures; and what more is requisite according to your own showing? Please then, Rev. Sir, to tell me *what* denominations are to be considered " Protestants;" for if Dr. Channing and the faculty of Cambridge, be not entitled to the appellation, I am at a loss to know who are.—Are the Friends Protestants? The Shakers, Swedenborgians, Baptists, are they Protestants? In a word, tell me what denominations constitute what you understand by "the Protestant religion." It is not for me to determine, among such learned people, which denomination is right and which is wrong. Show me the *boundaries* of the "Protestant religion," and I shall not transgress them. Narrow your definition to whatever limits you please—and then prove that the religion professed by those whom it encloses, and the religion of Christ are the same thing. If you will not do this, you had better give it up.

4. " Had the Reformers themselves, and if *not* could they transmit to their successors any MINISTERIAL AUTHORITY?" To this you give answer " that whatever authority *our* church possessed in this way was imparted to them." But our church *recalled* this authority, in their suspension and excommunication, and a *new* supply was necessary. Whence was it derived? And if not derived at all, it follows on your own admission, that the Protestant clergy differ from the laity only in the colour of their dress and the diversity of their occupation. Will you clear up this point? *Can* you do it?

When you insinuate that I have misquoted the Reformers, you should be prepared to sustain the charge. Your lengthened quotation from Luther does not alter the sense of mine, which was to show that he denied *free will in man*, denied the *possibility* of keeping the commandments, or of *doing good works*. But his own writings indicate his doctrine much more correctly than any commentary of those who, ashamed of it, would accuse me of perverting his meaning. " A person, says he, that is baptised cannot, though he would, lose his salvation by any sins how *grievous soever*, unless he refuses to believe.—For *no sins* can damn him, but *unbelief alone*." (Cap. Bab. Tom. 2. fol. 74. 1.)

Again, " the Papists teach, that faith in Christ justifies indeed, but that God's commandments *are likewise to be kept*. Now *this* is directly to *deny Christ*, and *abolish faith*." (Tom. 5. Witt. ed. fol. 311.)

Is this passage designed to recommend good works? It requires greater penetration than I am possessed of, to discover any such meaning, either in this or the passage quoted at the close of your last letter. Now, Rev. Sir, be pleased to meet the arguments and authorities of this, and my last paper on the question of " the Protestant religion." In this it is made clear that your attempts to derive the Protestant religion from Christ by the channel of the Waldenses and the Greek church is as unprofitable to you, as it is amusing to the reader. Another effort, however, may be more successful, and we shall wait patiently to see what your next pen will bring to light.   Yours, &c.

JOHN HUGHES.

CONTROVERSY. No. XXVI.

IS THE PROTESTANT RELIGION THE RELIGION OF CHRIST?
Philadelphia, July 26th, 1833.

To the Rev. John Hughes.

Rev. Sir,—Busaeus, the Jesuit, gives this sage counsel to his disciples, "*avoid, if you can, controversy with an heretic, on the articles of faith!*" This wily apothegm has been the pole star of all your discussions. On the first great question, the rule of faith, after all your promises, you did never once *define* the Roman Catholic rule of faith; and even now the public know not (by any thing *you* have said,) *what* your rule *is*, except that it is *not* the Bible; and *not* the *Protestant* rule of faith. You began the controversy by requiring me to *prove* the canonical authority of the Bible. This was taken for *granted*, in the very terms of our debate; and it was puerile, deistical, and foreign to the question for you to insist on such a course. Yet I followed you again and again over the *ten heads:* and when they wax so frail and so weary that they die away, lo, you charge me with giving up our rule of faith, because I still insist that the *Bible* is our *only* rule. As if conscious of the very defenceless condition in which you left your rule, you continue to revert to the subject from letter to letter. Now if you are afraid to go forward with the present question, I will still meet you on your rule of faith, and give you an opportunity to defend your neglected friends "Unwritten Traditions," "the Apochryphal Books," and "the unanimous consent of the Fathers." Without this it is useless farther to notice your clamour on this subject. What takes away all apology from you is this, that you have *admitted* the Bible to be *a* rule; but you deny that the Bible *alone* is a *sufficient* rule. Even the vilest heretics have, as you allow, been so far respectful towards revelation, as to receive it as the true and sufficient rule of faith. But to the church of Rome belongs the disastrous distinction of refusing to the word of God its proper rank as our exclusive and infallible guide in matters of religion. You have, however, admitted that it is a rule. Here, then, we *agree;* but we differ in this, that you would add something to it to make it *perfect*. Surely, then, the duty lay on you to exhibit and to prove what that *something* is, without which the rule is not complete. We well know what that something is, but I have striven without effect to bring you out in the defence of it. In vain then do you insist that I have given up the Protestant rule, when I aver that the Bible is that rule, and that private interpretation is only the method of its use. But supposing the Protestant rule to be abandoned, the questions still return upon you, and call aloud for answer, *where* is the true rule? *What* is the true rule? *Why* do you withhold it?

As you lay so much stress on private interpretation, it may be well briefly to say something of *your* system on this subject. And here let me present the memorable admission, unconsciously made, in your last letter, by which all my charges of Deism are fairly confirmed. "You say 'the Bible is the rule; and common-sense interpretation the way to find the sense of the rule.' Your common-sense interpretation tells you, that transubstantiation is absurd and impossible; another's 'common-sense interpretation,' tells him that the incarnation and the deity of Christ are absurd and impossible ; a third man's ' common-sense interpretation,' tells him that the book itself is a book of contradiction, as plainly appears by the contradictory ' common-sense interpretations,' which Protestants give of it, and that, therefore, *revelation* is absurd and impossible." Now is not this to say that to "common-sense" the Bible has *no* meaning ? We as Protestants hold that men *may* err and *do* err in the interpretation of the Bible, as of other books : but that like other books it has a meaning, which is to be reached, as the meaning of other books is reached.— But you allow that " common-sense" may teach *any thing* from the Bible ; and may from the Bible prove the Bible false ! How strange that you by *private* interpretation insist so zealously for the fixed and c.ear meaning of Bellarmine, and yet thus treat the holy book of God !

With all the claims of the church of Rome to be the exclusive and infallible interpreter of the word of God, there is not to be found in he circle of human productions such crude, silly, and profane commentaries as those given by the Roman oracle. They have been for ages the alternate sport and wonder of the world I will give a specimen, which may at once inform and amuse the reader.

In the Decretals of Pope Gregory the 9th is the following commentary on Genesis i, 16 : " Pope Clement the 3d to the most illustrious Emperor of Constantinople, c. 6. Besides you ought also to have known that God made two great lights in the firmament of heaven, the greater light to rule the day and the lesser light to rule the night ; each of them great, but one the greater of the two. For the firmament of heaven, therefore, viz. the universal church, God made two great lights, that is, he appointed two dignities, which are the *Pontifical* authority, and the *kingly* power. But that which rules the day, that is to say, the *spiritual*, is the greater, and that which rules the *carnal*, the less ; so that the same difference may be discerned between the Popes and the kings, as between the *sun* and the *moon !*" Then follows this infallible and learned gloss ! "Since, therefore, the earth is seven times greater than the moon, and the sun is eight times greater than the earth, therefore the Pontifical dignity is *forty-seven* times greater than the regal dignity." After such arithmetical skill, such reach of astronomic science, such a profound and perfect commentary on the size and significations of the sun, moon, and firmament, can any man wonder at Mr. Hughes's devotion to the *interpretation* of the holy see ; or dispute the propriety of Gallileo's imprisonment by the Pope, because he held that the earth was *circular*, and *moved* around the sun ?

Again, as if to reduce the subject to the last absurdity, the church of Rome have a *Standing Committee*, to regulate and announce the legitimate meaning of the decrees of the Council of Trent. The difficulty of the case is this. The decrees were to be interpreted after they were published. Who was to do it ? Not the Council and Pope united, which (you say) are necessary to constitute infallibility ; for the Council was then dissolved, and near three centuries have passed, and no other has met. The Pope, you say, is not infallible ; nor is any individual Priest ! Who then shall int. p et ?

The best approach to it is the Standing Committee at Rome, headed by the Pope, and appointed by the Council to interpret its decrees. It still exists and sits stately at Rome. A collection of its "*sentences*" has recently been published in eight vols. quarto, by D. Zamboni. Now, query, are its interpretations fallible or infallible? They are not infallible, for you have distinctly told us that none but a General Council confirmed by a Pope can decree or interpret *infallibly*. But this committee is *not* a General Council; therefore its decisions are *fallible*. Yet they are *binding*. Here then is private interpretation, *(the radical delusion of Protestantism)* in the last resort, and after all the outcry against it, *adopted and used by the church of Rome!*— Then *fallible interpreation* is, and has been, the *exclusive* guide of your church since the Council of Trent, that is, for two hundred and seventy years; and still worse, this has *always* been its guide, except during the sessions of the Councils, and as soon as they rise, their decrees, like the Bible, pass over to the "radical delusion of Protestantism," viz. to *fallible interpretation*.

I said that you were true to the maxims of Busaeus, *to avoid controversy on the articles of faith*. If you did it much on the rule of faith, you do it *more* on the second question, now before us. In it, as in the other question, there are *some* points on which we are *agreed*. These of course, we are not called to discuss. There are other points in which we *differ*. Against these I *protest*. To these I have directed my first attention. I have already enumerated them, and exposed *your errors*, or a number of them. This I have done by right, and in order. But though you still shrink from the discussion of them, on them the question turns; and to them you must come, or your own church will exclaim that you have betrayed her interests. Why is it that you decline such a course? When you refused (in settling the terms of the controversy) to discuss this question, *Is the Roman Catholic religion the religion of Christ?* did you mean to keep the Roman Catholic religion *entirely* out of view? Was that your design when you accepted the *present* form of the question and refused the other? When it became my privilege to introduce the 2d question, and when you called on me to define the Protestant religion, did you imagine that *your* religion would be left untouched, and that I would allow the very end for which I engaged with you, to be frustrated by a Jesuit's arts? If you *did*, you will now find that such adroitness will not avail. If you did *not*, you will expect me to pursue the plan of argument already begun, and with some efficacy, if we may judge from your strong dissatisfaction.

I. In the order of discussion for the present letter, I proceed to expose *Extreme Unction as a daring invention of the church of Rome, which is not a sacrament of Jesus Christ, is a novelty in the church, and ruinous to the souls of men.* The decrees of the Council of Trent are to this effect. (Session 14. Chap. 1. Coun. Trent.) "This sacred unction of the sick was instituted, *as it were*, a true and proper sacrament of the New Testament by our Lord Jesus Christ, *hinted at*, indeed, by Mark, but recommended and preached to the faithful by the Apostle James, brother of our Lord. 'Is any man,' saith he, 'sick among you; let him bring in the Priests of the church, and let them pray over him, anointing him with oil in the name of the Lord; and the prayer of faith shall save the sick man; and the Lord shall raise him up; and if he be in sins they shall be forgiven him.'" James v. 14, 15. Chap. 2d. "The power and effect of this sacrament are explained in the words, 'the prayer of faith shall save the sick man; and the Lord shall raise him up; and if he be in his sins they shall be forgiven him.' For this power is the grace of the Holy Spirit; whose unction *cleanses away sins, if any remain to be expiated, even the last traces of sin.*" "And he sometimes obtains the restoration of his *bodily health*, if the same shall *further the salvation of his soul.*" Canon I. "If any shall say Extreme Unction is not truly and properly a sacrament *instituted* by Christ our Lord, and preached by the Apostle St. James; but that it is a human invention—Let him be accursed." Canon II. "If any shall say, that the holy anointing of the sick doth not *confer grace*, nor *remit sins*, nor relieve the sick; but that it hath long since ceased, as if the grace of healing existed only of old—Let him be accursed."

Having explicitly stated the doctrine of your church on this subject, I now assert: 1. *That Extreme Unction is not a sacrament of Jesus Christ, but a daring innovation of the church of Rome.*

Dr. Challoner, (a standard writer in your church,) in his "Catholic Christian," pp. 3, 4, thus defines a Sacrament. *Question.*—"What are the *necessary* conditions for a thing to be a Sacrament? *Answer*, 1st. It must be a sacred, visible, or sensible sign. 2d.—This sacred sign must have a power annexed to it of communicating grace to the soul. 3d. This must be by virtue of the *institution* of Christ." And he adduces the very words of Christ for the institution of the Lord's Supper and Baptism. Now will any candid reader take up the only two passages of the word of God, referred to for authority, and say that there is the least foundation for a Christian Sacrament? In Mark vi. 13. it is written, "And they (the twelve Disciples) cast out many devils, and annointed with *oil* many that were sick and healed them." Here was, plainly, a miracle by the use of *oil*. But it was to *heal* the sick, not to anoint them for *death:* and was no Sacrament. Christ was not *present* to institute it a Sacrament; the Apostles had no *authority* to do it; and not a word is said about a Sacrament. Indeed the Council of Trent seemed fully aware of this, for they say in the decree, " Being first *hinted* at by Mark vi. 13;" and "*as it were*, instituted." Is not the very language expressive of the consciousness of fraud, and of the absence of authority? *Is this the religion of Christ?* Is this your holy and infallible church? The other passage from James v. 14, 15. quoted above, is equally silent about the institution of a Sacrament. The unction referred to, was for the *healing of the sick;* the effect was peculiar to the days of miracles; and the whole intention, directly opposed to your decree on this subject, by which you make it *extreme* unction, or "the Sacrament of the dying." Now, the decree acknowledges that *James* did not institute, (as none but Christ could,) a Sacrament, in this unction: but that he only "*recommended and published it.*" The same decree also owns that in Mark vi. 13, it was not instituted but only "*hinted at.*" It results then that Christ did not institute it, therefore, it is *not* a Sacrament. And yet, your infallible church, gravely tells us, that the recommendation, by an Apostle, of a thing which never existed, *gives it existence;* and that a *hint* in one place, and an *allusion* in the other, are sufficient authority, for a Christian Sacrament. Who then, instituted this Sacrament? the church of Rome; and the act by which she performed it, is a rebellious innovation. The Rhemish translators, in their notes on Mark vi. 13, confess that Christ did *not* institute it, when they say, " It was a *preparative* to the Sacrament of Extreme Unction;" and they refer us to its *completion*, in James v. 14, 15.

2. We next notice an *insuperable dilemma, into which you are brought by this pretended Sacrament.* The Council of Trent says, (session 22d, c. 1.) " that it was not till the last supper that our Lord ordained the Apostles to be Priests of the New Testament." But the same Council decreed (Sess. 14. c. 3.) " that Bishops or Priests properly ordained by them, are the proper ministers of the sacrament of extreme unction." Then the Apostles were not *Priests* when they applied unction to the *sick*, Mark vi. 13.; and of course, it was *no sacrament.* Therefore, the council has *erred.* But if you say they *were Priests*, then the council still has *erred*, for it says they were *not* Priests till the last supper. So that either way the church has erred. Is this your infallible church, which cannot err in an article of faith? Does not the council curse all who reject it, (Canon 1. Sess. 7.) " Whosoever shall affirm that the sacraments of the new law were not *all* instituted by Jesus Christ our Lord, or that they are more or fewer than seven, namely, Baptism, Confirmation, the Eucharist, Penance, *Extreme Unction*, Orders, and Matrimony, or that any of these is not truly and properly a sacrament: let him be accursed." How strange does this profane anathema appear in contrast with the declarations of Augustin, " that the Doctors of this (6th) age, acknowledge only two Sacraments, Baptism and the Lord's Supper." Duo tantum Sacramenta theologi hujus ætatis agnoscunt.

3. *This pretended Sacrament and Purgatory, cannot, on your own principles, subsist together.* The decree, as quoted above, declares " that the power of this Sacrament is the grace of the Holy Spirit, whose unction cleanses away sins, if any remain to be expiated, even the *last traces* of sin;" and also, " that Christ has fortified the close of our existence with the Sacrament of Extreme Unction, as with a most *secure defence.*" The Catechism of the church, also states the same, at large; and tells us that " while penance is for the remission of *mortal* sins, the grace of this Sacrament remits *venial* sins; and is not to be administered until the penitent has confessed and has received" *(i. e.* the Eucharist.) But Purgatory, as we showed in Letter No. 24, is for the cleansing away of just such sins as these; as for example, "*from that part of the church which is in Purgatory,*" (Bellarmine.) Now, if Extreme Unction does the work at death, what need of Purgatory? Why atone over and over again; 1. by the blood of Christ; 2. by Extreme Unction; then 3. by Purgatory? Hence to say Masses for those who have died under Extreme Unction, *may make money* for the Priests, but is *deceiving* the people.

And if it be to make it more certain, then is not Extreme Unction an uncertain thing, and useless? Do they not destroy each other?

4. "But there is a greater cheat than this in the doctrine of Extreme Unction. Such, it is pretended, are the intention, efficacy, and virtues of this rite, that, if it be *necessary* to the salvation of the person who is anointed, that he should recover, he will; but if this be not necessary, he will not. Hence it follows: 1. That if the person recovers, he was in a state of damnation, after he was anointed. 2. That if he does not recover, he died in a state of salvation. Therefore, nobody was ever damned that was anointed at the hour of his death. Therefore, also, nobody that recovers had benefitted by any Sacrament he received before the unction; otherwise he would not have been in a state of damnation. Upon the whole, then, it is plain, as this Sacrament, like the rest, is said to operate, (ex opere operato, by its own power,) *whoever has a mind never to die*, needs only be *in a state of damnation when he is anointed.*"

5. One of the awful features of this invention of the Church of Rome is, that it encourages delay of repentance till the hour of death, and holds out at the grave, delusive and destroying hopes of heaven. At death, our great business is to die, not to *prepare* for it; that is the business of *life*. But by this institution, the dying sinner is encouraged to depend upon the *last act of a Priest* for the salvation of his soul. *Baptism*, as the Catechism of the Council of Trent informs us, remits *original* sin; *Penance*, remits *mortal* sins; and Extreme Unction remits *venial* sins; it also says that in *this*, as in the other Sacraments, the Priest is the *representative* of Jesus Christ; (See 6th Chap.) and the Council of Trent, (Canon 8th on the Sacraments) declares, "that grace is conferred by the Sacraments of the new law, by their own power." Put these doctrines together, and it results, that the Sacraments of the Church of Rome, in the hands of any Priest, are in and of themselves, sufficient to fit a man to die. Hence the work of the Spirit of God on the heart is wholly put aside; the object of faith is not Christ, but, as Mr. Hughes himself informs us, "the Holy Catholic Church," *i. e.* the *Priesthood* of the Church: the regeneration of the heart is not required, or if it be, it is *wrought* by the Priest and the Sacraments: and thus without saving faith or personal holiness, without repentance and the knowledge of the Saviour, the departing soul is absolved by the Priest, and by the application of oil to the *body*, his *soul* is dismissed a safe and fit candidate for heaven!

6. This institution is an utter *novelty* in the Church of Christ. The very language of the decree owns it to be an invention of men. Pope Innocent the 1st, calls it *a kind of sacrament*. Cardinal Cajetan, Chemmitius, Hugo, Peter Lombard, Alexander, Cassander, not to mention Augustine, and other Fathers, deny that it is a sacrament of Jesus Christ, and thereby show that it is a novelty in the church.

7. In fine, this article of faith entirely explodes your infallibility as a church. This is proved in the dilemma stated above. But still more, the Rev. Dr. Manning, a celebrated defender of your faith, in his "short method with Protestants," (pp. 20, &c.) thus writes:

'The Church of Christ can only be that which believes wholly and entirely the doctrine that was taught by Christ, and delivered by his apostles. That church that would teach any *one* point of doctrine contrary to the revealed word of God, which I call *heresy*, would not be the chaste spouse of Christ, but an *harlot* and the *school* of Satan, and the gates of hell would prevail against her." Mr. Hughes also, has said, (Letter No. 1.) "that the *doctrines* of Christianity have been regarded by the Catholic Church *from the beginning as fixed stars in the firmament of revelation.*" Then, as this doctrine was not from the *beginning*, the *Roman* is not the Catholic Church; and, by your own and Dr. Manning's showing, she is *heretical*, she is an *harlot*, and the gates of hell *have prevailed* against her!

II. *The Church of Rome is grossly idolatrous.* The Church of Rome worships, and commands the worship (not only of the consecrated bread, as we have already showed, but) of the cross of Christ, of the Virgin Mary, of the Saints, of relics and images. I have already proved in former letters that the Catechism of the Council of Trent has *omitted* that part of the second commandment which forbids the making and worshipping of images. Though you have disputed *this*, you have not denied that the versions used in various countries, either wholly drop, or criminally *suppress* the offensive parts. Indeed the very edition printed by Mr. Cummiskey in this city, recommended by four Arch-Bishops, and used, probably, in St. John's, *wholly omits* it. If not, it is easy to disprove it. These are expressive erasures. But we have *decrees* of Councils for idolatry. The 2d Council of Nice *established idolatry by law.* How stoutly its acts were opposed, in the bosom of the church, at that day, I need hardly inform you; and I suppose you also know that when the *emperors* would have put down idolatry, the *Popes* would not permit it; but enthroned idolatry in the heart of the church. The Council of Trent has reduced this worship, (though with some caution) to a system. Thus, (25th Sess.) it is said, " It is a good and useful thing, suppliantly, to invoke the saints, and to flee to their prayers, help and assistance;" " that veneration and honour are due to the *relics* of the saints, and that it is a useful thing for the faithful to honour these and other sacred monuments, and that the memorials of the saints are to be frequented, to obtain their *help* and *assistance;*" " that the images of Christ, of the Virgin, mother of God, and of other saints, are to be had and retained especially in churches, and due *honours* and *veneration* rendered them; that we are to *kiss them, uncover our heads in their presence, and prostrate ourselves;*" " that great advantages are to be derived from all sacred images,—because of the divine miracles performed by the saints;" " that *new miracles* are to be admitted, and *new relics* to be received, with the recognition and approval of a bishop," &c. It is remarkable, that the very language, word for word, in which the heathen, both of ancient and modern times, excused their idolatry, is used by the church of Rome. And what is still more remarkable, their worship of idols and Saints, and their abounding ceremonies, are derived in chief part from the ancient Pagans. Let any intelligent reader take up " Middleton's Letter from Rome, showing the exact conformity between Popery

and Paganism, or the religion of the present Rc
that of their heathen ancestors," and if he doe:
perusal a *Protestant* in his opinions on this sub
can in any sort escape the conviction of modern
and idolatry, he must be something of a *stock* hi

The church of Rome worships the cross of Chri
nas (your divine doctor) tells us, " *that the cros*
adored with *divine adoration ;*" " if we speak o
which Christ was crucified, it is to be worshippe
ship." (Aquin. 3. p. q. 25. Art. 4.) The follo
rised worship of the cross in the church of Rom
the Breviary, the book which contains the daily se
i. e. their *Book of Common Prayer*, sanctioned
universal use in the church; compiled by order
Trent; and enjoined with great strictness upon
ecclesiastical revenue, upon all the regular orc
Nuns; upon sub-deacons, Deacons, and Priests,
public or private, the whole service of each day fi
omission of any one of the eight portions of whi(
sists, is declared to be a *mortal* sin. This book (
ing idolatrous worship, page 330.

	The English t of the holy week
O crux Ave! spes unica!	Hail cross of hor
Hoc passionis tempore,	Now is the mour
Auge piis justitiam,	Improve religious
Reisque dona veniam.	The sins of crim

Specimens of idolatry equally direct may be ¡
the Missal, or Mass-Book of the church, not to m
examples which are found in your standard writ
this worship is given to the cross itself, yes, to t
senseless matter. There are probably more *relic*
on which Christ was crucified, now exhibited and
church of Rome, than would build a ship!

The Virgin Mary is also worshipped ; not o
worshipped. I observe you recognise this as a pa
education of your collier. (letter No. 5.) Father
to 128) says, " being truly our Saviour's mother,
as she was on earth, she still retains a sort of *natu*
his *person*, over his *goods*, and over his *omnipo*
Albertus Magnus says, by her motherly authority
him. She preserves from *heresy and error*, she (
procures a *good death* for her followers, has bro
purgatory ; we ought to render her religious hon(
to her images, as the *many miracles done by them*

In the " offices of the blessed Virgin," is this pr
and her son bless us !" Confession is made " to A
the blessed Virgin Mary," &c. &c. Absolution (s(
in the name of " the passion of our Lord Jesus Chr
of the blessed Virgin," &c. &c. Bellarmine clos
on this very topic with this idolatrous doxology.]
que matri Mariæ: " Glory be to God and the Virg

ther." In the Breviary (office of the blessed Mary,) she is hailed and worshipped, as the *gate of heaven;* she is implored to loose the bands of the guilty, to give light to the blind, to establish their peace and drive away all evil ; to make them holy, and to guide them safely till they see Jesus on high ! She is called the glorious mistress of the earth, and the queen of Heaven ! And this not by a transient fanatic, but in the book of common prayer, in which the daily exercises of the Roman church are performed ; which Mr. Hughes and every Priest is bound to use ; the standard book of worship, and the guide of the "*universal*" church. Is not this gross, unqualified creature-worship ? Could more be said to God ? Can *He* do more than is thus attributed to a *mere creature ?*

The worship of images in the Church of Rome is clearly idolatrous. But for want of room I omit the proof now, yet will return to it when you please.

As to relics it seems almost incredible to what an extent superstition and idolatry have been carried. These, as will be seen in the decree copied above, are to be religiously honoured, *in plain English, worshipped.* 11,000 are preserved in *one* church in Spain ; some of these are " several pieces of the most holy cross, on which Christ suffered; thirteen thorns from the *crown* He wore ; a piece of the manger in which he lay; a piece of the handkerchief with which the Holy Virgin wiped her eyes at the foot of the cross ; a thigh of St. Lawrence ; and the nails, and lance, and other instruments of Christ's passion," &c. &c. They show at Rome the heads of Peter and Paul, a lock of the Virgin's hair, a phial of her tears, some of the sponge, the rod of Aaron, and part of the ark of the covenant, though the latter the Jews never could find after the Babylonish captivity. The *emerald* dish on which our Saviour was said to have eaten his last supper, was taken to Paris by the ungracious French troops ; and the "Institute," on trial, found it a piece of *green glass.* They swear by these relics, they worship them avowedly, (as in the case of the cross) they consecrate them, dedicate *them* to God, and churches *to them*, and even trace miracles to *them.* I will not pursue the humiliating detail. But, surely, when the authority of the church enjoined, and the people practised such idolatry and superstition, it was time for *protests* to sound, and *Reformation* to begin. On *this whole subject* the Council of Constantinople, and the 2d Council of Nice, were directly at issue, though in close succession one after the other. They cannot both be *right.* One said Images must not be put in the churches, nor honoured by the people. The other rescinded their decisions, anathematized them, and erected and worshipped with new zeal the images which they had broken down. Which was right? Surely not both ? If either was wrong, your infallibility perishes !

III. *The Church of Rome is an enemy to human liberty, and has done all in her power to stifle it.* When you defined the Reformation to be "*the religion of free thinking about the meaning of the Bible; the religion in which every man has a right to judge for himself.*" (Letter 21.) you unwittingly disclosed the doctrine and spirit of your communion, viz. *that no man has a right to judge for himself*, but must receive what he is commanded to believe in *implicit faith*. The spirit of oppression begins in your church as soon as the child is born, and ends only with death—nay, if he will *not* submit, his "*soul after death* is *devoted*," as in the case of John Huss, "*to infernal devils*." The 7 Sess. 14 Can. Coun. Trent, thus lords it over the souls of men: "Whoever shall affirm that when the baptized children grow up, they are to be asked whether they will confirm the promises made by their godfathers in their name at their baptism; and if they say they will not, they are to be left to their own choice, and not to be *compelled* in the mean time to lead a Christian life, by any *other punishment* than exclusion from the Eucharist and the other sacraments, until they repent: let him be accursed." Then, is not every person baptized in your communion liable *to force*, (where it will be tolerated) *by punishment*, besides *exclusion* from the sacraments, *if he will not submit?* Surely! where, then, is this liberty? Is he not the slave of spiritual despotism whether he will or not! Baptism then becomes, as it has been truly said, *an indelible brand of slavery;* and the church claims her slaves wherever she finds them, and condemns them to perdition when they will not *submit;* and being the "*only true*" church, they are to *be forced into* her communion, or *damned out* of it. And as this is a *canon* of the church, involving *an article of faith*, so every true Catholic must *believe* it without doubt or faultering, viz. that *punishment* is to be *applied* to. compel belief. Again: suppose the unhappy subject, (say in Italy or Spain,) when "he grows up" resolves that he will *not* "confirm the promises made in his name by his godfather at baptism," we have practical demonstration of the treatment he endures. *The inquisition is at hand.* I have always failed to fix this *eye-sore* on *your* vision! You will not *see* it.— But the *public* will. The INQUISITION is a court of which the Pope is head; it is his tribunal, and is established throughout the world, wherever there are Roman Catholics, and where the government will tolerate it. These bloody tribunals arrest and punish, and torture, and condemn to death for *error* of *doctrine ;* not for transgressions of *civil* law, for they are professedly *spiritual* courts, and have to do with "*heretical pravity*." Yet they apply *force* from first to last. The interior of an inquisition is hell on earth. Not only have some of their victims escaped to tell us, but they have been thrown open by invading armies; and military leaders, more merciful than the ruthless inquisitors, have exposed to the gaze of an astonished world the scenes of alternate butchery and debauch, in which the ghostly fathers have glutted, as they respectively arose, their *zeal* and their *lusts*. The Bishop of Aire talks of "innocent victims whose numbers have been greatly exaggerated!" But who is an *innocent* victim? one who is not a heretic? Then if a man be a heretic, he *ought to be punished!* Yes—this is the conclusion necessarily. And then of the 150,000 who suffered in the Inquisition during fifty years, *some* were innocent victims? Does not this very defence establish my position, viz. that there is no real liberty of *person* or of *conscience* under the Roman Catholic religion? that to dissent is to be a *guilty* victim? And the alternative is submission *to*, or oppression *by* it! What is conclusive proof that the holy See sustains and approves the Inquisition is this, that it never has uttered one *word* or taken one *step* to put it down, though *one* word would have done it. Nay, so far from this, it has been the parent and the patron of it.

The spirit of Romanism is a spirit of *persecution.* This is necessary to its nature. This I have shown at large heretofore, and you have struggled in vain through many a captious and artful page to avert the testimony of bulls, decrees, and historical evidence to that effect.

The Church of Rome is the avowed enemy of the freedom of the press. I have proved this from the Pope's circular letter. You have not denied this. I have showed its restrictions on the translation, printing, sale, and perusal even of God's holy word. I have pointed you to the *Standing Committee* at Rome who *watch* and *purify* the press. But you find safety in silence. Let me present to you a decretal by the Lateran Council held at Rome. (Sess. 10. A. D. 1515, Leo X. presiding.)

"In the same session a decretal was issued concerning the printing of books, in the following form, viz. By order of the holy Council, we in fine, ordain and decree, that *no* person shall *presume to print*, or *cause to be printed*, any *book or other writing whatsoever*, either in our city (Rome) or in any *other* cities and diocese, unless it shall first have been *carefully examined*, if in this city, by our Vicar and the master of the holy palace, or if in *other cities* and dioceses, by the Bishop or his deputy, *with the inquisitor of heretical pravity* for the diocese, in which the said impression is about to be made; and unless also it shall have received, under their own hand, their written approval, given without price and without delay. Whosoever shall presume to do otherwise, besides the loss of the books, which shall be publicly burned, shall be bound by the sentence of excommunication." (Caranza, page 670.) By authority of the Council of Trent, this decretal and all others of a like kind are thus *confirmed*, viz. Rule 1. "*All books* condemned by the supreme pontiffs, or general Councils, *before the year* 1515, and not comprised in the present Index, are, nevertheless, to be considered as condemned." The creed also, as adopted by every Roman Catholic, requires all "to receive undoubtedly, *all things delivered, defined*, and *declared by the sacred canons and General Councils*, and *particularly* by the holy Council of Trent." These decretals, rules, &c. of Popes, and of Councils having been thus finally confirmed by your last and great Council of Trent, are now in full force; they bind every Roman Catholic upon earth; they involve an article of faith, and *must* be *believed;* they announce infallible law, and *must* be *obeyed;* to reject them is heresy; to obey them brings ruin to civil liberty; yet to the present hour they are in full operation wherever the Pope has sway. Now you have this alternative, *disclaim* these decrees, and you are not a Roman Catholic; *defend* them, and you are a traitor to your country. Will you defend the dogmas of infallibility and Papal supremacy at such a price?

To make this despotism over thought complete, and conscious that truth and testimony were against the "Mother church," the holy see has applied its pruning knife to trim down the *works* which were *allowed* to appear, and even the writings of the "Fathers" have been erased, and amended to bring them into harmony with your doctrines and decrees. Evidence on this subject is both abundant and strong. Some of it I have adduced already; more is at hand, if you will meet me on this point. *Why* you entirely evade this whole subject the public must, by this time, clearly understand. As it is a *painful* and *delicate topic* it might almost seem a matter of mercy to let it slumber. I must be permitted, however, to name it to you as an item which convinced the *Reformers* that *truth* was not your friend; that free inquiry would be the ruin of your church; and that liberty was to be sought in retiring from her iron grasp. At your pleasure we will examine this topic fully.

Once more, *civil liberty cannot flourish under the influence of the church of Rome.* It is to the Reformation we owe, under God, all the liberty now in the world. If you take the map of the world, and strike from it those states which are now eminently Protestant, how much civil liberty will remain? How much is there in Spain? How much in Austria? How much in Portugal? How much in Italy? In this our age the power of the Pope is broken: his political consequence is gone; and no wonder, (as is said in a letter lately written from Rome) it is currently foreboded in the *eternal city* that the present will be the *last Pope*. But where he reigns, and while he reigns, men cannot be free. It is impossible. Hence he must soon finally and irreparably fall; for he *will* not change, and the system cannot long survive that inextinguishable love of liberty and growing light of knowledge, which the God of providence and truth is sending forth upon the nations.

Here then are *three leading errors* in the *doctrine* as well as the *practice* of the church of Rome, showing her manifest departure from the religion of Christ, and calling aloud for Reformation, justifying, nay, forcing a *protest* from every friend of truth. I suppose your *discretion* will pass these by, as you have done the long catalogue of cognate errors already exposed in my previous letters. But our readers will not pass them; nor will your suffering cause find shelter in your silence.

I now proceed to notice your attack on the "Protestant religion."

And 1st. You have admitted fully (Letter No. 23.) "that what are called 'orthodox' tenets among Protestants are all found in the Catholic church;" and "that the Reformers in going out from the church carried them forth," such as "the doctrine of the Trinity and divinity of the Son of God, the doctrine of original sin, and the atonement through the death of Christ." (See your Letter, No. 22.) And (in the same letter) "you admit, *for argument sake*, that the religion of Christ, established in its purity by the Apostles, gradually became corrupt; and was finally restored to its primitive purity by the event called the Reformation:" you say "starting even from this extravagant supposition, you will find it a difficult task to prove that the Protestant Religion is the Religion of Christ." Now by first admission Protestants are "orthodox" in certain "tenets," and in such, they *agree* with *your* church, for "they brought them out of her."—By the second admission, the *other tenets* of your church being *errors*, it follows as an irresistible consequence, on your own principles, that "orthodox" "Protestants" are the only true Christians in the world. For you admit that all we hold, of the truth, we got from you; that all you *hold* which we *refused* to bring away is *false:* therefore, we *hold* all that is *true*, and what we reject is *false;* hence the discussion, on your part, is at an end.

2. As to the *character* of the Reformers, *your reasoning is absurd.*

If all you say of them is true, the case stands thus: They were *fallible* men; so *we* hold them to have been; and emerging from the long night of darkness and death which the Papacy had spread over Christendom, no wonder if they had faults, and errors too.— They are not our *guides*, but the Lord, and his Apostles, speaking in the Bible. They were *Reformers* such as often appeared in the Old Testament church, not to give a *new* religion, but to *restore* the old. We call no man "*Father,*" and only follow *them* so far as they follow *Christ.* Suppose they had all the defects you falsely charge on them, and held some opinions which were not true; yet as the Reformation was necessary, and the religion of Protestants looks to the *Bible* as the only infallible rule of faith and practice, it affects us not. But with your church it is far otherwise. A large party in it believes in the Pope's infallibility. This is especially the system of the Jesuits, and of Italy at large. Now on their principles your church is irreparably ruined. *Fifty apostate Popes* in one long black line, are mentioned, by one of your writers; many Popes, Baronius tells us, were elected and ruled by strumpets;——divers others came in by Simony; others still filled with their bastard progeny, the highest offices of the church; some dealt in poison and sorcery; one sacrificed to idols; several Popes reigned at once; a woman it is said once filled the Papal Chair; and incest, debauchery, civil war, and unnumbered crimes characterized the *Holy* See for more than a century. And, now, pray tell me, where was the infallible Head of the Church, and what sort of a church was that which sustained, and followed such monsters of iniquity? But if you say the Pope was *not* infallible, (as surely you must) what becomes of your argument under the second question, viz: "reviewing the doctrines and characters of the Reformers, is there any, even the smallest evidence, that the Spirit of God had aught to do with it?" Yet this is your *great* argument against the Reformation!— On your own showing then, the church of Rome does not hold the religion of Christ; to protest was a right; and reformation was a duty.

3. But *you have grossly slandered the Reformers.*

In the first place, it is very remarkable, that in many cases you studiously omit all references by which your quotations can be identified and exposed. In the next place, where you give the references, I have tried in vain to find some of the passages to which you refer. From this I cannot doubt that you quote second hand from Jesuit authors, with whom it is a duty to falsify when ecclesiastical utility requires it. In the third place, your glaring perver sion of Luther, which I exposed at the close of my last letter, is a living monument from which we learn how little reliance is to be placed on your quotations. I say this with regret; but what follows proves it necessary. In your Letter No. 23, you make Luther say, " let this be your rule in interpreting the Scriptures; whenever they *command* a good work do you understand that they *forbid* it;"— that is, Luther's rule was, to contradict Scripture and encourage bad works! Such was the language you made him hold. I quoted in answer, (to which I refer the reader,) the *whole* passage, when lo, we find the disjointed member of the sentence taking its place, *honestly*, and making Luther urge good works in God's strength, according to God's word, and to God's glory!—Pressed by the exposure, you venture in the last Letter (No. 25,) to give a new version of your quotation from Luther, and tell us " the sense of my quotation (from Luther) was to show that he denied *free will in man*, denied the *possibility* of keeping the commandments, or of *doing good works.*" This, truly, is strange self-conviction! You first pervert his meaning, and then deny your own statement. Such is the process by which you would expose the Reformation! Luther was but a *man*, and yet such a man as no slander can pull down. It is well for truth that he had other historians besides my Rev. opponent. Erasmus says, (see Tom. 3. in Epist. ad Albert,) " If I favour him, it is because he is a *good man*, a thing his very enemies acknowledge. This I observe that the best men are least offended with his writings." Frederic, Duke of Saxon, said, " Erasmus did truly point out Luther's two chief faults, that he meddled with the Pope's *crown* and the Monk's *bellies.*" Guiccard (His. Ital. l. 13. p. 380.) tells us, " many conceive that the troubles raised against Luther, had their origin in the *innocency of his life* and the *soundness* of *his doctrine*, rather than in any thing else." Sir James M'Intosh says, of Luther, (see Hist. of England, chap. 5. vol. 2.) " Martin Luther was of a character thoroughly exempt from falsehood, duplicity, and hypocrisy—it was fortunate also that the enormities of Tetzel, found Luther busied in the contemplation of the principle which is the basis of all ethical judgment, and by the power of which *he struck a mortal blow at superstition*, viz. ' men are not made righteous by performing certain actions which are externally good; but men must have right principles in the first place, and then they will not fail to perform virtuous actions:' the general terms which are here used, enunciate a proposition, equally *certain and sublime*, the basis of all pure ethics, the cement of the eternal alliance between morality and religion. *From the promulgation of this principle may be dated the downfall of superstition.*" And now shall we believe the illustrious historian or the interested priest? It were easy in the same way to defend the other honoured names, which you have held up, so falsely, to public infamy. We give the above only as a specimen, and design hereafter to do justice to their characters and writings.

4. *Your four questions* are assuming the place of *your ten heads*, and are progressively meeting their fate. You seem to have no ideas beyond them, and by repeating them again and again, even after they are all answered, make it apparent, that you intend no defence

of *your* doctrines, while you have little to say against our own. As to the Greek church, which is as ancient as your own, I did not, as you know, claim her as agreeing with ourselves in all points; but stated, what you also know, that she protested against purgatory, human merits, supererogation, forbidding the use of the Scripture, worshipping images, the sale of masses, extreme unction, and infallibility.—So far you will allow she was a *Protestant*. Your remarks on the Waldenses, are not worthy of notice. They entirely evade the abundant testimony brought by me, from your own writers. They contain nothing; and ex nihilo nihil fit. The dialogue with which you amuse your readers is *unanswerable*. You must have been reading Corderius's Colloquies, or the " Courtship of Cock Robin and Jenny Wren," when its fine conception was first imparted to your mind!

5. *The doctrinal unity of the Reformed*, as expressed without collusion, and almost simultaneously, is one of the most remarkable events in the history of the church. If, instead of cavilling over garbled extracts, from individual writers, you will take up these FORMULARIES, which were published over Europe at the commencement of the Reformation, you may see in them the Protestant religion. No less than TWELVE of these, containing essentially the same doctrines, are now extant. They are the Augustan, the Tetrapolitan, Polish, Saxon, Bohemian, Wittemberg, Palatine, Helvetian, French, Dutch, English, and Scotch Confessions. They issued at the call of God, from millions of minds in Germany, Switzerland, France, Holland, England, and Scotland. In due time, (and though you ridicule the sentiment which it conveys, yet let me say,) *if God permit*, I propose to show the essential harmony of many of these confessions with the word of God, with the earliest creeds, councils, and fathers, and also with each other; and thus to display the Christianity, antiquity, and unity of the Protestant religion. In contrast with this shall be made to appear, still more, the total *novelty* of your peculiar doctrines, and the abounding variations of Popery for 1200 years.

I terminate this letter with Bishop Jewel's famous challenge, which he often uttered, but which was never accepted. "If any learned man of our adversaries, or all the learned men that be alive, be able to bring any one sufficient sentence out of any old Catholic doctor, or father, or general council, or Holy Scripture, or any one example in the primitive church, whereby it may clearly and plainly be proved, during the first six hundred years, 1. that there were at any time any private masses in the world : 2. or that there was then any communion ministered unto the people under one kind : 3. or that the people had their common prayer in a strange tongue that the people understood not: 4. or that the Bishop of Rome was then called an Universal Bishop, or head of the Universal church: 5. or that the people were then taught to believe that Christ's body is really, substantially, corporally, carnally, or naturally present, in the sacrament: 6. or that his body is or may be in a thousand places or more at one time : 7. or that the priest did then hold up the sacrament over his head; 8. or that the people did fall down and worship it with godly honours: 9. or that the sacrament was then, or ought now to be, hanged up under a canopy: 10. or that in the sacrament after the words of consecration there remained only the accidents and shows, without the substance, of the bread and wine: 11. or that then the priest divided the sacrament in three parts, and afterwards received himself alone: 12. or that whoever had said the sacrament is a figure, a pledge, a token, or a remembrance of Christ's body, had therefore been adjudged for an heretic: 13. or that it was lawful then to have thirty, twenty, fifteen, ten, or five, masses said in the same church in one day: 14. or that images were then set up in the churches to the intent the people might worship them: 15. or that the lay people were forbidden to read the word of God in their own tongue: 16. or that it was then lawful for the priest, to pronounce the words of consecration closely, or in private to himself: 17. or that the priest had then authority to offer up Christ unto his Father: 18. or to communicate and receive the Sacrament for another, as they do: 19. or to apply the virtue of Christ's death and passion to any man by means of the Mass: 20. or that it was then thought a sound doctrine to teach the people that Mass, *ex opere operato* (that is upon account of the work wrought) is able to remove any part of our sin: 21. or that any Christian man called the Sacrament of the Lord, HIS GOD: 22. or that the people were then taught to believe that the body of Christ remaineth in the Sacrament as long as the accidents of bread and wine remain there without corruption: 23. or that a mouse, or any other worm or beast, may eat the body of Christ, (for so some of our adversaries have said and taught:) 24. or that when Christ said hoc est corpum meum, (this is my body) the word hoc (this) pointed not to the bread, but to an *invidium vagum*, as some of them say: 25. or that the accidents, or forms, or shows, of bread and wine be Sacraments of Christ's body and blood, and not rather the very bread and wine itself: 26. or that the Sacrament is a sign or token of the body of Christ that lieth hid underneath it: 27. or that ignorance is the mother and cause of true devotion—The conclusion is, that I should then be content to yield and subscribe "

Yours, &c. JOHN BRECKINRIDGE

CONTROVERSY. No. XXVII.

IS THE PROTESTANT RELIGION THE RELIGION OF CHRIST?
Philadelphia, August 2, 1833.

To the Rev. John Breckinridge.

Rev. Sir,—I have just read your last letter. It is remarkable for nothing, except a repetition of special pleading, petty sophistry, and, as usual, the *evasion of the question at issue*. It is superior, however, in style and good manners, (if not in argument) to most of its predecessors from the same quarter. When I saw myself *again* addressed by "Rev. Sir," which you had so long denied me, and marked the absence of deistical objection and flippant personality, I was tempted, for a moment, to question the identity of authorship. But this suspicion vanished from my mind the moment I read your classical allusion to the "courtship of Cock Robin and Jenny Wren."

It must have, long since, become manifest to every candid and sensible reader, that you utterly disregard the rules of this controversy, to the observance of which you were bound by your signature. How far this is honourable, I shall not take upon me to say. In the world, the man who makes an agreement and then violates, systematically, all its conditions, enjoys no enviable fame. "The rule of faith," and then the "Protestant religion" were the questions to be discussed, successively. "And the parties agree *respectively*, to adhere strictly to the subject of discussion for the time being, and to admit no second question until the first shall have been exhausted." If, as appears, you did not intend to fulfil this part of the agreement, I am at a loss to account for your having entered into it. As it is, however, no assertion of mine is necessary to show that you have given up your rule of faith, and that you shrink from the defence of the Protestant religion. On the former topic, the amount of your six months labour is this, that the Bible is the infallible rule of all those who are fortunate enough to arrive at the *true sense* of it. But that private interpretation, when it extracts from the sacred volume a *wrong* meaning is an "abuse." And that *relatively to all who are guilty of this abuse*, even the Bible is not an infallible rule!! Thus the infallibility of the Bible itself as a rule is made to evaporate under the chemical influence of your arguments. Every peculiar system of Protestantism looks upon itself as being the system of the Bible, and whilst each retorts upon the other, the *abuse* of the writen word of God, Mr. Breckinridge pleading in the name of all, bears testimony that those who are guided by the TRUE SENSE of the Bible are "infallibly right," but that those who with equal sincerity miss the TRUE SENSE, are infallibly wrong. Still he asserts that the Bible alone, interpreted by each individual for himself, is "the infallible rule of faith appointed by Christ."

As to the other question, it also, has been virtually abandoned.—The reader must have observed that you find yourself unable to answer my questions. I asked you to define the Protestant religion; and you could not tell me what it is. Arguments and authorities were adduced to show that it could not be the religion of Christ, and no attempt has been made to refute the arguments, or question the authorities taken from the writings of the Reformers themselves.—

You say you cannot find the quotations, and insinuate that they are spurious. This inclines me to believe that they were *new* to you, and that you are not so conversant with the theological discoveries of the 16th century as I had supposed. But if you will only take the trouble to designate the particular passage quoted in my letters which you cannot find, and call it spurious, I shall have great pleasure in marking the page and leaving the original work at the Coffee-house, or any other public place, for your inspection and that of the public.

In the mean time I shall place my unanswered questions touching the pretended divinity of the Protestant religion on record, and keep them as a standing advertisement. If they *cannot* be answered, Protestants whose love of truth, is greater than their hatred of the Catholic religion, will see how baseless is the fabric of their belief.—They will reflect how dangerous is their position, since they can find NO Christians agreeing with them in doctrines, from the days of Christ until the coming of Luther, and very few since.

Mr. Breckinridge says that *" the Protestant is the religion of Christ."*

If so, I call upon him 1st. To tell me what the Protestant religion is?

    2. I call upon him to say what society of Christians ever taught this pretended " religion of Christ," previous to the Reformation?

    3. I call upon him to say, whether Christ revealed ALL *the doctrines of the Protestant religion, beginning with the best* IMAGE *of his church, Episcopalianism, and terminating with the most consistent of Protestant sects, the Unitarians?—and if not, how* MANY *denominations, out of the whole, belong to the* TRUE *Protestant religion, the religion of Christ?*

    4. I call upon him to show whether the Reformers received any NEW *ministerial authority, after the withdrawal of that which they had received from the church?*

    5. I call upon him, in case no such NEW *authority was received, to show that the Protestant clergy, so called, have any divine right to exercise the Christian ministry, more than other educated laymen?*

These are the questions by which the touchstone of truth will be applied to the divinity of the Protestant religion. If it can stand *this test*, you will gain the point, but if *not*, it will be impossible to conceal the deception.

Let Princeton, and all the clergy set about the solution of these difficulties; which stand between the Protestant religion and the religion of Christ. They are too well founded, as you cannot but know, in the principles of Christian theology to be overturned by ridicule. You cannot take them up one after another, and give that *unequivocal* reply, which would satisfy any mind seriously disposed to inquire for the truth. And as long as you will not attempt it, then they stand cutting short the claims of the Protestant religion to be what you said it was; the religion of Christ. To all you time to ruminate on these difficulties of your position, I shall now proceed to show that the doctrine of the Eucharist as held in the

Catholic church, is an integral part of the Christian Religion; and that Protestants in rejecting it, have deprived themselves of the last and best pledge of a Redeemer's love. This Sacrament, which by Protestants is called the Lord's Supper, was instituted on the night on which he was betrayed, the eve of his passion, as if he would select that moment, for the most sublime exercise of his divine charity and omnipotence. Is it then an article of Christian Revelation that the body and blood of Christ are contained in the Catholic Sacrament of the Eucharist? This is the question; for as to the *mystery* of doctrine it is not greater than those of the Incarnation, Trinity, or Deity of Jesus Christ. Has it been revealed? In answer to this question we will have to examine the evidences.

It is remarkable, that among Protestants, those sects whose founders had never been raised to the order of Priesthood in the Catholic church, were the most disposed to reject the reality of Christ's presence in the Eucharist. Luther maintained this doctrine till his death; the first bishops and clergy of the English Government church, maintained, or at least pretended to maintain it, in like manner. Whereas Calvin, who, though brought up a Catholic, was not a Priest, rejected it from the first, conscious that the *priestly ordination* was necessary to consecrate the species. Still, Rev. Sir, even in your Presbyterian Confession of Faith, which has not been "amended" since the year 1821, there is much mystery and much to impress upon the untutored communicant an idea that he is receiving something more than mere bread and wine. "Our Lord Jesus, in the night wherein he was betrayed, instituted the Sacrament of his *body and blood*"......(page 124.) " Worthy receivers, *outwardly* partakers of the *visible* elements in this Sacrament, do then also inwardly by faith, really and indeed, yet not carnally and corporally, but spiritually, receive and feed upon Christ crucified, and all benefits of his death: the *body and blood of Christ* being then not corporally or carnally in, with, or under the bread and wine; yet as *really*, but spiritually, present to the faith of believers in that ordinance, as the *elements* are, to their outward senses." (Page 127-8.)

On the same page it is said, that unworthy receivers " are guilty of the body and blood of the Lord to their own damnation"—and that without great sin they " cannot partake of these *holy mysteries*."

Here then is a strange compound of double-meaning language, " outward elements"—" body and blood of Christ"—" spiritual feeding"—" not discerning the body of the Lord"—" holy mysteries"— connected with what? With the belief of a real presence? not at all; but with a piece of bread and a cup of wine, over which an unauthorised minister has pronounced an abortive benediction!! The blessing of the minister produces no change whatever, and if I understand the language of your creed, the bread and wine, received with the same dispositions *any where*, are as much the Sacrament of the body and blood of Christ, as they are after a fruitless and inoperative blessing in the Presbyterian church or meeting-house. The communicant is taught that he receives nothing but bread and wine; and yet, that in being guilty of the bread and wine, he is guilty of the body and blood of Christ; for not discerning what has no existence.

viz: the body of the Lord in bread and wine!! What is the meaning then of all this strange language? This affectation of a real presence, with the simultaneous denial of it, and the positive doctrine of a real absence. But take it altogether, I find it quite as unintelligible as the Catholic dogma of the Eucharist.

The same kind of mysterious double-meaning hangs round the sacramental bread and wine of all the other Protestant denominations. The people generally, imposed upon by this language, have a vague idea, in spite of their teachers, that, in receiving the Sacrament of the Lord's Supper, they receive something more than mere bread and wine.

When the Reformation, as it is called, of the 16th century set about rending the seamless and unbroken garment of the church, (which amidst the corruptions of the age, the vices of the people, and the scandal of degenerate ecclesiastics, still preserved the "one Lord, one faith, and one baptism," which she had received from her divine founder,) the work of sacrilege was carried on with such daring irregularity, that even the form of "casting lots" was dispensed with. Luther first raised the standard of error; and set the whole Christian world at shameless defiance. His example and doctrines encouraged others to bolder innovations; and it was not long after his attempt to drag the Pope, from the seat of his spiritual supremacy, when a brother Reformer undertook, by a similar license to drag the Saviour of the world from the throne of his divinity. But the denial of the real presence, had escaped the father of the Reformation, and was reserved for the famous, or rather infamous, Carlostadius. He began by teaching that when Christ said "this is my body," he pointed to himself as he sat at the table; and not to the eucharistic species which he gave to the apostles. On this, he quarrelled with Luther; married a woman; made war on education; joined himself for a time to the fanatical Ana-baptists under Nicholas Stork; wandered about through Germany for several years, and finally died at Basle in 1541. Melanchton describes him as an impious and brutal fellow, and testifies that he broached this error, out of jealousy and hatred of Luther. (In Epist. ad Mycon.) Zuinglius embraced the doctrine of Carlostadius, and fought the battles of his party against the "Ecclesiastics of Wittemburg," with great fury and success. Hence it was that Luther declared by way of funeral oration on his brother Reformer; "Zuinglius is dead and damned, having desired like a thief and a rebel to compel others to follow his *error*," viz. the denial of the real presence in the Eucharist. In fact Zuinglius draws a terrible character of himself. "I cannot," says he, "conceal the fire that burns me, and drives me on to incontinence, since it is true that its effects have already drawn on me but too many infamous reproaches among the churches." (In Parenæs. ad. Helvet Tom. 1. d. 113.)

The controversy about the *real presence* between the Lutherans and Zuinglians was in this fervid condition when a new personage made his appearance on the theatre of the Reformation. John Cauvin, or Calvin, born in 1509, and instructed in Protestantism by his teacher of Greek, Wolmar was destined to throw Zuinglius in the shade, and to rival if not eclipse the great Luther himself. He published the text book of Calvinism, called the "Institutions," at Basle, near the grave of Carlostadius. He denied the "real presence." Becoming master at Geneva, his disciples denied it also—for Calvin was a man whose infallibility was not to be disputed, except at the risk of the stake and faggot. It was from Geneva that the church of England derived her present doctrine on the eucharist, during the golden days of her "Calvinistic articles," to which Doctor Miller alluded, as quoted in a former letter, with such triumphant reference —telling us that they (the Calvinistic articles) had kept the English church *almost* pure, for *nearly* one hundred years. Wise men, however, sometimes see the same objects in very different aspects.— Bishop Bancroft, in reference to the same Calvinistic derivation of doctrine, says, "Happy, a thousand times happy our island, if neither English or Scot had ever put foot in Geneva, if they had never become acquainted with a single individual of these Genevese Doctors." (Survey of pretended Holy Discipline.)

Here then is the course and brief history of the Protestant doctrine —rejecting the real presence of Christ in the eucharist. From America we trace it to England; from England to Geneva; from Geneva to Basle; from Switzerland to Germany, where, according to Melanchton, it originated with the "brutal fellow" Carlostadt, who broached it out of pure hatred to Luther. The circumstances under which this warfare was commenced, at the Black Bear, where Luther lodged, are so disgraceful and profane, that I shall pass them over in silence. The curious reader may consult the recent work of Thomas Moore, chapter xlvi. page 241, where the references are given. The war of the Sacrament being once declared among the Reformers, became the source of deadly strife, duplicity, stratagem, and intrigue among the belligerents. "In vain," says the writer, to whom I have just referred, "did Bucer by tricks and evasions, and it is painful to add, Melanchton, succeeded in maintaining, for a time, a false and feverish truce between the parties. But art so gross could not long continue to deceive; all compromise was found to be hollow and hopeless, and, at last, the three great eucharistic factions, the Lutheran, Calvinistic, and Zuinglian, all broke loose in their respective directions of heresy—each branch again subdividing itself into new factious distinctions, under the countless names of Panarii, Accidentarii, Corporarii, Anabonarii, Tropistœ, Metamorphistœ, Iscariotistœ, Schwenkenfeldians, &c. &c. &c., till, to such an extent did the caprice of private judgment carry its freaks, on this one solemn subject, that an author of Bellarmine's time counted no less than TWO HUNDRED *different* opinions on the words, "*This is my body.*"— Thus the Protestants in attempting to escape the "hard saying," which gave offence to the Caphaarnites, found themselves unable to agree on any other explanation. Hence the duplicity of the language in which it is expressed in most of the Protestant formularies, of which your Confession as amended in 1821, furnishes no mean specimen.

Protestants therefore can trace the doctrine of the sacrament, in which, according to their books, Christ is really present, and really absent at the same time—as far back as 1524 to Carlostadt, to whom belongs the glory of having originated it. Beyond him, ALL believed in the real presence of Christ in the Eucharist. You have been bold enough, Rev. Sir, in utter ignorance, or in utter contempt of Christian antiquity and the testimony of innumerable writers, to assert that our belief was introduced in the 13th century, A. D. 1215. Even this, however, shows that it was the general faith for 300 years before the Reformation. But let us see whether the doctrine had not been believed in every age from the days of Christ. Now, Rev. Sir, if this doctrine of the real presence and transubstantiation, be " as young," to use your own language, as 1215, how does it happen that Berengarius wrote against it, nearly two hundred years before it was born? How does it happen that Scotus Erigenus had written against it, in the reign of Charles the Bald, some two hundred years before Berengarius?—And that the schismatical held it before their separation from the church in the 9th century—and continue to hold it to this day? How comes it that the Paulician Heretics of the 7th century rejected transubstantiation, if as you learnedly assert, transubstantiation was not known in the church until the year 1215? How was it that the Manichæans rejected this doctrine in the 3d century? And approaching nearer still to the pure fountain of Christian faith, how is it, that the Gnostic heretics denied it in the very first age of the church? These heretics professed to believe in Jesus Christ, and his doctrine, propounded by their *private judgment.* They hold that Jesus Christ suffered only in *appearance,* and that it was not his real flesh but a *fantastical* body, which suffered and bled on the cross. It seems that they also had an accountable aversion to the doctrine of the real presence of Jesus Christ in the Eucharist, and this, too, if we may believe Mr. Breckinridge, 1200 years before that doctrine was introduced! St. Ignatius says of them in the very first century, " they abstain from the Eucharist and from prayer, *because* they do not acknowledge the *Eucharist to be the flesh of our Saviour Jesus Christ,* which suffered for our sins, and which the father by his goodness resuscitated." Rejecting therefore this gift of God, they die in their disputes. (Ep. ad Smyrn. p. 36. Tom. ii. P. P. Apost. Amstelœdami 1724.) Here, the father makes the flesh of our Saviour Jesus Christ, in the Eucharist, to be identically the same, which suffered on the cross, and arose from the dead. Jesus Christ had equally identified his flesh in both. " This is my body, which is given for you....This is my blood of the New Testament, *which* shall be shed for many. It was not *bread* that was given, neither was it *wine* that was shed for many. Now these Gnostics would not have abstained from the Protestant Eucharist of mere bread and wine. There is nothing in it, that would have offended them. But they were offended at the Catholic doctrine of the real presence of the flesh of Christ in the sacrament. It clashed with their heresy, and therefore they abstained from it. How then, Rev. Sir, could you have exposed yourself so far as to assert that our doctrine on this subject originated in the 13th century, when even the wanderings of the human mind in the mazes of heresy during all the preceding ages of the church prove its existence from the very origin of Christianity, and since it is known to every man acquainted with ecclesiastical history that in rejecting it, Carlostadt only renewed the errors of the Docetæ and other branches of the Gnostic heresy broached and branded in the Apostolic age itself. To this heresy we are indebted for the evidence thus furnished of the primitive belief of the real presence of Christ in the mystery of the Eucharist. " There must be heresies," said the Apostle " that they also who are *approved* among you may be made manifest." (1 Cor. xi. 19.)

To the same cause we are indebted, for another brilliant but apparently accidental testimony in the second century. St. Irenæus who was trained in the doctrine of the Redeemer, by St. Polycarp, the disciple of St. John, uses the *real presence* of Christ in the Eucharist, as an argument against other heretics of his time, who denied the resurrection of the flesh. He compares it with the manner in which the *vine* and *wheat* are propagated, to furnish the matter of the Eucharist before the consecration." And as, says he, a section of the vine laid in the earth produces fruit in due season, and in like manner the grain of corn is multiplied, by the blessing of God, which afterwards is used for the benefit of man, and receiving on it the *word of God*, becomes the Eucharist, *which is the body and blood of Christ:* so our bodies, nourished by that Eucharist, and then laid in the earth, and dissolved in it, shall, in due time rise again." (Iren. Adver. Har. L. V. c. 11. p. 395. 397. 399.) Tertullian in like manner, says, " our flesh is fed with the body and blood of Christ, that the soul may be nourished with God." (De Resurrectione Carnis, chap. viii. p. 569.) In the 3d century, Origen speaking of the doctrine of the church, says, " In former times, baptism was obscurely represented in the cloud, and in the sea; but now regeneration is in kind, in water and the Holy Ghost. Then, obscurely, manna was the food; but now in kind, the *flesh* of the word of God is the true food ; even as he said, *my flesh is meat indeed, and my blood is drink indeed."* (Hom. vii. in Num. Tom. ii. p. 290.)

In the 4th century among a host of others, take St. Cyril of Jerusalem : " the bread and wine, says he, which *before* the invocation of the adorable Trinity, were nothing but bread and wine, *become*, after this invocation, the body and blood of Christ." (Catech. Mystag. L. N. 4. p. 281.) Shall I multiply these quotations ? It is unnecessary, but I will give you the testimony of the great first Reformer himself, to show the " unanimous consent of the fathers" on the subject of the Eucharist, and to show the extent of the delusion under which Protestants, and *perhaps* their ministers, labour when they ascribe the origin of this doctrine to your famous epoch, "1215."

He is defending his own opinion against those, who, making use of the liberty, which he had promulgated, of expounding the Scriptures by their own judgment, denied the real or corporeal presence. " That no one among the Fathers," says Luther, " numerous as they are, should have spoken of the Eucharist, as these men do, is truly astonishing. Not one of them speaks thus: *there is only bread and wine:* or, *the body and blood of Christ are not present.* And, wher.

we reflect how often the subject is treated and repeated by them, it ceases to be credible; it is not even possible; that, not so much as once, such words as these should have dropped from some of them. Surely it was of moment that men should not be drawn into error. Still, they all speak with such precision, evincing that they entertained no doubt of the presence of the body and blood! Had not this been their conviction, can it be imagined that, among so many, the negative opinion should not have been uttered on a single occasion? On other points this was not the case. But our sacramentarians, on the other hand, can proclaim only the negative or contrary opinion. These men, then, to say all in one word, have drawn their notions neither from the Scriptures nor the Fathers." (Defensio verborum—Cœnæ, Tom. VIII. p. 391. Edit. Wittemb. 1557.)

Such is the testimony of Martin Luther, who elsewhere speaks of the Eucharist as the "ADORABLE Sacrament." He tried with all his might to discard this belief, chiefly, as he tells us, because by so doing he should greatly vex the Pope. "If Carlostadt, or any one else, says he, could five years ago have convinced me, that in the sacrament there is nothing but bread and wine, he had wonderfully obliged me! For with great anxiety did I examine this point, and labour with all my force to get clear of the difficulty; *because* by this means I very well know that I should terribly incommode the Papacy. But I find I am caught without hopes of escaping. For the text of the Gospel is so *clear and strong*, that it will not easily admit of a misconstruction." (Epist. ad Amic. Argia. Tom. 7. p. 502. Witt. Ed.)

What is this text of the Gospel by which Luther "found himself caught without hopes of escaping?" We may suppose in the first place the language of St. Paul, who received his doctrine of the Eucharist by a special revelation from Jesus himself, after the ascension; which would have been unnecessary if it merely taught him the Protestant mystery, viz.: that bread and wine, are bread and wine. He taught that men by the unworthy reception of the sacrament were guilty of judgment, or damnation to themselves; "not *discerning* the *body* of the Lord." (1 Cor. x. 16, and following verses.) Now if the body of Christ was *not* in the Sacrament, how could men "*discern*" it there? Again it is to be admitted that Jesus Christ would not be guilty of duplicity in the teaching of his doctrines. When, after the miraculous multiplication, of the loaves and fishes, he introduced (John vi) the doctrine of the bread from heaven, even his own flesh and blood, to be miraculously multiplied for the life of the world, the Protestants who heard him, were scandalized; they exclaimed then, as they exclaim still, "this is a hard saying, and who can hear it"....and many of them then, as now on account of it, "went back and walked no more with him." He declared that he would give them his flesh to eat; they understood him to mean his flesh; and in the unbelieving spirit of Protestantism they inquire, "how can this man give us his flesh to eat?" This was the moment for the Son of God to have undeceived them, by telling them that he did not mean his flesh but merely some bread and wine. This doctrine would not have surprised them. But instead of softening it, by explanation, he confirmed the first declaration by adding, "Amen, Amen, I say unto you; unless you eat the flesh of the Son of man, and drink his blood, you shall not have life in you. He that eateth my flesh and drinketh my blood, hath everlasting life: and I will raise him up at the last day. For my flesh is meat indeed; and my blood is drink indeed. He that eateth my flesh, and drinketh my blood, abideth in me, and I in him," (verses 54, 55, 56, 57.) Now if those Protestant disciples who were scandalized at this language of our Lord, had misunderstood his meaning, was he not bound to remove from their minds the erroneous impression which his own words had produced? Did he use this language to drive them away from him? Did he, who would leave the ninety-nine in the desert to go after the one which had been lost; did he, I say, banish the sheep already in the fold, from the pastures of life, by speaking of " flesh and blood," (to be communicated in a mysterious manner, which *as yet* he had not revealed,) and allowing them to understand " flesh and blood," if he meant only " bread and wine ?" Protestants are *obliged* to admit that he did; and this admission, so injurious to the character of Jesus Christ, is the first implement borrowed by the Deists to sap the foundation of Christianity. If Christ's meaning had been that which Carlostadt invented for the Protestants, would he not have removed or explained the difficulty about "giving his flesh to eat," instead of confirming it, with the emphasis of repeated and solemn affirmation? Would he not have said, "Amen, Amen, I say unto you, unless you eat the *bread* of the Son of man and drink his *wine*, you shall not have life in you. He that eateth my bread and drinketh my wine hath everlasting life: and I will raise him up at the last day. For my bread is meat indeed, and my wine is drink indeed. He that eateth my bread and drinketh my wine, abideth in me and I in him." If he had said, or meant this, we should not have heard of those Protestant disciples " who went back and walked no more with him." In almost every verse of the chapter he reproaches them, not for misunderstanding his words, but for the want of belief. But they would have misunderstood him, if his meaning had been bread and wine, and in that case too, we are unable to conceive how *faith* is necessary to believe that bread and wine, are bread and wine. He spoke of his flesh and blood; he meant his flesh and blood; *all* that heard him, understood him to have spoken of his flesh and blood; and when the Protestants of that day, frightened by the " *how* can this man give us his flesh to eat," " went back and walked no more with him ;" he turned to the twelve and said to them, "will ye also go away?" And Simon Peter answered him (in the name of all) Lord to whom shall we go? thou hast the *words* of eternal life. And *we have believed*, and have known that thou art the Christ the Son of the living God." (68, 69, 70.) Peter understood the mystery of the Eucharist proposed in this discourse of Christ, as little as the rest, but he *believed* as Catholics do, that Christ could not *deceive;* and therefore he withstood the " honest, common-sense interpretation, lauded by my Rev'd opponent, and urged with great plausibility, against Jesus Christ himself, by the Protestants of Capharnaum.

What was spoken in this chapter, is actually accomplished in the institution of the holy Eucharist. "And whilst they were at supper, Jesus took bread, and blessed and broke, and gave to his disciples, and said; Take ye and eat, THIS IS MY BODY. And taking the chalice, he gave thanks; and gave to them saying: Drink ye all of this. For THIS is my blood of the New Testament, *which* shall be shed for many for the remission of sins." (Math. xxvi. 26, 27, 28) "And whilst they were eating, Jesus took bread and blessing broke, and gave to them, and said: Take ye, THIS *is my body*. And having taken the chalice, giving thanks, he gave it to them and they all drank of it. And he said to them: "THIS *is my blood* of the New Testament, WHICH *shall be shed for many.*" (Mark xiv. 22, 23, 24.) "And having taken bread he gave thanks, and brake, and gave to them saying: THIS *is my body* WHICH is given for you: *Do this* for a commemoration of me. In like manner the chalice also, *after* he had supped, saying: *this is the chalice,* the New Testament in my blood, which shall be shed for you." (Luke xxii. 19, 20.) "For I have received of the Lord, that also which I delivered to you, that the Lord Jesus, the night in which he was betrayed, took *bread,* and giving thanks, broke, and *said*, take ye and eat: THIS *is my body* WHICH *shall be delivered for you;* do this for a commemoration of me. In like manner also the chalice, after he had supped, saying: This chalice is the New Testament in my blood: this do ye, as often as you shall drink it, for a commemoration of me. For as often as you shall eat this bread and drink this chalice, you shall show forth the death of the Lord, till he come. Wherefore whosoever shall eat this bread or drink this chalice of the Lord unworthily, shall be guilty of the body and blood of the Lord. But let a man prove himself, and so let him eat of that bread and drink of the chalice. For he that eateth and drinketh unworthily, eateth and drinketh judgment to himself, not discerning the Lord's body." (1 Cor. xi. 23, 24, 25, 26, 27, 28, 29.)

Now according to the Protestant doctrine of the eucharist, when ever the word " body and blood" occurs in these passages, we are to understand " bread and wine." Consequently, since Christ spoke of the chalice as of the "blood, *which* was to be shed for many for the remission of sins," we are to understand that we have been *redeemed* by the giving of bread and the shedding of wine. There is no escaping this consequence, on the Protestant principle. Having shown above that the *Protestant* doctrine of the Eucharist, denying the real presence, originated in the hatred and jealousy which the fame of Luther, roused in the breast of his would-be *rival*, Carlostadt, (as Melanchton testifies,) having shown by the testimony of the Holy Fathers, that the Catholic doctrine of the real presence was held by the church, and rejected by the heretics of the first age—that is 1200 years before the date assigned by Mr. Breckinridge—I shall allude briefly to the ruinous bearing which the Protestant Eucharist has on the divinity of Christ, and the whole system of Christianity.

1. Of all the wonders operated by Jesus in the institution of his religion, the only one which a mere creature deputed by God *could*

not accomplish, is that which subsists in the real presence, in the Eucharist. This doctrine then is the shield of his divinity. He might have accomplished all the miracles that Protestants believe of him, and yet be nothing more than what the Socinians represent;—but to accomplish the miracle which we contemplate not with the eye of the body, but with the eye of faith, in the mystery of the holy Eucharist—he must have been God. To *creatures* deputed by God, some *power* was given, but to Christ ALL POWER both in heaven and on earth—and it was in the Eucharist alone that this ALL power was exercised. This connexion between the real presence in the Eucharist, and the Divinity of "the word," was quoted by St. Irenæus in the 2d century. (Adv. Hor. L. 4. c. 18. No. 4.)

2. Jesus Christ must have foreseen the terrible consequence of the language he made use of in reference to the Eucharist. He must have foreseen the error, into which his immediate disciples were about to fall, and which was to be entailed on the church until the coming of Andreas Carlostadius—who to reform the church, merely invented a new gesture for Christ, making him point to his own breast, when he said, "*this* is my body." Did Christ foresee this supposed error of the real presence? If he did, it being founded on his own express words, he was bound by his promise to the church (Math. xxviii. 19.) to prevent it becoming general:—if he did not foresee it—then goes his divinity by the board. When the Unitarians urge this argument, how can the other Protestants answer it?

3. The Apostles warned the Christians of future errors, such as the denial of the reality of the flesh of Christ, his divinity, and the resurrection, &c. But against the supposed error of the real presence of Christ in the Eucharist, which according to the acknowledgment of eminent Protestants was believed from the second century, they take no precaution; though according to the Protestant doctrine of bread and wine, it changed the religion of Christ into a religion of impiety.

4. According to the Protestant hypothesis, the religion of Christ became the falsest religion of earth, and what he preached, was perverted into a system of idolatry almost immediately after his ascension into heaven. Did the eternal Son of God become man, to establish a religion so short-lived, so degenerate, and so idolatrous as this supposes? Christians adored Christ's body in the Eucharist; and if the Eucharist were mere bread and wine, it follows, that from the beginning the followers of the cross were idolaters. Such are the destructive consequences, if the Protestant doctrine were true.

But on the other hand, admit the doctrine of the church—bend the stubborn neck of what you call "honest common-sense interpretation," to the yoke of faith, believe that Jesus Christ has love to design and omnipotence to accomplish what he declared—this is my body—this is my blood—and you will escape the horrible consequences of the Protestant system. Then you will recognise "the hidden manna," in the sacrament,—the wisdom of God, in mystery. Then you will understand the meaning of "Christ, a Priest for ever

2 S

according to the order of Melchesidec." Then you will understand the connexion between this priesthood—communicated at the last supper, "*do this* for a commemoration of me,"—and the "ALTAR of which they have no right *to eat* who serve *the tabernacle;*"—you will perceive the "clean offering," from the rising to the setting of the sun, among the Gentiles, as foretold by Malachy, (i. 10, 11,) and in the sacrifice of the mass, the death of the Lord, in the language of St. Paul, "shown forth till he come." Then you will find your faith according with the language and institution of Christ, the apostle of the Gentiles, the apostolical fathers, the whole Christian church of all nations and ages, except a few straggling sects of heretics in the by-ways of antiquity. Then order, beauty, consistency, and stateliness will appear in the edifice of Christianity But deny the real presence, and it will experience the fate of Jerusalem—not a stone shall be left upon a stone. Protestant Germany at the present day, is the sad proof that what I have here asserted, is not speculation, but *history*. But who can believe such a doctrine? I answer, all those who deem Jesus Christ worthy of belief. That infidels should disbelieve it does not surprise me.

But I cannot understand it? I answer, you can understand it as well as you can the Trinity—or the union of the divine and human nature in the person of Jesus Christ. When you study mathematics you *reason*—but in revelation you believe. But is it possible that Jesus Christ can be seated at the right hand in heaven, and yet be whole and entire under each of the consecrated hosts in the world? I answer, Jesus Christ is God—he has said so, and therefore it is possible, and infallibly certain. But think of the indignities to which he is exposed? I answer, that they are not greater than those which he suffered when he was sold by his disciple, buffeted and spit upon by his people, scourged and crucified. His body in the Sacrament can suffer no more—can die no more—it is the glorified body of the cross, still offered up to perpetuate the sacrifice of Calvary in a different manner—to "show forth the death of the Lord till he come." But if an insect or reptile consume the host? I answer, the consequence is nothing more horrible than if an insect or reptile consumed some portion of the adorable blood which flowed from his wounds as he hung upon the cross. But if arsenic be mixed in the elements of the eucharist they still remain after the consecration? I answer, that Christ appointed bread and wine, to be operated on by the words of consecration—and not *arsenic*. But Mr. Breckinridge says that this doctrine is "as young as the year 1215? I answer, that if Mr. Breckinridge says queer things, it is for himself and those who sympathise in his prejudices to see to it. But he says also that if this doctrine be true, we cannot believe our senses? I answer, that St. Ambrose refuted this objection 1400 years ago, (De Initiandis cix. Tom. IV. p. 350, 351.)—And that Mr. B. must have forgotten both his natural philosophy and his New Testament when he repeated it. The senses judge only of *appearances;* and we read in a book which Protestants profess to respect that the Holy Ghost *appeared* in the shape of a dove.

There is no end, however, to objections. Objections against the real presence the Incarnation, the resurrection of the body, the Trinity of persons in the Godhead, and the immortality of the soul are equally numerous, and equally plausible, if that every thing and nothing which my Rev. opponent calls "honest, *common-sense* interpretation," is to be the arbiter of belief. Who can comprehend any of them? There are nevertheless one or two objections common among Protestants from whom we might expect better things, and which I shall here notice as well for their want of truth, as their want of decency.—Catholics are represented as adoring bread and wine in the Eucharist, which is expressed by calling the Sacrament a "wafer." This ungenerous trick of our opponents is unworthy of Christians. They know that we adore no "wafer," that our adoration is directed to Jesus Christ, believed to be truly present under the *appearances* of bread and wine. But I lament to have read in the course of this correspondence the expressions, "that we make our God and eat him," it sounds like the buffoonery of Tom Paine. It is unworthy of a Christian origin, and I leave it even to sensible Protestants whether a doctrine resting on the arguments of this letter should have been treated of in language so coarse, and so indecent. How many gross questions may not the infidels ask touching the sacred person of Jesus Christ, by imitating the licentious pen of a zealous, but indiscreet, polemic. Such language shocks the feelings, but does not touch the faith, of a Catholic reader. It may make him weep to see Jesus Christ insulted, as he conceives, on the Sacrament of his love, but it only binds him more intimately to the object of his faith, and of his affection. He knows that what Protestant incredulity calls "making God," is the act which Christ commanded. "Do this for a commemoration of me." He knows that what Protestant prejudice or indecency calls "eating God," is the act of religious obedience to him who said, unless you eat of the flesh of the Son of man and drink of his blood you cannot have life in you, and who said in like manner, "take ye, and eat, *this is my body*."

Now, Rev. Sir, although I have been obliged to pass over testimonies sufficient to fill a volume, establishing the constant belief of the real presence in the eucharist, still, I make bold to assert that all the ministers in America cannot furnish as much positive evidence from all the documents in existence in support of the mere bread and wine of the Protestant Sacrament, as this letter contains, imperfect as it is. They may say that the word "signify" is not found in the Hebrew, and that Christ consequently used the words "this is" instead of "this *signifies* my body." Zuinglius actually made this change in the text. But what do they make of Jesus Christ—when they represent him opening the door to supposed error, which he foresaw, merely because the Hebrew was a jejune language!! For want of a suitable expression, the Son of God laid the foundation of perennial idolatry in his church!!! And after all the New Testament was written in the Greek tongue, not the Hebrew. Truly Protestants must be easily satisfied in their doctrines. They may say that the Fathers often applied the terms, *figure, sign, symbol, antitype, bread* and *wine*, to the eucharist even after consecration.—It is true they ap plied these terms to the exterior appearances—but this only proves, that under these *signs, symbols*, &c. they believed the substantial existence of the thing signified, viz: the flesh and blood of Jesus Christ. Hence, none were allowed to participate of the Eucharist who did not first "ADORE." All the ancient liturgies, heretical as well as Catholic, with the exception of some few sects, contain the doctrine of the Eucharist as it is believed at this day in the Catholic church. That of the Apostles, those of St. Basil and St. John Chrysostom, the ancient Gallican liturgy, the Mozarabic, the Nestorian, the Jacobite of Syria, the Copht, the Ethiopian are all identically the same with the Roman Missal, on that doctrine which you have made to originate in the 13th century, A. D. 1215. I will allow any gentleman who is a scholar, and desirous to verify what I assert to compare them, at my house. But where can the Protestant doctrine of mere bread and wine find testimony to support it? Would to God, that Protestants would reflect in the soberness of genuine piety, on the mutilated Christianity which their fathers in the ardour of religious strife have bequeathed them. They would not reject the substance for the shadow as they have done.

However, you have to prove that the Protestant religion is the religion of Christ, and perhaps you have furnished yourself by this time, with the long expected arguments. You have closed your last letter by invoking the aid of Bishop Jewel, and quoting a list of requirements which is long and arrogant enough. But you should recollect that his Panegyrist and Biographer, Dr. Humphreys, admits that the good Bishop "spoiled himself *and his cause*" by the *boldness* of his *challenges*. It might have been well if you had seen this, before you issued yours. Besides Jewel, on his death bed, directed his chaplain to make known after his decease "that what he had written, he had done against his own knowledge and conscience, only to comply with the state, and that religion which it had set up." (Dr. Smith's Prudential Balance, published in 1609, page 54.) In appealing to the Episcopalians, then, for aid, you might have made a happier selection than Bishop Jewel   Yours, &c

JOHN HUGHES

CONTROVERSY. No. XXVIII.

IS THE PROTESTANT RELIGION THE RELIGION OF CHRIST?

Philadelphia, August 9th, 1833.

To the Rev. John Hughes.

Sir,—You complain for the second time, in your last letter, that I have "*long denied you*" the title of "Rev'd. Sir." I assure you, it was as far from my intention to rob you of your honour, by *omitting* it, as it is now to flatter your weakness and vanity by *inserting* it. I have uniformly addressed you thus, "the Rev. John Hughes;" and surely the repetition (in immediate succession,) of "Rev'd. Sir," is both a violation of good taste, and a useless tautology. I see, however, that the little urchin at the press who attached two ††'s to your name, in my last proof sheet, understood your wishes better than I do. But I would respectfully admonish you, that the title *once* written, frowns upon him "who seeks honour of men :" and that it is not on the number, or magnificence of our titles, but on the spirit with which we fulfil our ministry, that our supreme care should be bestowed. But personal arrogance is not the only characteristic of the introduction to your last letter. The tone of denunciation and bigotry seems to rise, as the cause you advocate sinks; and you supply the defect of argument, with the increase of pretension. You tell us "that NO Christians agreed with Protestants in doctrines, from the days of Christ until the coming of Luther, and *very few* since." It is no *new* doctrine with your church to consign all men, out of her communion, to eternal woe. It is an article of your creed, that "none can be saved," who do not hold the Roman Catholic faith : and " the Canon Law" makes it "necessary to salvation for every human being to be subject to the Roman Pontiff." While the people stand amazed at the unparalleled bigotry and intolerance of Romanism, they must at least approve your candour, in applying these doctrines to the *unhappy* millions of American Protestants.

That this is the universal spirit of the system, whenever it is honestly disclosed, or forced out by controversy, may readily be gathered from the monuments of the Papacy in every age and country where it has had a being. Take for example the notes on the Rhemish translation of the New Testament. The text is the same with the New Testament of the Doway Bible, lately republished in this country. These notes have been prudently suppressed in that edition. The following are specimens. Note on Heb. v. 7. "The Translators of the English (Protestant) Bible ought to be abhorred to the depths of Hell." Note on Gal. i. 8. Perverting and commending a passage from Jerome, they say, "the zeal of Catholic men ought to be so great towards all heretics, and their doctrines, that they should give them the anathema, though they are never so dear to them ; so as not even to spare their own parents." Luke ix. 55, 56. The Samaritans had rejected Christ ; and the indignant disciples asked Him, if, like Elias, they should "command fire to come down from Heaven and consume them." "But he turned and rebuked them, and said, ye know not what manner of spirit ye are of ; for the Son of man is not come to destroy men's lives, but to save them." On these passages, and in direct contradiction of our Lord, the commentary remarks: "Not justice, nor all rigorous punishment of persons is here forbidden, nor Elias's fact (conduct) reprehended; nor the *Church*, nor Christian Princes blamed for putting heretics to death." Rev. xvii. 6. "The blood of *Heretics* is not the blood of Saints; no more than the blood of thieves, man-killers, and other malefactors; for the shedding of which blood by order of justice no commonwealth shall answer." Rev. ii. 6, 20, 22. "Of all things, Christian people, especially Bishops, should hate heretics, that is, their wicked doctrines and conditions.........As Lutherans, Zuinglians, &c. &c. " He (Christ) warneth Bishops to be zealous, and stout against the false Prophets, of *what sort soever*, by alluding covertly to the example of holy Elias that in zeal killed four hundred and fifty false prophets." John x. 1. " Arius, Calvin, Luther, and all that succeed them in room and doctrine, are thieves and murderers." Acts xix. 19. " A Christian man is *bound* to burn or deface all wicked books, of what sort soever; especially *heretical* books. Therefore the *Church* hath taken order against all such books."

This is the *charity* of Rome. These are the doctrines upon oath, of every Roman Priest, whatever be the honied words of liberality and love which distil from his lips, or run from his ready pen. And we may see what we have to hope for in America, if by the skill of the Jesuits, this last refuge of civil and religious liberty shall be violated and controlled by the Pope of Rome.

I proceed still further to exhibit the grounds of our *protest* against the *doctrines, corruptions, &c.* of the church of Rome. And,

I. The abounding and shocking immoralities, either tolerated by the church of Rome, or directly produced by her institutions.

In a church where absolute subjection to her supreme head, is the very touch-stone of orthodoxy, authority cannot be wanting to correct and punish vice. By a single act, one Pope abolished the immense power of the Jesuits; by another act, another Pope has recently revived that infamous order in all its force. Authority to reform is therefore not wanting. And yet, as I have in part already shown, in several unanswered letters, the church of Rome had become so corrupt in *its morals* that the whole world was crying out for several ages for a Reformation. This too, was not a temporary, local, or partial corruption. It had existed *for ages before* the Reformation: it was *universal*, extending to all parts of the world, and to all orders in the church, beginning at the Popes and Cardinals, Bishops and Priests: it was *deep* and *dreadful*, striking at the foundation of morals; so that religion lay expiring on the altar, by the hands of her Priests. The history of the immoralities of your Popes, Prelates, and Priests alone would fill a volume. We give (in addition to those recorded in previous letters) only a few examples. Erasmus (Ann. in. Epis. ad Tim. c. 3.) writes: "If any one consider the state of these times, how great a part of mankind the multitude of monks take up; how great a part the collection of Priests and clergymen; and then consider how few out of so great a number truly preserve chastity of life, with how great scandal most of them are openly incestuous, and incontinent, into what kinds of lusts, innumerable of them degenerate, he will perhaps conclude it were convenient that those who are not continent, may have the freedom of public marriage, which they may purely and chastely, and without infamy, maintain." Gerson (De vita Spirit. Animae Lec. 4.) affirms " that unchaste Priests must be tolerated or no Priests can be had." Clemangis (De Corrupt. Eccl. stat. p. 15.) writes that *the Priests openly kept concubines at a stated price paid to the Bishop*. In Germany this system was carried so far, that the *licenses* to do so, were *forced* even upon those who did not wish them, that the tax might not be lost; and in Switzerland (Sleidan Com. 1. 3.) every new Pastor was required to take a concubine that he might not endanger the *families* of his charge. The Bishop of Saltzburg (Onus Ecclesiac chap. 22.) tells us that " the nunneries in his time were as publicly prostituted as the common brothels." Sunt propatula ut ipsa loca veneris. Thurnus (a Roman Catholic Historian, B. 37. p. 766, A. D. 1566) says, that when Pope Paul 5th, thought of putting down the *public brothels* in Rome, and expelling the courtezans the city, the senate of Rome, *instigated privately by the clergy, interceded with him not to do it:* and they added this reason, that if such a crowd of *unmarried Priests* were left in the city *without* these evil women, it would be impossible to preserve the chastity of their families." This shocking state of things among the Priests of the Holy City was nearly half a century after the Reformation of Luther had begun. Nor let it be supposed that this was done without approval. It was defended and sustained by example, license, and even by publicly avowed principle. It was tolerated when REFORM was called for from every throne, and from all parts of the world. It is notorious that the Pope of Rome *licensed* brothels and built stews in the city of Rome, and at one time he drew from them an annual revenue of 20,000 ducats; the crowd of such women in the keeping of the priests was immense; and the revenue collected week after week, was taken from the *chest* in which the *price of iniquity was cast*, and divided equally between the houses, the women, and the Popes! If you would have more full references, they are at hand. Bellarmine, sustained by Coster, Pighius, Cardinal Hosius, and Cardinal Campegius, does not hesitate to declare " *that it is a greater evil (i. e.* under a vow of celibacy) *so to marry than to commit fornication.*" Est majus malum sic nubere, quam fornicari. (Bel. b. 2 De Monachis c. 34.) and the reason which he assigns for this is its own best comment, viz. "because she who thus marries renders herself incapable of keeping her vow; but she who commits fornication is not incapable." Quia quae ita nubit, reddit se inhabilem ad votum servandum; quod non facit, quae fornicatur. I need not here remind you of the incest of Paul the 3d, the sodomies of Julius the 3d, and the vile commerce of Innocent the 10th with his brother's wife, Olympia. Abbott Gualdi pronounces his amours almost without a parallel for scandal and illicit love. John Casa, Archbishop of Beneventum, and legate of the Pope, published an apology for sodomy; and Gualter Mapes complains that the Priests *used to suspend the salvation of females at confession, upon the condition of yielding to their infamous wishes!* Horror and shame alternately possess me while I record these enormities. But if the *perusal* makes us shudder and blush, what must the *perpetration* of them have been?

We said that these immoralities were in part, produced by the peculiar institutions of the church. We alluded to the monasteries, nunneries, vows of celibacy, and especially the celibacy of the clergy. Strange as it may seem, these institutions and vows, were professedly established and enforced to advance piety, and secure purity of life. But in this as in most cases where men attempt to be wiser than God, the result has been of the most disastrous character. We would not be understood indiscriminately to condemn a life of voluntary celibacy. " Both virginity and marriage were states of innocence, and of paradise. Christ has consecrated both, having been born of a virgin, and yet of a woman who was then betrothed and afterwards married." The Council of Trent not only encouraged monastic vows, but *enforced* celibacy on the clergy. This is both a novelty and an innovation in the church of God. The word of God declares, Heb. xiii. 4. "*that marriage is honourable in all.*" The church of Rome on the contrary *forbids* it to her clergy. The word of God declares that " a bishop must be the husband of one wife." Tit. i. 6. The church of Rome forbids it; and dares to put asunder what God has joined together, separating the priest or bishop from his lawful wife, and anathematizes those who dissent from her decree. Chrysostom, on the last named Scripture, makes this decisive comment : " the apostle prescribed this passage to this end, that he might stop the mouths of heretics who reproached marriage ; declaring thereby that marriage is no unclean thing, but so honourable that a married man may be exalted to the sacred throne of a bishop." (Hom. 2. c. 1. ad. Tit.) It is very remarkable that the Apostle Paul in immediate connexion with his definition of a Bishop's qualifications (among which he mentions that he must be the husband of one wife, 1 Tim. iii. 2.) predicts the coming of seducing spirits who should depart from the faith, " FORBID TO MARRY, *and command to abstain from meats.*" I leave the application for yourself, reminding you that the early heretics, viz: the Manichees, Nicholaitans, &c. unite with the church of Rome and the followers of Joanna Southcote and Jemima Wilkinson in more modern times, in " FORBIDDING TO MARRY." Radolpho Pio-di Carpo, an Italian Cardinal in the Council of Trent, when various princes pressed the propriety of the priests marrying, told the Council in a speech, " this inconvenience would follow from it, that having house, wife, and children, they will not depend on the Pope, but on the prince; and their love to their children will make them yield to any prejudice of the church, and they will seek to make the benefices hereditary, and so in a short time the authority of the Apostolic See will be confined within Rome." (Hist. Coun. Trent. B. 5.) It was the abounding corruptions of the church of Rome, and especially of Rome itself, that made the candid Roman Catholic author of the " Onus Ecclesiae," call Rome " the seat of the Beast, the church of the wicked, the kingdom of darkness, sustained by simony and ambition, filled with covetousness, a GULPH OF CRIMES." (Chap. 21.)

You have been pleased, entirely to overlook the long extracts which I made, in letter No. 18, addressed to Pope Paul the 3d, by four Cardinals, and four other distinguished Prelates, at his own request, containing a picture of the church, drawn by the hands of its friends, which for deformity and crime finds not a parallel in the history of the world. I also gave you large extracts, in Letter No. 20, from the address of the Bishops at Banonia to Paul the 3d, and referred you, for this shocking but faithful sketch, to Verjerius and Wolfius. I pointed you also to the "*one hundred grievances*" of the German States, detailing the corruptions of the church, and calling for reform. But nothing can break the profound and wise silence which you have decreed upon this subject. Without further enlarging upon it now, I would direct our readers to the "Provincial Letters" of Pascal, in which, though himself a Roman Catholic, he exposes with the pen of a master, the casuistry of the Jesuits in destroying the *foundation of morals*. There, within a short compass, it is clearly shown, how the order of the Jesuits, who are now in high favour at Rome, make truth, and sacred oaths, and loyalty, and justice, and chastity, and principle, in all its forms, give way to their refined interpretations and infamous doctrines. And yet I find that on the last Sabbath day the President of Georgetown College, District of Columbia, delivered in St. Joseph's church in this city, *a Panegyric* (according to public notice) *on St. Ignatius Layola, founder of the society of Jesuits!!!* How well has St. Chrysostom said, (In 1 Tim. hom. 5.) "When men lead corrupt lives it is impossible they should keep themselves from falling into perverse doctrines."

II. *We would next exhibit the forged miracles, and the legalized superstitions of the church of Rome*

We have already, in a previous letter, made reference to the authority of the Breviary as the book of common prayer in the Church of Rome. The Latin edition of this work, now before me, revised by three Popes and of unquestioned authority, is a very fountain of the grossest frauds and superstition. I find for example under the festival appointed for the 15th day of October (pages 1011, 1012) in honour of the Virgin Saint Teresa, the following narrative. "She burned with so strong a desire for chastising her body, that although disease seemed to deter from it, she inflicted on herself the severest pains and penalties by the use of hair-cloth, chains, pricking-nettles, and likewise by most severe flagellations: and sometimes while rolling herself on thorns, she would thus hold communion with God; '*O Lord, I must afflict myself or die.*' Being premonished of her death, she breathed out her *most pure* soul to God in the form of a dove, aged sixty-seven, in the year 1502. Jesus Christ appeared to her, as she was dying, surrounded by bands of angels; and immediately a lifeless and barren tree, which stood near to her cell bloomed forth. Her body continues *incorrupt* until this day, (the 18th century) circumfused in a sacred fluid, and is worshipped with religious veneration. She was made illustrious by miracles wrought by her, both before and after death. Gregory the 15th has canonized her." Here we see *flagellation* and other self-inflicted punishments recommended, and the most notorious frauds, gravely put upon the people, in their standard prayer book, for real miracles.

It is related of Dionysius in the same book, "that after he had been beheaded he took his head in his arms, and carried it no less than two thousand paces." (See Breviary 1007 p.)* In the festival of August the 1st, in honour of *the chains* of St. Peter (p. 877) is the following narrative. "Eudoxia the wife of the Emperor Theodosius the younger, being on a pilgrimage at Jerusalem, received among other presents, the chain with which the Apostle Peter was bound by Herod. Eudoxia with pious veneration, sent this chain to her daughter, who was then at Rome, who carried it to the Pope, the Pope in return showed her another chain with which the same apostle had been bound by Nero. As soon as the two chains were brought together, it came to pass that they instantly flew to each other, and the links formed one chain as if welded by art." In honour of so great a miracle, the church instituted the festival "*ad vincula.*" In the proclamation of the jubilee for 1825, the Pope expressly mentions this chain as an inducement to the faithful to visit Rome, that they might kiss it, and secure the indulgences peculiar to such miracles and relics, &c. In pages 971-2, are recorded the feasts and miracles of St. Januarius, living and dead. We are seriously told on the authority of the infallible church, that "by means of his dead body which was preserved at Naples, an eruption of Mount Vesuvius that was spreading desolation far and wide, was miraculously extinguished. What is still more illustrious, his blood, some of which is preserved in a glass phial a Naples, in a coagulated state, when brought within reach of the Martyr's head, is immediately *liquefied*, and *boils up* as if recently shed; and this miracle may be seen even at *the present time.*" That there may be no question about this record, I give the original. Praeclarum illud quoque, quod ejus sanguis, qui in ampulla vitrea concretus asservatur, cum in conspectu capitis ejusdem Martyris ponitur, admirandum in modum collique—fieri, et ebullire, perinde atque recens effusus. Ad haec usque tempora cernitur. Great as is this miracle, the chemist's test has been studiously resisted. It would be easy to settle this question by such a trial, and *real* miracles invite inquiry. But the Pope is too wise to hazard an experiment, and yet it is a miracle professedly of fifteen hundred years standing, and is at this day sanctioned by the Roman Breviary and celebrated in the public worship of the whole church. When the French troops first occupied Naples, this miracle, which is *annual*, failed to occur; with the design of agitating the people and producing an injurious impression towards the French. But the French general sent a positive order to the saint to do his duty under the pain of making an example of the priest if he failed. He promptly obeyed: the miracle was immediately *wrought!*

Once more: The translation of the house of Loretto from Palestine to Italy, is recorded in the collect of that festival, even in a direct address to the Deity. It is pretended, that this house, in which the Virgin Mary was born at Nazareth, was translated by angels in the 13th century across the Sea into Dalmatia, and afterwards into Italy, where it now stands under the name of "our Lady of Loretto's

Chapel." When the question arises about the truth of the miracle and the identity of the house, the Bulls of Popes are adduced to confirm the faith of the doubting. With such frauds are the bigoted and deluded millions deceived, and by such attestations does the infallible church confirm the truth of her doctrines, and the holiness of her character. The following prophecy, (2 Thess. ii. 3—10,) though penned in the first century, is as true to the life, as if it had been written by an *eye-witness.* " Let no man deceive you by any means: for that day shall not come, except there come a *falling away* first, and that *man of sin* be revealed the son of perdition; who opposeth and exalteth himself above all that is called God, or that is worshipped; so that he, as God, sitteth in the temple of God, showing himself that he is God. Remember ye not, that when I was yet with you, I told you these things? And now ye know what withholdeth that he might be revealed in his time. For the mystery of iniquity doth already work; only he who now letteth, will let, until he be taken out of the way, and then shall that wicked be revealed, whom the Lord shall consume with the spirit of his mouth, and shall destroy with the brightness of his coming: Even him, whose *coming is after the working of Satan, with all power and signs, and lying wonders, and with all deceivableness of unrighteousness* in them that perish; because they received not the love of the truth that they might be saved."

Besides the false miracles thus attested by the Church of Rome, the rites, ceremonies, and observances of the church are characterized by the grossest superstitions, and exhibit a ritual-worship derived directly from the Pagans. The celebration of the Mass, the burning of tapers, the whole system of processions, the use of holy water, their exorcisms, beads, rosaries, &c., their talismans, amulets, and Agnus Dei, their lustrations, blessing of beasts, &c. &c., constitute one deforming assemblage of heathenish superstition. Look for example at the style of Baptism as contrasted with the simple institution of Jesus Christ. " The Priest in the first place calls for a lighted candle; he then procures some holy water, he next calls for salt, which has been exorcised, some water, tow, the oil-box, &c.; he then prepares a solution of salt and water for the aspersion of the child, much in the way in which holy water is made, describing hieroglyphics with his hand, and pronouncing at the same time some cabalistic words in Latin. Next he commences expelling the Devil from the child, he then puts salt into his mouth, besmears the eyes, nose, and ears of the child with spittle, and after pouring water on the child's head, rubs sweet oil on its crown and shoulders."

We spoke of talismans, amulets, &c., as sanctioned by the Church of Rome. Take as a specimen the Agnus Dei, or little image of a Lamb, made of a compound of virgin-wax, balm, and consecrated oil, which they hang about the neck, like the Heathen, to preserve them from diseases, evil spirits, &c. The Pope consecrates the Agnus Dei, in the first year of his Pontificate, and afterwards every seventh year, on Saturday, before low Sunday, with many solemn ceremonies. The pretended properties and virtues of these talismans are described by Pope Urban V. (who sent one of them to Constantinople to be presented to the Emperor,) in the following inimitable lines:

> "Balsamus et munda cera cum Chrismatis unda,
> Conficiunt Agnum quod munus do tibi magnum.
> Fulgura desursum depellit, omne malignum.
> Peccatum frangit, ut Christi sanguis, et angit.
> Pregnans servatur, simul et partus liberatur.
> Dona defert dignis, virtutem destruit ignis.
> Portatus munde, de fluctibus eripit undae."

I refer these infallible and lofty lines for poetical rendering to the pen of your *holy* poet, cidevant, Tom Moore. Our readers for the present must be satisfied with the following plain English translation. "They prevent the ill effects of thunder and lightning, they preserve pregnant women from miscarriages, and procure a happy delivery. They grant spiritual gifts to the worthy. They extinguish fires and preserve from drowning."

In the last pages of the Missal, whose leaves you doubtless turn over every day as a Priest at the altar, there are contained exorcisms and benedictions for salt, and water, and for the mingling of these, for sheep, for bread, for fruit and other food, for candles, places, houses, beds, ships, sacerdotal robes, &c. &c. We give as an example the *exorcism of water*. "I exorcise thee O creature of water, in the name of God † the Omnipotent Father, and in the name of Jesus † Christ his Son, our Lord, and by the virtue of the Holy † Ghost; that thou mayest become exorcised water, and may prevail in chasing away the power of the evil one, and be able to supplant and expel him and his fallen angels, by the merit of the same Jesus Christ our Lord." *The prayer of consecration.* "O Lord be present to bless our invocation and infuse into this element, thus prepared by many fold purifications, the virtue of thy benediction: that this thy creature made subservient to thy mysteries, may have the effect of divine grace in expelling devils and diseases: that in whatever houses or places of the faithful this water may be sprinkled, all noxious uncleanness may cease: let no pestilent spirit or corrupt air abide in them: let all the snares of the evil one come to naught: and if there be any thing which threatens the safety or quiet of the inhabitants, may it be *chased away* by the sprinkling of this water," &c.

From these most painful and humiliating details I gladly turn away, asking, if any church enjoining such heathenish rites and superstitious ceremonies as these, and sustaining them by such barefaced impostures called miracles, can be the true, the only true, the holy and infallible church of Jesus Christ, out of which there is no salvation? These are some of the errors and evils, against which we *protest*, and for whose *reform* our fathers plead in vain!

III. As you profess to have in the Church of Rome the unbroken and exclusive succession from the Apostle Peter to the present time, I will next examine this claim.

I have, already, proved (see letter No. 22,) that the *supremacy* of the Pope is an anti-christian usurpation of which the Scriptures are wholly silent; and whose *origin* is found, ages after the death of Christ. But even on your own principles, Bellarmine allows (B. 2. c. 1. of the Pope,) "The right of succession in the Popes of Rome is founded in this, that Peter, by Christ's appointment, placed his seat at Rome, and there remained until his death."

1. But there is no certainty whatever that Peter ever was at Rome. The Scripture is wholly silent about it. Paul was there once and again; and in his epistles written from Rome he records a long list of names, and among them even a *refugee-slave;* but not a word of POPE PETER. The Rhemish Commentators are so anxious to prove this from Scripture, that they say *Babylon,* from which Peter wrote his first epistle, was *Rome.* But if this be so, then confessedly, Rome is the anti-christ mentioned in Revelations, 16 and 17th chapters.

2. Allowing that Peter was at Rome, there is not a shadow of proof that he had his *seat* there, or that Christ appointed him to be Bishop of Rome. The Bible is wholly silent on this subject also. Yet surely in fixing the imperial seat, and appointing the monarch and head of the universal church, we might expect it to be full and definite, saying, " this is the place," "this is the man," " hear ye him." So far from this, Peter had quite another sphere. His field of labour was far, far away from Rome; and his office as an Apostle, made it impossible for him to be a Bishop, or to be local, or to have a successor at all.

3. The Apostle John survived Peter some 30 years. Hence the succession, if any, must come from John, or else the Pope who succeeded Peter was the head of the church, and above an Apostle. But you do not pretend to trace succession from John; and your own doctrines lead you to deny that the successor of Peter was superior to John. Therefore your succession is irreparably ruined at the threshold. If not, will you please to explain this dilemma?

4. It is not agreed among yourselves whether Linus, or Clemens, or Cletus, or Anacletus succeeded as *second* Pope. The Fathers are divided about it; so are your standard authors. *Bellarmine owns this to be the fact.* Here then, the succession fails again, at the *third* link.

5. What were the *character and doctrine*, of these pretended successors of Peter. There were fifty Popes in a line, says Genebrard who were *Apostates.* Baronius tells us that strumpets elected several Popes, whom they also ruled, having driven away the *true Popes, and that their names were written in the catalogues of the Popes only to note the times.* These testimonies have been brought forward before; but you lack " *intention,*" and therefore they are of no avail. Bellarmine says, (Book 4. c. 14. on Popes,) "that at the Council of Constance there were three who claimed to be Popes, John XXIII., Gregory XII., and Benedict XIII.; each having very learned advocates; and it could not be readily decided which was the true Popes." Again, (in his B. 2. c. 19. of Councils) he says, " a doubtful Pope is reckoned no Pope." Since then there were *false Popes,* and *apostate Popes,* and *several Popes at once,* who being *doubtful,* were *no* Popes, is not the *succession* of your church forever gone? And then as to the *doctrines* of these Popes, what were they? Ambrose saith, " they have not the *succession* of Peter, who have not his *faith.*" (Ambrose de Poenit. B. I. c. 6.) Gratian has practised a fraud upon this passage, making it read " seat"

of Peter, instead of "faith" of Peter. This is owning that "in faith" the succession was gone. I have heretofore mentioned several heretical Popes. Their contradictions of each other, and their departure from the faith of the church, are matters of such notoriety that you will not deny them. If you do, I can name them at will. I will here only advert to Liberius, the Arian Pope. And I ask you, did he or did he not, sign the Arian Creed? Yes, or no? He *did*, as your own historians confess, publicly adopt the Arian Heresy. Then while he was an Arian, what became of the Apostolical succession? when the Head of the universal Church as you declare him to have been, became radically, and avowedly a Heretic, either his heresy made his office vacant, or else he continued the Head of the Church. If the former, then the succession was *broken* for *want* of a Pope. If the latter, then your succession is kept up through the *Arian line*, and by the destruction of the true faith.

6. The succession in your church is ruined by the schisms and electoral variations of the Papacy. Geddes enumerated twenty-four schisms. Mayer and Baronius twenty-six; and Onufrius thirty, which is the common estimate. The *second* schism in the Papacy lasted for three years. It arose between Liberius and Felix, both of whom were *Arians;* yet *now* both, are on the calender of Roman saints! The *seventh* schism distinguished the Popedoms of Silverius and Vigilius. Silverius obtained the Pontificate by simony, and was supplanted by Vigilius, by similar means. They were rival Popes, occupying professedly the Papal chair at the same time. According to canon law, as well as common sense, this was impossible; and yet the schism, nullified the succession. Formosus and Sergius disgraced the Papacy, divided the church and destroyed the succession, by the *thirteenth* schism. About this time a number of the Popes were monsters upon earth. Stephen, who succeeded Formosus, violated his grave, and insulted his dead body, as we have already related. John the tenth rescinded in turn the acts of Stephen; and Sergius again the acts of John, restoring the ordinations of Stephen and annulling the ordinations of Formosus. Amidst these conflicts, schisms, and mutual abrogations of each other's Pontifical ordinations and acts, where was the succession, either of the Popes, or of the clergy? In the 11th century Pope Sylvester, Pope John, and Pope Benedict, all reigned at the same time, exhibiting a specimen of a Papal Cerberus. The great western schism, being the *twenty-ninth* division, lasted for fifty years, and extended through the reigns of Urban, Boniface, Innocent, Gregory, Clement, and Benedict. Rival Popes reigned at Avignon, and Rome, and distracted the church and the world with schism and revolution, with atrocious crimes and unbounded wretchedness. Amidst these *thirty schisms*, where is the *Apostolical* succession? Amidst ordinations and counter-ordinations, and ordinations recalled, where was the succession of the *clergy?* Papal succession thus lies buried in a heap of ruins, and is attended with more difficulty than "the quadrature of the circle or the longitude at sea." And yet you boast of your unbroken succession from the Apostle Peter, and array with empty pageantry

from letter to letter your objections against the rights of Protestant ministers to preach the gospel of Jesus Christ.

7. In the age of Liberius and Felix, the rival *Arian* Popes, the Church of Rome, and the church at large, also became Arian. The Tyrian Synod convened by the Emperor, A. D. 335, adopted the Arian creed, and excommunicated Athanasius, the champion of truth. The Synod of Antioch also degraded this great man. The Synod of Arles in 3 3 sustained the heresy of Arius, and condemned Athanasius. In 355 the Synod of Milan, a *Western Council*, and composed of several hundred members, formally denounced the *true faith*. Thus western and eastern Christendom united to espouse Arianism. The Sirmian Council issued three creeds. The second of these, A. D. 357, was without mixture Arian, and this was confirmed by Pope Liberius. Du Pin gives this testimony, and is sustained by Hilary, who calls this formulary " the Arian perfidy ;" and by Athanasius, Jerome, Sozomen, &c. &c.

Here then the Papal Church in its head and in its representatives at Sirmium *apostatized from the true faith*, and adopted at large a fatal heresy. The Council of Arminium met in 359, and was composed of from four to six hundred Bishops. It seemed to begin well, but ended in subscribing the semi-Arian Creed and making the Son of God a *creature*. About this time Arianism filled the world. Sozomen, Jerome, Gregory, Basil, Prosper, Baronius, and Bede acknowledge this. Arianism was thus sanctioned by Popes, Councils, and the Church at large. From these undeniable facts we draw the following conclusions. (1.) The true succession of the Church of Rome is irrecoverably lost amidst the apostacy and heresy of her Popes and Bishops, unless you trace it in the Arian line. (2.) As the head and great body of the church, both generally, and in Councils were radically heretical, *separation* was not only the *right* but *duty* of the faithful. Arianism was subscribed by the Pope, and sustained by the Councils; the Emperor directed all his power to persecute the orthodox, and establish heresy: the pulpits and the churches were filled with Arians; and Athanasius himself was condemned and excommunicated. In these circumstances God's people must either *subscribe to heresy*, and be subject to daily contamination themselves, or else *separate themselves*. They chose to separate themselves. In the *manner* of this separation they had no more choice, than they had in the *duty* of it. Their number was as one to a thousand. Every decree and question was carried against them. Thus outnumbered, and the Pope against them, their only choice was to retire; nay, they were denounced and excommunicated; they fled to the forests; they held their religious assemblies in the fields; they withdrew from the contagion of the corrupted church. And for this the orthodox fathers commend them. But on your principles they were bound to stay: they had no right to go The Arians had authority from God to force their faith upon them, and to " unfrock" even Athanasius for refusing to subscribe their abominable creed. But if the church at large may become so corrupt in faith or morals, or both, as to leave the faithful no choice but heresy or separation, then separation is a *duty;* and then, also, wicked excommunications can have no binding authority: *for that which makes it* a *sin* to *conform, also nullifies the excommunicating act.* It is the church which goes out; and she carries with her the institutions and blessings of her divine head. You evade this reasoning, by denying that the church can *err.* But *facts* confute you. You say that God has promised that the gates of hell shall not prevail against her. True: and the very way to fulfil it is to separate the good from the evil; as Athanasius did from the Arians, and the Reformers from the Pope of Rome. That promise is that a church shall always exist, but not *an infallible* one; and it was made to the *Catholic,* not the *Roman* church! The true Catholic church *cannot fail.* But the *Roman,* which never was the Catholic church (and was not *called* so for ages after the death of Christ,) was threatened with excision by the Apostle Paul, Rom. xi. 20—22. "Thou standest by faith—otherwise thou also shalt be cut off."

We have now reached the second era in this discussion, viz. your attempt at a defence of some of your peculiar doctrines. The very fact that you feel it necessary to do so, after what you have heretofore said, is a fine index to the present state of the discussion. From a crowd of pressing difficulties on Supremacy, Indulgences, Purgatory, Idolatry, Extreme Unction, etc. etc. you select for defence the doctrine of Transubstantiation. In your argument we meet the newly christened "defender of the faith," Thomas Moore, at almost every step. In his "Travels in search of a Religion," he found it convenient to *pass by* the word of God, agreeing no doubt with you, (in your discussion on the "rule of faith") that when left to speak for itself, IT does not teach the religion of Rome. If, in his travels, he had visited Rome, or touched at the Inquisition, or met the Council of Sirmium, or mingled with the Council of Constance, he might have given a very different report. At the latter place, he might have relieved the severity of theological discussion by the more agreeable communion of those fifteen hundred *fair* companions who attended the *holy fathers;* and have found a market for his "amatory poetry," as well as materials for the defence of the infallible church. I do not blame you, however, for availing yourself of every help in time of need. His book has nothing *new,* save the *service* to which it led him. But to proceed. It is not a little surprising that in a defence of Transubstantiation covering five columns, you should not only begin with the fathers (instead of the Bible) but should also entirely evade the testimony of your writers, and the body of my arguments given in Letter XXIV. You will permit me to invert the order of discussion, by beginning with the Scriptures. And first, in regard to John, 6th chapter, where it is thus written: "Except ye eat the flesh of the Son of man and drink his blood ye have no life in you," verse 53. On this passage you attempt to found the doctrine of Transubstantiation. But observe (1.) if this be taken *literally* it will prove that Christ's body was changed into bread, and not the bread into his body; for he expressly says, "this is the bread which cometh down from heaven," verse 50. But your doctrine is the reverse of this, viz. that the *bread* is changed into his *body.* Of course this passage gives no support to your doctrine. Besides, this discourse was delivered more than a year before the institution of the last supper, and (as Cusanus, Biel, Cajetan, Tapper, Hessels, Jansenius, all Roman Catholic writers, allow) had no reference to that sacrament. (2.) In verse 32, 33, Christ expressly tells us, that the bread he is here speaking of *came down from heaven;* but his natural body was born on earth, and had never been in heaven; and the bread which you say is changed into his body, "is of the earth earthly." It follows, therefore, that Christ did not here refer at all to the sacrament. (3.) Such was the virtue of the bread here spoken of, that whoever ate of it had eternal life, " if any man eat of this bread he shall live forever," v. 51. If then, Christ here speaks of the last supper, it follows, that all who partake of it, are forever saved. But this your own dogmas contradict. Therefore, on your own principles Christ spoke not of the Eucharist. (4.) Whosoever eats not *this bread is lost for ever.* " Except ye eat the flesh of the Son of man ye have no life in you," ver. 53. Then, if this passage refers to the Lord's Supper all are damned who do not partake of it. Will you follow your false logic to such an issue? And again, Christ said, ver. 53: " Except ye drink of the blood of the Son of man, ye have no life in you." But the cup is forbidden to the laity by your church under a heavy anathema. Then if Christ is here speaking of the Eucharist, all the laity in the church of Rome are lost for ever, and that by the express law of said church. Therefore, if your argument be true, you must restore the cup to the people, or destroy all their souls. (5.) Christ expressly tells us that this is throughout, a *figure*, and has not a literal but a spiritual meaning; that it is not an external eating and drinking with the mouth, but an internal and spiritual participation effected in the soul of the believer, *through* a living faith, and *by* the quickening spirit of Christ. The Jews understood Christ literally and grossly, just as Roman Catholics do now; but he openly rebuked them for their carnal stupidity, in mistaking his meaning. " This is that bread which came down from heaven; not as your fathers did eat manna.........It is the spirit that quickeneth, the flesh profiteth nothing; the words that I speak unto you, they are spirit and they are life. But there are some of you that believe not," vs. 58, 63, 64. Such is the obvious destruction of your doctrine as founded upon this passage. But that you may see that this interpretation is agreeable to antiquity, I will adduce the testimony of the Fathers. Eusebius, (Lib. 3. Ecclesiast. Theologiæ, Cont. Marcell.) Speaking of the above words of Christ, in paraphrase, he says, " Do not think that I speak of that *flesh* wherewith *I am compassed* as if you must *eat* of *that ;* neither imagine that I command you, to *drink* of my sensible and *bodily blood:* but understand that the *words* which I have spoken unto you are *spirit* and *life.* So that those very words and speeches of his, are his flesh and blood." Augustine, (In serm. ad. infan. de Sac. apud Bedam.) " It is no way to be doubted by any one that the faithful are made partakers of the body and blood of Christ, when they are made members of Christ in Baptism; and they are not estranged from the *communion* of that bread and that cup, although before they eat that bread and drink that cup, they depart out of this world, being united to the body of Christ; for they are not deprived of the *participation and benefit of the Sacrament when they have found that which the Sacrament* doth *signify.*" And again, (in Evang. John, Tracts 25, 26, 50.) " how shall I send up my hand into heaven and take hold on Christ sitting there ! *Send thy faith and thou hast hold of him.* Why preparest thou thy *teeth* and thy *belly ? Believe, and thou hast eaten. For this is to eat the living bread; to believe in him.* He that believeth in him *eateth.* He is *invisibly* fed, because he is invisibly *regenerated.* He is *inwardly* a babe, *inwardly renewed; where he is renewed, there he is nourished.*"

How plain is it then, that the Fathers dissented from the carnal and senseless construction of your church; and how affecting is the evidence, that the spirituality of religion and the quickening grace of God's Holy Spirit, are as little understood by the Roman priesthood, as they were of old by Nicodemus and the unbelieving Jews.

I regret that the limits of the present letter forbid me to enter farther on the confutation and exposure of your use of the Scriptures and the Fathers in your defence of Transubstantiation. While I refer our readers to what you have left unanswered on this subject in my Letter No. XXIV. I pledge myself to do this at large, if my life is spared, in my next letter.

When I quoted for your perusal, the challenge of Bishop Jewel, it was rather to invite your attention to his reasoning, than his character; and you must be aware that you do not answer the one, by attacking the other. It is true, even as you have said, that he once confessed " he had written what he had done against his own knowledge and conscience, only to comply with the state, and the religion which it had set up." When Mary of bloody memory, ascended the throne of England, and re-established, by her memorable persecutions and cruelties, the religion of Rome, Jewel was hunted down, and compelled either to renounce his religion or go to the stake. " His cowardly mind," as he himself confessed, yielded in the hour of danger and temptation to a forced conformity. It is to *this* he refers in the language which you adduce. And yet with unaccountable license, you make it appear, at the close of your letter, that he renounced the Protestant religion !! Over such deliberate misrepresentations, I would for your office sake, if truth and justice did not forbid, throw a veil which should hide it from the eyes of men. You have used the same liberty (as I have heretofore shown) with the writings of Luther; and your silence on this subject in the last letter seems to confess that it could not be defended. The frequency of such occurrences in your letters, afflicts and amazes me.

But to return to Bishop Jewel, allow me once more to propose for your consideration and answer, the direct questions which his famous challenge contains. Are they incapable of answer ? Are they not simple, pertinent, and decisive ? I pray you, that you will not again pass them by. I remain, yours, &c.

JOHN BRECKINRIDGE.

P. S. As the time originally specified " in the rules," for the continuance of this controversy has now elapsed, it is due to the public and the parties, that the following correspondence should be made known. I accordingly publish it below. It sufficiently explains itself without the need of comment.

Princeton, N. J. 26th July, 1833.

Rev. John Breckinridge,

Rev. Sir,—Allow me in this way to remind you that the period for which the Controversy was to continue has now just elapsed. The letter now in press ends the six months, beyond which, according to mutual agreement, the correspondence was not to go.

If, however, it should be deemed proper by the disputants to prosecute the discussion still further in the columns of the Presbyterian, it will be necessary that there should be previously a personal arrangement and definitive limitation of time, between yourself and Mr. Hughes.

A reply, addressed to the care of the publishers, will be esteemed by me as a favour.

An exact duplicate of this letter is carried by the same mail to the Rev. Mr. Hughes, in pursuance of that impartiality which it has been my endeavour to maintain.

Respectfully yours,
James W. Alexander,
Ed. of the Presbyterian.

To the Rev. John Hughes,

Sir,—On my return from Baltimore this morning, I received a letter from the Editor of the Presbyterian, reminding me that " the period for which the Controversy was to continue has now elapsed," and saying, that " if the disputants should deem it proper to prosecute the discussion still further in the columns of the Presbyterian, it will be necessary that there should be previously, a personal arrangement, and definitive limitation of time between yourself and Mr. Hughes."

In view of the above suggestions, it becomes my duty to say to you, that it rests entirely with yourself to close or continue the discussion.

It will not be necessary for me to commence my autumnal tour, earlier than the 1st of October; in the mean time therefore, I am entirely at your service. And if *after* that time, you feel disposed to prosecute the Controversy still further, I shall be happy to meet you in a public oral discussion; or if you think *prudent* to decline that, I shall *at all times* hold myself in readiness to attend to your communications (through the press) of a more permanent and connected character.

I remain your ob't. serv't.
John Breckinridge.

Philadelphia, August 1, 1833.

To the Rev. John Breckinridge.

Rev. Sir,—I have already complied with the requisition of Mr. Alexander, by a note to the publishers—in which I have stated my intention to continue the controversy as long as may be desired. You will have it in your power to fix the "limitation" when and where you may deem it convenient. Your obedient servant,

JOHN HUGHES

August 1st, 1833.

CONTROVERSY. No. XXIX.

RULES.

The undersigned agreeing to have an amicable discussion of the great points of religious controversy, between Protestants and Roman Catholics, do hereby bind themselves to the observance of the following rules:

1. The parties shall write and publish, alternately, in the weekly religious papers, called the Presbyterian, and a Roman Catholic paper, to be furnished by the first of January. It being understood that the communications shall be published after the following plan:—One party opening the first week, the other party replying the next week, and every piece to be republished in the immediately succeeding number of the Roman Catholic paper. The communications not to exceed four columns of the Presbyterian, nor to continue beyond six months, without consent of parties.

2. The parties agree that there is an infallible Rule of Faith established by Christ, to guide us in matters of religion, for the purpose of determining disputes in the Church of Christ.

3. They moreover agree, that after giving their views of the Rule of Faith, they shall proceed to discuss the question, "Is the Protestant religion, the religion of Christ?"

4. The parties agree respectively, to adhere strictly to the subject of discussion, for the time being, and to admit no second question, until the first shall have been exhausted. Each party shall be the judge when he is done with a subject, and shall be at liberty to occupy his time with a second topic, when he is done with the first, leaving to the other party the liberty of continuing to review the abandoned topic, as long as he shall choose; subject, however, to be answered, if he introduce new matter.

5. Mr. Hughes to open the discussion, and Mr. Breckinridge to follow, according to the dictates of his own judgment.

Philadelphia, December 14th, 1832.

JOHN BRECKINRIDGE,
JNO. HUGHES.

IS THE PROTESTANT RELIGION THE RELIGION OF CHRIST?

To the Rev. John Breckinridge.

Rev. Sir,—*Mr. Breckinridge says that "the Protestant is the religion of Christ."*

If so, I call upon him 1st. To tell me what the Protestant religion is?

2. *I call upon him to say what society of Christians ever taught this pretended "religion of Christ," previous to the Reformation?*

3. *I call upon him to say, whether Christ revealed* ALL *the doctrines of the Protestant religion, beginning with the best* IMAGE *of his church, Episcopalianism, and terminating with the most consistent of Protestant sects, the Unitarians?— and if not, how* MANY *denominations, out of the whole, belong to the* TRUE *Protestant religion, the religion of Christ?*

4. *I call upon him to show whether the Reformers received any* NEW *ministerial authority, after the withdrawal of that which they had received from the church?*

5. *I call upon him, in case no such* NEW *authority was received, to show that the Protestant clergy, so called, have any divine right to exercise the Christian ministry, more than other educated laymen?*

Now I call upon you to answer these questions. Take them up, one after the other, and give to each of them, that simple, candid, and ingenuous answer that each of them demands. You are bound to do this. Otherwise, it will be said of you, in the figurative language of Scripture, "this man began to build, and *was not able* to finish." My own opinion is, that you are afraid—that you see the difficulties of the case, and endeavour to shun them. But there are venerable brethren and fathers in the Presbyterian church, learned professors, men in ripe age and knowledge, inquire of *them* "what is the Protestant religion?" Let them answer successively *the other questions.*

If, however, neither you, nor they *can* answer them, then it follows that, whether you acknowledge it or not, you are driven out of the field on the present question. 1st. Because you cannot *defend*, what you cannot *define*. 2. Because you cannot discover so much as one village that professed, *previous* to the soi-disant Reformation, the doctrines of *any sect* of Protestants. 3d. Because you cannot defend Protestantism in the *gross*, and yet you dare not *divide* it. 4th. Because the Reformers had no ministerial authority. 5th. Because, consequently, they *could not* transmit any ministerial authority to their successors.

The peevish little disquisition, on epistolary etiquette, with which you commence your last letter, is very curious. It would seem that you are determined to chastise the "bad taste" and "useless tautology" of your friends in Princeton, who address you just as I do, "Rev. Sir." Why is the Rev. Mr. Alexander, whose letter you *publish*, guilty of this supposed "bad taste?"

And even some of your own letters, (some at least that have your signature,) are guilty of that "repetition," which, as the magister elegantiarum, you pronounce to be a "violation of good taste and a useless tautology!" How was this? But the whole amounts to this, that when you condescended to address me by the title of "Rev. Sir," you were courteous *by mistake*, and the opening of your last epistle is your apology for having been polite. For the rest, you should be assured *by this time*, that nothing from your pen can awaken vanity, or provoke resentment in the bosom of your opponent.

This same paragraph winds up with an attack on the pretended uncharitableness of the Catholic religion, touching the doctrine of exclusive salvation. You seem to feel that the prejudice of Protestants, on this and other subjects is now your only dependence, and accordingly you try to stir it up in your favour. Catholics, as you know, or ought to know, believe that out of the *true* church there is no salvation. But they hold, as *explicitly* belonging to the true church, all those who are members of the great, primitive, and Catholic society of Christians in communion with the Apostolical see of Rome; besides, they hold, as belonging *implicitly* to the true church, all those who do what God requires of them according to the measure of grace, knowledge, and opportunity which they may have received. Hence even among Protestants there may be members of the *true church*, not indeed because they are Protestants, but because by the inscrutable permission of God, they have been brought up in *invincible ignorance of the truth*, which they would embrace, if they knew it. But it is manifest that this plea of *invincible ignorance*, is the only one that can excuse a rational being for rejecting the revelation of Christ. Can Protestants say that *their* ignorance is invincible? Can their ministers, more especially say so? I judge them not, God will judge. And at his tribunal the plea of chance, party attachment, or prejudice, which binds them to one sect or another, will not be admitted.

Now let us state the "exclusive salvation" of Presbyterianism, and see whether it is not more "bigoted," contracted and "intolerant," than ours, which I have just described. I will not *misrepresent* as you have done. But I shall quote from your own *last* "Confession of Faith," as *amended* in 1821, (page 111.) "The visible church........consists of all those throughout the world, that *profess* the true religion, *together with their children;* and is the kingdom of Jesus Christ, the house and family of God, *out of which there is no ordinary possibility of salvation.*" This doctrine secures heaven to Presbyterians "and their children," and denies the "possibility of salvation to all the rest of mankind, Protestants as well as Catholics. And yet you talk about "bigotry!" This doctrine dooms the whole Christian world to perdition, except Calvin and the chosen race of which he became the father, some 1500 years after Christ!! And all Protestants, who have not Calvin for their religious progenitor, are doomed to the same destruction. I would advise that the confession be again "amended."

But then I shall be told that the Catholic church will not extend the right hand of fellowship to any other. Certainly not—and this is one of the marks of her divinity. She could not be the church of Christ, if she ceased to proscribe the systems invented in the 16th century, by a few of her own apostate children. She would be unworthy of her celestial origin, if she could stoop to Luther's religion or to Calvin's, and say "Hail, Sister! Thou *also* art heaven-born like myself!" Truth is unchangeable—I will say more, it is essentially intolerant; in history, in mathematics, in medicine, in jurisprudence—so that when the culprit forfeits his life to the insulted laws of his country, he perishes by the *intolerance of truth*. But error, on the contrary, may be tolerant towards its kindred error, and the liberality of Protestantism, as far as it exists, is the evidence that the whole system is bottomed on conscious uncertainty. Thus Protestantism subsists by excitement, or else degenerates into that frigid indifference to all religious truth, which is the incipient stage of infidelity. It has charity for deists and atheists, but not for Catholics, just as Pagan Rome was tolerant to every thing but Christianity. This gentle spirit of Protestantism cannot contend against the Catholic church, without being reminded of its own recent and spurious origin. Hence those who write against the primitive faith, and in defence of that nondescript called "Protestantism," are almost invariably observed to lose their sense of good manners, propriety, decency, and even *self-respect*, which should never be forgotten. They believe in mysteries as well as Catholics; and yet they ridicule Catholic mysteries just in the same language which DEISTS use against their own. They read our books and pervert them, just as DEISTS read and pervert the Scriptures. Their arguments are *deistical*, and yet they pretend to be Christians by excellence! They insult Jesus Christ in the mystery of the *Eucharist*, and thereby teach the DEISTS to insult him in the mystery of the Incarnation.—The former doctrine being even more fully attested by Scripture than the latter. They find, on mature reflection, that in their immortal hatred of the Catholic church they do the work of the deists. They stoop to every thing, however low and vulgar, that may sustain the credit of their floating systems, as they are tossed to and fro by every wind of doctrine.—And seem to regret, as a misfortune, that the moorings of the Catholic church are fixed, unchangeable and eternal.

If any one, Rev. Sir, is tempted to suppose that this picture is overcharged, I refer him, for the correction of his mistake, to the contents of your last letter. The perusal of it must have been painful to your best friends. They must have been *mortified*, to perceive the advantages which it yielded to your opponent, when, instead of dignified controversy, such as the question called for, they saw you descend to the filthiest topics, couched and amplified in the filthiest terms known to the English language. It might have been expected from the pen which composed the Report of the Magdalen Society in New York, some time ago; but from the Rev. John Breckinridge with his *name*, it was *not* expected. Delicacy must have blushed, and cast the paper away. And even among your own people, I venture to assert that no *lady* will acknowledge to have it read. I had laboured from the commencement to hold you up, and *compel you* to be dignified; and, at this advanced stage of the discussion, judge how it grieves me to perceive that I have toiled in vain! But I have the satisfaction to assure you, that if you are determined to sink, you shall not drag me with you: you shall go down *alone*, when I can support you no longer. In retailing, therefore, the scandals wherewithal Protestant calumny has endeavoured to blacken the character of the Popes and the church, you may safely calculate on *impunity*. The region to which *you* have descended, is to me unapproachable. The very indelicacy of your position shall protect you. And though I shall leave you "alone with your glory," still I cannot help exclaiming over you, more in *pity* than in triumph, "O! how the mighty hath fallen." I have no hesitation, however, in asserting that your statement of immoralities at Rome, (which I dare not repeat) is as false as your manner of expressing it is disgusting. Name the page of the *Catholic* historian, who states what you have asserted, and I pledge myself again to *expose you*. But how are we to expect the truth of history from a pen, which, in desperation, corrupts the sacred text of Scripture itself. Let me give an instance. "The word of God declares," (you say,) that "a bishop MUST BE the husband of one wife." Titus i. 6. Now we turn to your reference and read, from St. Paul, that you have corrupted the word of God, since the apostle says no such thing!!! St. Paul had NO WIFE, and how could *he* say what you make him say, viz. that "a bishop MUST BE the husband of one wife." The verse merely declares, in substance, that those who had been *twice* married, were thereby disqualified for the office of Bishop, but the word "must be" is your own addition —according, indeed, with the *practice* of Protestant ministers, if not of St. Paul.

With these observations I might close my letter, since the whole of your letter, besides the vileness of the topics you treat of, is entirely foreign to the question. But having space, I shall fill it up with such matters as I deem proper. And first, it cannot be called a digression, if I make a few remarks upon the course which our Episcopal friends have thought proper to adopt, in reference to this controversy.

Some months ago, when Bishop H. U. Onderdonk's " CHARGE on the RULE OF FAITH," appeared as a succedaneum to your labours, I felt it my duty to publish a "*Review*" of it. That the review, by exposing the *false premises* of the charge, destroyed the great body of the Bishop's conclusions, was manifest to all those who *are acquainted with the principles of sound reasoning*. And I have occasion to know, that Episcopalians themselves, who read *both productions*, formed the same opinion, and regarded the *subject* of the charge, as an unseasonable interference in a pending discussion. The Review was treated by the Episcopal press as very weak; hopes were expressed that no notice should be taken of it; and a paper called the Episcopal Recorder, apparently in a fit of bad humour, accused me of having *challenged* the Bishop to a " personal controversy;" a statement, by the way, which was utterly *unfounded in truth*. Still the circulation of the Review was checked by every underhand manœuvre that could be resorted to without palpably betraying the motive. In one instance a bookseller, (as I have been told) who enjoyed some sectarian *patronage*, was actually forbidden to keep it for sale. And yet the Review was a weak production, not worthy of a reply. When you *cannot answer* an argument, say it is too weak to deserve refutation.

Now, however, the Review has become the subject of *anonymous* " observations," in the August number of the " Church Register;" and were I to judge these " observations" by the style of the " charge," I should say that both came from the same pen. But the author deems it prudent to conceal his name, and I allude to his essay principally on that account. He does not refute the arguments of the " Review;" nor yet vindicate the fallacies and contradictions, which had been pointed out in the language of the " charge." He merely cavils with fine spun prolixity. He merely nibbles at the substance of the " Review." And after you have read the whole of his " observations," spread over fourteen pages, you rise from the perusal with but vague and confused ideas of the conclusion which the author himself intended to establish. He treats the matter under the following heads:—

I. " Appellations;"—and contends that it is right to call us by the nickname, " Romanists." Now the English Bishops in the House of Peers call us " Roman Catholics," except when they speak in derision with a view to insult. And if the author of the " observations" were asked whether an Episcopal Bishop is a *Catholic Bishop*, he is too modest, I am sure, to answer in the affirmative. But Protestants pay us a *high compliment*, when they seek to shake off their own name, and to clothe themselves with ours. The thing, however, is ridiculous and impossible.

II. " Tradition; various meanings." This is no new idea. Almost every word in our language has " various meanings."

III. " Tradition; not valueless." What is its value? What says the author of the " observations," " we hold, for example, that *Episcopacy* has ample testimony in these (traditional) records." What will your *ruling Elders* think of this? Just admit tradition, as far as may be necessary for the purposes of the Episcopal Church: and behold—" Tradition; *not valueless.*"

IV. " Tradition; its elementary nature." What? " Hearsay," says the author! Then the preaching of Christ, and the Apostles; the miracles and doctrines of Christianity; are nothing but " hearsay;" which does not change its " *elementary* nature," by having *been afterwards committed to writing*. Does the Church Register not see that this consequence follows from its assertions?

V. " Tradition, the Council of Nice." Under this head, the author merely quotes Mr. Milnor in opposition to Mr. Hughes, and modestly abstains from deciding between them. He speculates on the probable *ages* of the Bishops, who attended the Council; and represents Mr. Hughes as contending that they *excluded the testimony of Scripture*, in condemning the heresy of Arius. Mr. Hughes, fortunately, never *said*, never *meant to say*, any such thing.

VI. " Tradition; its fallibility." Here the author contends that whereas the Scripture was " added and advantageous," therefore, Tradition is fallible. This is vicious reasoning. St. John's Gospel was "*added*," and it does not therefore follow that the other three were fallible. The Review itself had disposed of this sophistry.

VII. "Infallibility." Under this head the author breaks down the bulwarks of the Christian Religion; and tells the Infidel that Christ appointed a church to be the perpetual witness of divine truth, and yet that *this Church, thus appointed, may deceive him!* If so, for what purpose did Christ appoint it?

VIII. " Infallibility; its consequences." Here the author seems to imagine that the world is undone, unless men agree to strip Christianity of its pretensions to " infallibility," and reduce it to the uncertainty of a doubtful problem. For this service, also, the Deist will be *grateful*.

IX. " Faith, Infallibility; Opinion." Under these three words the author takes pains to exclude faith in *its theological sense*, and contends that both Catholics and Protestants must be satisfied with " opinion." This also is giving the right hand of fellowship to Deists and Atheists. For if Christianity be founded *on mere opinion*, it rests on the same identical basis, which supports infidelity and Atheism.

But there is one position assumed by the author of these " observations," which goes farther towards the impeachment of Christianity, than any thing that I have ever seen, even from a Protestant pen. It is under the head of " infallibility." The author has discovered that the inspiration of the Apostles, was of an " *intermittent*" character! *Periodical infallibility*, the author is willing to grant them. But in the *intervals*, he tells us that even the Apostles were *capable of erring*, in their interpretation of the Gospel!!!! Here then, is a desperate alternative resorted to, in order to prop up the "Charge," and meet the arguments of the " Review." Another writer would have explained the 11th verse of the 2d chapter to the Galatians, without destroying the inspiration of the Apostles. The fault ascribed to Peter was not the *teaching of erroneous doctrine*, as our "Observer" would make appear, but the sanctioning of a practice which might impede the progress of the Gospel among the Gentiles, and was therefore inexpedient. The fault was of *practice*, and not of *preaching*. And the author of " observations" should have *observed* this, before he ascribed it to the absence of *inspiration*. But he has denied the infallibility of the Apostles. He is a *Christian*, and I leave him to his own reflections on the injury he has done to the character of the Christian religion.

In taking leave of the " Church Register," I would beg leave to state that I have no disposition to engage in controversy with Episcopalians. But they should not *provoke* it. They mistake their *interest*, and forget their position on the theological map, whenever they provoke a controversy with Catholics. They can triumph over Presbyterian antagonists in every contest;—but they should recollect that they are indebted for the victory, to the use of weapons which they *borrow from the Catholic Church*—and the moment they provoke a controversy with *that church*, whose attributes they have appropriated to themselves, they shall experience a prompt exposure and defeat. They shall be found on the field as naked and defenceless as any other sect of Protestants. The host of witnesses by whose testimony they bear down their Presbyterian adversaries, will *desert* and be arrayed against them in every contest with Catholics. They have, however, good people; learned and respectable clergy. Their mode of attacking Catholics is, at least, more genteel, if not more successful, than that which Presbyterian ministers adopt. They preserve decency, when they write against us. Still it is true, however paradoxical it may appear, that whilst they have more of *truth* they have less of *consistency*, than any other *Protestant* denomination. In *this* respect they are directly the opposite of the Unitarians. But without enlarging—I have only to say that the author of the " Charge" on the " rule of faith," and of " observations" in the " Church Register," has *come to your aid*, in a way which I cannot help regarding, as equally indelicate and unprofitable. *Indelicate*, because *you* were the self-proclaimed champion of Protestantism; and *unprofitable*, because he has not succeeded in the attempt one whit better than yourself.

With regard to your often repeated *assertion*, that transubstantiation was introduced A. D. 1215—your silence in the last letter I construe into a tacit *acknowledgment* of your mistake. Starting from that epoch I had traced the doctrine upwards to the apostolic age, the apostles, and Christ himself. And instead of *contradicting the testimonies* adduced, you wonder that I did not *begin* with the Bible! But I *ended* with it. I gave abundant Scripture. And instead of meeting my arguments and reasoning, you merely *cavil at the words employed by Christ*, as in fact, the incredulous Jews, who heard him, did. Again, you ascribe to Catholics gross notions of

Christ's real presence in the Eucharist—as if he subsisted in the *manner* of a natural body, with sensible flesh and blood. This is an *old device* of Protestants. Where honest argument is impossible, they have recourse to misrepresentation. What Catholics *believe*, what all Christians believed before Carlostadius, what I placed in my last letter beyond the reach of refutation is, that the body and blood of Christ are truly and really present under the appearances of bread and wine in the sacrament of the Eucharist. This presence is effected by the *Omnipotence of God*, and in virtue of the institution of Jesus Christ. "*Do this* for a commemoration of me."

I shall fill up the remainder of this paper, by establishing the eucharistic sacrifice of the new law—commonly called the mass. *Sacrifice* is the supreme action of religion—in which, by offering up to God, something in a state of immolation we *visibly and publicly recognize him as the master of life and death, and the sovereign Lord of all things*. From the beginning of the world, this *action of religion* was commanded and observed among the people of God. All the ancient sacrifices of the Jews had reference to that of Christ, upon the cross, and, on the altars of his church. This *latter*, is not a *new sacrifice*, or *another victim;* but it is the same sacrifice of Calvary, perpetuated in an unbloody manner, by Christ's divine appointment; by which, according to the prophecy of Malachy, "from the rising of the sun to the going down of the same, the name of the Lord is great *among the Gentiles;* and in every place there is sacrifice; and there is offered to his name a clean oblation." Mal. i. 11. The same in which the *death* of the Lord, in the language of St. Paul, is shown forth till he come. Now pray what *other* sacrifice is there among the Gentiles, that corresponds with the Prophet's prediction, except the eucharistic sacrifice of the Catholic church? —which is literally offered from the rising till the setting sun. And how else is the "death of the Lord shown forth *till he come,*" except in the mystic shedding of Christ's blood in the eucharistic sacrifice of the altar?—*even as he commanded*. St. Paul alludes to the Priesthood of Christ in direct and positive connexion, not with the *bloody sacrifice as it was on the cross*, but as it is in *the Christian eucharist*. He showed that the priesthood of Christ was not according to that of *Aaron*, but of MELCHISEDECH. And what do we read of him? "Melchisedech, the King of Salem, bringing forth BREAD AND WINE, for he was the PRIEST of the most high God; and he blessed him." Gen. xiv. 18. Do you not perceive then, Rev. Sir, that in the institution of the holy Eucharist, Jesus Christ actually exercised this priesthood of Melchisedech, by changing "bread and wine," into his own body and blood, and in distributing in this mysterious manner among his Apostles the flesh of the victim, even before its immolation on the cross! "Take ye, and eat." "*This is my body.*" "*This* is my blood *which shall be shed for many unto the remission of sins.*" "*This do* for a commemoration of me." By this act he annulled the priesthood of Aaron, and substituted that of Melchisedech. And accordingly from that day the *Jewish* sacrifice has not been offered——whereas the Christian sacrifice, according to the Priesthood of Christ, and order of Melchisedech, has existed, and does exist wherever the *unreformed* religion of the Redeemer is known from the rising till the setting sun. Hence St. Paul instructs the Hebrews in the *difference between the Jewish and the Christian* sacrifice. Having described elsewhere, the *order* of the Christian priesthood, as *superior to that of Aaron*, he tells the Jews, "we have seen an ALTAR, whereof *they* have no power to *eat* who serve the tabernacle." Heb. xiii. 10. If it be said, that he alluded to the " sacrifice of praise," mentioned in one of the subsequent verses, I reply that St. Paul could not hinder or make it unlawful for the Jews to participate in *such* a sacrifice. He spoke of the *sacrifice* of the *new* law; of the ALTAR on which the body and blood of Christ was offered, under the *appearances* of BREAD AND WINE, by the *new* priesthood according to the order of Melchisedech. Hence we find the early Fathers bearing unanimous testimony to the *existence of this doctrine*, and *this belief*. And every one of them pointing to the eucharistic *sacrifice* as the fulfilment of Malachy's prophecy, quoted above. St. Justin Martyr, almost, if not quite contemporary with St. John the Evangelist, says, "Christ instituted a *sacrifice* of bread and wine, which Christians offer up in every place," and immediately *quotes* the Prophet Malachy i. 11. (Dialog. Cum. Tryphon.) Irenæus the disciple of Polycarp, says, " Christ, in consecrating bread and wine, had instituted the *sacrifice* of the new law, which the church received from the Apostles, *according to the prophecy of Malachy*." (Iren. L. iv. 32.) St. Cyprian calls the eucharist, " a true and full *sacrifice*," and adds that " as Melchisedech offered bread and wine, so Christ offered the same, namely, HIS BODY AND BLOOD." (Epist. 63.) All the later Fathers speak the same language—as the learned Centuriators of Magdeburg indignantly acknowledge.

Here, then, we find that in the days of St. Paul, St. Justin, Irenæus, Cyprian, and *onward* till you arrive at the Reformation, the religion of Christ had its Priesthood, its altar, and its *sacrifice*, which sacrifice was then, and still is, offered up by the Catholic church in every place among the Gentiles. Why then has Protestantism, in its blind career, abolished and destroyed them all? Where does it pretend to fulfil the *prediction of Malachy*, touching the " sacrifice and clean oblation among the Gentiles?" Where is its Priesthood? Where does it perpetuate the immolation of Calvary, " showing forth the death of the Lord till he come?" Where is its "*altar?*" Where are the body and blood of the Lord, which it affects to talk about, whilst it boasts of having nothing left but a piece of bread and a cup of wine?

But then, the " Popish mass !" Yes, such, indeed, is the appellation of insult bestowed by Protestant apostacy on the Eucharistic sacrifice of the new law, foretold, as we have seen by the prophet, instituted by Jesus Christ himself, and believed by *all the Christians in the world* before Martin Luther! But then it detracts from the merits of the *one sacrifice of the cross?* No—it is the same sacrifice continued in a supernatural manner, by which the church daily, throughout the world, presents to the eternal Father, the same victim of atonement and propitiation for the sins of men, in which she shows forth the death of the Lord till he come; and in which our souls are nourished with the body and blood of the Lord. "But Mr. Breckinridge says that it is idolatrous." Poor Mr. Breckinridge does not understand it. He says *this*, because others have said so before him, and *ignorant* Protestants think so. "But how can the Priest bring Christ down from heaven by the words of consecration?" I answer that Christ does not cease to be in heaven by being present in the Eucharist. And since he was pleased so to appoint and ordain in the sacrament of the Eucharist, how can the Protestant minister *prevent* him? "But Mr. B. says that this doctrine of a sacrifice in the Christian church was an invention of the middle ages. So he said of the real presence, 1215 was the point beyond which he would not go, but I brought the testimony of all the preceding ages against him, and now he speaks no more about 1215. "But Protestants worship in spirit and in truth." They *say so;* but it is after their own manner, and not as the early Christians worshipped. "But if the Eucharistic sacrifice was a part of the Christian religion, held at all times, and by all Christians previous to the Reformation, how came the Protestants to abolish it?" That is a question which I shall proceed to answer.

It will be recollected that, in the first place, Calvin was not a priest, and consequently had no *power* either to consecrate or offer sacrifice. Hence it is, that the Presbyterian ministers call themselves *bishops* (overseers) and not priests, having never received any ministerial authority, more than their founder, for the performance of any priestly function. Luther, on the contrary, being a priest, continued to believe in the real presence, and to claim the power of consecrating until his death. But if Carlostadt and Zuinglius provoked the implacable resentment of the great Reformer by denying the real presence, without *his permission;* he was determined to enjoy the undivided glory of abolishing the sacrifice of mass. However, he had no idea, it seems, of abolishing it until after he had heard the arguments brought against it, in a dispute which he held with the Devil on the subject. He quotes the disputation at length in which he argued strongly for the mass, but he was finally obliged to yield to the superior reasoning of his infernal Tutor, and the mass was *accordingly* abolished. Protestants, I fear, will not be edified at discovering such intimacy, between the father of the Reformation, and the father of lies. But I only quote what *Luther himself recorded in his writings* (Wittem. ed. (1558.) vol. vii, p. 228, 229, 230.) Here then we see how and why the Eucharistic sacrifice, was proscribed by the two great divisions of Protestantism on the continent of Europe. It was soon after this abolished in England by *act of Parliament*, and by similar means was it suppressed in other countries.

Before these events *all the Christian countries in the universe*, believed in the Eucharistic sacrifice of the Mass, as Catholics still believe in it. And yet Protestants are generally as ignorant or as unmindful of *these important facts*, as if *their* doctrine of mere *bread* and *wine* had originated with the Apostles, instead of the Reformers. This was so far from being the case, that Luther in writing against those who began to deny the real presence of Christ in the Eucharist, says "the Devil seems to have mocked mankind in proposing to them a heresy so *ridiculous* and *contrary to Scripture,* as that of the Zuinglians." (Op. Luth. Defens. Verb. Cœnæ.)

Having thus established the doctrine of the Eucharistic Sacrifice of the new law, instituted and appointed by Jesus Christ, believed by the church, and rejected by the Reformation about three hundred years ago.—I shall now make a few remarks on what Protestants call denying the cup to the laity. They accuse the church of dividing the Sacrament, and administering it in a manner contrary to the command of Christ. In both charges, however, they are deceived by their deceivers. For in the first place, Christ is present, whole and entire, under *each* of the species of the Sacrament, as much as under *both.* Consequently there is no division of the Sacrament; since the laity receive in the communion, under the form of bread, that same body and blood of the Lord, which the Priest receives, in the *action of sacrificing* on the altar, under the separate forms of both bread and wine. But they (Protestants) contend that, in as much as Christ, at the last Supper, administered this Eucharist under both forms, therefore, say they, all persons are bound to receive under both. "Drink ye all of this." To this I reply, that Christ in these words addressed the *Apostles* and *Ministers* of the church, whom he appointed to *consecrate and offer the sacrifice,* which he had just instituted. " *This do* for a commemoration of me." The words "drink ye," and "this do," are addressed to the *same* persons. And if the *former* be a precept, to the laity, as well as to the ministry; it will necessarily follow that so is the *latter;* and yet Protestants do not allow the laity to *consecrate,* or pronounce what they call the "blessing" over *their* Sacrament of mere bread and wine. Why not? if both were precepts.

But it is said that in the earlier ages of the church, communion was administered to the laity in both kinds. I answer, so it was: but the great question is, was the administration of it under both kinds, taught to be *essential* for the reception of the Sacrament? I say no. And the proof is, that it was frequently even then administered only under *one kind.* Will Mr. Breckinridge deny this? If he do, I shall take pains to *instruct* him. If he do, I shall quote, beginning with the second century, Tertullian, St. Dyonisius, of Alexandria, St. Cyprian, St. Basil, St. Chrysostom, &c to prove that he is as much *mistaken,* as when he said, that " Transubstantiation was as young as 1215." It will be easy to show him that learned Protestants have admitted this fact. Among others, the Protestant Bishops Forbes, White, and Montague, of England, not only admit the fact, as to *the ancient practice of the church,* but acknowledge that the *authority* for giving the communion under *both* kinds, is rather from *tradition, than from Scripture!* Cassander and Grotius, make similar acknowledgments on the subject.

If you are not satisfied with these, I shall have the pleasure of introducing you to the Calvinistic Synod of your own brethren, held at Poictiers, in France, 1550. Where it was decreed that "the *bread* of the Lord's Supper ought to be administered to those who cannot drink *wine.*"..... (Lord's Supper, C. iii. p. 7.) Even the acts of Parliaments which established the communion under *both kinds* in

England, made it *lawful* to administer in one kind *only*, when necessity required. (Heylin's Hist. of Ref. p. 58; and Sparrow's Collection, page 17.) What have you to say against all these witnesses? Here are the united testimonies of early Fathers, Episcopal Bishops, Protestant Parliaments, and even a *Presbyterian Synod*, all against you? What will you have to say for yourself?

But it may be asked why Protestants, in the face of such evidence, still declaim against the Catholic usage on this point, whereas they themselves, have thus acknowledged it to be matter of *discipline*, subject to the regulation of a Synod, or of a Parliament? In answer to this, I can only say, that the Reformers seemed to have had no rule, to guide their spirit of change, except the rule of mere gratuitous opposition;—first turned against the Church by *them all ;* and then, by each, against the other. Thus, for example, on the subject now treated of, Luther tells us, "if a Council ordained or permitted *both kinds*, in spite of the Council, says he, *we* would take but *one*, or *neither*, and curse those who should take both." (Form. Miss. Tom. II. p. 384. 386.) This glory of *originating*, seems to have been common to all the Reformers; and there is no other reason why the Reformation might not have been confined to Lutheranism; except that Zuinglius and Calvin would have been subordinate in Saxony, instead of being (as ambition prompted,) *supreme* in Switzerland ; *seconds* in Wittemburg, instead of *firsts*, in Zurich and Geneva. Hence they disagreed in almost every thing except in hostility towards the Church, and more especially towards the Pope. But for the rest, they quarrelled regularly; wrote against, and reviled each other; and if we *believe what they have written*, it will be difficult to escape the conviction that, a more impious or wicked set of men never insulted heaven, by pretending to espouse the cause of religion on earth. If we look along the line of their labours from Luther at one end, to Socinus at the other, we will see Revelation made to run the gauntlet, and the body of Christian doctrine rudely torn, limb from limb. The object was to cut out the cancer of Popery from the breast of religion, and thus, the daughter of God, brought under the operation of every "reforming" quack, who had *nerve* enough to apply the knife, was wounded, with gash after gash, as she passed from one to the other, until the steel of Socinus touched her heart, and she expired! Such has been the work of the Reformation: and Mr. Breckinridge says, that the work of the Reformation is "the religion of Christ!!" Not only this; he has actually *promised* to *prove* it!!

I do not mean to say that the Reformers *never* agreed. Dudith, one of their number tells us, that they sometimes agreed in drawing up a "Confession of Faith," but he does not forget to add, that they quarrelled about what they had written, almost before the ink was dried on the paper. There is another remarkable instance in which I find six Reformers, including Bucer and Melanchton, agreeing with the great leader of the Reformation. Now as these men are the fathers of the Protestant religion, and as you are about to show that "the Protestant religion is the religion of Christ," I deem it proper to submit the case for your consideration.

I allude to the "indulgence" granted by these new Popes of Germany, to the Landgrave of Hesse, by virtue of which his Royal Highness was authorized to be the husband of "two" wives at the same time. They however took the precaution to recommend that it should be done as secretly as possible. And accordingly, his Royal Highness did marry a second wife, Margaret de Saal, in March, 1540.

Now, Rev. Sir, do not insinuate that this *fact* is without foundation, it is known to all the learned men of Europe and America, and if any one is curious to *see the documents here referred to*, I shall have great pleasure in submitting to his perusal a copy in Latin and French of this infamous correspondence, as well as of the marriage contract; attested by the regular notary public, as taken from the imperial archives. When, therefore, you set about redeeming your *pledge*, by attempting to prove that the religion of the Reformation is the religion of Christ, do not forget this decision of the Reformers in favour of polygamy. You have said that "indulgences are a bundle of licenses to commit sin," and here is a *Protestant* "indulgence," corresponding exactly with your definition. If you wished to know the meaning of a *Catholic* "indulgence," you might have learned from our catechisms, or any Catholic child in the street, that it is "the remission of *canonical penance*, or of *temporal punishment*, which often remains after the guilt of eternal punishment of sin have been remitted in the sacrament of penance."

When you waste your time, in attempting to break the illustrious chain of apostolic succession which links the present Bishop of Rome to the first Apostle, you cannot imagine how much you *expose yourself*, in the judgment of those who are acquainted with ecclesiastical history. The year "1215" was nothing to it. Equally ludicrous is your assertion that the Catholic church adopted the Arian heresy;— *that* church, always in communion with the See of Rome, *branded* Arianism, Nestorianism, Pelagianism, Lutheranism, Calvinism, Socinianism, and every other "ism" from the commencement of Christianity, that presumed to corrupt the doctrine of which she was the guardian, and which she received from the Apostles and from Christ. In a word, you had better return to the defence of the "Protestant religion." Tell us WHAT it is. How we shall know it by its doctrine. Does it acknowledge Prelacy? Does it deny infant baptism? Does it *destroy* free will? Does it teach that men are damned and saved by the *absolute force* of predestination?

Tell us where it was.... and by whom it was possessed before Luther. Tell us from whom the Reformers received authority to make a new religion. Was it from men? They were *disowned* by all the Christian world. Was it from God? Then where are their miracles? Whence do the *present clergy* of Protestantism derive their *ministerial* character? Have they a single evidence to show that they are not mere laymen, vested with titles which are essentially defective. These, Rev. Sir, are the main questions. These are the *crucible*, from which the Protestant religion cannot pass, and to which, you are manifestly afraid to trust it. Come up then, I pray you, to the task you have assumed, and meet the question. Let us decide it, and proceed to other matters. But if you cannot, because the thing is *impossible*, then give it up, and let some other question be placed at the head of your letters. You have promised to come forward with your arguments letter after letter, and if you *cannot* find arguments to prove that " the Protestant religion is the religion of Christ," let me know it, and I will cease to press you on the matter. I now request the publishers to place the *rules of the discussion*, at the head of every letter, in order that all men may see your disregard of the *name* with which you signed them. My letter No. 23, is *unanswered*, it is a letter not of abuse, but of solid argument, founded on testimonies which cannot be called in question. Permit me to request that you will read it again, and try to answer it. Reflect on the arguments and evidences, and do not allow the exhausted patience of your Protestant readers to suppose that the Protestant religion is not susceptible of at least, *some sort of defence*. You perceive how badly you have succeeded, by straying from the Protestant religion, and taking your stand against the real presence at the year " 1215," with the bold assertion that the doctrine was unknown before that epoch. In reference to the sacrifice of mass, and communion under one kind, your discursive pen has been equally unfortunate.

Return then, Rev. Sir, I pray you, to "the question." The whole community of our readers are crying " Question," " Question." Take up the difficulties stated at the head of this letter, and by removing them, show us that " the Protestant religion is the religion of Christ." Yours, &c

J᠎ᴜɴ Hᴜɢʜᴇs

CONTROVERSY. No. XXX.

IS THE PROTESTANT RELIGION THE RELIGION OF CHRIST?
Philadelphia, August 22, 1833.

To the Rev. John Hughes,
   Sir,

>   A pious, sensible, and well-bred man,
>   *Will* not insult me; and no other, *can!*

The exposure (in my last letter) of the *immoralities, forged miracles and superstitions, of the Church of Rome,* seem deeply to have disturbed you. They are new things to most of our fellow-citizens; and yet they are so true, so shocking, so incapable of explanation or defence, that I do not wonder you are agitated by such disclosures. I can both pardon and pity you, for the rude and ungentlemanly explosion which ensues.

There are two very important facts, however, connected with this tirade against me. The first is the undesigned denunciation which you utter against your own church, in thus wantonly assailing me. In all I have said on the subject of "immoralities" *in the Church of Rome,* I used the very language of your own authors. Let the reader turn to my Letter (No. XXVIII.) and he will see this to be literally true. I once thought of giving these Roman Catholic authorities in the original Latin, or other *unknown* tongue, from a desire to spare the feelings of our readers; for most truly as you have said, the narrative is "a Magdalen report." It is a report, by your own writers, of the debauches of Popes, and the infamy of Priests, and Monks, and Nuns, in a church calling itself *holy,* and sending to perdition all who dissent from her. I blushed while I read them; I shuddered while I transcribed them. But the object was to make these *evils known,* and the only choice was between *suppressing* them, or giving them, as I did, in the *language of the country.* But if they have been perpetrated in your church; (as your standard-authors say,) and if you are so *shocked* at my extracts from their histories, how much more should the *deeds themselves* revolt you? Then, when you *denounce me* for *exposing* these enormities, do you not (though unconsciously) pass the heaviest sentence against the institutions and the clergy of your church, by whom they have been committed?

The other important fact is this; that you give this pledge: "I have no hesitation however, in asserting, that your statement of the immoralities at Rome, (which I dare not repeat) is as false as your manner of expressing it is disgusting. Name the page of the Catholic historian, who states what you have asserted, and I pledge myself to expose you." (Letter No. XXIX. 2d column.) This, indeed, is a most auspicious promise; and I meet you at once, with the following *Roman Catholic historians. Thuanus,* Book 37, page 776. A. D. 1566; as cited in my last letter, "where the writer states that the Senate of Rome, instigated by the clergy, interceded with the Pope not to expel the courtezans from Rome, adding as a reason, that if he did, the chastity of their families would be endangered by the Priests." Barronius's Annals, Tom. X. pages 765, 766. A. D. 908. Where this Roman Catholic historian informs us, "that Theodora, a courtezan of noble family, obtained supreme control in Rome, that she expelled the lawful Popes, and put violent and nefarious men into the Papal chair; that Pope Sergius III. committed adultery with her daughter; and their son John, the offspring of their crimes, was afterwards Pope himself; he says they were apostate Popes, and not Apostolical; calls the times deplorable; and the scandal overwhelming; says the church was governed by strumpets; and forgotten by God." He quotes also various Roman Catholic authors in proof, viz.: Luitprand, Sigebert, Auxilius, Adam, &c. Dupin, *a Roman Catholic historian*, Vol. 4. Cent. 10. Chap. 2.; confirms the above disgusting narrative; and gives also at the same time a history of the Popedom, during the *holy* lives of Popes Formosus: Stephen VI.; John IX.: Benedict IV.; Sergius; John X.; Leo VI.; Stephen VII.; John XI.; John XII.; &c. which for blood, debauch, murder, rapine, and manifold villany, exceeded the *worst days* of Heathen Rome. Of Sergius he says, " this man is esteemed a monster, not only for his ambition, and the violent proceedings he was guilty of, but on account of his loose morals." He had a bastard son who was afterwards promoted to the Popedom, as John XI. " He tells us this John was a monster; Stephen the VI. was strangled; Romanus was a Pope a few months; Theodorus only twenty days; and Leo V. forty days; Sergius *usurped* the Holy See, imprisoning his predecessors; John XII. was a slave to vice and debauch." The same writer (Vol. 7. c. 16. page 14.) says, " Pope Alexander VI. died August 17, 1503, by the poison which he had prepared for another, loaded with the iniquities of himself and his natural son Cæsar Borgea." I present to your consideration this picture. These are specimens of the POPES.

As to the Priesthood at large, and also the Monasteries, Nunneries, &c., and the *immoral* doctrines as well as lives of the Clergy, Jesuits, &c. I have in several successive letters given full, satisfactory, unanswered, and unnoticed authorities. To them I now refer you. If they are not sufficient, *enough* is in reserve. The worst, the half has not been told!

Now according to your promise, I call on you to meet these testimonies from Roman Catholic historians. Do it with candour, and without evasion, so that the community may see before we close this discussion, *one* example from your pen, of *ingenuous* thinking, and an elevated love, not of victory, but of truth.

In my last letter I exposed the palpable rebellion of the Church of Rome against the laws of God, on the subject of the celibacy of the clergy. You make no other reply than the following, which supplies with insolence, the lack of argument. " But how are we to expect the truth of history from a pen, which, in desperation, corrupts the sacred text of Scripture itself."

Here we have a sample of your usual disingenuousness. In 1 Tim. iii. 2. it is written in your standard Bible, " Oportet ergo Episcopum irreprehensibilem, esse unius uxoris, virum." This is correctly translated in our English version, " a Bishop *must* be blameless, the husband of one wife." Again in Titus i. 6. " If any (Bishop) be blameless, the husband of one wife." Will you compare these verses and say then, with reckless disregard of truth, that I corrupt the *sa-*

rred text, when your own Bible confronts you? Does not this distinctly declare that a Bishop *may* marry; that if he *should he must be the husband* of one wife! And in Titus i. 6. the reference is not to a Bishop who *once* had a wife, but who was living in that relation when the Apostle wrote, viz. " if a Bishop *be*—the husband of one wife." *Peter* " the first Pope," *had a wife*, though Paul had not; and Paul writes, " marriage is honourable in all." But your church forbids marriage to her *clergy*. Is not this fighting against God? While the word of God thus extends to ALL the privilege of matrimony, your Bellarmine says, (I hope you will notice this also in your next letter.) " It is a greater evil to marry than to commit fornication," *i. e.* for those under a vow of celibacy. (Bell. b. 2. De Mon. c. 34.) and Cardinal Campegius (Apud. Sleidan. b. 4.) openly declared before the magistrates of Strasburg; " that it was a greater sin for Priests to marry than to keep several concubines in their own houses." Quod sacerdotes mariti fiant, gravius esse peccatum, quam si plurimas domimeritrices alant!

We come next to the charge of bigotry, and an intolerant, exclusive spirit. In proof of this I adduce the *creed* of your church, the declaration of a Pope, and the Rhemish Translators at large. As you *deny* none of these, we are, I suppose, to take them for granted. Your rejoinder, in charging a *similar* spirit on the Presbyterian church, is of a piece with your extracts from Tertullian, the works of Luther, Wesley, and the life of Bishop Jewel. In citing a paragraph from the 25th chap. of our Confession of Faith, which I insert below, *entire*, you leave out that part which is put in italics. It is as follows: " The visible church, *which is also Catholic, or universal, under the Gospel (not confined to one nation as before under the law)* consists of all those throughout the world, that profess the true religion, together with their children; and is the kingdom of the Lord Jesus Christ, the house and family of God, out of which there is no ordinary possibility of salvation." On this passage thus mutilated you make the following extraordinary comment. " 'This doctrine secures heaven to Presbyterians and their children, and denies the ' possibility' of salvation to all the rest of mankind, Protestants as well as Catholics. And yet you talk about bigotry." Perhaps no conclusion was ever drawn having less connexion with its premises. It is utterly gratuitous and wantonly perverse. So far from being *exclusive*, the name of Presbyterian is not mentioned in this paragraph. The definition takes away all limits more narrow than " the universal church under the Gospel;" and it makes the church to " *consist*," not of Presbyterians, but " of all those throughout the world that profess the true religion, together with their children." In the very next chapter, also, is the following distinct condemnation of all narrow feelings and bigoted opinions. " Saints by profession, are bound to maintain a holy fellowship and communion in the worship of God; and in performing such other spiritual services as tend to their mutual edification; as also in relieving each other in outward things, according to their several abilities and necessities, which communion, as God offereth opportunity, is to be extended unto all those, who, in every place, call upon the name of the Lord Jesus." In chap. 1. of book 1. form of government sec. 5. it is written, " they (*i. e.* the Presb. ch.) believe that there are truths and forms, with respect to which, men of good character and principles may differ. And in all this they think it the duty, both of private Christians and societies, to exercise mutual forbearance towards each other." Such is the spirit of liberality and love which our standards proclaim, and in which our people glory. Thus it is that we delight to extend the right hand of fellowship to all who love our Lord Jesus, and say " *hail sister*" to every church that " holds the head," that is Christ. To you we leave the service of making the truth " *intolerant.*" It is a discovery reserved for the Papacy ; and you glory in your shame when you connect such contradictions. Now in contrast with the above extracts, hear the doctrine of the church of Rome. The canon law declares " it is necessary to salvation for every human being to be subject to the Roman Pontiff." The creed of the church, by which all its members are bound, under a solemn oath, professes, " that without the true faith of the Roman Catholic church, none can be saved." Mr. Hughes says, letter 27, " *no Christians* agreed with Protestants in doctrine, from the days of Christ until the coming of Luther ; *and very few since.*" Of course very few Protestants are saved ! Indeed this is more than intimated, in the succeeding paragraph. If this be so, then truly it is one of the *greatest calamities* that ever befell the American Protestants, that you have been selected to " preach up to them" " the only true church ;" for at every step, you confirm them more and more in *fatal error !* I will only add on this topic, that to this day, once every year, the Pope at Rome, publicly, and *in full form, excommunicates all Protestants ;* and absolution is refused to all those who *harbor these heretics, who read their books*, &c. &c., and all ecclesiastical persons (Mr. Hughes included) are required to publish the Bull, that the faithful may know its contents !

I would now resume the discussion on *Transubstantiation*. This, with its adjuncts is undoubtedly one of the distinguishing, and radical doctrines of the church of Rome. You have presented it at large, in Letter No. 27. Before proceeding to examine your arguments I will refresh the memory of the reader by giving the doctrine in the words of your church. The Council of Trent at its 13th Session thus decreed touching the doctrine of Transubstantiation. "In the first place, the holy Council teacheth, and openly and plainly professeth, that our Lord Jesus Christ, *true God and man*, is truly, really, and *substantially* contained in the pure sacrament of the holy Eucharist, *after* the consecration of the bread and wine, and under the species of those sensible objects." " *By the consecration* of the bread and wine there is *effected* a conversion of the whole substance, the bread into the *substance* of the body of Christ our Lord, and of the whole substance of the wine into the substance of his blood, which conversion is fitly and properly termed by the Holy Catholic Church, *Transubstantiation.*" " If any one shall deny that in the most holy sacrament of the Eucharist, there are contained truly, really, and substantially, the *body* and *blood*, together with the *soul and divinity of our* Lord Jesus Christ ; or say that he is in it only as a sign or figure, or by his power, let him be accursed." The following extracts from the Catechism of the Council of Trent, part 2d, Chap. the 4th, define the method of consecration, &c. &c. " Here the pastor will also explain to the faithful that in this sacrament not only the true *body* of Christ, and *all the constituents of a true body*, as *bones* and *sinews* (velut ossa et nervos) but also Christ, whole and entire are contained."—The Catholic Church, then, firmly believes, and openly professes, that in this *sacrament the words* of *consecration accomplish three* things ; first, that the *true and real body of Christ*, the *same that was born of the Virgin*, and is *now seated at the right hand* of the Father in heaven, is *rendered present* in the holy Eucharist; secondly, that however *repugnant* it may appear *to the dictate of the senses*, no substance of the elements remains in the sacraments ; and thirdly, a natural consequence of the two preceding, and one which the words of consecration also express, that the accidents which present themselves to the eyes, or other senses, exist in a wonderful and ineffable manner, *without a subject*. All the accidents of bread and wine we see ; but they inhere in no *substance*, and exist independently of any. The substance of the bread and wine is so changed into the body and blood of our Lord, that they altogether cease to be the substance of bread and wine." " The accidents cannot inhere in the body and blood of Christ ; they must therefore, *above the whole order of nature*, subsist of themselves, inhering in no subject." Finally, the efficacy of the consecrating act, depends upon the *intention* of the officiating priest, so that if he lacks the intention, to Transubstantiate, no change takes place, and the bread and wine remain the same, (see 6th chap. Coun. Tr. Can. 11.) " Whoever shall affirm that when ministers perform and confer a sacrament, it is not necessary that they should at least have the *intention* to do what the church does, let him be accursed."

In defence of this doctrine, you adduced in letter No. 27, the 6th chap. of John. In letter 28, I exposed so fully your improper use of that passage, that you seem to have abandoned its further aid in defence of Transubstantiation. Your application of it to the defence of the *real* presence, is refuted by two Popes, four cardinals, two archbishops, five bishops, and doctors, and professors of divinity to such a number as to make in all no less than thirty Papal writers, who deny that the 6th chap. of John gives any support to Transubstantiation. The only other portions of Scripture which you adduce in support of this doctrine, are found in the account of the institution of the Eucharist given by Matthew, Mark, Luke, and Paul. The Douay and English translations used in this country, differ so little from each other in these passages, that either will suffice to exhibit the language of institution. We give them in our translation.

Matthew xxvi. 26—29. " And as they were eating, Jesus took bread and blessed it, and brake it, and gave it to the disciples, and said, take, eat; this is my body. And he took the cup, and gave thanks, and gave it to them, saying, Drink ye all of it. For this is my blood of the New Testament, which is shed for many, for the remission of sins. But I say unto you, I will not drink henceforth of this fruit of the vine, until that day when I drink it new with you in my Father's Kingdom." Mark xiv. 22—25, differs from Matthew only by adding, "and they all drank of it." Luke xxii. 19—20, adds: "'This do in remembrance of me." 1 Cor. xi. 23—27. "The Lord Jesus, the same night in which he was betrayed, took bread; and when he had given thanks, he brake it, and said, Take, eat; this is my body, which is broken for you; this do in remembrance of me. After the same manner also, he took the cup, when he had supped, saying, This cup is the New Testament in my blood; this do ye, as oft as ye drink it, in remembrance of me. Wherefore, whosoever shall eat this bread, and drink *this* cup of the Lord, unworthily, shall be guilty of the body and blood of the Lord."

I. The question between us is not, *whether* Christ be present in this Sacrament; but *how* he is present. Evangelical Protestants all allow, as their standards clearly evince, that Christ is *spiritually* present; and the truth of Christ's words recorded above, they undoubtedly believe. But they utterly deny that the bread and wine are by the consecration of a priest changed into the very, the real body and blood "bones and sinews" of Christ, so that the bread and wine no longer remain; but under their appearance is contained that same Christ who was born of the Virgin, together with his soul and divinity. This we deny to be meant in the words of the institution. In fact it is upon the *wrong interpretation* of these passages that the proof of transubstantiation rests. Here observe, there is no necessity of taking the words *literally*. You admit that there are *figures* used in the Bible. Why then take these *literally?* When the Apostle tells us (Ephesians v. 30.) "We are members of Christ's *body*, of his *flesh*, and of his *bones;*" and calls it "a great mystery"—is it *literal* or *figurative?* Surely he does not mean to say the *bones* and *flesh* of Christ are *substantially* in every believer? When Christians are said, (Hebs. vi. 4.) "To be made *partakers of the Holy Ghost*," are we to understand that they are *really deified?* Or (1 Cor. x. 17.) "We being many, are *one bread and one body*." Does it mean that all Christians are first compounded into one *body*, and then that body is transmitted into one great *loaf?* Yet literally taken it must be so? You will not deny that *figures* may be used in a *sacrament*. For this is the very nature of a sacrament, to be an outward sign and figure of some invisible grace and benefit. Besides, the words of this sacrament are replete with figure. When it is said, "this cup is the New Testament in my blood," *there* is a figure; viz. the *cup* is put for the *wine;* for if it be *literal*, then the *cup* is changed (and not the wine;) and the cup is changed into the *New Testament*, and not into *Christ's blood*. Or if you say that it is the *wine* which is changed into a Testament, then we have this absurdity, viz. that the *testator*, is also the *testament*. But you will not deny that it is by a *figure* that the cup is called the New Testament. I ask, then, why it may not be by a figure, that the wine is called the blood of Christ, and the bread his body? Again, these words "this cup is the New Testament in my blood," plainly show that what is *in* the cup is not *really* the blood of Christ. For suppose "*this cup*" to mean "*this blood*," then we make Christ say "this blood is the New Testament in my blood;"

that is, the blood of Jesus Christ is *in* the blood of Jesus Christ. In order to avoid this absurdity, Bellarmine actually makes *two sorts* of blood of Jesus Christ. (Book 1. chap. 11. of the Eucharist.) The conclusion, then, is irresistable, that since *literally* taken, it makes *nonsense*, it is spoken in a *figure*. Besides, if the words " this is my body," are to be taken literally, then the bread is changed into the body of the *Priest*, and not the body of Christ, as it is the Priest who speaks. For your church holds, that the *Priest* (tanquam gerens personam Christi,) *personates Christ*, when he repeats the words of consecration; and that they operate what they signify. Hence it is the *priest's body* and not *Christ's*, which is wrought into the Sacrament; and the priest's body which the people *worship*. If not, then the words of consecration, were only *historical*, and used in a *figure*. Observe still further, that the words are not, " this *shall be* my body," nor " this is *made*, or *shall be changed into my body*," but " *this is my body*." Now the word " *this*," can refer to no other substance, than that which was present when our Lord spoke that word. But the only substance which was then present was *bread*. This is acknowledged by your own authorities. In the gloss upon Gratian, (De Consecrat. Dist. Cap. 55.) it is said, " it is impossible that *bread* should be the *body* of Christ." Bellarmine also owns, (Book 1. chap. 1. on the Eucharist) " that these words, viz. ' this is my body,' must be taken *as a figure*, bread being the body of Christ in *signification*, (significative) or else it is plainly *absurd* and *impossible;* for it cannot be that *bread* should be the *body* of Christ." It clearly appears, then, that when Christ said " this is my body," he meant it *in a figure*. Hence, in Luke 22. 19, it is written : " He took *bread* and gave thanks and gave it unto them saying, *this is my body*, which is given for you, this do in remembrance of me." Now what did he call his body, but that which he *gave* to his disciples? What did he give to them, but that which he *broke?* And what was it he broke, but what he *took?* And does not Luke tell us, in so many words that he *took bread?* Then was it not of the *bread* he spoke when he said " *this is my body ?*" But could bread be his body in any other way than as a sacrament, in a figure, or as he expressly tells us, a *memorial* of his body? The Apostle Paul puts this subject beyond doubt, (in 1st Cor. 10. 16.) " the bread which we break, is it not the communion of the body of Christ." Is not this a distinct declaration, that the *bread* is the *body* of Christ? And if so, did not Bellarmine rightly say that we must understand it *figuratively*, since it is impossible that bread should be *literally* the body of Christ? Let it not be said that Paul meant that which *once* was bread, but now is the *real* body of Christ; for he says " the bread which we *break;*" and you own that the real body of Christ cannot be *broken*. So that it is bread and only bread which is meant in the words of institution; and therefore, when Christ said " this is my body," he spoke of it *sacramentally*, and in a *figure;* and not of his *real* body.

This is, if possible, still more plain in the other part of the Sacrament. Matth. xxvi. 27, 28. " He took the cup and gave thanks, and gave it to them, saying, drink ye all of it, for this is my blood of the New Testament;" or as Luke and Paul recite it, " this cup is the New Testament in my blood." Now your church acknowledges, that Christ delivered these words, *before* the act of consecration; and therefore, before the *change* took place. Hence it was *wine*, which he called his blood; it was *wine* of which he said, "drink ye all of it;" or as he also called it "the fruit of the vine." Now since you must confess that it is impossible for *wine*, or the *fruit of the vine* to be *really* the blood of Christ, and since notwithstanding, Christ *called* it his blood *before* consecration, he could have meant nothing else than his blood in a *figure*, or sacramentally.

It appears then, incontestably from an examination of the words of the institution, that the doctrine of Transubstantiation is not taught in them; that so far from this, it reduces the language of Christ to inextricable difficulties and absurdities to put such a meaning on his words; and that the only consistent and intelligible sense of which they are capable is that which evangelical Protestants give them. It is remarkable also, how strictly our interpretation accords with the usage of the sacred writers. Thus, Genesis xli. 26. "The seven good kine *are (i. e.* represent) seven years; and the seven good ears *are*, seven years." Daniel vii. 24. " The ten horns out of this kingdom *are (i. e.* signify) ten kings that shall arise." 1 Cor. x. 4. "They drank of that spiritual rock which followed them, and that rock *was* (represented) Christ." Rev. i. 20. "The seven stars *are* (represent) the angels of the seven churches; and the seven candlesticks *are* (represent) the seven churches." Matth. xiii. 28, 39. "The good seed *are* (represent or signify) the children of the kingdom; the tares *are* (signify) the children of the wicked one: the enemy *is* (signifies) the devil; the harvest *is* (signifies) the end of the world; and the reapers *are* (signify) the angels." With such undoubted testimony from the word of God, who can question it, that when Christ says, "this is my body," he means this *represents* my body. We here subjoin a very striking example from Augustine (De doctrin. Christian, Lib. 3. cap. 46.) which speaks volumes as to your false doctrine of Transubstantiation, whether you found it on the 6th chapter of John, or on the words of institution. "If, says he, the saying be perceptive, either forbidding a wicked action, or commanding to do that which is good, it is *no figurative* saying; but if it seems to command any villainy or wickedness, or forbid what is profitable and good, it *is figurative*. This saying, ' except ye eat the flesh of the Son of man, and drink his blood ye have no life in you,' (John vi. 53,) seems to command a *villainous*, or *wicked* thing; it is therefore a FIGURE, enjoining us to *communicate* in the *passion* of our Lord, and to lay it up in dear and profitable *remembrance*, that his flesh was crucified and wounded for our sakes."

From the above examination, how clear is the proof, that the word of God entirely fails you in sustaining the doctrine of Transubstantiation. But to show you that this is not merely a Protestant statement, let me point you again to Roman Catholic authorities. Bellarmine admits, (Book III. chap. 23. on Euch.) " though the Scripture quoted by us above seems clear to us, and ought to convince any man who is not froward, yet it may justly be doubted whether it be so, (that is, whether Transubstantiation can be proved from Scripture) when the most learned and accute men, such as Scotus in particular, hold a contrary opinion." Cardinal Cajetan, a famous Roman Catholic writer, says, (Notes on Aquinas, p. 3. q. 75. Art. 1. &c.) "The other point which the Gospel has *not expounded expressly*, that is the change of the bread into the body of Christ; *we have received from the church.*" And again, "There appears nothing in the Gospel to compel any man to understand these words, '*this is my body*,' in a proper sense. Nay, the PRESENCE (of Christ) which the church holdeth, *cannot be proved*, unless the declaration of the church be added." These words are expunged from the Roman edition of Cajetan, by order of Pope Pius V. !!! It is also undeniable, that Durand, Ocham, and the Cardinal of Cambray, Gabriel Biel, Cardinal Contarinus, Melchoir Cane, and Fisher, Bishop of Rochester, a martyr of your church, unite with Scotus, in granting that the doctrine of transubstantiation *cannot be proved from Scripture.* And now, here we might rest our cause. For if the word of God will not sustain transubstantiation, in vain do you go to the *authority* of the church, or the testimony of the Fathers. But we will meet you at all points.

II. *We come then next to the testimony of the Fathers.* On this subject we remark: 1. That their unanimous consent is necessary to prove an article of faith in your church. It is a part of your rule of faith (See Creed of Pius IV.) "never to take, or interpret the sacred Scriptures, otherwise than according to the *unanimous consent of the Fathers.*" Of course, if the Fathers are *divided* on this subject, they avail you nothing. 2. It will abundantly appear in what follows, to say the least, that the *body* of their testimony is entirely against transubstantiation. 3. If this be true, then it cannot, on your own principles, be an *article of faith* in the church of Christ. 4. If you deny this, then all the Fathers who agree with Protestants were *Heretics.* But of the many cited below, who denied the real presence, none was on that account excommunicated as a heretic. Then it follows that all such were Protestants in their principles, and that our doctrine was not only tolerated, but professed and held at large by the Fathers of the church. 5. Such *liberties* have been taken by your church with the writings of the Fathers, and the pruning knife and various forgeries have been so frequently resorted to, that every testimony *in our favour* is to be esteemed incontrovertible indeed. 6. The fathers often used strongly figurative language, in speaking of the Eucharist; and the writings of some *late* in the history of the church, savour of the real presence; but mingled with much contradiction and absurdity. With these remarks we proceed to examine their authority on this subject, by way of contrast with the doctrine of the church of Rome. 1. The Fathers differ from the church of Rome in determining what that thing is which Christ calls "*my body.*" We have seen above, that the gloss on Gratian and Bellarmine, (and we might add Salmeron, Kellison, and Vasquez,) explicitly state that the word "*this*" cannot refer to the *substance* of the *bread*, for they say, bread cannot be the body of Christ Now the Fathers expressly tell us that bread *is* Christ's body. Hence it must be in a *figure* as Protestants believe. Irœneus, in the second century, (Adv. Hæres. L. 5. c. 2.) says, "Our Lord confessed the cup which is of the creature to be his blood, and the bread which is of the creature he confirmed it to be his body." Clement of Alexandria, second century, writes, (Pædag. Lib. 2. c. 2.) "Our Lord blessed the wine, saying, take, drink; this is my blood, the blood of the grape; for the holy river of gladness (that is, the wine) does alegorically signify the word *(i. e.* the blood of the word) shed for many for the remission of sins." Tertullian, (Lib. 4. Advers. Marcion, c. 40.) thus writes, "the bread that he took and distributed to his disciples, he made it his body, saying, 'this is my body,' that is, the *figure* of my body." So likewise Cyprian, Eusebius, Origen, Cyril of Jerusalem, Jerome, Chrysostom, Augustine, &c. and the seventh General Council at Constantinople, confirm the above testimonies. Here then we have a decisive proof that the ancient Fathers considered Christ as speaking in a *figure*, when he said " this is my body," and of course they rejected the doctrine of transubstantiation.

2. The Fathers, contrary to the doctrine of transubstantiation, make the bread and wine to be the *Sacrament, sign, type, and image of Christ's blood and body.* Origen (Com. in Math. 15.) speaking of the Eucharist, says, " this much may suffice concerning the *typical* and *symbolical* body." Isodore, speaking of the bread and wine, (De. Off. Ecc. l. i. c. 18.) says, "these two are visible, but being sanctified by the Holy Spirit, they pass into a *sacrament* of his divine body." Augustine calls the Eucharist (In Psal. 3.) "a banquet in which he commended and delivered to his disciples the *figure* of his body and blood." The words of the office of Ambrose (Lib. 4. de Sac. c. 5.) are very striking. " Wouldst thou know that the Eucharist is consecrated by heavenly words? Hear then what the words are. The Priest says, make this oblation to us allowable, rational, acceptable, which is the *figure* of the body and blood of our Lord Jesus Christ." In the present canon of the Mass (a confession that transubstantiation is new) the words *figure of the body*, are altered to read, *may it be made to us the body*, fiat nobis corpus. Eusebius (Lib. 8 Demon. Evang.) thus writes, "Christ delivered to his disciples the *symbols* of his divine economy, requiring them to make an *image* of his body." Ambrose says, " none can ever have been an *image* of *himself;*" and Cyril of Alexandria says, "a *type* is not the *truth*, but rather imports the *similitude* of the truth;" and Gregory Nyssen, "an *image* would be no longer such, if it were altogether the *same* with *that* of which it is an image." And yet the church of Rome ventures the following anathema, " whosoever shall deny that in the most holy sacrament of the Eucharist there are truly, *really*, and *substantially contained* the *body* and *blood* of our Lord Jesus Christ, together with his soul and divinity, and consequently, Christ entire; but shall affirm that he is present therein only in a *sign* or *figure*, or by his *power:* let him be accursed." 3. The Fathers directly contradict the church of Rome in this, that they say Christ's body is eaten *spiritually*, whereas the

church of Rome says that Christ's body is eaten, *literally* and *carnally*. Berringer, A. D. 1059, recanted the *Protestant* doctrine before the General Council of Lateran, under this proscribed form, "that the *true* body of our Lord Jesus Christ, not only in the *sign* and sacrament, but in truth, is *handled* and *broken* by the Priest's hands, and *ground by the teeth* of the faithful." We have seen above how St. Augustine declares that it is a "crime," and "horrid thing" to speak of "eating Christ's real flesh;" and therefore he explains it *spiritually*. Origen says, (Hom. 7. in Levit.) "not only in the *Old* Testament is found the *killing letter;* there is also in the *New* Testament a letter that *kills* him who does not *spiritually* consider what is said. For if thou follow this according to the letter which was said, 'unless ye eat my flesh and drink my blood,' *this letter kills*." Macarius (Homil. 27.) "They which are partakers of the visible *bread* do *spiriturlly* eat the flesh of the Lord." Augustine (In Psl. 98.) represents our Lord as saying "understand spiritually what I have spoken. Ye are *not* to eat *this* body which ye *see*, nor to *drink* that *blood* which they *shall shed*, who will crucify me. I have commended a *certain sacrament* to you, which, if *spiritually* understood, will give life to you; and since it is necessary this sacrament should be *visibly celebrated*, yet it must be *invisibly understood* by you." This is the very language of evangelical Protestants. What makes this position still more clear, is that the Fathers make Christ as *really* present in baptism, as in the eucharist. Thus Chrysostom, (Cat. ad. Illum.) speaking to those who were to receive baptism, says, "you shall be *clothed* with the purple garment dyed in the Lord's blood." Fulgentius (De. Bapt. Aethiop. Cap. Ult.) writes, "neither need any one at all doubt that then, every believer is made *partaker of our Lord's body and blood*, when he is made a member of Christ in baptism."

4. The Fathers deny the *substantial presence* of Christ's natural body in the Eucharist, and thus differ wholly from the church of Rome. This may be proved from the writings of Ambrose, Augustine, Cyril, Chrysostom, Gregory, Nazianzen, &c.

5. The Fathers positively assert that the *substance* of the bread and wine remains *after* consecration, which is directly the reverse of transubstantiation. In Theodoret's Dialogues 2. it is written "after sanctification the mystical *symbols* do not *depart* from their own *nature*, for they *remain* still in their former *substance* and *figure* and *form*, and may be *seen* and *touched just as before*. But they are understood to be that which they are made, and are believed and venerated as being what they are believed to be." (Dial. 1.) "He (Christ) honoured the visible *symbols* with the *appellation* of his body and blood, not *altering* nature, but to nature adding *grace*." The same may be proved from Peter Martyr, Chrysostom, Pope Gleasius, Facundus, Origen, Cyprian, Irenæus, Ambrose, Augustine, &c.

The multiplication of particulars and of proofs would be endless. But from the Fathers it may abundantly be gathered, that transubstantiation was not the doctrine of the early church. They contradict the church of Rome about the nature and properties of bodies; they deny that "accidents" or properties can exist without a subject, that is, the appearance of bread, without its *substance;* they deny that our senses can deceive us in the Eucharist; they deny that any but the faithful *can* eat "Christ's body;" the absurd use of the word *species* in your church was unknown to them; they professed no *miracle* in the Eucharist such as you do, but make it a *spiritual* mystery; they gave the cup to the people, as well as the bread; they never elevated the Eucharist that it might be adored; they took no care to *reserve* what remained of the consecrated elements after administration, and they allowed the people to make what use they pleased of them; and they even used to send the elements from one Bishop to another as a token of peace; strange use, impious custom, if indeed it was the *real* body of Christ! In all these things they differed wholly from the church of Rome; and by these differences showed that they believed not the doctrine of transubstantiation. I hope hereafter, to have the opportunity of presenting the argument from the Fathers to the community at full length, either in a public discussion with you, or if you *decline* this, in a form which will give room for ample citation of authorities. In the mean time let me say, in reference to the work of Thomas Moore (from whom you seem chiefly to draw your testimonies,) that there is not a more garbled, dishonest and superficial view of the writings of the Fathers, in any language.

III. The doctrine of Transubstantiation is not only against the Scripture and the Fathers, but it is *contrary to reason, and contradicts all our senses.* Bellarmine himself acknowledges, (Book 2. chap. 12. De Eucharist) "we might be accounted fools truly, if *without the word* of God, we believed the *true flesh* of Christ to be eaten with the *mouths* of our bodies." But we have shown conclusively that it is believed *without* the authority of God's word. Hence on his principles it is an absurdity. When you attempt to put this doctrine by the side of the Trinity, the Incarnation of Christ, &c. you compare the most opposite and dissimilar things. There is not a mystery, or a doctrine of Christianity that is contrary to reason. In saying therefore, "when you study mathematics, you *reason*, but in revelation you *believe*," you can mean, I suppose, nothing more than Bellarmine does, (Lib. 1. cap. 7. De Just.) "that faith is better defined by *ignorance* than *knowledge.*" In revelation, as in mathematics, we reason upon *facts*, communicated in the one case through God's *word*, in the other through his *works*. When his word reveals facts which connect themselves with his works, they do not contradict each other. It is not a contradiction to say that Jesus Christ was a perfect man and yet God, though the revelation is *above* our reason. But it *is* a contradiction to say that a piece of bread can become a perfect man, "bones, sinews, body and soul;" that the man Christ Jesus, who is in Heaven, should at the same time be *bodily* in the bread, nay, in ten thousand pieces of bread, in ten thousand places at the same time; that the bread should be turned into the *substance* of Christ, and yet nothing of the bread become any of Christ, either as to matter, form or properties; that the bread should yet be so changed into Christ's substance as to cease to be bread, and still retain the *appearances* of bread, so that there should be a long, broad, thick, white, heavy, moist, active, passive *nothing ;* that there should be length and nothing long, breadth and nothing broad, thickness and nothing thick, whiteness and nothing white, weight and nothing heavy, &c. &c. ; that this strange something nothing, seeming bread and not bread, the body of Christ yet seeming bread, should be eaten and pass into our blood and should be a body, and yet not diminished, and be living in heaven entire and unbroken, while all this is going on upon earth, is, I say, an infinite absurdity. Yet this is a part of the doctrine of Transubstantiation. Again, the proof of miracles rests on the testimony of the senses. Hence when Christ rose from the dead, he said to unbelieving Thomas, "*handle* me and see, for a spirit hath not *flesh* and *bones* as ye see me have." All the miracles of the Bible appeal to the senses of men ; that is *not* a miracle which the senses cannot *discern;* and that it is not a true miracle which *contradicts* the senses. Hume's argument in favour of infidelity proceeds upon the denial of the testimony of the senses ; and if Transubstantiation be true, he cannot be confuted. Now the senses say that the bread is still bread, and the wine, still wine, after all your consecration ; therefore there is no miracle, or the senses would *discern* it ; it is not the flesh of Christ for the senses all say it is *bread*. When, therefore, you say I have " forgotten my philosophy," you discover that the philosophy of the Bible, and of Newton and of Bacon, and of common sense, all are with me. Your church seemed to feel this difficulty in its canons and its catechism. Thus the Catechism says, "*however repugnant it may appear to the dictate of the senses no substance of the elements remains in the sacraments.*" In fact, in the whole account of the Eucharist, there are almost as many absurdities as words. When you refer to the Holy Ghost appearing at the baptism of Christ in the form of a dove, you not only forget your philosophy, but pervert your Bible. The Holy Ghost never had a *human body:* He appeared in the form of a dove ; and we do not deny that God may manifest himself in a visible form. But the cases are not parallel. If it had been said, that what appeared to be a dove, was a *man*, and yet had all the *external appearances* of a dove, and that this *same man*, which appeared a dove to John at Jordan, was at the *same time* in Heaven on the Throne a real man, then you might have claimed it for an illustration.

It is a remarkable fact that the ancient heathen, Jews, and Infidels, such as Celsus, and Porphyry, Lucian, Julian and Trypho, who used all their wit and cunning to oppose the doctrine and worship of Christians, and who attacked by name the doctrines of the Trinity, the Sonship of Christ, his Incarnation, Crucifixion, and our Resurrection, *as absurdities*, never once noticed the doctrine of the *real* presence, which surely is the mystery of mysteries. From this it is evident that the doctrine was not then known. This is the more clear from the fact that Julian was once initiated into the Christian Church, and therefore, knew all their doctrines and mysteries ; yet he attacked all the rest and never *named* this. But on the other hand, just about the time at which Transubstantiation was *adopted*, A. D. 1215, Jews and Mahommedans, and others, with great fulness and frequency, attacked this doctrine. Averroes, a Mahommedan, whom we quoted in a former letter, saying, " that Christians first *made* their God, then *ate* him," lived in the same age with Innocent III. and the Lateran Council, which introduced this doctrine, sat under Innocent. Now we object not to the doctrine because Mahommedans, Jews, &c. opposed i. but because they never opposed it *before*, though they opposed whatever they thought absurd *before* that age; and have opposed *this* doctrine ever since that age; therefore, we infer that in that age it was *adopted*. There is also this singular fact, that the *taking away* of *the cup* from the people immediately followed the adoption of Transubstantiation. As the wine (by this doctrine) is Christ's *real* blood, so the use of the *cup* exposed it to be *spilt*; and besides as the blood is said to be in the *body*, so the *cup* became useless. He that runs may read and understand this.

IV. We notice briefly the origin of this doctrine. The last remark goes far to prove its recent date. Scotus, a Roman Catholic writer, (as Bellarmine owns) states "that it was not an article of faith before the Lateran Council, A. D. 1215." It is false when you charge me with saying that this doctrine was not held before 1215; but I still assert that it was never an *article* of faith before. In proof of this I refer not only to Scotus, but to Tonstal, to Durand, Erasmus, and Alfonsus a Castro. Erasmus says, (De Hæres, B. 8.) "that it was *late* before the church *defined* Transubstantiation, which was *unknown* to the *ancients*, both name and thing." And now I challenge you to produce any proof that it was enacted an article of faith before 1215. It was agitated for some time before; it was matter of *discussion* in the church till the year 1059, when Berringer recanted the *truth* on this subject; in 1079 his recantation was *amended*; and finally, after a world of strife, through several ages, the doctrine was promoted into an article of faith in 1215.

V. Your objections are so trivial and puerile, that they scarcely deserve notice. You say, "if the body of Christ was not in the Sacrament how could men *discern* it there?" I answer, can you *discern* the body *after* Transubstantiation? Is not the very word "*species*" used in your Church to cover the absurdity of saying Christ's *flesh* is there, though we *discern* only *bread?* Truly, if the evidence of Christianity had rested on such miracle as no man can *see*, we should all have been without a religion! *We* discern Christ *spiritually; you* worship the bread and superinduce *idolatry* upon the Eucharist.

You say: "to *creatures* deputed by God some *power* was given, but to Christ *all power*, both in heaven and in earth, and it was in the Eucharist alone that this *all power* was exercised." Strange indeed! Christ " exercised this all power" in the only way in which, from the nature of the case, nobody could see, feel, or know that it was exercised! Other miracles, you say, creatures could work by delegation; other miracles as raising the dead, passing the Red Sea, &c. &c., spoke for themselves, and were seen as soon as done. But this miracle, which " *all*" Christ's power and his "*alone*" could operate, is dumb and invisible; none ever discerned it, or ever can; and in order to know it, you must tell us it has been done, and we must disbelieve our *senses* in order to believe *you*. Besides, are not all miracles, by the power, and to the glory of Christ? And does not this pretended miracle degrade his humanity, and Deify the operating Priest? And does it not destroy all miracles to believe this miracle? If this be true all others *may* be false, for this falsifies all those senses on which the truth of other miracles rest. You say Christ and his Apostles did not warn Christians of the error of Transubstantiation, though they spoke of other errors that were to arise; and you more than intimate that Christ was "*guilty of duplicity,*" if Transubstantiation be false. Such profanity needs no comment. But I ask, did Christ and his Apostles warn Christians of the Protestant error of *denying* the real presence? Did he not warn them of "seducing spirits;" of "their lying wonders;" of their "changing the truth of God into a lie;" "exalting themselves above God;" "forbidding to marry," &c. &c.? These prophetic warnings are so direct and clear, that they are written in as sun-beams on the Vatican at Rome.

VI. As the *real* presence of Christ depends upon the *intention* of the Priest who consecrates; (See the Canon already quoted) and as Bellarmine owns, (Book 3. Chap. 8 Justn.) "no man can be certain, with the certainty of faith that he receives a true Sacrament; because it depends on the minister's intention to consecrate it; and none can see another's intention;" it follows irresistibly that to worship the consecrated wafer exposes every member of your Church to continual and gross idolatry. For how can you be certain? And if you are not certain, how dare you worship it? For if it be not truly consecrated, you encourage, and you practise gross idolatry.

VII. It would be quite amusing, if it did not call up, along with that feeling, others more serious, to find you claiming the *ancient Liturgies*, as teaching Transubstantiation. I here venture to assert that there is *not one word* of truth in all you have said on that subject; and I am prepared to prove what I say whenever you please. So far is what you say from being true, that the Mass, decretals, and glosses of the Church of Rome do much to *overthrow* Transubstantiation, as I will show in my next letter, if you deny it; and so confessed is this, that the Mass has been *altered* so as to *change* the *ancient* Liturgy, (which was *against* Transubstantiation) to *make* it *speak for* it. There is another fact on this subject, which speaks volumes in behalf of the *Protestant* doctrine. It is that the ancient Syrian Christians, called St. Thomas's Christians, because evangelized by the Apostle Thomas, and who have come down with the Bible in their hands from the days of the Apostles, reject *Transubstantiation*, as well as "the *Apochryphal books,*" which your church has foisted into the canon. For these, and other *Protestant* doctrines, their Breviary, Book of Homilies, &c. were condemned by a Roman Catholic Synod held in Goa, India, A. D. 1599. But more of this hereafter. May I not then retort the question, " what have you now to say for yourself?"

Thus we see that on every point Transubstantiation is a false, shocking, novel doctrine. With Transubstantiation falls the sacrifice of the Mass. Upon Transubstantiation, every thing important and decisive in the church of Rome may be said in a degree to hang. It is on account of its importance, and dreadful evils that I have entered so largely into the discussion of it. Having not room to take up your remarks in the last letter on the sacrifice of the mass and communion in one kind, I for the present refer our readers to my exposure of them in letters No. 22 and 24.

And now the *doctrine* of *truth* which remains on the subject of the Eucharist, is the simple and sublime institution founded by Jesus Christ, practised by the earliest Christians, taught by the Fathers for the first six hundred years, and now held and practised by the great body of Protestants in Europe and America, which makes the elements of bread and wine to be symbols and figures of the body and blood of Christ; which gives the bread and the wine to all who commune; which makes saving faith the qualification to partake profitably, and to discern the spiritual presence of Christ in his sacrament; and which is the only rational and consistent construction that can be put upon the words of institution. Luther's doctrine called " consubstantiation," retains a remnant of his Papal errors, as his great mind was in *transition* from the absurdities of the real presence towards the simple and beautiful institution of Jesus Christ. But whatever his doctrine was, it is radically different from yours, whose enormous evils his eyes were opened to behold.

You lug in " the review" of your review of " Bishop Onderdonk's charge on the Rule of Faith," *as if you had nothing to do beside*. When I called you out on *tradition* you declined to appear. Now you would *divert me* from unveiling to an astonished nation, the true history and real doctrines of the Papacy. But no, no! Our respected Episcopal brethren do not need my humble help. I suppose you never read Tillotson nor Barrow, nor Usher (" whose authority" I know your church has never loved, nor met) nor Stillingfleet, nor Sherlock, nor Patrick, nor Wake, whom Bossuet could *not* forget. Go read them and be humble!

The personal vanity displayed in your notice of this review makes me ashamed of you. And then to repeat the wretched tale of " a bookseller (as you have been told) having been forbidden to keep it for sale!" Have you forgotten the Index Expurgatorius at Rome, for pruning books, and prohibiting their perusal and sale, yes, even of the Bible? May I ask who this bookseller is? May I call for the name of your informant? Surely I have more right to do so, than you had to demand the Rev Mr. Burtt's? Who then are these whose scandals you retail and publish against the Episcopal community?

In my next letter, if my life is continued, I will classify and extend my answers to your stereotype stale questions. They have already been replied to. But you shall not complain of my silence. In the mean time I ask an answer to the following enquiries, viz :

1. Did Pope Liberius subscribe the Arian creed, yes or no ?
2. Did the councils of Sermium and Ariminum adopt Arian creeds ?
3. Does the validity of ordinations, administration of the sacraments, &c. depend on the *intention* of Popes, Bishops, and Priests ?
4. Was there ever a time when there was a schism in the Popedom, when several persons claimed to be popes at once, and it was not certainly known who was the true pope; and were there ever any *false* popes ?
5. Do you approve the decrees of councils, rules of the Index, and bulls of popes against the freedom of the press ? Is there not *now* a committee at Rome who may, and do, prohibit to all the church the printing, sale, and reading of any books they please ? If so, do you approve of this ?
6. Why is *money* paid for indulgences, masses for the dead, and in aid of souls in Purgatory ?
7. Was it right to *abolish* the order of the Jesuits ? Was it right to *restore* it ? The same two questions also touching the Inquisition ?
8. If the Jewish church was infallible why do you reject all *her* traditions ? These questions bear directly on the controversy. An explicit answer to them will gratify the community, many of whom are surprised that you *evade* so many subjects brought before you; and it will also much oblige your obedient servant, JOHN BRECKINRIDGE.

CONTROVERSY. No. XXXI.

IS THE PROTESTANT RELIGION THE RELIGION OF CHRIST?
Philadelphia, September 24, 1833.

To the Rev. John Breckinridge.

Rev. Sir,—Mr. Breckinridge says that "*the Protestant is the religion of Christ.*"
If so, I call upon him 1st. To tell me what the Protestant religion is?
2. I call upon him to say what society of Christians ever taught this pretended "*religion of Christ,*" previous to the Reformation?
3. I call upon him to say, whether Christ revealed ALL the doctrines of the Protestant religion, beginning with the best IMAGE of his church, Episcopalianism, and terminating with the most consistent of Protestant sects, the Unitarians?— and if not, how MANY denominations, out of the whole, belong to the TRUE Protestant religion, the religion of Christ?
4. I call upon him to show whether the Reformers received any NEW ministerial authority, after the withdrawal of that which they had received from the church?
5. I call upon him, in case no such NEW authority was received, to show that the Protestant clergy, so called, have any divine right to exercise the Christian ministry, more than other educated laymen?

In my last letter I promised to "expose you," in case you would mention "the page" of any Catholic historian who states what you had asserted, respecting the immorality of the Popes and clergy of Rome. You have complied with your part of the condition, and now, it is for me to fulfil *mine*. You give two extracts; and refer me to the pages where they are to be found. The one is from "Thuanus, Book 37. p. 776." The history of Thuanus has been condemned at Rome by two public decrees; the one of November 9, 1609; the other of May 10, 1757; from which fact, the reader may see with how little propriety he deserves to be called a "Roman Catholic historian." He was, says a modern author, Paquot, "an audacious writer; the implacable enemy of the Jesuits; the calumniator of the Guises: the copyist, flatterer, friend of the Protestants; and was far from being even just *(parum æquus)* to the Holy See, the Council of Trent, or any thing Catholic." But *hostile as he was*, I am not certain that the extract given in your letter is contained in his work; which is not in my possession If it is to be found in the city, I shall examine it. Among Catholics, however, he is any thing but an *accredited* historian.

You mention as another *Catholic historian*, Dupin. We disown him; and for the following reason. His secret papers were examined on the 10th of February, 1719, at the Palais Royal, and it was found, as Lafitau testifies, that in his correspondence with Archbishop Wake, of Canterbury, on the subject of a re-union between the English and Catholic churches, he was ready to give up the following points. 1. Auriacular Confession. 2. Transubstantiation. 3. Religious Vows. 4. The fast of Lent and abstinence. 5. The supremacy of the Pope. 6. The Celibacy of the Clergy; having probably anticipated you in discovering that a Bishop " must be" the husband of one wife. But it is clear, that a man who could so far *betray the Catholic Religion*, is not entitled to the credit or appellation of a Catholic historian. From him, however, you give no extract.

But Baronius *is* a Catholic historian. You refer to " the page" of his Annals for A. D. 908. From this you give an extract: I have consulted the text, and find: 1st. That you suppress *that* part of the passage, which, so far from criminating the legitimate Popes, absolutely vindicates them from your charge. 2d. That you absolutely FALSIFY Baronius, (if indeed you ever saw the original,) by making him say the very contrary of what he has said. To put the matter to rest, I shall *mark the pages*, and leave two copies of Baronius, one in Latin, and the other in Italian, at the Athenæum on Thursday morning, together with a copy of your letter, for the curious to compare the one with the other. The public will then see which of us is to be " exposed." If the American people pride themselves on their love of TRUTH, these little matters will open their eyes to the impositions that have been practiced upon them and their fathers. They will see to what an extent their credulity has been abused, on the subject of the Catholic religion. They will see, moreover, that you EVADE the *only question* for which you had pledged yourself: viz. whether " the Protestant Religion be the Religion of Christ?" I furnished ample arguments founded on the authority of the Reformers themselves to prove the contrary. This was in Letter, No. XXIII. Will *they* ever be answered? Is not the author of your last able to refute them? If not; but hold: here is something like a renewal of the promise.

" In my next letter, if my life be continued, I will classify and extend my answers to your past, stale questions." Here, then, is a promise at last, and I hope the " stale" questions will be satisfactorily disposed of. If you had answered them sooner, they would not be " stale."

In the first column of your last letter you return to your " Magdalen Report," but with less of indecent language than had been employed on a former occasion. You do me great wrong, however, when you insinuate that I wished to insult you. I merely stated, with a view to the improvement of your style, that you had given offence to modesty and delicate sentiment, by the elaborate grossness of your descriptions. For this, you should not be displeased with me. I merely held up the mirror of public taste, and instead of attempting to " break the looking glass," you should have endeavoured to correct the deformities (if any) that were reflected by it, until at length, you might look upon the image of your pen without feeling yourself " insulted."

It is true that our own writers have lamented, and do lament the existence of immoralities. But this is common to all denominations. And if it be an argument against the truth of a religion, the deist may quote the example of Judas, and use it against the doctrines of Christ. There are, and have been, immoral men of every religion, and yet I know of no religion that does not profess to condemn im morality. But the man who practises the duties of the Catholic religion is found to be an example of every virtue that can adorn humanity. How then can that religion be made accountable for transgressions that are committed in contempt of her authority and in violation of her precepts? Is Christianity to be held responsible for the crimes of men, calling themselves Christians? Certainly not. So neither is the church accountable for the crimes of individuals. This is manifest to every mind endowed with common sense. When, therefore, you speak of scandalous men in the church, you speak of men who are self-condemned by the very doctrines which they profess. They are Protestants in *morals*, by despising and trampling upon the moral precepts of their religion. But pray do Presbyterians stand so immaculate in public estimation, that you are warranted in wielding the weapons of reproach with so large an assumption of sectarian righteousness? Are there no instances of depravity among your people, your pastors, and ruling elders? Are not "publicans and sinners" sometimes found under the Pharisee's mantle? Are there no "*convictions*" among you, except those of the spirit? If not, you have a right to "cast the first stone." I merely suggest these inquiries to your recollection, leaving it to some pen more reckless than mine to go into specific criminations. Materials are not wanting, and *the public are aware of it.*

Now certainly it is not the *celibacy* of the Protestant clergy that gives occasion to these scandals. Their ministers may be, or as you have discovered "MUST BE" the husband of one wife; and even this does not always protect them from the tongue and the type of scandal. How is this?

Again :—if the details of impudicity be a favourite theme, why did you pass over those of "Brother McDowell's Journal," and other Protestant documents by which it appears that in the city of New York no less than "ten thousand" females have forgotten to be virtuous? And yet New York is a city, in which Protestant ministers are superabundantly numerous, basking in the sunshine of popularity and emolument. This state of morals is certainly not owing to the celibacy of the clergy. Is it to be ascribed to the Protestantism of New York? The analogy of *your* reasoning would lead to that inference.

As to the charge that the Catholic church forbids marriage, it is untrue. She teaches in the very language of St. Paul, that marriage is honourable in all. She holds, however, that there is a holier state, which *is free* for those who, by the divine grace, are called to embrace it. The law of her priesthood enjoins celibacy and chastity, but no one is *compelled* to enter into the ministry of her sanctuary. If they wish to marry, they do well. She does not choose them for her clergy. If they wish not to marry, they do better, freeing themselves from solicitude "about the things of this world, how they may please their wives." But in neither case is there any compulsion. At some future time I may enlarge upon the subject, but at present I merely state the fact to show that you either did not know or did not choose to represent fairly, the doctrine of the church. It is certain that the marriage of Luther and his associates was a shocking scandal even to their followers. And Dr. Miller goes so far as to recommend celibacy among the Protestant clergy, but evidently with the conviction on his mind, that his advice will not be followed. He thinks for example that neither Wesley nor Whitefield should have engaged in matrimony. But the fact is that Protestant clergymen seem to feel it as an inward reproach, that they can furnish no such examples of self-denial, as those which are witnessed in the Catholic priesthood. They feel, that in the trying duties of the ministry, they *dare not* expose their lives, as the Catholic clergy do. When pestilence is in the city, they fly to the country, and when the voice of reproach from their own people pursues them, they take refuge behind their wives and children " according to law." If the example of the Catholic Priests is pointed at, to shame them by the comparison, it only fills them with additional hatred towards clerical *celibacy*. " A Bishop" *must be* " the husband of one wife," and to say the contrary is, you tell us, " fighting against God."

Now, in the Catholic church, the vow of celibacy and chastity, voluntarily assumed, is binding, and constitutes a moral incapacity on the part of those who have taken it, to enter into matrimonial engagements. Such is the case which you select from Bellarmine, in which he contends, as you cannot but know, that the marriage is essentially *null* and *void*. The Catholic religion teaches that the vows of the Priest in his ordination, which he makes by his own free will and choice, are an absolute impediment to any marriage vow, *subsequently* made. To illustrate the case, then, cited from Bellarmine, I would ask you whether an act of conjugal infidelity, in a married person, is as great a sin as polygamy? In other words, whether the Landgrave of Hesse was more guilty in his libertinism, being the husband of only *one* wife, than he was afterwards, when for the peace of his conscience, and " by virtue of an indulgence" from the Reformers, he became the husband of *two ?* Whilst speaking on this subject I may as well direct your attention to a permanent " indulgence," (I mean according to your definition, " license to commit sin,") which I find recorded in your Confession of Faith, in favour of polygamy. In cases of adultery, " or such wilful *desertion* as can in no way be remedied by the church or civil magistrate," the injured party may obtain a divorce, and *with the approbation of the church* enter into a *new* contract of marriage ! ! (See chap. xxiv. p. 110.)

If the church had gone a little farther, and to this " wilful desertion," added " incompatability of disposition," as another cause for dissolving marriage, it would have anticipated the morality of the French Revolution, and even of Miss Wright.

Touching the bigotry and intolerance of the Presbyterian creed, I am glad to see that they are becoming antiquated, if we may credit your magnificent professions of liberality. But with regret I add, that in reference to Catholics, you make an assertion, which, in justice to his Holiness and myself, I must say it is not true. " Once every year," you tell us, " the Pope at Rome, publicly, and in full form, excommunicates all Protestants ; (not true) and absolution is refused to all those who harbour these heretics, who read their books,

&c. (not true) and all ecclesiastical persons, Mr. Hughes included, are required to publish the Bull that the faithful may know its contents," (not a word of truth in it.) How can you write such tales ! But it *is* true that once every year the Pope at Rome, and all the clergy throughout the world, pray to Almighty God for the conversion of all those who are under the delusion of heresy, as well as Jews and Pagans, that they may be gathered from their wanderings, into the unity of faith and into the one sheepfold of Jesus Christ. This is probably what you have mistaken for excommunication.

The Catholic belief is, that out of the true church there is no salvation. But besides those who *profess the true religion*, it considers as implicit members of the church, those who, *invincibly ignorant of the truth*, yet have so upright and sincere a heart towards God, that they would embrace the truth if they knew it. It holds, that those who sin without the law (except by their own fault) shall not be judged by the law. Has Presbyterianism so much charity ? Let us see.

The church, says the Confession of Faith, "consists of all those *throughout the world*, who *profess the true religion."* This is the house of God, "*out of which there is no ordinary possibility of salvation."* Now let us see how large a portion of the human race your doctrine excludes from this "house of God," and to how small a number it reduces the elect. 1st. All the *Jews* since Christ, and all the *Pagans since and before.* 2. All *Mohammedans, Greeks, schismatics,* heretics of the east, and Catholics, whom it expressly denounces as "Idolators." Here then all are lost but Protestants. But 3d, how will *they* fare ? The Synod of Dort, which you hold, condemned Arminianism as heresy. Of course those who hold Arminian doctrines do not 'profess the true religion,' and are shut out, consequently, from the "house of God." Now it is known to all men that 4th, most of the Episcopalians, and 5th, most of the Methodists are on the side of Arminianism, consequently *they* are excluded. 6. Lutherans are, for the error of *consubstantiation.* 7th, the Drs. Brownlee and Cox of New York, have proved to the satisfaction of all the Bishops in the General Assembly, that the Quakers are not even *Christians,* consequently they are done for. As for 8th, Unitarians, 9th, Universalists, 10th, Swedenborgians, and others; it would be out of the question to cherish even a hope for them. This, Rev. Sir, is the charity of the Presbyterian doctrine. Let any man who has common sense see, whether these consequences do not flow from the definition of "the church," "out of which there is no ordinary possibility of salvation," as laid down in your Confession of Faith, "amended" in 1821. Which is the more exclusive ?— Which, the more charitable towards *involuntary and invincible* error? Let those who have eyes and understanding decide.

Your objections to the dogma of the Eucharist, are but the repetition of those which have been urged a thousand times before, and a thousand times refuted. You pass over most of the arguments adduced in my Letter No. 27, to which I beg leave to refer the reader, that I may avoid the necessity of repeating what has already been said You admit that Berringer was condemned as an heretic for denying the doctrine of Transubstantiation in 1059, and yet by a contradiction which I shall not pretend to explain, you assert that Transubstantiation was *not* a doctrine of the church until "1215." That is, a man is condemned by the whole church for denying a doctrine which did not exist!! Now this fact *alone* would prove its existence, unless, indeed, you can persuade men into the belief of a *paradox*. Here, then, you furnish all requisite testimony against yourself. The question is not of the *word* Transubstantiation, as used by the Council of Lateran, but of the *doctrine* which it expresses. Did that doctrine exist before the Council? I say it did, you say it did, since you admit that Berringer was condemned in 1059 *for denying it*. Here then we are agreed. For the rest, your quibble is like that of the Socinians who contend that the divinity of Jesus Christ was not believed in the primitive church, because the words "Consubstantial with the Father" were first used by the Council of Nice, not for the purpose, as you know, of creating a new doctrine; but on the contrary, for the express purpose of DEFENDING a doctrine which had always been believed.

But it is not in this alone that we can trace the exact similarity of your reasoning, to that of the Socinian. It pervades the whole of your objections. To illustrate this allow me to state some of your difficulties in juxta-position with those of the Unitarian argument as sustained by Professor Norton in his "Statement of Reasons" against the Trinity and the divinity of Jesus Christ. In his preface, he *apologises* for writing against a doctrine which he regards as exploded by all *sensible* men, for its absurdity. He means the Trinity. To prove this he does every thing that you do, to show that Transubstantiation should be exploded by sensible men.

He quotes the Scriptures as abundantly and as *figuratively* as you do. He cites passages from the Fathers as confidently as you do. He contends that the Trinity is as great an absurdity as Transubstantiation, and the weapons which *you* wield against the one, *he* wields against the other.

The arguments in both cases are neither more nor less than deistical. Mr. Breckinridge applies reason to the doctrine of Christ's real presence in the Eucharist—Mr. Norton to the doctrine of *three* persons in *one* God. Yet God, says the Bible, out of stones *could* raise up children unto Abraham.

Mr. Breckinridge.
"It is not a contradiction to say that Jesus Christ was a perfect man, and yet God, though the Revelation is *above* our reason."

Mr. Norton.
"The doctrine that Jesus Christ is both God and man, is a CONTRADICTION in terms." (Title of a chapter.)

Mr. Breckinridge.
The doctrine of Christ's *real* presence in the Eucharist proved to be *false* from Scripture.

Mr. Norton.
"The proposition that Christ is God, proved to be *false* from Scripture." Title of Sect. III.

Mr. Breckinridge.
"The doctrine of Transubstantiation is not only against the Scriptures and the Fathers, but it is contrary to *reason*, and contradicts all our senses."

Unitarian.
The Deity of Jesus is not only contrary to Scripture, but it is contrary to reason, and contradicts all our senses. We *see, hear, feel, smell,* and (if possi-

Mr. Breckinridge.	*Unitarian.*
"Thus we see that Transubstantiation is a false, shocking, novel doctrine."	ble) *taste*—a MAN, and yet you, Mr. Breckinridge, contrary to Scripture and reason, and ALL our senses, require us to believe that he is God! Thus we see that the divinity of Christ is a false, shocking, and novel doctrine. "Will any one at the present day *shock* our feelings and understanding to the uttermost, by telling us that Almighty God was incarnate in an *infant*, and wrapped in swaddling clothes?" Norton, p. 31. To show how "*shocking*" this doctrine is, he quotes Dr. Watts. "This infant is the mighty God, Come to be SUCKLED and *adored*."

Now, Rev'd Sir, put your invention to the torture, and see whether a single argument can be raised against the *pretended* unreasonableness of Transubstantiation, that will not hold against the Incarnation. The one is as contrary to reason as the other. Did I not then, rightly define Protestantism "as the middle ground between ancient Christianity and modern Deism, combining certain elements of both, and unable to defend itself against either?" Let *reason* be the rule, and tell me which is easier to be believed; that GOD was an *infant*, "suckled and adored," or that the body and blood of Christ are, by the Divine Omnipotence, truly contained under the appearance of bread and wine? You believe that "Omnipotence, Omniscience, and Omnipresence, were wrapt in swaddling-clothes, and abased to the homely usages of a *stable* and a *manger;*" "that the artificer of the whole universe turned carpenter (I quote from an orthodox Protestant sermon,) and exercised an inglorious trade in a little cell!" "That the eternal God could be subject to the meannesses of hunger and thirst, and be afflicted in all his appetites." "That the *Creator*, *Governor*, and *Judge* of the world, was abused in all his concerns and relations; *scourged*, *spit upon*, *mocked*, and at last *crucified!*" ALL THIS you believe, if you believe the divinity of Jesus Christ; and yet you reject Transubstantiation because your *reason* forsooth, cannot comprehend it. Can it comprehend the mysteries just stated?

Now for your objections under their respective heads.

1. You begin by stating that "Evangelical Protestants all allow, as their standards clearly evince, that Christ is *spiritually* present, and the truth of his words recorded above (this is my body, this is my blood,) they undoubtedly believe." Let me then take you at your words, "Christ, you say, is *spiritually* present." By this I understand that the spirit, soul, or divinity of Christ is present. If it does not mean this, it means nothing. This presence of Christ, as to the *fact*, is roundly stated; but as to the *manner*, it is qualified by the word 'spiritually.' Now this statement goes far towards the Catholic doctrine. For Christ is both God and man; and if he is present *at all*, it follows that he is *corporally* as well as 'spiritually' present. Will you separate the soul of Christ from the body of Christ, and say that he is present

'spiritually,' and absent *corporally?* This presence of Christ is connected with the locality of the Lord's supper; of course it is a *specific* presence; and we are told that "Christ is present 'spiritually;' that is, *all but his body.*" Your Confession, page 127, tells us that, at the reception of the bread and wine, this absent body and blood, are " spiritually present to the faith of believers in that ordinance as the *elements themselves are, to their outward senses.*" A body absent—present! Christ the man-God " really present," without his body! His body and blood *present* spiritually; but not corporally! Do you understand it, Rev'd Sir? I do not.

If it mean that *indefinite* presence, which was promised to "two or three gathered together in his name," then we can comprehend it. But that *Christ* should be really present in a *special manner*, as you assert, and your standards teach of the Lord's supper, and yet be present, *whole Christ*, WITHOUT A BODY, is above comprehension. You, however, make the statement, and from you we must wait for the explanation. The real presence as revealed by Christ was indeed a " hard saying," which the Jews sought to escape by " walking *no more* with him," and the Protestants endeavour to evade by an explanation which spoils a *mystery*, and substitutes a paradox.

> The literal sense is hard to flesh and blood;
> But *nonsense* never could be understood.

Now the argument or objections which you make against the mystery of the Eucharist under the first head, are from your interpretation of Scripture. Their amount is this: the Scriptures often speak figuratively, *therefore* the words of Christ, both in the 6th chapter of St. John, and in the institution of the Eucharist, are to be understood figuratively. Here again is the reasoning of the Unitarian whenever you quote the passages that establish the divinity of Christ. They are, he says, to be understood figuratively. But there is one brief reply. When Christ said, " I am the door," " I am the vine," &c. those who heard him understood him to speak figuratively. But when he said "I am the living bread which came down from heaven," "The bread which I will give is my flesh for the life of the world," " unless you eat the flesh of the Son of man, and drink his blood, you cannot have life in you," &c. his *hearers understood him to speak* literally, and if that was an error, as you say, his language gave rise to it, and his silence, when they objected that it was "a hard saying," confirmed them in it. Therefore his language was not figurative. Figurative language would not have offended them. He reproached them for their incredulity, he suffered them to go away; therefore they understood him literally. And it is because Protestants do not believe, that they also go back and walk no more with Jesus, unless he will accommodate them with a figurative explanation, which he refused to his own disciples.

But in the institution, he took bread and literally fulfilled what he had promised. He *blessed* and broke and gave to them; saying, take ye and eat, this is my body, which is given for you....This is my blood *which* shall be shed for many unto the remission of sins."

It was not the *figure* of his body that was given for us on the cross; it was not the *figure* of his blood which was shed for us. Therefore he spoke of his real body and blood, and his language was *literal* and *not figurative*. And consequently Protestants, in appealing to figure, oppose the language and conduct of Jesus Christ, at every point of the promise, and of the institution of the holy Eucharist.

As to the pretended " absurdities and inexplicable difficulties, which you find in Christ's words," according to Catholic interpretation, I must refer you to a *higher* tribunal. But the plain Scripture is, " this is my body; this is my blood." And these *plain words of Scripture*, you tell us, are " absurd," unless we understand the *contrary* of what they assert; so as to read " this is *not* my body, but *bread* which is given for you;" this is *not* my blood, but *wine*, which shall be shed for many unto the remission of sins." This amendment of Scripture may relieve Jesus Christ from the imputation of having used " absurd" language, *if you will have it so*, but in that case I ask, is the Scripture *plain and intelligible* to all ?

The attempt to convert St. Augustine, Bellarmine, Cardinal Cajetan, Bishop Fisher, &c., into Protestants on this subject, is what I would call overdoing the business. It proves your *courage*, not your cause. Bellarmine asserted that the doctrine of the real presence and Transubstantiation *are clearly proved from Scripture*, but he admitted the possibility of a man's reading the Scripture, *clear and plain as its language is*, without being convinced. Just as you would say, that however clearly the divinity of Christ is revealed, it may still be doubted whether "a man who is not froward" will be convinced of it, by reading the Scriptures.

Again, the passages which you quote from St. Augustine, (De Doct. Christ. Lib. 3. c. 46.) and from Theodoret, (Dial. 2.) and other passages from Origen, Ambrose, Isidore, Chrysostom, &c. which you copy from the Calvinistic objections of Claude and Aubertin, in their controversy with Nicole, are ambiguous, *taken by themselves;* but taken with *other passages*, from the same Fathers in which, as I shall presently show, the Catholic doctrine of the Eucharist is *clearly stated*, they are quite intelligible. If you wish to see a full and complete refutation of all these ambiguous passages of the Fathers, I refer you to the third volume of " Perpetuite de la Foi;" in which they are triumphantly vindicated against the false meaning ascribed to them by the Calvinistic ministers. If you have not this work, I shall have great pleasure in loaning it, and you will see that these passages, which express neither the Catholic, *nor the Protestant* doctrine on the Eucharist, are reconcileable *only with the former*. Some of them, even as quoted by yourself, are a condemnation of the Protestant doctrine. For example, St. Isidore speaking of the bread and wine says, " these two are visible, but being sanctified by the Holy Spirit, they *pass into* the Sacrament of his divine body." This language from a Catholic pulpit would be understood. But how would it sound in the First Presbyterian Church *on a Sacrament Sunday ?* If the minister were to speak of the bread and wine " PASSING INTO" any thing, but what it was before, would not the people accuse him of teaching something very like " Transubstantiation." And yet *this* is made an *objection;* and the rest are like it. Let us try another, which you quote from Theodoret.

"After sanctification the mystical symbols do not depart from their nature, for they remain still in their former substance and figure and form, and may be seen and touched just as before." All this is true *as to appearances:* but he goes on to show that *notwithstanding* these *appearances,* "they (the Eucharist) are understood to be *that which they are* MADE, and are *believed and venerated* (*or* " ADORED") as being what they are *believed* to be." Would you venture to hold even this language to a Presbyterian congregation? If you did, they would say that you are half a Papist, at least; and you would be called to account for your sermon. And yet these are the PROOFS that the Fathers held the doctrine which you preach!!! Even the ambiguous language of the Fathers, is irreconcileable with the Protestant Lord's supper of mere bread and wine. Even your own quotations are against you.

The *exceptions* which you profess to find, as to the "unanimous consent of the Fathers" on the Catholic faith of the Eucharist, have as much foundation in reality, as the contradictions which the Deist pretends to discover in the comparison of the four Gospels. In both cases there are *apparent* disagreements. But to proceed. After having claimed the testimony of Scripture by qualifying the *affirmative words* of Christ, with a *Protestant negative,* making him say " no, this is not my body," instead of what he actually said, " this *is* my body; this *is* my blood." You appeal to the Fathers under your second head, for you " will meet me at all points." By this you would persuade our Protestant readers that the Fathers held the doctrine of mere bread and wine as they do. Now to our Protestant readers I leave the decision of the case, let them judge between us."

You state as a consequence from other statements, " that the Protestant doctrine (viz. mere bread and wine) was not only tolerated, but professed and held at large by the Fathers of the church." What say the Fathers on the subject? Hear them.

Hear St. Ignatius, in his epistle to the faithful of Smyrna: "These heretics abstain from the Eucharist and the oblations, *because* they do not acknowledge the Eucharist to be *the flesh* of our Lord and Saviour Jesus Christ, which suffered for our sins, and *which* the Father resuscitated by his goodness." Who were the " Protestants" *then?* St. Ignatius or these heretics?

"How, says St. Irenæus, can they, (other heretics) be assured that the bread over which they have given thanks, is the *body* of the Lord?" (Adver. Hær. Lib. 4. c. 34.) And again, no less than three times he repeats " the Eucharist is the body of Jesus Christ, and it is *made so* by the word of God." (Ibid. L. 5. c. 2.) This was in the Apostolic age, long before the year " 1215."

St. Jerome, " But as for us, let us hearken *to* what the Gospel tells us, that the bread which the Lord broke and gave to his disciples, *is the body of our Lord and our Saviour,* since he said to them; take and eat, this is my body." (Epist. ad Hedib.)

St. Chrysostom says, " The blessed chalice is the communion of the blood of Jesus Christ, it is very terrible, because that which is in the chalice is that *which flowed from the side of Jesus Christ*" (Hom. 24. Epist. 1. ad. Cor.

St. Ambrose says, "He (Jesus) took bread into his holy hands; *before* it is consecrated it is bread, *after* the words of Jesus Christ have been applied to it, *it is the body of Jesus Christ*. Hear what he says to you, take and eat; this is my body. The Priest says, the body of Christ; and *you* answer, Amen; that is, it is true; let your heart be penetrated with what your mouth confesses." (De Sacr. Lib. 4. c. 5.) Would any minister dare to pronounce these words of the Fathers in a Protestant pulpit? And yet you, Rev'd Sir, would persuade the poor people, that the doctrine of mere bread and wine, which Carlostadt invented in the sixteenth century, and bequeathed to Protestantism, was the doctrine of the Fathers!!!

St. Cyril of Jerusalem, speaking of the consecrated chalice, asks "who shall dare to say that it is *not* his blood?" (Catech. 4.)

Origen. "When you *receive the body of the Lord*, you take all possible precaution that not the smallest part of it should fall." (Hom. 13. in Exod.)

Cyril of Alexandria. "Jesus Christ *returns* and *appears* in our mysteries invisibly as God, visibly in his body, and he gives us to *touch his holy flesh*." (Comment in Joann. p. 1104.)

The Council of Nice decreed "that neither canon nor custom has taught, that they (deacons) who have themselves no power to offer (*i. e.* in the sacrifice of mass) should give the *body of Christ* to them (viz. Priests) who have that power." (Canon xviii.)

St. Athanasius says: "Our sanctuaries are now pure, as they always were; having been rendered venerable by the *blood alone of Christ*, and embellished by his worship." (Apol. adver. Arian. T. 1. p. 127.) "Take care, then, he says, (in another place) take care, O Deacon, not to give to the unworthy the *blood of the immaculate body*, lest you incur the guilt of giving holy things to dogs." (Serm. de Incontam. Myst. T. ii. p. 35.)

St. Ephrem of Edessa. "Abraham placed earthly food before celestial spirits, of which they ate, (Gen. xviii.) This was wonderful. But what Christ has done for us greatly exceeds this, and transcends all speech, and all conception. To us, that are in the flesh, *he hath given to eat his body and blood*. Myself incapable of comprehending the mysteries of God, I dare not proceed; and should I attempt it, I should only show my own rashness." (De. Nat. Dei. T. iii. p. 182.)

St. Optatus of Milevis, says, "What is so sacrilegious as to break, to erase, and to remove the altars of God, on which yourselves made offerings. On them the vows of the people and the members of Christ were borne. For what is the altar, but the seat of the body and blood of Christ? What offence had Christ given, whose body and blood at certain times, do dwell there? This huge impiety is doubled, whilst you broke also the chalices, the *bearers of the blood* of Christ." (Contra Parmen, (the Donatist,) Lib. vi. p. 91, 92, 93.)

Now, Rev. Sir, if Donatists, or other persons were to destroy all the communion tables, and all the cups for the sacramental vine in the whole Protestant world, would any Protestant complain of it, in the language of St. Optatus? And yet you would persuade the people that Protestants and the Fathers, believed the same doctrine touching the sacrament, and that the Catholic dogma was introduced, A. D. "1215."

St. Basil. " About the things that God has spoken, there should be no hesitation, nor doubt, but a firm persuasion, that all is true and possible, though nature be against it. Herein lies the struggle of faith. The Jews therefore strove among themselves, saying: How can this man give us his flesh to eat? Then Jesus said to them: Amen, Amen, I say unto you, unless you eat the flesh of the Son of man and drink his blood, you shall not have life in you. John v. 53, 54." (Regula viii. Moral. T. ii. p. 240.)

You say the Fathers did not understand the 6th chapter of St. John as relating to the Eucharist. If you wish to correct this mistake, you have only to consult Origen, (Hom. in Num 16.) Cyprian (de cæna Dom. Lim. 1. Coutr. Judeos, c. 22.) Hilary, (Lib. de Trin.) Basil, (de Reg. Moral.) Chysostom, (Hom. 41. In Joann.) Ephiphanius, Hœres 55.) Ambr. (Lib. 4. de sacr. c. 5.) Augustine, (de Pecc. Mr. Lib. 1. c. 20.) Jerome, (Comm. in cap. 1. Ep. ad Ephes.) *All* the Fathers, all the *Christians* of all ages, understood the 6th chapter of St. John of the Eucharist, except the Protestants; and when they attempt to explain it *otherwise*, they make awkward business of it.

When the Fathers speak of bread before the consecration, they mean bread; when they call it bread *after* the consecration, they mean the body of Christ under the appearance of bread, and so Catholics at this day are accustomed to call it the *bread* of life. This is proved by their *adoring* that which was contained under the appearances of bread and wine. Hear St. Augustine :

"And because he (Christ) walked in the flesh, he also gave us his very flesh to eat for our salvation; but no one eat this flesh unless he adores it before hand......so far are we from committing sin by *adoring* it, that we should commit sin in not adoring it." (St. Aug. in Psalm 98.)

St. Cyril. "Jesus Christ does not quicken us by the participation of his spirit only, but also by giving us *to eat the flesh which he assumed.*" (De Incar. p. 707.)

St. Augustine. " God gives us to eat truly *the body in which he suffered so much.*" (In Psalm 33.) And again, " We receive, says he, with a faithful heart and *mouth*, the *mediator between God and man*, the man Christ Jesus, who has given us *his body to eat*, and his *blood to drink, although it seems a more horrible thing to eat the flesh of a man*, than to slay him, and to drink human blood, than to shed it." (Contr. Adværs. leg. et. proph. Lib. 2. c. 9.) St. Chrysostom. " The body of Jesus Christ is placed before us that we may *touch it.* ' O how I should desire, many of you exclaim,' says he, (addressing his audience) ' how I should desire to see the form of his (Christ's) countenance and of his clothes.' God has granted you *more*, for you *touch* HIMSELF, you *eat* HIMSELF." (Hom. 83. in Matt.)

Here, Rev. Sir, was your objection about eating God, more than seven centuries before "1215," and "Avenoes, the Arabian philosopher." Was St. Chrysostom, were the believers whom he addressed *in this language,* Protestants? And yet you would persuade the people that the Fathers held the *figurative sense,* the mere bread and wine of Protestantism!!! No; the *rationalism,* that is, in other words, the infidelity of Protestantism, would be *shocked* at the language of the Fathers, because it was and is, the language of the Catholic church. Protestant ministers, (if indeed they are aware of it themselves) dare not repeat in their pulpits, the doctrine of the Fathers in their own words. The people would discover that the Fathers were *Catholics,* and that no Christians *ever held* your doctrines before the days of Carlostadius and Luther. What would they say, if to convince them that the Fathers held the doctrine of "Evangelical Protestants" on the Eucharist, you were to quote the following testimony from St. Augustine. "Who could understand, my brethren, says this Father, how that saying, 'he was borne in his hands;' could be accomplished in a man. For a person may be borne by the hands of another, but no one is borne in his own proper hands. We cannot understand this according to the letter of David, but we can understand it of Jesus Christ. *For* Jesus Christ *was borne in his hands* when speaking of his very body, he said, this is my body: *for he bore his body in his hands.*" (In Psalm 33.) How would the General Assembly stop their ears if any one were to propose this "hard saying," as the doctrine of "Evangelical Protestants," and yet *you* have asserted that they hold the same doctrine with the Fathers, on the Eucharist! This was the belief of the *Church* when St. Augustine preached some fourteen hundred years ago; it was the belief of the *Church,* when St. Ignatius reproached the Heretics with refusing to acknowledge that the Eucharist was the FLESH of our Lord Jesus Christ, seventeen hundred years ago; it *is* the belief of the *Church* this day. Were the Fathers Protestants?

St. Augustine. "It has pleased the Holy Ghost that in the honour of this great Sacrament, the body of Jesus Christ should *enter into the mouth of the Christian* before all other meats." (Epist. ad Januar.) Do we not still receive *fasting?*

St. Cyril. "Since Jesus Christ is in us, by his *proper flesh,* we shall assuredly rise again." (In Joann. L. 4. p. 363.)

Again Cyril of Jerusalem. "That which *appears* to be bread is *not bread,* although the *taste* judge it to be bread, but it is *the body of Jesus Christ:* and that which appears to be wine, is *not wine,* although the *taste* testifies that it is, but it is the *blood of Jesus Christ.*" (Catech. 9.) Have I given enough to show Protestants how far they have been deceived by their books and their ministers, (I do not say intentionally) when it is *pretended* that the Fathers of the first six centuries were not Catholics? Here are *positive* statements of the Christian belief of the Eucharist in *their* days. Was it the Protestant belief? Mere figure; mere bread and wine? Let any sensible Protestant reader compare these testimonies with what his minister tells him of the bread and wine of the Lord's Supper, and ask himself in the presence of God, whether the Protestant doctrine is not diametrically opposed to that of the Fathers of the first six centuries?

Under the third head, you bring up the objection of *reason and the senses*. But the example of the Jews at Capernaum, of the Socinians, and Deists among ourselves should teach you, that *in the mysteries of the Christian Revelation* these are but sorry guides. We may reason on the question whether a mystery has been revealed; and if the *evidence* be sufficient, to convince us that it *has;* then we BELIEVE. By reason you cannot understand the *mystery of the Trinity*. By the senses you can discover nothing of the Saviour's divinity, when, hanging on the cross he cried out, " My God, my God ! Why hast thou forsaken me." But this mode of attacking a mystery is sufficiently exemplified in the introduction. The Presbyterian selects *one* dogma; the Unitarian another; the Universalist a third; but all work with the *same weapons*. When you deny that the " real presence" of the Holy Ghost, under the forms and appearances, length, breadth, thickness, and all the external properties of a dove, is a parallel case with "the real presence" of Jesus Christ, under the forms and appearances of bread and wine you affect to discover a difference which but few minds, except your own, can perceive. The ground, it seems, of this difference is that Christ, "*as man,*" *cannot* (what !) be present on the earth; " he is seated on his throne in heaven." But have you forgotten that, notwithstanding all this, he appeared to St. Paul on his way to Damascus ? If you have, I refer you to Acts ix. 17. Christ did not cease to be on his throne, by appearing to St. Paul on the way; therefore his body can be in two places at once, and if in two, so in a million of places, and yet be at the right hand. His body is spiritual, that is, endowed with the properties of a spirit. Can you tell what those are? Can you say that such a body *cannot* exist under the *appearances* of bread and wine ? When the Deist retorts your argument, against the Bible itself, what will you have to reply ? When you tell him that the Holy Ghost descended in the form of a dove ; "what !" he will exclaim, " that there should be a long, broad, thick, white, heavy, moist, active, passive, feathered flying, *nothing ;* and that this strange something nothing, seeming; dove, and not a dove, the Holy Ghost, and yet seeming a dove, should descend on a man in the Jordan, and yet be living in heaven entire and quiescent, while all this is going on upon earth, is, I say, *an infinite absurdity*." Pardon me, Sir, he will continue, the expression seems harsh, and the objection savours of levity, ridicule, and, as you Christians would say, *blasphemy:* but *to the honour of Deism*, I must inform you that I learned it from a *Christian minister*. It is your own, extracted literally from your Letter No. XXX. on "Transubstantiation." How will you meet this Deist? Will you have the courage to destroy *your own child ?* And if you would, will you have the *power?* Has not the press made it immortal? And if you disown it, will it not be adopted by the Deists, and arrayed against its *Christian* parentage.

When you call Transubstantiation a miracle, and institute a parallel between it and the miracles which prove the truth of Christianity, do you not grossly (I will not say intentionally) deceive your readers? These being intended as proofs were addressed to the senses. The miracle of the Eucharist is like the miracle of the Incarnation, acknowledged by FAITH, made known, not by *taste, hearing, sight, smell,* or *touch,* but *by the Revelation of Jesus Christ.* Hence the Jews are reproached by him because they would not *believe,* and the Protestants do not *believe.* But the Apostles believed, the apostolic Fathers believed, the Catholic church, of whose faith they are witnesses, believed, and believes. So that when you say "Hume cannot be confuted, if Transubstantiation be true," you impose grossly (without intending it, I hope) upon the *ignorance* of Protestant readers. Christ proposed a mystery, and you wish to *prove by* your *senses,* that he does not *deceive!!!* Catholics are not so distrustful. Jesus Christ has *said so,* that is enough. The *true, real body and blood of Christ* exist in the sacrament of the Eucharist, not in the natural manner in which they existed on the cross, but in the spiritual, supernatural manner in which they existed, when they were given at the last supper, or when they entered the room where the disciples were, *the doors being closed.* (John xx. 19.) He said to Thomas, "a spirit hath not flesh and bones as ye see me to have." Yet we find that he, having "flesh and bones" which were touched by St. Thomas, entered an apartment, *the doors being closed!* How could an entrance into a closed apartment be effected by *a human body consisting of flesh and bones, which all could see and touch?* The Bible states the fact—does the philosophy of Bacon and of Newton explain it? Can you, Rev. Sir, explain it? Did Christ's body penetrate through the wall, or the door? Then, there were *two bodies* existing in the *same space* at the *same time!* Here then are two facts: 1. That the body of Christ was at the same time in two places, viz. in heaven and on the way to Damascus. 2. That the body of Christ existed in the same space which was occupied by the *closed* door or *wall,* through which he entered the apartment, where the disciples were: By both of which it is *proved,* that the body of Christ is *not* under the government of *natural* laws, and therefore, that your argument, founded on the laws that govern bodies in their *natural condition,* whilst it *proves nothing against the real and substantial presence of Christ in the Eucharist,* is a FLAT CONTRADICTION OF THE BIBLE, in the *two cases* referred to, and comes mal-a-propos from an *evangelical* Protestant. Neither is it correct in philosophy. For we know nothing of SPACE, abstractedly from the relations of bodies existing in their *natural condition;* nor of TIME, except by the succession of perceptible events. Of the manner therefore, in which *spirits,* or the *spiritual body of Jesus Christ,* are effected by *time* and *space,* permit me to say that you and we are all equally and *utterly ignorant.* And yet with a mind ignorant of what is *space*—ignorant of what is *time*—ignorant of the relations which *they bear to the spiritual body of Jesus Christ*—ignorant of the properties of that body, you rise up against the *express* and *reiterated* declaration of the Saviour, against the doctrine of all the Fathers, and of THE WHOLE CHRISTIAN WORLD before, and except the Protestants; and in the plenitude of all this *ignorance,* you scan the attributes of the *eternal God,* circumscribe the ocean of Divine Omnipotence, by *your* ideas of time and space, and proclaim that the real presence of the body of Christ in the mystery of the Eucharist is "an infinite absurdity!!!" Deists, Rev. Sir, never made a more *arrogant, perverted,* or *fallacious* use of reason, than this is. Reason *knows nothing* of these matters, except as they are revealed; and the haughty little blunderer may return to its nut-shell, convinced of its own *impotence,* and satisfied that the son of God *would not have required of us to believe* any thing which is absurd. So much for the deistical objection of *reason and the senses.*

Under this head also, you introduced the *silence* of the enemies of Christianity in the primitive church; having nothing to hope from the Fathers, *said,* on the subject, you expect something from what the *Jews, Pagans,* and *apostate* Christians did *not* say. "Celsus, Porphyry, Lucian, Julian and Trypho, would have written (as Protestant ministers do) against the doctrine of Christ's real presence, if it had been believed in *their time* as it is now in the Catholic church." Answer 1. The knowledge of the Christian mysteries, and the administration of the sacraments was inviolably concealed from Jews and Pagans by the "discipline of the secret," for an account of which you may consult Bingham and Mosheim, though they are not the *best* authority. 2. I have proved already from the Fathers, that the belief of Christ's *real flesh* in the Eucharist *did* exist. 3. The charge made *against* the Christians of "*murdering a child, and eating its flesh in their secret assemblies,*" proves that the Jews and Pagans had a confused vague knowledge of the *doctrine of the Eucharist.* 4. With regard to Julian the apostate, we cannot know whether he wrote against the doctrine or not, since his *theological* works *have been lost.* St. Cyril in his preface tells us, that he had written *three* books against the Christians. Of the contents of them we know nothing, except a *part of one* to which Cyril replied. Who knows then, that in the others he did not prove himself a *sound Protestant* by attacking the Eucharist, and pronouncing it an "infinite absurdity?" It is like his language.

The IV. head is on the origin of the doctrine. *Here you deny having asserted* " *that the doctrine of Transubstantiation was not held before the year* 1215." I am glad to see you deny your assertions, but it would be more magnanimous to recall them and acknowledge that you were *mistaken.* But the matter has been already sufficiently disposed of, in the introduction.

V. Head you ask "how we can *discern* the body and blood *af-*

ter consecration?" I answer, by *faith*. By believing with St. Augustine that "*it is the body of Jesus Christ in which he suffered*," and with St. Ignatius that it is "*the flesh of Jesus Christ*," with St. Chrysostom that "what is in the chalice is what *flowed from his side*," and with Christ himself that it is "*his body and blood*." And now I ask you how can Protestants *discern* it *at all?* Since they will not allow *even faith* to believe that the "body of the Lord" is there. Would St. Paul require the Corinthians to discern the body of the Lord in the sacrament, if the body of the Lord were not really and truly there, though in a supernatural manner, impervious to the senses? No, certainly.

You ask, "does not this pretended miracle degrade Christ's humanity, and deify the operating Priest?" I answer first, that it is a miracle, *which faith alone can appreciate*, and that your language is a *gross imposition on the ignorance of Protestants*, when you *speak of it as a miracle for the senses to judge of.* Is this intentional? and if it be, is it *honest?*

I answer secondly, that the priest offering "the sacrifice," acts *as the minister* and *by the authority of Jesus Christ*—just as you profess to do, when you *preach the Gospel.* Is this "deifying" either the priest or the parson? Can you be serious when you employ *such expressions?* I answer thirdly, that so far from *degrading* the Catholic doctrine of the Eucharist, *glorifies*, the Saviour's humanity, and the Saviour himself. Because we *believe* in his *veracity* when he said "this is my body," and the flesh which the Jews *seeing scourged* and *spit upon*, that same the Catholics ADORE *without seeing*—as if to atone for the insults.

VI. Head. Under this you make a difficulty respecting the priest's "intention." To this I reply that there is no ground to suppose, that a priest who administers a sacrament should have the intention *not* to administer. In heaven, or on earth, in time or in eternity, there is no *motive* for him to withhold his intention, and deliberate wicked actions *without any motive or inducement*, are not to be presumed. The Presbytery that ordains a Calvinistic minister, *would* constitute thereby a *real* minister if *it depended on intention*, and whenever we say that it does not, we predicate on the absence, *not* of intention, but of *power*. The Presbytery cannot give, what it does not possess—however much it may intend it.

VII. and last head. Here you affect to be amused at my claiming the ancient Liturgies as teaching (the doctrine of) Transubstantiation, and venture to assert that there is not one word of truth in all I have said on that subject. I must say that you never "ventured" on a more hazardous experiment in your life—the appeal to the Fathers not excepted. I have not room *here* to quote the words of those liturgies. But at a proper time I shall lay them before the public, and let Protestants see with THEIR OWN EYES, *how grossly they are imposed upon*, when they are told, that before Luther there *ever were Christians* that believed as they do. In the mean time I shall mention *two facts* which will show how little of Protestantism is in these Liturgies.

In the early part of the seventeenth century the Duke of Saxony had been persuaded that Protestantism, vainly sought for in the primitive church, was to be found abundantly in the ancient liturgies of the heretics in the east. Accordingly he sent an eminent oriental scholar, John Michael Vensleb to examine. This examination resulted in his CONVERSION TO THE CATHOLIC FAITH. Afterwards, he travelled in the east, and procured no less than five hundred manuscripts for the French King's Library. One of these, the Liturgy of Dioscorus, Patriarch of Alexandria, was published in London in 1661. He had been the pupil of the celebrated oriental scholar, Ludolf. A similar discovery in the examination of the Eastern Liturgies, caused the CONVERSION *to the* CATHOLIC FAITH of Vigne, a *Calvinistic minister of Grenoble*, about the same time. (Le. Brun vol. 4. p. 467.) These two *facts* are ample proof, that on the Eucharist all the liturgies of the east and west, teach the *real presence* by the change of the bread and wine into the body and blood of Jesus Christ. This I shall make appear at large.

I have now answered the arguments of your letter to the satisfaction, I trust, of the public, if not of its author. Did the Fathers, up to St. Ignatius, in the very age of the Apostles, hold, or did they not, the Catholic doctrine of the real presence of the glorified body of Jesus Christ in the sacrament of the Eucharist? If they *did not*, then take up, one after the other, the passages I have quoted, and tell us what they mean. If they did—then Catholics are right, and Protestants are wrong, on your own admission, for you claimed the Fathers, and professed yourself ready "to meet me at all points." If then the Fathers, up to the apostolic age, held the *true* doctrine, does it not follow that Protestants have been led to forsake the *faith* of Jesus Christ? Let them *reflect* on it.

I have no objection to the compliments which you pay to the great men of the Episcopal church. But you might have left the name of "Usher" out, and substituted those of Drs. Bowen and Cooke of Kentucky, and of Mr. Briton, of New York, who have so triumphantly vindicated, at least, *one* article of Catholic belief against the errors of Presbyterianism. These names I know are not in good odour at Princeton, but their triumph is not the less complete on that account.

The Bookseller who was forbidden to keep my review of Bishop Onderdonk's charge for sale, is the Agent of the Baptist Tract Depository, and my informant is Mr. Fithian, whose note see below. Now I shall answer your questions by number.

To the 1st. I say that Pope Liberius did not sign the Arian Creed in *the Arian sense or meaning*.

To the 2d, that no council, recognized by the Catholic church, ever "adopted" the Arian Creed. For the errors of other councils or general assemblies, the church is not accountable.

To the 2d. I reply, I have answered it already, the VI. head.

To the 4th compound question, I answer 1st, that there were pretenders to the see of Rome, besides the rightful occupant, and in *this sense* there were schism in the Popedom—2, that *Catholics* have no difficulty in knowing who was the true Pope, and 3, that a *false* Pope is no Pope.

To the 5th. about the freedom of the press at Rome, and the "Prohibiting Committee" which you are pleased to *imagine* for the benefit of "all the church," I answer, that the latter does not exist, and the former is a question on which every man may abound in his own sense.

To the 6th. I answer, that money given to a priest for any sacred function is not given, and cannot lawfully be received as an *equivalent*, but either as alms, deeds, or for support, on the principle that they who serve at the altar should live by the altar.

To the 7th. I answer, that *in my opinion*, religion and science suffered by the suppression of the Jesuits, and that both are gainers by their restoration. This opinion is founded on the fact that they are hated for their zeal, and admired for their learning by all the *infidels* in Europe. As to the Inquisition, it may have been a good thing —*abused*.

To the 8th and last, I answer that so far as the traditions of the Jewish church had reference to the ceremonial law, they expired with it. So far as they regarded proof of Jewish *faith* before the coming of Christ, I do not reject them.

Yours, &c.   JOHN HUGHES.

As the publisher of "the Review," I supplied a number of Book sellers with it on commission; among others, the Depository of the Baptist Tract Society. As I was personally acquainted with them generally, I called in occasionally to inquire if I should send more, &c. and was informed by the Assistant Agent that the number which I had sent them was all sold, *but orders had been given him not to receive and offer for sale any more.*   M. FITHIAN

CONTROVERSY. No. XXXII.

IS THE PROTESTANT RELIGION THE RELIGION OF CHRIST?

Philadelphia, September 7th, 1833

To the Rev. John Hughes.

Sir,—In my last letter I produced the distinct testimony of three several Roman Catholic historians, in support of my charges against the infamous lives of the clergy and Popes of Rome. This was done in answer to your challenge, to the following effect, viz. "Name the page of the *Catholic* historian who states what you have asserted, and I pledge myself again to *expose you.*" (Letter No. XXIX.) And now when these connecting authorities are adduced, how do you meet them?

Thuanus you reject, saying that he was twice condemned at Rome by public decrees, in 1609 and 1757. Were these decrees issued by General Councils, approved by Popes? If not, they are of no weight in this question. But they were not, for the *last* Council (that of Trent) sat more than fifty years before the *first* of these dates! How then can you say that he is *not* a *Catholic* historian? Does the *Church* condemn him? Has he not written the truth? Yes; and it is for this that you reject him, as you did Bellarmine when his testimony became insupportable, though you informed me *once,* that he was a standard writer in the church of Rome. Dupin was my *second* witness. You answer, "we disown him!" So you do the Bible, as a rule of faith; and for the same reason, that *it does not teach Romanism, if left to speak for itself.* Dupin *not* a "Catholic historian!" And why? Because he does not deny or conceal the corruptions of Popes, Prelates, and Priests. "He is your enemy because he tells you the truth." This is a summary method of disposing of an author; not forsooth, because what he says is proved to be *false;* but because he condemns the party whose history he writes, and because the condemned party finds fault with him for doing it.

But you are forced to own that my *third* witness, Baronius, "*is* a Catholic historian."

Here then we join issue.

On this reference, you speak so unlike a gospel minister, or Christian gentleman, that I assure you I feel ashamed to be dragged before the community in such company. After language which shows a desperate and infatuated state of mind, you propose the following extraordinary course—

"To put the matter to rest, I shall mark the pages, and leave two copies of Baronius, the one in Latin, the other in Italian, at the Athenæum on Thursday morning, together with a copy of your letter for the curious to compare the one with the other. The public will then see which of us is to be exposed."

From such a trial I shrink not, except for the indecent coarseness and vulgarity with which it is proposed to be made, and at which every honourable mind must revolt. The volume and my friend were at the Athenæum at the appointed hour; and by referring to the *Postscript* you will see that *I was fully prepared to meet you at* "*all points.*" But the passage in Baronius to which I referred you, was *only one of a hundred* furnished by this "Catholic historian." He relates, for example, that Pope Alexander VI., A. D. 1492, (see Baronius' Annals, Vol. 19, p. 413 et seq.) was elected by Cardinals, some of whom were bribed, some allured by promises of promotion, and some enticed by fellowship in his vices and impurities, to give him their suffrages. He refers to various authors who complained that he was (insignem stupris) famous for his debauchery; he tells us of his vile example (pessimo exemplio) in keeping (pellicem Romanam Vanoziam) a Roman strumpet Vanozia, by whom he had many children; that he conferred wealth and honours on them, and even created one of them, Cæsar Borgia, (an inordinately wicked man,) archbishop of the church. The same writer (Vol. 11th. p. 145, &c.) records the election of Benedict the 9th, at the age of twelve years, which he says was accomplished by *gold*, and he calls it ("horrendum ac detestabile visu") "horrible and detestable to behold:" yet he adds that the whole Christian world acknowledged Benedict, without controversy, to be a true Pope. This man he represents as a monster of iniquity, and relates, that after death he appeared to a certain Valcus in a hideous shape, and informed him that he was doomed to everlasting woe!

Once more: the same author (vol. 10. pp. 742, 3.) informs us at large of the villanies and infamous conduct of the notorious Pope Stephen the 7th. The following sentence conveys the history of his unparalleled wickedness in a single line. Ita quidem passus facinorosus homo quique ut fur et latro ingressus est in ovile ovium, laqueo vitam adeo infami exitu vindice Deo clausit "Thus perished this villanous man, who entered the sheep-fold as a thief and a robber; and who in the retribution of God, ended his days by the infamous death of the halter." There have been probably not less than *two hundred Popes* whose lives furnish in a greater or less degree confirmation of the charges which I have already made. There is not in the history of human crime such a catalogue as is furnished by the lives of the Popes. No list of Mahommedan or Syracusan tyrants—no annals of human barbarity, debauch, and infamy—no history of any age or any people furnish such a picture of depravity. Let any reader consult Baronius, or Boyer, or Dupin, or Thuanus, or even the popular Encyclopedias of the day, and he will find our description abundantly sustained. When, therefore, you speak of "Magdalen Reports," and refer to the history of crime in our country, remember, that the infamous women of whom you speak are not *Protestants;* and that it is the Protestant church which is seeking their reform; while on the other hand the history which I have given above, is the history not only of your Priesthood, but of your *Popes.*

I. Your defence of the celibacy of the clergy, carries its own exposure with it. You say, "as to the charge that the Catholic church forbids marriage, it is untrue." But in the next sentence you own, that "the law of her Priesthood enjoins celibacy and chastity, but no one is *compelled* to enter into the ministry of her sanctuary." But pray who authorized her to *make a law* enjoining celibacy on the

Priesthood? The Bible says "marriage is honourable in *all*;" but the church of Rome says it is *not* honourable in the Priesthood. The Bible confers on Bishops, in so many words, the privilege of marriage; whereas the church of Rome in so many words forbids it, and anathematizes those who dissent from her. This is what I call "fighting against God;" it is in fact nothing less than *cursing* God. If, as you say, "no man is *compelled* to enter the ministry" in your church (which, however, is far from the truth in Spain Italy, &c.) yet do you not *compel* those whom God may call into the ministry, to abandon their families or else stay out of the Priesthood? And I ask is not this tyranny; is not this the most daring species of oppression and rebellion against God? Your defence of Bellarmine is a full exemplification of the spirit and corrupt principles of the Jesuits. Bellarmine as cited by me contends "that it is a greater evil to marry under the vow of celibacy than to commit fornication;" you say that "under such a vow, marriage is essentially null and void;" and you ask "whether an act of conjugal infidelity in a married person is as great a sin as polygamy?" Bellarmine's reason for his opinion is that one who is married *after* a vow of celibacy is incapable, for the future, of keeping the vow, whereas one who commits fornication may quit it and return to his vow. Now on your principles, as marriage under a vow is "null and void," it follows that the *wife* may as properly be forsaken as the *mistress;* therefore Bellarmine's reason can have no weight. And then we are brought to this, that a Priest who cannot or will not keep his vow of celibacy, had better keep a *mistress* than get a *wife!* This is the reasoning, and this the morality of the Rev. John Hughes! Is it to be wondered at then, that the Priests of the church of Rome are often found to be *fathers*, though they have no *wives?* When you charge our Confession of Faith with giving a *license to commit sin* (see Confession of Faith, chap. 24.) as it grants divorce in case of adultery, you forget that you *condemn* the Lord of Glory, for he has said (Matt. xix. 9.) "whosoever shall put away his wife, *except it be* for fornication, and shall marry another, committeth adultery." Here is a full warrant for divorce in the case supposed.

On the subject of intolerance and exclusive salvation, you seem to be conscious in your late letter that your church cannot be defended; and your last, though fruitless effort, is to prove that the Presbyterian church is as intolerant as your own. But it is a failure to the extent of being even ludicrous. So far from excluding other denominations of Christians from heaven, we cherish the hope that God numbers many of his own children among those who are subjected to the despotism of the Pope; but we are free to acknowledge, that this hope almost expires when we reach the Priesthood of your church. The records of past ages and the daily developments of the present time, tell us in a language which we cannot misunderstand, that the clergy of your church, taken as a body, have been and are the most guilty and most dangerous men with whom this fallen world has ever been cursed. You deny that once every year the Pope of Rome excommunicates all Protestants, and refuses absolution to their abettors, harbourers, readers of their books, &c. I know not whether most to wonder at your assurance or your ignorance. Cardinal Tolet (Istruct. sacred. cap. 20, 32.) tells us with the most copious distinctness that this is the fact. Can it be possible that you have never seen or heard of the famous Bulla Coenae in which the Pope annually curses Protestants as I have said; claims power over kings, denounces all governments who tax Papists without his consent, who harbour heretics, furnish them with arms, read their books, &c. &c. Strange that you have never heard of this Bull, though it requires *you once* a year to *publish* it to the faithful!

II. We next proceed to notice your ineffectual effort at the defence of transubstantiation. You struggle in the toils of truth and self-contradiction in which you have been caught, with a pertinacity and desperation which would excite compassion if you were labouring in a better cause. A brief notice of the several particulars is all that is necessary, for you have met none of my arguments, and as will soon appear, have still more deeply involved yourself. You attempt to prove me guilty of contradiction when I admit that Berringer was condemned for denying transubstantiation in 1059, while I say that it was not an article of faith until 1215. But do you remember that in Berringer's day, amidst the controversies on this disputed point, even the terms in which the parties expressed their opinions were not fixed? Berringer's first recantation, (before a Council in which the *majority* held the real presence) was in such crude and shocking language as the following; "the true body of our Lord Jesus Christ is broken by the Priest's hands, and ground by the teeth of the faithful." But the party *for* transubstantiation afterwards found that his recantation was *worse* than the former *Protestant* doctrine which he held; so after many years his recantation was *amended;* and he finally returned to his first opinion, and was backed in it by half the church. Any one acquainted with the history of the church must know as Scotus, and Tonstal, and Durand, and Erasmus, &c. (all Roman Catholic writers) informs us, that until 1215, it was a disputed question sustained on each side with great warmth, that the church allowed her members to hold either side without censure; and that even after it was decreed in 1215 to be a doctrine which *all* must believe, it was received on *authority* and not from the Bible. So we are informed by Cajetan, Scotus, Durand, Ocham, Biel, Contarinus, Melchior, Cane, Fisher, &c. all Roman Catholic writers. Bellarmine, Bruys and Sirmond tell us that Pascasius in the 9th century was the first author who *expressly* wrote on the real presence. Bertram answered him; yet he was no heretic, and for two hundred years his work was circulated and not condemned. This said work was revived after the Reformation in support of Protestantism by the Reformers. After this, Cardinals, the Pope and the Committee of the Index at Rome denounced Bertram's book; yet Mabbillon in 1680 proved beyond all doubt that it was the genuine work of Bertram. Do not such facts incontestibly prove the *novelty* of transubstantiation; and the antiquity of the Protestant doctrine?

1. Your renewed attempts to derive this doctrine from the Scripture grow worse and worse at every step. If you take the words

"this is my body" literally, why will you not also take literally *all* the remaining words of institution, viz. "this *cup* is the *New Testament* in my blood?" Why did you not answer my argument on this point? Have you not one word then to say in reply to all that was presented in my last letter showing the absurdity of your interpretation of Scripture? Must not the public and even your own people see and own that you abandon the Scripture defence of your doctrine? Is not the Bible against you? When you give us, letter after letter, teeming columns of perverted testimonies from the "Fathers," and furnish only a solitary line from the word of God, what can such dearth of Scripture mean but that Scripture is against you?

2. As to the Fathers, even admitting that *some* of them are for you, then by your own rule of faith as you have not their "unanimous consent," their proof is of no value to you. This is a point of which you are manifestly afraid, and which you have never touched though presented to you in my letter, No 1. In your last letter you barely say as follows: "The exceptions which you profess to find, as to the 'unanimous consent of the Fathers' on the Catholic faith of the Eucharist, have as much foundation in reality, as the contradictions which the Deist pretends to discover in the comparison of the four Gospels. In both cases there are *apparent* disagreements." If by this you mean to say that "the Fathers" are as *unanimous* as the four Gospels, then surely you ought never again to speak evil of the Deist. Yet this is all you say in defence of their unanimity. I have proved in my last letter that the Fathers, as a body, rejected transubstantiation. But to settle this question and give you the opportunity of making out their unanimity in support of your doctrine, let me here summarily present to you a few specimens. If you will reconcile them to your doctrine of the *real* presence, then will I concede that the Fathers are yours. But until you do, by your own confession, your *rule of faith* rejects this doctrine. Besides when some of the Fathers *appear to agree with you* in calling the bread the '*body and the flesh*' of Christ, &c. meaning the sign of his body and flesh, they can be reconciled to *our* views; but when they call it 'a figure of his body,' and say 'the nature of bread still remains after consecration,' that 'it is wicked to say we eat the *flesh* of Christ,' &c. they *cannot* be *reconciled* with your doctrine. *Therefore they either contradict each other, or all of them are for us.*

Augustine, whom you claim, (De doctrin. Christian, Lib. 3. cap. 46.) thus writes:—If the saying be perceptive, either forbidding a wicked action, or commanding to do that which is good, it is no *figurative* saying; but if it seems to command any villany or wickedness, or forbid what is profitable and good, it is *figurative*. This saying, 'except ye eat the flesh of the Son of man and drink his blood, ye have no life in you,' (John vi. 53.) seems to command a *wicked* or *villanous* thing; it is therefore a FIGURE, enjoining us to *communicate* in the *passion* of our Lord; and to lay it up in dear and profitable *remembrance*, that his flesh was crucified and wounded for our sakes." Chrysostom (Epis. ad Gæsarium Monachum.) says,

"Christ is both God and man: God, for that he cannot suffer; man, for that he suffered. One Son, one Lord, he, the same without doubt, having one dominion, one power of *two natures;* not that these natures are consubstantial, seeing each of them does retain, without *confusion* its *own properties*, and being two are not *confused* in Him. For as (in the Eucharist) before the bread is consecrated, we call it bread; but when the grace of God by the Priest has consecrated it, it has no longer the *name* of bread, but is counted worthy to be called the Lord's body, although the *nature* of bread *remains* in it, and we do not say that there are two bodies, but one body of the Son: so here, the divine nature being joined to the (human) body, they both together make one Son, one person; but yet they must be acknowledged to remain without confusion, and after an indivisible manner, not in one nature only, but in two perfect natures."

The Eutychians, against whom this Father wrote, denied that Christ had *two* natures, that is, that he was truly a *man* and truly *God* also. Now he uses the example of the Eucharist to illustrate the two *natures* of Christ; and argues, that though " the nature of the bread remains the same" after consecration, and the nature of Christ's body in Heaven remains the same, yet they are both called his body; *so* the manhood of Christ and the Godhead of Christ remain each unchanged, though they are both together called *one* Son of God. What he says would be inapplicable and absurd, if the bread be *really* changed into the body of Christ. Tertullian (Adv. Marcion. L. 4. c. 40,) says, " Christ taking the bread and distributing it to his disciples, made it his body, saying, this is my body, *i. e.* this is the *figure* of my body! Now it would not have been a *figure* or representation of Christ's body, if Christ's body had not been a *true* and *real* body." Marcion, against whom Tertullian wrote, denied that Christ had a true body, and held, that it was one only in *appearance*. Tertullian proves that he had a *real* body, in the above passage, by showing that the bread in the Eucharist was a *figure* of his body, and the argument was this: how could a phantasm or shadow which was not a *real* body, have a *figure* to represent it? Now suppose Tertullian to have believed the doctrine of Transubstantiation, then his argument would have been in the highest degree absurd. Nay, Marcion might have turned it directly against him; for he would have retorted thus: " You say that the accidents and *appearance* of bread subsist in the Sacrament without the *substance* of bread. Why then could not the accidents and appearance of a body subsist in Christ without the *substance* of a body?" There could not be therefore a stronger proof that Tertullian rejected Transubstantiation. Epiphanius, (In Anchorat.) " We see that our Saviour took in his hands, (viz. bread,) and having given thanks, said, this is mine, and that; and yet we see, that it is not equal to it, nor like it; not to the *incarnate image*, not to the invisible Deity, not to the lineaments of members; for this (the bread) is of a *round* form, and *insensible* as to any power." Once more; Augustine, (De utilit. Pœnitentiæ Cap. 1.) "The Apostle says that our fathers, not the fathers of unbelievers, not the fathers of the wicked that did eat and die, but *our* fathers, the fathers of the faithful, did eat spirit-nal meat, and therefore the same, (with us.) For there were such there, to whom Christ was more tasteful in their heart than manna in their mouth. Whosoever understood Christ in the manna did eat the same spiritual meat we do. So also the same drink, *for the rock was Christ.* Therefore they drank the same drink we do, but spiritual drink, that is drink which was received by *faith*, not what was swallowed down the body. They ate therefore the same meat, the same to those that understand and believe; but to them that do not understand, it was only that *manna*, only that *water*." And just after this he says, " it is the *same* Christ, though under the different form of words, ' *Christ to come*,' or that *has* come ;" (Venturus, et venit; diversa verba sunt, sed idem Christus.) Here it is manifest that this Father did not believe in Transubstantiation. In explaining the Apostle's declaration in 1 Cor. x. 3—4. as to the manna and the water and the wilderness, he tells us " that our fathers did spiritually eat and drink of the same Christ with ourselves ;" but if *our* eating *now* be Christ's *natural* body, then *their* meat and *ours* was *not* the same; for as Christ had not then taken flesh upon him, those fathers in the wilderness could not have eaten it in a *carnal* sense. This is made more obvious by his Tract 45, in John, where he says, " the *signs* are varied, *faith* remaining the same. There the *rock* was Christ; to us that which was laid on the altar is *Christ;* and they drank of the water that flowed from the rock for a *great Sacrament* of the same Christ; and what we drink the faithful *knew*. If you regard the *visible species*, it is another thing; if the *intelligible signification*, they drank the same spiritual drink." If this be not good Protestant doctrine, I know not what is. The usages also of the Fathers show in the most striking light that they did not believe in the *real* presence. Anciently it was the custom to give what remained of the consecrated bread to little children for food; sometimes they burned it in the fire; they even made plasters of it for the sick; they sent it from one to another as a token of communion; and they sometimes mixed the consecrated wine with ink for writing things of importance. Does this look like the real body and the real blood of Christ? Could the Fathers thus sacrilegiously treat the Son of God? Impossible ! It is clear that they held no such belief as yours. How unlike this were these usages to those of the present church of Rome. With you, if a drop of the wine be spilled, it must reverently be licked up; if a mouse run away with a crumb of the bread, the whole church is in commotion; " if a Priest vomit the Eucharist he must swallow it again." Such being the difference of usage, and such the clear testimonies of the Fathers, let me once more refer their opinions to your re-consideration.

3. Under the head in which you attempt to meet my objections to Transubstantiation, " as contrary to reason and contradictory to the senses," I know not whether you are most feeble or most prolix Your parallel between Professor Norton's objections to the Trinity, and mine to the real presence, is only remarkable for this, that you seem to prefer the sacrifice of the Trinity to the surrender of Transubstantiation. It is surely a most profane parallel. But the *contrast* between the Trinity and Transubstantiation, is perfect in all its

parts. 1. There is not a word of Scripture for the real presence: whereas it is redundant in favour of the Trinity. 2. Transubstantiation is contrary to reason and contradictory to the senses: whereas the Trinity does not the least violence to either. I would ask *you* if the doctrine of the Trinity *does* contradict the senses? Your whole argument then, as derived from the Unitarian is this—the Unitarian *says* the Trinity is contrary to reason, which Mr. Hughes does not believe; therefore Transubstantiation is not contrary to reason and the senses. A noble syllogism truly! Is it *impossible* for your *false* doctrine to contradict reason and the senses, because a Unitarian says a *true* doctrine does? In reference to Hume I still insist, that if Transubstantiation be true he *cannot* be confuted. You seem not to understand his system. He found prepared to his hand a false philosophy, which in violation of common sense denied first principles. Previous philosophers had denied the existence of *matter*. And who can *prove* it? It is self-evident; nothing is clearer to prove it by; we look to the senses for the proof of it. Proceeding on the same false principle, *he* denied the existence of *spirit*. If you grant his principle, it is impossible to answer his arguments. Now *as* his error *started* with the absurdity of contradicting the senses, and rejecting their testimony about the existence of matter, *so* Transubstantiation, in the same way contradicts the senses by saying that bread ceases to be bread, and has only the *appearance* of bread, when all our senses tell us it is still bread. We prove it to be bread as we prove the existence of *all* matter, *on the testimony of the senses*. We feel it, we taste, we smell it, we see it, that it is very bread, after all your consecrations; and the moment that you admit that it is not *bread*, Hume steps in, and on the same proof, may deny the existence of *all matter*. Whoever, therefore, takes your ground, if a thinking and consistent man, must launch into the wide sea of universal scepticism. Hence it has happened, as in Spain and South America at this day, that multitudes of your priests are *infidels*, as well as men of pleasure, in the worse sense of the terms; for your doctrines lead to it. And hence too the mass of your people are as *superstitious* as the Hindoos themselves; their confused views of the body of Christ are transferred to all things around them; and wizzards, and witches, and saints, and angels, and devils possess all objects, and people the creation; and holy water, and amulets, and relics, and images, and crosses, and beads, and agnus Dei's, and exorcisms abound; and they must have something around the neck, or in the bosom, at all times, to save them from devils, witches, fevers, fires, shipwrecks, &c. &c. Here I cannot but remark on the shocking way in which you express your ideas of the incarnation of the Son of God. You speak of "omnipotence, omniscience, and omnipresence, wrapt in swaddling clothes;" "the artificer of the universe turned carpenter;" "the eternal God subjected to the meanness of hunger and thirst;" and you adopt this as your creed by saying, " ALL THIS you *must* believe, if you believe the divinity of Jesus Christ." No Sir, I do not believe one word of it, and it is an insult to the God of heaven to connect such expressions with his august nature. I believe that the *man* Christ Jesus was thus exposed, and that the eternal God was and is united to the *man* Christ Jesus; but that *God* could not be born or suffer, or die any more than " his divinity, together with the soul and body of Jesus Christ," could be called into a piece of bread by the incantations of a priest, and then be eaten by the mouths of men. Again, even allowing that the *body* of Christ was really and carnally present in the Eucharist, it would still be gross idolatry to worship *it*. For I would ask, what is the proper object of divine worship but the divine attributes and perfections? To worship the *body* of Christ alone, is idolatry, as much as to worship a stock, or stone, or any mere creature. We worship Christ as *God:* but you worship the *flesh* (as you call it) of Jesus Christ. Is this not downright idolatry? For you do not merely adore *God* in the communion, but you " elevate the host," i. e. the consecrated wafer, (not *God*, for you cannot *handle and elevate* an infinite spirit) and you " adore" what you *elevate*. So that even if it *be* Christ's body, you are guilty of gross idolatry; and if it be not, of course, it is idolatry; so that taken either, or any way, to worship it is idolatry. Your ideas of matter are surely of the most extraordinary kind, and as dangerous to Christianity as they are absurd in themselves. The truth of Christianity was suspended by its author, on his resurrection from the dead. Now if his body did rise, it was and *is* a body still; and though *refined*, not a *spirit*, for Christ said, *"handle me and see,* for a spirit hath not flesh and bones, as you see me have." Luke xxiv. 39. And yet you venture to say " his body can be in two places at once; and if in *two*, so in a *million* of places, and yet be at the right hand. His body is *spiritual:* that is, endowed with the *properties* of a spirit." Let Augustine (Epist. 57. ad Dardan) answer you. "Take places away from bodies, and the bodies shall be *no* where: because they shall be no where, they shall *not be at all."* He thought that an omnipresent *body*, was *no* body. A *body* present in a *million* of places at the same time! Is not this a precise equivalent to the Eutychean heresy which denied that Christ had a body at all? "A body endowed with the *properties* of a spirit!" Is not this absurd? Is it not to say that it is *not* a body, for the *properties* of a spirit, make a *spirit;* and a *body* is *that* which has not the properties of a spirit. Do you not then in fact take the ground of the Swedenborgians, and Shaking Quakers, and deny the *bodily* resurrection of Christ, making it all *spiritual?* You most strangely appeal to John xx. 19. " When the doors were shut, where the disciples were assembled for fear of the Jews, Jesus came and stood in the midst." This you apply to prove, that as Christ must have come *through* the door, or the *wall*, therefore the body of Christ existed in the same space which was occupied by the closed door or wall. Surely you will not call this infallible interpretation. Do you forget that Christ had power to open the door by miracle, as the prison doors, shortly after this were opened and shut again by the angel of God, who liberated the apostles without disturbing the keepers? Acts v. 19. Do you forget that Christ had power miraculously to open a passage for his body through the door or wall, and close it again? Do you forget that matter having all the properties of matter, may be transmitted through other matter and yet neither occupy the place of the other, as light passing through a pane of glass? You adduce Christ's appearing to Paul on his way to Damascus, as a proof that his body was in two places at the same time. Christ also appeared to Stephen, Acts vii. 56, who said "behold I see the heavens opened and the Son of man standing on the right hand of God." Pray tell me *where* is the right hand of God? Have you any proof that Christ was not at his right hand when he was seen by Paul? Until you make this appear, your reasoning upon the passage is but a begging of the question we are discussing. I observe in all your remarks about our ignorance of space and time abstracted from the natural relation of bodies, you exclude the bread. Now the bread in our hands is certainly in its *natural* relation, both as to *time and space;* and whatever we do *not* know, this we do know, that it is bread, possessing all the properties of bread, *after* as well as before consecration; and as such, we handle, and break, and eat it; and being such, it is *not* the body of Christ. This we know. You attempt in vain to meet my exposure of your illustration, drawn from the descent of the Holy Ghost upon Jesus Christ at his baptism. I ask, was the Holy Ghost ever incarnate, or is he now? And can you then still insist that the case is parallel; or that the visible manifestation of Deity is the same thing, or a similar thing to the Transubstantiation of bread into a human body, a human soul, and the Divinity, yet retaining every *appearance* of bread?

4. Your remarks on the doctrine of intention; on the early silence of Jews, Pagans, and apostate Christians, about Transubstantiation; on the Eucharist as a miracle, and yet *no* miracle, since all miracles are palpable to the senses; are mere evasions, and call for no reply. My arguments on these topics stand just where they did, except that your failure to meet them shows their strength. As to the ancient Liturgies, I am prepared to meet you on that question when you please. I would only here ask you, whether the Mass used in your church is not altered so as to differ materially from the ancient Liturgy on the subject of the real presence? If you deny it, I will prove it.

III. Having now, as I suppose, effectually disposed of Transubstantiation, I proceed briefly to expose the sacrifice of the Mass, which you attempt to defend in Letter No. XXIX. This doctrine is the legitimate offspring of Transubstantiation, as we have already remarked, and of course falls with it. But it is worthy of a separate notice, especially as you own that it is the *chief* business of your clergy to offer up this sacrifice. The doctrine of your church is, "that the *same* Christ who once offered himself by his blood, on the altar of the cross, is *contained* in this *divine sacrifice,* which is celebrated in the Mass, and offered without blood; and the holy Council (of Trent) teaches that this is *really propitiatory*, and made by Christ himself:" "the *victim* and the Priest are the same Christ our Lord:" "in the Mass there is offered to God, a true, proper, propitiatory sacrifice for the living and the dead." (See Council of Trent, 1st and 2d chapters on the Mass; the Catechism on the Eucharist, and Creed of Pius IV.; also in Letter No. XXIV.)

Against this "blasphemous fable," as it is called in the articles of the Church of England, we have already (See Letter No. XXIV.) said much which you have left unanswered. We now add: 1. This is properly no sacrifice, because every real sacrifice supposes the death of the victim, and also its oblation to God. But the Council of Trent confesses as quoted above, that it is an *unbloody* sacrifice; and the Apostle Paul tells us, Heb. ix. 22. "that without shedding of blood is no remission." It follows therefore that it is *no* sacrifice, and especially not *propitiatory*, though the Council calls it so. Your standards confess that there is no *destruction* of life in the sacrifice of the Mass. The *bread* is destroyed, but bread cannot be a victim. How then can you call it a sacrifice? Again, there is no oblation; for there can be no offering up of Christ, if Transubstantiation be false; and we have abundantly proved that it is. 2. If the mass be a true sacrifice, then Christ did at the last Supper offer up his body and blood as a true propitiatory sacrifice, to God *before* he offered himself on the cross. You acknowledge that you offer in the Mass what Christ offered in the Supper; then if the Mass be a true sacrifice, Christ must have offered himself as a sacrifice to God in the Supper *before* he suffered on the cross. Of course Christ laid down his life *before* his death; that is, he offered himself *twice*, which is an absurdity. But it is clear that Christ did not *shed* his blood at the *Supper*, and without shedding of blood there is no proper sacrifice. The Mass therefore, cannot be a propitiatory sacrifice. 3. We are expressly told in Hebrews that Christ made but ONE propitiatory sacrifice of himself to God. Thus it is written, Heb. x. 11–14. " Every Priest, (Jewish) standeth daily ministering and offering *oftentimes* the same sacrifices which can never take away sins: but this man (Christ) after he had offered ONE sacrifice for sins forever sat down on the right hand of God; for by ONE offering he hath perfected forever them that are sanctified." And again, verse 10; " we are sanctified through the offering of the body of Christ ONCE." Here there is a definite statement that Christ was offered but *once;* yet in your Church, by the sacrifice of the Mass you profess to offer him *daily,* and in different parts of the world, *millions* of times every year. The churches in Madrid, alone in about one century, offered Christ 558,921 times, at the price of £1,720,437, for relieving from Purgatory, 1,030,305 souls!! Truly this is changing the temple of God into a house of merchandise; and this at last is the secret magic of the Mass. But the word of God makes not the least mention of Christ's sacrifice being offered again on earth after his death, or of repeating it in the Mass. So far from this we are told, Hebrews ix. 12. "that by his own blood Christ entered into the holy place, having obtained *eternal* redemption for us." 4. The Apostle plainly contradicts the doctrine of the Mass when he lays down the principle, that if Christ be *offered often* he must *suffer often*. (Hebrews ix. 25, 26.) "Nor yet that he should *offer himself often*, as the High Priest entereth into the holy place every year with blood of others; for then must he *often have suffered* since the foundation of the world; but *now once* in the end of the world hath he appeared to put away sin by the sacrifice of himself." If then you *really* offer

Christ, you *renew* his *sufferings* and *repeat* his *death*, by every sacrifice of the Mass. Yet you call it an *unbloody* sacrifice, and deny that Christ really *suffers;* though you say you offer the *same* victim that died upon the cross. Thus do you contradict yourselves, and do violence to the word of God. 5. The Mass makes an external visible sacrifice of a thing that is perfectly invisible; for it is Christ's body which you say is the *matter* of the sacrifice in the Mass; and yet this matter is not seen nor perceived by any of the senses. If Christ had thus offered himself on the cross, who would have known it? It would have been the offering of a *shadow* and not a *substance* to God. You might just as well have an invisible Priest, and an invisible altar. It is a gross absurdity. 6. It is not to this day determined in the Church of Rome what is the *essence* of this sacrifice, and wherein the true *sacrificial act* should be placed. The subject is involved in inexplicable difficulties. To put this to the test, I now ask you to tell me in your next letter wherein they consist? Now what sort of sacrifice must that be which none explain, which none understand, and which none can tell whether it consists in the oblation, the consecration, the breaking or eating of the elements? 7. Your own mass book, though altered from the ancient Liturgy, still goes directly in the face of such a sacrifice as you profess to offer, in several of its parts; and appears to be a strange compound of ancient truth, and modern errors. It is easy to make this manifest if you call for it. Yet this is the sacrifice by which you help souls out of purgatory. As if conscious that it could not be defended, you have left untouched my refutation of purgatory presented many weeks ago. Upon this profane and unscriptural institution have you hung the hopes of innumerable millions of souls. For this doctrine you bring no Scripture proof. Of the three passages in Genesis, Malachi, and Hebrews, not one has the least reference to the subject. I have much more to say on this subject which I now omit for want of room, and am prepared to show from Scripture, and antiquity, and reason, that this innovation, so *profitable* to the Priests, and so *ruinous* to the souls of the people, is utterly anti-Christian. IV. We come next to consider your defence of the Roman church *for taking* the *cup* from the people in the Eucharist. Your first reason is that Christ is present, whole and entire under *each* of the species of the sacrament. But the force of this depends, as you are aware, on the truth of Transubstantiation; and I think that by this time the community are satisfied that this is a slender thread on which to suspend such an innovation. Our Lord must have known the nature of his sacraments as well as you do, and yet he commanded the *cup* to be used, as well as the bread.

2. You contend that when Christ said "drink ye all of this," and "this do in remembrance of me," he addressed Apostles and Ministers only; and therefore if the people are to have the cup, the people also are to "consecrate and offer the sacrifice which he had just instituted." Yet you admit below "that in the earlier ages of the church the communion was administered to the laity in both kinds." Then on your admission it follows, that the church in the first ages understood Christ to confer on the laity the right of administering the

sacrament of the supper. But this you deny; and of course contradict yourself; I ask then why the early Christians gave the cup to the laity? But again the Council of Trent in so many words, says "that it was not *till* the last supper that our Lord ordained the Apostles to be Priests of the New Testament;" and you say the same. I ask then, were the Apostles *Priests* when they applied "the sacrament" of *extreme unction* to the sick? (Mark vi. 13.) If they were, then they were made Priests *before* the last supper; for none but Priests can administer sacraments. But you say they were made Priests *at* the last supper. If so, it follows that *extreme unction* was not a sacrament. But your church says it *is* a sacrament. Then the church has *erred*, and is infallible Yet if it be a sacrament, instituted by Christ, as you say, then the Apostles administered it *before* they were priests, or if you say, they were priests, *before* the last supper, then the church has *erred*, for she says they were not. 3. It appears then that the Roman church has, after all, violated an express law of Christ. For He said "drink ye all of it," to those to whom he said "take, eat;" and if you may do away the "*cup*," so may the "bread;" and if he meant the *Priests* only to have the "cup," he meant the priests only to have "the bread," and so there is no sacrament. You own "that in the earlier ages," they gave the cup to the laity. Why? And why alter the practice? Is not the *change* an insult to Christ? You say it is not "essential" to give the cup. How dare you say so when Christ *ordered* it to be done? And you his *priest* to administer his sacrament? Not *essential!* to do what Christ has fixed by a standing law, and in a holy sacrament! The Councils of Lateran and Trent own that the cup was primitively received by the people; but gravely tell us that for good and sufficient reasons the church has by *law* changed it; and has added an anathema to him who disputes the Church's authority!

4. By this act you nullify the Lord's Supper. You *divide* what Christ *united*, viz. the cup from the bread. Now as you drop one *half*, you destroy the entire institution. The Eucharist is never, no never, celebrated in your church. You not only *pervert* it by the pretended *sacrifice*, when it is *no* sacrifice, but you *destroy* it, by dropping one-half, and the more *important* part, if there be a difference. And now I call on you to prove your right to do so; and to show that the *earliest* antiquity gives to this criminal mutilation, nay, destruction of the Eucharist, the least countenance

V. We come next to your stereotype questions. These have at different times been answered by me already; and I doubt not to the satisfaction of every reasonable man. Your motive for their frequent repetition, is but too evident. The course of discussion which I had adopted under the general question, viz. "*Is the Protestant Religion the Religion of Christ*," led me in the first place to expose the errors and corruptions of the church of Rome. From the nature of the question this was the only consistent line of argument. In pursuit of this plan, I have exposed in a long series of unanswered arguments and historical facts, the false doctrines and abominations of the church of Rome. Instead of meeting me on this ground you have continually been crying out for the "question," the "question," desirous, no doubt, to call me off from points which your pen could not defend, and whose discussion your cause could not endure. To prevent an endless and indeterminate controversy, I waived the points on which we *agreed;* and selected those on which we *differed.* On these *disputed* points the controversy between us turns. *You* hold these disputed points to be essential as a part of the religion of Christ; whereas *we protest* against them as errors and innovations. I fully stated these disputed tenets in my definition of the Protestant Religion in letter No. XX.; and since that time have been engaged in confuting the chief part of them. To illustrate this; we *agree* that Christ is the head of the church; but you *add* the supremacy of the Pope. I have shown his supremacy to be a anti-christian usurpation. When this Papal excresence is cut off, the Christian, Protestant headship of Christ *remains.* We *agree* that the Bible is a rule of faith; but you add to it the apochryphal books, unwritten tradition, an infallible interpreter, and the unanimous consent of the Fathers. I exposed your additions, and showed that they are unchristian novelties. The Christian, Protestant Rule of Faith remains. We agree that God is the proper object of religious worship; but you add to this, gross idolatry, in the worship of the cross, the consecrated bread, the Virgin Mary, angels, saints, pictures, relics, and images. I exposed this idolatry; the Christian, pure, Protestant worship of *God* alone remains. We agree that Christ instituted the two sacraments of Baptism and the Eucharist; but you corrupt these two, and add *five* more. I have exposed these your corruptions and additions; the Christian, Protestant sacraments remain; and so of the other points of difference, whether it be of your *additions to,* or *subtraction from,* the Religion of Christ. At every step, therefore, in this discussion, (besides my direct replies, at the close of several of my letters,) I have been answering your interrogatories by assailing and confuting those doctrines of your church against which we PROTEST.

But to be more particular. You ask, 1. *"What is the Protestant religion."* Answer. It is the religion of the Reformation, in contradistinction from the Roman Catholic religion, as it concerns doctrine, and morality, government, discipline, and worship. It is the religion which is exclusively derived from, and consistent with, the *Holy Scriptures as the only infallible Rule of Faith and practice:* and which *protests* against the errors and corruptions of the church of Rome. After all your vain cavils, this definition is clear, minute, and just. You object that *Deists protest* (see Letter No. 23,) against the Roman Catholic Religion. True; but I *defined* the points on which we protest; and they, in important respects, differ from the protests of Deists; for Deists protest against those points in which we *differ* from you; and Deists protest also against those points in which we *agree* with you. You object again to the definition "that our religion is derived exclusively from the Holy Scriptures, because we derive it by private interpretation." But how else shall we derive it? I have fully proved that your infallibility is a figment, that your rule of faith is a failure and a fraud; that the right use of reason, under the guidance of God, is the only way; and that as to abuses, your forcing the sense of Scripture and the conscience of men, have led to greater abuses than private interpretation ever did, with this difference against you, that if men *abuse* private interpretation, that is not the fault of our *rule*, or *our method* of using it; whereas, your enormous abuses of the Bible are by *authority*, and your church must answer to God for all the violence she has done to conscience, reason, and his holy word. Once more, you object to the definition, that " our religion is consistent with the Holy Scriptures," and say that " every sect claims the same for its notions." It is true; but are *claims* facts? Do false claims destroy true ones? False prophets claimed inspiration; does that destroy the evidence of Paul's inspiration? False Christs arose; does that falsify the true Christ? The truth of a definition depends upon the proof of a conformity between the thing defined and the terms; and I have proved the justness of my definition in the progress of this discussion. If heretical sects *do* claim conformity to the Bible, they pay more respect to it than the church of Rome does, for she professedly violates Bible law by taking the cup from the laity in the Eucharist; by using prayers in an unknown tongue; by forbidding priests to marry; by making a sacrament of extreme unction, &c.

2d Question. " I call upon you to say, what society of Christians ever taught this pretended ' Religion of Christ' previous to the Reformation ?" This question was answered at large in Letters No. XX. and XXIV. I answer that the *name* Protestant is *new*, but not the religion. The name Roman Catholic is also new, as well as absurd. Neither name is found in the Apostles' creed, or any early creed; and the Roman church was not even *called* Catholic for ages after the Apostles' days. Protestant is a new name for the old religion of Christ, which was given to those who *protested*, at the Reformation, against the corruptions of that religion by the church of Rome. Every society of Christians on earth from the days of the Apostles to the Council of Nice, held the doctrines of the Protestant Religion ! All the churches founded by the Apostles (including Rome) beginning at Jerusalem, in Asia, Africa, and Europe, held essentially, the doctrines of the Protestant church until the Council of Nice; as may be seen by comparing the formularies issued by the Reformers with the Apostles' creed; the Athanasian creed; the Nicene creed, and the writings at large of the Ante-Nicene Fathers. In order to test this, will you be so good as to take up these formularies and compare them, first with these monuments of antiquity, and secondly, with the word of God? After Arius arose, the church by degrees became corrupted with his heresy; and finally Liberius the Bishop (Pope) of Rome, signed the Arian creed; several Councils adopted Arianism; and finally, as Hilary informs us, Arianism was spread throughout the whole world. Still a remnant was left according to the faithful promise of Christ to his church, which professed the true religion; and from age to age, till the glorious Reformation in the sixteenth century, the doctrines of the Protestant church, though persecuted by the church of Rome, were cherished [as I have shown in previous letters] by faithful witnesses to the truth. The Syrian Christians to whom I have often in vain invited your attention, who were never connected with or subject to the church of Rome, who reject your canon of Scripture; who were condemned by your Archbishop for holding Protestant doctrines, and who derived from Apostolical days their Bible and their creeds, are a living monument to the Christianity of Protestantism, and to the innovation and corruptions of the church of Rome. It is also notorious, that the Christian churches in England and Ireland, held the Protestant doctrines in their essential purity, *before* and *when* the first emissaries of the church of Rome, invaded them, and began to proselyte them to the Roman Hierarchy.

Question 3d. "I call upon you to say, whether Christ revealed all the doctrines of the Protestant Religion, beginning with the best image of your Church, Episcopalianism, and terminating with the most consistent of Protestant sects, the Unitarians? and if not, how many denominations out of the whole, belong to the true Protestant Religion, the Religion of Christ?"

Answer. In your Letter No. XXIII. you make the following acknowledgment, viz: "touching what are called 'Orthodox' tenets among Protestants, I have to observe that they are all found in the Catholic Church. These doctrines always existed in the Church; and the Reformers in going out from the Church, carried them forth." Now, we agree with you, that some who call themselves Protestants are not Orthodox in their faith; and you agree with us that there are 'orthodox' Protestants. I refer you again (as in Letter 26) to the *Formularies* which were drawn up and published by the Reformed church in the 16th century. There were no less than 12 of these, viz the Augustan, Tetrapolitan, Polish, Saxon, Bohemian, Wittemberg, Palatine, Helvetic, French, Dutch, English, and Scotch Confessions. These doctrinal standards exhibited the Christian Theology and unity of the flower of Europe as to its *character*, and of half its population as to *number*. They were issued as by one simultaneous movement; they agreed essentially with each other; and with one consent threw off the despotism, and corrupt doctrines of the church of Rome. Protestantism pervaded Norway, Sweden, Denmark, Poland, Prussia, Germany, Transylvania, Hungary, Switzerland, France, Holland, England, Ireland, Scotland; and soon reached the continents of Asia, Africa, and America. That there have been and are many sects calling themselves Protestants, whose doctrines are heretical, who are not Protestants, and with whom we cannot symbolize, Evangelical Protestants are as free to admit as yourself, and cease not to deplore it. But this is not peculiar to Protestantism. No church has so abounded with sects as the church of Rome; and not an error has arisen in the Protestant church, which finds not its parentage or its likeness in your church. You have this great advantage over us, that by the Inquisition, or the stake, or a crusade, or some tremendous interdict, you compel uniformity; but our people are subject to no such bodily pa'ns and *penalt'es*, and persecutions, and stakes. And this also, that the capricious and polluted bosom of the church of Rome can contain all sorts of wickedness, and can tolerate all sorts of irregularities if her peculiar dogmas and dominion are but recognized. Thus her Priests, as in South America and Spain, may spend the afternoon of the Lord's day in the cock-pit or at the gambling-table, if they only *say mass* in the morning; and the convenient morality of the Jesuits can cover and excuse any sin, even fornication, or murder, so that the Pope be acknowledged, and Protestants abhorred. Now we cannot do so, and hence we often are to called *d'vide* from us, for errors, or immoralities, those who give rise to some *new* but small sect. Yet after all, the different denominations of Protestant Christians, as Episcopalians, Baptists, Congregationalists, Methodists, Moravians, and Presbyterians, agree far more nearly with each other than the various sects now existing (as I shall prove in my next letter) in the church of Rome. But if the Reformed church is made responsible for the many heresies and sects with which you charge her, I ask who is responsible for the many heresies and sects which arose in the church of Rome at the Reformation? Why did half the population of Europe forsake the church of Rome and break into various sects? You say the fault was in those who broke off. Why then is it not the fault of those who break off from the Protestant church? You affirm that these sects and heresies in the Protestant church are produced by our Rule of Faith. Then, query, if your rule of faith be so perfect, why did so many sects and heresies arise in your bosom? Such are the inconsistencies and absurdities involved in your system.

The 4th and 5th questions regard Protestant ordination. Want of room compels me to delay an answer till the next letter, in which, Providence permitting, I will give one at large. I observe that you have omitted a 6th question, once numbered in the series, touching the character of the Reformers, in these words, "Take the Reformers as they have been described by themselves, *is it clear* that *they* were the men whom God would have selected to purify the church?" This question was returned upon you in the wicked lives of the Popes with such effect, that you voluntarily withdrew it from the list of your auxiliaries.

But I must, before I close, notice *your answers* to *my* questions. 1. You say that "Pope Liberius did not sign the Arian creed in the *Arian sense* or mean ng." This is a mere evasion. I ask in *what sense did* he sign it? 2. What councils does your church recognize, and by what rules is she guided, if she reject the Councils of Sermium, Ariminum. &c.? 3. I repeat the question concerning "the intention of Popes, Bishops, and Priests;" supposing they do. as they may, lack *intention*, are their acts valid? It is not true that "they have no motive to withhold intention." Your answers to the remaining questions are highly important, and shall be exposed in my next. Let me here remark, that your approbation of the Inquisition, your high tribute to the Jesuits, and your shunning an answer on the freedom of the Press, are approaches to the true spirit of Popery, at which I hope our readers will distinctly look; and from which the most important results are promised. Allow me to add the following questions to those which you have left unanswered in your last. Is there any evidence of the Pope's Supremacy before the Council of Nice? Were the Apostles Priests when they administered Extreme Unction, Mark vi. 13. Has the Pope a right to put a kingdom under interdict, or to depose a monarch or chief magistrate? Did the second Council of Pisa decree a reformation in *faith* or not? Did the Council of Lateran in 1215 pass an anathema against those rulers who should *tax Ecclesiastics?* Is not the second commandment dropped from the Catechism which are in *common* use in your Church in Europe and in America? Have not "The Fathers" been altered and pruned by authority in your church? Are the Missal and the Breviary authorized and standard works? When you have answered these, we shall have additional light on the policy and principles of the Roman Church. I remain, Yours, &c.

JOHN BRECKINRIDGE.

P. S. Last Thursday morning, Mr. Hughes, according to his promise deposited his copy of Baronius in the Athenæum, for the inspection of the public, accompanied with a paper, of which the following is a correct copy. My copy of Baronius, which is page for page the same as his, was laid beside it. As no notice was published in the daily papers of the fact, or the reason of it, it attracted, I believe, very little notice. I have too much reason to think that this was exactly what Mr. H. wished.

MR. HUGHES' NOTES.

"*Theodora.*—Baronius tells us, paragraph 6, that she was the mistress of Albertus Marquis of Tuscany, who at that time could tyrannize over Rome by means of *the Fort of St. Angelo*, of which he was *master.* Consequently, he could expel lawful Popes and put in usurpers, just as his *mistress directed.* Was it fair in Mr. B. to suppress this?

"*Sergius.*—Baronius tells us that the monster Sergius was a usurper, and was sustained in his usurpations by said *Albertus.* And moreover, that all the *scandals* referred to, were by *these creatures of a tyrant.* "Perpetrata sunt ista ab invasoribus et intrusis!! verum *legitime creati Romani Pontifices* ista vehementer sunt execrati." § 3. Was it fair then to suppress this?

"*Apostate Popes and not Apostolical.*"—Baronius says this in reference to the *illegitimate and tyrannical manner* in which they had been thrust into the place of the lawful Popes. Was it fair to suppress this?

"Baronius tells us the church was "disgraced" (infamari) by strumpets. Mr. Breckinridge translates it "governed" by strumpets. Is this fair?

"Baronius occupies the whole of the seventh paragraph to prove how manifestly the *providence of God appears in the preservation* of his church in those days of tyranny, scandal, and disorder. He argues that it would have been rent asunder, "had not God with his supreme watchfulness preserved its safety and integrity," "*nisi Deus ejus incolumitati et integritati summa vigilantia prospexisset.*" He says it was the *invisible hand of God which sustained the Church,* and that nothing else could sustain it under the shocking scandals of those wicked tyrants and intruders which he had just described.

"Does not Mr. Breckinridge, then, assert what is untrue in making Baronius say that the church was orgotten by God? Did he ever see the original?
N. B. The Italian copy is but an abridgment."

As this appears to be a proper occasion to dispose of this matter, I must trespass a little longer on the patience of my readers by submitting the following answer to the above notes.

In my last letter I answered as follows:

1st. "That Theodora, a courtezan of noble family, obtained supreme control in Rome."

PROOF.

Baronius, Vol. X. p. 766. § 5. Audisti temporis hujus deploratissimum statum, cum Theodora senior nobille scortum monarchiam (ut ita dicam) obtineret in urbe?

Hast thou heard of the most deplorable state of this time, when Theodora the elder, a noble courtezan, obtained (so to speak) supreme control in the city?

Mr. H. leaves this assertion untouched. Baronius unfortunately is too explicit.

2d. "That she expelled the lawful Popes and put violent and nefarious men into the Papal chair."

PROOF.

Baronius, ibid. § 6. Exquibus tantarum invaluit meretricum imperium ut pro *arbitrio* legitime creatos dimoverent pontifices et violentos ac nefarios homines illis pulsis intruderent.

By which means these courtezans acquired such power that at their *pleasure* they expelled the lawfully constituted popes, and put violent and nefarious men into their place.

Mr. H. says that "Albertus could expel lawful Popes, and put in usurpers, just *as his* MISTRESS *directed*." (This mistress was Marozia, one of the *noble* daughters of the *noble* Theodora.) Here we agree. Popes have been deposed, and others appointed at the direction of a courtezan. I would like to know whether these facts are stated in the Italian translation of Baronius, which Mr. H. promised to deposit at the Athenæum, for the inspection of the public, but which he withheld, on the ground of its being only *an abridgment?* It might have scandalized the devout Italians to read such things about their Holy Mother.

3d. "That Pope Sergius III. committed adultery with her (Theodora's) daughter, and their son John, the offspring of their cr mes was afterwards Pope himself."

PROOF.

Luitprandus, quoted by Baronius, ibid. § 5. Harum una Marozia ex Papa Sergio......Ioannem qui.....sanctæ Romanæ Ecclesiæ obtinuit dignitatem nefario genuit adulterio. Joannes undecimus ex Marozia scorto Sergii Pseudopapæ filius papa creatur. See Index to Vol. X.

One of these daughters, Marozia, by a shocking adultery, had a son John by Pope Sergius, who afterwards obtained the dignity of the Holy Roman Church. John XI. son of the pretended Pope Sergius, by Marozia a courtezan, is made Pope.

Uncontr .dicted *for a good reason.* But Mr. Hughes says Sergius was an *usurper.* I grant it, and so were all his predecessors and successors. But I would ask, did not this usurper hold the Papal chair at least three years? Were not he and his bastard son John XI. who was likewise an "usurper," acknowledged by the Catholic church as its only visible head? Did they not perform the functions of Pontiffs in consecrating Bishops, &c.? If they were not true Popes, then the line of succession was broken, and all the consecrations and episcopal acts performed by them were null and void. How does Mr. H. know that *he* himself has not received his ghostly authority from this tainted source?

4th. "He (Baronius) says they were Apostate Popes, and not Apostolical."

PROOF.

Baronius ibid. § 4. Cumtamen eosdem sedis Apostolicæ invasores non Apostolicos sed apostaticos esse dicendos, Ecclesiastica benedisposita censuit disciplina.

Whereas in the judgment of sound ecclesiastical discipline such invaders of the Apostolical See should be called not apostolical but Apostate.

Not denied by Mr. H. I have not suppressed a word of the passage or context here. See assertion second.

5th. "Calls the times deplorable." See 1st.

Admitted by Mr. H. by "expressive silence."

6th. " And the scandal overwhelming, says the church was governed by strumpets and forgotten by God."

PROOF.

Baronius ibid. § 7. Quis ista considerans non obstupescens, scandalumqua patiens putarit, Deum oblitum Ecclesiæ suæ, quam meretricum arbitrio permiserit infamari?

Who in view of these things would not be amazed and shocked, and think that God had forgotten his church, which he had thus given up to the infamy of being governed by strumpets?

Baronius says that the Church was disgraced by the *government* of strumpets, (infamari arbitrio meretricum.) And here I cannot but admire the *courage* of Mr. H. in asserting under his hand that I had translated infamari *governed*. Did he not know, or did he think that the intelligent gentlemen who visit the Athenæum would not discover that Baronius uses the word *arbitrio*, "*will, pleasure, rule, power.*" See Ainsworth. "Did he ever see the original?" Alas, for the cause that needs such a subterfuge! It is not only once or twice that Baronius makes the same assertion. On page 779. § viii. he says, quæ tunc facies sanctæ Ecclesiæ Romanæ? Quam fœdissima, cum Romæ *dominarentur* potentissimæ æque ac sor didissimæ meretrices! Quarum arbitrio, &c. "What was then the aspect of the Holy Roman Church? How foul, when courtezans at once the most powerful and most sordid, *governed* Rome?"

With respect to the assertion "that God had forgotten his church," Baronius acknowledges that it would be a rational conclusion in any one who would consider these things But with much Jesuitical ingenuity he goes on to show from the fact that no schism nor heresy occurred in the church, in consequence of these scandalous corruptions, that this is the true church of God! A more palpable sophism was never conceived. It only proves that it was '*like priest, like people.*' For if there had been any virtue in the community, a church which had thus forsaken God, and been forsaken by him, would have become " a bye-word and a hissing." Moreover, Baronius, speaking of the Pontificate of John X., another "usurper" who obtained the chair by the influence of his paramour Theodora, and held it sixteen years, says " Dormiabet tunc plane alto (ut apparet) so pore Christus in navi." "Surely Christ was then sound asleep in the ship, as is evident." Do not these expressions warrant the assertion that Baronius said " God had forgotten his church?" At all events Mr. H. should be the last person to deny that God had forgotten the Roman Catholic Church, unless it could exist *without a head*. For he tells us in his last letter that " *a false* pope is no pope." Baronius, whom he acknowledges to be good authority, calls John X *pseudopapa, pseudopontifex, a false Pope* So that for sixteen years there was no *Pope!* If the Catholic Church was the Church of God, where was his care of it all this time? Had he not *forgotten it?* J. B.

The following letter speaks for itself.

To the Rev. John Breckinridge.

Sir,—Having observed in the papers of this morning a card signed by M. Fithian, as the publisher of the Review of Bishop Onderdonk's charge, in which reference is made to me, it becomes my duty to say that his statements are incorrect. Immediately after the letter of Rev. Mr. Hughes appeared, in which he says, " In one instance a bookseller who enjoyed some sectarian patronage was actually forbidden to keep it for sale," I was called upon by the said Mr. Fithian to ascertain whether the information that he had given, and which led to the above statement, was correct. I told him that it was not, and this he must have known when he gave the card to which his name is annexed, and which appeared many days after our interview. I was never forbidden to keep it for sale, I have never received orders of any kind whatever on the subject, nor am I aware that it was ever known by the members composing the Board, that I had received the work at all. Any one acquainted with the nature of this institution, must see that even if *orders had been given*, the statement of Rev. Mr Hughes makes a false impression on the public mind. I am not a *bookseller* in the sense in which that term is ordinarily understood; but an *agent* employed in a religious institution. I can therefore neither "enjoy" nor receive "*patronage;*" nor be influenced in the discharge of my duties by the fear of losing it. The object of the Baptist Tract Society is the diffusion of what that denomination considers truth. All its agents and concerns are under the direction of a Board of Managers. The supplying of the Depository with other works than those issued by the Society, is under the direction of a Committee of that Board. But in the case of the Review no orders whatever were given by the Board, nor by the Committee respecting the sale of it at first, or the discontinuance of it. I received and sold the copies that were left with me on my own responsibility, and declined receiving any more upon the same, and by that responsibility I am willing to stand.   A. S. LANGLEY,

Assistant at the Depository of the Bap. Gen. Tract Society

Philadelphia, Sept. 5th, 1833.

CONTROVERSY. No. XXXIII.

IS THE PROTESTANT RELIGION THE RELIGION OF CHRIST?
Philadelphia, September 13th, 1833.

To the Rev. John Breckinridge.

Rev. Sir,—Mr. Breckinridge says that "*the Protestant is the religion of Christ.*"

If so, I call upon him 1st. To tell me what the Protestant religion is?

2. I call upon him to say what society of Christians ever taught this pretended "*religion of Christ,*" previous to the Reformation?

3. I call upon him to say, whether Christ revealed ALL the doctrines of the Protestant religion, beginning with the best IMAGE of his church, Episcopalianism, and terminating with the most consistent of Protestant sects, the Unitarians?—and if not, how MANY denominations, out of the whole, belong to the TRUE Protestant religion, the religion of Christ?

4. I call upon him to show whether the Reformers received any NEW ministerial authority, after the withdrawal of that which they had received from the church?

5. I call upon him, in case no such NEW authority was received, to show that the Protestant clergy, so called, have any divine right to exercise the Christian ministry, more than other educated laymen?

You will not be surprised that the five "stale questions," should still stand at the head of my letters, as I shall show in the sequel, that you have not answered any of them; and moreover, that they cannot be answered to the satisfaction of any dispassionate or reasonable mind.

With regard to the authority of Thuanus and Dupin, as Catholic writers, it is rejected for reasons which I have already stated; and from the fact of its rejection you are at liberty to draw your inferences as you think proper.

In reference to Baronius, I had simply accused you of falsifying the text in your quotation. I supposed then, that you did it through ignorance; but the book has since been laid open to public inspection, and you have the courage still to repeat what every scholar who examined the original, must acknowledge to be *untrue*.

In my postscript I shall give the translation of Baronius; so that even the uneducated may see what must be your situation, when you first quote falsely, and being advised of it, repeat the assertion, under circumstances which go far, as I shall show, to prove that you must *have known it was unfounded*.

But, Rev'd. Sir, I hope you will not be offended, if I direct your attention to some things in your letter, which can hardly fail to be regarded even by your friends, as a reprehensible want of courtesy on your part. For example, when you tell me that you "are ashamed (perhaps not without *reason*) to be dragged before the public in such company;" do you forget that your controversial challenge was addressed to "Priests and Bishops," and that you condescended to admit my claims as a "responsible correspondent?"

Again, as regards what you call " superstition," you compare Catholics with " Hindoos." Now the Catholics (accustomed to insult) can forgive you this, but Protestants themselves will say there is no *argument* in such phrases.

Again, since you have sent your "friend to the Athenæum," when (and perhaps *because*) I did not expect him, it is but fair that he and you should have another and a *better* opportunity.

Be it known, therefore, that a reward of five hundred dollars is hereby offered, to any friend of Mr. Breckinridge, or any other person, who shall find, in the 10*th volume of the writings of Baronius, a certain quotation, which he, the said Mr. Breckinridge, published with inverted commas, in Letter No. XXX. of the pending Controversy; and which he, the said Mr. Breckinridge, professed to have found in, and taken from, the said* 10*th volume. If Mr. Espy, Mr. Parker, Teachers of Languages, and Mr. M'Elhenny, (all Protestants,) or any two Professors of languages in any College, in America, shall attest that said passage has been found, the subscriber hereby binds himself to pay five hundred dollars to the finder. The said* 10*th volume of Baronius shall remain at the Athenæum, open for inspection during one week after the publication of these presents.*

Now, Rev'd. Sir, let "your friend" get ready, whilst I proceed to notice whatever deserves to be noticed in your letter, of which, by the way, the continued perversions of authorities form the principal part.

The case of Bellarmine you still affect not to understand. I have explained and vindicated it in my last letter, and to that explanation I refer the reader. It is not necessary for me in *every* letter to extricate my arguments and reasonings from the confusion in which it may suit your convenience to involve what you cannot answer or refute. Touching the " license to commit sin," the Protestant INDULGENCE which I pointed out in your " Confession of Faith," you have thought fit to be silent. It was not founded on the case of adultery; but on the liberty to obtain a divorce and marry another wife or husband, in consequence of such " wilful desertion (by the *true* wife or husband) as can in no way be remedied by the church or magistrate." Here there is no mention of "adultery"—"wilful desertion" is recognised *as sufficient to authorise Polygamy!!* This is pretty morality. Neither is it the opinion of individuals. It is the doctrine of the Presbyterian church proposed in her Standard of 1821. Does the Scripture say any thing of this case of " wilful desertion," and yet your ministers are obliged to receive the " standard" as the *summary of the Scriptures.*

As to the intolerance of Presbyterianism, I established it by logical demonstration in a way which bids defiance to all your *gratuitous* assertions to the contrary. As long as my arguments are unanswered, I need not return to the subject. *You say* it is liberal, I have proved the contrary from its own standard testimony. I am content therefore to leave the matter as it is.

The same observation applies to your review of my arguments on the Eucharist. Not a single argument of mine have you touched; not a single authority have you disputed. You had appealed to

Scripture. I showed that Scripture *positively states* the Catholic dogma, as it is believed in the church. You had appealed to the Fathers. I showed that all the Fathers of the first six hundred years believed and taught with the church and with the Scriptures. You had appealed to reason and the senses. I showed that the doctrine of the real presence of Christ in the Eucharist, like *other mysteries*, is believed *by virtue of Revelation*. And that having been *revealed*, it rests, not on the testimony of reason, or what you call by that name, but on the *omnipotence* and *veracity* of God. With God it is perfectly reasonable. But I have so little cause to be *dissatisfied* with your late production, that I willingly leave the matter to the sincere judgment of our readers. Let them compare letter with letter and see whether a single difficulty has been raised by you, not excepting the *deistical sophisms* which you have introduced, that has not been answered or anticipated in the arguments of my last.

For the information of the reader, however, I shall make a few remarks by way of explanation. I have already observed, that in the primitive church the doctrine of the Eucharist was concealed from Jews, Pagans, and even Catechumens, until *after* their initiation by the sacrament of Baptism. This practice was derived from the doctrine of Jesus Christ directing that holy things should not be given to dogs, nor perils placed before swine. (Matt. vii. 6.)

It was derived from this practice: "To you, he said, is given *to know* the mysteries of the kingdom of God, but to the rest in *parables*." (Luke viii. 10.) And again, "I have many things to say to you, but you cannot bear them *now*." (John xvi. 12.) So also after his resurrection, "He opened their understanding, that they might understand the Scripture." (Luke xxiv. 45.) In the Acts, the celebration of the mysteries of the Eucharist is referred to, in a way which indicates that it was not to be exposed to the Jews or Pagans " continuing daily in the temple, and *breaking bread*, from house to house, they took their meat with *gladness* and *simplicity* of heart." (ii. 46.) " And it came to pass, whilst they were at table with him (after the resurrection) he took bread, and blessed, and brake, and gave to them......and how they knew him in the breaking of bread." (Luke xxiv. 30 and 35.) So in like manner St. Paul—" And I, brethren, could *not speak to you* as to spiritual, but as to carnal. As to *little ones* in Christ, I gave you milk to drink, not meat: for you *were not able* AS YET: but neither are you now able: for you are *yet* carnal." (1 Cor. iii. 1, 2.) Thus Justin Martyr in his "Dialogue with Trypho" the Jew, refers to the Eucharist as the SACRIFICE of the new law, spoken of by Malachy, of bread and wine in commemoration of Christ's passion, because the *mystery* of that sacrifice was not to be exposed *to Jews*. We have the testimony of Clemens Alex. (lib 1. Stromatum,) of Tertullian (Apol. c. 7. and lib. 2. ad uxorem,) of Origen (Hom. 9. in Caput. 16 Lev. No. 10.) of the Apostolical Constitutions (lib. 3. cap. 5.) of St. Cyril of Jerusalem, (Pref. ad. Catech. No. 12.) of St. Basil (lib. de Spir. s. c. 27. No. 66.) In short, of Gregory Nazianzen, St. Ambrose, St. Epiphanius, St. Chrysostom, St. Augustine, St. Cyril of Alex. Theodoret, of all the Fathers to prove that in their discourses *to mixed assemblies*, while either Pagans, Jews, or even Catechumens were present, they spoke of the holy Eucharist with *caution and concealment*, so that whilst the faithful, who were initiated, *knew the mystery*, the knowledge of it should be withheld from the profane, lest being as they were carnal, they should be scandalized and scoff at it, as Protestants do now. They said in the figurative language of our blessed Redeemer, that holy things were not to be given to dogs, nor perils cast before swine. It was on *such occasions* they used those ambiguous expressions, by which Protestant books and Protestant ministers would persuade the people that the Fathers did not believe the Eucharist to be *flesh and blood* of Jesus Christ. Hear St. Cyril of Jerusalem. "We declare not to the Gentiles the hidden mysteries of the Father, Son, and Holy Ghost; nor do we speak *openly* of the mysteries of the Catechumens: but we frequently employ *obscure expressions*, that they may be understood by those who are *already instructed*, and that the *uninstructed* may not be injured by them." (Catech. vi. No. 29.) It is of these "obscure expressions" that Protestants take advantage, when they would persuade the people that the Fathers believed in mere bread and wine. But I showed in my last letter the doctrine of the Fathers and of the primitive church, by their instructions to the faithful *initiated*, in which there was no necessity for concealment, and in which, they consequently teach the doctrine of the real presence of the body and blood of Jesus Christ in the Eucharist *so strongly and so unequivocally* that no Protestant minister would dare to repeat their expressions in his pulpit.

Now I maintain that this very concealment of the Eucharist from Pagans, Jews, and Catechumens is *by itself*, a powerful proof of the Catholic doctrine. For in the first place, if it were mere bread and wine, what *motive* could there exist to conceal it? 2. When they were accused of "murdering a child, and *feasting on its flesh* in their assemblies," it would have been easy and natural to refute the calumny, and say that it was *merely a little* bread and wine they took figuratively in memory of Christ's body and death. But this they never said; even when they were *tortured*, as was sometimes the case, to force them into a confession of what it was! 3. They would not have celebrated the Eucharist with doors inviolably closed, for even the High Priest would not be scandalized, at seeing them eat bread and drink wine; though he might be, if he saw them adoring the flesh of Jesus Christ in the Eucharist as they invariably did (see my last letter) before they received it. But their positive testimony, when speaking to the faithful *alone*, leaves no room to doubt on the subject. So much so that Zuinglius, in reading the Fathers, acknowledges that on every page in which they referred to it, he found nothing but "*bread of life*," "*flesh of Christ*," "*body and blood of our Lord Jesus Christ.*"

How well then, would it be, for Protestants and their ministers, to hearken to the beautiful advice of St. Chrysostom. "Let us believe God in all things, and gainsay him not, although what he says *appears to be contrary to the testimony of our eyes and our reason.* Let the authority of his *word* supersede the testimony of our eyes and our reason. Since, therefore, his word said, "this is my body," let us *rest satisfied and believe,* let us behold it with the eyes of faith." (Hom. iv. in Joan.)

The principal exception which you make to the arguments of my last letter is that, "admitting some of the Fathers to be for the real presence," I have not their unanimous consent. I answer, that I have. They *all* taught, and believed, as Catholics do. But say you, St. Augustine tells us, that "when the Scripture seems to *command a wicked thing* it is to be understood *figuratively.*" Thus of the words 'unless you eat the flesh, &c.' Answer. In this St. Augustine speaks not of the *substance* of the Eucharist. He speaks of the *action* or manner in which the flesh of Christ was to be received. If the Jews understood the precept *to eat,* in the literal or natural sense, it would lead to a wicked consequence, viz. tearing the flesh from the bones of Christ and so eating it. He points out the error of the Capharnaites: they understood Christ to speak of his flesh, in this they were right, but they imagined that it was to be eaten, in the *gross manner* of human, natural flesh, instead of the supernatural manner, *in which it exists in the Eucharist,* and he showed, that in the *former* sense "the Scripture would seem to command a wicked thing," and in so much was not to be understood literally. How you could have read the passage and not *know* this, or knowing, not mention it, I am at a loss to conceive. But read the testimonies from St. Augustine in my last letter, and you will be compelled to acknowledge, in your own mind at least, that he was the *believer* and *adorer* of Christ's body in the Eucharist.

Again you quote Tertullian. But the context shows that you pervert him. The scope of his passage is to show that, according to the Prophet Jeremiah, bread had been the *ancient* "figure," of Christ's body. To prove this, he quotes the words of the institution to *show that the figure of the prophet had received its* fulfilment, adding immediately, the words which you suppress, "figura autemnon *fuisset,* nisi veritatis esset Corpus," that is, "but it (the bread) *would not have been* a figure, if it (the holy Eucharist) were not the body in truth." Why did you mistranslate this?

You mention Erasmus as asserting that until the year "1215" the Catholic doctrine of the Eucharist was a disputed point. You give no quotation, but I shall, to show how far you have injured him by the assertion. "Since the ancients," says he, "to whom the church, not without reason, gives so much authority, *are all agreed in* the belief, that the true substance of the body, and blood of Jesus Christ is in the Eucharist: since, in addition to all this, has been added the *constant* authority of the Synods, and *so perfect an agreement of the Christian world,* let us also agree with them in this heavenly mystery, and let us receive here below, the bread and the chalice of the Lord under the veil of the *species,* until we eat and drink them without *veil* in the kingdom of God. And would that those, who followed Beringarius in *his* error, would follow him in his repentance." (Præf. in Tract. de Euch.) Is this the language of a man who held that the Catholic doctrine of the Eucharist was a disputed point till the year "1215?" We should have had another article in our rules, couched in something like the following terms: "It is understood between the parties, that Mr. Breckinridge shall make as many unfounded assertions and false quotations as onfidence, *without experience,* may dictate; and that Mr. Hughes shall have nothing to do, but go after him and refute them."

In your quotation from Epiphanius (In Anciorat,) you again suppress the part that goes against you. He was showing that man is made after the likeness of God, although the resemblance is not perceptible to the senses. This he shows by comparison with what appears to the senses in the Eucharist. It does not *sensibly resemble* the body of Christ. But referring in the *very next sentence* to the words of Jesus Christ in the institution of the Eucharist, he says, "there is no one who does not believe them; *for* he that does not *believe it to be himself truly* (ipsum verum) falls from *grace* and *salvation.*" Why was this suppressed?

Did the Fathers believe that the body of Christ cannot be in two places at once? So says Mr. Breckinridge: but hear St. Chrysostom. "We always *offer* the same *victim,* (here is the sacrifice) not as in the old law, sometimes one and sometimes another: but here it is always the same, for which reason there is but *one sacrifice: for if the diversity of places,* in which the sacrifice is offered, multiplied the sacrifice, we should have to allow that there were *many Christs.* But there is but one Christ, who is *entire here,* and *entire there,* possessing still but one body: for which reason there is but *one sacrifice.*" (Hom. in Epist. ad Hœbr.)

This language, Rev. Sir, indicates the true belief of the real presence as it is in the church, and as it was from the beginning of Christianity. Carlostadius, however, originated a contrary doctrine, or rather opinion, and Protestants go with Carlostadius. It is the belief of a mystery; nothing greater, however, than what Protestants *who believe* the Scriptures, acknowledge respecting the presence of Christ's body on the way to Damascus, or its entrance into a *closed* apartment. The latter difficulty you have solved by an explanation which may be *original,* but it is not very ingenious. "Christ could remove out of the wall or door, space for his body to enter by, and then close it up again!!" This of course explains the mystery.

When you take offence at "Omnipotence wrapped in swaddling clothes," you forget that I quoted the expression from a *Protestant sermon!*

On the couplet of Watts,

> "This infant is the Almighty God
> Come to be *suckled and adored,*"

you make no comment. But when you come out boldly, and proclaim that to adore Jesus Christ as man, "would be gross IDOLATRY," you show the downward tendency of Protestantism. Protestants *generally,* adore Jesus Christ without distinguishing between his divine, and human nature, which are hypostatically and inseparably united in the person of Christ. Your separation of them savours strongly of *Nestorianism;* and I should not answer for your safety if you had proclaimed this "idolatry" in Geneva, during Calvin's days. All the "Old School" Protestants have acknowledged that if the body of Christ be in the Eucharist, it is to be adored in it. This is precisely the point which Beza and the first Calvinists urged against the Lutherans, who taught the real presence, and yet did not require adoration. (Beza de Cœna Dom. p. 270.) (Balæus in Exam. Recit. p. 220.) And Chemnitius, himself a Lutheran, says: "There is no one doubts but that the *body of Christ* is to be ADORED in the Supper, unless he who doubts or denies with the Sacramentarians that Christ is really present in the Supper." (Exam. Con. Trid. Sess. 31. c. v.)

Still a "new light" has beamed on Mr. Breckinridge, and he has discovered that these Protestants and all who believe with us that the body is to be adored wherever it is, no less than his divinity, "are gross idolaters." Then the Reformers were idolaters. What will the Unitarians, Rev. Sir, say to all this? Will they not begin to look upon you, as one of their own? Although I am persuaded that you are not.

You once threatened us with the testimony of the ancient Liturgies, on the subject of the Eucharist; but you have withheld them on second reflection, having been admonished, probably, by some one more correctly informed, that you were treading on dangerous ground. There is one, however, the Syrian Liturgy of the "Christians of St. Thomas," (Protestants if we may believe Mr. B.) to which you invite my attention. By this I understand you to *give up* the others, and if so, you are wise.

About the year 1500 the Portuguese having doubled the Cape of Good Hope, penetrated into India, and to their amazement these Christians of St. Thomas, were found on the coast of Malabar. This was reported in Europe, and gave rise to much speculation; but unfortunately it was made known that their faith had been corrupted by the errors of Nestorianism. They were heretics; and the Reformers, who had just separated from the faith of the church and of the world, took it into their heads that, of course, they were Protestants. La Croze, a Protestant, wrote a treatise to maintain this supposition, under the title of "History of Christianity in India." But Assemini (Biblioth. Orient. Tom. 4. c. 7. § 13.) refuted La Croze's book, and convicted him as usual in such cases, of twelve or thirteen gross misrepresentations. Their errors were condemned by the Catholic Archbishop of Goa, but the *denial of the real presence* was not among them. In their Liturgy, to which Mr. B. refers, are found the following words:

"With hearts full of respect and fear, let us all approach the MYSTERY *of the precious body and blood of our Saviour*......and now, O Lord, that thou hast called me to thy holy and pure ALTAR, to offer unto thee this living *and holy sacrifice*, make me worthy to receive this gift with purity and holiness." At the communion the Priest says, "O Lord, my God! I am not worthy, neither is it becoming that I should partake of the *body and blood of propitiation*, or even so much as *touch them*. But may thy word sanctify my soul and heal my body." In the thanksgiving after communion, he says, "strengthen my hands which are stretched out to receive the holy one......Repair by a new life, the bodies which have *just been feeding on thy living body* ......God has loaded us with blessings by his liv ing Son, who, for our salvation, descended from the highest heavens, clothed himself with our flesh, has given his own flesh, and mixed his venerable blood with our blood, a mystery of propitiation." (Renaudot's Latin translation.)

Such is the language of the Liturgy of those "Christians of St. Thomas," to whom Mr. B. has referred as holding the Protestant doctrine of mere bread and wine! The Catholic missionaries among them had nothing to correct in their belief of the real presence. And to show what kind of Protestants they were, it is sufficient to state that they believed in the remission of sins by the Priest's absolution; held three Sacraments, Baptism, Holy order, and the Eucharist; and taught that in Christ there were two persons, the divine, and human: that the divinity dwelt in Jesus, as in a temple. Are these the doctrines of Protestants? So much for those pure and unpopish Christians of St. Thomas and their LITURGY.

When you say that Christ *commanded* the cup, and that we " nullify" the Sacrament, you must have forgotten, that in my Letter, No. XXIX. I gave, besides other, and better proofs, the Protestant authority of a Presbyterian Synod in France, and an act of British Parliament, to prove the contrary. Read, I pray you, the arguments there adduced, and either answer them, or be silent. Assertions are cheap, and cost *too* little to deserve that I should repeat the same arguments and authorities, as often as you make them.

In refuting your attempt to answer the "stale questions," I shall have occasion to show how far the unsuspecting Protestant reader is liable to be led astray by your representations. 1. To the question " what is the Protestant religion," you answer as before, " it is the religion of the Reformation." This is no definition, unless we know what the religion of the Reformation is. When you enumerate, in another part of your letter, the denominations that constitute " the Protestant religion," you expose the definition. For if " Episcopalians, Lutherans, Moravians, Baptists, Methodists, Congregationalists, and Presbyterians," constitute " the religion of Christ;" then, " the religion of Christ" should be made up of *contradictions!!* Did Christ infuse *such contradictions* into his religion? To say that " it is exclusively derived from the Bible, as the only infallible rule of faith and practice," is not a definition; but an assertion, which *remains to be proved*, and the truth of *which, I utterly deny*. Every sect claims the Scripture for its notions. This you admit, and ask whether "claims are facts,"—whether " false claims destroy true ones?" I answer No, and therefore " the false claims" of the Reformation, could not destroy the *true* claims of the Catholic church. She was, and had been, from the beginning of Christianity, in possession of the Scriptures and their meaning. So that turn it as you will, every new aspect only shows more clearly that " the Protestant religion" mocks the powers of definition. What is it?

In reply to my second question, you *say* that "every society of Christians on earth from the days of the apostles to the Council of Nice, held the doctrines of the Protestant religion." Here there is something tangible, and since you appeal to the test of comparison, between Protestant and primitive doctrines, I shall try you by it.

The Ante-Nicene Fathers and *ancient liturgies* were all Protestant, you have told us. Then of course you will have no objection to correct your doctrines, if it should happen to be different from theirs. Liturgy of Jerusalem—" We *offer* thee, O Lord, *this* TREMENDOUS AND UNBLOODY SACRIFICE." " Send down thy most holy Spirit on us and on these holy gifts; that he, by his holy, kind and glorious presence, may *make this bread the holy body of Jesus Christ.*" Answer, "Amen." "And this chalice the precious blood of Jesus Christ." Answer, "Amen." Is this the doctrine of our *modern* Protestants on the sacrifice of Mass? No. They call it a "blasphemous fable."

The Liturgy of Constantinople. At the communion the deacon says, "Father, give me the holy and precious body of our God and Saviour Jesus Christ." The priest in giving it says, "I do give thee the precious, holy, and most immaculate body of the Lord God, our Saviour Jesus Christ, for the remission of sins and eternal life." The deacon then confesses his unworthiness, and concludes with these words, "O Thou! who art goodness itself, forgive all my sins, *through the* INTERCESSION *of thy unspotted and ever Virgin mother.*"

Here is the *intercession of saints* inaddition to the *sacrifice* and the *adoration*, as marked in the same page. Are these the doctrines of our *modern* Protestants?—yet Mr. B. claimed the Liturgies!! The one just quoted from, ascribed to St. Chrysostom, is used by the western GREEKS, Mingrellians and Georgians, by the Bulgarians, Russians, Muscovites, and all the Melchite Christians.

The Alexandrian and Coptic Liturgy, used by the Jacobite Copts of the east *for more than* 1200 *years*, at the oblation has :—"O Lord Jesus Christ....bless this bread and this chalice, which we have placed on the sacerdotal table: sanctify them, consecrate them, and CHANGE them in such manner, that this bread may BECOME the *holy body*, and that what is mixed in the chalice, may BECOME *thy precious blood.*" A little before the communion, the people prostrate and adore it. At the profession of faith, the priest says: " This is the most holy body, and the pure and precious blood of Jesus Christ, the Son of God. This is, in truth, the body and blood of Emmanuel our God. Amen. I believe, I believe, I believe, and I confess to the last breath of life, that this is the life-giving body of thine only begotten Son."....Is it thus that modern Protestants " *belive?*" This liturgy goes back 600 years before " 1215," and 900 before the Reformation. It is the testimony of our *adversaries*—who erred on other points and were cut off from the church.

The Liturgy of St. James (Syriac version,) "Bless us, O Lord, by this holy *oblation*, this *propitiatory sacrifice*," which we offer to God....a "blasphemous fable," says Mr. Breckinridge, which I proved by referring to the Fathers before the Council of Nice, and to " the *ancient Liturgies ! ! !*"

As for those " Christians of St. Thomas," in India, their doctrine on the Eucharist is the Catholic doctrine, as we have seen. But besides that, they venerated the crucifix, made the sign of the cross, *fasted from food on certain days*, and *abstained from meat* on others, celebrated festivals in honour of the blessed Virgin, and prayed for the dead. (Le Brun. Tom. III. Dis. xi. Art. 15.) They hold not, therefore, the doctrines of Protestantism. The learned Protestants Grotius, (votum pro pace,) and Bishop Bull, (vol. i. p. 342,) give up the Liturgies, as far as Protestantism is concerned, and the few extracts here made, show they were as correct as they were candid. Still Mr. Breckinridge asserted " that there was not one word of *truth*" in my statement touching the ancient Liturgies. If I have *proved* the contrary, the reader will appreciate the veracity and politeness of my opponent, as they deserve.

Let us now glance at the Protestant Fathers before the Council of Nice. Take for example the invocation of Saints; and let us hear Origen. " O ye *saints of heaven*, I beseech you with sorrowful sighs and tears, fall ye at the feet of the Lord of mercies for me a miserable sinner." (Origen Lament.) Would Mr. Breckinridge join in prayer with this (Protestant?) Father ?

Irenæus. " As Eve was seduced to fly from God, so was the Virgin Mary induced to obey him, that *she* might become the *advocate* of her that had fallen." (Adver. Hœres. L. V. c. 19.)

On the subject of *Tradition* and the Scriptures, let us see if they agree with the doctrine of *modern* Protestants. Hear St. Clement of Alexandria, (second century.) "They (Heretics,) make use indeed of the Scriptures; but then they use not *all* the sacred books; those they use are corrupted; or they chiefly *use ambiguous passages*. They *corrupt* those truths which agree with the inspired word, and *were delivered by the holy Apostles and teachers*, opposing the *divine tradition* by human doctrines, that *they may establish heresy*. But it is clear from what has been said, that there is *only one true church*, which is alone *ancient;* as there is but one God, and one Lord." [Strom. Lib. vii. p. 891. 896. 899. Edit.Oxon. 715.] Is it thus that Mr. Breckinridge *distinguishes heresy ?*

On penance and satisfaction, what said these Protestants of Mr. B. ?

Tertullian addressing the sinner, "Thou hast offended God, but thou canst be reconciled; thou hast a God to whom thou canst *make satisfaction*, and who desires it...Believe me the less *thou spare thyself* the more will God spare thee." St. Cyprian against those who *mitigated the austerity of penance*, "What do they intend by such interference ? unless it be that Jesus Christ is less appeased by pains and satisfactions !" (Ep. ad Com. 55.) Is this the doctrine of *modern* Protestants?

Did those ante-Nicene Fathers know any thing of "indulgences?" We are not to understand Protestant "indulgences," however, for of these they knew nothing. In the Catholic church an indulgence is " the REMISSION of canonical penance, or temporal penalty, which often remains due to sin *after* the guilt and eternal punishment have been remitted in the sacrament of penance." To prove the exercise of such remission, by indulgence, I refer you to Tertullian, (Lib. de pudicit, c. 21, 22. p. 1014) to Cyprian,(Ep. 27. p. 39. and Ep. 29. p. 41, 42.) I refer to the Council of Ancyra, in 314, (Conc. Gen. L. i. Cant. v. p. 1458.) All these were before the Council of Nice !

Did these Fathers, whom Mr. B. has converted into Protestants know any thing of Purgatory? Hear Tertullian, directing "*Oblations* for the dead on the anniversary day." (de Coron. Milit. p. 289.) Again, "Reflect," says he, to *widowers*, "for *whose souls you pray*, for whom you make *annual oblations*." (Exhort. ad Cast. c. xi. p. 942.) Is it thus that our *modern* Protestants speak of the duty of praying for the dead?

St. Cyprian. "Our predecessors prudently advised, that no brother, departing this life, should nominate any churchman his executor; and should he do so, that no *oblation should be made for him*, nor SACRIFICE offered for his repose"....(Ep. 1. p. 2.) These are some of Mr. Breckinridge's (supposed) Protestants before the Council of Nice!! These 'Protestants,' speak of '*oblations*,' then, they believed in the sacrifice of mass, which exists still in the Catholic church. They prayed for the dead: then, they believed in *purgatory*. Be assured, Sir, that the General Assembly would not extend the right hand of fellowship to those primitive witnesses of the christian faith. They were *Catholics*, and the man who says they were any thing else, only *proves*, by the assertion, that until he is better acquainted with ecclesiastical antiquity, it were wiser not to speak of them at all. This was before the Council of Nice. Tertullian calls the Pope in his days, the "*supreme* pontiff, the Bishop of Bishops." (de pudicitia cap. 1.) "Remember, he adds elsewhere, that Christ gave the keys to St. Peter, and *through him* to the church (Scorp.) St. Cyprian speaks of the Pope in his day as occupying "the chair of St. Peter in the head church, from which proceeds the unity of the Priesthood." (Ep. 55. ad Cornelium.) How, says he again, can any one imagine himself to be in the church, *if he forsake the* CHAIR OF PETER, *on which the church is founded*. (De Unit Eccl.) Now, Rev. Sir, since, as you say, all the Ante-Nicene Fathers were Protestants, it is to be hoped you will learn to speak of the See of Rome as they did. Tell your congregations with St. Cyprian, that if they forsake the "chair of Peter," they cannot belong to the true church.

Eusebius of Cæsarea, describing the funeral of Constantine, says, "the ministers of God, surrounded by the multitude of the faithful, advanced into the middle space, and with prayers performed the ceremonies of the divine worship. The blessed prince, reposing in his coffin, was extolled with many praises; when the people, in concert with the Priests, not without sighs and tears, *offered prayers to heaven for his soul;* in this manifesting the most *acceptable service* to a religious." (De vita Constant. L. iv. c. 71. p. 667.) Is it thus that our *modern* Protestants bury their dead? Do they pray to heaven for the *soul of the deceased?* St. Ephrem of Edessa, addressing his brethren on the approach of his death requests them to remember him after his departure. "Go along with me," he says, "in psalms and in your prayers; and please constantly to make *oblation* for me. When the thirtieth day shall be completed, then remember me; *for the dead are helped by the offerings of the living.*" (In Testam. T. iii. p. 294.) Do Protestants say this?

St. Cyril of Jerusalem. "Then (he is speaking of the liturgical service of the church) we pray for the holy fathers and bishops *that are dead;* and in short for all those that *are departed this life* in our communion; *believing that their souls receive very great relief, by the prayers that are offered for them,* while this HOLY and TREMENDOUS VICTIM (i. e. Christ in the Eucharist) *lies upon the* ALTAR." (Catech. Mystag. v. n. vi. vii. p. 297.) Do Protestants hold this doctrine, of prayers for the *departed*, round an *altar*, with a *victim lying on it?*

St. Ambrose (Serm. in Psal. clxviii. T. ii. p. 1073) St. Epiphanius (Hæres. T. i. p. 911.) St. Jerome (ad Jovin ii. L. i. p. 538.) In a word all the fathers testify that prayer for the dead was the practice of the Christian church, and founded on the doctrine of that middle state of *temporary* suffering and purification, which is called purgatory. St. Augustine states the doctrine as distinctly as it could be stated by the present Bishop of Rome or of Philadelphia. " Before the most severe and last judgement," says he, "some undergo *temporal punishments* in this life; some after death; and others both now and then. But *not all that* SUFFER after death, are condemned to *eternal* flames. What is not expiated in this life, to some, is remitted in the life to come, so that they may escape eternal punishment." (De Civ. Dei. L. 21. c. 13. vol. 5. p. 1432.)

St. John Chrysostom. "*It was ordained by the Apostle,* that, in celebrating the *sacred mysteries,* (viz. the sacrifice of mass) the DEAD should be remembered; for they well knew, what advantage would be thence derived to them. Will *not God be propitious,* when he looks down on the whole assembly of the people raising their hands up to him; when he beholds the venerable choir of the priests, and *the sacred* VICTIM *lying on the altar.*" (Homil 3. in Ep. ad Philip. T. xi. p. 32.) Were these Protestants? Then why do not Protestants believe as they did?

With respect to EXTREME UNCTION, St. James says: " Is any one sick among you? Let him bring in the Priests of the church, and let them pray over him, anointing him *with oil in the name of the Lord:* and the prayer of faith shall save the sick man and the Lord shall raise him up, and if he be in sins, *they shall be forgiven him.*" (v. 14, 15.) This *Scripture* has lost its meaning among Protestants. It so offended Luther that he expelled the whole Epistle from the canon of Scripture, calling it "an Epistle of Straw," and unworthy of an Apostle.

The testimonies of the Fathers *referring to the text for the proof* and practice of " Extreme Unction" are equally clear and numerous. The text itself however is so plain, that those who disbelieve or pervert its testimony, would not be convinced even if "one were to rise from the dead." The apostles were not priests, neither was it "extreme unction" they administered in the case referred to. Mark. vi. 13.

Let us now see what was their doctrine on the SUPREMACY OF THE POPE. The faith of the Catholic Church is, that Jesus Christ invested St. Peter with prerogatives of superiority above the other Apostles. To the twelve he imparted general powers, but to Peter special and personal prerogative. The language which he addressed to Peter was not addressed to the other Apostles, either collectively or individually.

The college of the Apostles were addressed by their divine Master in their *collective* capacity, but Peter, in the singular number, and in language which included none besides. For *proof* of this, see Matth. xvi. 15, 16, 17, 18, 19. Luke xxii. 31, 32. John xxi. 15, 16, 17. Did the Fathers on these passages believe as Mr. Breckinridge would persuade us they did?

But I would first ask, if Christ had not meant to impart superiority to Peter in the external administration of his spiritual kingdom, the church, why address him *singularly* above all the rest? The *general commission* given to *all* would have been sufficient.

Tertullian, Irenæus, and Origen, the best witnesses of the faith, during that period of the church, in which we have your *assertion* for believing that "all Christians were Protestants," I mean before the Council of Nice, attest the superiorty of Peter. Origen, commenting on the words "I will give to THEE the keys of the kingdom of heaven," says: "This was done before the words whatsoever ye shall bind, &c. were, in the 18th chapter, uttered. And, truly, *if the words of the Gospel be attentively considered*, we shall there find that the last words were *common* to Peter, and the others; but that he former spoken to Peter, imported *distinction* and *superiority*." (Comment in Matth. Tom. xiii. p. 613.)

I might quote innumerable other passages to show that this superiority was recognized in St. Peter and his successors in the See of Rome, from the Apostolic days until this hour, and that the denial of its existence was, as we have just seen, incompatable with the *communion of the church.* It is true, that St. Paul withstood Peter, but this proves nothing except the zeal of the one and the meekness of the other; the matter besides had no reference of faith, and did not involve any question of superiority. It is true, that St. Cyprian withstood Pope Stephen, on the subject of baptism administered by heretics; but here again the question was not about the Pope's superiority, which Cyprian distinctly recognized, since he advised this same Pope to exercise *his supreme authority* in correcting certain abuses which existed among the *Bishops in Gaul.* It is true, that in every age the Popes have received counsel, and sometimes severe reprehension from those who acknowledged their spiritual supremacy. The letters of St. Bernard to Pope Eugene, are as remarkable for their freedom and almost *severity,* as they are for the evidence that their author considered himself as addressing the vicar of Jesus Christ, and visible head of the church upon earth.

But Mr. Breckinridge says that even one of the Popes, Gregory the Great, denounced John, Patriarch of Constantinople for assuming the title of Universal Bishop. Answer. He did, because it *belonged* to the Bishop of Rome, to Gregory himself, who in the very same place claimed and exercised the rights of Universal Bishop. In that very letter he asserts that the Bishop of Constantinople is subject to the See of Rome, and adds "when Bishops commit a fault, I know not what Bishop is *not* subject to it."

What did those Fathers believe respecting *ceremonies*? Jesus

Christ used them, when he mixed clay and spittle and spread it on the eyes of the blind man. Also when he touched the ears of the deaf man with spittle. Both instances might furnish theme for Protestant ridicule, as well as any ceremonies used in the church. But let us see whether Mr. Breckinridge's "Protestants, before the Council of Nice," were *averse* to ceremonies, as their would-be descendants. Tertullian says, speaking of the Christians of the 2d century " whenever we move; when we enter and go out; in dressing and washing; at table, when we retire to rest, during conversation, *we impress on our forehead the sign of the cross.*" (De Corona Milit. c. iii. iv. p. 289.) Would it not sound odd to hear Mr. Breckinridge at the commencement of his *next sermon* saying to the people, " My Brethren, let us begin like our Protestant Fathers before the Council of Nice, by making the sign of the cross upon our foreheads, in the name of the Father, Son, and Holy Ghost." He might go on to encourage them by the following quotation from St. Augustine. " It is not without cause that *Christ would have his sign impressed on our foreheads*, as the seat of shame, that the Christian should not *blush* at indignities offered to his Master." (Enar in Ps. xxx. 7. viii. p. 73.) What would the congregation say to this specimen of Ante-Nicene Protestantism?

Here then we have the testimony of these *(supposed)* Protestants before the Council of Nice as well as after, by which it appears that they believed as Catholics on the *Eucharist, Penance, Indulgences, Purgatory, Prayers, and the Eucharistic sacrifice of Mass for the dead,* the *supremacy* of *Peter* and his *successors* in the See of Rome, *Ceremonies* even down to the *sign of the cross*, which the Pagans ridiculed in their days, as the Protestants do in ours.

All this proves that the second of my " stale questions," in which " I called upon you to say what society of Christians ever taught this pretended " religion of Christ, previous to the Reformation?" is still to be answered. You once referred to " the Waldenses and the Greek church." But I exposed the ignorance betrayed by this answer, so effectually, that you did not venture to repeat it. After some three months, you have again returned to the "stale questions," and just told us that "every society of Christians on earth, from the days of the Apostles, to the Council of Nice, held the doctrines of the Protestant Religion!!!" When you were determined to make an *assertion* so extraordinary, you should have adduced something like proof. Even " Usher's authority," would have been better than none. But in addition to the evidence just produced, let me ask did " every society of Christians on earth," pass into *Popery at the time of the Council of Nice,* and yet so effectually conceal the change, that neither themselves, nor the rest of mankind *knew any thing about it?* What ancient history mentions it? *Where did it begin? Who was its author? How did it spread?* What fine *Protestants* they must have been, to give up the pure doctrines of Calvanism, without a struggle; and become Roman Catholics, *without* being *conscious of the change!!* They must have gone to bed Protestants, and got up Papists, having forgotten that they had ever been any thing else!! But this is not all. How is it that in the days of their "pure Protestantism," they furnished such anti-protestant testimonies of their belief in *all the doctrines* on which the children of the Reformation disagree with Catholics—even to *making the sign of the cross?* an act which their would-be descendants sometimes denounce as the "mark of the beast." *The Fathers were Catholics;* believing in the doctrines, and glorying in the *Unity, Holiness, Catholicity,* and *Apostolicity* of the *Catholic* church. Their language glows with eloquence, when they pointed to these her attributes, which are exclusively *peculiar to the church of Christ.* The weapons with which *they* confounded heresy in their day, have been transmitted from century to century, in the unbroken succession of the ministry, and constantly been employed for the same purpose.

But he must be very indifferent about his reputation as an ecclesiastical scholar, who ventures to assert that the Fathers were Protestants, either "before the Council of Nice," or after. Such *bold strokes* of the pen evince too great a *disproportion* between a man's knowledge and his zeal. They may do, however, when entrusted exclusively to the partial inspection of Protestant criticism. In writing theological epistles to Presbyterian ladies, for example, you may make Latin quotations, and take an extract from a Protestant Archbishop, as in the case of Usher, to show that Catholics are idolators, *by the admissions of their own writers!* But when you condescend to invite "priests and bishops" into the field of discussion, the case is materially altered; and where you assert, for instance, that the Fathers were Protestants, you merely give your opponent an occasion to *prove* the contrary. This I have done, in the present case, to the satisfaction, I trust, of every sincere reader. So that it will be necessary to search *again* for that unheard-of society of Christians, that professed the doctrines of Protestantism, previous to the Reformation. And because no such society *ever existed*, the "stale questions" will remain *unanswered*, and unanswerable to eternity. The consequence is, that if the Religion of Christ was professed in the world before the sixteenth century, it is not, and it cannot be, that which *Protestantism in the mass,* or any sect in particular, has professed since the Reformation.

The 3d question was that in which "I called upon you to say whether Christ revealed ALL the doctrines of the Protestant Religion, beginning with Episcopalians and ending with Unitarians?"

To this Mr. B. opposes a remark of my own in which I admitted the existence of "orthodox doctrines among Protestants." But my remark was intended to show that for all the orthodox doctrines that exist among Protestants, they are indebted to the *tradition or constant teaching of the Catholic church,* and *not* to private interpretation of the Scripture; since Unitarian Protestants, on the contrary, reject some of those doctrines, contending, with arguments which Presbyterians at least, can never answer—that they are *no. contained in the sacred volume.*

This observation he converts, with much more ingenuity than in genuousness, into an admission on my part, "that there are orthodox Protestants." I never said so. I merely said that there are some orthodox "doctrines" among Protestants. Presbyterians believe in the Trinity; Unitarians, in the existence of God—both *doctrines* are orthodox. Yet both denominations are heterodox, the latter for denying the Divinity of Christ, the former for teaching that Christ did not die for all, and that God created some men under the UNAVOIDABLE NECESSITY OF *being damned.*

By transferring the word "orthodox," to Protestants, instead of "doctrines," Mr. B. attempts to shake off all those Protestant denominations which *he* condemns as heterodox, and rallies a few sects under his own perversion of my words. He goes so far as to include "Episcopalians, Lutherans, Baptists, Congregationalists, Methodists, Moravians, and Presbyterians," in "the religion of Christ," but here his charity seems to fail. Why he should exclude the Quakers, Swedenborgians, Universalists and Unitarians, I am, as no doubt they will be, utterly at a loss to conceive. Do not all *these* profess to follow the *true* doctrines of the Reformation, as well as Mr. Breckinridge? Are they not threading the labyrinth of Scripture by the same "rule of faith" as himself? Be this as it may, he has not enumerated them among the sects that compose the Protestant religion, alias the religion of Christ.

But, Rev. Sir, considering the doctrinal CONTRADICTIONS, by which even the sects you mention are divided from one another, will any reasonable man say that Christ could have revealed ALL their *doctrines?* If Baptists are right, as you admit, must not Presbyterians be *wrong?* Can the same Jesus Christ be the author of *both* doctrines? Does the same Bible teach both? Do any two of these denominations teach alike on all points? Do any two congregations hold identically the same doctrines? Does not the whole amount to this—that every Protestant believes exactly what he pleases?

When you talk of "various sects," in the Catholic church, you evidently forget that a few lines before, you had *acknowledged the contrary*, and ascribed our "uniformity" of belief to "compulsion." Now even this will not account for our uniformity in countries where compulsion cannot reach us. In England, Scotland, Ireland, and North and South America we are uniform in faith, and are increasing by conversions from Protestantism, so much so, that all the bigots of the land affect to be *frightened* at the rapid growth of popery. Do they not from the pulpit and the press endeavour to perpetuate *prejudice* and *excite hatred against Catholics and their religion?* Are we not denounced by even your Reverend self, as idolators? And still we are uniform and increasing! Is *this* by compulsion? THE UNITY OF CATHOLIC FAITH, in all ages, and throughout the world, is one of the marks of its *Divine origin.* Protestants, on the contrary, have never ceased to divide and sub-divide since their separation from the church.

They set out with the principle that Scripture is plain. Then, it would be expected that all should understand it alike. But no: Luther and Carlostadius, and Zuinglius, and Socinus, and Calvin quarrelled, on the very threshold of the Reformation, about the *meaning of Scripture.* The battle, after three hundred years, is still going on among their descendants, less fiercely indeed, because the parties are now scattered over a larger surface of ground, and of doctrine.

The Reformers felt and foresaw all this; and whilst they preached the right of *private*, they substituted public, interpretation of Scripture in the form of "Creeds and Confessions of Faith." Yesterday they set at defiance the authority of the whole Christian world, and to-day they prescribe on a piece of parchment, what their own followers are to believe! Mr. Breckinridge alludes with apparent complacency to those *Creeds* of Protestantism, and singularly enough, lays considerable emphasis on their *number*. He says they were twelve. But would not *one* be better than twelve? And why make so many?

There was, 1st. The Helvetian Confession, drawn up in Basle in 1536. *Amended* and enlarged in 1566. Then there was, 2d. The Calvinistic Confession, drawn up by Beza, and presented to Charles IX. in 1561. Then there was, 3d. The *English* Calvinistic Confession, drawn up in 1562, and published under Elizabeth, in 1571. Then, 4th. The Creed of Scotland, by Parliament, in 1568. Then, 5th. The Belgic Confession, 1561, approved in the Synod of 1579, and confirmed in that of Dort, 1619. Then, 6th. The Calvinistic Confession, in Poland, composed in the Synod of Czenger, in 1570. Then, 7th. That of the four imperial cities presented to Charles V. in 1530. In the same year was, 8th. The Augsburg Confession, drawn up by Melancthon. Then, 9th. The Saxon Confession at Wittemburg, in 1551. Then, 10th, *Another* in the sacred city, presented afterwards at the Council of Trent. Then, 11th. The Confession of Frederic, published ten years after his death, in 1577. There were several others, all published within the short period of forty years. And *all these* for what, if the Scripture was plain, and every man had a right to judge of, for himself? Now it is evident that these confessions VARIED in doctrine, one from another; otherwise, *one* would have been a *model* for the rest. All these confessions were by the *Lutherans and Calvinists alone*. But we have, since then, had the Westminster Confession, which was to have been the *last;* and the reader will recollect, that when I quoted it some time ago, Mr. Breckinridge advised me of my *mistake*, and informed me, that certain "OFFENSIVE PASSAGES," had been expunged out of it "some fifty years ago." The *present* standard of Presbyterian Orthodoxy, professes in its title page, to have been "*amended*" in the year 1821. How soon it will require to be amended again, no one can tell. But judging by the decay of *old* doctrines, and the growth of *new* ones, the period cannot be distant. It has run a long time now, nearly twelve years!

Such are the *harmony* and *unchangeableness* of Protestant doctrine! Can these cotemporaneous and consecutive *contradictions* of doctrine, constitute "the Religion of Christ" even though they had existed previous to the Reformation?

Mr. Breckinridge also tells how rapidly Protestantism, "this (supposed) religion of Christ," spread in Europe, Asia, (!!!) Africa (!!!) and America. As history has not made us acquainted with its triumphs either in *Africa* or *Asia*, we must be content to notice those which it boasts of in Europe. It is a fact, however, founded on the general authority of the Protestant Dr. Heylin's History of the Reformation, *that Protestantism was introduced into every country in Europe, either by the rebellion of the subjects, or the tyranny of the governments.* Take Heylin's History, and the map of Europe, and see whether a *single exception* can be found. Its footsteps in every direction were marked with bloodshed and desolation, when it wanted *power,* and with oppression after *power* had been obtained. But Mr. Breckinridge will say that *this* was owing to the persecution it suffered. I *deny* the assertion; but even if it were true, he should remember that " *the* Religion of Christ" waited patiently through a martyrdom of persecution for three hundred years, and never unsheathed the sword, nor raised the arm of rebellion against its *Pagan persecutors.*

Protestantism in its establishment, did not trust much to its own evidences. It did not wait to gain its ascendency over the minds of men by the influence of gentle persuasion. It owes its propagation more to the corrupt passions of men, than to any other cause. It flattered princes, and magistrates; by making them *heads,* and as your standard has it, "*nursing Fathers*" of the church. It flattered the lusts of faithless ecclesiastics, by teaching them that celibacy was contrary to the law of God. It flattered the pride of the multitude by telling them that each one of them, could understand the Scriptures *better* than *all the Fathers, Councils, and Pastors of the Catholic church.* It formed intrigues with civil power; worked by revolution and violence; rewarded its votaries with the spoils of sacrilege, torn from the *Catholic Clergy, Convents, Monasteries, and churches.* Read the Protestant Doctor Heylin, and you will see the proof of what is here stated.

Is it not then, somewhat surprising that *you* should have referred to the spread of Protestantism in Europe, as a *proof* that it is " the Religion of Christ;" whereas the very reference furnishes evidence of the contrary! Has it not been propagated by violence, and maintained by *acts of Parliament ?*

If then, as Mr. Breckinridge asserts, "*the* Religion of Christ" is composed of "Episcopalians, Lutherans, Baptists, Congregationalists, Methodists, Moravians, and Presbyterians," I ask him whether Christ revealed *all* the doctrines, on which these denominations are divided? Until he has answered this, my third " stale question" remains; and what he *has* said is only the evasion of the difficulty. As to the fourth and fifth questions about the nullity of Protestant ordination, they seem to have taken him by *surprise,* although they are as " stale" as the others. " Want of room, compels him to *delay* an answer until the next letter, in which, *Providence permitting,* he will give one at large." But is it not curious, that room should be wanting? And that after nearly three months of evasion, the answer to a preliminary question should still be crowded out for " *want of room ?*"

    Yours, &c.   JOHN HUGHES.

P. S. Translation of the eighth paragraph in which Mr. B. makes the author say that the church "was goverened by strumpets and forgotten by God."

" Who, considering these things, would not be scandalized, and think in amazement, that God had forgotten his church, which he permitted to be disgraced at the will, (or caprice) of strumpets? So indeed the holy Fathers sometimes complained, the suggestion whether God had forsaken his church, sometimes striking their minds, whilst they saw the church almost overwhelmed by towering waves from every side. For hear the great Basil thus oppressed with the sense of these evils, writing as follows to the Alexandrians: ' But this thought has come to these speculations of my mind; whether the Lord has entirely forsaken his churches, &c. whilst for example (which our own Bede also says) the church is sometimes not only afflicted but also disgraced by such oppressions from the Gentiles, that (if it were possible) her Redeemer would appear to have deserted her for a season, &c.' The lamentation of the church is the voice of the mourning dove: ' I am forsaken and alone.' *But not so*, because it is in these evils particularly that we recognise the more earnest vigilance of Divine Providence towards his church, and the closer *indwelling* of his protection, solicitude and care. For although such great evils prevailed through this whole century, and scandals multiplied, still there was no one found to seperate on this account from the church of Rome, by schism, or rise against her by heresy; but all, in every part of the world, united by the bond of faith, continued in the covenant of obedience. So that the saying of Nahum is applicable; '*why do you think* against the Lord? He will effect a consummation, a two-fold tribulation shall not arise.' For whilst the church was labouring under these evils, she was not suffered to be divided by schisms, nor torn by the deceptions of heresies, but God preserved all the faithful in obedience to her. Which certainly would not have been the case if God had not provided with supreme vigilance, for her safety and integrity; in such a manner that the farther he seemed exteriorly to have withdrawn from her, so much the more do we recognize his interior presence supporting her with his hand, lest, agitated by the shocks of wicked men, she should be overthrown. Who will deny but this is to be considered as miraculous? For, if something be thrown in the fire and is not consumed by it, we acknowledge greater power of God, than if the same thing is preserved, being remote from fire. And as St. Paul says, ' the fire shall try every man's work of what kind it is;' certainly the evidence of the fact proves it to have been the work of God, when the Roman church, to which so many firebrands were applied, could not be consumed to destruction, and reduced to nothing. The declaration and promise of Jesus Christ to the See of Peter, ' that the gates of Hell shall not prevail against it, has clearly stood, and will stand forever immoveable.' "

Is this, Rev. Sir, saying that the church " was forgotten by God?"

In the former letter, your quotation ran thus : " That Theodora, a courtezan of noble family obtained supreme controul in Rome; that she expelled the lawful Popes and put violent and nefarious men into the Papal chair, that the Pope Sergius III. committed adultery with her daughter, and their son John, the offspring of their crimes, was afterwards Pope himself; he says they were apostate Popes, not Apostolical; calls the times deplorable; and the scandal overwhelming; says the church was governed by strumpets, and forgotten by God."

This quotation, it will be remembered, you made under the *threat of exposure*, and from its unfairness the reader may infer what must be your quotations when you are under *no such advisement* of impending exposure. The reader would suppose that this quotation was taken out of one place in the original, that the context was unbroken. But no. Mr. Breckinridge made it up of scraps taken out of four different paragraphs of a folio page, divided. The first scrap is from the 5th paragraph, the 2d scrap from the 6th, the 3d scrap from the 5th again, the 4th scrap from the 4th paragraph, the 5th scrap from the 5th again, and the 6th scrap from the 7th paragraph. All these he transposes as suits his purpose; tacks them together, and produces, *without indicating a single breach of context*, the quotation, as it stands above! Has not Protestantism found in him, an *able* defender? One it may be proud of? But this is not all.

The words of the author to which he refers for the penultimate are "scrap," "meretricum arbitrio infamari," by which Baronius says, that God permitted the church " infamari," to be disgraced, "arbitrio," at the caprice "meretricum," of strumpets. But Mr. Breckinridge takes a short cut; and makes Baronius say that the Church was " *governed* by strumpets." Nor is this all yet. He makes Baronius say that the Church " was forgotten by God; whereas Baronius not only does *not* say this, but *says directly the contrary!* And Mr. Breckinridge has the blushing modesty, to refer to the first words of the 7th paragraph, and call it the "proof" (See Mr. B's. last postscript,) of an *untruth;* and which he *must have known to be an untruth*, if not when he first uttered it, at least, when he attempted the *deception of proving it;* since, with the same pen he rates Baronius as a 'Jesuit,' because he (Baronius) *goes to prove, on the contrary, that the Church was not forsaken by God!* This proves that Mr. Breckinridge must have known at the time what Baronius said: and *knowing* this, how could he have the blushing modesty, as I said before, to write the word "proof," when he himself *furnishes the evidence* that he knew the assertion to be proved, was *untrue?* Does not all this look strange? Does Protestantism require such defence? If it does, you may say of it, on reviewing the labours of your pen, what Hector said of Troy,

———————Si Pergama dextra
Defendi possent, etiam, *hac* defensa fuissent.

J. H.

To the Rev. John Hughes.

As the note from Mr. A. S. Langley, appended to the Rev. Mr. Breckinridge's last letter, is calculated to carry abroad a conviction of falsehood against me, I feel it a duty which I owe to myself to assert that the impression made upon my mind, on his declining to receive any more of the Review was, that he had been forbidden to keep it for sale. Now, if Mr. L. had allowed me the benefit of misconception of what he *did* actually say, in reference to the sale of the Review, I should have remained satisfied with the guilt of having indiscreetly mentioned the circumstance through an error of my own understanding. M. FITHIAN.

Sept. 13th, 1833.

CONTROVERSY. No. XXXIV.

IS THE PROTESTANT RELIGION THE RELIGION OF CHRIST?

Philadelphia, September 20th, 1833.

To the Rev. John Hughes,

Sir,—I consider it worth all the labour and trial to my feelings connected with this controversy, to have brought to the view of the American people the true system of the church of Rome, in her treatment of the Bible. What I peculiarly value in these disclosures is, that they have been made by her professed advocate in the progress of this discussion. First, you asserted that the Bible was not a sufficient rule of faith, though God revealed it for that very end: next, you contended that it had no fixed meaning without an *authoritative* interpretation: then you conceded that if left to itself it did not teach the doctrines of the Papacy; and finally, you almost abandon its use, and retreat to the forlorn hope of 'the Fathers.' If you had written in *Italy* or *Spain*, you might with more frankness have spoken your whole mind. You would have owned that for these and other reasons (as I have proved already) it stands at the head of 'Libros Prohibitos;' *prohibited books at Rome*. With Pighius you might have called it (see Hierarc. Lib. 3. c. 3.) 'a nose of wax which easily suffers itself to be drawn backward and forward; and moulded this way and that way, and however you like;' or with Turrian, 'a shoe that will fit any foot, a sphynx's riddle, or matter for strife;' (calceus utrique pedi aptus, sphyngis ænigma, materia litis;) or with Lessius, 'imperfect, doubtful, obscure, ambiguous, and perplexed:' or with the author, ' De Tribus veritatibus;' ' a *forest* for thieves, a *shop* of heretics;' lucus Prædonum, officina Hæreticorum. These are honest *Romans;* but such candour would not have suited the latitude of an enlightened, and Bible-reading people.

Finding that you renounced the defence of the Apocrypha, and the use of the Bible, I followed you to 'the Fathers,' 'whose unanimous consent' you declared to be in your favour, and which is made in your creed, a part of the rule of faith, 'according to which the sacred Scriptures are to be received and interpreted.' Now we Protestants reverence the *earliest* Fathers; and though we hold them to be fallible, and not unanimous, sometimes fanciful, erroneous, and pruned and corrupted by your church; yet we still find the body of their testimony *with* us, and especially on fundamental doctrines. I think after the last four letters, the community are prepared to admit these two positions: 1. That you depend far more on *the Fathers*, than on the Bible; and 2, that their '*unanimous consent*' if it has a being, is by no means in *your* favour. But whatever *you* may *assert*, presuming on the fact that very few of your readers have access to them, it will not be denied that other Roman Catholic writers are as learned and honest as yourself. Let us see what they say of some of the very Fathers whom you claim, and on the very doctrines in proof of which you quote them. Cardinal Baronius, ' who is a Catholic historian,' (Vol. I. p. 275. Sec. 213, Ann. 34.) thus writes: 'Although the most Holy Fathers, whom for their great learning, we rightly call the Doctors of the church, were indeed above others, imbued with the grace of the Holy Spirit, yet the Catholic (Roman) church does not always, in all things follow their interpretation of the Scriptures.' Bellarmine, (De Verbo Dei Lib. 3. c. x.) 'It is one thing to interpret the law as a *Doctor*, and another thing, as a Judge: for expounding as a Doctor learning is required: as a Judge, *authority*. For the opinion of the Doctor is to be followed so far as *reason* persuades; that of the Judge, from *necessity*.......Wherefore in their commentaries, Augustine and the other Fathers supply the place of teachers; but the Popes and Councils, of a *Judge* commissioned by God.' Cardinal Cajetan, [in Gen. 1.] 'We must not reject a new sense of the Holy Scriptures because it differs from the ancient Doctors; but we must search more exactly the context of Scripture; and if it agree [Si quadrat] praise God who has not *tied* the exposition of the sacred Scriptures to the sense of the ancient Doctors.' Such are the principles laid down by three of your Cardinals, *two* of whom have received your sanction. Now let us for a moment see their application. Bellarmine [De Amiss. Gra. B. 4. c. 15.] tells us, that ' the immaculate conception' of the Virgin Mary though not an article of faith, is not to be condemned; and 'that they who do it resist the decrees of Trent, and of two Popes; and are not to be considered as Catholics.' Yet your Bishop Cane says, [Theol. b. 7. c. 1.] 'All the Holy Fathers with one voice (uno ore) affirm the blessed Virgin to have been conceived in original sin.' Here they flatly contradict each other, and if Bellarmine is right, *none* of the Fathers were Roman Catholics: or if wrong, the Council of Trent *erred*. Which do you choose? Cardinal Cusanus (Exerc. lib. 6,) writes, ' certain of the ancient Fathers are found of this mind, that the *bread* in the sacrament is *not transubstantiated*, nor *changed in nature*.' Yet Mr. Hughes claims *all* the Fathers for this doctrine! Who shall be believed, the learned Cardinal, or the Priest *expectant?* Bellarmine cites Ignatius (as Mr. Hughes did) *in proof of the real presence*. (Lib. 2. c. 2. De Euch.) But when we adduce Ignatius to prove that the *cup* is to be given to all, in the sacrament, viz. on his epistle to the Philadelphians, ' one bread is broken for all; *one cup* is distributed to *all :*' Bellarmine rejects the author, saying, ' *not much faith is to be put in the Greek copies of Ignatius !*' (Euch. b. 4. c. 26.) Augustine especially is grossly trifled with in this way. He says (De Mor. Eccles. c. 36.) 'I know certain worshipers of tombs and pictures whom the church condemneth.' Bellarmine remarks on this (De Imag. c. 16.) ' Augustine wrote this book soon after his conversion to the Catholic faith !' On the famous passage against Transubstantiation cited by me from Augustine in which (see 1 Cor. x. 3. 4.) he speaks of the *manna*, and the *rock* Christ: Maldonat the Jesuit thus remarks: ' I am verily persuaded that if Augustine had been living in these days and had seen the Calvinists *so* interpret St. Paul, he would have been of another mind, especially being such an enemy to heretics.' (In John 6. n. 50.) Augustine says, (contro duos Eps. Pelag. &c.) ' The *works* which are done *without faith*, though they *seem* good, are turned into *sin*.' Maldonat says of this: ' We may not defend that opinion which the Council of Trent did of late justly condemn; although the great

Father St. Augustine seemed to be of that opinion.' (Com. in Matth vii. 18.) Here is a Roman Catholic author, of at least as good title to infallibility as Mr. Hughes, who condemns Augustine, the 'great Father,' and held him up as contradictory to, and condemned by the 'great Council' of Trent! Augustine (Deverbo Dom. serm. 13,) on the words of Christ, 'Thou art Peter, and on this rock I will build my church,' says, 'The rock was Christ.' Stapleton answers (Princip. Doc. lib. 6. 3.) 'It was a human error caused by the diversity of the Greek and Latin tongue, which either he was ignorant of, or marked not.' Bellarmine (b. 1. de Pont. c. 10.) condemns the Father, saying, 'Augustine was deceived by his ignorance only of the Hebrew tongue.' Bishop Cane (Loc. Theo. l. 7. c. 3,) owns that 'the ancient Fathers sometimes err, and against the ordinary course of nature bring forth a monster.

I could fill sheets with these exceptions to the Fathers. But it is unnecessary. Here then we clearly discover that in the judgment of a crowd of Roman Catholic authors, some of whom you have publicly approved, the Fathers *often* err; they contradict each other, they oppose the Catholic (Roman) faith, they are ignorant of the learned languages, they speak like Calvinists, they misunderstood Christ, they are fanciful, they are not to be followed, the Council of Trent condemned them, and as for their 'unanimous consent,' it is fiction which was never found; while 'the Bible is a nose of wax,' the Fathers have as many faces as Proteus, and are to be used or rejected as occasion may require, or their varying opinions permit. When we add to this, that the Fathers have been altered and many of their works *erased and Romanized*, it would seem indeed a slender and unstable foundation, to build a *religion* on; especially when their 'unanimous consent' is your rule of faith.

Never did sons treat Fathers so uncourteously as the loyal Jesuits treat the ancients, while they torture them into their service, or chastise them for their Protestant partialities. Like the ancient necromancers (Isaiah viii. 19—21,) who forsook 'the law and the testimony' of God, they roam through the 'wilderness' of the Fathers 'hungry and hard bestead and fret themselves,' while they search in vain for their *unanimous consent* in support of the Papacy. As the Scriptures fail you in the time of need, so we find the Fathers cannot help you; and the higher you rise in antiquity the more decidedly Protestant do they become, until the last traces of Romanism disappear amidst the better light of the ante-Nicene Fathers. Before I dismiss this subject it is due to myself to say, notwithstanding all your peevish charges and unworthy reflections, that I have suppressed nothing in my various extracts from the Fathers which to my knowledge, in the least degree favoured your cause, or injured mine. So far from this, ample matter of the strongest kind in my favour, has been omitted to make room for other departments of the argument. If their writings could be presented in unbroken connexion, the argument against you would appear in tenfold strength. It is you who profitably insulated sentences and figurative terms uptorn from their natural relations and true coherence. Your readers cannot forget Tertullian, and Wesley, and Luther, and Jewel, who were made by you to speak a language so foreign from their meaning by the citation of disjointed extracts. Even in your last letter, while charging me with such unfairness, you leave unnoticed all the strong passages and enlarge upon those which seem to you most easily explained, like feeble commentators who skip the hard places, and are profound and redundant on those which are easy.

II. I may here, as properly as elsewhere, allude to your last and feeble struggle for Transubstantiation. You say, 'I maintain that this very concealment of the Eucharist from Pagans, Jews, and Catechumens, is by itself a powerful proof of the Catholic doctrine.' You allude in this sentence to what has been called the secret discipline of the early church, *i. e.* the custom which originated in the second century of withholding the mysteries of Christianity from those who were not initiated. You say, 1st. 'if it were mere bread and wine, what motive could there exist to conceal it?' Answer, here you take for granted, that the *only* thing concealed was the doctrine of the Eucharist. Yet, two sentences above, Cyril, of Jerusalem, whom you cite, distinctly contradicts you; for he says, 'we declare not to the Gentiles the hidden mysteries of the Father, Son, and Holy Ghost.' Then the Trinity, the Incarnation, &c. were *among* these mysteries? I return then your question upon you, and ask what motive they had to conceal *these* mysteries? Besides there is no evidence (as Faber triumphantly shows in his answer to the Bishop of Aire,) that the doctrine of the Eucharist was among the doctrinal mysteries at all. Cyril does not even mention it in the passage just quoted. Of course your inference falls to the ground.

2. You say, 'when they were accused of murdering a child and feasting on its flesh in their assemblies,' it would have been easy and natural to refute the calumny, and say that it was merely a little bread and wine they took figuratively in memory of Christ's body and death. But this they never said; even when they were tortured, as was sometimes the case, to force them into a confession of what it was.' Here you are still more unfortunate than before. The fact is directly against Transubstantiation. During the persecution at Lyons, A. D. 177, 'the Pagans wishing to ascertain the secret ceremonial of the Christians, apprehended their slaves, and put them to the torture. Impatient of the pain, and having nothing to tell which might please their tormentors, the slaves, who had heard their masters say that the Eucharist was the body and blood of Christ, forthwith communicated this circumstance. Whereupon the tormentors, fancying that it was *literal* flesh and blood served up in the mysteries of the Christians, hastened to inform the other Pagans. These immediately apprehended the martyrs, Sanctus and Blandina, and endeavoured to extort from them a confession of the deed. But Blandina readily and boldly answered, how can those who through piety abstain even from lawful food, be capable of perpetrating the actions which you allege against them?' These are the words of Iræneus preserved by Ecumenius. Those slaves, and the Pagans whom they had informed, *mistook* the doctrine of the Eucharist as the Jews did, and you *do* now, supposing the Christians to feed on

real flesh. But these Christians denied from first to last that it was *literally flesh and blood* which was served up for them. Was not this a denial of the real presence? Could they in truth have *denied* that they did eat literal flesh if they had believed Transubstantiation? How then, this argument can help your cause I confess myself wholly at a loss to determine. 3. You add, ' They would not have celebrated the Eucharist with doors inviolably closed, for even the High Priest would not be scandalized at seeing them eat bread and drink wine, though he might if he saw them adoring the flesh of Jesus Christ.' It would have been hard indeed for them to close their doors to conceal a doctrine which they did not believe, and which until ages after was never heard of! They closed their doors because they were persecuted, as well as because of their mysteries; and they were persecuted, and they worshipped with closed doors long *before* they were charged with eating human flesh. As to the Jews and High Priest, it was *worshipping* Christ as God which scandalized the Jews before the Eucharist was instituted; and you have sense enough to know, that the early Christians might worship Christ as we do now, without worshipping the bread. The Jews would have been scandalized by the Protestant doctrine as much as the Papal, excluding however the dreadful absurdity and idolatry of Transubstantiation.

You must have been nodding over your midnight lamp, when you make me to say, that ' Christ could remove out of the wall or door, space for his body to enter by, and then close it up again.' My words were, ' do you forget that Christ had power miraculously to open a passage for his body through the door or wall and close it again?' Besides this perversion you entirely omit the preceding and the succeeding illustrations drawn from the miraculous opening of the prison doors for the Apostles; and from the transmission of light through a pane of glass. But it is plain that you write for those who from prohibitions and the fear of light read your letters alone, and see my arguments as they are reflected in distorted forms from your pages only. The couplet from Watts, to which you refer, needed no comment. In expression it is most unhappy; yet as conveying the doctrine that He who was born of a woman was also God, I fully subscribe to it; and we are willing to bear all the censures to which you subject us for refusing to worship the *body* of Christ, if separated from his *divinity*. It is his divinity which we adore; and believing his divinity and humanity inseparably blended in the person of Jesus Christ, we worship him. But the doctrine of Transubstantiation is idolatrous because it worships his *body* alone; and as I proved in my last letter, you are guilty of idolatry whether the doctrine be true or false. But why are you silent on the argument brought against you from Hume? Why do you not defend your doctrine from the proof of leading to infidelity, or else give it up? And where is the expected answer to my seven separate exposures of the sacrifice of the mass? Can you not meet them? And yet own that it is your *chief* business to offer this sacrifice? Will you leave your *chief* business and your chief *gain* thus unsheltered in the field of argument? And where is now your communion in one kind? Have you nothing to say for this daring act? Must not our readers see that it is no answer to all I have said on this subject to remind me that a Protestant Synod in France once said half-communion was right? Neither you nor I hold to the infallibility of a Protestant Synod. You leave us then to sing the mournful coronah of these departed doctrines; while you take up the lamentation of the poet,

"Come then expressive silence, muse their praise."

How you will next look your friends in the face during the sacrifice of Mass, or withhold from them again the cup in the Eucharist, it must be for conscience and pained memory to answer. You have at least this consolation uttered once by way of *comfort*, 'You could do no more; for you have done all you could.'

As to the ancient Liturgies, every scholar knows that they are replete with forgeries of the church of Rome. The Liturgy attributed to St. Peter, mentions St. Cyprian, who died some two hundred years after Peter! Cardinal Bona owns it to have been spurious. The Ethiopic Liturgy, attributed to St. Matthew, speaks of the Synods of Nice, Constantinople, and Ephesus, which were held centuries after Matthew's death. St. James's Liturgy speaks of *Monasteries*, which every one knows originated ages after his day; and it quotes from Paul's Epistles, most of which were written after James's death. The ceremonies mentioned in these Liturgies were also wholly unknown in the Apostles' days. If you say these things were *added* to them in after ages; then why not those too on Transubstantiation? They did not exist at that day; but allow they did; then, as they have been *corrupted*, what proof do they afford you? As to the Liturgy of the Jacobites which you adduce, it is strange that their book of Homilies and Breviary, should contradict their Liturgy; and still more strange that the Roman Catholic Inquisition at Goa, should condemn these books for rejecting '*Transubstantiation*;' and yet that their Liturgy should contain this doctrine. As to your own, you do not deny that it has been altered to suit your doctrine; for whereas the ancient form ran thus, 'make this oblation to us allowable, rational, and acceptable, which is *the figure of the body and blood of our Lord*,' it is now changed to read thus, 'that the oblation *may be made to us the body and blood of our Lord*;' dropping 'FIGURE' from the ancient form which was plain Protestant doctrine. Who then can trust to your testimonies?

III. As the matter of the present letter is necessarily multifarious, we may as properly here as any where, canvass your answers to my several questions.

1st Question. 'Did Pope Liberius subscribe the Arian creed?' Mr. Hughes' answer. 'I say that Pope Liberius did not sign the Arian Creed in *the Arian sense or meaning*.' It is obvious that this answer is a most disingenuous evasion; I therefore repeated the question in my last letter, wishing to know in *what sense* Liberius *did* sign it. But the oracle is dumb; it gives no response to this question. I have already proved (in Letter No. 28,) that this Pope did adopt the Arian Creed. It may be proper, however, here to add, that Dupin with his usual candour, says, (page 62, vol. 2.) 'Liberius did not only subscribe the condemnation of St. Athanasius, but he also consented to an Heretical Confession of Faith.' The sainted Hilary (In Fragm :) says of the Confession of Faith signed by Liberius; ' this is the Arian perfidity. I anathematize thee and thy companions, O Liberius, and again, and a third time I anathematize thee.' Athanasius confirms the relation of Hilary, and denounces the apostacy of Liberius, ' who through fear of death, subscribed.' Jerome, in his Catalogue and Chronicon, states the same fact; so also Fortunatian, Philostorgius, Damasus, and Sozomen; and in more modern times Platina, Eusebius, Mezeray, Bruys, Petavius, &c. &c. all testify to the same fact. From these statements there result two conclusions. 1. The head of the infallible church from whom, according to Mr. Hughes, all right to preach the Gospel and administer its sacraments proceed, and to whom ' every creature must be subject in order to be saved,' apostatized into damnable heresy. 2. It appears, I regret to say, how little faith is to be put in the statements of my Rev. opponent, who flatly contradicts the testimony of antiquity on this subject.

2d Question. ' Did the Councils of Sirmium and Ariminum adopt Arian Creeds ?' Mr. Hughes's answer. ' No council recognized by the Catholic church, ever adopted the Arian Creed. For the errors of other councils or general assemblies, the church is not accountable.' This reply is curious enough. It involves, however, the admission that the said Councils did adopt the Arian heresy. This I have already proved (see Letter No. 28,) and as *one* of them was certainly approved by the Pope, so on your own definition it was an infallible council ; and therefore it is an article of faith in the Roman church, binding on all her members at this day, that Jesus Christ was *not* God, that his divinity is a *figment*, and *Unitarians* are *right*. It is a striking fact, which I hope to have the opportunity soon of publicly proving, that it is not agreed in the church of Rome which *are* infallible councils ; and there is just as much evidence that the Pope and council who adopted the Arian Creed were infallible, as that the Council of Trent was.

3. ' Does the validity of ordinations, administrations of the sacraments, &c., depend on the *intention* of Popes, Bishops, and Priests ?' Mr. Hughes's answer. ' In heaven or on earth, in time or in eternity there is no *motive* for him (the Priest) to withhold his intention ; and deliberate wicked actions *without any motive or inducement*, are not to be presumed.' This is strange logic indeed! The Council of Trent must have thought very differently when they enacted as follows : (6th Chap. 11th Canon.) ' Whosoever shall affirm that when ministers perform and confer a Sacrament, it is not necessary that they should at least have the *intention* to do what the church does, let him be accursed.' Bellarmine must have thought differently, for he says, (Lib. 3. c. 8. Justif:) ' no man can be certain with the certainty of faith that he receives a true Sacrament; because it depends on the minister's *intention* to consecrate it; and none can see another's intention.' Now if all Popes and Priests be not perfect and infallible they *may* lack this intention. Your answer concedes, impliedly, that if they *should* lack it, evils must result. The

fact is, we have divers examples of sacrilegious Priests and concealed Jews, who have owned at their death that during their whole Priesthood in the Roman church, they *never* had, in any of their consecrating acts *that intention* which the church of Rome prescribes. Then in such cases these men having many thousand souls under their care must, on your own doctrine, have ruined them all. The infants they appeared to baptize, were not baptized, therefore by your creed they are lost; when they *appeared* to consecrate the bread in the Eucharist, they did not, and therefore the thousands to whom they administered it were guilty of idolatry; no marriage ceremony performed by them was valid, therefore all who were thus united by them lived in adultery, and their children were illegitimate; all their uses of Extreme Unction were fraudulent, therefore all who died under their hands are lost forever; the innumerable souls in Purgatory for whom they offered up the sacrifice of the Mass are still held there, because, from lack of intention, it was no real sacrifice. The same remarks may be extended to every Bishop and every Pope. A Pope, centuries ago, may have lacked intention in conferring orders, and all the Bishops, and all the Priests who derived orders from him, remained *laymen* for life, because he lacked intention; and all their acts were invalid: the sacraments they administered were null and void, so were their ordinations; and the innumerable millions of souls to whom they and their successors administered from age to age were lost, and the ten thousand Priests and Bishops who got their ordination from this poisoned source, acted without authority, and the Rev. Mr. Hughes may be one of them. Who can tell? Surely Pope Sergius III; Pope John XI; Pope Alexander VI; (whom Baronius owns a true Pope) could not have had *intention* to do their duty in any of these acts; and yet from these filthy fountains the stream of ordination has flowed in successive centuries through all the Roman church, and down from generation to generation of the Priesthood unto the Rev. Mr. Hughes himself! Catharin, Bishop of Minori, stated this evil with appalling force before the Council of Trent. 'Behold (says he) here, how by the wickedness of a minister, we find in one sole act a million of nullities in Sacraments.....If it should *happen* that a Priest who hath charge of four or five thousand souls, should be an unbeliever, but withal a great hypocrite, and that in the absolution of penitents, and the baptism of little children, and the consecration of the Eucharist, he should have a *secret intention not to do* what the church doth, we must conclude the little children damned, the penitents unabsolved, and all deprived of the fruits of the holy communion.' Father Paul, the Roman Catholic historian of the Council of Trent, says, (B. 2. p. 226.) ' the divines (of the Council) did not approve this doctrine, yet were troubled and knew not how to resolve the reason; but they still defended that the true intention of the minister was necessary, either actual or virtual.' If then, there is the least *certainty* in any sacrament or ordination of the church of Rome, or if there is the least satisfactory proof that the living Pope, Cardinals, Archbishops, Bishops, Priests, and Deacons of the church of Rome embrace one single ordained man, who has 'any divine right to exercise the

Christian ministry more than other educated laymen;' (See Mr Hughes' 5th Question,) then I will own that it is possible to prove, and right to believe an impossibility.

The 4th question, on the subject of schisms in the Popedom, plurality of Popes, &c. Mr. Hughes has also evaded; but my previous letters have so fully laid this subject bare, that I need not dwell on it here.

My 5th question, touching the liberty of the press, and the 'prohibiting committee' at Rome, Mr. Hughes thus obliquely touches. " About the freedom of the press at Rome, and the 'Prohibiting Committee' which you are pleased to *imagine* for the benefit of 'all the church,' I answer, that the latter does not exist, and the former is a question on which every man may abound in his own sense." Here, then, you again deny an historical fact. The Council of Trent, in its 25th session, enacted that a Committee which that body had appointed, acting for the council and under the Pope, should draw up and publish an Index of books which were to be prohibited to the whole church. This committee did accordingly draw up such an Index, and published it, accompanied by ten most tyrannical rules sanctioned by the Pope, and binding on *all* the church. This Committee is permanent, and from year to year has added to their work, until now the Index which is only a catalogue of prohibited books, makes a large volume. I have a copy of this book now in my possession, printed at Rome A. D. 1787, by order of the Pope. In the title page it is written, ' In this edition are inserted in their proper places, the books recently prohibited, even to the year 1787.' The Brief of the Pope, of the same date, and the ten rules of the standing Committee, are prefixed to the work, as also Decrees concerning prohibited books, Instructions, Constitutions, &c. for regulating the press. The Pope tells us in his Brief, that the said Index is binding on all persons, every where, under pain of such punishment as is therein and elsewhere denounced. In this base book we find such works as Locke's, Milton's, Galileo's, &c. &c., and in fact all writings containing any thing contra-religionem Catholicam, 'against the Catholic Religion.' Thus is a war of extermination waged by the authority of the church against letters, liberty, and conscience; and thus does the church of Rome shrink in conscious error and by wicked means from free inquiry; and thus is Mr. Hughes exposed when he denies that such a Committee exists. This book is open for inspection at the Education Rooms, No. 29 Sansom street, where gentlemen may call and see for themselves. The 4th rule which we have often quoted, prohibits the having, or reading, or selling of *God's holy word* in any living language, except by a written permission from the Inquisitor, or Bishop, with the advice of a priest or confessor. In Letter No. 26, I presented at large a decree of the great Lateran Council against the freedom of printing, which you have never noticed. The first rule of the standing committee at Rome, condemns all books which had been condemned by the Popes or general Councils, *before* A. D. 1515; the creed of Pius IV. confirms all previous canons and decrees of General Councils, and of course this decree against the freedom of the press; and the reigning Pope de nounces the liberty of the press as 'that fatal license of which we cannot entertain sufficient horror.' From these facts it appears that the liberty of the press is proscribed by the decrees of Councils and acts of Popes, which are binding upon every Roman Catholic on earth; and that a standing committee exists at Rome, (of which Mr. Hughes is ashamed, and which he has the hardihood to deny) to enforce these decrees against personal and civil liberty. In your answer you utter this extraordinary sentence: 'About the freedom of the press, at Rome, every man may abound in his own sense.' Then it seems you are afraid to condemn these decrees, lest haply you be found fighting against Rome; and you are afraid to defend them before the American people, who justly consider the freedom of the press the palladium of their civil and religious rights. Will not such evasions convince a free people that your system is at enmity with the freedom of the press? Are not such unmanly subterfuges anti-American as well as anti-Christian? What! an American citizen decline approving the liberty of the press? Is it not apparent that you are afraid of the subject, and that the Papacy and the republic cannot flourish together?

In answer to the seventh question, you say, 'I answer, that *in my opinion*, religion and science suffered by the suppression of the Jesuits, and that both are gainers by their restoration. This opinion is founded on the fact that they are hated for their zeal, and admired for their learning by all the *infidels* in Europe. As to the Inquisition, it may have been a good thing *abused*.' This is an ominous avowal! I have before me the Bull or Brief of Clement the 14th, dated A. D. 1773, for the suppression of the order of the Jesuits. In the course of this Bull the Pope tells us that notwithstanding his own, and his predecessors efforts, the most violent contentions pervaded nearly the whole world concerning both the doctrines and morals of the Jesuits, and that these dissensions especially from without, were created by accusations against the society for amassing wealth; that to his great grief, all the remedies applied by him to restore the peace of the church had failed, so that these clamours against them daily increasing, at length seditions, tumults and scandals occurred, which weakened and dissolved the bonds of Christian love, and violently inflamed the minds of the faithful with party animosities and rancour; that at length the king of France, the king of Spain, the king of Portugal, and the king of the two Sicilies, who had once been famous for their great liberality to the Jesuits, expelled them from their kingdoms, finding that to be the only way to heal the divisions by which their Christian people were torn even in the bosom of the Holy Mother Church. He proceeds to say, that lasting peace could not be restored to the church while the society existed; that it had ceased to do the good for which it was established, and that the laws of prudence, and the best government of the universal church, required him to extinguish and suppress the order of the Jesuits; which he accordingly did. This, you will mark, was only *sixty* years ago; and it was done for the above reasons, not by 'infidels,' but by the *head of the Universal Church*, and became a law binding on the conscience of all the faithful. How Mr. Hughes will settle this question with the Pope, it is not for me to say. These Jesuits have in succession been expelled from almost every kingdom upon earth. Bishop Taylor, in his Dissuasive from Popery, has proved, with masterly skill, that their principles and practices are incompatible with the safety of governments, destructive of Christian morals, and even of Christian society, where they prevail. Pascal, who was himself a Roman Catholic, has written his Provincial Letters for the purpose of exposing the detestable principles and infamous morals of the order of the Jesuits. The Jesuit's Catechism is another work, which in a large volume exposes their enormities, intrigues, assassinations, dissolute principles, and dangerous influence in the church and state. Their own Secreta Monita, ' secret instructions,' now published in this country, in a separate volume, having been providentially brought to light, expose their true character upon their own showing. This Society has recently been *revived* by the Pope, as a fit instrument to aid the Papacy in its expiring struggle. The successive revolutions of Europe have shaken the Papacy to its centre; the advancing light of the age, the increasing love of liberty among the people, and the repeated conquests which they have made of their dearest rights, both civil and religious, from *priest*-craft and *king*-craft in the old world, have lessened beyond measure the power of the Papacy, and left crowds of off-cast Priests and Jesuits without employment. These men, in augmenting numbers, are seeking our shores. The fall of the Papacy in Europe thus gives it a temporary impulse in our beloved country. These are the accessions of which you boast: not proselytes from Protestants, as you would have us think, but the dregs of Jesuitism cast from Europe upon our country. Once, guileless Protestants confided their children to the training of these men. But it is becoming apparent that they will do so no more. Let them work their machinations; but Protestant parents have learned, at length, not to trust a Jesuit with the formation of their children's minds and hearts. I speak of the *Priesthood* and not of the people of your church. The people are the most enlightened Roman Catholics on earth. We have much to hope from the influence of liberty and Gospel light upon them: and even now you retain their allegiance by hiding from their view the real deformities of the Papacy; and by repressing, without ceasing, that aspiration after religious liberty which has begun to glow in the breasts of all men.

Your apology for the Inquisition shall stand as its own exppressive comment. ' May have been a good institution !' And can you say this in the face of your country? Have you read its history? Have you counted its racks? Have you heard the groans of its innumerable victims? Have you examined its filthy seraglios? Paul the IV. called it the ' battering-ram of heresy ;' and the Rev. Mr. Hughes, in a late letter, talked of the Roman church as having ' *branded*' every heresy. I wish that my limits allowed me to give the history of the institution, that I might tell my country of its crusades, its inquisitors, and its victims, (who are only considered *innocent* when, by mistake, a Papist is arrested for a Protestant;) of its warfare against the press, the Bible, the morality of the Gospel and the rights of man. Let my readers consult Baker, or Limborh, or Geddes, or Lavalle, or the Key to Popery. or *any* history of those countries in which it has been established, if they would learn *how* (as Bellarmine says) *the church destroys Heretics, and how useful the Inquisition is.* In the mean time, let it not be forgotten that the Rev. Mr. Hughes says, ' it may have been a good thing abused.' Perhaps the next most dreadful engine of tyrannic power beside the Inquisition and the crusade, is the Papal Interdict. This is no less than stopping the connexion between Heaven and a whole state or nation that has offended the Pope. This tremendous censure has been executed in France, Italy, and Germany, not to mention the famous effort of the Pope to crush the Republic of Venice, for daring to interfere with the property of Ecclesiastics within that state. Hume, who surely was not a friend to Protestants, (See Hist. of England, Chap. XI. reign of John,) gives us the following fearful account of the Pope's Interdict on that realm : " The sentence of interdict was at that time the great instrument of vengeance and policy employed by the court of Rome; was denounced against sovereigns for the lightest offences ; and made the guilt of one person involve the ruin of millions, even in their spiritual and eternal welfare. The execution of it was calculated to strike the senses in the highest degree, and operate with irresistible force on the superstitious minds of the people. The nation was of a sudden deprived of all exterior exercise of its religion : the altars were despoiled of their ornaments; the crosses, the relics, the images, the statues of the Saints were laid on the ground ; and, as if the air itself were profaned, and might pollute them by its contact, the Priests carefully covered them up, even from their own approach and veneration. The use of bells entirely ceased in all the churches ; the bells themselves were removed from the steeples, and laid on the ground with other sacred utensils. Mass was celebrated with shut doors, and none but the Priests were admitted to that holy institution. The laity partook of no religious rite, except baptism to new-born infants, and the communion to the dying; the dead were not interred in consecrated ground ; they were thrown into ditches, or buried in common fields ; and their obsequies were not attended with prayers or any hallowed ceremony. Marriage was celebrated in the church yards ; and that every action in life might bear the marks of this dreadful situation, the people were prohibited the use of meat, as in Lent, or times of the highest penance ; were debarred from all pleasures and entertainments, and even to salute each other, or so much as to shave their beards, and give any decent attention to their person and apparel. Every circumstance carried symptoms of the deepest distress, and of the most immediate apprehension of divine vengeance and indignation." The Pope afterwards proceeded to excommunicate the King ; next, to absolve his subjects from the oath of allegiance, and to declare every one excommunicated, who had any intercourse with him ; he promised John's throne to the King of France, who raised an army to secure it ; and it was not until John had resigned England and Ireland to the Pope, and agreed to pay the annual tax of one thousand marks, as feudatory to the Pope, that he was permitted again to wear

3 K

his crown. Here is the blessedness of Papal domination; 'A GOOD INSTITUTION ABUSED!'

A word upon your answer to the 8th question, in which you say, 'so far from this (that is, the Jewish traditions) regarded the proof of Jewish *faith*, before the coming of Christ, I do not reject them.' You owned in a previous letter that the Jewish church was infallible, until superseded by Christ; of course all their traditions to that time were infallible. And now, from the above answer it follows, that the Jewish tradition of the canon was true; for this regarded their *faith* at the very foundation. But they rejected the Apocryphal Books. Hence, your church errs in holding them. Again, it was a Jewish *tradition* touching *faith* that the Messiah was to be a temporal Prince; even Christ's Apostles, when first called, held this *article* of faith. Hence, on your admission, this doctrine, though so absurd and false, must be true. I need not multiply points; but it is a fact, that the Jewish traditions were better supported than those of your church; and yours and theirs must stand or fall together. As Jesus said of theirs, so it is true of yours, that you 'make the word of God of none effect by your Traditions, teaching for doctrines the commandments of men.' (See Mark, 7th chap.) The character of *these* questions induced you, I suppose, to pass in silence those which remain. They are certainly *unanswerable* on your principles. Let me simply repeat them here almost without comment as *unanswered* by you.

Is there any evidence of the Pope's supremacy before the Council of Nice? I answer, no. The 6th canon of the Council of Nice, passed A. D. 325, puts the Bishop of Alexandria, the Bishop of Antioch and of Rome, on the same footing. Has the Pope a right to put a kingdom under interdict, or to depose a monarch or chief magistrate? No: and yet the Pope claims it; Popish writers defend it; Popes have often done it; and Mr. Hughes is afraid of the question.

Did the second Council of Pisa decree a Reformation in *faith* or not? It did. Did the Council of Lateran, in 1215, pass an anathema against those rulers who should *tax ecclesiastics?* It did: there is a decree on that subject. Is not the second commandment dropped from the catechisms which are in *common* use in your church in Europe and America? I have proved that it is. Have not 'the Fathers' been altered and pruned by authority in your church? Yes· there is ample evidence of the fact. Are the Missal and the Breviary authorized and standard works? They are; but Mr. Hughes seems ashamed of the latter.

To the only remaining question, viz: 'Were the Apostles priests when they administered Extreme Unction, Mark vi. 13?' You answer: 'The Apostles were *not* Priests; neither was it Extreme Unction they administered in the case referred to, Mark vi. 13.' The Council of Trent (Sess 14. Can. 1.) expressly says, 'that Extreme Unction was instituted by our Lord Jesus Christ;' and you allow that none but Jesus Christ *could* institute a sacrament; yet you say 'It was not Extreme Unction they administered,' Mark vi. 13. Pray then when was it instituted? If not then, Christ never did it; for this is the only mention of it in all the Gospels; and James did not and could not institute it in his epistle; for it was not competent to an Apostle to do such a thing. So it appears that there is, on your interpretation, no such sacrament. Again; the Council of Trent says, (Sess. 16, chap. 1.) 'this sacred unction was first intimated by Mark vi. 13,' but you say this was *not* extreme unction; wherefore you contradict the Council of Trent. Finally there is a dilemma here from which it is impossible to escape; for if this sacrament was instituted Mark vi. 13. (as it was, if ever) then the Apostles administered a sacrament not being Priests; but the Council of Trent says, (Sess. 14. chap. 3.) 'Bishops, or Priests properly ordained by them, are the proper ministers of the sacrament of extreme unction;' and yet they say (Sess. 22. chap. 3.) 'that the Apostles were *first* made Priests at the last supper.' Here then, while you contradict the council on one point, it contradicts itself on another; and which ever way you take it, the council has erred.

IV. Having now seen how you answer *some* of my questions, and wholly pass by others, I proceed to reply to the fourth and fifth in your series; they are in substance this: Did the Reformers receive any new ministerial authority after the withdrawal of that which they had received from the church; and if not, had they any divine right to exercise the Christian ministry? The proper answer to these questions turns on the settlement of a previous question, viz: 'had the church of Rome the right or power in this case to withdraw their ministerial authority?' When Athanasius was deposed, 'unfrocked,' as you say, by the Arian bishops, had he a right to preach or not? If he had not, then the Arian majority in the church did right in deposing him for holding the divinity of Jesus Christ. But you will hardly defend them. It was an unlawful stretch of power, and he was not actually deposed, nor his ministerial power really recalled. Then the principle is plain, that *when a church deposes ministers of Christ for refusing to preach ruinous errors, and refusing to submit to oppressive usurpations, the deposing act is null and void.*

If a minister of Christ be deposed for refusing to sin, the deposition is null and void. If this be not true, then you hold that a man *must* sin, knowing it to be sin; and that Christ has given the church the right and power to *make* a man sin, or to depose him if he will not. It is therefore strictly a question of fact. If the Reformers *protested* without *cause*, it was *heresy;* and if they left the church without cause, it was *schism:* if they *had* cause, then the *church of Rome* was guilty both of heresy and schism. Now, I have, in a long series of almost unnoticed expositions, proved that there *was* cause to *protest*, and necessity to *separate:* I showed that a Reformation had been for a long time needed deplorably in faith and morals: the latter was acknowledged by all: the Council of Pisa declared the former; and the necessity of Reformation became an *article of faith:* that a false canon of truth, and a false rule of faith and practice were forced upon our fathers: that the Pope was a spiritual tyrant and usurper of Jesus Christ's place and authority: that the doctrines of grace were universally corrupted, and that all the members of the church were required to believe these errors, and her ministers to preach them; that they were required to practice gross idolatry in the worship of saints, images, relics, and even *bread*, or be *cut off* from the church; that force was applied by the inquisition, by crusades, by censors of the press to compel uniformity, implicit faith, and unqualified submission; that all who disbelieved were in danger of the confiscation of their goods, excommunication, interdicts, and the stake; that there was no liberty of conscience; that even the word of God was torn from the people by *law;* and that all the errors which I have exposed in these letters, were forced upon the people and the preachers. Now, if these things were so, it was their right, their duty to *protest;* and when *forced* on them, to *separate.* Indeed, they had no choice; the church of Rome would not let them stay in her communion. Look at John Huss, Jerome of Prague, Luther, &c. &c. She burnt the two former; she sought to burn Luther, and failing to do that, excommunicated him; that is, *forced* him from her. Then I say, it was the *right*, the *duty*, the *necessity* of the case to go out of her. But if this be once admitted (and I have fully proved it) then they carried their ministerial authority with them; and you might as well say that the Apostles had no right to preach after the Sanhedrim *silenced* them, nor Athanasius after the Arian majority of the council *deposed* him, as to say that the church of Rome, under such circumstances, could recal the ministerial authority of the Reformers. But still farther; by her errors, and tyranny, and vile immoralities, the church of Rome herself became *heretical*, and was guilty of *schism;* she it was who divided Christ's body, and *left* the true church, as the Arians did in the days of Athanasius. The true church depend not on numbers (once it was all assembled in an upper chamber in Jerusalem,) but on the holding and preaching of God's truth, and administering Christ's sacraments as he commanded. Besides, millions of God's people, and hundreds of his ministers united with the Reformers, and left the corrupt church of Rome. If these things be so, and I have proved them, then the deposing of the Reformers was an *empty* and a *wicked act;* and therefore they claimed, as they needed no *new* authority; *they had all they required or ever had.* 2. On your own principles, the act of ordination leaves '*an indelible character.*' The Council of Trent, session 23, canon 4. decreed 'that a character is impressed (by ordination) and that he who was once a priest can never become a layman again.' Hence, you hold that the acts of a person ordained, though a heretic, are valid; though cut off, deposed, and even an atheist, he is still *indelibly* a minister of Jesus, and his acts are still valid, and he begets a like character to his own or the ordained persons, and though both parties sin in the act, yet the act is valid. If so, the Reformers did not lose their indelible character, and they had power to *communicate* the same to others. Therefore, what you gave them you *could* not take away, on your own principles.

3. There is not a church on the globe in which the ordination of ministers is so *defective* as the church of Rome. 1. You call orders a '*sacrament.*' But there is nothing in its nature like a sacrament; not one word in all the New Testament to rest it on. I defy you

to bring *one text*, or *one fact* to prove it. 2. Priests in your church are ordained to offer up Jesus Christ in the mass, and you say, 'it is the *chief business of a Priest to offer sacrifice*.' Yet I have proved in my last letter, and you have not disputed one of the points, that this sacrifice is blasphemous, anti-christian, and unfounded. Your *chief business*, therefore, for which you are ordained, does not exist. You might just as well, for all the ends of ordination, ordain a man to search for the philosopher's stone, or to find out *perpetual motion*. The business of Aaron's priesthood was to offer up sacrifices, but of *Christ's* ministers to 'preach the word,' to publish salvation, to administer his true sacraments; to serve (not lord it over) but serve the church, and seek to save the world. 3. The manner of ordination in your church is grossly heathenish, and wholly unlike the simple 'laying on of the hands of the Presbytery,' (1 Tim. iv. 14.) practised in primitive days. A more unmeaning mummery can hardly be invented or conceived.

4. And then you have *seven* orders of ministers. Now there is not one word for *all* these in the Bible; and you know it full well.

5. The ordination of your church is wrapped in utter uncertainty. I refer, in proof of this, to my discussion in this Letter on 'intention.' I refer again to my Letter, No. XXVIII. where it is shown that the Papal succession cannot be made out; that is, never existed: and that you *do* not, to this day, know, nor can you know, a *false* from a *true* Pope. Yet your ordination hangs on his button, and distils through his polluted hands.

Your only reply to this was—that try in vain to break the golden chain which connects the chair of St. Peter with the present Pope! Finally, see what your *own* Baronius (on the *famous* page 766 of 10th vol.) makes Segebert say from Auxilius. 'Auxilius writes a dialogue under the persons of Infensor and Defensor, confirmed by divine and canonical examples, against the intestine discord of the church of Rome, forsooth concerning the ordinations, and ex-ordinations, and super-ordination, of the Popes; and of the ex-and super-ordination of those ordained by them.' In such giving, recalling, and confounding ordinations by false Popes and true, who could be certain of his scrip or staff? Who could tell whether the Pope who authorized his ordination, or the Pope who recalled it, was the true Pope? Yet in divers cases after one Pope was deposed, or died, his ghostly successor nullified *all* his acts of ordinations; and, in return, on his removal, his acts of ordination were thus treated. And for *fifty years* there *were two* reigning Popes, one at Avignon and one at Rome, who excommunicated and anathematized, and deposed each other, and all their respective followers; and of whom we can say this good thing at least, that *they always spake truth when they denounced each other.* But under such circumstances, who can unravel the riddle of this mangled subject; or trace his ordination with any certainty through this Cretan labyrinth?

Before, therefore, you question our authority to preach, look better to your own; and let your holy lives, your faithful preaching, your success in saving souls, be added as the living seals to your ministerial authority. If you *can* make your own out, we have all that *you* ever had. But since the Reformation, it is a grave, and to say the least, a debateable question, whether yours is a church of God *at all.* God said to his people at that day, ' *come out of her ;*' and they came. Jerusalem had her Pella; the church of Rome, had the Reformation. Let God's people come out of her. He who returns to her ' loves darkness rather than light.'

V. Your exceptions to my twofold answers to your first, second, and third questions, need scarcely any additional notice. The inquiry, as to the existence of Protestantism *before* Luther, and *where,* and *when,* (besides my previous replies) may thus be finally settled. You admit that the doctrines taught by the Apostles, and recorded in the Bible, are true Christianity—so do I. We both also allow that these doctrines have been, according to Christ's promise to his church, held and taught by the true church ever since. Then if *your* present doctrines contradict the Bible, at every step, and if *ours harmonize* with it, it follows, that we are the true church, and that our doctrines have been taught and held in every age. But I have proved this at large, as to both faith, and morals, and worship; I have showed the Pope to be a usurper; that ' indulgences were a bundle of licenses to commit sin,' and that heaven is set up for sale by them; I have exposed the anti-christian and idolatrous character of Transubstantiation, the sacrifice of the Mass, and adoration of the Host;—I have disproved purgatory, extreme unction, your false doctrine of human merits, and priestly absolution: I have proved that sheer idolatry, immoralities the most gross, persecution, the destruction of personal, religious, and civil liberty, crusades, inquisitions, &c. involving the murder of some 50,000,000 of men, women and children, were not only tolerated, but made lawful and necessary in your church; in a word, I have showed, that your church has corrupted the very Bible itself, by spurious books, false interpretations, and unfounded traditions, and even dared to say that God's *word* would, and did *injure* his creatures, and prohibited it to the people. In contrast with all this, I have presented the Protestant doctrines, and morals, and worship, as harmonizing with the word of God. Now if this has indeed been made out (as I think it has) then it follows, that the Protestant religion was taught by the Apostles, and of course has been held by the true church in every age; whereas your doctrines were not taught by the Apostles; are novelties and corruptions; and the true church never did, does not, and cannot hold them. My arguments, for many letters, have borne steadily on the accumulative proof of this position; and, if well founded, the conclusion is irresistible. As to Protestant *unity,* I stated that the various denominations mentioned in my last letter, were more united with each other, than the Papal church in successive ages. I stated also, that the twelve Confessions of Faith issued at the Reformation all presented essential and wonderful unity. The fact that they were *many* and yet *agreed,* without trick or force, is far better proof of honest and real unity, than the forced *uniformity* of all your people in the one creed; and as these twelve creeds agree in the *truth,* and as your people agree in *error,* so *their unity* is Christian unity, but yours, like that of Jews or

Mohammedans, if ever so great, being unity in error, is the *more dangerous*. Again, if *any one* of the many Protestant communions be a true church, my argument against you is still sound and good ; and those in *error* may be *reformed*. But if you are wrong, it is not only universal heresy, but a desperate one. For, as you claim to be infallible, so you are incapable of Reformation, and the case is *without remedy*. The Bible foreshows in lines clear as light, that your church must be destroyed, for she rejects reform, and is therefore incurable. The Jews themselves shall be rec ,vered, ' and grafted in again ;' but the church of Rome ' shall be cut off.' Who can read the 11th chapter of Romans, or the 2d chapter of 2 Thess. or the book of Revelations, and doubt that the church of Rome is to be cast off ? It is a curious fact, that in Malta, and even Rome itself, it is a common opinion (not an *article* of faith) that the present will be the last Pope. Prophecy travails in the speedy dissolution of the Papal dominion.

VI. I promised in my last letter to say something of the *sects and variations* of your church. These are subjects replete with matter, and require volumes for their elucidation. *Since* the Council of Trent, and especially since the Reformation which tore the jewel from the Pope's crown, and delivered better than half of Europe from his dominion, and poured a flood of light on the world, necessity and growing weakness have compelled more union ; and the progress of the Reformation has shed its twilight even on the Vatican. Thus, in self-defence some excesses have been reformed, and more union engendered. But look at the church before the Reformation ; yea, look at her parties and opinions even now. It is not agreed to this day, which are the general councils, there are parties on this subject ; nor whether the Pope be infallible ; nor where infallibility is lodged ; nor whether the Pope has power over both swords, to depose princes, &c. &c ; nor whether *all* the human race were born in original sin ; nor in what the true consecrating act in Transubstantiation consists ; nor in what the matter and essence of the sacrifice of the Mass consists ; nor what the infallible Traditions are ; nor whether the Pope be above a Council, or a Council above the Pope ; all these have their parties in the church of Rome at this day. It is true, (as at the council of Trent,) where they cannot agree, they call them *opinions ;* and where they can, *doctrines*. But this is absurd. On this plan, the Protestant communions, named in my last Letter, are now more united, than the present church of Rome. But again, if we ascend into earlier days we shall find *old* Rome and *new*, far, far at odds. The Council of Nice, A. D. 325, put the Pope on a level with the other leading Bishops ; and Pope Gregory called the title of Universal Bishop, (not as Mr. Hughes says, in the Bishop of Constantinople's, but in *any* hands,) the mark of anti-christ. Now, the Pope is universal monarch, and head of all Bishops. Is not this a vast variation ? The Council of Laodicea decreed, " we ought not to leave the church of God, and go to invoke angels, (Angeli.) But as this directly *forbids* what the Council of Trent directly commands ; so it has been *changed* to read, *Anguli-corners ;* i. e. ' *worship corners.*' By this, and other forgeries and erasures, H. Boxhorn, Professor of Divinity, at Loraine, had his eyes opened, and left the church of Rome forever. (See his 3d book, de Euch.) The church of Rome *once* gave the cup to the laity in the communion, *now* she takes it away ; once she and all the church prayed in the known tongue of the people, and Paul expressly forbids an unknown tongue, unless accompanied by an interpreter. (See 1 Cor. xiv.) Once too, the Bible in the church of Rome was in the *known* tongue of the people, and open to all. Now the church-prayers and Bible, are in the *unknown tongue*, and the church curses those who condemn it. There have been four different systems of infallibility, at different times and places : 1. That of the Pope ; 2, that of the Council ; 3, the Pope and Council ; 4, that the universal church was the *seat* of infallibility. There have been also three systems as to the nature of the Pope's supremacy: 1, a Presidency; 2, a Monarch; 3, a God on earth. There have been three systems of image worship: 1, Their use as a help to devotion: 2, the *lower* worship of them: 3, the same worship of them as of the *originals* represented by them. And three *periods* us to Priests' marriage: 1, It was allowed; 2, forbidden under Gregory VII.; 3, preference of fornication to it, and permission to keep concubines. Also there are now three parties as to the *doctrine* of celibacy: 1. That it is a divine interdict; 2, only a human institution, though binding and good; 3, (as now in France,) that celibacy is useless and injurious. Once the church of Rome gave the Eucharist to infants as necessary to their salvation; now she forbids it. Once she held the doctrine of the millennium; afterwards she stoutly rejected it. In these two last she not only varied, but on one side or other must have *erred*. Now is not this the very essence of variation, and party dissensions in the bosom of the Roman church?

She boasts of never *changing*, and Jerome says (Præf. to Evang.) 'What changes is not true; verum non esse quod variat. Was there ever such versatility and variation? Yet this is the unchangeable church, reigning in the eternal city. Finally, once *confession* of sin was public in the church of Rome, and the penitent was referred for pardon to God Now the *priest* pardons, and to him *confession* is made in *private*. He is now like a common sewer, the depository of all the sins of all his people. What an effect must it produce on the priest's soul, and what a power does it give him over other men, and then he *must* keep every villain's secret, and pardon the villain confessing. The questions asked at confession, are enough to ruin a chaste mind. I wish you would publish them. I have a list of them in Spanish; but I dare not render them into English. Even 'The Christian's Guide,' published by Mr. Cummiskey, Philadelphia, and in use here, under the Bishop's approval, contains in its 'Table of sins,' such matter, as no man should, on any account, permit his child to see, and which no lady ought to read, much less use in confession. Yet the penitent is directed to consult this very 'table of sins,' in preparation for confession; and at it to confess all her sins. I forbear to publish this horrible catalogue.

VII. I had desired to say something of the EFFECTS OF THE REFORMATION, in proof of its divine origin and intrinsic excellence. Whoever would be truly informed on this subject, should read "Villers on the Reformation," lately reprinted in this city by Messrs. Key & Biddle, in the Christian Library. We may read the influence of the Reformation in the history of Spain contrasted with Holland, Italy with England, Portugal with Scotland, or Mexico and the South American States with our own happy country. Here in broad extent and for successive generations, the two systems have been exhibited in their practical effects. The first named state in each of the above contrasts, is Papal, the last Protestant. And now, where is most freedom, most happiness, most moral dignity, most science, most national greatness? We are indebted to the Reformation under God, for the rights of conscience, for civil liberty, for the revival of letters in chief part, and for the circulation of the Bible for the virtue and piety of the people, and the eternal salvation of innumerable souls. The love of power is the very genius of the papacy, and it rises on the ruins of holiness, light and liberty. In our country as elsewhere, the liberties of the people must expire with the general prevalence of Popery. But it is impossible it should prevail if Protestants are only true to their master, and to their principles. We glory in the principles of universal toleration. Truth wants no help but its own power, directed by the hand of its author. It must finally triumph; it will at last prevail. Magna est veritas, and prævalebit.

In my imperfect efforts to assert its evidences, and to vindicate its sacred doctrines, I have at every step felt my own unfitness for so great a work; and should never have ventured to assume such a task, had it not been forced upon me.—During the progress of this discussion, I have been absent from home half the time; and during the whole, engaged in an arduous and perplexing agency. I say this not for my own, but the cause's sake. But I have done what I could. As the second limit set to the time for continuing the controversy has now been reached, the future renewal, or final close of the discussion, will be referred to the decision of my Rev'd opponent.

JOHN BRECKINRIDGE

P. S. I have but a few words to say in answer to your Postscript. It will be perceived that the first five assertions are admitted to be correctly quoted from Baronius, as you do not give us a word to the contrary 'That this silence arises from inability, rather than want of will, to prove their incorrectness, is too evident to those who observe how eagerly you catch at a straw in endeavouring to disprove the sixth. It avails you nothing to object, that the quotation is given as a continuous passage, and therefore 'unfair,' when our readers know, and you know, that I referred for it to *two full pages*, 765, 766. The only question is, Is every fact contained in this passage proved to have been stated by Baronius? For an answer to this question, I am willing to appeal to any man, who has a competent knowledge of the original, and whose judgment is not perverted by sectarian influence. Let any such man read the proofs I gave in the Postscript to my last letter, compare them with the context in the original, and then say whether the *facts* I have stated on the authority of Baronius are not fully made out by reference to the ages quoted. Whether it was, or was not, the opinion of Baronius, that 'God had forgotten the (Roman Catholic) church' is a matter of very little importance, while the *facts* which he states, clearly prove that such was the case, as I have shown in my last; and the *object* of *your call*, as well as the point of my proof, was the depravity of the Popes. On this you said you would expose me. It is rather amusing to see, to what a pitiful shift you are driven, to disprove the sixth assertion quoted from Baronius, 'that the church was governed by strumpets.' Have you forgotten that you stated in your '*Notes*' left at the Athenæum, that Albertus 'could expel lawful Popes, and put in usurpers, just as his *mistress directed?*' Was not the church then governed by a strumpet? But while ringing your changes on the word *arbitrio*, did you forget, or think your readers would forget, that I quoted from Baronius, such unequivocal expressions as '*cum Romæ* DOMINARENTUR....*meretrices*' when strumpets GOVERNED *Rome*—'*cum Theodora...scortum* MONARCHIAM...*obtineret in urbe*', when *Theodora a strumpet held* SUPREME CONTROL *in the city*—'*invaluit meretricum* IMPERIUM,' *the* SOVEREIGNTY *of strumpets prevailed!* Will you please to construe these expressions word for word, as you have *meretricum arbitrio infamari?*

But now I come to the very essence of your Postscript. You tell your readers that this quotation was made by me '*under the* THREAT *of exposure!!*' and intimate that it would have been much more 'unfair,' if it had not been made under such awful circumstances! '*Risum teneatis, amici?*' I fear I shall be set down as one under the guilt of *mortal sin*, and destitute of all grace; but truth compels me to confess, that from the beginning of this controversy, to the present time, I have not for a moment had the fear of the Rev. John Hughes, nor of his '*Lord God the Pope*,' before my eyes! No, Sir, I thank my God, that the time is not yet come, and it is my grand object in this controversy to keep that day far off, when the '*THREAT*' of a Roman priest can make me tremble for my reputation, my liberty, or my hopes of heaven. Even the Bulls of your master become very harmless animals, when sent to pasture on our happy soil. Your arrogant and impotent *threats* only show what you *would* do, if you *could*.

> "O, tua cornu
> Ni foret exsecto frons, quid faceres quum
> Sic mutilus mintaris?"—Hor.

> "If you can *threaten* now, what would you do,
> Had not the horn been rooted out, that grew
> Full in thy front?"

J. B.

CONTROVERSY. No. XXXV.

IS THE PROTESTANT RELIGION THE RELIGION OF CHRIST?

Philadelphia, October 3d, 1833.

To the Rev. John Breckinridge,

Rev. Sir: By a note received from the Editor of the Presbyterian, I am informed that your letter closed the controversy, and this communication is admitted by the courtesy of the editor, to remove the " semblance of partiality." Of course, I am bound to acknowledge this courtesy, and I shall avail myself of it, simply for the purpose of correcting the erroneous statements of your last letter.

1. You charge me as follows—"You asserted that the Bible was not a sufficient rule of faith, though God revealed it for that very end: next you contended that it had no fixed meaning without an *authoritative* interpretation: then, you conceded that if left to itself, it did not teach the doctrines of Papacy; and finally, you almost abandon its use and retreat to the forlorn hope of the Fathers."

Every sentence in this statement is a misrepresentation. In the first place, I never said that God had appointed the Bible for the "very end" that it might be the sufficient or only rule of faith. On the contrary, the errors and opposite doctrines which Protestants deduce from it, are the proof that God did *not* appoint it exclusively for this end. If he had, it would be understood in the same sense by all—since God *cannot be the author of those contradictory doctrines which Protestants profess to find in the Bible.*

2. I *never* said that the Bible "has no fixed meaning without an authoritative interpretation." But I said, and argued, that without an authoritative interpretation, men *cannot be assured* of what that "fixed meaning" is. Because, (as we see among Protestants,) Unitarians, Universalists, &c. &c. have as good a right to charge their errors to the Bible as the Presbyterians themselves. Every one has the right to *unfix* the *true* meaning of the Bible and substitute his own favorite folly, error, opinion, and fanaticism. This is what I said, what I supported, and I think, established under the head of the rule of faith.

3. I never said that the Bible does not teach the Catholic doctrines, "if left to itself." Left to itself, it is "the Bible on the shelf"—and teaches nothing. Rightly *interpreted*, it teaches Catholicity—Wrongly *interpreted*, it *is made to teach* a thousand doctrines, which it does not contain—Calvinism, Socinianism, or any other *ism*, which the interpreter, for the time being, may happen to prefer.

4. I have not abandoned the use of the Scriptures for the testimony of the Fathers. On all the questions I have shown that the Scriptures and the Fathers spoke the same language—that the doctrines of Catholicity are supported by the testimony of both; and that the opinions of Protestantism are not drawn

from the Bible, but from the Protestant mode of interpreting the Bible, of which the Fathers knew nothing.

Finally, you would make me say that the Bible is a "nose of wax," a "shoe that fits any foot," &c. &c. To all which I reply, that the Protestant rule of interpretation makes of the Bible just whatever the interpreter thinks proper. This you did not deny, but thought to account for, by saying that such interpretation is the "*abuse* of the Bible." It is, at all events, the Protestant rule of faith, as I have had occasion to show under the first question. I have no hesitation in stating that, according to the use which Protestants make of it, the Bible may be called a musical instrument, on which every sect of Protestants may play its *own* favorite tune. Which sect is right? Who can tell—when all have the same patent of interpretation, and each claims the Bible in opposition to all the rest? Who is to decide among them?

Having thus corrected your misstatement, and misrepresentation of *my* arguments, I shall follow you to your next twofold position—which "*you think* the community are prepared to admit," viz: 1. That I depend far more on the Fathers than on the Bible: and, 2. That their "unanimous consent," if it has a being, is by no means in my favour."

To the first of these positions I answer, that the Catholic doctrine is established on the evidence of the Scripture—the attestations of the Fathers—the testimony of all the ancient Liturgies, of the heretics themselves—the testimony of the Syrian Christians, (whom you *once called* "Protestants,")—of the Greek church—of all the eastern sects—in fine, of all Christians, from the preaching of Christ, to the days of Martin Luther. And, *this being the case*, it follows, that either "the Protestant religion is NOT the religion of Christ," or else, that the religion of Christ had no PROFESSORS in the world before the days of Martin Luther. All this accumulated testimony shows that the Catholic doctrines were the doctrines of the Bible, down to the sixteenth century; and that no Christians, in *the whole world*, understood the Bible to teach the doctrines which Protestants profess to find in it.

As to the "UNANIMOUS CONSENT," it is undeniable. You find that all, who speak on the doctrines now disputed between Catholics and Protestants, are clear and unequivocal in their testimony in our favour. They do not indeed, *always* speak equally clear. But whilst *you* may cite passages that are *obscure*, and which, by themselves, might harmonize with EITHER *doctrine*, I have cited others, which settle the matter of their belief—on the real presence of Christ in the Eucharist—the sacrifice of the Christian Liturgy, called the mass—the invocation of saints—prayers for the dead—purgatory—fasting—sign of the cross—supremacy of St. Peter, and his successors in the visible government of Christ's church upon earth; and, in short, of all the doctrines which the innovators of the sixteenth century have rejected. These testimonies, clear and *unequivocal*, may be found in the quotations of my last two letters, taken from the writings of the Fathers—both *before* the Council of Nice, and *after*, for the first five hundred years of the Christian church. Neither were they of one country alone, but taken indiscriminately from Asia, Europe, and Africa. You seem to admit that there is no way of evading their powerful testimony on these matters, except by a grammatical quibble on the word, "unanimous consent." Taking it for granted that there are exceptions, you infer that these exceptions destroy the force of the rule. The great body of testimony must go for nothing, provided that, by the *distortion* of his language, you can make it appear that any *one* Father disagreed from the rest. In fact you cannot find such disagreement. All have not, it is true, expressed themselves *equally* plain ; nor have the same Fathers, in *all* the parts of their works ; but when so great a number of them have expressed themselves so clearly and so strongly in attestation of the Catholic doctrines, as they still exist in the church, the "consent" of ALL is rendered "unanimous," by the acquiescence of the rest.

We do not profess to receive our belief from the Fathers, as if they were the authors of it. They are only the channel through which it descended, but the fountain is Jesus Christ. They are the witnesses of what was the belief of the church, at the times when *they lived and wrote.* And as Protestants pretend that the primitive church believed as *they* do, we quote the Fathers to show, on the contrary, that the belief of the church was then what Catholics still hold. Thus, Reverend Sir, you appealed to the Fathers ; and having selected the tribunal, one should suppose that you would consent to be judged by it. But no. The moment I furnish their verdict, you attack their authority, and say that their writings have been "erased and Romanized!!" Then why did you appeal to them? But the Fathers have been recognized by the University of Oxford ; and is it possible, that the learned body of Protestants who presided at their publication, would palm on the world writings which have been "erased and Romanized?" Again, how could the church "erase and Romanize" these writings in the hands of *her enemies?* They have been preserved by the various sects of heretics, separated from the communion of the church, some of them, since the very days of the Fathers. They have been preserved by the Greek Schismatics—would *they* suffer their copies to be "erased and Romanized?" Does not the fact of your having uttered this charge, under your present circumstances in this controversy, imply the consciousness, that the Fathers are *against you*— whilst the charge itself is refuted by its own absurdity?

Mr. B., after all these expedients resorted to—for the purpose of sustaining his cause, with great apparent gravity makes a new assertion, and tells us that...." the higher we rise in antiquity, the more decidedly Protestant do they (the Fathers) become, until the last traces of Romanism disappear amidst the better light of the Ante-Nicene Fathers." Does Mr. B. imagine that the *quotations* of my last letter, taken from the writings of the Ante-Nicene Fathers are to be overturned by empty declamation, and mere assertion, without the least proof? Does he suppose that those proofs, which are undeniable, are already forgotten by our readers? In reference to the authorities quoted by *him*, and which I had occasion to expose, he assures us that nothing unfair, was done by him, "*to his knowledge.*" He then, no doubt, copied from others, who wrote for Protestants *only*, and whose false or garbled quotations, passed unexposed, and even unsuspected. It was on this account, at an early stage of the controversy, I advised him to beware of his quotations; and it is but a poor plea for the false quotations which he has since put on record, to say now that, indeed, it was not done " to his knowledge." As an offset, however, he arraigns me in connexion with the authorities quoted by me from Tertullian, Wesley, Luther, and Jewell. Now I refer the reader to the particular passages, in which I quoted from these writers, and he will see that you, Rev'd Sir, revive a charge, which was promptly resented, and triumphantly refuted in each particular instance. Such charges come with a bad grace from you, inasmuch as they are not only unfounded, but have been already refuted. Of Tertullian's, you may recollect that you misrepresented the *object for which it was adduced as a proof*—and that the charge of garbling was refuted by my correcting your misrepresentation of my argument. Of Wesley, I proved, from his own writings, all I had asserted. Of Luther, the same. Of Jewell, I spoke on the strength of authorities which you did not dispute. These being the facts of the case, our readers will not be imposed upon by your *gratuitous* charge against me, of garbling, mistranslations, perversions, and *false assertions* of authorities ;—charges, which have been not only *preferred*, but UNDENIABLY ESTABLISHED AGAINST YOURSELF.

Not less curious is the manner in which you allude to my proofs of Christ's real presence in the holy sacrament of the Eucharist. You had pretended that the Protestant doctrine could be found, at least in the LITURGIES of the ancient Heretics of the East ; as if men could not err from the UNITY of Christ's religion, without necessarily falling into the Protestant doctrines. Now I have shown the belief of the Catholic church on all the doctrines that appertain to the Liturgy, viz. : The SACRIFICE of the Eucharist—the REAL PRESENCE of Christ's body and blood, after the consecration, under the appearance of bread and wine ; the PRIESTHOOD of the new law ; the ALTAR, the VICTIM, in the *unbloody* manner—the INVOCATION OF SAINTS ;—the sacrifice and prayer for the DEAD, as well as the living. Such is the testimony of these *neutral* documents, which are neither Catholic nor Protestant, but which, being preserved by the *enemies of the Catholic church*, from the very first ages of Christianity, must be received by all candid men, as unimpeachable vouchers for the primitive belief of Christians, on these points. For, these sects would not borrow their liturgy, *after the separation*, from their *enemies*, the very church which had excommunicated them. Consequently, the liturgies and the doctrines which they contain are to be referred to a date *anterior* to the separation. They all agree with the Catholic church ; and it must be this conviction, and the argument which it furnishes, that have obliged my opponent, after having *claimed* these liturgies for the Protestant side, a few letters since, to shrink now from their withering testimony against him, and tell the public that, indeed, "every scholar knows them to be replete with forgeries of the Church of Rome!!!" Why then did he claim them? And having claimed them, without knowing their contents, why now does he make a bad cause worse, by charging them with "forgery?"

He then turns to a new question and says they were not written by the authors to whom they are ascribed. This is nothing to the purpose. It is known that the first liturgies were not, for a long time, *committed to writing at all*. And the name of St. Cyprian, in the liturgy ascribed to St. Peter, is no proof that the substance of it, as relates to the *Eucharistic sacrifice*, had not been taught by St. Peter. The Scriptures furnish a case in point. The Book of Deuteronomy is ascribed to Moses, yet the last chapter contains an account of his death and burial, which shows that this part was written by some other. This turning away from the doctrine to the *authorship* of the liturgies, is in keeping with all the rest. But the implicit *acknowledgment* of all the documents of antiquity being adverse to Protestantism, is easily gathered from your charges of "forgery," "erasure and Romanizing," and the interrogatory with which the whole winds up, "who then can trust your testimonies?"

After having established the Catholic belief, by arguments founded on the testimony of the Holy Scripture; by the very incredulity of the Jews at Capharnaum when the doctrine was first proposed; by the plain and positive words of the Redeemer, in the institution of the Sacrament; by the testimony of St. Paul, who warned the Christians against the sin of eating or drinking the body and blood of the Lord unworthily; by the testimony of the apostolic Fathers, Ignatius in particular, who states that the Heretics of that age abstained from the Eucharist, *because they would* not acknowledge it to be the "FLESH OF CHRIST;" by the unanimous consent of the Fathers, both before and after the Council of Nice; by the very testimony of the enemies of the Catholic church, the Greek schismatics and heretics of the East generally; by *all the liturgies* in the world, before the days of Carlostadius, with whom the Protestant doctrine of mere bread and wine began:—after all this, to which no positive testimony has been opposed, it is curious, I say, to perceive the tone of *nonchalance* with which you introduce "my last and *feeble* struggle for TRANSUBSTANTIATION!" Do you suppose, Rev. Sir, that this manner of affecting to see no strength in evidences which you cannot deny, and arguments which you cannot answer, will not be duly appreciated by the intelligence of our readers? Do you suppose that such a *mass of testimony* is to be outweighed, in the public mind, by your naked assertion?

You say, that it is I who profit "by insulated sentences" from the Fathers, and that "if their writings could be presented in unbroken connexion, the argument against me would appear in tenfold strength.' Then, Rev. Sir, it was your business to give some specimens of this "unbroken connexion." But let us test the truth of your *ipse dixit,* even on this. St. Chrysostom is one of those, whom Protestants are pleased to claim as friendly to their opinions. Allow me, then, to give an extract from a sermon which he preached at Antioch in the year 386, (Hom. 61.) and mark well its doctrine

"It is necessary, my dear brethren, to learn what is the MIRACLE, wrought in our mysteries, why it has been given to us, and what profit we ought to derive from it? We are all but one body, the members of his flesh and bones. Let us *who are initiated*, follow what I am about to say. In order then that we may be mixed up with the flesh of Jesus Christ, not only by love, but *really and truly*, he has given the food that effects this prodigy, being desirous thus to manifest the love he bears us. For this purpose he has *mixed and incorporated himself* in us, in order that we might form but one with him, in the same manner as the members form but one body, being all united to the same head. In fact, those who wish to love tenderly, always wish to be but one with the object of their love..... Wherefore, like lions which inhale and breathe forth flames, let us leave this table, having ourselves become formidable to the devil, reflecting on our head, and the love he has so wonderfully and manifestly shown us. Mothers not unfrequently put out their children to be nursed by strangers, 'but I, says he, (Christ) feed my children with my *own flesh :* I myself am their food : for it is my desire to ennoble you all, and to give you an earnest of future blessings. Giving myself to you, as I do, in this world, I shall be able, with much more reason, to treat you still better in the other. I wished to become your brother, for you I have taken flesh and blood; and *now, moreover*, I give you this flesh and blood by which I am become of the same nature with yourselves.' This blood produces in us a brilliant and royal image: it prevents the nobleness of the soul from suffering, when it frequently sprinkles and nourishes it....This blood is spread through the soul, as soon as drunk : it waters and fortifies it. This blood, when worthily received, puts the devil to flight : it invites and introduces to us the angels and the Lord of the angels.... This blood, being shed, washed and purified the world....And if in the capital of Egypt, the symbol of this blood, being merely sprinkled on the door-posts, possessed such virtue and efficacy, *the truth and reality is infinitely more efficacious*......If death so much feared the *figure* and the *shadow*, how much, let me ask you, will it not fear the *reality ?*....Thus every time we partake of this body and taste this blood, let us think that HE who sitteth in heaven and whom the angels adore, *is the self-same* whom we taste and receive here below."

"But what! Do you not see that these vessels, upon the ALTAR, are of dazzling brightness and purity ? Our souls ought to be still more resplendent with purity and sanctity. And why so ? Because if these vessels are so well polished, it is on our account ; they can neither taste nor feel Him whom they *contain*, but we *must certainly*.

"Consider, O man! the royal table is laid out, the angels attend : the King himself is *present :* and thou remainest in a stupid indifference ! Thy garments are soiled, and thou carest not ? But they are clean, thou wilt say. Well, then, ADO IT and communicate."

Here is the "miracle" stated, the *caution* of the secret discipline *removed*, because he spoke to the "*initiated ;*" the true body and blood of Jesus Christ, presented, '*adored*," and *received in the Eucharist*. This is the "unbroken connexion," which you told us is so favourable to the Protestant "bread and wine." This, too, is from one of those Fathers over whose testimony you charged me with having passed lightly. Would you venture to preach this doctrine in any Protestant pulpit in the city? The people would stare, for matters have changed as regards *their* mere shadow, of that adorable mystery of the Eucharist, which a Chrysostom proclaimed with such fervent eloquence to the people of Antioch, 1400 years ago. Pronounced in a Catholic pulpit, however, it would be listened to as the ordinary doctrine of the church, which teaches now, as she taught when she numbered the Chrysostoms, the Augustines, the Ambroses, the Cyrils, the Gregories, the Jeromes, the Cyprians, the Irenæuses, and the other lights of primitive Christianity among her disciples, her doctors and defenders, against the heresies of wicked men.

Let us now look into that "better light of the Ante-Nicene Fathers," in which we are told that the "last traces of Romanism disappear." To avoid repetition, I request the reader to turn to my last letter, and he will see what Mr. Breckinridge calls "Romanism," strongly asserted in the testimonies of the Ante-Nicene Fathers there quoted. But I will add one quotation more, from Justin Martyr, who was put to death in the year of our Lord, one hundred and sixty-six. In his apology to the Emperor Antoninus Pius, he says, describing the celebration of the mysteries,—" Our prayers being finished, we embrace one another with the kiss of peace. Then to him who presides over the brethren, is presented bread, and wine tempered with water, having received which, he gives glory to the Father of all things in the name of the Son and the Holy Ghost, and returns thanks, in many prayers, that he has been deemed worthy of these gifts. These offices being duly performed, the whole assembly, in acclamation, answers, *Amen;* when the ministers, whom we call Deacons, distribute to each one present a portion of the blessed bread, and the wine and water. Some is also taken to the absent. This food we call the Eucharist, of which they alone are allowed to partake, who believe the doctrines taught by us, and who have been regenerated by water for the remission of sins, and who live as Christ ordained. Nor do we take these gifts as common bread, and common drink; but as Jesus Christ, our Saviour, made man, by the word of God, took flesh and blood for our salvation: in the same manner, we have often been taught *that the food which has been blessed by the prayer of the words which he spake,* and by which our blood and flesh, in the change, are nourished, IS THE FLESH AND BLOOD OF THAT JESUS INCARNATE. The Apostles in the commentaries written by them, which are called Gospels, have delivered, that Jesus so commanded, when taking bread, having given thanks, he said: '*Do this in remembrance of me: This is my body.*' In like manner, taking the cup, and giving thanks, he said: ' This is my blood:' and that he distributed both to them only." (Apol. 1. p. 95. London Edit. 1722.)

This testimony was given about *half a century* after the death of St. John the Evangelist, and it is so strongly Catholic, that no Protestant would dare to repeat it in his pulpit, except as "one of the errors of Popery." I might multiply quotations from the Fathers, into the extent of a volume. But what I have already produced, must suffice, especially as you have nothing positive to oppose them with—for I confess that three sentences of St. Justin, St. Ignatius, Tertullian, or St. Cyprian, who were the almost immediate successors of the Apostles—three sentences from any of these, attesting the real presence of Christ's flesh in the Eucharist, has more authority in my mind, than a thousand letters filled with Mr. Breckinridge's cavils, objections, and assertions.

On communion under one kind, I refer him to Letter No. XXIX., where I showed by arguments, also *unanswered,* that the same reasoning which would make it the *right* of all to receive under both kinds, would equally make it the r ght of all *to consecrate.* Until Mr. B. shall have condescended to notice my arguments, as *I stated them,* I shall not consider his objections of mere *assertion,* worthy of further reply.

Mr. Breckinridge says, that I " take it for granted, that the only thing concealed (by the discipline of the secret,) was the doctrine of the Eucharist." I never said any such thing, nor did I ever take it for granted. This answer will be sufficient.

He says, "that there is no evidence that the doctrine of the Eucharist was among the doctrinal mysteries at all." Now, with all due deference to Mr. Faber, from whom Mr. Breckinridge copies the *assertion*, I shall show that they are both mistaken. St. Augustine, I should suppose, is a better witness than either. "What," says he, "is there hidden in the church? The Sacraments of Baptism, and the EUCHARIST. The Pagans see our good works, but not our Sacraments." (1 in Psal. 103.)

Mr. B. says the "*discipline of the secret* originated in the second century." Tertullian says in his Apology, "It is the common law of all mysteries to keep them secret." And common sense shows, that this discipline would have been useless, if the Pagans or uninitiated, had, *at any time* previously, been acquainted with these mysteries.

Immediately after this, Mr. B. falls into another train of blunders and misrepresentations by following Mr. Stanley Faber. Blandina the slave was tortured to make her disclose the "SECRET" of the Christian mysteries. She replied, says the original, "*liberê et scité*," that is, "freely and prudently;" which Faber translated "freely and boldly." Irenæus, who relates the affair, was praising the constancy of these martyrs, and the *prudence* of Blandina, who, though a slave, answered so *prudently* that she betrayed nothing of the Christian mysteries. Mr. Faber puts the word "boldly," instead of "prudently," or "adroitly," in order to make it appear that Blandina had nothing to confess. Mr. Breckinridge follows Mr. Faber, and neither, unfortunately for their argument, follows exactly the truth.

Mr. Breckinridge in reference to this, says, "these Christians denied from first to last that it was LITERAL flesh and blood which was served up to them. Was not this," he asks, "a denial of the real presence?" Not at all, Rev. Sir—Catholics believe in the real presence, and in transubstantiation now, as they did when Blandina was tortured—and yet they do not say they eat "*literal* flesh." They do not, as Mr. B. constantly *misrepresents*, hold that the flesh of Christ is present in the Eucharist, in the *natural condition* of human flesh. This I have repeatedly explained in the course of these letters. But still he does not hesitate to borrow the artifice of Mr. Faber, in order to make the doctrine appear shocking to the minds of Protestants. For this, even the purity of our language must be sacrificed, to put forth the solicisms of " LITERAL flesh" and " LITERAL blood." The object of this is to reflect on Protestant minds, ideas of gross misconception—which will operate *instead of argument*. We never hear of a "*literal*" house, a "*literal*" loaf of bread, or a "*literal*" stage-coach drawn by "*literal*" horses. The word "literal" cannot be applied to a *material* object. Yet these gentlemen would barbarize the language, in order to pervert the doctrine of the Eucharist which they cannot refute. [See St. Aug. *De verp Apost.* Serm. 2.]

Mr. B. says I perverted his argument touching the manner of Christ's entrance into the closed apartment where the disciples were. His words, he says, were these:—

| "Do you forget that Christ had power miraculously to open a passage for his body through the door or wall, and close it again.' | I made him say, "that Christ could remove out of the wall or door, space for his body to enter by, and then close it up again." |

I willingly submit it to the reader whether I have perverted, or Mr. B. has accused me of it, without cause. He then refers to a subject which he ought to wish *forgotten*, and insinuates still that there is a "prohibition" to read his letters. Does he forget, or does he suppose that the public forgets, the manner in which he crept out of this false and unfounded charge, by exposing his friend Mr. Burtt to the pity, or the contempt of our common readers?

Then, as if frightened at the Nestorianism of his former letter, Mr. Breckinridge shrinks back from his declaration that "it was *idolatry* to worship the body of Jesus Christ." But shunning Nestorianism, he seems to lean to the heresy of Eutyches, and tells us that "the Divinity and humanity are inseparably *blended* in the person of Jesus Christ." A *better* theology would have taught him to say that the two natures are "inseparably *united.*" Even at Princeton, I am persuaded this distinction would be recognized. He says, that in transubstantiation we worship the "*body alone.*" I reply, that when he thus asserts what is *untrue*, he must expect to be contradicted. We worship Jesus Christ; his human and divine nature being inseparably united in the mystery of the holy Eucharist as in that of the Incarnation.

As to his "exposures of the sacrifice of mass," I can see only his assertions for them. I have seen no refutation of my arguments and authorities on that subject. He casts an imputation on my motives, by calling the sacrifice of mass "my chief gain." In reply to this indelicate allusion, I have only to repeat, that if I could consent to give up my soul for 'gain,' I should become a Protestant at once. So far as the advantages of this world are concerned in the matter, the scale greatly preponderates in favour of Protestantism.

Now we come to 'POPE LIBERIUS.' On this, I have only to say, that whether he signed the Arian creed or not, is a matter of very little moment to the present question. He might have signed it, and yet from the act, none of those awful consequences which Mr. Breckinridge is pleased to imagine, must necessarily follow. Besides even Mr. Breckinridge, whilst he accuses him, ascribes the act to *compulsion*, 'through the fear of death.' Neither was Athanasius condemned, even by the Arians, as a *Heretic*, but only as a disturber of the peace. What Liberius is charged with having done, was not the act of a free agent—since (if done at all) it was done 'through fear of death'—as even his enemies acknowledge. Though this persecuted Pontiff had done what is charged, you must remember that the *defect* consisted, NOT in signing a creed in which the Arian heresy was approved, but in signing a creed in which that heresy was NOT expressly condemned. The word 'consubstantial' of the Nicene Council, was omitted, and this omission was used by the Arians as a *proof* that Liberius had approved their doctrine, which, in fact, he condemned, with the sufferings and constancy of a martyr.

With regard to the Councils of Sirmium and Ariminum, I have only to reply as before, that no council acknowledged by the Catholic church, signed the Arian creed. None but Mr. Breckinridge could discover in this answer, the 'admission that the said councils *did* adopt the Arian heresy.' He can extract admission and deduce consequences, no matter what is said. He follows this pretended admission to its pretended consequences, and in two or three sentences makes it appear, that 'therefore, it is an article of faith in the Roman church, binding on all her members at this day, that Jesus Christ was *not* God, that his divinity is a figment, and Unitarians are right.' The Pope signed the *Catholic* council which condemned the *Arian heresy;* 'therefore' Catholics are bound to believe the doctrines—which their church condemned!!! This is *patent* logic. But Mr. Breckinridge is not the first of that race, who

> Without the *care of knowing* right from wrong,
> Always appear decisive, clear, and strong,
> Where others toil with philosophic force,
> Their nimble nonsense takes a shorter course,
> Flings at your head conviction in a lump,
> And gains remote conclusions at a jump.

Next in order, comes the doctrine of 'INTENTION,' in which Mr. Breckinridge follows the lucubrations of a Mr. Waddle, who has been put on a fair way to immortality as an author, by the insertion, in the Catholic Miscellany, and triumphant refutation of his—twaddle. On this, also, I repeat, that until Mr. Breckinridge can produce some *motive* or *interest*, in heaven or on earth, in *time or in eternity*, for a Priest's setting his mind deliberately in opposition to the 'intention' of the church, in the administration of the Sacraments, his objection is utterly inadmissible. Supposing that Baptism, according to the Presbyterian mode is administered, *on the stage, in mockery*, would the SACRAMENT be administered? The answer of this will justify the decision of the church, upon this point. Luther, in one of the propositions condemned by Leo X. maintained that a Sacrament was validly administered even though the Priest did it in jest: (*non serio, sed joco*.)

Against this error, the church renewed, in the council of Trent, the doctrine which had been defined before, in the council of Florence in the year 1439, viz. that the sacraments should be administered according to the intention of the church, or according to the end for which Jesus Christ instituted them. Still, even if a clergyman should intend to cheat the recipient of the sacrament, (which is not to be admitted) yet the consequences would not be such as Mr. B. so pathetically describes. In one part of his letter, he treats the sacrifice of mass as 'idolatry;' in another, he makes the delivery of souls from purgatory depend on the validity of this 'idolatrous' act! Such, and similar consequences does he draw from his own *imagination.* His objections are founded on his ignorance of the Catholic doctrine, or his powers of perverting it. In order, however, to show this, let me suppose for argument sake, the particular case which he imagines, yet it will not follow, as he pretends, that, according to our doctrine, 'little children are damned.' For we do not consign unbaptized infants to eternal damnation, as *Presbyterians do* all except those who 'profess the true religion, and *their* children.' Again, in the sacrifice of mass the multitude would not 'be guilty of idolatry,' as *he* pretends; 'for no Catholic teaches that the mere external symbols are to be adored.' (Bellar. Lib. 4. de Euch. c. 29.) Neither would ' the marriage ceremony be invalid,' as he pretends; nor for want of extreme unction, 'would all who died under their hands be lost for ever.' All these are false consequences, which you deduce, not from our doctrine, but from ignorance or the misrepresentation of it. But the supposition is not to be admitted, seeing that men are not *gratuitously wicked;*—and that, for the sacriligious wickedness here supposed, there is no motive, in time or in eternity.

Then comes the 'popular misrepresentation' about the 'LIBERTY OF THE PRESS AND THE INQUISITION.' Touching these topics, Mr. B. dilates with no inconsiderable powers of declamation. But declamation is a sorry expedient in grave theological controversy. The church of Rome might be opposed to the Liberty of the Press, and yet, it would not follow, as a necessary consequence, that 'the Protestant religion is the religion of Christ.' Mr. B. should not have forgotten the fines and imprisonment enacted by Presbyterians against such as should read the *Episcopal Common Prayer Book.* This fact, among others, proves that the church to which he belongs was the tyrannical enemy of the Liberty of the Press, when she had power to control it; and, that she would be so again, if she had the power, is the decided conviction of many enlightened Protestants in this country.

As for the committee at Rome, whose prohibition of books, Mr. B. asserts, is binding on the whole church,' I have only to answer, that if he will take pains to be informed on the subject, he will find that there are many countries in which the prohibitory Index is not acknowledged—for example, France, England, Ireland, and our own country. Of course, in saying that he has '*exposed me,*' it happens that he has only 'exposed himself.'

He says that THE BIBLE is on the prohibitory Index. He should have added, in truth and candour, that it is the *Protestant Bible,* in particular, and not the Bible, in general, as his statement would lead the reader to suppose. This prohibition is quite natural, when it is recollected that Catholics regard the *Protestant* Bible as a spurious version, mistranslated, and containing only a part of the sacred Scriptures. Throughout his letters, Mr. B. has kept up this *unfounded* accusation, that the church is inimical to the perusal of the sacred Scriptures. It may be well to state a few facts to show how false is this charge, and how groundless is this Protestant clamour, kept up without cause.

The Catholic church, by whose ministry, and to whose faith, ALL the nations of the earth, that have abandoned Paganism, were converted, has always been zealous to disseminate the sacred Scriptures among her children. Witness the fact, that so early as the fourth century, St. Augustine testifies that 'the number of those who had translated the Scriptures from the *Hebrew* into the *Greek* might be computed, but that the number of those who had translated the *Greek* into the *Latin* ' *could* NOT be computed." At that period, Latin, we should observe, was the language of the Western Empire.

Again, in 1552, when the Maronite Christians returned to the communion of the church, under Pope Julius III. a new edition of the *Syriac* version was printed at Vienna, and transmitted to Syria.

Pope Paul III. in 1548, published at Rome an *Ethiopic* version of the New Testament in Ethiopic, for the use of the Christians.

In 1591, an *Arabic* version of the whole Bible was published at Rome. And in the year 1671, another edition, in three volumes, folio, of the same version, from the press of the Propaganda.

Again, in 1591, an *Arabic* version of the four Gospels was printed at the Medicean press in Rome, for the use of the Arabic Christians in communion with the church.

Even in the *Chinese* language, notwithstanding it is so difficult and so few can read it, a harmony of the four Gospels was prepared by the Jesuits, and is mentioned with praise by the British and Foreign Bible Society in their first Report.

The fact is, that as soon as printing was invented, the church availed herself of the discovery, for the purpose of multiplying copies of the Scripture in every language. Luther's translation in Germany in 1522 and 1530, had been preceded nearly a century, 1. By the *Catholic* edition of Fust, printed at Mentz in 1462. 2. By that of Bemler, printed at Augsburg, 1467. And, 3. By the FOUR versions which Beausobre mentions in his 4th book of the History of the Reformation.

The French *Protestant* version is that of Olivetan, assisted by Calvin, published in 1537. It had been *preceded* by different *Catholic* versions. *First*, the New Testament by Julian the Augustinian Monk, printed in 1477. 2. A version of the whole Bible, by Guyards des Moulins, printed 1490. 3. By that of Estaple, who printed the New Testament in 1523, the Old Testament in 1528.

The Italian *Protestant* version was printed in 1562. It had been preceded by, 1, the *Catholic* version of Malermis, in 1471. 2. By that of Brucciofis, in 1532; on which the Protestant translation was generally founded.

In Belgium, the first Protestant translation was that of Luther, published in 1527. It had been preceded by a Catholic version of the four Gospels, printed in 1472; and by another Catholic version of the whole Bible, printed at Cologne, in 1475; and again at Delft, in 1477; at Gouda, in 1479, and both at Antwerp, in 1518. It is useless to extend the testimonies; when it is well known that in Italy alone, and with the Pope's approbation, more than TWENTY editions of the Bible, have been published in the vulgar tongue.

With these facts on historical record, is it not surprising to hear ignorant Protestants, misleading other Protestants yet more ignorant than themselves, by the false charge against the Catholic Church, that she is hostile to the Scriptures? The rules established subsequently, by the church, to regulate the use of the Holy Scriptures, were dictated by the glaring abuse to which the sacred volume was exposed in the hands of the Protestants, during the fanaticism of the Reformation. These abuses are acknowledged by learned Protestants, no less than by Catholics. A learned minister of the English Protestant Church, describes some of these excesses, and accounts for them, as Catholics do, not by charging the Scriptures as the source of impiety, but by showing that they are liable to be misunderstood, when left to the ignorance and daring rashness of mere private interpretation. As an example, he says—" The private judgment of Munzer discovered, in Scripture, that titles of nobility, and large estates were 'impious encroachments on the natural equality of the faithful,' and he invited his followers to examine the Scriptures whether these things were so? They examined—praised God—and proceeded with fire and sword, to the extirpation of the ungodly, and the seizure of their property. Private judgment, also, thought it discovered, in the Bible, that established laws were 'standing restraints on Christian liberty;' that the 'elect were incapable of sinning,' and might '*innocently* obey all the propensities of nature.'

" John of Leyden, laying down his thimble, and taking up his Bible, surprised the city of Munster, at the head of a rabble of frantic enthusiasts, proclaimed himself 'King of Zion,' and ran naked through the streets, vociferating that 'whatever is highest on earth, would be brought low, and whatever is lowest, should be exalted.' To keep his word, he made his common executioner, his minister of state; and his minister of state, his common executioner. Improving on the example of the Patriarchs, he 'took unto him' fourteen wives at once, affirming, that 'Polygamy was Christian liberty, and the privilege of the Saints.'" (Thoughts on the tendency of Bible Societies, p. 8.)

When Europe presented spectacles of this kind, wherever the Reformation prevailed, and when the actors referred to texts of Scripture for the justification of their *doctrines* and *conduct*, was it not natural, nay more. I would ask the sober judgment of Protestants, was it not even wise in the church, to establish regulations for the right use of the sacred Scriptures? But the facts submitted above amply vindicate the church from the ignorant and unfounded charge of being hostile to their dissemination: even if we had not the express declaration of Pope Pius VI. who, in a letter to Martini, on his translation of the Bible into Italian, says: "that the faithful should be excited to the reading of the Holy Scriptures; for these are most abundant sources *which ought to be left open to every one*, to draw from them purity of morals and of doctrine, to eradicate the errors which are widely disseminated in these corrupt times." (See this letter prefixed to every Catholic Bible.)

If Mr. Breckinridge were better informed, he would know that the placing of a book on the Index at Rome, does not necessarily imply the condemnation of the *whole work*. And if Locke, Milton, Galileo, and so forth, be on the catalogue, it is not because the authors were *good* poets, or philosophers, but because they were *bad* theologians. But I am at no loss to conceive the opinion which the intelligent reader will form of my opponent's acquaintance with the history of literature, when he reads the following assertion. "This is a war of extermination waged by the authority of the church against LETTERS, liberty, and conscience!" Thousands of *learned* Protestants, enemies of the church, no less than Mr. Breckinridge, have acknowledged, that to the zeal of the church, and to the labours of the monks, the world is indebted at this day for the preservation of ancient literature. As for "liberty" and "conscience," they are words which Mr. Breckinridge plays off, to catch the popular sympathy. I contend, and in the course of these letters have shown, that "liberty," and "conscience," never had a deadlier enemy to struggle against, than Presbyterianism *in power*. Then he appeals to a "free people;" as if engaged to carry a favourite candidate at an election, instead of furnishing arguments to show that "the Protestant Religion is the Religion of Christ."

Next follows his attacks on the "JESUITS," in which, instead of admitting with the candour of a generous mind, that such a society is not to be condemned for the vices of a few of its members—he attacks them *in globo*. He repeats the slanders with which they were attacked by the *infidels* of Europe; for it is their glory, that *infidels* have always laboured for their destruction. This is proved by the private correspondence of Voltaire and D'Alembert, in which, plotting the destruction of Christianity, these patriarchs of Deism, acknowledged that there was no hope of success, unless the Jesuits were first put down. Every base artifice was resorted to, to blind the judgment, and rouse the enmity of kings and governments, against the society. The Pope who suppressed it, made no charge of immorality against them; but acted with a view to avert the hurricane of civil persecution, which their enemies had excited against them, from every quarter. With reference to their persecution, by the Portuguese government, a liberal Protestant says, speaking of their college in Pernambuco: "Reader, throw a veil over thy recollection for a little while, and forget the *cruel, unjust*, and *unmerited censures* thou hast heard against an unoffending order. This palace was once the Jesuits' College, and originally built by those charitable fathers. Ask the aged and respectable inhabitants of Pernambuco, and they will tell thee, that the destruction of the Society of Jesuits, was a terrible disaster to the public, and its consequence severely felt to the present day."

"When Pombal took the reins of government into his hands, virtue and learning beamed within the college walls. Public catechism to the children, and religious instruction to all, flowed daily from the mouths of its venerable priests. They were loved, revered, and respected throughout the whole town. The illuminating philosophers of the day *had sworn to exterminate Christian knowledge*, and the college of Pernambuco was doomed to founder in the general storm. To the long-lasting sorrow and disgrace of Portugal, the philosophers blinded her king, and flattered her prime minister. Pombal was exactly the tool these sappers of every public and private virtue wanted. He had the naked sword of power in his own hand, and his heart was as hard as flint. He struck a mortal blow, and the Society of Jesuits, throughout the Portuguese dominions, was no more."—(*Wanderings in South America*, &c. By Charles Waterton, Esq. p. 82.)

When the Jesuits can point to testimonies like the above, in a hundred *Protestant* authors, the authority of any one of whom is equal, at least, to that of Mr. Breckinridge, they may bear with great equanimity those slanders, propagated against them in Europe by the *sworn enemies* of the name of Christ, and of which, it was the singular honour of the society to be the distinguished victims.

Mr. B. tells us that "once, guileless Protestants confided their children to the training of these men. But it is becoming apparent they will do so no more." This unlucky sentence shows us an *ulterior motive* for the attack on the Jesuits. And for the consolation of my Reverend opponent, I can assure him, that so far from this being the fact, the number of Protestant students in the Jesuits' college in Georgetown, is, of late, much augmented, and daily increasing. Some, and not a few, of the most learned and distinguished citizens of our country, *prefer* that Institution for the education of their sons. And so long as the public mind is imbued with *knowledge* and *discernment*, the education imparted in a college of Jesuits will be preferred to that which Presbyterian institutions are in the habit of administering. Much calumniated as the Jesuits have been, even their enemies have acknowledged them to be the most learned body of men that ever laboured in the work of education.

We are next introduced to the INQUISITION, on which Mr. B., like his predecessors, is quite pathetic. Of this I said, "it may have been a good institution—*abused*." And I am sure that there is nothing criminal in this reply. Now its abuses I condemn as much as Mr. B. himself. But it is manifest he has derived his knowledge of the Inquisition, not from any critical, candid investigation of the institution, or of the circumstances which must be taken into consideration, to form even a just idea of it. Protestants, generally, imbibe their notions of it from distorted portraits of hostile writers.

If Mr. B. wishes to be correctly informed, let him consult the history of the Inquisition by Count Le Maistre, which may be purchased at Mr. Cummiskey's book store, in Sixth street, above Spruce. Until he gives some proof that he has read some author not avowedly hostile, what I have said is sufficient in reply to charges founded either on ignorance or misrepresentation. For the information of the reader, however, I would remark, that the doctrines of the Catholic religion and the tribunal of the Inquisition are essentially distinct, the one from the other—which is proved by the fact, that only in two or three countries in the whole Catholic world, was the Iquisition ever established.

But does Mr. B. forget that, as has already been shown, Protestants put to death their fellow Protestants, for exercising the mere liberty of conscience? Does he forget the Protestant, as well as Catholic blood, shed by the Presbyterians in Geneva, Holland, England, Ireland, Scotland, and New England itself? Does he forget the barbarous acts of the British Parliament and Scotch Assembly against the Catholics, during a period of three hundred years? What were all these but the "Inquisition," under other and more refined names? Does he forget the "scavenger's daughter," and other instruments of torture, used in the Tower of London, by Elizabeth and her successors? Does he forget that the eighth act of the Presbyterian Assembly of 1699, directed, "that *according to the former acts of assemblies* and acts of parliament, the *names* of Popish priests and Jesuits, and trafficing Papists, and of those who have sent their children to Popish colleges and countries, be given in to each provincial synod and by them transmitted to the *respective magistrates*, to the effect that they *may be proceeded against according to law*." What is all this but the Inquisition—under other names?

But what after all is the object of these questions about the liberty of the press, the Jesuits, the Inquisition, &c. &c.? The object is manifest. Unable to prove that "the Protestant religion is the religion of Christ," or to answer my arguments in proof of the contrary, he endeavors to divert public attention from the *real* question, and to entrench himself in a position better suited to his resources—where he hopes to sustain himself, if not by argument, at least, by the prejudices of popular feeling. To this popular feeling he thinks to betray me, by putting me on the defence of the Jesuits, the Inquisition, and so forth. He seems to have taken the hint from the policy of those who said, "Master, is it lawful to pay tribute to Cæsar or not?"

Next in order are the "JEWISH TRADITIONS," of which I said that, "so far as they regarded the proof of the Jewish *faith*, before the coming of Christ, I do not reject them." From this answer, Mr. B. draws the inference, that, "of course *all* their traditions to that time were infallible." I answer no; but only those that appertained to the "*proof* of the Jewish faith." These our Saviour did not touch, in his rebuke to the Pharisees, but only those *false traditions* which did not appertain to the "proof of their faith." Why was it necessary to change the answer? If fairly dealt with, it excludes all the false consequences which he deduces from his own perversion of it.

Mr. B. asks, "is there any evidence of the POPE'S SUPREMACY, before the Council of Nice?" *He* says no—*I* answer yes. And I refer him to the proofs which I have already adduced from the writings of St. Cyprian, Irenæus, and other Ante-Nicene Fathers, and which he has not denied, nor yet attempted to refute. But another "evidence" is the fact, that in the first century, while some of the Apostles were still living, a dispute, which arose in the church at Corinth, was referred to Pope Clement, Bishop of Rome, and settled by his authority. The epistle which he addressed to the Corinthians on the occasion is still extant. In it he calls the "divisions which had just appeared among them, impious and detestable." He says, "to Fortunatus" (who had carried their appeal to him) "we have added four deputies: send them back as speedily as possible in peace, *that we may be informed of the return of union and peace among you,* for which we pray without ceasing: and that we may be enabled to rejoice at the re-establishment of good order among our brethren at Corinth." This very appeal, from Corinth to Rome, and this sending of "deputies" to settle the dispute, are at once, the recognition and the exercise of the Pope's supremacy. But to this, and the several instances already mentioned, we might add many others still. Eusebius tells us, that Irenæus remonstrated with the Pope, Victor, against the excommunication of the Bishop of—Asia. "He becomingly also," says Eusebius, "admonishes Victor, *not to cut off whole churches of God,* who observed the tradition of an ancient custom." (Chap. 24. p. 209-210.) Does not this *entreaty* acknowledge his supremacy? All this was before the Council of Nice.

Mr. B. asks, "did the second Council of Pisa decree a Reformation in faith or not?" I answer, that no Catholic Council—no *Council acknowledged by the church,* ever decreed a Reformation in *faith.*

He asks, "did the Council of Lateran pass an anathema against those rulers, who should *tax ecclesiastics?*" I reply that it *expressly* referred to extortions exacted from ecclesiastics by petty tyrants, contrary to the immunities secured to them by previously existing laws.

With regard, finally, to "Extreme Unction," Mr. B. infers that in as much as I have not specified the *time* of its institution, as a sacrament, therefore it was not established at all. I answer, that the fact of its existence is clearly established by the the text of St. James, quoted in my last letter. And besides, his reasoning is not only illogical, but anti-scriptural; since St. John tells us that "there are also many other things which Jesus did," which are not written. Mr. B. charges me with "contradicting the Council of Trent." The Council says, "this sacrament was first intimated in Mark vi. 13." And I said that it was not administered then. Where is the contradiction? Neither did an Apostle institute it. But an Apostle, St. James, in the fifth chapter of his epistle, *attests its existence,* and enjoins the use of it. The Council does not contradict itself, as Mr. B. says, but he invents a supposition for the Council, and draws the pretended contradiction from his own invention, on the one side, and from what the Council really did say on the other; on these he forms his "dilemma from which," he says, "it is impossible to escape!" But "*if,*" says he, "this sacrament was instituted, Mark vi. 13. (as it was, if ever) then the Apostles administered a sacrament, not being priests; but the Council of Trent says that Bishops and Priests are the proper ministers of this sacrament." Whence he concludes that the Council contradicts itself. Now the Council did not say that it was instituted or administered in Mark vi. 13, but only "intimated." Which proves that the Council did not err, did not contradict itself, but merely contradicts Mr. Breckinridge.

Before I pass to the various attempts of Mr. B. to answer the five "stale questions," which appertain immediately to the topic of discussion, I must be allowed to make a few General Remarks. The first is, that, from the commencement of the controversy, instead of preserving *unity* of subject, in that simple, but lucid order which men who write with the love of truth are studious to preserve, he, *in open violation of the rules subscribed by himself,* has continued to crowd letter after letter with matter altogether extraneous from the subject. Every succeeding letter from his pen is but a more confused repetition of the same subjects, on which, from the 2d to the last, he has continued to ring the changes. If he had, as he was bound to do, given but one, or, at most, two subjects in each of his letters, allowing me to do the same, then our letters might have been equally instructive, to both Catholics and Protestants. But this did not suit Mr. B. When I argued on the Rule of Faith, he argued on persecution, purgatory, &c. &c. When I argued against the pretensions of the Protestant religion, he argued against the Jesuits and the Inquisition, although "the Rule of Faith," and "the Protestant Religion" were the only subjects on which, until *they* should be exhausted, he was authorized by a *mutual engagement,* to write. What says the world of those who deliberately break their engagements?

Again, in upright controversy, no man charges on the cause of his opponent doctrines or principles, which his opponent disclaims, as not belonging to the cause. Yet has Mr. B. compelled me again and again to disclaim the same falsely imputed principles and tenets. He has acted throughout, on the assumption, that he knows the

Catholic religion better than I do, and that he is to be believed in preference: although, in so many instances I have convicted him of ignorance respecting it, and of the natural consequence of ignorance—misrepresentation. Of his false quotations *in general*, I shall not say any thing. A flagrant instance, is still fresh in the memory of the public—in the case of Baronius.

Finally, he writes a letter, in which he re-asserts objections and arguments that have been answered by facts, authorities, and reasoning, in the progress of the discussion—*asserts* that they have not been refuted, and with this letter, *proposes to close the controversy!!* Now I have the right to *reply*, and the reader will perceive that I have replied without broaching either *new* matter, or new arguments.

Besides the fact that Mr. B. has crowded all the sophistries of all his letters, into *this last* production, to which, it seems, he took it for granted that I would not claim the right of replying, he issues in it a recommendation to the public, of many of the vilest productions that have ever been written against Catholics and their religion. I may mention, as a sample, the pretended " Secreta Monita" of the Jesuits, a work which even the bigoted Leslie Foster, acknowledged, in the British House of Commons, to be a "forgery," got up by their enemies. It was worthy of Princeton to have published this "forgery," and of the Presbyterian clergy to recommend this infamous work to the "American people," as containing a *faithful expose* of the secret maxims of that calumniated body. If he wished his Protestant readers to be acquainted with the doctrines of the Catholics, to learn how *wicked they are*, he should have told them to read approved Catholic books, *explaining* their doctrines, and giving reasons for their belief. But he recommends, instead of these, the "Secreta Monita," a forgery, and the "Key to Popery," whose very title indicates its enmity. Sincere minds will see through the object of all this.

But what has become of THE QUESTION, in the mean while? "Is THE PROTESTANT RELIGION THE RELIGION OF CHRIST?"

1. Mr. B. has never ventured to tell us what the Protestant Religion is?—Except that it is "the Religion of the Reformation." This is defining a thing by itself—and according to this, a man has only to protest against the Catholic church—then he is a member of the Protestant Religion; and, what is the same thing, (if we may believe Mr. B.) a member of the Religion of Christ! All this, simply by protesting against Popery!

2d Question: "Did any society of Christians, previous to Luther, ever PROFESS the doctrines of Protestantism in general, or of any sect of it, in particular?

Mr. B. in his last letter proceeds to the final settlement of this question. "You will admit," says he, "that the doctrines taught by the Apostles, and recorded in the Bible, are true Christianity—so do I." All correct. "We both allow also," he continues, "that these doctrines have been according to Christ's promise to his church, *held and taught by the* TRUE *church ever since.*" All correct again; so far I could not have framed a better argument on the *Catholic* side. For since the doctrines of Christ have been "held and taught" at all times by the *true church*, as he acknowledges;—and, since he cannot find in the *whole world*, previous to Luther, a society of Christians who "held and taught" as Protestants do, therefore, the claims of Protestantism to be the true religion of Christ, are cut off, by his own argument. But let us see the conclusion which *he* draws from the above premises. "Then," says he, "IF your doctrines contradict the Bible at every step, and IF ours harmonize with it, it follows that we are the true church, *and that our doctrines have been taught and held in every age.*" Then, he goes on to show that the "IFS" on which the sophistry of his conclusion turns, are no obstacle—"I have proved—I have proved—I have proved"—as though he had in fact "proved" any thing, except his inability to prove what he had undertaken to prove; viz. "that the Protestant Religion is the Religion of Christ." He first said that the Waldenses,—then, the Greeks,—then, the Ante-Nicene Fathers "held and taught" the doctrines of Protestantism. I leave it to the reader whether, in every instance, I have not proved the contrary. At last he retreats to the Bible, (just as Unitarians do,) and *tells us*, that the Protestant doctrines are the doctrines of that divine book, (which I deny) therefore they must have been "*held* and *taught*" by the true church, from the commencement, although he cannot tell by whom or where!

3d Question: "Whether Christ revealed ALL the doctrines of Protestantism, beginning with Episcopalianism and ending with

Unitarianism." This remains as it was before his last letter. He does not venture to repeat the assertion, that Christ could have revealed contradictory doctrines.

4th Question: "Whether the Reformation received any new ministerial authority, to supply the place of that which the church recalled from them, in their excommunication?" To this he replies, that "IF a minister of Christ is deposed for refusing to sin, the deposition is null and void." This is not the question. The question is, by what new MINISTERIAL AUTHORITY did the Reformers *create new* religions? For no society of Christians, as we have seen, ever "held and taught" their doctrines before.

This has been acknowledged by the Reformers themselves. Luther says expressly, that "for a long time he stood ALONE." Calvin, in his letter to Melancthon in 1552, says, "we have been obliged to separate from THE WHOLE WORLD." This is undeniably manifest. Whence then, " standing alone," *excommunicated by the church,* and " separated from the whole world"—whence their NEW AUTHORITY? It was not from men. If it was from God, God would have sealed this *new* work with the power of miracles. Did the the Reformers ever prove by *this* test, that God had sent them? Erasmus, who was acquainted with them, says, "they could not so much as cure a lame horse." By their own admission they separated from the church, and by their own doctrine, they are condemned for this crime alone. Calvin tells us, that "to separate from the church, *is to renounce Jesus Christ.*"..... Then, Calvin, himself, must have " renounced Jesus Christ," having, as he admits, " separated from the whole world."

The condemnation of Athanasius by the Arians, furnishes no parallel to the case of the Reformers. He was deposed by the violence of those Heretics, from whom he had received *no authority.* But the Reformers were excommunicated by the very church which had ordained them, and joined themselves to *no other society.* Therefore, they had no authority themselves, and consequently could not transmit it to their successors.

In treating this question, Mr. B. labours, first, to show that ordination and ministerial authority in the Catholic church is, to use his favourite expression, a "figment," and then he contends that the Reformers in their suspension and excommunication, could not be deprived of this same 'figment,' and *thus* proves that Presbyterian ministers are something more than mere laymen!! On this point I give him over to the rigid logic of Drs. Bowden, Cooke, Brittan, and others, who, whilst they vindicate Catholic ordination on the one side, prove to a demonstration on the other, that Presbyterian ordination is a "figment" indeed. "Where there is no Episcopal ordination," says Dodwell, "there is NO MINISTRY; NO SACRAMENT; NO CHURCH. *Men are out of the covenant of Grace, and hope of salvation.*'

5th Question. The fifth question appertains as a corollary to the solution of the fourth. Since it is manifest, as we have seen, that the first Reformers had received no " NEW *ministerial authority,*" it follows that the original deficiency has not been supplied to their successors at any subsequent period. Consequently, the right by which the Protestant clergy exercise the ministry, is merely an assumption, founded on a *human* origin, but not derived from God, by any visible order of derivation. The *ordinary mission and authority* were cut off by their defection from the Catholic church; and there were no extraordinary mission and authority; for these are known only by the evidence of miracles, to which the Reformers, very wisely, never pretended.

Mr. B. unable to answer, in a satisfactory manner, these five questions, is powerful in his criminations against Catholicity. He sees nothing but sects in the Catholic church; yet when I called upon him to show so much as two Catholics in the whole world, professing a different belief on any article of faith; he could not find them. Throughout the universe, Catholics are as united in *their faith*, as if they dwelt under the same roof. The distinction between faith, opinions, and mere local customs, has been pointed out.

Towards the close of his letter, he makes an allusion to the "table of sins," and whilst he pretends that no parent should permit his child to read it, he seems to forget that there are passages in the Bible, which, on his own principle, it is quite as improper for children to read, or hear, or *understand*.

The last flourish of his letter is on the "EFFECT OF THE REFORMATION." He says, "we are indebted to the Reformation, under God, for the rights of conscience, for civil liberty, for the revival of letters, in chief part, and for the circulation of the Bible, for the virtue and piety of the people, and the eternal salvation of innumerable souls." All this is popular declamation, most of it untrue, and contradicted by learned Protestants themselves. The "salvation of souls," ascribed to the Reformation is the only thing worth refutation. Mr. Haldane, a Protestant, in his Second Review of the British and Foreign Bible Society, represents the Protestants, not only of Germany, but Sweden, Norway, Finland, Prussia, Hungary, Holland and France, as consisting almost entirely of Arians, Socinians, Neologists, Rationalists, and Deists. Does this, I would ask Mr. B., look like "the salvation of innumerable souls?" The editor of the Presbyterian corroborates the above position by telling us that the mother churches of Calvinism in Geneva are sinking into "Atheism." The Protestant Brandt, in his History of the Reformation, says, in reference to morals......that " vice, persecution, hatred, envy, and self-love, have prevailed among them, (the Reformed;) that every body *accommodates the word of God to his own prejudices;* and has a gospel of *his own making.*" (Roache's Abridgement of Brandt, vol. i. p. 3.) Does this look like the "salvation of innumerable souls?" But I have already given the testimony of the Reformers themselves to prove that morals deteriorated by the Reform.

Mr. B. has repeatedly made reference to those portions of the Holy Scripture which Protestants call Apocryphal. Now, in my letter No. 13, I showed by unanswered proof and testimony, that the objections raised by Protestants to those books, are equally strong against all the deutero-canonical books. Let him take, and refute *those arguments.*

With regard to the charge which he *renews* of SUPPRESSING THE SECOND COMMANDMENT, (as Protestants divide the decalogue) I have simply to reply that it is false and unfounded. There is only one copy of the catechism (and that is not in general use) in which it is not expressly and fully stated. He denies that it is in the " CATECHISM OF THE COUNCIL OF TRENT," and calls for the page. Let him read page 332, and he will learn the truth of a fact which he has denied. But let the candid acknowledgment of learned and eminent Protestants reprove the ignorance or malice that prefers such a charge.

Doctor Heber, in his Bampton Lectures, says, " We ourselves are not altogether guiltless of FALSELY imputing to the Catholics, in their public formularies, the systematic omission of that commandment which we make the second in the decalogue......This accusation has been brought forward by some who *ought to have known better.*"

Dr. Parr says, " I should be ASHAMED of urging against them any FALSE *accusation* of disingenuous omission, or unauthorized arrangement of the decalogue." (Dr. Parr's Character of C. J. Fox, vol. ii. p. 129.)

I have now done—and I submit it to the reader whether my opponent has not utterly failed to prove either " the Protestant Rule of Faith," or that " the Protestant Religion is the Religion of Christ." He has indeed urged against the Catholic church the misrepresentations of three hundred years, wielded with all the force which ignorance of, and prejudice against our REAL doctrines, could impart. But what has he done besides? Even in this, has he ever planted his foot in a *fixed position,* from which he has not been driven by the force, not of assertion, but of facts, authorities, and argument? Even in point of literary courtesy and polite language, I do not shrink from the candid judgment of the Protestant reader himself. It is to be admitted, that when he quoted authorities, which are *untrue,* I said *they were "untrue."* But for this, the blame belongs to *him,* and not to *me.* For the rest, Rev. Sir, with all good wishes for your better knowledge of the holy, but calumniated religion, which you have assailed, as well as for your happiness,

I remain your obedient servant,

JOHN HUGHES.

CORRESPONDENCE.

Philadelphia, September 19th, 1833.

To the Rev. John Hughes,

Sir,—When I accepted your offer of a public controversy, I proposed to you the alternative of a connected discussion in successive volumes, or of a public oral debate. You declined both of these, however; and, after much difficulty and delay, the present plan was finally adopted, under a limitation of six months. The reason of this limitation was the nature of my present occupation, which requires me to be absent from home a greater part of the year. By the indulgence of the Board of Education of the Presbyterian church, in whose service I am engaged, I was enabled to add two months to the six already devoted to you. These have now expired; and my duty imperatively calls me to leave the city and travel at large through the country for several months.

As I am very solicitous, however, to continue and complete this Controversy, I now propose to you a public discussion of the remaining topics, as soon after my return as may be convenient for the parties. In this way, and in this alone, we can in a few successive days investigate every subject which it may be desirable to discuss. I now claim this arrangement, not only as due to me in justice, but in the exercise of that choice which you conceded to me in your note of August 1st, (See Appendix to Letter No. XXVIII.) where you say, " you will have it in your power to fix the limitation, when and *where* you may deem it convenient." I now fix it on the Rostrum, before the American people. If you decline this proposal in view of the above facts, it must be considered as the expression of a desire to retire from the defence of your cause.

An early and explicit answer is requested.

I remain your obedient servant,

JOHN BRECKINRIDGE.

P. S. You will be so kind as to receive the bearer, the Rev. William L. M'Calla, as fully authorized by me to negotiate the proposals of this letter, and all things connected with it, or resulting from it.

J. B.

Philada. Sept. 21, 1833.

To the Rev. John Hughes.

I have received with extreme regret your *verbal* reply to my letter of the 19th inst. in which you wholly decline my proposal to finish the pending Controversy in a public oral discussion.

In existing circumstances, therefore, my letter of the 25th will close the Controversy, until my return from the tours incident to my office, at the present season of the year. If, however, you desire its unbroken continuance, I offer to you as a substitute (according to your own suggestion, in view of possible interruptions on my part) the Rev. William L. McCalla during my absence. If Providence permit my return, as I hope, after some weeks, I shall be prepared, and disposed to resume the discussion in such a way as may be agreed upon between us. And I hereby assure you that nothing shall hinder me (if God permit) from bringing this whole subject before the American people.

I remain your obedient servant,

JOHN BRECKINRIDGE.

Philada. Sept. 23d, 1833.

To the Rev. John Breckinridge.

Rev. Sir,—In reply to your letters of the 19th and 21st inst. I have to inform you, that I see no reason why we should depart from the form and medium of Controversy which we have used hitherto, and which was agreed upon between us after mature deliberation and repeated conferences. It is unnecessary here to state the reasons that induced me to prefer conducting the Controversy in the form of letters, nor will the public be at a loss to divine your motives for now declining that mode, as it must be evident that in an oral discussion, you would have the opportunity of quoting authorities in a manner to suit your own purpose, when it would not be in the power of your opponent to detect and expose you, as has been successfully done in a variety of instances. It would seem as if you considered yourself justified in overturning our rules and regulations *in globo*,—having contrived to evade and violate them in detail, during the progress of the Controversy. But, Sir, I am not to be made a party to such proceedings. It was through the press you first assailed the Catholic Church. Through the press you circulated your memorable challenge to "Priests and Bishops." Through the press I have, thus far, successfully exposed your incompetency to defend your cause, except by misrepresentations of doctrines, or perversions of authorities—and through the press I shall continue to submit the case to the judgment of a discerning and enlightened public, until the final close of the Controversy. If your business carry you abroad, you are free to discontinue when you please, and to resume when you find it convenient to do so.—But you must not deprive me of my right to return the arrow which you shoot—in retreating. When you return, you may resume the contest, and I shall be prepared to receive you.

In the mean time, I have to assure you, that I have not sent any "verbal reply" to either of your letters. Yours, &c.

JOHN HUGHES.

Philadelphia, September 28, 1833.

To the Rev. John Hughes.

Sir,—I have received your answer of the 23d, to my communication of the 21st; and have also seen your note to the publishers of the Presbyterian asserting your purpose to reply to my Letter No. 34. It is difficult for me to tell you, how painful it is to me, on the point of my departure, to see you pursuing so unworthy a course; or to frame an apology for it. As you wrote the *first* letter in the series, so it is clearly my place, as *respondent*, to write the *last*. Yet you insist on writing the *last* as well as the *first*. If it requires *two* of your letters to answer *one* of mine, then can any one be at a loss to draw the inference? What renders your desperate condition still more apparent is, that you seek the exercise of so unjust an advantage at the moment of my departure, and not only insist on a *supernumerary* letter, but would deny me the right of responding to it, even through a friend—while necessary absence renders it impossible for me to do it in *person;* while yet you first *suggested* this very arrangement in view of my possible interruptions; and while, with the resolution of despair, you refuse to meet me on the Rostrum. When you charge me with seeking an oral debate that I may shun your examination, and exposure of my authorities, you forget that a cart-load of 'authorities,' might attend each of us to the stage; and that this will be the very place to confront and expose false references. I am so accustomed to the language of insult from you, that it now passes me, with no other emotion but pity, and regret that I am constrained to sustain a Controversy with one who defends his cause at the expense of his character. Your praise might now appear almost a reason for self-examination; and while I can appeal to God, and my country, for my character, and to your own monuments for the truth of all my citations, I shall continue to construe your personal attacks, as the last struggles of a system which has ceased to be defended by argument and truth. My reasons for proposing a public debate were these.—I desired, from the *very* first, a discussion which could be presented in a body, (as in a book) that all our arguments might rapidly, and together, be examined and reviewed. But for this you proposed to substitute the columns of a daily newspaper!

The next best form and the nearest approach to the former, is a public debate. This, besides passing before our hearers in a few days, the whole matter of controversy, might be speedily furnished, and then allow me room for other duties which call me much abroad. Either of these methods is better suited to both these ends, than a protracted newspaper discussion, which may become interminable, and afford to you the occasion of incessant evasions. On the Rostrum I could bring you to the point, and confront you before the people, where cowards lose their shelter, sophists their veil, and Jesuits their power to dally and deceive.

Being now, in the providence of God, called away for a season, as you insist on still another letter, I must leave you *under the care* of my gallant friend, during my absence. I shall request him to do no more than is necessary, in replying to your forthcoming letter, if you persist in so unjust an *act*.

In closing this communication, I beg you to bear in mind, that your fond hope of my "retreat," cannot be realized, however consoling such an event might be to you, at the present crisis. In the *existing posture* of the discussion, I can scarcely believe that any one (much less yourself,) will construe my absence into "a retreat," especially when our first arrangements were made in view of that absence, and when I spontaneously added two months to the six originally fixed on as the limit of the Controversy. I hope, however, soon to have it in my power to give a practical refutation to so uncandid and false a charge. If my life should be contiuued by a merciful God, I shall promptly be at hand, prepared to press the discussion to its legitimate close, in any form consistent with my present mode of life, whether on the Rostrum, or in permanent volumes, or in the weekly papers, either *with* you or *without* you. I remain, yours, &c.

JOHN BRECKINRIDGE.

[From the U. S. Gazette.]

MISTATEMENT CORRECTED.

Perceiving in the letter of Rev. John Breckinridge (No. 6 of the Controversy) the following paragraph, I deem it due to the public, as well as to myself, to give it the earliest and most unequivocal contradiction.

"I have been informed that Bishop Kenrick did, on the 17th February last, in St. Mary's church (Philadelphia), publicly warn the people against reading this controversy."

Not having on that or any other occasion made the remotest allusion to the pending controversy, and not having even in private given, to any individual whatever, any such warning, I declare the information to be utterly groundless. Given under my hand this 13th day of March, 1833.

† FRANCIS PATRICK KENRICK, Bp. &c.

N. B. Understanding that the above mistatement was contained in the letter, I sent the contradiction of it to the office of the *Presbyterian*, on Monday between 2 and 3 o'clock, that it might appear together with the letter then in press; but to my surprise, no notice is taken of it in that paper published this morning.

MR. LANGLEY'S LETTER.

To the Rev. John Breckinridge.

Sir,—Having observed in the papers of this morning a card signed by M. Fithian, as the publisher of the Review of Bishop Onderdonk's charge, in which reference is made to me, it becomes my duty to say that his statements are incorrect. Immediately after the letter of Rev. Mr. Hughes appeared, in which he says, "In one instance a bookseller who enjoyed some sectarian patronage was actually forbidden to keep it for sale," I was called upon by the said Mr. Fithian to ascertain whether the information that he had given, and which led to the above statement, was correct. I told him that it was not, and this he must have known when he gave the card to which his name is annexed, and which appeared many days after our interview. I was never forbidden to keep it for sale, I have never received orders of any kind whatever on the subject, nor am I aware that it was ever known by the members composing the Board, that I had received the work at all. Any one acquainted with the nature of this institution, must see that even if *orders had been given*, the statement of Rev. Mr. Hughes makes a false impression on the public mind. I am not a *bookseller* in the sense in which that term is ordinarily understood; but an *agent* employed in a religious institution. I can therefore neither "enjoy" nor receive "*patronage;*" nor be influenced in the discharge of my duties by the fear of losing it. The object of the Baptist Tract Society is the diffusion of what that denomination considers truth. All its agents and concerns are under the direction of a Board of Managers. The supplying of the Depository with other works than those issued by the Society, is under the direction of a Committee of that Board. But in the case of the Review no orders whatever were given by the Board, nor by the Committee respecting the sale of it at first, or the discontinuance of it. I received and sold the copies that were left with me on my own responsibility, and declined receiving any more upon the same, and by that responsibility I am willing to stand.

A. S. LANGLEY,
Assistant at the Depository of the Bap. Gen. Tract Society.

Philadelphia, Sept. 5th, 1833.

To the Rev. John Hughes.

As the note from Mr. A. S. Langley, appended to the Rev. Mr. Breckinridge's last letter, is calculated to carry abroad a conviction of falsehood against me, I feel it a duty which I owe to myself to assert that the impression made upon my mind, on his declining to receive any more of the Review was, that he had been forbidden to keep it for sale. Now, if Mr. L. had allowed me the benefit of misconception of what he *did* actually say, in reference to the sale of the Review, I should have remained satisfied with the guilt of having indiscreetly mentioned the circumstance through an error of my own understanding. M. FITHIAN.

Sept. 13th, 1833.

www.ingramcontent.com/pod-product-compliance
Lightning Source LLC
Chambersburg PA
CBHW020833020526
44114CB00040B/605